The Graceful Lie

a method for making fiction

for Violet, with love

1/99

"When a child lies, he often believes himself. He weaves a fantasy around the behavior that is acceptable to him. Fantasy becomes a means of expressing those things that he has trouble admitting as reality."

— V. Oaklander

MP

The Graceful Lie
a method for making fiction

Michael Petracca
University of California at Santa Barbara

Prentice Hall
Upper Saddle River, New Jersey 07458

Library of Congress Cataloging-in-Publication Data

The Graceful lie : a method for making fiction / Michael F. Petracca.
  p. cm.
Includes index.
ISBN 0-13-287418-0
  1. College readers.   2. English language—Rhetoric—Problems,
exercises, etc.   3. Fiction—Authorship—Problems, exercises, etc.
4. Creative writing—Problems, exercises, etc.   I. Petracca,
Michael,
PE1417.G636   1999
808.3—dc21   98-7709
                                                          CIP

Editor-in-Chief: *Charlyce-Jones Owen*
Senior Acquisition Editor: *Maggie Barbieri*
Editorial Assistant: *Joan Polk*
AVP, Director of Manufacturing and Production: *Barbara Kittle*
Production Liaison: *Fran Russello*
Project Manager: *Pine Tree Composition*
Prepress and Manufacturing Buyer: *Mary Ann Gloriande*
Cover Design: *Kiwi Design*

This book was set in *10/12 Palatino* by Pine Tree Composition, Inc.,
and was printed and bound by *Courier
Companies*. The cover was printed by *Phoenix Color Corp.*

© 1999 by Prentice-Hall, Inc.
Simon & Schuster / A Viacom Company
Upper Saddle River, New Jersey 07458

Printed in the United States of America
10 9 8 7 6 5 4 3 2 1

ISBN: 0-13-287418-0

Prentice-Hall International (UK) Limited, *London*
Prentice-Hall of Australia Pty. Limited, *Sydney*
Prentice-Hall Canada Inc., *Toronto*
Prentice-Hall Hispanoamericana, S.A., *Mexico*
Prentice-Hall of India Private Limited, *New Delhi*
Prentice-Hall of Japan, Inc., *Tokyo*
Simon & Schuster Asia Pte. Ltd., *Singapore*
Editora Prentice-Hall do Brasil, Ltda., *Rio de Janeiro*

To my *other* parents: Annie and Mike Lorimer, who—with quick wit, refinement, and a warm billiards room—keep alive a connection to the family of my youth; Ingeborg Comstock, loving mom when this orphaned kid needed one, best mixed-doubles partner ever, generous trader of Monopoly properties, perpetual embodiment of grace; Hilaire Ingram, who understands the Buddhist principle that life is suffering almost as well as I do, and leads the way to graceful acceptance; the memory of Richard Ingram, egg farmer, political pundit, loving pop and grandpop, and the coolest stiff man ever; and Marshall Sweet, cousin/brother who sanely and whimsically fathers me more than he knows.

Contents

Preface

The principle of art is to pause, not bypass. The principle of true art is not to portray, but to evoke. This requires a moment of pause—a contract with yourself through the object you look at or the page you read. In that moment of pause, I think life expands. And really the purpose of art—for me, of fiction—is to alert, to indicate to stop, to say: Make certain that when you rush through you will not miss the moment which you might have had, or might still have. That is the moment of finding something which you have not known about yourself, or your environment, about others and about life.

—Jerzy Kosinski

Literary inspiration is often mistaken for indigestion.

—Sue Grafton

As a boy I was a natural liar. I told my parents I was going to play outside, then lurked in the laundry room, where I pretended the washer and drier were overweight space-robots. I told by seventh-grade phys. ed. teacher I had benign paroxysmal positional vertigo (I found the cool-sounding disease in one of my mom's old medical textbooks) when in actuality I was scared of doing an overhead pullover on the gymnastics highbar. I told the business manager at Ethan Allen Junior High I was selling French-dip sandwiches in the cafeteria, then pocketed the money for myself, thereby augmenting my parents' meager allowance by several bucks a week. I told my high school sweetheart, Jannisue Saxon, that I was going surfing, when I was really riding the waves of benign paroxysmal bliss with Diana Bucci, a sophomore modern-dance major at UCLA. I'm not proud of any of this, and as a grown man I might have followed my little personality disorder to an unhappy conclusion. I might have become a convicted embezzler or a philandering husband or a city councilman who shoplifts garden shears from home-improvement stores. Instead, I turned my lying tendencies to more healthy ends, by becoming a writer.

Now I've created this book that teaches other people how to achieve grace through fictionalizing. Before I contracted to write *The Graceful Lie*, I had some serious reservations. I had just finished working on a nonfictional title and didn't relish the notion of committing another two years to a project that seemed at the outset . . . well, not terribly creative. I wanted to start a new novel, not write a book about writing a novel. A fiction-writing text might turn out to be informative—maybe even inspirational to some aspiring writers—but it wouldn't engender in me the kind of mad illogic and blissful surprise that fiction writing does. Nevertheless, some inner voice hinted that I might find meaning in the project: an intrinsic value greater than the almost-generous advance money and the added resumé line.

I had been a full-time university lecturer in academic and creative writing for the past fifteen years, so I knew I'd have a few things to say on the subject. I also had bookshelves full of novels and short stories I had read and kept. Every time I moved into a new place (a restless, itinerant youth, I used to average a two moves a year), I would have to schlep all those books along with me. Friends would mock my little library. "Lose the books," they used to laugh, "and save thousands in chiropractic bills." Some even accused me of showing off, as though I were trumpeting my erudition by an external signifier: the Wall of Fiction. Being a brat—a delightful childhood quality I never outgrew, unlike my lying—I came up with a smartass answer to shut them up. "Books are my friends," I would tell the detractors. "Better than my real friends, even."

When I started writing *The Graceful Lie,* though, I realized my real reasons for having kept all those books around. Subconsciously, I must have known I'd someday need to mine them for evidence: quotations and paraphrases to support the abstract assertions in *The Graceful Lie*. More importantly, I came to realize that the books—and by extension their authors—really *were* friends in a state of permanent absentia. If a friend is a person whom one knows, likes, and trusts to the point of sharing intimate details of one's life, a person with whom one is allied in a struggle or cause, and/or a person with whom one shares a profound connection bordering on the spiritual . . . then I was immeasurably close with hundreds of people whom I had never met—yet who diverted me (Sue Grafton), moved me to tears

(Alice Walker) and laughter (Joseph Heller) and nausea (Jean-Paul Sartre) and violent rage (Pete Dexter) and psychotic fugue states (William Burroughs); who tripped me out (Ursula LeGuin) and took me to ecstatic heights (Virginia Woolf) and depths of depravity (Hunter Thompson); who blurred gender categories (Maxine Hong Kingston), and tweaked my sense of sexual identity (Kathy Acker); who suggested I was not alone in viewing the world as utterly absurd (Kurt Vonnegut), benignly indifferent (Albert Camus), unfathomably cruel (Jerzy Kosinski), yet possessed of mystic depths (Gloria Naylor), moral ambiguities (Anne Rice), and the potential for spiritual redemption (Nikos Kazantzakis); who validated my excesses (Henry Miller), yet supported my impulse to elevation of spirit (Chaim Potok)—and a thousand other writers I can't mention here, because we have a paper shortage in the country right now.

When one works in (or near) a university English department, the literary theorists—cultural critics, new historicists, textual geneticists and so on—sometimes deride one's reveling in the soul of literature. Onto such behavior, they slap a label that's lately fallen into disfavor among academics: *belletrism,* the appreciation of literature on its own merits, not for the ways in which it provides textual evidence for political or social theories. For me—fringe academic that I am—the author-to-reader connection is the true grace, the numinous power of fiction. By bringing me back to this realization, writing *The Graceful Lie* turned out to be not merely a practical career move, but a life's work: the culmination of several decades' worth of reading, writing, teaching, and thinking about fiction. When the cosmic motes settle, the transformative power of language is as close as this agnostic Jewish/Catholic/Zen Buddhist kid ever gets to religion, I guess. In *The Graceful Lie* I get to teach the word(s) . . . without, one hopes, ever stooping to preach.

There's an additional benefit in writing a book of this kind: I get to choose fictional pieces from my favorite writers as end-of-chapter readings. While I obviously cannot include all the novelists and short story writers who have delighted me over the years, I've tried to provide a representative sampling . . . and not just "literary" authors, either. In my reading life, I try to alternate between "serious" fiction—pieces that have been canonized, or are soon-to-be-canonized by the critical community—and popular genre titles . . . especially mysteries. I ground myself in popular fiction partially because it's my job as a pop-culture critic (see, for example, the recent book *Common Culture,* written with UCSB colleague Madeleine Sorapure), but more importantly because I'm a hog for a well-constructed *noir* thriller or detective procedural with wry, snappy dialogue. While I admire experimental and literary fiction that expands one's sense of what is possible with language, that works the same lexalchemic juju as the best poetry, I also have immense respect for popular authors. Certainly there are supermarket novelists who crank out horribly cliché-ridden prose with formulaic plots, and who might therefore deserve to be called hacks and wordwhores who've sold out the muse in exchange for a pouchful (all right, in some cases a *big* pouchful) of coin. But many more pop fiction writers, I think, manage to capture the mass imagination while paying attention to the aesthetic potentialities of language, the sublime complexity of a well-constructed storyline. In *The Graceful Lie,* then, you'll find a charming mix of the literary and the popular. You'll see Dr. Hunter S. Thompson lying down next to May Sarton (as frightening an image as I've ever typed), mystery writer Sara Paretsky sharing chapter space with Ernest Hemingway and Grace Paley. I sincerely hope this book will delight you by providing an eclectic reading experience, while giving you friendly and practical instruction in the methods of writing prose fiction.

ACKNOWLEDGMENTS

Because I'm such a dogged cuss, I could have written this book without anyone's help. If I had done so, I'd probably be composing this preface from Atascadero State Hospital for the Criminally Insane's lockdown ward today, not my writerly garret warmed by crackling wood stove. I'm therefore extremely grateful to the many folks who helped along the way. I want to thank my editor, Maggie Barbieri, for her calm, good sense, insightful commentary, elastic deadline policy, and diplomatic handling of the occasional permissions crisis. Special thanks to Muriel Zimmerman, Director of the Writing Program at the University of California at Santa Barbara, who has been an unflagging supporter of my fiction and who singlehandedly makes it possible for me to hold a full-time teaching gig while writing books at the same time. Thanks likewise to Richard Whitney, Undergraduate Chair at Antioch University, Santa Barbara, who makes it possible for me to teach fiction workshops to the diverse, inquisitive, energetic and always inspiring students on that campus. Thanks to Richard Helgerson, who gave me the opportunity to teach fiction writing to undergraduate students in the UCSB English Department's now-defunct creative writing emphasis. Thanks to the countless students who taught me, and to the interns and volunteers who derived valuable experience—or at least lines on their resumés—from helping me research, revise, and generate student-friendly exercises and discussion questions for *The Graceful Lie:* Elizabeth Anderson, Uta Ayala, Chucky Byerson, Evelyn Chiaverini, Matt Gilbert, Risa Goldstein, Doug Graham, Jamie Haser, Kim Lund (whose gymnastics story appears in Chapter 2), and Stephen Martin.

Finally, exxes and oes to anybody who ever discussed this project with me, or listened to me whine about how I don't have enough free time anymore, or encompassed my essentially hermetic nature without dissing me, or checked moles for changes, or tractioned my neck with a towel slung under the skullbone, or gave me a certain mystery writer's unlisted phone number, or blew out the circuits with fine second-line rhythms, or discussed that recurring dream about the satanic entity who flies through walls, or appeared mysteriously one day in 1981, gave unconditional love for fifteen years and then disappeared mysteriously in 1997, or didn't tease me for eating Gerber's strained summer squash (yum!), or set me up with a computer system customized to my peculiar brand of gimpiness, or read the lesbian young adult story to verify its accuracy and suitability, or used woo-woo new-agey techniques to balance my neural energies, or made me chicken noodle soup (not from the can) when the literary stresses wore down my resistance to student-borne virions, or turned me on to Durrell when I was twenty, or read and responded to chunks of draft material from *The Graceful Lie* . . . including Stephen Barcia-Bacon, Bonnie Beedles, Gordon Black, Blake Brown, Kelley Camp, James Coffey, Mark Comstock, Keith Coplin, Mark Ferrer, Linda Ferro, Jane Freeburg, Ana Inés Heras, Kenna Hickman, Hilaire Ingram, Jan Ingram, R.N., Judy Kirk, John M. Landsberg, Little Feat, Carl and Stella Herzig, Penelope Maddy, Minou Petracca, Berwyn Moore, Peter Mortola, Frances Maria Petracca, Stella Nell-Akoni, Michael Ryan, Mark Schlenz, Tara Sweeney, Marshall Sweet, Lauren Wyeth. I am immensely grateful to all of you.

The Graceful Lie
a method for making fiction

PART I: A METHOD FOR MAKING FICTION

1

Introduction

THE GRACEFUL LIE: GOALS AND CHARACTERISTICS OF FICTION

In the preface to his fictional dream-journal, *The Burning Tapers,* novelist Carlo Zeamba calls narrative prose the Graceful Lie, because "in fiction, the imagination creates worlds blessed with more beauty and horror than the everyday world can possibly reveal to us." In this passage, Zeamba suggests that even though creative writing contains made-up elements—fictions, "lies,"—it embodies essential human truths in ways that other kinds of written expression can't.

Of course, all writing is creative. Whether they're producing computer manuals, anthropology essays, poetry, or novels, writers replace blank space on a page or computer screen with words organized toward some purpose. However, the activity that is broadly labeled "creative writing" in college catalogues and instructional texts like this one—and the activity of creating prose fiction in particular—does differ from other kinds of writing in significant ways.

Academic writing, for example, does an excellent job of presenting a main point (a thesis, as your freshman composition teacher may have called it) and developing that point logically, using illustration, example, and maybe some researched source material. Likewise, a piece of reportage in the Sunday *Times* Metro section may describe a random shooting or city council meeting as objectively as possible, given the limitations of a single writer's point of view, and any biases or hidden agendas the writer may have. Newspaper writers learn to address themselves to the "five W's of journalism": *who* was involved in the story, *what* happened, *when* did it happen, *where* did it happen, and *why*, namely the factors leading up to the incident in question. By narrowing their focus to these five questions, journalists hope to arrive at some relative objectivity about a certain incident in the real world.

By contrast, creative prose often presents a range of perspectives on characters and the issues they confront, leaving the reader with several possible interpretations about what the piece means. This ability to evoke a range of intellectual responses and sense impressions separates creative writing from expository or academic prose, which may be imaginative and inventive but usually has a central point or thesis. The quality of being open to interpretation, which literary critics call *ambiguity,* is generally a desirable trait in art. It means that a certain artifact has been rendered by the author (or painter, hip-hop songwriter, composer, and so on) in a complex and multifaceted way, so that the reader might have numerous "correct" interpretations of it. Thus free of the constraints imposed by focusing on a thesis and the linear development of ideas, fictional creation gives the writer an opportunity to present life as complex, elusive, exhilarating, joyful, chaotic, grief-filled, terrifying, delicious . . . perhaps even pointless. In fiction, the writer may pretend to be reporting events objectively, or may shamelessly render her creation fantastic, dreamlike.

The main goal of the fiction writer, then, is not necessarily to present "reality" (whatever that is!) objectively, but to create an internal reality that is convincing to readers. Most fiction writers agree on this central point. Novelist David Lodge, for example, explains the writer's central task this way:

> I have always regarded fiction as an essentially rhetorical art—that is to say, the novelist or short-story writer *persuades* us to share a certain view of the world for the duration of the reading experience, effecting, when successful, that rapt immersion in an imagined reality . . .

Author and instructor Stephen Minot echoes this sentiment, noting that fiction is an "untrue story in prose." Fiction cannot be criticized for being "untrue," says Minot, but rather judged on whether it *seems* true. According to Minot, good fiction is the "reshapement of real life," a process which he calls "Virtual Invention" (113). These quotations point to a shared belief among novelists and short story writers, who insist that it's perfectly legitimate to "lie" in fiction—to allow the imagination to invent happenings, places, and characters. In fact, creating a believable "lie" will make your writing "graceful," capable of generating real, transformative power.

JUST WRITE: ZEN AND THE FICTION PROCESS

Fiction embodies some conventions that have worked for centuries to keep readers coming back for more. All stories use words. They usually (but not always) involve some human characters, and they describe events in time—events that frequently involve some kind of conflict. However, it's impossible to write a "how-to" book for fiction writing as one would write a recipe book for the rural cuisine of southern France or a repair manual for Volkswagen engines, because fiction has no strict, inviolable rules and structures.

For example, the traditional, Aristotelian plot structure, involving periodic buildup and release of tension, is often used by novelists and is an absolute *must* with most movies produced today. But writers (see the Literary Fiction chapter later in this book) also create "stories" that resist Hollywood-style plot-point construction and upset readers' expectations of conventional narrative elements, such as linear time flow and satisfying closure. Furthermore, creative writers frequently exercise *creative license* by flaunting the formal mechanical rules, such as correct grammar. Look no further than the sentence before the last one, for a concrete example of this phenomenon. Because I thought it sounded good, I chose to begin the sentence with the conjunction, "but"—a definite no-no according to Mr. Pidgeon, your starchy junior high school English teacher, but perfectly acceptable in creative writing.

Having no fixed, inviolable body of rules to follow can be a profoundly liberating experience. For many people, writing stories or novels allows for a soul-satisfying, unfettered discharge of creative energy. Taken a step further, writing fiction may even assume the form of meditative practice, if the writer approaches the process with such intention. Natalie Goldberg, a popular and articulate proponent of this approach to fiction, likens the writing process to Zen Buddhist practice. She quotes a certain Japanese master:

> Katagiri Roshi said, "Capability is like a water table below the surface of the earth." No one owns it, but you can tap it. You tap it with your effort and it will come through to you. So just practice writing, and when you learn to trust your voice, direct it. If you want to write a novel, write a novel. If it's essays you want or short stories, write them. In the process of writing them, you will learn how. You can have the confidence that you will gradually acquire the technique and craft you need.

In other words, writing is its own instruction, and the process, not the literary product, becomes its own reward. When you achieve the mental state of childlike receptivity described by Goldberg and others (see the Bradbury essay, "How to Keep and Feed a Muse" at the end of this chapter), you will respond to stimuli as though for the first time. Should you let yourself remain in the present moment, your mind devoid of paradigms and accompanying self-criticism, you may find the words emerging effortlessly and sometimes in a rush.

At such times, you'll feel as though you were touched by the finger of God, or "channelling" the spirit of Jane Austen, or as though you were a craps-shooter making ten passes in a row, to the appreciative shouts of the circled players. As Goldberg says in *Writing Down The Bones,* "Basically, if you want to become a good writer, you need to do three things. Read a lot, listen well and deeply, and write a lot. And don't think too much. Just enter the heat of words and sounds and colored sensations and keep your pen moving across the page." By freeing yourself from any expectation of creating a critically acclaimed literary product, and by discarding (or at least suspending) the "rules" of traditional narrative prose, you can enter a state of enlightened detachment, existing and composing with no gaining thought whatever. Paradoxically, some of the "best" literary creation may arise from letting go of your desire to create good literature.

COLICKY BABY MUSES: SOME BUMPS ALONG THE PATH

There is much to commend in the philosophy/practice of Goldberg et al. It works...not just in the sphere of writing but as a general approach to everyday living as well. All writers—whether beginners or grizzled professionals—would do well to keep Katagiri Roshi's simple but profound instruction in mind, to remind them of the ideal state of mental preparedness for writing. Unfortunately, very few among us are boddhisattvas, paragons of Buddhist enlightenment. Even when we uphold the highest ideals for our writing practice, the experience may not always be enjoyable.

Sometimes, for instance, the words emerge not as a blessed stream but rather as a chaotic jumble. Rather than being visited by a gentle and nurturing muse who descends from the heavens, bathing the artist in divine inspiration, you may find yourself amidst a swarming riot of muses—call them creative impulses or inner voices, if you have a psychological bent—vying for attention at the same time, like colicky babies: loud and demanding. At other times, despite your best intentions, the words won't come at all. Anne Lamott, in her delightful, irreverent, and frequently self-revealing *Bird By Bird,* says of this phenomenon,

> We all often feel like we are pulling teeth, even those writers whose prose ends up being the most natural and fluid. The right words and sentences just do not come pouring out like ticker tape most of the time.

This particular hardship is called writer's block, and almost every writer suffers from it from time to time. The exercise at the end of this chapter—

and the one at the end of Chapter 2 of this book—provide some effective (I hope) solutions to this problem.

Finally—even when you've achieved a certain status as a professional—the writer's life is not all glamour, appearances on the "Tonight Show" and chauffeured limousines to gala book signings. E. Annie Proulx, herself a much-celebrated contemporary novelist, comments,

> How many recognize that there is another, darker side to the writing life—risk, stress and peril? You may have noticed how often a new book, usually a first novel or a collection of short stories or poems, appears, followed by three or four decent notices saying, "Thumbs up! Virgil Blitz is a writer to watch!" yet a few months later the book is gone, off the shelves, no paperback appears and the name Virgil Blitz is never seen nor heard again. I can tell you something—Blitz is dead in a ditch somewhere, adrift on an ice floe, trampled in a Missouri hog panic. Another writer lost.

In this passage, Proulx suggests that for every writer who is channeling genial phrases in a blissfully meditative state, there are several writers struggling mightily with various aspects of the writer's life. If "all life involves suffering," as Zen monk Daisetz Togiryo said, then writing is definitely part of life, because it's often a pain.

The writing process demands a nearly impossible mix of honesty, imagination, spontaneity, pointed concentration, attention to the minutest of details, rigorous discipline. Any attempt to speed up the creative process, to force or cajole the muse, will make the fictional text stilted, unnatural, grotesque. You will find yourself having times when your prose springs forth effortlessly, but other times when you feel nearly paralyzed by blocks, disorganization, self-doubt. My purpose in writing this book is to maximize the former, by providing you with practical methodologies and structures, along with some gentle pats of encouragement and sympathy . . . and to minimize the latter, by providing exercises that will keep the words flowing by juicing your muse, and by keeping you focused on your personal goals as a writer—goals that will probably change and evolve over time.

LITERARY MOTIVATION: A SQUID IN YOUR FACE

If writing fiction can be meditative and centering, but also awful, frustrating, and even—as Proulx suggests—hazardous to your health, then a reasonable person might ask: Why do it? The answer varies from writer to writer, from writing teacher to writing teacher, from academic theorist to . . . well, you get the point. From the theoretical perspective, educational psychologist Peter Mortola suggests a deep, underlying motive for constructing narratives. He asks,

Have you ever noticed that friends who have the most disastrous vacations are also the ones with the best stories afterward? This is because sitting on the beach at Waikiki all day may be relaxing, but that's exactly what we would expect. Now sitting on a Waikiki beach and having a squid thrown at you by a local is much more interesting, simply because we didn't expect it. It is an experience that counters our "norms of the way things should be." Breach, trouble, conflict, disequilibrium, surprise: life is full of these, and we make sense of those things, to ourselves and others, through writing/telling a good story.

Mortola says that human beings—from our pre-literate past right up to the present—have always told stories, in order to ascribe meaning, order, logical framing, to an existence that is frequently disordered and maybe inherently meaningless. In this way, narrative has historically (and probably prehistorically, too) taken on a quasi-religious significance in people's lives and serves that same function today.

That significance assumes a variety of forms for different people. Some write for personal reasons: for the pleasure derived from the writing act itself, or for the uncovering of poignant self-discoveries. Other people derive satisfaction from sharing their inner worlds—as represented through their stories—with readers . . . either through publishing their work in literary journals or small presses, or in person, at workshops and classes. Some people belong to that dedicated corps of fiction-writing professionals, who put food on their tables by satisfying the wildly diverse tastes of the reading public with romance novels, soft-core stories, creative-nonfictional magazine articles, and so on. Finally, there are those who engage in the fiction-writing process to discover whether they are the fortunate few who can put pen to paper (or pixel to computer screen) and end up with a title on the *New York Times* bestseller list.

To this list of literary motivations, I would add that some writers—a deranged minority, perhaps—feel a certain compulsion to do it. They can't *not* write. Lamott refers to a friend of hers who tells himself every morning, "It's not like you don't have a choice, because you do—you can either type or kill yourself." This writer—and, by extension, all people who define themselves as writers—really *doesn't* have a choice; for him, it's write or die. I suppose I am another of this breed. For me, writing is not always the meditative practice that Goldberg describes in *Writing Down The Bones,* and sometimes it feels worse than a long morning with the oral surgeon. But the bottom line for me is that, difficult as the writing process may sometimes be, I'm more unhappy when I'm not doing it.

Before you proceed with the nuts-and-bolts exercises in this text, it may be useful for you to identify your own goals as a writer. If your goal is to become a professional fiction writer, you will necessarily approach your writing process differently than if your goal is to write for private, personal expression, and you will probably focus on different elements described here. For instance, if you want to publish short stories or novels, you will pay close attention to the chapters on plot, characterization, point of view, and perhaps some of the fictional subgenres, such as young adult fiction, science fiction, or postmodern fiction.

If, on the other hand, your goal is primarily self-expression and self-discovery, then you may pay closer attention to the sections on description, showing rather than telling, setting, and diary/creative nonfictional writing. The exercise at the end of this chapter will help you identify your goals, so that you can make informed choices about the fictional areas on which you want to concentrate, as you begin your own writing process.

WHY THE WORLD NEEDS THIS CREATIVE WRITING BOOK

There are literally dozens of excellent books on creative writing. I know they exist in great numbers, because I have several stacks of creative writing books on the table next to me, and I'm counting the individual texts: twenty-eight . . . perhaps less than half the creative writing books available at bookstores today. I know most of these are excellent—well-written, informative, even inspirational—because I've read them, and in *The Graceful Lie,* I occasionally quote them to develop certain points I make throughout this text.

Sometimes, when I'm suffering from a nasty case of writer's block, I look at my stacks of creative writing books—a brightly spangled, tumble-down wall like some Roman ruin spray-enamelled with graffiti—and ask myself whether the world needs another writing book. My brief, depressive's answer is: It doesn't. The world needs people to stop dumping industrial solvents into its oceans and a hands-off policy on tropical rainforests. Humankind needs more universally available medical care, food and shelter, and some healthy, gunpowder-free outlets for our innate aggressiveness; and fiction writers, in order to improve, need to do nothing more than to read lots of stories, and to write, write, write . . . just write, in the words of the Zen master.

My longer and perhaps more accurate answer, however, is that the writing process *is* one of those healthy outlets that can improve the human condition to some considerable degree. If people are prey to dark motives, rages, and aggressive urges, then the arts generally—and creative writing high among them—exist as pure and constructive means of discharging impulses both base and joyful . . . thus circumventing the random incident of freeway road-rage, a physical confrontation between spouses, the schoolyard fight that might otherwise escalate into a bloody discharge of Glock pistols and semiautomatic rifles, maybe even diplomatic hostilities between bordering countries. I recently read a bumpersticker on a battered, paint-worn Volkswagen bug. It read, "Art saves lives." While my inner cynic says that's an overly simplistic answer to all the world's problems, I'm just ideal-istic enough to endorse the spirit and intention of that bumpersticker's au-thor. Art increases understanding, and understanding can't help but save lives.

That's where all the creative writing books come in. People want to write, because—even if they don't see themselves as potentially bestselling authors—they intuit that writing might be a healthy creative outlet. Unfor-tunately, those same people often have doubts about their worth as writers, and their ability to maintain a regular writing practice. Texts such as *The Graceful Lie* can boost people's confidence in themselves as creative individ-uals who have rich personal histories. Furthermore, writers and would-be writers benefit from being reminded of certain fictional truths, from a vari-ety of voices—Goldberg's, Burroway's, Minot's, mine—in the same way that chainsmokers benefit from being reminded by physicians, newspaper articles, hour-long televised specials, obituary notices, Cancer Society stud-ies, and Surgeon General reports that inhaling two packs of unfiltered Camels a day may not leave them in optimal health. If we hear certain mes-sages enough times, and from enough credible people, we may actually change our behavior. In that way, *The Graceful Lie* represents one of many valid approaches to the fiction process, each with its own particular empha-sis.

Some texts concentrate exclusively on various techniques of story writing and elements of effective narrative construction, while others focus on the process of imaginative creation without much (or any) attention to the effect that writing might have on readers. *The Graceful Lie* differs from all the other books on my computerside table, simply because it contains *my* ideas about what's useful and motivating to writers, based on long experi-ence as a novelist, short story writer, and university-level fiction writing teacher. I would never be so reckless as to say my approach is better than that of John Gardner, Natalie Goldberg, David Lodge, Anne Lamott, all he-roes of mine in different ways. In fact, *The Graceful Lie* undoubtedly contains echoes of texts I find particularly genial, while adding original insights, ex-ercises, models, as well as a comprehensive organizational framework.

As regards the latter point—organization: following the overview of fiction presented in this chapter, *The Graceful Lie* will provide you with some practical suggestions for getting started and a discussion of the writer's daily routine. The succeeding five chapters deal with specific elements of narrative prose creation: plotting theory, story construction, characteriza-tion, description, and revising. The second broad division of *The Graceful Lie* will provide detailed instruction in a range of fictional modes. "Guest" au-thors who are recognized experts in each of these subgenres will present the chapter material in the second half of the book: prose poetry (Gary Young); creative nonfiction (Christopher Buckley); young adult fiction (Francess Lantz); science fiction (Harlan Ellison and John M. Landsberg); mystery fiction (Sue Grafton); historical fiction (Leonard Tourney); and literary fiction (Barry Gifford). Each chapter will also provide two or three selections of published work that exemplify each fiction-writing task under consideration, along with exercises that build upon each other from one chapter to the next. Following this sequence, you'll gradually and organically develop competence and confidence in yourself as a maker of fiction.

The Love of Books
Gloria Naylor

In answering the question of how she became a writer, when she grew up never reading any writing by a black woman like herself, Gloria Naylor describes how her mother inspired her love of books and education, reminds us of the importance of public education and libraries for all children, particularly poor ones, and traces the subjects of her fiction to her own roots: "You write where you are. It's the only thing you have to give. And if you are fortunate enough, there is a spark that will somehow ignite a work so that it touches almost anyone who reads it." Naylor has written screenplays, short stories, and four novels, among them *The Women of Brewster Place, Mama Day,* and *Bailey's Cafe.*

Any life amounts to "organized chaos": biologically we are more space than matter and that matter consists of careening atoms always in flux; psychologically we are minute electrical charges, running from the brain to the spinal cord, the organs, the hormonal systems. Sitting apart from that is a consciousness that orders, to our specific preferences, any given reality at any given time. A long way of saying: our lives are what we make them. And definitely our "writing lives," which is miming life in both its execution and its product. And so to make sense of the senseless, writers reach for metaphors to explain—to themselves and others—exactly what it is that they do. Those metaphors and the resultant explanations are value-laden; they spring from our specific culture and our personal politics.

Why do I write? The truth, the unvarnished truth, is that I haven't a clue. The answer to that question lies hidden in the same box that holds the origin of human creativity, our imperative need as a species to communicate, and to be touched. Many minds for many years have busied themselves trying to unlock that box, and writers, for the most part, are quite happy to allow the literary critics, anthropologists, psychologists, and biologists to argue interdiscipline and intradiscipline while they stay out of the fray. And when writers are invited in, they'll reach for some shorthand, some metaphor, to throw quickly into the ring so they can get back to doing—for whatever reason—what they do best.

I normally reach for a poem called "The Unclaimed," by Nikky Finney, a young African-American woman who evokes the spirit of all the women in her past "whose names do not ripple in neon lights or whose distinctiveness has yet to be embedded on printed paper." These women, the poet tells us, were never allowed time to pamper themselves in front of mirrors or even time to cry. They were women who sang over stovetops and washtubs; scribbled poems on bits of paper and dinner napkins—women who acted out the drama of their lives unsung and forgotten. And so she concludes:

> for all that you were
> for all that you always wanted to be
> each time i sign my name
> know that it is for a thousand like you
> who could not hold a pen
> but who instead held me
> and rocked me gently
> to the creative rhythms
> i now live by

I elect to trace the untraceable, my passionate love of books and my affair with the written word, back to my mother, who was also an avid lover of books. She and my father were from sharecropping families and grew up in the 1930s in Mississippi. She was not allowed to use the public libraries; and purchasing books was out of the question for her. What many young people tend to forget today, in the age of excessiveness and of almost ingrained waste that we have in consumerist America, is that books were once a luxury for people until the advent of the ten-cent novel which ultimately evolved into the paperback. Most people, especially working-class and poor people, were not able to buy books so they depended on the public libraries. That was why Ben Franklin instituted the free lending library, hoping to give the children of the working class at least a competitive edge with the children of the upper classes, who could afford to have books.

My mother was one of eight children and her family worked collectively on a farm from Monday to Friday to bring in the requisite crop—for them it was cotton. Since this was in the South, in the Bible Belt, it meant that Sunday was spent in church—all day. Saturday was then the only free time my mother had. So while her sisters and brothers went off to town to spend their time, she would hire herself out in someone else's field on her free Saturdays. For that labor, she received fifty cents a day but it was her fifty cents. At the end of the month she had two dollars and she would take that two dollars and send away to book clubs. And that's how she got her reading material.

She made a vow to herself that she would never raise a child in the South. It is ironic that when my parents, in 1949, moved north to New York City, they left behind a region that would eventually become a place much more conducive for African-Americans to hold power than the place to which they fled. But who was to know the future? My mother only knew her past. And her history spoke loud and clear: if you were poor, and if you were black in Tunica County, you were not going to read. She always told my sisters and me that she was not ashamed of her background—it was no sin to be poor. But the greatest sin is to keep people from learning to dream. And my mother believed that books taught the young how to dream. She knew, of course, that she would not be eradicating racism from her life by moving, as Malcolm X said, "from down South to up South." But she was aware that, in New York City at least, her tax dollars would go to support public institutions that would be open to her children.

Because we grew up without much money and a whole lot of dreams, we spent a great deal of time in the public libraries. The law in New York was that a child had to be able to write their name in order to get a juvenile library card. But before my sisters and I had even attained the age of literacy, my mother would take us on these pilgrimages to the library. They live in my mind as small dark rooms with heavy wood bookcases and the heavy desks of the librarian, who looked like Olive Oyl. My mother would say, "Do you see all these books? Once you can write your name, all of these books will be yours. For two weeks. But yours."

I had to get much older to understand why she took us on those pilgrimages. While indeed it was to educate us, I think it was also to heal some place within herself. For me it made the library a place that was quite familiar, a place that was even welcoming. I was eager to be able to qualify to enter those doors. I was eager to discover whatever mystery was within the ink upon that paper, because also within me—and this had to be genetic—was a fascination with the written word. I used to love the feel and the heft of a book. In those days, they were made with a certain kind of glue and when you broke the binding you could smell that special glue. I'm not saying I was getting high off that glue. There was just this wonderful, earthy smell to it.

My mother didn't know then and, of course, at four or five I didn't know that I was on my way to being a very shy and very repressed adolescent. Books were to be my only avenue out of the walls my emotions built around me in those years. I felt trapped within my home and trapped within school, and it was through the pages of books that I was released into other worlds. I literally read my way from the A's to the Z's in the children's section of the library. I can still see that two-shelf row of books, and it ran the whole length of the room. Louisa May Alcott's, I recall, was the first set of books—*Little Women,* and *Little Men,* and *Jo's Boys,* and *Under the Umbrella*—she wrote a whole slew of books following those young women from adolescence into adulthood. I can remember reading all the way through to the last author because there was another set of books by Laura Ingalls Wilder—*Little House on the Prairie, Little House in the Big Woods, Those Happy Golden Years.* Once again following a young girl in her coming-of-age from adolescence all the way into adulthood and marriage. It was the world through which I lived.

I don't believe this would have been enough to have created a writer, although most writers first begin as avid readers. But a writer needs something else—a conscious connection between the validity of their personal experiences and the page. My shyness kept me from communicating verbally, to the point that my teachers thought perhaps I was slow. The theory of education in those years—the fifties and early sixties—held that a well-rounded child participated in class. That meant raising your hand, which for a child like me meant to break out in a cold sweat. The idea that I had to step forth and give voice to something was a nightmare.

My mother, seeing that I was not a talker and understanding that indeed I was, of the three girls, perhaps her most gifted child (the teachers came to understand that later as well because I always excelled in the written tests) went out to Woolworth's and bought me one of those white plastic diaries. I think they went for something like ninety-nine cents in those days, and stamped on it in gold leaf was "One Year Diary"—the kind with the cheap lock your sister could open with a bobby pin. My mother said, "You know, Gloria, I'll bet there are a lot of things going on in the world you don't understand and I'm sure there are even things going on in here in our home that might be troubling you, but since you can't seem to talk to your father and me about these things, why don't you write them down in here." She threw the book on the bed and was wise enough to leave the room, and not belabor the point. I picked up the diary and I did just that, I proceeded to write down all the things that I could not say.

From the age of twelve I made the vital connection between inarticulate feeling and the written word. Whatever went into those original pages are not eternal keepsakes, they are not classic thoughts, but they were my feelings, it was my pain, and the pain was real to me at twelve years old. And we wonder about the rise in teenage suicides. It is because adults resist believing that whatever the demons are, if they're twelve-year-old, thirteen-year-old, fourteen-year-old demons, they are *real*. I know; I had them.

Through the luck of the draw of having a very wise and perceptive mother who happened to match what I needed with the gift of that diary, my life was saved. Because those feelings were going to come out. I was going to speak one day. But the horrifying question is, In what language would those feelings have been expressed? I paraphrase Toni Morrison in *Sula:* An artist without an art form is a dangerous thing. It is probably one of the most dangerous things on this earth. And being a female in the 1960s, I would have, I think, directed that destruction inward as opposed to outward. But instead, I filled up that diary, and then proceeded to fill up the spare pages in my loose-leaf notebook at the end of the school year with my ramblings that slowly turned into poems. The poems slowly evolved into *Twilight Zone*–type short stories—I have always been enamored somehow with the mystical and the idea of alternative realities, and began writing supernatural stories even as an adolescent.

But it took until I was twenty-seven years old for me to believe that I had the faintest chance of being a writer. I went through my adolescence and young adulthood being told that black people did not write books. How did this come about? I was a kid who read to the tune of a book a day, who had been "discovered" by her middle-school teachers, who plied me with extra reading, which I would take home on the weekends. In those hundreds of texts that I read, there was nothing about black Americans or by black Americans. Those authors weren't on the shelves in the public libraries in New York City, and they definitely weren't on my standard junior high school or high school curriculum. If black people had written books, would I not have read them? Would I not have been taught them? If Gwendolyn Brooks had indeed won the Pulitzer Prize the year she did, 1950 (ironically the year I was born), should she not qualify as a talented enough American writer to be on my syllabus?

We do not have to say to our children, "You are nothing." We don't have to stand up in an auditorium, on a parade ground, and blatantly shout out to them, "You have nothing to give." We have done this much more effectively, through silence, through what they do *not* see, through what is *not* there when we parade before them what we declare is worthy. It is a very effective message. It was the one that I received. And I received it from well-meaning people, who thought I was bright, I had a future, I had promise. It took the unrest in the sixties and the kids then in their late teens and early twenties, who were willing to put their careers on the line, their lives on the line—and some lost them at Jackson and Kent State—in order to give birth to the educational institutions that began to exist in the mid-seventies. Ones which taught what America really was, that provided an education that edified and represented the entire citizenry. This was the gift that they gave me. And so by the time I entered Brooklyn College, once again an institution supported by public funds, there was an Africana Studies Department, a Women's Studies Program, Chicano Studies (as they were called in those years), Asian Studies. And I then was able to encounter the works of Ralph Ellison, Toni Morrison, Nikki Giovanni, James Baldwin, Richard Wright, Zora Neale Hurston . . . the list goes on and on. We're not talking about people who deserved a Black Literature Day or a Black Literature Hour in our curriculums. These are names that will be here in the year 3000, because they have helped to define not only American literature, but world literature. I owe those young people who spilled their blood in the sixties a huge debt of gratitude, because by learning that there was this heritage of writers behind me, and specifically black female writers, when I looked in the mirror there was the image I desperately needed to see. What I had seen previously was no image. Slowly, by completing my diet with these books, an outline was filled in. And that outline did not say that black was beautiful, it did not say that black was ugly. It said simply: you are. You exist. It reverberated enough to give me the courage to pick up the pen. And it's what finally validated me.

My first novel, *The Women of Brewster Place,* literally began that very semester at Brooklyn College when I discovered that there was a whole history of black writing in America; and that I had foremothers and forefathers who stood behind me with the ghosts of their excellence. And I was determined that if I had only one novel in me, I was going to write about what I had not had, in those twenty-some odd years of literacy, the privilege to read about. I was going to write all about me. And I knew that if I just chose one female character, one protagonist, she could not do justice to the diversity of the black female experience in America. One woman couldn't do it all. So I hit upon the structure of having different chapters devoted to the lives of different women. I can remember making a mental list of how they would differ. They were to vary, beginning with something as superficial as their skin colors. I know it's not currently in vogue but I do like the word "colored." Because when I look around, that's what I see—colored people—pink on up in the European American; then moving from alabaster to ebony in the black female. We also range from being devotedly religious to almost irreligious. We are young and old. We are political, nonpolitical. We even differ in our sexual preferences. So on this dead-end street, I had hoped to create a whole panorama of what it meant to be black and female in America. To claim and to validate as many lives as I possibly could. To give them each the dignity that I felt they each deserved. To this day I still call that book—which is now fifteen years old—my love letter to the black woman in America. But it first began as a love letter to myself. And by beginning with what was indeed a very visceral and personal statement it had reverberated and touched women all over the world. I have received letters from as far away as Japan, from Korean women who inform me that they are a minority within that society. They saw their own grandparents and aunts on that dead-end street.

Every writer must articulate from the specific. They must reach down where they stand, because there is nothing else from which to draw. Therefore were I to go along with the traditional view that the Western literature began with Homer (a good argument to the contrary is the subject of another essay)—Homer didn't write about the Romans, nor the Phoenicians, nor about the Huns. He wrote about the Greeks because that's what he was. Shakespeare wrote about Elizabethan Englishmen. He put them in the Caribbean, he put them in Denmark, he put them in Verona—but they were all Elizabethan Englishmen. Joyce wrote about the Irish; Philip Roth writes about the Jews, Maxine Hong Kingston about Chinese-Americans. You write where you are. It's the only thing you have to give. And if you are fortunate enough, there is a spark that will somehow ignite a work so that it touches almost anyone who reads it, although it is about a very specific people at a very specific time. And so that's what I attempt to do with my work—to reach down where I am and to articulate those lives. I could spend my entire life, what I have left of a natural life span, writing only about the Brewster Places in America and never exhaust that which is universal to it.

What I plan to do though with the rest of my life is indeed to communicate with images. They will not always be written images. I love working for the stage. I will write for film. I will always have stories to tell. They may not be good stories, they may not be bad stories. But I would like to believe that I will always tell honest stories and that to the lives that come to me I will somehow do them justice.

POINTS TO CONSIDER ABOUT "THE LOVE OF BOOKS"

1. According to this piece, why did Naylor decide to become a writer? Was it a conscious decision? What specific psychological and social forces conspired to turn her into a writer? What forces—similar and different to Naylor's—conspire to make *you* want to write fiction?

2. Why does Naylor begin this reflection on the importance of reading and the writing process with a mechanistic description of human beings as "careening atoms always in flux" and "minute electrical charges"?

3. Explain the literal meaning of the words and explore the possible underlying meanings of the poetry excerpt that Naylor quotes in her piece:

> for all that you were
> for all that you always wanted to be
> each time i sign my name

know that it is for a thousand like you
who could not hold a pen
but who instead held me
and rocked me gently

What does it mean? What does the poem say to Naylor . . . and to you?
Why does the author of the poem not use punctuation or capital letters?

4. Naylor says of her mother's "pilgrimages" with her children to the library, "While indeed it was to educate us, I think it was also to heal
some place within herself." Explain these dual motivations in the author's mother.

5. What is the relationship between Naylor's youthful shyness and her later
becoming a writer, according to this prose piece? What function did the
diary serve for the author as a young person?

How to Keep and Feed a Muse
Ray Bradbury

It isn't easy. Nobody has ever done it consistently. Those who try hardest,
scare it off into the woods. Those who turn their backs and saunter along,
whistling softly between their teeth, hear it treading quietly behind them,
lured by a carefully acquired disdain.

We are of course speaking of The Muse.

The term has fallen out of the language in our time. More often than
not when we hear it now we smile and summon up images of some fragile
Greek goddess, dressed in ferns, harp in hand, stroking the brow of your
perspiring Scribe.

The Muse, then, is that most terrified of all the virgins. She starts if she
hears a sound, pales if you ask her questions, spins and vanishes if you disturb her dress.

What ails her? you ask. Why does she flinch at the stare? Where does
she come from and where go? How can we get her to visit for longer periods of time? What temperature pleasures her? Does she like loud voices, or

soft? Where do you buy food for her, and of what quality and quantity, and what hours for dining?

We might start off by paraphrasing Oscar Wilde's poem, substituting the word "Art" for "Love."

> Art will fly if held too lightly,
> Art will die if held too tightly,
> Lightly, tightly, how do I know
> Whether I'm holding or letting Art go?

For "Art" substitute, if you wish, "Creativity" or "The Subconscious" or "Heat" or whatever your own word is for what happens when you spin like a firewheel and a story "happens."

Another way of describing The Muse might be to reassess those little specks of light, those airy bubbles which float across everyone's vision, minute flaws in the lens or the outer, transparent skin of the eye. Unnoticed for years, when you first focus your attention on them, they can become unbearable nuisances, ruptures in one's attention at all hours of the day. They spoil what you are looking at, by getting in the way. People have gone to psychiatrists with the problem of "specks." The inevitable advice: ignore them, and they'll go away. The fact is, they don't go away; they remain, but we focus out beyond them, on the world and the world's ever-changing objects, as we should.

So, too, with our Muse. If we focus beyond her, she regains her poise, and stands out of the way.

It is my contention that in order to Keep a Muse, you must first offer food. How you can feed something that isn't yet there is a little hard to explain. But we live surrounded by paradoxes. One more shouldn't hurt us.

The fact is simple enough. Through a lifetime, by ingesting food and water, we build cells, we grow, we become larger and more substantial. That which was not, *is*. The process is undetectable. It can be viewed only at intervals along the way. We know it is happening, but we don't know quite how or why.

Similarly, in a lifetime, we stuff ourselves with sounds, sights, smells, tastes, and textures of people, animals, landscapes, events, large and small. We stuff ourselves with these impressions and experiences and our reaction to them. Into our subconscious go not only factual data but reactive data, our movement toward or away from the sensed events.

These are the stuffs, the foods, on which The Muse grows. This is the storehouse, the file, to which we must return every waking hour to check reality against memory, and in sleep to check memory against memory, which means ghost against ghost, in order to exorcise them, if necessary.

What is The Subconscious to every other man, in its creative aspect becomes, for writers, The Muse. They are two names for one thing. But no matter what we call it, here is the core of the individual we pretend to extol, to whom we build shrines and hold lip services in our democratic society. Here is the stuff of originality. For it is in the totality of experience reckoned with, filed, and forgotten, that each man is truly different from all others in the world. For no man sees the same events in the same order, in his life. One man sees death younger than another, one man knows love more quickly than another. Two men, as we know, seeing the same accident, file it with different cross-references, in another part of their own alien alphabet. There are not one-hundred elements, but two billion elements in the world. All would assay differently in the spectroscopes and scales.

We know how fresh and original is each man, even the slowest and dullest. If we come at him right, talk him along, and give him his head, and at last say, What do you want? (Or if the man is very old, What *did* you want?) every man will speak his dream. And when a man talks from his heart, in his moment of truth, he speaks poetry.

I have had this happen not once but a thousand times in my life. My father and I were really not great friends, until very late. His language, his thought, from day to day, were not remarkable, but whenever I said, "Dad, tell me about Tombstone when you were seventeen," or "the wheatfields, Minnesota, when you were twenty," Dad would begin to speak about running away from home when he was sixteen, heading west in the early part of this century, before the last boundaries were fixed—when there were no highways, only horse paths, and train tracks, and the Gold Rush was on in Nevada.

Not in the first minute, or the second, or the third minute, no, did the thing happen to Dad's voice, did the right cadence come, or the right words. But after he had talked five or six minutes and got his pipe going, quite suddenly the old passion was back, the old days, the old tunes, the weather, the look of the sun, the sound of the voices, the boxcars traveling late at night, the jails, the tracks narrowing to golden dust behind, as the West opened up before—all, all of it, and the cadence there, the moment, the many moments of truth, and, therefore, poetry.

The Muse was suddenly there for Dad.

The Truth lay easy in his mind.

The Subconscious lay saying its say, untouched, and flowing off his tongue.

As we must learn to do in our writing.

As we can learn from every man or woman or child around us when, touched and moved, they tell of something they loved or hated this day, yesterday, or some other day long past. At a given moment, the fuse, after sputtering wetly, flares, and the fireworks begin.

Oh, it's limping crude hard work for many, with language in their way. But I have heard farmers tell about their very first wheat crop on their first farm after moving from another state, and if it wasn't Robert Frost talking, it was his cousin, five times removed. I have heard locomotive engineers talk about America in the tones of Tom Wolfe who rode our country with his style as they ride it in their steel. I have heard mothers tell of the long night with their firstborn when they were afraid that they and the baby might die. And I have heard my grandmother speak of her first ball when she was seventeen. And they were all, when their souls grew warm, poets.

If it seems I've come the long way around, perhaps I have. But I wanted to show what we all have in us, that it has always been there, and so few of us bother to notice. When people ask me where I get my ideas, I laugh. How strange—we're so busy looking out, to find ways and means, we forget to look *in*.

The Muse, to belabor the point then, is there, a fantastic storehouse, our complete being. All that is most original lies waiting for us to summon it forth. And yet we know it is not as easy as that. We know how fragile is the pattern woven by our fathers or uncles or friends, who can have their moment destroyed by a wrong word, a slammed door, or a passing fire-wagon. So, too, embarrassment, self-consciousness, remembered criticisms, can stifle the average person so that less and less in his lifetime can he open himself out.

Let's say that each of us has fed himself on life, first, and later, on books and magazines. The difference is that one set of events happened to us, and the other was forced feeding.

If we are going to diet our subconscious, how prepare the menu?

Well, we might start our list like this:

Read poetry every day of your life. Poetry is good because it flexes muscles you don't use often enough. Poetry expands the senses and keeps them in prime condition. It keeps you aware of your nose, your eye, your ear, your tongue, your hand. And, above all, poetry is compacted metaphor or simile. Such metaphors, like Japanese paper flowers, may expand outward into gigantic shapes. Ideas lie everywhere through the poetry books, yet how rarely have I heard short story teachers recommending them for browsing.

My story, "The Shoreline at Sunset," is a direct result of reading Robert Hillyer's lovely poem about finding a mermaid near Plymouth Rock. My story, "There Will Come Soft Rains," is based on the poem of that title by Sara Teasdale, and the body of the story encompasses the theme of her poem. From Byron's, "And the Moon Be Still as Bright," came a chapter for my novel *The Martian Chronicles*, which speaks for a dead race of Martians who will no longer prowl empty seas late at night. In these cases, and dozens of others, I have had a metaphor jump at me, give me a spin, and run me off to do a story.

What poetry? Any poetry that makes your hair stand up along your arms. Don't force yourself too hard. Take it easy. Over the years you may catch up to, move even with, and pass T. S. Eliot on your way to other pastures. You say you don't understand Dylan Thomas? Yes, but your ganglion does, and your secret wits, and all your unborn children. Read him, as you can read a horse with your eyes, set free and charging over an endless green meadow on a windy day.

What else fits in our diet?

Books of essays. Here again, pick and choose, amble along the centuries. You'll have much to pick over from the days before the essay became less popular. You can never tell when you might want to know the finer points of being a pedestrian, keeping bees, carving headstones, or rolling hoops. Here is where you play the dilettante, and where it pays to do so. You are, in effect, dropping stones down a well. Every time you hear an echo from your Subconscious, you know yourself a little better. A small echo may start an idea. A big echo may result in a story.

In your reading, find books to improve your color sense, your sense of shape and size in the world. Why not learn about the senses of smell and hearing? Your characters must sometimes use their noses and ears or they may miss half the smells and sounds of the city, and all of the sounds of the wilderness still loose in the trees and on the lawns of the city.

Why all this insistence on the senses? Because in order to convince your reader that he is *there,* you must assault each of his senses, in turn, with color, sound, taste, and texture. If your reader feels the sun on his flesh, the wind fluttering his shirt sleeves, half your fight is won. The most improbable tales can be made believable, if your reader, through his senses, feels certain that he stands at the middle of events. He cannot refuse, then, to participate. The logic of events always gives way to the logic of the senses. Unless, of course, you do something really unforgivable to wrench the reader out of context, such as having the American Revolution won with machine guns, or introducing dinosaurs and cave men into the same scene (they lived millions of years apart). Even with this last, a well-described, technically perfect Time Machine can suspend disbelief again.

Poetry, essays. What about short stories, novels? Of course. Read those authors who write the way you hope to write, those who think the way you would like to think. But also read those who do not think as you think or write as you want to write, and so be stimulated in directions you might not take for many years. Here again, don't let the snobbery of others prevent you from reading Kipling, say, while no one else is reading him.

Ours is a culture and a time immensely rich in trash as it is in treasures. Sometimes it is a little hard to tell the trash from the treasure, so we hold back, afraid to declare ourselves. But since we are out to give ourselves texture, to collect truths on many levels, and in many ways, to test ourselves against life, and the truths of others, offered us in comic strips, TV shows, books, magazines, newspapers, plays, and films, we should not fear to be seen in strange companies. I have always felt on good terms with Al Capp's "Lil Abner." I think there is much to be learned about child psychology from "Peanuts." A whole world of romantic adventure has existed, beautifully drawn by Hal Foster in his "Prince Valient." As a boy I collected and was perhaps influenced in my later books by the wonderful middle-class American daily strip "Out Our Way" by J. C. Williams. I am as much Charlie Chaplin in *Modern Times* in 1935 as I am Aldous Huxley's reader-friend in 1961. I am not one thing. I am many things that America has been in my time. I had enough sense to keep moving, learning, growing. And I have never reviled or turned my back on the things I grew out of. I learned from Tom Swift, and I learned from George Orwell. I delighted in Edgar Rice Burroughs's *Tarzan* (and still respect that old delight and will not be brainwashed from it) as today I delight in the C. S. Lewis's *Screwtape Letters*. I have known Bertrand Russell and I have known Tom Mix, and my Muse has grown out of the mulch of good, bad, and indifferent. I am such a creature as can remember with love not only Michelangelo's Vatican ceilings but the long-gone sounds of the radio show, "Vic and Sade."

What is the pattern that holds all this together? If I have fed my Muse on equal parts of trash and treasure, how have I come out at the farther end of life with what some people take to be acceptable stories?

I believe one thing holds it all together. Everything I've ever done was done with excitement, because I wanted to do it, because I loved doing it. The greatest man in the world for me, one day, was Lon Chaney, was Orson Welles in *Citizen Kane,* was Laurence Olivier in *Richard III.* The men change, but one thing remains always the same: the fever, the ardor, the delight. Because I wanted to do, I did. Where I wanted to feed, I fed. I remember wandering, stunned, off a stage in my home town, holding a live rabbit given to me by Blackstone the Magician in the greatest performance ever! I remember wandering, stunned, in the papier-mâché streets of the Century of Progress Exhibition in Chicago in 1933; in the halls of the Venetian doges in Italy in 1954. The quality of each event was immensely different, but my ability to drink it in, the same.

This does not mean to say that one's reaction to everything at a given time should be similar. First off, it cannot be. At ten, Jules Verne is accepted, Huxley rejected. At eighteen, Tom Wolfe accepted, and Buck Rogers left behind. At thirty, Melville discovered, and Tom Wolfe lost.

The constant remains: the search, the finding, the admiration, the love, the honest response to materials at hand, no matter how shabby they one day seem, when looked back on. I sent away for a statue of an African gorilla made of the cheapest ceramics when I was ten, said statue a reward for enclosing the wrapper from a package of Fould's Macaroni. The gorilla, arriving by mail, got a reception as large as that given the Boy David at his first unveiling.

The Feeding of the Muse then, which we have spent most of our time on here, seems to me to be the continual running after loves, the checking of these loves against one's present and future needs, the moving on from simple textures to more complex ones, from naïve ones to more informed ones, from nonintellectual to intellectual ones. Nothing is ever lost. If you have moved over vast territories and dared to love silly things, you will have learned even from the most primitive items collected and put aside in your life. From an ever-roaming curiosity in all the arts, from bad radio to good theatre, from nursery rhyme to symphony, from jungle compound to Kafka's *Castle*, there is basic excellence to be winnowed out, truths found, kept, savored, and used on some later day. To be a child of one's time is to do all these things.

Do not, for money, turn away from all the stuff you have collected in a lifetime.

Do not, for the vanity of intellectual publications, turn away from what you are—the material within you which makes you individual, and therefore indispensable to others.

To feed your Muse, then, you should always have been hungry about life since you were a child. If not, it is a little late to start. Better late than never, of course. Do you feel up to it?

It means you must still take long walks at night around your city or town, or walks in the country by day. And long walks, at any time, through bookstores and libraries.

And while feeding, How to *Keep* Your Muse is our final problem.

The Muse must have shape. You will write a thousand words a day for ten or twenty years in order to try to give it shape, to learn enough about grammar and story construction so that these become part of the Subconscious, without restraining or distorting the Muse.

By living well, by observing as you live, by reading well and observing as you read, you have fed Your Most Original Self. By training yourself in writing, by repetitious exercise, imitation, good example, you have made a clean, well-lighted place to keep the Muse. You have given her, him, it, or whatever, room to turn around in. And through training, you have relaxed yourself enough not to stare discourteously when inspiration comes into the room.

You have learned to go immediately to the typewriter and preserve the inspiration for all time by putting it on paper.

And you have learned the answer to the question asked earlier: Does creativity like loud or soft voices?

The loud, the passionate voice seems to please most. The voice upraised in conflict, the comparison of opposites. Sit at your typewriter, pick characters of various sorts, let them fly together in a great clang. In no time at all, your secret self is roused. We all like decision, declaration; anyone loudly for, anyone loudly against.

This is not to say the quiet story is excluded. One can be as excited and passionate about a quiet story as any. There is excitement in the calm still beauty of a *Venus de Milo.* The spectator, here, becomes as important as the thing viewed.

Be certain of this: When honest love speaks, when true admiration begins, when excitement rises, when hate curls like smoke, you need never doubt that creativity will stay with you for a lifetime. The core of your creativity should be the same as the core of your story and of the main character in your story. What does your character want, what is his dream, what shape has it, and how expressed? Given expression, this is the dynamo of his life, and your life, then, as Creator. At the exact moment when truth erupts, the subconscious changes from wastebasket file to angel writing in a book of gold.

Look at yourself then. Consider everything you have fed yourself over the years. Was it a banquet or a starvation diet?

Who are your friends? Do they believe in you? Or do they stunt your growth with ridicule and disbelief? If the latter, you haven't friends. Go find some.

And finally, have you trained well enough so you can say what you want to say without getting hamstrung? Have you written enough so that you are relaxed and can allow the truth to get out without being ruined by self-conscious posturings or changed by a desire to become rich?

To feed well is to grow. To work well and constantly is to keep what you have learned and know in prime condition. Experience. Labor. These are the twin sides of the coin which when spun is neither experience nor labor, but the moment of revelation. The coin, by optical illusion, becomes a round, bright, whirling globe of life. It is the moment when the porch swing creaks gentle and a voice speaks. All hold their breath. The voice rises and falls. Dad tells of other years. A ghost rises off his lips. The subconscious stirs and rubs its eyes. The Muse ventures in the ferns below the porch, where the summer boys, strewn on the lawn, listen. The words become poetry that no one minds, because no one has thought to call it that. Time is there. Love is there. Story is there. A well-fed man keeps and calmly gives forth his infinitesimal portion of eternity. It sounds big in the summer night. And it is, as it always was down the ages, when there was a man with something to tell, and ones, quiet and wise, to listen.

A CLOSING NOTE

"The first movie star I remember is Lon Chaney.

The first drawing I made was a skeleton.

The first awe I remember having was of the stars on a summer night in Illinois.

The first stories I read were science-fiction stories in *Amazing*.

The first time I ever went away from home was to go to New York and see the World of the Future enclosed in the Perisphere and shadowed by the Trylon.

My first decision about a career was at eleven, to be a magician and travel the world with my illusions.

My second decision was at twelve when I got a toy typewriter for Christmas.

And I decided to become a writer. And between the decision and the reality lay eight years of junior high school, high school, and selling newspapers on a street corner in Los Angeles, while I wrote three million words.

My first acceptance came from Rob Wagner's *Script* Magazine, when I was twenty.

My second sale was to *Thrilling Wonder Stories.*

My third was to *Weird Tales.*

Since then I have sold 250 stories to almost every magazine in the U.S., plus writing the screenplay of *Moby Dick* for John Huston.

I have written about the Lon Chaney-and-the-skeleton-people for *Weird Tales.*

I have written about Illinois and its wilderness in my *Dandelion Wine* novel.

I have written about those stars over Illinois, to which a new generation is going.

I have made worlds of the future on paper, much like that world I saw in New York at the Fair as a boy.

And I have decided, very late in the day, that I never gave up my first dream.

I am, like it or not, some sort of magician after all, half-brother to Houdini, rabbit-son of Blackstone, born in the cinema light of an old theatre, I would like to think (my middle name is Douglas; Fairbanks was at his height when I arrived in 1920), and matured at a perfect time—when man makes his last and greatest step out away from the sea that birthed him, the cave that sheltered him, the land that held him, and the air that summoned him so that he could never rest.

In sum, I am a piebald offspring of our mass-moved, mass-entertained, alone-in-a-New-Year's-crowd age.

It is a great age to live in and, if need be, die in and for. Any magician worth his salt would tell you the same."

POINTS TO CONSIDER ABOUT "HOW TO KEEP AND FEED A MUSE"

1. Why does Bradbury characterize the Muse as "she"—a female presence? Does this relate exclusively to the classical roots of the term, or might he be suggesting certain archetypal characteristics (some might say sexist stereotypes) traditionally associated with women—or both?

2. Bradbury makes a comparison between the Muse and "those little specks of light, those airy bubbles which float across everyone's vision, minute flaws in the lens or the outer, transparent skin of the eye." What point about literary creation is implied in this analogy? Does this point in any way undermine the notion of "keeping" the Muse, as suggested in the title of this piece?

3. What specific activities does Bradbury "list" for nurturing the creative faculty? Can you add any other activities that work for you, and might work for others, to "diet" the subconscious?

4. According to the author, why is it so important for you to improve "your color sense, your sense of shape and size in the world . . . " along with "the senses of smell and hearing"? What does this suggest about the writing of fictional settings and characterizations?

5. In the "closing note" to this piece, Bradbury lists a number of "firsts" and other accomplishments; what is his rhetorical (i.e., persuasive) intention in appending "How to Keep and Feed a Muse" with this list? What does he mean by the statement at the end: "I am a piebald [means spotted or patched in color, by the way] offspring of our mass-moved, mass-entertained, alone-in-a-New-Year's-crowd age."?

WRITING ACTIVITIES: INTRODUCTION

Freewriting is a friendly method for exploring ideas, recording sense impressions, and increasing your fluency as a writer. An English professor and composition theorist, Peter Elbow, originated this technique, suggesting that students could avoid the horror of writer's block by writing whatever came into their minds, and/or reporting external sounds, smells, sights, as well as physical feelings.

The only rule in freewriting, as described by Elbow—and Rule #2 of the fiction writer's handbook—is to keep writing. All other rules and formal considerations—grammar, punctuation, spelling, logical sequencing, thematic focus—go out the window temporarily with this exercise. Just keep writing, and if you find yourself unable to think of anything to say, merely write, "I find myself unable to think of anything to say," or, "This is an extremely stupid exercise," or, "I hate Peter Elbow," over and over. You will eventually get bored with the repeated phrase, and your subconscious mind will begin to supply some new insights and sensations—perhaps ones that you didn't even know you had: happy surprise!

Freewriting can be focused or unfocused. In the unfocused freewrite, you merely sit with a blank piece of paper or a new word processing file and let the words come, with no particular topic to explore. The typical unfocused freewrite by a student in a classroom setting might sound like this:

> Our teacher has a cold today and he looks like a rag-muffin—red nose,
> watery eyes, mussed hair—but I don't want to hurt his feelings b/c after
> all he's here instead of at home where he should be. I hope hes not a
> walking petri dish of germs, since I'm sitting in the front row! I felt the
> fall today and my longjohns are out of hibernation, they warm my arms
> & legs & make me feel alls well in the world even though there's a possi-
> bility of germ warfare in the middle east i read in the paper today. Cold
> today, end of the world tomorrow. Well I guess its all a part of the deal
> on this bumpy road of life, balance of good and evil the age old story
> and all that. Here's one thing I know for sure its rice pudding and only
> rice pudding i want in this moment & if I ever get done with this exer-
> cise i'll head down to the U. Center cafeteria for some rice pudding—
> damn good for institutional food, good for ANY food ANYWHERE!!
> Rice pudding could make people so happy that theyd forget about all
> their differences and realize we're all in the same boat, b/c everybody
> loves pudding, so rice pudding could bring the wld together once and
> for all.

Note the abrupt changes in focus, the lack of scrupulous attention to
spelling and grammar, the rambling, obsessive fixation on the sociopolitical
implications of rice pudding. By contrast, in the focused freewrite, you
write as a means of exploring and opening up a certain idea or issue. A five-
minute focused freewrite by a student responding to the question, "What is
your favorite television program, and why?" in an American Popular Culture course, might come out this way:

> Modern American television ranks somewhere up there on the list of
> pastimes right behind having an enema. Social themes explored in the
> afternoon sitcom, I hope, fail to depict an accurate view of modern
> young adulthood. If today's teens are actually as petty and cruel as a
> great number of the midday entertainment (if they can be called that)
> shows predict, then the current state of interpersonal relationships, if
> measured by turbulent ratings, would send our seismic anomaly equip-
> ment to the repair room. If, however, we have not yet come to a point
> where our youth are seeking petty revenge with unrelenting fist, then
> shows such as those in question are only reinforcing negative behaviors.
> If programs such as the Discovery Channel, the Weather channel and
> other non-biased, non-stereotyping forms of communication were being
> broadcasted, T.V. may have proved to be a wonderful invention. As it is,
> unfortunately the power of T.V. is being misused to serve as a harbinger
> of cheap entertainment.

This freewrite has certain elements in common with the previous one: shifts
in focus, run-on passages, imaginative leaps. It also features some unusual
verbal constructions, such as "right behind having an enema," "seismic
anomaly," and "harbinger of cheap entertainment." This is typical of the
freewriting process. When you allow your subconscious mind free access to
paper or computer screen, it will often reward you with startlingly original

phrasings: Some you may end up using in your final drafts, others you will eventually discard as excessive, confusing, or inconsistent with the tone you're trying to establish in your fictional piece.

Your first exercise in *The Graceful Lie* asks you to spend an hour engaged in the freewriting process: do three separate twenty-minute focused freewrites, in response to at least three of the following questions:

- Why am I engaged in this writing process at this moment? Why would I choose to do this exercise over taking a healthful walk or eating a Twinkie?
- What specific emotions and physical sensations am I experiencing as I do this exercise? Do I find the writing process enjoyable or dreadful, or a combination of the two?
- What do I hope to achieve by making a commitment to engage regularly in the writing process?
- What areas of my personal experience can I use to give my fiction an air of validity?
- What are my strengths as a writer or as a creative/ imaginative person? What is my greatest fear about making a commitment to fiction writing? What about the writing process do I anticipate enjoying?
- Who are some of my literary heroes? Would I like to write in a style that emulates any of these people? Are there certain types of writing I've read that I didn't particularly like and would prefer to avoid emulating?

I strongly suggest that you *not* attempt all three freewrites during the same sitting. You will probably have more positive results (and less severe hand and/or brain cramping) if you write for twenty minutes, take a break of several hours' duration, and then start the next freewrite. This non-writing downtime will give your subconscious mind a chance to recharge itself, so that you'll begin each freewrite with a fresh perspective and maximum creative energy.

When you've finished the freewriting portion of this exercise, you may want to go around the class and read your freewrites aloud . . . or not. Since freewriting tends to be a highly personal business, some people may feel reluctant to share revealing passages with relative strangers—in other words, classmates—especially early in the quarter or semester, when the class hasn't yet evolved into a supportive learning community. It 's perfectly acceptable to pass on reading your work aloud at this point, if you so choose. After everyone has had a chance to read, it might be illuminating to follow the reading with some discussion: List the various motivations that class members have for writing fiction. You might even come up with some additions to the list of motivations provided in this chapter.

2

First Things

CONCRETENESS, RISK, AND THE JOY OF FAILURE

My father was a television writer in the early 1960s. He had a tiny, dark office in what was then the tallest building in Santa Monica, California: a black and gold deco-angular tower that's since been leveled and replaced by a frozen yogurt parlor. My father occupied the top floor of this building eight hours a day, six days a week. On those special occasions when I joined him at work—usually when my mother tired of hearing my plastic soldiers fire burp-gun blasts at each other—I would amuse myself with silent war games on the scarred hardwood floor, while Dad hunkered down in front of his paintworn Smith-Corona. He had used that venerable typewriter for so many years that each key had filmed over with a layer of caked sweat, making it impossible to see the letter on any but the least-used keys, like z and x and the numbers. Sometimes my father would take time out from his writing to bend down and give me a kiss, his beard stubble coarse against my cheek, the scent of cigar smoke clinging to him like mortality, his fingers black from fingering sheets of carbon paper all day long.

What does this brief description of Joe Petracca and his office have to do with a chapter on getting started as a fiction writer? In writing prose of any kind—whether a science fiction story or a book on how to write a science fiction story, it's always a good idea to balance your abstractions (that is, ideas and concepts) with concrete descriptions that readers can grasp with one or more of the senses. In the foregoing paragraph, for example, I created a visual, auditory, tactile, and olfactory impression of a nonfictional character, my father, to provide a sense-break from my lengthy intellectualizing about the writing process. Furthermore, the passage illustrates one of the basic Rules (#3) of the writing workshops I teach: Have a healthy fear of taking risks, but take them anyway. I've read lots of chapters in lots of creative writing books. Not one of them started with a description of the author's father's cigar breath. It may be that nobody ever started a chapter that way before because it's a dumb idea, but conversely it may be a genial notion that nobody considered until this very moment. The genius scenario has my vote.

For originality's sake, I encourage students to indulge even the most outrageous of creative impulses. Break the rules of grammar for effect, invent words, flaunt formal conventions, foil readers' expectations: These subversive activities keep the writing process interesting and—dare I say it?—fun. Furthermore, you'll sometimes even end up with a passage worth keeping . . . like the foregoing passage about my father, which my editor obviously decided wasn't too precious or self-serving, or she would have slashed it and you wouldn't have had the opportunity to read it just now.

Of course, taking risks inevitably leads to some spectacular flops as well. For an example of the latter, I need go no further than the previous chapter of *The Graceful Lie*, which, you'll remember, contains a description of a pile of books as "a brightly spangled, tumbledown wall like some Roman ruin spray-enamelled with graffiti." In my first draft, the phrase was much more gaudy—"a brightly spangled, tumbledown wall like some Roman ruin spray-enamelled with graffiti, papered with political broadsides and spattered by clown vomit"—to which my editor replied with her usual bluntness: "The content and style are fine, but I don't get the political reference, and 'clown vomit' frankly turns my stomach. Lose it, or I'm going to quit this job and go to work in a FotoMat."

My editor was right [*as always—ed.*]. I had been shooting for a chaotic, over-the-top, splash-of-confetti-with-an-edge kind of image, but I ended up with a foul conceit suggesting a circus geek who pukes M&Ms. Following my editor's suggestion, I cut the phrase, and the reading world is a better place for its absence. Still, I can't fault myself for having indulged the impulse to aim for an entirely new way to create a description of a pile of books, as that's one of my goals as a writer: to find felicitous new ways to express timeless and universal human perceptions and themes. In pursuing this elusive goal, you'll sometimes succeed, but more often you'll fail . . . and that's O.K. Such failure may actually be growthful for you as a writer, like falling repeatedly on your rump while learning to snowboard, or throwing two hundred teacups on the Zen pottery wheel before you get one "right." As Samuel Beckett says in *Worstward Ho* (part of a trilogy of prose pieces written late in his life): "No matter. Try again. Fail again. Fail better."

Words to live—and write—by.

AVOID THE HEARTBREAK OF SAGGY PROSE: YOUR WRITING TIME

Just as there are no fixed rules for creating a story, so every writer must discover the most effective time, location, and tools for writing. It is axiomatic among writers and writing teachers that one should try to write at roughly the same time, and for approximately the same number of hours, every day. Professional writers often carve out a full workday that they devote exclusively to their craft, since writing provides their bread, butter, mortgage, and Rolls-Royce payments. For a contemporary example, prolific mystery writer Robert Parker says that he needs "essentially, a 9-to-5 writing schedule" to produce his novels. Ditto my father, as illustrated above. However, for most of us whose writing must be secondary to other professional or academic activities, a full day of writing isn't an option. We have to work our writing time around the demands of work, school, and householding.

Many writers, even professional ones, tailor their schedules to the nonliterary demands their lives place on them. French Caribbean novelist Maryse Conde says of her writing schedule:

> I get up at five o'clock, and I work until twelve. At twelve, I go down and cook some food for my husband and myself; and since it is very hot in Guadeloupe at that time, I take a siesta until three P.M., and from three to seven, I work again. I don't work at night because I have very bad eyes. I developed something in one of my eyes, and I have to be very careful. So I don't work by electric lights. I work during the day. I work every day unless I'm sick or a member of my family or friends are visiting.

As Conde suggests here, it's quite possible—if not always easy—to observe a rigorous writing schedule while meeting the various demands of life and honoring one's physical or geographic limitations.

A practical, general rule for your writing schedule should be the following: Set aside a chunk of time that you can manage every day, without—and this is the central point—having it become an additional stressor in your life. If you try to jam three hours of writing into an already-too-busy schedule, writing will become just another taxing chore, and you will eventually break your schedule. I guarantee it. Furthermore, the quality of your writing will suffer. As Gabriel Garcia Marquez, Nobel laureate from Colombia, has observed on this point, "The big problem for most writers who don't earn enough to be able to write full time is that they write in their spare time, in other words when they are tired. This is literature produced by tired men.". . . and, the modern critic might add, by tired women.

To avoid producing the kind of saggy prose that Marquez describes, set up a realistic schedule for yourself, and make sure you write when you're relatively refreshed . . . ideally when the subconscious mind is most accessible to you. For the latter reason, I choose to write every morning, when I am closest to dreams. Other writers work late at night, when they're relaxed, have had some rest from the work day (and perhaps a nice glass of '88 Merlot), other members of the household are asleep or watching Letterman, and sleep is not far off. Whatever your unique life situation may be, the regular-writing-time axiom is a crucial one and should be followed rigorously, if it's at all possible for you. Even if your schedule seems impossibly busy, identify a daily (preferably including weekend days?) block of time that is exclusively reserved for writing, even if it's only a half-hour or an hour a day, and let that time have the meditative quality described in the previous chapter.

It's remarkable how much you can accomplish, even if you only write for a brief stretch every day, on a regular basis. For example, writing for two or three hours every morning, I end up with approximately one page of rough draft-quality prose per day (unless I'm mired in one of those salt-marshy writer's block periods). Averaging that page a day, I wind up with around three hundred and fifty pages of manuscript material at the end of a year . . . enough to edit into a novel of average length (or a fiction how-to book like this one, or a college composition textbook, or several short stories, magazine columns, and pieces of popular culture criticism), at the relatively modest investment of a few hours a day.

Of course, that's just me. Daily writing production varies greatly from person to person, depending on number of hours scheduled for writing per day, temperament (hyperactive versus kicked-back), rate of metabolism, level of caffeine intake, typing speed, onset of carpal tunnel symptoms, and so on. I know from long experience that I am not a quick writer. I am a long-distance plodder, like to turn a sentence around fifty times before going on to the next one. That is to say, before going on to the next sentence, I like to turn a sentence around fifty-one times. I must therefore make peace with my single modest page at the end of every writing session. At the other end of the spectrum, there are those naturally prolific writers you hear about, glib wordsmiths who can crank out a novel in a few months or less. Nineteenth-century novelist Anthony Trollope is reputed to have written four manuscript-quality pages of fiction an hour—or an average of around twenty pages a day (!)—during the lengthy span of his career. For a pop-cultural example, mystery writer Ed McBain (whose real name is Evan Hunter) says of his own prodigious output, "I used to do ten pages a day. Now I try to do about forty pages a week. I've cut down a bit." At the rate of forty usable pages a week, one could write several books a year. However, Trollope and McBain are the genius exceptions. Most people can expect that their natural writing output will probably fall somewhere between a half-page and three pages a day, if they stick to a regular schedule.

At this moment, I find myself regretting that I raised the issue of daily page production at all, as it contradicts the process-oriented Zen approach I recommended in the first chapter. I bring up the issue of page quantity only to illustrate that one can produce a substantial amount of writing with a minimal daily writing regimen. I therefore need to caution strongly against counting pages as a regular practice. My suggestion to you would be this: While it's useful for some people (especially people who write articles that are supposed to conform to certain length requirements) to hold a page- or word-number goal in the recesses of their minds, it's far more important simply to write during the time you allot for yourself.

Whether you can only manage a half-hour a day—or whether you decide to quit your job, rent a solitary garret in the attic of an ivy-covered Victorian cottage, and write twenty-three hours a day—adhere religiously to your chosen routine, so that writing becomes as much a habit as brushing your teeth. If you find yourself belonging to the former camp—people who can realistically devote less than an hour a day for writing—that's fine: This book provides models for some shorter fictional forms, such as the prose poem, that you can complete in a relatively short time, and with a great deal of personal satisfaction.

The bottom line for the time/quantity discussion is this: As much as possible, avoid focusing on product, especially during the first-draft phase. Just commit to whatever number of hours is realistic and enjoyable for you, and write. If you want to concern yourself with the public readability and critical worthiness of your work, save that for the revision process.

HERMITS ANONYMOUS: WHERE TO WRITE

A book such as this one can't provide a prescription for the optimal writing environment—the space most conducive to creating fictional prose—because people's circumstances and preferences vary widely. Some writers have the enviable ability to sit down anywhere and write. Creative nonfiction author Kelly Cherry, for example, reports in the brief biography accompanying her *Writing the World* that "she writes wherever she is." Like Cherry, certain writers can write on crowded buses in Khartoum, or during soccer matches in Birmingham, or at the kitchen table while their kids are gleefully (and loudly) playing Chutes and Ladders underfoot. The latter group actually derive comfort from being enveloped in the warm bosom of family, and this sense of well-being informs their composition process.

Similarly, many of my college-level creative writing students insist that they have no problem writing in their dorm rooms or cramped apartments, while roommates are conversing loudly in the same room, or next-door neighbors are pumping Rage Against the Machine at top volume on the stereo. In fact, some writers tune out the distractions of daily life by wearing headphones and playing their favorite tunes at top volume—creating their own personal cacophony that envelopes and apparently energizes them. One of my students, Dave Pevker, said recently during office hours:

> I crank some tunes like Feral Suicide at eleven-plus on my headphones and my mom's all, "That's just noise, Davey," and I'm all, "I know it's noise, Moms, but it's MY noise, and it helps me to, like, clear my mind, you know what I'm saying?"

It may not make sense to Dave Pevker's mother—and it probably wouldn't work for me—but Dave has found an effective way to keep his mind "clear" for imaginative creation. Whatever works, keep doing it . . . as long as it doesn't do long-term damage to your eardrums.

By contrast, many writers require an ample measure of quiet aloneness. Some even demand a total withdrawal from the world, in order to achieve the frame of mind necessary for the sensitive and timid imagination to emerge, like a young damselfish poking tentatively from the craggy recesses of a tropical reef. We reclusives (I proclaim myself a member of this group: Hi, my name is Mike, and I'm a friendless loner . . .) accomplish this delicate balancing act with a variety of ingenious solutions. Fiction writer Alix Kates Shulman, for example, actually spends half the year on an island and the other half "in the world," writing and engaging in feminist politics. For those of us whose professional and/or personal commitments keep us from spending half the year on an island, a local "getaway" writing space may serve as a happy compromise. Some people, as illustrated at the beginning of this chapter, rent office space and hole themselves up there, while others (like myself) set aside a separate writing room within their homes—a space where loved ones are admitted only by using a secret knock and at great peril to themselves.

Even if you're a college student who shares living quarters with roommates, it's possible to define a few square feet of desk space, or a corner of the library that you visit regularly, as quasi-sacred writing territory. The amount of space you carve out for your writing isn't important. Most people don't need a Polynesian island or a tower office to achieve a writerly frame of mind. The important thing, whether you have a reclusive or more expansive writing temperament, is to write consistently, in a place that is conducive to freeing up your imagination.

THE GREAT YELLOW PAD DEBATE

Throughout most of this century, writing was either done by hand—with pencil/pen on paper—or with a typewriter. For those readers born after the Beatles broke up, the typewriter was a clever device that resembled the front end of a Jeep and produced typeset-looking characters by means of a keyboard that actuated a set of bars, which in turn struck a piece of paper through an inked ribbon. If one wanted to produce multiple copies of a document, the writer used thin sheets of "carbon paper" coated on one side with a dark pigment—hence the screenwriter's blackened fingers at the beginning of this chapter.

Nowadays, that quaint, antiquated contrivance has been replaced on most writers' desks by the personal computer, which uses the same keyboard setup as a typewriter but has a number of significant advantages over traditional methods of generating text. Using word processing software, the writer can revise "on the fly," experimenting with a variety of word combinations in one sentence before going on to the next. As Myron C. Tuman writes in a recent issue of *Computers and Composition,*

> With word processing, it becomes as easy to revise a text as to leave it alone; indeed, most of the playful aspects of the computer only come into play when we begin manipulating text we have already entered.

Similarly, the fiction writer can revise drafts of manuscript material without having to retype the whole novel or story over again, as one had to do in the "old days" . . . in other words, fifteen years ago. The computer allows one to check for typing and spelling errors, which even the most meticulous proofreaders and former spelling-bee champs inevitably commit. It offers an almost endless variety of page-formatting options, including fonts, italicized and boldfaced text, typeset-quality em-dashes (—), simplified indentation for block quotes such as Tuman's passage in this paragraph, and so on. Computers allow for easy (and usually reliable) storage and transmission of text files. Additionally, they can help individuals with hearing, vision, and speech impairments and learning disabilities to become independent writers.

Personally, and at the risk of sounding like an evangelical tech-nerd, I swear by computer-aided writing. In fact, I probably would never have written a novel had it not been for computer technology. Before the popular availability of home PC's, I wrote and published mainly poetry. Because my style of writing lends itself to continual revision—and because poems are very short—I could retype many drafts of them before ending up with final draft copy. When I got my first Apple IIe, though, everything changed. I quickly realized that I could produce a more extended mass of writing, even a book-length manuscript, and revise it without having to retype draft after draft. That single revelation gave me the impetus I needed to start my first novel, and the rest is literary history, at least in my own mind. Many writers are not so enamored of word processing, or computer technology in general. Across the world, in fact, there is a small but vocal movement of individuals who call themselves (or who are called by the media) neo-Luddites, "a group of anti-technologists who view the digital revolution with a sense of horror and dread," in the words of popular journalist Steven Levy. Just as certain individuals resisted the effects of the industrial revolution during the nineteenth and early-twentieth centuries, so neo-Luddites see computers as potential agents of dehumanization, depersonalization, and social control.

Adherents to the hardcore neo-Luddite party line are relatively few, but there are significant numbers of people who—while not viewing computers as the devil's plaything—nevertheless have serious reservations about the effect of computers on the current state of writing and publishing. For some people, this antipathy to computer-aided writing is personal: They simply don't like sitting in front of cathode-ray tubes for extended periods of time. College student Jeff Bixby, writing in the University of Washington *Daily*, says that he doesn't use a word processor because "I can write faster than I can type," and adds: "Our parents and teachers have told us all our lives that TV ruins our eyes. What? Sitting two feet from a computer screen won't?"

Like Bixby, a significant number of people feel more comfortable handwriting their manuscripts and then retyping the hand-produced material into final draft form. Israeli author Amos Oz, for example, prefers to write in longhand, without the help of a word processor, because he likes "strolling around his room" while composing his text. For other writers, the no-tech approach gives them a sense of connection with a simpler and more organic past, when the writer had a more tangible physical connection to words. Certain contemporary writers are so invested in hand-producing fictional text that the yellow lined pad seems to have taken on an almost mystical importance. Priscilla Lampkin, a noted writer of regional creative nonfiction, says,

> I love the legal pad. Revel in its secure firmness and accommodating flexibility, its color of cornflowers blowing in a field. Happy but not hysterical yellow. The predictable row of lines, like storm swells moving in from the Pacific and taking form as they pass over the continental shelf—these promise order, regularity, perhaps even naughty blue restraint. Subtle but staunch and unrelenting rule. The legal pad is the new-pressed papyrus or blank marble tablet of the imagination, and I wouldn't think of writing a single blessed word without one.

Lampkin's description of the yellow pad is the most extravagant I've read, but she is not alone in favoring them. Numerous writers prefer pen and paper to word processors, because they feel that generating text by hand is more genuinely authorial. Other people resist computers because of the implication they carry for the future of publishing and literary scholarship. In researching this topic, I've run across a surprising number of students and collectors of manuscripts who worry that in the future, word processors will eliminate drafts of novels and stories, thus depriving critics of valuable insights into certain writers' literary processes.

Furthermore, there exists a concern—especially among publishers and editors—that word processing and desktop publishing will flood their desks with amateurish manuscripts, thereby making it much more difficult to discover truly "worthy" pieces of writing. Social critic George Slanger laments in the *Midwest Quarterly* that the tedious process of typing and retyping used to form a natural barrier between publisher and an author. "Only those with something important to say (or a secretary) could penetrate it," he says. Nowadays, the argument goes, all those people who own—or will own—computers will be cranking out reams of mediocre draft material, making the jobs of editors and publishers next to impossible.

From the publisher's perspective, the latter argument may have the ring of annoying truth, but my job in this book isn't to bring added convenience to editors' lives. [*But it's a healthy impulse for writers to stay on our good side—ed.*] My job, as I see it, is to make the writing process as easy and pleasurable for you as possible, and perhaps to give you some guidelines for writing "worthy" prose, the kinds of fiction editors will be likely to favor. One of my prescriptions for making your writing life easier is to work with a word processor, if you can afford or have regular access to one.

If you know from experience that you're naturally more comfortable handwriting your prose and typing it later—or if you're a yellow pad-carrying neo-Luddite (a political stance with which I sympathize, by the way, although I confess to being personally enslaved to the dark forces of cyber-culture)—then it would be foolish for me to insist that you process words electronically. You've already discovered a text-generating technique that works well for yourself, and that technique will become the practice that you employ during your regular writing time, and in your writerly space. If, on the other hand, you don't despise all things high-tech or aren't a confirmed hand-writer, I strongly recommend composing directly to the computer.

Practically stated, word processing gives you the highest probability for generating language with fluency, revising your prose effectively, and producing error-free final copy in quantities sufficient to send out to editors or agents, if publishing is your final goal. And if that means publishers' desks end up buried in manuscripts . . . well, they'll just have to hire more junior editors, which will boost the economy and keep all those recently-graduated English majors off the streets—a boon for all concerned.

WRITE WHAT YOU KNEW

You now have: a cozy attic room with ivy winding around the windows (or an unswept corner of a vacant downtown industrial warehouse); a desk with a comfortable, ergonomically designed captain's seat (or an aluminum-legged, Formica-topped breakfast table with a stern taskmaster of a straight-backed oak library chair); a Tandoori 2002 computer system with 96 megs of RAM, word processing software, built in voice-recognition capability, spellchecker, grammar checker, thesaurus, and sixty-thousand-word dictionary (or a pad of lined paper with a number-two Eberhard Faber pencil—preferably sharpened); and a regular chunk of time you will routinely devote to your writing (unless it's Grover Cleveland's birthday, and you're much too busy celebrating). You have a writing space, a schedule, and appropriate materials. You're ready to start making stories. All you need is a subject. This is where some people get stuck.

Creative writing students often lament that they don't know what to write about. "My life is boring," they say. "I go to work, come home, make dinner, watch T.V. I don't know anything about spies or pirates or detectives or explosives. What could I write about that anybody would be interested in reading?" Likewise, college-age writers may complain, "I'm too young, I haven't done anything interesting yet. All I do is go to school, do homework, party sometimes. Who wants to read about a bunch of kids drinking and getting sick?"

The short answer to that question is: nobody . . . unless you write about drinking and getting sick very, very well. The longer answer also embodies the seventh most popular axiom in the creative writing teacher's quiver of Rules to Write By. That axiom is: Write what you know. In other words, write from your own experience. Your present life may seem as though it consists mainly of unexciting routine and repetition—not the stuff from which gripping plots are built—but even if you're "only" twenty, you have a wealth of experiences, including childhood ones, on which to base wonderfully evocative settings, fascinating characters, realistic dialogue, and situations that have the ring of universal truth. As a contemporary and popular example of this approach, Richard Price—author of the critically acclaimed *Clockers*, among numerous other hard-edged fictional pieces—"advises would-be writers to source out material from their own childhood to write great stories," according to a recent article in the *Paris Review*.

This isn't to say that you have to start out writing nothing but girl-meets-dog stories. You may have a science fiction or mystery piece already fully plotted in your mind or outlined on your computer, and you've just been waiting for the time and place to get started on it. If that's the case, then go for it, following some of the formal recommendations made in succeeding chapters of this book. But if you find yourself staring blankly at your computer screen or yellow pad, then I'd suggest that you begin at the beginning—yours. As Lamott says, "Start with your childhood . . . Plug your nose and jump in, and write down all your memories as truthfully as you can." From such memories can emerge powerful stories with gripping plots and important themes.

Keep in mind, however, that at some point in your writing process, you will undoubtedly find yourself moving from the primordial pools of childhood/adolescent experience, onto the solid ground of the present. When you start writing every day, according to the schedule suggested above, you'll naturally begin to develop a writer's frame of mind. You'll discover that your present life—the one that you thought was hopelessly mundane and predictable—is actually rich, overbrimming with story-worthy episode and deep feeling. You will gradually learn to recognize and collect all the poignant interpersonal connections, the absurd small talk, the richly comical blunders, the grief-charged losses, the heated human conflicts that occur in the course of your daily life—experiences that you may register, record, and later incorporate in your fiction. In my experience, the personal journal is the most effective way to begin recording daily occurrences that might find their way into fictional constructs. The exercises at the end of this chapter will get you started with the journal-keeping process.

Journal of a Solitude
May Sarton

OCTOBER 11*th*

The joke is on me. I filled this weekend with friends so that I would not go down into depression, not knowing that I should have turned the corner and be writing poems. It is the climactic moment of autumn, but already I feel like Sleeping Beauty as the carpet of leaves on the front lawn gets thicker and thicker. The avenue of beeches as I drive up the winding road along the brook is glorious beyond words, wall on wall of transparent gold. Laurie Armstrong came for roast beef Sunday dinner. Then I went out for two hours late in the afternoon and put in a hundred tulips. In itself that would not be a big job, but everywhere I have to clear space for them, weed, divide perennials, rescue iris that is being choked by violets. I really get to weeding only in spring and autumn, so I am working through a jungle now. Doing it I feel strenuously happy and at peace. At the end of the afternoon on a gray day, the light is sad and one feels the chill, but the bitter smell of earth is a tonic.

I can hardly believe that relief from the anguish of these past months is here to stay, but so far it does feel like a true change of mood—or rather, a change of *being* where I can stand alone. So much of my life here is precarious. I cannot always believe even in my work. But I have come in these last days to feel again the validity of my struggle here, that it is meaningful whether I ever "succeed" as a writer or not, and that even its failures, failures of nerve, failures due to a difficult temperament, can be meaningful. It is an age where more and more human beings are caught up in lives where fewer and fewer inward decisions can be made, where fewer and fewer real choices exist. The fact that a middle-aged, single woman, without any vestige of family left, lives in this house in a silent village and is responsible only to her own soul means something. The fact that she is a writer and can tell where she is and what it is like on the pilgrimage inward can be of comfort. It is comforting to know there are lighthouse keepers on rocky islands along the coast. Sometimes, when I have been for a walk after dark and see my house lighted up, looking so alive, I feel that my presence here is worth all the Hell.

I have time to think. That is the great, the greatest luxury. I have time to be. Therefore my responsibility is huge. To use time well and to be all that I can in whatever years are left to me. This does not dismay. The dismay comes when I lose the sense of my life as connected (as if by an aerial) to many, many other lives whom I do not even know and cannot ever know. The signals go out and come in all the time.

Why is it that poetry always seems to me so much more a true work of the soul than prose? I never feel elated after writing a page of prose, though I have written good things on concentrated will, and at least in a novel the imagination is fully engaged. Perhaps it is that prose is earned and poetry given. Both can be revised almost indefinitely. I do not mean to say that I do not work at poetry. When I am really inspired I can put a poem through a hundred drafts and keep my excitement. But this sustained battle is possible only when I am in a state of grace, when the deep channels are open, and when they are, when I am both profoundly stirred and balanced, then poetry comes as a gift from powers beyond my will.

I have often imagined that if I were in solitary confinement for an indefinite time and knew that no one would ever read what I wrote, I would still write poetry, but I would not write novels. Why? Perhaps because the poem is primarily a dialogue with the self and the novel a dialogue with others. They come from entirely different modes of being. I suppose I have written novels to find out what I *thought* about something and poems to find out what I *felt* about something.

OCTOBER 17ᵗʰ

The long warm autumn has come to an end—hard frost last night, a cold gray sky. When I woke it was snowing! These are only flurries, but what a change! I picked the last nasturtiums yesterday. They are shriveled now, and even the parsley has been "touched." I have the very last bunch of garden flowers on my desk—a few yellow marigolds, one pale yellow and pink rose, and two others in bud. Now it will have to be florists' flowers with their awful sameness, none of the delightful home-grown mixtures of the spring, summer, and fall.

It has been next to impossible to keep at this journal lately because I am writing poems and they take the marrow of my energy. Things stir and buzz in my mind but do not get sorted out on paper. Today I want to think a little about loyalty, and it is a fact that I can think something out only by writing it. It is interesting that there is very little about loyalty under that heading in the *Oxford Book of Quotations* or in Bartlett; yet it must be one of the crucial concepts having to do with human relations, closely connected with trust. I am accused of disloyalty because I talk about things that many people would keep to themselves, and especially because I may discuss with people who "should not know" a human situation in which I am involved. I am not at all discreet about anything that concerns feeling. My business is the analysis of feeling.

It is the same with money—both human problems and money flow out of this house very freely, and I believe that is good. At least, it has to do in both cases with a vision of life, with an ethos. Might there be a valid distinction to be made between gossip (re human affairs) and boasting (re money) and this free flow in which I believe? I am always so astonished, after all the years when I had none, that I now have money to give away that sometimes I may speak of it out of sheer joy. No one who has inherited a fortune would ever do this, I suspect—*noblesse oblige*. No doubt it is shocking to some people. But I am really rather like a child who runs about saying, "Look at this treasure I found! I am going to give it to Peter, who is sad, or to Betty, who is sick." It reminds me of the old days with Kot* and James Stephens when we made up endless fantasies about what we would do when we were rich . . . and being *very* rich then meant not having to worry about every week's expenses! Being very rich so far as I am concerned is having a margin. The margin is being able to give.

---

*S. S. Koteliansky.

I do not feel disloyal when I talk about my own life or that of the many others who pour in here in one way or another. What I am loyal to, I hope, is something more complex, i.e., I would not *use* things I know about anyone's private life to further my own ends. That would be both indiscreet and disloyal. But I believe we learn through the experiences of others as well as through our own, constantly meditating upon them, drawing the sustenance of human truth from them, and it seems natural to me to wish to share these *aperçus,* these questions, these oddities, these dilemmas and pangs. Why? Partly, I suppose, because the more one is a receptacle of human destinies, as I have become through my readers, the more one realizes how very few people could be called happy, how complex and demanding every deep human relationship is, how much real pain, anger, and despair are concealed by most people. And this is because many feel their own suffering is unique. It is comforting to know that we are all in the same boat. Into this house comes the despair now of many middle-aged women, to take one example.

I myself am engaged in trying to maintain a not altogether simple or easy human relationship in love that I talk about with true friends, for illumination. It has been immensely comforting lately to talk with D and to share what we are each learning through pain about our loves. I feel honored that we can talk as we do, and I do not feel it disloyal to the partners in each case. Why? Because it is "pure." We are sharing our experience in order better to understand it. D and I surely recognized each other the first time we talked some months ago. I have not felt this intimacy based on instant "recognition" so strongly since I first knew Bill Brown, thirty or more years ago. D and I are the same breed of cat, responsive and sensitive close to the surface, willing to give ourselves away. Such people rarely lead happy lives, but they do lead lives of constant growth and change. Gerald Heard's saying "he must go unprotected that he may be constantly changed" always comes to mind when I am speaking of what it is to be a poet and to go on writing poetry beyond the meridian of life. It is costly, so one has to hug very hard those like Bill Brown and D whom one has recognized.

DECEMBER 1st

The darkness again. An annihilating review in the Sunday *Times*. I must have had a premonition, as I felt terribly low in my mind all weekend. Now it is the old struggle to survive, the feeling that I have created twenty-four "children" and every one has been strangled by lack of serious critical attention. This review is simply stupid. But what hurts is the lack of respect shown by Francis Brown in not getting a reviewer who had some knowledge of my work and would be able to get inside it with sympathetic understanding. It is odd that nonfiction appears to get a better break these days than fiction. On a deeper level I have come to believe (perhaps that is one way to survive) that there is a reason for these repeated blows—that I am not meant for success and that in a way adversity is my climate. The inner person thrives on it. The challenge is there to go deeper.

What a lonely business it is . . . from the long hours of uncertainty, anxiety, and terrible effort while writing such a long book, to the wild hopes (for it looked like a possible best seller, and the *Digest* has it for their condensed books) and the inevitable disaster at the end. I have had many good reviews and cannot really complain about that. What I have not had is the respect due what is now a considerable opus. I am way outside somewhere in the wilderness. And it has been a long time of being in the wilderness. But I would be crazy if I didn't believe that I deserve better, and that eventually it will come out right. The alternative is suicide and I'm not about to indulge in that fantasy of revenge.

Somehow the great clouds made the day all right, a gift of splendor as they sailed over our heads.

POINTS TO CONSIDER ABOUT MAY SARTON'S DIARY ENTRIES FROM *JOURNAL OF A SOLITUDE*

1. What does writing mean to Sarton, as expressed in these diary entries? Is it merely a job or something more? What function does this specific form—the diary—serve for her? Cite specific examples from the text to support your assertions.

2. What, according to the author, is the difference between poetry and prose? What personal and/or social functions does each of these literary vehicles serve, in Sarton's opinion. What are your own feelings and thoughts about this distinction?

3. These diary pieces are excerpted from a longer diary collection entitled *Journal of a Solitude.* What role does solitude play in the writing process, according to the author? How important is solitude in your own writing process?

4. Each of these pieces contains some description of natural setting: for example, "The long warm autumn has come to an end—hard frost last night, a cold gray sky" in the October 17th entry. Why does Sarton include this description of external setting? Is it just an aside, in the same way that the weather report complements a television newscast, or is there a more important—possibly even thematic—reason for including this external description?

5. List all the possible functions this diary serves for Sarton, and cite examples from her writing as evidence for each of your points. To Sarton's list of diary functions, add some of your own: how do you (if you already use diaries)—or might you (if you haven't already incorporated the diary into your daily writing practice)—use the diary to help you progress as a writer . . . and even to develop as a person?

Hellish Speed . . . Grappling with the California Highway Patrol . . . Mano a Mano on Highway 61

Hunter S. Thompson

Tuesday, 12:30 P.M. . . . Baker, California . . . Into the Ballantine Ale now, zombie drunk and nervous. I recognize this feeling: three or four days of booze, drugs, sun, no sleep and burned out adrenalin reserves—a giddy, quavering sort of high that means the crash is coming. But when? How much longer? This tension is part of the high. The possibility of physical and mental collapse is very real now. . . .

. . . but collapse is out of the question; as a solution or even a cheap alternative, it is *unacceptable.* Indeed. This is the moment of truth, that fine and fateful line between control and disaster—which is also the difference between staying loose and weird on the streets, or spending the next five years of summer mornings playing basketball in the yard at Carson City.

No sympathy for the devil; keep that in mind. Buy the ticket, take the ride . . . and if it occasionally gets a little heavier than what you had in mind, well . . . maybe chalk it off to forced *consciousness expansion:* Tune in, freak out, get beaten. It's all in Kesey's Bible. . . . The Far Side of Reality.

And so much for bad gibberish; not even Kesey can help me now. I have just had two very bad emotional experiences—one with the California Highway Patrol and another with a phantom hitchhiker who may or may not have been who I thought it was—and now, feeling right on the verge of a bad psychotic episode, I am hunkered down with my tape machine in a "beer bar" that is actually the back room of a huge Hardware Barn—all kinds of plows and harnesses and piled-up fertilizer bags, and wondering how it all happened.

About five miles back I had a brush with the CHP. Not stopped or pulled over: nothing routine. I always drive properly. A bit fast, perhaps, but always with consummate skill and a natural feel for the road that even cops recognize. No cop was ever born who isn't a sucker for a finely-executed hi-speed Controlled Drift *all the way around* one of those cloverleaf freeway interchanges.

Few people understand the psychology of dealing with a highway traffic cop. Your normal speeder will panic and immediately pull over to the side when he sees the big red light behind him . . . and then we will start apologizing, begging for mercy.

This is wrong. It arouses contempt in the cop-heart. The thing to do— when you're running along about a hundred or so and you suddenly find a red-flashing CHP-tracker on your trail—what you want to do then is *accelerate*. Never pull over with the first siren-howl. Mash it down and make the bastard chase you at speeds up to 120 all the way to the next exit. He will follow. But he won't know what to make of your blinker-signal that says you're about to turn right.

This is to let him know you're looking for a proper place to pull off and talk . . . keep signaling and hope for an off-ramp, one of those uphill side-loops with a sign saying "Max Speed 25" . . . and the trick, at this point, is to suddenly leave the freeway and take him into the chute at no less than a hundred miles an hour.

He will lock his brakes about the same time you lock yours, but it will take him a moment to realize that he's about to make a 180-degree turn at this speed . . . but you will be *ready* for it, braced for the Gs and the fast heel-toe work, and with any luck at all you will have come to a complete stop off the road at the top of the turn and be standing beside your automobile by the time he catches up.

He will not be reasonable at first . . . but no matter. Let him calm down. He will want the first word. Let him have it. His brain will be in a turmoil: he may begin jabbering, or even pull his gun. Let him unwind; keep smiling. The idea is to show him that you were always in total control of yourself and your vehicle—while *he* lost control of everything.

It helps to have a police/press badge in your wallet when he calms down enough to ask for your license. I had one of these—but I also had a can of Budweiser in my hand. Until that moment, I was unaware that I was holding it. I had felt totally on top of the situation . . . but when I looked down and saw that little red/silver evidence-bomb in my hand, I knew I was fucked. . . .

Speeding is one thing, but Drunk Driving is quite another. The cop seemed to grasp this—that I'd blown my whole performance by forgetting the beer can. His face relaxed, he actually smiled. And so did I. Because we both understood, in that moment, that my Thunder Road, moonshine-bomber act had been totally wasted: We had both scared the piss out of ourselves for nothing at all—because the fact of this beer can in my hand made any argument about "speeding" beside the point.

He accepted my open wallet with his left hand, then extended his right toward the beer can. "Could I have that?" he asked.

"Why not?" I said.

He took it, then held it up between us and poured the beer out on the road.

I smiled, no longer caring. "It was getting warm, anyway," I said. Just behind me, on the back seat of the Shark, I could see about ten cans of hot Budweiser and a dozen or so grapefruits. I'd forgotten all about them, but now they were too obvious for either one of us to ignore. My guilt was so gross and overwhelming that explanations were useless.

The cop understood this. "You realize," he said, "that it's a crime to . . ."

"Yeah," I said. "I know. I'm guilty. I understand that. I knew it was a crime, but I did it anyway." I shrugged. "Shit, why argue? I'm a fucking criminal."

"That's a strange attitude," he said.

I stared at him, seeing for the first time that I was dealing with a bright-eyed young sport, around thirty, who was apparently enjoying his work.

"You know," he said, "I get the feeling you could use a nap." He nodded. "There's a rest area up ahead. Why don't you pull over and sleep a few hours?"

I instantly understood what he was telling me, but for some insane reason I shook my head. "A nap won't help," I said. "I've been awake for too long—three or four nights; I can't even remember. If I go to sleep now, I'm dead for twenty hours."

Good God, I thought. What have I said? This bastard is trying to be human; he could take me straight to jail, but he's telling me to take a fucking nap. For Christ sake, *agree* with him: Yes, officer, *of course* I'll take advantage of that rest area. And I can't tell you how *grateful* I am for this break you want to give me. . . .

But no . . . here I was insisting that if he turned me loose I would boom straight ahead for L.A. which was true, but why *say* it? Why *push* him? This is not the right time for a showdown. This is Death Valley . . . get a grip on yourself.

Of course. Get a grip. "Look," I said. "I've been out in Las Vegas covering the Mint 400." I pointed to the "VIP Parking" sticker on the windshield. "Incredible," I said. "All those bikes and dune buggies crashing around the desert for two days. Have you seen it?"

He smiled, shaking his head with a sort of melancholy understanding. I could see him thinking. Was I dangerous? Was he ready for the vicious, time-consuming scene that was bound to come if he took me under arrest? How many off-duty hours would he have to spend hanging around the courthouse, waiting to testify against me? And what kind of monster lawyer would I bring in to work out on him?

I knew, but how could he?

"OK," he said. "Here's how it is. What goes into my book, as of noon, is that I apprehended you . . . for driving too fast for conditions, and advised you . . . with this written warning"—he handed it to me—"to proceed no further than the next rest area . . . your stated destination, right? Where you plan to take a long nap . . ." He hung his ticket-pad back on his belt. "Do I make myself clear?" he asked as he turned away.

I shrugged. "How far is Baker? I was hoping to stop there for lunch."

"That's not in my jurisdiction," he said. "The city limits are two-point-two miles beyond the rest area. Can you make it that far?" He grinned heavily.

"I'll try," I said. "I've been wanting to go to Baker for a long time. I've heard a lot about it."

"Excellent seafood," he said. "With a mind like yours, you'll probably want the land-crab. Try the Majestic Diner."

I shook my head and got back in the car, feeling raped. The pig had done me on all fronts, and now he was going off to chuckle about it—on the west edge of town, waiting for me to make a run for L.A.

I got back on the freeway and drove past the rest area to the intersection where I had to turn right into Baker. As I approached the turn I saw . . . Great Jesus, it's him, the hitchhiker, the same kid we'd picked up and terrified on the way out to Vegas. Our eyes met as I slowed down to make the corner. I was tempted to wave, but when I saw him drop his thumb I thought, no, this is not the time . . . God only knows what that kid said about us when he finally got back to town.

Acceleration. Get out of sight at once. How could I be sure he'd recognized me? But the car was hard to miss. And why else would he back away from the road?

Suddenly I had two *personal* enemies in this godforsaken town. The CHP cop would bust me for sure if I tried to go on through to L.A., and this goddamn rotten kid/hitchhiker would have me hunted down like a beast if I stayed. (Holy Jesus, Sam! There he is! That guy the kid *told* us about! He's back!)

Either way, it was horrible—and if these righteous outback predators ever got their stories together . . . and they would; it was inevitable in a town this small . . . that would cash my check all around. I'd be lucky to leave town alive. A ball of tar and feathers dragged onto the prison bus by angry natives. . . .

This was it: The crisis. I raced through town and found a telephone booth on the northern outskirts, between a Sinclair station and . . . yes . . . the Majestic Diner. I placed an emergency collect call to my attorney in Malibu. He answered at once.

"They've nailed me!" I shouted. "I'm trapped in some stinking desert crossroads called Baker. I don't have much time. The fuckers are closing in."

"Who?" he said. "You sound a little paranoid."

"You bastard!" I screamed. "First I got run down by the CHP, then that *kid* spotted me! I need a lawyer *immediately!*"

"What are you doing in Baker?" he said. "Didn't you get my telegram?"

"What? Fuck telegrams. I'm in *trouble.*"

"You're supposed to be in Vegas," he said. "We have a suite at the Flamingo. I was just about to leave for the airport. . . ."

I slumped in the booth. It was too horrible. Here I was calling my attorney in a moment of terrible crisis and the fool was deranged on drugs—a goddamn vegetable! "You worthless bastard," I groaned. "I'll cripple your ass for this! All that shit in the car is *yours!* You understand that? When I finish testifying out here, you'll be *disbarred!*"

"You brainless scumbag!" he shouted. "I sent you a telegram! You're supposed to be covering the National District Attorneys' Conference! I made all the reservations . . . rented a white Cadillac convertible . . . the whole thing is *arranged!* What the hell are you doing out there in the middle of the fucking desert?"

Suddenly I remembered. Yes. The telegram. It was all very clear. My mind became calm. I saw the whole thing in a flash. "Never mind," I said. "It's all a big joke. I'm actually sitting beside the pool at the Flamingo. I'm talking from a portable phone. Some dwarf brought it out from the casino. I have total credit! Can you grasp that?" I was breathing heavily, feeling crazy, sweating into the phone.

"Don't come anywhere near this place!" I shouted. "Foreigners aren't welcome here."

I hung up and strolled out to the car. Well, I thought. This is how the world works. All energy flows according to the whims of the Great Magnet. What a fool I was to defy him. He knew. He knew all along. It was He who sacked me in Baker. I had run far enough, so He nailed me . . . closing off all my escape routes, hassling me first with the CHP and then with this filthy phantom hitchhiker . . . plunging me into fear and confusion.

Never cross the Great Magnet. I understood this now . . . and with understanding came a sense of almost terminal relief. Yes, I would go back to Vegas. Slip the Kid and confound the CHP by moving *East* again, instead of

West. This would be the shrewdest move of my life. Back to Vegas and sign up for the Drugs and Narcotics conference; me and a thousand pigs. Why not? Move confidently into the midst. Register at the Flamingo and have the White Caddy sent over at once. Do it right; remember Horatio Alger. . . .

I looked across the road and saw a huge red sign that said BEER. Wonderful. I left the Shark by the phone booth and reeled across the highway into the Hardware Barn. A Jew loomed up from behind a pile of sprockets and asked me what I wanted.

"Ballantine Ale," I said . . . a very mystic long shot, unknown between Newark and San Francisco.

He served it up, ice-cold.

I relaxed. Suddenly everything was going right; I was finally getting the breaks.

The bartender approached me with a smile. "Where ya headin', young man?"

"Las Vegas," I said.

He smiled. "A great town, that Vegas. You'll have good luck there; you're the type."

"I know," I said. "I'm a Triple Scorpio."

He seemed pleased. "That's a fine combination," he said. "You can't lose."

I laughed. "Don't worry," I said. "I'm actually the district attorney from Ignoto county. Just another good American like yourself."

His smile disappeared. Did he understand? I couldn't be sure. But that hardly mattered now. I was going back to Vegas. I had no choice.

POINTS TO CONSIDER ABOUT "HELLISH SPEED . . ."

1. Thompson sets this piece up like a diary or journal, complete with an initial date and time. How much of what follows is "real"—a faithful reporting of actual events—in your opinion, and how much is added for effect? If a diary contains fictional material, does it still deserve to be called a diary, or should it be called something else?

2. This piece begins in present tense ("I recognize this feeling . . .") and then shifts into past tense ("The cop seemed to grasp . . .") about a third of the way into the story. Why does Thompson make this temporal shift? How does this affect the diary-like tone of the piece?

3. Do you believe that the narrator of this piece is actually Thompson, or a caricature of the author, exaggerated for rhetorical effect? What clues can you find in this piece that would support your opinion? What is your

"gut" reaction to the narrator—do you find him sympathetic or repellent? What was Thompson's intention in creating a narrator of this kind?

4. How does the tone of this piece differ from that of May Sarton's diary excerpts in the previous example? What specific details of language, what literary devices, and what narrative events contribute to the tone that Thompson creates in this chapter from *Fear and Loathing in Las Vegas?*

5. Toward the end of this piece, Thompson's narrator says, "Register at the Flamingo and have the White Caddy sent over at once. Do it right; remember Horatio Alger . . . ." Who is Horatio Alger, and what thematic point about this story—and the entire text of *Fear and Loathing in Las Vegas*—does this allusion suggest? In what ways does this story comment satirically on the myth of the "American dream"?

My Turn
Sara Paretsky

At four the little girl's hair is a frizzy mass, a knot of tight curls around her head instead of the fine straight silk of other girls her age. Her mother makes one forlorn attempt to set it right, to put it in pincurls and smooth it out. But when the bobby pins come out, instead of the glossy curls the mother hoped for the daughter's frizz now stands up wildly all over her head.

'Witch! You're a witch!' Her older brother dances in a circle around her, pointing and doubling up in laughter.

The little girl scowls fiercely. 'I *am* a witch,' she says menacingly. 'And witches know everything.'

The brother's laughter collapses. He races to the kitchen, calling to his mother, 'Sara says she's a witch and witches know everything. She doesn't really know everything, does she?'

The mother soothes him and tells him of course not, that his sister was just making it up. That was my first story.

The Witch of the Seahouse lived in a beautiful stone house on a deserted beach. The water shimmered as if under moonlight even during the day. The Witch of the Seahouse used to come to me when I was very little, but afterwards she was replaced by the evil Witch of the Moon, who lived only in the dark, including the darkest part of my brain. After the day of my hair the Witch of the Seahouse never came back to me.

Soon after that my mother, weary of my unruly frizz and the tears at shampoo-time, cut my hair close to my head. If I tried letting it grow out my father would mock me at dinner, telling me I looked like a sheepdog and to get it cut. I wore it short for many years, like my four brothers, like a fifth son.

In the stories I told in my head my hair was long and straight and glossy. In real life I was the Witch of the Moon, a monster. I struggled unsuccessfully for years to overcome the differences of appearance, of personality, of sex, that seemed to mark me as a monster both at home and in the world beyond.

It was only as I got older and began to absorb the example of my mother's cousin Agnes that I came to see myself differently. It took a long time to realize you could be independent, have a strong will, be a woman—and be human, not an evil witch. (And it wasn't until I read Woolf's 'Professions for Women' two years ago that I realized how universal the conflict between being angel and monster is for women who write.)

When I was little Agnes frightened me: she embodied too many strange qualities anathema to the world I lived in. I grew up in Kansas in the golden age of America, in a society where everyone had a defined place, where everyone knew right from wrong—and what happened when you forgot.

We had mandatory prayer (Prostestant) in our public schools. The same schools barred blacks from college-track courses. In those golden days they knew better than to agitate about it. Abortion was a crime. Only bad girls had sex outside marriage—whereupon they reaped their inevitable punishment since such contraceptives as existed weren't available to unmarried women.

Best of all, we little girls knew we were destined to be mommies. We didn't worry about careers. Except for some married teachers the only women who worked were those too strange or too unfortunate to get husbands. And they were secretaries or waited tables in the coffee shops.

Our dreams were of our weddings. When Roxanne Farrell 'had to get married' in our sophomore year of high school, to us the most tawdry part was that she bought her trousseau at Woolworths. Good girls who waited until they graduated from high school or college bought fancy bridalwear at the Plaza in Kansas City.

Agnes—unmarried, travelling where and when she wanted (as I write this she's seventy-one and trekking in Nepal), living not with a husband but a woman friend—was an embarrassment to be hidden from the neighbours.

Everything about her was labelled in red, danger, especially the fact that she was unmarried by choice. 'Who would want her?' my father demanded. 'She's too bossy—what man wants to be pushed around?'

With her friend Isabel she ran a girls' school, the first time I ever heard of a woman running her own business. Something about that made my father guffaw in a nasty way. 'Girls, of course she surrounds herself with girls. If she could get herself a real man she wouldn't be afraid of a few boys.'

My father had a way of saying things like that that made you feel you were an imbecile if you didn't know what he was talking about. We would whisper our questions—in case he treated them with contempt we could pretend we hadn't said anything.

'Why not?' I whispered now.

'The girls are irremediable,' said my mother, as if that was an answer. 'No one else can make them behave except Agnes.'

I still didn't understand, but knew better than to probe further.

When Agnes dropped in out of the blue—as she did from time to time on all her relatives—my father treated her with a nervous deference. It made me think she had great power—not only could she make irremediable girls behave but she even controlled him. My father terrified all of us, but in a way, her power over him frightened me even more: he would mock her behind her back but to her face, against his will, he was forced to obsequiousness.

Male writers such as Sartre and Bellow have recorded knowing early in life that their destiny lay in literature. Bellow knew he was 'born to be a performing and interpretive creature', Sartre that he was born for words.

I call myself a writer, but feebly, without conviction. Where did they get this sense, I wonder? Were their childhoods spent like mine? I wrote from an early age, but I knew that, as in all fields, literature belonged to men. The history and biography we studied in school told tales of the deeds of men. We learned to speak of the aspirations of mankind and of 'man's' inhumanity to man'—his inhumanity to woman not being worth recording.

And the literature we studied was all written by men. If they were like me, Bellow and Sartre may not even have known that women wrote in a serious way, that the first novelist to treat psychology as a significant force in human lives was a woman. Sartre's boyhood was spent with Flaubert, Cornelius, Homer, Shakespeare. Bellow went to Anderson, Dreiser, Edgar Lee Masters, Vachel Lindsay.

The books Sartre's grandmother read were feminine, he says, and he was taught by his grandfather to deem them inferior. By an odd chance I was taught the same lesson. We studied only one novel by a woman in my school—and her first name was George. Although I wept over *Little Women*, the moral of Jo March's life is that little girls must put aside the dream of literature to perform the higher duty of looking after their families.

Did their childhoods resemble mine in other ways? Was Jean-Paul or Saul's first responsibility to look after the little children—to spend summer vacation and evenings after school taking them for walks, changing their diapers, feeding them, reading them their stories? Did their fathers tell them their works were derivative, that they lacked the genius necessary for originality? Did their mothers assure them that the work their sisters did was superior to anything they could ever do, that the future lies with girls, not boys? Can destiny swim in such waters?

All my childhood dreams were directed to the present, specifically to escaping it, until I learned escape wasn't possible. My older brother and I would look at a picture of a ship at sea or a beautiful island, some strange wonderful place we wished to be. We would hold hands and run toward the picture, and by wishing hard enough be transported into it. More often we climbed on to the two hitching posts in front of our house—remnants of the days when visitors had horses to tie up. After turning around three times we jumped, landing in a magic world where we fought dragons and loving elves came to our rescue.

The walls of my bedroom were papered with cabbage roses and behind the roses lay a corridor, a long hall whose windows looked on perpetual sunlight. After going to bed I could get into this corridor and live a life of total secrecy.

When I was eight my mother had a baby. While she was pregnant I dreamed of having a sister, but she produced another boy to go with the two she already had. She put the baby in my room and told me to look after him.

I had longed for a doll that cried real tears—I'd seen one at Grand Central Station when we moved from New York to Kansas and had always wished for one. They gave me my brother and said I would like him much better than a doll. In fact, they gave him my dolls to break, since I was now too grown up to want them. Getting a baby to look after ended my magic worlds. In my stories I was still a princess but I knew now they were stories and would never come true.

When I was seven my mother stood me on a chair next to the kitchen counter and had me bake a cake and cookies for my father and brothers, beginning a weekly baking stint that lasted until I left their house at seventeen.

Sartre writes he knew his mother existed to serve him. I raised the two babies born when I was eight and thirteen and cleaned the house every Saturday. I would have made somebody a good old-fashioned kind of wife. It wasn't that I fought my destiny—it just somehow side-stepped me.

Maybe my hair saved me, cropped close to my head when everyone else wore hers long—it made me look too strange. Or maybe it was my stories—I wanted a man from one of my stories, not the pimply, self-absorbed ones who came to dorm mixers. Or maybe it was a message absorbed from Agnes—against my will at first, then later with great eagerness.

The summer I turned ten, on one of her abrupt visits, Agnes learned I was writing a story. She asked me to read it to her. She sat in the living room and listened with total attention. It still seems unbelievable to me that a grown woman could really *want* to spend an hour hearing a young girl read a story. She didn't offer any literary criticism. I don't even remember her saying anything. Just that she sat and listened.

Sartre records how his mother used to go into transports over his writing, showing his boyish 'novels' to neighbours and to her father, with whom they lived. She would stand over his shoulder while he wrote, in ecstasies over his imagination. It was one of her intimates who named writing as young Jean-Paul's career when he was seven or eight. His cousins were told they would be engineers.

Both of my parents had stories to tell, their sides, in an unending feud, and both would make use of my writing to help them make their points—my mother wanting me to write poems describing her entrapment, my father, stories proclaiming his unlauded glories. But beyond that my words created so little interest that my mother tells me my father burned all my childhood papers in some housekeeping frenzy or other. I keep hoping she got it wrong. I spend hours feverishly hunting through her attic for some story, some diary, a remnant that will connect me with my past, that may tell me what dreams I used to have. Nothing comes to light. Despite my anguish I'm relieved that the forced bondage of my words to my parents has also vanished.

Agnes's listening to one story was not enough to give me a sense that my future lay in words. It was enough, though, to keep me writing.

After Agnes listened to my story I would lie in bed imagining my parents dead and me adopted by her, taken into her school where there were only girls.

The dream took on new dimensions the following year when we moved to a house in the country five miles from the town of Lawrence. At first I loved it: I finally had my own room and we went to a two-room country school—just like in *Understood Betsy* or *On the Banks of Plum Creek*. Later I came to hate it. My parents' fights intensified and the isolation of the country made it easy to seal me off completely from friends my own age, from any activities but school and housework.

The main line of the Santa Fe crossed the road at the bottom of the hill on the outskirts of Lawrence. There wasn't any crossing gate or bell and every now and then the Kansas City Chief, roaring around a blind curve toward San Francisco, would annihilate a family.

Mary and Dave would be arguing, not paying attention to the road or to the tracks. The crash would be appalling. We'd be at the house, of course, my four brothers and I, lounging around reading or maybe playing softball. We should have been doing a dozen chores—mowing the lawn (my older brother's job), vacuuming (mine), changing the baby's diapers (mine again) or sorting the bottles out of the trash to take to the dump (my brother). 'I don't need a dishwasher,' Mary used to tell visitors, 'I have two right here.' And she would point at my older brother and me.

When we heard the car in the drive we leaped into action, attacking our chores—there was hell to pay if we were found loafing in bourgeois self-indulgence. And then we saw it was the sheriff's car, the red light flashing. We raced over to see what he wanted, me grabbing the baby and carrying him along on my hip.

The sheriff looked at us very kindly. He said maybe we should go sit down. He had something very serious to tell us. There'd been an accident and we were orphans now. Was there someone we could call to look after us? Of course not, we already did any looking after there was to do, but we couldn't tell him that, and anyway, of course, we were underage, we needed guardians.

I would go to Agnes, to the school for irremediable girls. Even though she only took girls I would have to bring the two little boys with me, they were mine to look after (they thought I was their mother. When they started kindergarten they didn't know what 'sister' meant—they didn't know that was me: they thought they had two mothers.) I didn't care where the other two went, they could look after themselves.

We looked solemnly at the sheriff, conjuring up tears out of shock, but we couldn't believe it had really happened: we were really orphans. Just like *Anne of Green Gables* or *English Orphans.* Our future changed miraculously.

And then Mary and Dave would come up the drive, still arguing, not dead at all, and we would leap into activity that was never quite frenzied enough. My older brother could never get tasks quite right, or the tasks set for him would change between when they were assigned and when he did them, and most of the yelling went his way. The rest of us slid upstairs.

Agnes didn't come to see us again after the summer she heard me read. Maybe she grew too busy, or maybe the number of fights in our house and their ferocity drove her away. I don't know. Maybe it was simply her paying so much attention to me—it might have frightened my father into telling her she couldn't come again.

He thought she was a lesbian, of course, although I only realized that later. WOMAN ON THE LOOSE! WEIRD WOMAN OUT OF CONTROL! That was the headline on my father's face when he talked about Agnes. It was out of the question for me to live with her—he wasn't going to risk losing control of me.

I've never known if she was a lesbian or not, even when I came to spend more time with her: it's never seemed particularly important. One thing I found out about Agnes was that her mother died when she was ten, died giving birth to a baby that didn't survive long, either. Agnes was

named for her mother, who gave her her wedding ring as a memento when
she knew she was dying. I don't know how that affected Agnes, but it
would have frightened me out of marriage. (When I got married she insisted I take her mother's ring. I'm still not sure if that gift portends good or
ill; just in case, I never wear it.)

Agnes took a more active role in my life after I moved to Chicago. She
appeared to me suddenly, a *dea ex machina,* during my first winter there. Although she didn't stay there long, Chicago is where she ran to when she
was twenty, away from the care of a family that took more than they gave.
She might have come to see me, looking for her younger self.

I was twenty-one then, fat, ungainly. I'd never had a boyfriend and,
aside from my three room-mates, I didn't have many women friends in
Chicago, either. My room-mates and I shared a dismal apartment on the
south side—six rooms for a hundred and sixty-five dollars a month and all
the cockroaches we could eat. We killed two hundred and fifty of them one
night, spraying the oven where they nested and stomping on them when
they scampered out. You'd have to be twenty-one to want to count the
bodies.

It was never warmer than fifty-five in the building and that was a
most bitter winter. The city code says it has to be at least sixty-two during
the day. We'd get building inspectors out who would solemnly measure the
air. Then they'd learn the landlady worked as a precinct captain for the
Daley machine and their thermometer miraculously would register fifteen
degrees higher than ours.

I had gone to Kansas for the Christmas holidays and was back several
days before my room-mates. Carrying my heavy suitcase up the stairs to the
apartment entrance I blundered into the doorjamb, knocking the wind out
of myself. I dumped my suitcase down and sat on it, not even going inside,
so miserable with my fat, my clumsiness, my loneliness that I hoped I might
just die right there.

My two youngest brothers would care, of course, as would my friend
Kathleen, but my parents wouldn't even come to the funeral. I'd been active
in community organizing both in Chicago and Lawrence; admiring community leaders came to the service to pay me homage. In my coffin I looked
like a Botticelli angel, miraculously slender with long soft golden curls. The
picture moved me to tears.

'What's wrong with you?' It was Agnes. I hadn't seen her come into
the unlit stairwell.

I was so startled that I lost my balance and fell to the floor with a crash
of suitcase and legs. 'Nothing,' I muttered. 'I didn't know you were going to
be here.'

I was terrified I'd been told and had forgotten—during this very low
point in my life people were always telling me things that I didn't seem to
hear.

'Neither did I. I called Mary to get your phone number and she told me you were just getting back to town today. Sorry if I frightened you.'

I got back to my feet somehow and unlocked the apartment door. Just navigating the strip from the hall to the living room was an agony—I ran into the jamb once more and was so nervous that I tripped over the suitcase. Agnes made no comment then or later on my shambling, awkward gait, nor on the freezing apartment which stank of mould and Raid.

She took me out to dinner, just her—Isabel hadn't come on this particular trip—and made me feel alert, witty, intelligent. She assumed I had an adult understanding of people—from the waiters to the US Congress to my own parents—and I responded with what seemed to me to be enormous sophistication. Late in the evening she told me I had beautiful hands and should plan to do something fine with them, and to this day, in the disgust I can't overcome for my body, I look at my hands with a loverlike admiration.

After that I used to visit her and Isabel. In those days you could fly on student-standby for some trivial price and I'd go in the summer and during the Christmas holidays. She didn't run the school any more. In the wake of Title VII legislation she'd been asked to take a role in shaping education policy. And she thought perhaps the country was changing in some way that would make it easier for little girls, that they wouldn't need special schools any more. Now she's not so sure, but in that era we all had heady dreams.

I've never stopped walking into doorjambs, but Agnes trained me to do it with my head up, without apologizing. She and Isabel taught me some of the basics that I'd never gotten the hang of, such as how to feel at better ease inside my own body. As a teenager I'd tied down my breasts, ashamed of their betrayal, their announcement that I was a girl. Agnes taught me, if not to love them, at least to live with them. Most of all she and Isabel taught me how to listen when other people talked, by listening to me with interest.

Agnes didn't ask about my stories and I was too uncertain about them to remind her of the day she'd listened ten years before. I kept thinking I should go to medical school, become a surgeon to justify her faith in my hands. Or perhaps a painter, but painting is such a public art. You can write a story and no one will know you've done it, but when you paint a picture it's apparent that you've been doing something, even if you only keep it in the privacy of your home.

A few years later I finally showed Agnes one of my stories because I couldn't explain in any other way the lives of some people I cared about, yet who troubled me. She was amazed—she didn't know I still wrote—she thought my academic work had taken that place in my life. She praised my writing and made me feel it might be something fine, like my hands. She urged me to try to publish my tale and told me about the burgeoning feminist magazines that nurtured women's art. I sent my story out and *Women: A Journal of Liberation* accepted it.

I'd published one other story, when I was eleven, in the *American Girl*. They had a section called 'My Turn' for contributions by readers. My entry was a story but they printed it as nonfiction, an uneasy sign to me that it wouldn't have made the grade if they'd known it was original, creative. Until Agnes urged me I never tried sending any of my other writing to publishers.

After *A Journal of Liberation* published my story, the romance I wove in my head was that I would write a book, a novel, and that it would be published. It took six more years before I was strong enough to make that dream happen: It was then that I started work on my first book, *Indemnity Only*.

I haven't seen Agnes for some time now, since 1982 when she came to celebrate the publication of *Indemnity Only*. Although I still hear from Isabel I find it painful that Agnes thinks I no longer need her.

For me the hardest part of telling stories is crossing the line from private words to public ones. When I write for myself alone the words come freely, but when I know someone else will read them they're like water squeezed from a stone. I think I still need Agnes, to give me more confidence in my voice, but she's spending her time with other irremediable girls whose troubles seem more serious—not running her school again, but seeking them out as she sought me.

Still, I've finally let my hair grow out. I've even learned to like my wild frizz. It gives me some assurance that I, too, may yet come to be a wild woman, not under anyone's control.

I've written five novels, all of them featuring a woman named VI Warshawski, a detective who lives alone but whose close friend is a doctor some twenty years her senior named Lotty Herschel. People sometimes ask if VI is me, if Lotty is based on someone real. They're not: you can't put real people in a book, at least I can't—if I try to describe a real person's idiosyncrasies and make a fictional character act the way that a real person would, everything becomes wooden. The action can't flow naturally because my imagination is penned in by how that living person would have acted.

But VI and Lotty are real, of course, because the only basis for imagining people is people. Even if VI isn't me, Lotty isn't Agnes, their relationship is real. Everyone needs an Agnes so that she can find her own voice, so that her stories don't die in her head.

POINTS TO CONSIDER ABOUT "MY TURN"

1. Why does Paretsky include her "Witch of the Seahouse" story at the beginning of this selection? What specific functions—both narrative and thematic—does Paretsky hope to accomplish by including a brief narrative piece at the beginning of "My Turn"?

2. How does Paretsky use material from her childhood as subject matter for "My Turn"? What specific youthful incidents does the author use as the foundation for this reminiscence-based prose piece?

3. What emotional needs did fictionalizing fill for the young Paretsky, according to this piece? What additional functions might it serve now? Compare Paretsky's underlying motivations for being a writer with your own.

4. How does the author describe the sociopolitical climate of America during the time she was growing up? How is this description of setting particularly relevant to thematic points which Paretsky raises in this piece?

5. Paretsky grew up to become one of this country's most popular authors of mystery fiction, and one of the first mystery authors to feature a woman as protagonist. What "clues" can you find in this evocation of a writer's childhood that would point to her later profession and successes?

✜ WRITING ACTIVITIES: FIRST THINGS

Writers read extensively, they pay close attention to the goings-on in their lives, and they write regularly. One form that combines all three of these activities is the personal journal. Journals may serve a number of different purposes, depending on the individual needs of the writer. Some literary-minded people, for example, record their responses to the reading they're doing, in order to deepen their engagement with the text they're reading, and to make notes on style and content—thus broadening their palette of styles, influences, references.

One especially useful means of responding to writing is something I call an "Interactive Reading Journal." Interaction, in its practical, logical sense, means the art or practice of examining ideas by a spontaneous exchange of arguments. This is exactly what you will do in your interactive journal. Begin by dividing a sheet of paper into two vertical columns (or set your word processor on two-column mode, as in the example below). Label the top of one column, "Quotation," and the top of the other column, "Reaction." As you read, record into the "Quotation" column any phrase or sentence that seems especially relevant, challenging, thought-provoking, illogical, misguided, aggravating, spiritually enlightening, or plain idiotic. Then, in the "Reaction" column, freewrite (see exercise at the end of Chapter 1) some responses to the passage: your own thoughts, gut reactions, flights of fancy, sense impressions. Your responses don't have to be presented grammatically or logically, just honestly.

At the end of a chunk of read text—a short story, a chapter in a book, for example—you might want to write some general commentary on it, in a brief paragraph. Here is an example of the Interactive Reading Journal, in this case a reader's response to this chapter of *The Graceful Lie:*

Title: Chapter 2 of *The Graceful Lie:* Beginnings

Author: Michael Petracca

QUOTATION

REACTION

p. 34: "Across the world, in fact, there is a small but vocal movement of individuals who call themselves (or who are called by the media) neo-Luddites, 'a group of anti-technologists who view the digital revolution with a sense of horror and dread,' in the words of popular journalist Steven Levy."

Hmm . . . I did not know that. I don't think I'm a neo-Luddite—I just think I'm deathly afraid of computers because nobody ever showed me how to use one—and I hate reading instructions! Maybe it's time to learn? Next year . . .

p. 39: ". . . college-age writers may complain, 'I'm too young, I haven't done anything interesting yet. All I do is go to school, do homework, party sometimes. Who wants to read about a bunch of kids drinking and getting sick?'

Some broad generalizations here. He seems to be implying that people my age do nothing but party—which is true for my roommate Janine but not me. I like the idea of using my childhood for material, though—I have a story I want to start right now, about my pet turtle I had in the fifth grade.

p. 37: "[But it's a healthy impulse for writers to stay on our good side—ed.]"

This guy's editor is REALLY starting to get on my nerves. I don't even believe it's his editor—I think it's him trying to be funny—maybe it was cute one time, but drop it or I'm going to have to slap you!

This chapter is about getting started as a writer—some suggestions for time, place, what to use, that kind of thing. Some of this stuff seems pretty common sense, but I think for me the chapter is definitely worthwhile, as a kind of a kick in the butt to get started—especially the scheduling part. I also never heard anybody rave about yellow pads before—funny! I'm a confirmed procrastinator, so the schedule thing is really important for me—maybe I'll actually do it this time. I wish he had talked more about how to make a story out of a journal—plot and that kind of stuff. Maybe he'll do that in the next chapter. If he doesn't, then I want my $ back!!

You can use an interactive journal to annotate any text, including short stories and novels that you find relevant in some way. Perhaps the most important single activity for the fiction writer is the constant reading of fictional prose. In the course of your extensive reading, you will undoubtedly come across passages you want to use as jumping-off points for focused freewrites or as germs of ideas for stories, or as models of certain stylistic features with which you want to experiment, or as inspirational mottoes you want to stick on your refrigerator with a little flower-magnet. Keeping this kind of interactive journal is an excellent way of recording those readerly reactions, so that you don't forget them later.

Another journal form is the diary or personal log. This is a kind of daily, extended freewrite: either unfocused—reporting spontaneously on the day's events and/or feelings and physical sensations in the present moment—or focused on a specific incident in the past... earlier in the day, a week ago, or many years previous. The latter can serve as the basis of a short story or even a more extended fiction. Here, for example, is a student's journal entry on a childhood incident—a thirty-minute exercise that, with a little revision, could become a fine short story or "flash fiction."

I am a very small person. I am also a very independent, strong-willed woman who does not like to be treated like she cannot make decisions for herself. When I was five I was just a miniature version of the same woman I am today.

I remember being at gymnastics practice one Saturday morning when one of the coaches asked me to come over with her group for a minute. I walk over to her group of big kids and she tells me she wants me to climb the rope and show these kids that they can do it too. They all were probably twice my size and weight and they were looking at me like "yeah right, like this little shit can climb the rope without using her legs." I was always uncomfortable when coaches put me on the spot like that. They just didn't understand what kind of pressure it was for a little kid to have to show other kids up. Well, their looks of doubt probably would have made anyone else jump at the chance to prove them wrong, not me. Nesa, my coach, pulls me over next to her and asks me again to climb the rope. I manage to squeak out a meek, "no." She looks at me real confused and asks again. I say "no" with my hands twisting in knots behind my back and my little shoulders shaking back and forth real slowly like I'm trying to be cute. No luck. She's mad now and she picks me up and practically throws me into the rope so I have no choice but to grab hold or fall on my butt in front of everyone. So I hold on and climb that damned sweaty stinky rope as fast as I can. I reach the top, clink the stupid bell and climb back down half way then slide down with my hands the rest of the way. I land with a big plop on the big squishy blue mat and jump off again in one swift motion. I tell her hurriedly that I need to go to the bathroom. I run out of there as fast as I can and go upstairs and pack all my little gear into my gym bag and take off.

I am now a five-year-old fugitive, on the run from who knows what. I'm going home to my mommy who would never embarrass me or make me feel different from everyone else, or so I thought then. So I'm just past the railroad tracks making my way home, which by the way is at least fifteen or so miles from the gym which was way back out in this industrial zone with nothing around but fields and empty warehouses, but I know exactly where I'm going. I've driven this way many times before. As I'm mapping my way home in my head this van comes pulling up next to me real slow like. This guys sticks his furry head half out the passenger window and asks if I need a ride anywhere. I say "no" which seems to be my word of the day. Next thing I know the van slows down more and I am pretty damned scared now so I take a sharp right and start running down this steep embankment. I hear the van come to a grinding halt and the hairy guy jumps out and starts chasing me. Even though he's fat he catches up with me in about three steps and grabs me from behind. I start screaming so he sticks his grimy, nicotine-stained hand over my mouth. I bite down as hard as I can until I taste his blood on my lips but this doesn't help my case any. He throws me into the van and jumps over me to the driver's seat and drives off like a race car driver. I try to jump out the door but we were going too fast. He sees this attempt and locks the doors on his little side panel thing. So now I am trapped. Just then I see my coach driving behind us in the side mirror. I am unsure of what to do now. If I start making noise he'll know we are being followed. Lucky for me the window is down just enough for me to stick my puny arm half out the window and start waving it like I'm just playing. You know how your arm flies with the wind when you're driving fast down the freeway, it just goes up and down like waves. Well I start doing this kind of, seeing as my arm is only half out the window it looks more like I'm in spasms. The stinky hairy man sees my arm and tries to shut the window. This is when I see my mother come bulleting down the other side of the street, driving like the dickens. Nesa starts weaving her car back and forth behind the van and my mother flips a bitch right in the middle of a crowded intersection, just missing the center divide. Nesa comes along the driver's side of the van yelling like a mad woman. This guy is starting to get scared now, and mad. He starts swearing and banging on the steering wheel. I'm sitting there screaming my head off clutching my gym bag like it's going to save me or something. My mother is right on our tail now, she's trying to drive up next to my side except there are a bunch of trees there next to the road. Nesa has pulled back a little because of the oncoming cars and the guy is looking back at her over his left shoulder. We're now coming to a big intersection and he starts to go faster instead of slowing down for the red light. This clunky grandpa mobile takes a left turn right in front of us so he swerves to the right and at the same time unlocks the door and throws me right out the passenger side. My mother screeches to a halt, just missing a tree. She jumps out of the car and grabs me while we see Nesa sail by on hot pursuit of this maniacal asshole. My mother grabs me and throws me in the car. She locks the doors and we head straight to the hospital. I try to tell her I'm fine, just a little scratch but she won't listen.

It turns out that Nesa had noticed I was missing only after a couple of minutes. She had gone to check on me because she knew that I was upset and realized I was gone. She called my mother who had no idea what was going on but seeing as this wasn't the first time I had run away my mom came straight there. I didn't think I had done anything wrong. I have always been a very strong-willed person and also one of those who feels they are somewhat invincible, but to this day I still can't get into a van.

In some cases, your journal writing will yield stories that spring fully-formed from the imagination and need little revision. The above journal example is rough in spots, with abrupt shifts from past to present tense, incomplete characterizations (such as the character of Nesa), some repetitive word selections, and so forth, but it is basically sound, with excellent narrative tension and a voice kind of like that of J. D. Salinger's youthful main character in *The Catcher in the Rye*. At other times, your journal writing will not yield anything that looks remotely like a story. Nevertheless, it may contain a graceful turn of phrase you can include in future work, or a charged idea or sense impression that you want to develop in later writing sessions. For those reasons, I advise that you make journal writing a part of your regular writing practice, if it's at all consistent with your temperament. The goal of journal keeping is to strengthen your skills as an observer and recorder of events past and present.

TEN SAMPLE JOURNAL PROMPTS

The previous student example was based on a journal prompt I give sometimes in creative writing workshops. Here it is:

- Write about the most harrowing experience you can recall from your childhood.

Take a half-hour, try that one yourself and see what you come up with. If you find the activity worthwhile and want to try writing some more focused journal entries, here are nine more prompts to keep you going for a while:

- Describe your third-grade teacher. What kinds of things did s/he wear? How did his/her voice sound? What kinds of funny quirks did s/he have?

- Think back on the first place that you can remember living in, and describe yourself there: the furniture, the floor plan, the people around you, the house pets, the insect life—whatever specific details spring to mind.

- Consider the most recent thing that made you laugh out loud and write about it. If possible, recall a stimulus that was *not* generated by an artifact of mass media, such as a television sitcom.

- Write about the first sexual or romantic feelings you can recall having, including details of place. Write about a singularly frustrating sexual encounter, or a singularly rewarding one.

- Describe today's lunchtime meal as though you are a restaurant critic charged with reviewing its preparation, presentation, taste impressions, and so on.

- Recall somebody that made you angry in the past week, and imagine yourself doing something to that person—exacting revenge, performing religious absolution, engaging in an extended session of psychotherapy.

- Describe the space you are occupying at this moment, concentrating first on the area closest to you and moving gradually outward for twenty feet . . . and *no farther.* Include details of smell, sound, touch, and even taste, as well as obvious visual impressions.

- Write about the last time you vomited: the events leading up to the dreadful activity (it's my least favorite thing to do in the world!), and the act itself.

- Describe all the hats you have ever owned, from the earliest to the most recent. If those hats in some way emblematize certain phases in the development of your personality, discuss that as well.

Of course, you don't need such prompts for a satisfying journal practice. Focused exercises of this kind are simply a means to expand the content range of your daily writing. Similarly, you can use the journal to experiment with a variety of styles, voices, perspectives. Write one entry in the voice of Hemingway, another in the style of the Bible. Write one entry that contains a cliché in every sentence, another that has three curse words in every sentence. Write a three-page journal entry that is one long sentence, another that contains no sentence longer than five words. Write one entry in the third-person plural ("They're all pounding the sidewalk as though . . .") and another in third-person singular ("He first became aware of sex while sitting in a warm bathtub . . .").

As you become more experienced in the journal process, you will start coming up with your own prompts and using the journal in ways that are most useful to you. Some writers use logs, lists, and notebooks as a means of generating draft material for short stories and novels. For a concrete example of the way professional writers use journals to keep them on track with a story and to flesh out plot elements, setting description and characterization, see Sue Grafton's working journal for *M is for Malice* in Chapter 11 of *The Graceful Lie*. Other writers use journals primarily as verbal lubrication: By writing in this way every day, they develop fluency, a certain confidence that when they sit down to write, words will come out. Still others use the diary as a means of sharpening their observational skills, recording details of life events both significant and poignantly mundane. And finally, in some cases—if it's focused, evocative, honest, and insightful, or poised on the edge of madness—journal writing may even stand on its own merits as a valid, publishable creative form, as in the examples by May Sarton and Hunter S. Thompson.

3
Making Stories

GARDENER CRUSHED BY METEOR!...OR, HOW TO HOOK YOUR READER

At the end of this chapter, you will find a story, "Cockroach Miracles, Solvent Dreams," that appeared in a journal several years ago. I decided to include one of my own short pieces in this text because I don't have to pay myself anything. More importantly, though, I use my story to illustrate certain key points about plot construction, because I constructed it and therefore know exactly how it was constructed.

Consider these two synopses of "Cockroach Miracles, Solvent Dreams":

1. Wearing worn leather gloves, I work in my garden. I have the satisfaction of setting up a drip irrigation system, joining lengths of PVC tubing connected to a hose-faucet. When I turn on the water, all the tiny drip emitters work, releasing water gradually to thirsty plants. The pittisporum, morning glories, rosemary, cocoa palms are all happy for the drink, and I'm happy for them. I put away my gardening tools and go into the kitchen for a nice glass of lemonade.

2. Bob Donohoe was setting up a PVC drip system, when he noticed something unusual in the sky. It turned out to be a rogue meteor hurtling toward earth, in the direction of Bob Donohoe's garden. In an instant, Bob reflected on his life, which was filled with superficial successes. Wanting to continue living, Bob tried to ward off the meteor with his hands. This was a futile gesture, as meteors are massive and move very fast. The meteor crushed Bob Donohoe to death, and then God explains why he allowed this to happen to Bob.

Scenario 1 is a story, a chronological sequence of events without any central theme, narrative hook, momentum, or payoff. In this case, it's a story based on personal experience, when I worked as a gardener to help pay my way through college. It describes a nice time outside, some communion with nature, the satisfaction of a job well done. This description might work nicely as a paragraph in *Better Homes and Gardens*. But if I were to develop it into a short story, it would be boring. Nobody would read it . . . or if they did, they'd wake up some hours later asking, "So what?"

    The second scenario is a plot. It draws upon elements of Scenario 1 for its subject matter but features the same recipe that most successful fiction writers use to engage readers. It has a central character with whom the reader can identify to some degree. It places its protagonist in places and situations that cause some kind of interpersonal friction or physical danger— in this case, an encounter with a force of nature, a meteor. It builds that narrative tension until it reaches critical mass . . . after which some kind of resolution follows: a long-winded God explaining why bad things sometimes happen to boring people.

    While many writers use the terms *story* and *plot* interchangeably, the distinction between Scenario 1 and Scenario 2 is useful, because it places writers in distinct methodological camps, based upon their individual goals. If, for instance, after completing the exercises at the end *The Graceful Lie*'s first chapter, you discovered that your main goal as a writer is to become more personally expressive, or to use your writing as a means of uncovering key elements of your psyche—in short, if you're writing for yourself and not for publication—then there's no reason why you should write plotted fiction that will hook readers, as Scenario 2 does. You're writing primarily for yourself, which is a fine and worthy goal in itself.

    If, on the other hand, you'd like to see your work in print some day, then you definitely need to consider giving your stories some kind of plot structure. Janet Burroway in *Writing Fiction* succinctly summarizes the distinction:

> A story is a series of events recorded in their chronological order. A plot
> is a series of events deliberately arranged so as to reveal their dramatic,
> thematic, and emotional significance.

While I might disagree with the phrase "deliberately arranged," as you will gather from the examples below, the notion that—unlike stories—plots work by engaging readers on several levels is an especially useful one, and will be the foundation for the ensuing discussion of narrative structure.

CONSCIOUS VERSUS UNCONSCIOUS PLOTTING

The Organic Approach

For the purposes of this discussion—and your starry future as a successful fiction writer—we will define *plot* this way:

> A plot is a conscious or unconscious sequencing of fictional events that uses one of numerous possible opening setups, subtle introduction of background material, narrative tension and subsequent resolution to keep readers engaged with the narrative from the beginning to the end of a given text.

The key to successful plotting, then, is to keep readers interested, so that they will want to keep reading. There is nothing new about this basic concern. The ancient (384–322 B.C.) Greek philosopher, Aristotle, called plot the most important element in the imitation of human action, and went so far as to assert that an effective dramatic sequence can exist "without character but not without plot." This key narrative concept has been considered and debated by rhetoricians and romance novelists, philosophers and porn authors, literary critics, television sitcom reviewers, playwrights and Hollywood B-movie hacks throughout human history, and everybody has a slightly different take on how best to construct a plot that works. However, everybody agrees on the simplest and most basic tenet of plot construction (fiction Rule #8): Hook your readers and keep 'em reading, by whatever means necessary.

Within the above definition of plot, you may notice the words "conscious or unconscious sequencing." This differs slightly from Burroway's "deliberate" definition of plot and hints at two fundamentally different approaches to constructing story lines in prose. At one end of the spectrum you find writers who use an *organic* approach to putting together their fiction. They envision a cast of characters, place them in settings and situations guaranteed to create some interpersonal tension, and then sit back and watch the fireworks, recording the plot twists as they emerge naturally from their fictional people's confrontations. Regarding this process, Anne Lamott insists,

> I say don't worry about plot. Worry about the characters. Let what they say or do reveal who they are, and be involved in their lives, and keep asking yourself, Now what happens? The development of relationship creates plot.... Your plot will fall into place as, one day at a time, you lis-

ten to your characters carefully, and watch them move around doing
and saying things and bumping into each other.

Alice Walker once described the creation of her novel *The Color Purple* in just
the way that Lamott describes. She had no clear sense of the direction her
plot would take, or of her novel's eventual outcome; rather, she imagined
Celie, Shug Avery, and Mr. _____, her central characters, to have certain key
personality traits; she invested them with fictional life so that they became
fully rounded characters; and then she let the plot spin out on its own, from
her characters' inevitable conflicts and passionate engagements. Throughout this process, Walker made herself almost a passive, "unconscious" observer, a quasi-scribe of the imagination, rather than taking the more proac-
tive role of architect, building contractor and bricklayer in the construction
of her story.

For writers like Lamott and Walker, who let their plots unfold spontaneously and even unconsciously, the writing process is one of continuous
discovery. About her writing, and the *organic* approach in general, Walker
has said: "Expect nothing. Live frugally . . . on surprise." Such a philosophy
can lead to some exhilarating moments: One's characters may become so invested with imaginative life that they feel as close (and sometimes as demanding) as one's own family members.

However, the organic approach to story creation also has some potential pitfalls inherent in it. Such an approach can occasionally lead to idiosyncratic, disjointed, or digressive plots that present difficulties to readers and
editors. Even the critically acclaimed Walker is not immune to this tendency. Literary critic Bonnie Braendlin recently said of Walker's *Temple of
My Familiar,*

> [it] is a path-breaking novel for its development of ideas and themes, but
> is criticised for its confusing amalgamation of narrative techniques and
> styles. Walker's novel expresses valorization of the African-American
> with emphasis on idealism, maternalism, and spirituality. However, her
> problematic style and narrative strategy deter an easy understanding of
> the novel.

It may be that Walker intended the plot structure and style of *The Temple of
My Familiar* not to be "easy." Perhaps she purposely used multiple voices
and fractured narratives in order to create a sense of diversity within the
collective human consciousness, since the latter was one of the subthemes of
her book. Whatever the author's intention, such narrative incoherence can
be considered a serious flaw if it truly does "deter an understanding" of the
writing. Especially for beginning writers—whose prose does not yet command the attention Walker's writing is afforded by dint of her reputation—
such "problematic style and narrative strategy" are probably good things to
avoid, if you want editors or workshop peers to read beyond the first few
pages.

Another problem built into the organic method of story construction is that, when you "expect nothing" as Walker suggests, sometimes you get nothing. As discussed in the first chapter of *The Graceful Lie*, most writers will inevitably have days, sometimes even weeks, during which they receive no happy surprises in the form of spontaneous exposition, no gripping dialogue or conflicts that arise from the interactions of their characters, no heart-pounding climaxes and satisfying resolutions. People who use the organic method of plot construction may therefore have days when the generation of a story line comes to an abrupt stop, and they find themselves staring at the screen, or doing freewrite after freewrite, in hopes that the story will pick up momentum again.

The Structural Approach

To forestall the problems of errant plot lines and writer's block—or because a more organized approach comes naturally to them—many writers use the *structural* method for constructing stories. That is, they carefully and consciously construct a framework for their plots before they write the story. This approach has both a practical and affective (i.e., emotional) advantage over the organic approach. Practically, there is no way their plots can digress or unravel, because they have carefully constructed a narrative framework before they have written a single word of their short story or novel.

Furthermore, the structural approach makes writer's block a lesser concern, because the writing process doesn't have to be linear and sequential. Having built a solid plot framework, the writer can plug chunks of text into that structure, as auto workers might add door panels, windshield wipers, and upholstery to the basic chassis as it moves down the assembly line. If, for example, your description of the island of Corsica isn't flowing naturally during the exposition phase of your plot's development, you can suspend that task and re-focus your energies on another phase of the plot: the motorcycle chase that leads up to your tale's climax, or even the calm rendering of the setting sun with which you resolve your fictional piece.

Most authors of popular fiction take the structural approach to writing fiction, because of its practical advantages. Prolific mystery author Elmore Leonard, as one example, says that the central goal for writers is to "know where you are going." According to Leonard, "I write plotted fiction. First I sit down with a journal and write out the idea I want to develop." Most of his pre-writing research, Elmore says, is primarily focused on specific issues of plot, and his characters—unlike those of Walker—take on fictive life only when they begin to occupy a position in the plot.

Similarly, historical novelist Patrick O'Brian insists that he always begins one of his fictional pieces by first conceiving a central plot. He comes up with a very rough outline of his story's narrative direction and then imagines a "number of possible actions"—different tacks his story could take, with very different complications and resolutions—and from this list of possibilities he chooses the story line he thinks will be the most compelling for readers. This is very typical of fiction writers who choose the structural approach, and may serve as a model—outline, explore alternatives, flesh out the most promising story line, revise—for your initial stabs at plot construction.

Choosing a Method

There is no more merit or honor or excellent karma that accrues from choosing one of these approaches over the other. The structural approach is sometimes criticized for being less "creative" than a more spontaneous, organic approach, but it actually allows for much imaginative activity within the plot framework, which can itself be flexible and open to modification, not rigid and limiting. It can also allow for meaningful themes and complex, layered meanings inherent in the narrative order.

The organic approach, likewise, gets slammed sometimes because it's too haphazard and unpredictable, leading to unfocused, incoherent, meandering prose. In fact, however, organically composed plots frequently end up having very traditional-looking plot structures. Our novelistic example, *The Color Purple,* if you graph its plot points, has: an opening (the lynching of Celie's father); much exposition (e.g., Celie's mother's mental instability, marriage to a man who is mainly interested in her property); an extended middle typical of complex novel plots (the departure to Africa of Celie's younger sister, the protagonist's abuse at the hands of Mr. _____, the arrival of Shug Avery); some high points (the consummated love of Celie and Shug, the realization that her sister Nettie had for years been writing Celie letters that Mr. _____ had kept hidden); and a resolution (Celie's intimacy with Albert—the former Mr. _____, whose personality has improved markedly—and the reunion with her sister and her own children). Clearly, even though Walker conceived and executed the novel organically, it ended up with a "traditional" structure—one that might appear (to someone who wasn't familiar with her composition process) carefully premeditated and which follows the traditional "rules" of successful plotting.

Assuming, then, that the organic and structural approaches are of approximately equal validity and utility, I'd suggest starting with the more organized method I outline in Chapter 4, to give yourself the best chance of writing a tight, gripping plot. In doing so, may find that you're a natural-born structural plotter, and you may spend the rest of your writing life with index cards or outlining software. However, you may also discover, after spending some time as a meticulous pre-plotter, that you begin to evolve naturally toward a more organic approach. Mystery writer Robert B. Parker, who has averaged a book a year for many years, describes that developmental process in his own life:

> For the first dozen or so books I worked from an outline. Then, when I did the Chandler book [*Mystery author Raymond Chandler (1888–1959) never finished the novel he called* The Poodle Springs Story. *It was completed by Parker and released as* Poodle Springs—*ed.*], I tried to be as Chandleresque as possible. He never outlined, so I didn't. I just got the idea and let the characters lead the way. Since then I have done so in each book. The outline was a great psychological support for a while. Working from an outline, I always knew where the story was going next, but it became a limitation. I stuck too close to it.

Toni Morrison similarly describes a hybrid structural/organic approach that she used to write one of her most critically acclaimed novels:

> In *Jazz* . . . I put the whole plot on the first page. . . . I wanted the story to be the vehicle which moved us from page one to the end, but I wanted the delight to be found in the moving away from the story and coming back to it, looking around it, and through it, as though it were a prism, constantly turning.

Even if you're positive you're always going to work as a free-flowing organicist, I strongly suggest you read, study, and internalize the following structural plot material anyway. The unconscious mind moves in mysterious and wonderful ways, and a deep-down understanding of the workings of effective plots will undoubtedly inform the unfolding of your stories, even if you don't intend it.

TO THOSE WHO ARE ABOUT TO SHOCK, I IMPLORE YOU . . .

When teaching plot development to writers' workshops, I break the structural method down into four stages—opening, exposition, midpoint and resolution—distilled from time-tested theories Aristotle set out in the *Poetics*, combined with the innovations and inventions of a number of dramatic theorists, novelists, playwrights and screenwriters, and teachers, and tested on many students. Most successful fiction features significant development in each of these structural areas, although some pieces will dwell more heavily on certain points, and some—especially experimental or postmodern narrative—will skip certain of these areas entirely.

For instance, one of the hallmarks of postmodern fiction is the resistance to satisfying closure or resolution: the last stage in the traditional plot. Postmodern novels may therefore have no resolution, or many resolutions that add up to no resolution. Many contemporary authors dismantle and revise the predictable movement of narrative in just this way, so that we find a novel such as John Fowles' *The French Lieutenant's Woman*, which uses multiple endings to suggest the fictional power of the narrator and to undercut the "reality" of the fictional world being created. An anti-resolving conclusion such as Fowles's may leave the reader confused and/or thrilled by the artistic unusualness and originality of the piece, and potentially mind-expanded after the last page has been turned.

Not conforming to the expectations of traditional plot structure looks especially appealing to many beginning writers, who often want to write something that distinguishes itself by startling or even shocking readers. Originality and shaking up the system are both noble and worthy goals, because rattling the status quo is Item One on the job description of artists and young people. Unfortunately, it's difficult to shock the modern reader with weird plot constructions and edgy subject matter, because we've become somewhat jaded as readers.

We've read William Burroughs' cut-up novels (e.g., *The Soft Machine*) which he created in part by throwing sentences down a flight of stairs; seen Quentin Tarantino's *Pulp Fiction*, which contains interwoven, recursive loops of narrative; laughed our fool heads off while watching a television sitcom that's admittedly "about nothing" ("Seinfeld"), been disturbed by the ending of Thomas Pynchon's *Gravity's Rainbow*, which is belatedly shown to have been a motion picture within the textual world of the book.

We've gladly subjected ourselves to stories about suicidal drunks (John O'Brien's *Leaving Las Vegas*), serial murderers who have sex with their dead victims (Cormac McCarthy's *Child of God*), brothers who fall madly in love and have sex with their milk-cow (*Darling* by William Tester), people spooning and eating brains from the skull of a live monkey (T. Coraghessan Boyle's "Descent of Man"), heroin addicts having sex in men's room stalls (William Burroughs's *Naked Lunch*), people who tickle the backs of their throats with feathers to transport themselves to hallucinatory alternate worlds (Jeff Noon's *Vurt*), and on and on.

Modern writers have pretty much covered the bases when it comes to experimental plot and outrageous subject matter. This isn't to say that you shouldn't innovate structurally or contribute your unique vision to the evolving literary culture. Rather, I'm suggesting that you read extensively in the traditional and contemporary/postmodern canon (it's fun!) and study the next chapter's presentation of traditional plot basics (it's less fun but good medicine), as partial preparation for writing the next new thing.

ONE MORE THING ABOUT "RULES" . . .

To close this overview of story construction, let me address a question students reasonably ask at some point during our discussion of plot. "Do we need to think about all these rules when we're writing stories?" somebody in a workshop always wants to know. "All this conscious sequencing and Aristotle and stuff makes me nervous and gives me a headache. It seems like it gets in the way. You said, 'Just write,' but if I'm worrying about all these rules then I get really frustrated and I want to do anything else *but* write."

"That's a reasonable reaction," I tell my students with teacherly supportiveness. Then I give them advice, a solution, fiction writers' Rule #4: "Learn the rules so well that you don't have to think about them." I know this is a valid response from firsthand experience. I started my first novel, *Doctor Syntax*, with the passage,

> A slow death by nagging: My mother would kill me if she knew I was dogging *Doctor Syntax*.

In creating that first sentence, I never consciously decided, "Well, today I think I'll elect to use the *in medias res* opening setup technique." It's very clear to me, in retrospect, that I intended to plop the reader directly in the middle of the protagonist's quest for his valuable lost book, thereby establishing forward movement immediately. Even though I wasn't thinking about the entire "list" of opening possibilities, I did in fact have them stored away as part of my writer's technical palette, and I drew upon those rules unconsciously to create that genial first sentence.

Here's how the process works, I think: Once you learn the "rules" of fiction and read lots of books that work by these rules, they become lodged in your brain forever, like that memory of the time Lucius Soames pushed you down the stairs in the second grade, or the Pepsodent toothpaste jingle. Then you draw on them, often unconsciously, when a creative decision presents itself. An illustration less frivolous than that of the toothpaste jingle might be my friend Mark Comstock, who is a jazz and R & B guitarist. There was a period in Mark's life when he decided he needed to play scales to improve his improvisational technique. Being an extreme sort of guy, my friend Mark withdrew from the world, took a room in the seediest flophouse in Santa Barbara (it's not all lovingly restored missions and upscale boutiques where I live). There he applied himself to the enterprise of practicing scales and studying music theory, which he did with Buddhist concentration at least ten hours a day, every day.

After a couple of years Mark Comstock emerged from the Southern Hotel, pale, gaunt, and unshaven. I went to hear Mark's new band at Cafè Bla and was instantly aware of a change in his playing. In his solos, it was clear that he had cultivated a more personal, even poetic voice that simultaneously drew upon and transcended jazz tradition. He had a new melodic ease, technique of uncommon purity, phrasings I'd never heard before, from him or anyone else, a controlled impressionism, as it occurred to me. In between sets, I commented to Mark about the change in his playing and asked how his two years as a scale-playing and theory-studying hermit had affected him.

"I used to think about chord changes in the middle of tunes, or whether my fingers were going to go where I wanted them to," he told me. "Now I just hear a line in my head, and I play it."

The fictional "rules" presented here work in exactly the same way. You study the techniques. At the same time, you read stories and novels that exemplify these techniques. You go to Schwarzenegger movies, read comic books, watch television sitcoms, attend the Ashland Shakespeare festival. You start freewriting, brainstorming, outlining. When the time comes to make a creative choice, all of these experiences influence your subsequent action in subtle but powerful ways. The imagination selects automatically from your internalized catalogue of technical and stylistic possibilities. You don't think about the rules. You just write.

Cockroach Miracles, Solvent Dreams

Michael Petracca

Bob Donohoe nipped off a length of quarter-inch rubber tubing and laid it out between the two clumps of dwarf rosemary he had just planted. Bob was in the final stages of a summer-long landscaping project. He had pick-axed his entire front lawn, ripped out as many twiny grass runners as he could, and run a feeder line off his old sprinkler system—all in preparation for installing drought-tolerant native California shrubberies and an underground drip system to keep them irrigated. The drought had been going on for three years, and some experts predicted Fiesta City's reservoirs would presently be tapped if people didn't take drastic measures. Bob had always felt embarrassingly suburban firing up his Toro gas mower and pushing it around on Saturday afternoons, so digging up his yard hadn't been as drastic a measure for Bob as it might have been for a true lawn enthusiast, the sort of person who derives pleasure from spreading nitrogen-rich fertilizers. Still, the project had been a hellish lot of work.

Now the end was in sight. Bob dipped one end of the PVC tube segment into a small brown bottle labeled MIRACLE SOLVENT! taking care not to get any of the corrosive and potentially carcinogenic liquid on his fingers. He fitted the tip of the tube into a cylindrical plastic drip-emitter, where it stuck fast; the solvent worked instantly, just as the label had

Cockroach Miracles, Solvent Dreams" by Michael Petracca from *Manoa*, Volume 3, Number 2, Fall 1991. Copyright © 1991 by Michael Petracca.

promised . . . not a miracle, perhaps, but satisfying. After troweling a shallow trench in the sandy topsoil, Bob placed the fitted pipe lengthwise along seven inches of narrow cut, and then he stopped to rest. He stretched out on a redwood chaise, which was shaded from the early afternoon sun by the back of the house and looked up at the sky. The sight that confronted Bob Donohoe was without precedent in his experience, although it aroused his curiosity more than his concern at first. Bob saw, or thought he saw, a spot in the middle of the sky, something like a fish egg: a single dark point in the middle of a gelatinous, shimmering plasma field the approximate size of a pencil eraser.

All succeeding perceptions took place in a fraction of a second, the time it might take for a human eyelid to traverse several millimeters of corneal surface in mid-blink, or for an earwig's heart to beat. In that minutest of passages, Bob saw the egg grow in size, its dark nucleus dilate with astonishing rapidity until it blocked out the sun and the vast disk of the sky, so that it appeared for a frozen instant as though an immense, breathing cowl undercast with ferrous crags and hummocks had suspended itself directly over the supine Bob Donohoe, or that the dark belly of an enormous motionless beast had settled over the earth. Brain waves don't have to travel very far, and they travel very fast; therefore, Bob actually had an opportunity to let fly two thoughts as he observed this rare phenomenon, just before he ceased to exist in his most recent form: first, My God! (which got my attention, even though he meant it in a purely secular sense, Bob never having prayed in his life and not about to start now); and second, At least I don't go out alone. True enough: this would not be a solitary but rather a mass exit featuring Bob, all Bob's neighbors, their pets, their pets' various parasitic guests, all the neatly tended gardens in the neighborhood along with all the rotting, untended weedy patches and every other living thing in the unincorporated portions of Schooner Valley and beyond.

Bob had always detested the idea of death, not so much because it connoted any future nonexistence as because it carried an implication of defeat. Expiring intubated on your hospital bed in the oncology ward, skewered upon your steering column or caught by cardiac arrest in mid-orgasm: wherever contingency happens to place you in your last moments, you lose; and everybody else—even those closest to you and suitably bereaved— can't help feeling a bit of elation at having survived you . . . a galling state of affairs, especially to people who pride themselves on being winners, as Bob did. If you overlooked his blasted marriage to the former Carolee Stern, who was now the only herbal homeopath in Durango, Colorado, you could consider the short life of Bob Donohoe as having been a string of victories: never had colic; had been able to form a cursive "e" several months earlier than most toddlers; was named spelling monitor by his second-grade teacher, Miss Millward; had been the best volleyball server in his fourth-grade class at Harding School, earning himself the nickname "Carburetor"; won two ribbons, a second and a fourth, in the all-city junior chess tournament; although too short to compete as a member of the varsity in high school, had taken first in the Cee pole vault two years running; was, because of his decent grades, placed in a special program that allowed certain gifted students to attend university courses during their senior year in high school; graduated Phi Beta Kappa, Cum Laude, from the College of Letters and sciences at UCLA; received a partial fellowship to attend graduate school in speech pathology at Cal Poly; had received a tenure-track posting in the Speech and Hearing Center at the University of California at Fiesta City, where he now worked as a clinician; and had numerous professional victories, including his most recent, in which Bob helped heal the vocal cords of a Spanish department teaching assistant, whose advanced glottal fry had rendered him virtually incapable of lecturing for more than thirty minutes without excruciating pain and loss of voice. Not a list of Nobel accomplishments, Bob might be the first to admit, but noteworthy enough to make dying seem bitter default by contrast. However, winning and losing become irrelevant conditions if your city gets pulverized by a random cosmic event, since there's nobody around to gloat. Despite the momentary comfort occasioned by this last (and I do mean last!) realization—the same sort of relief that participants in a suicide pact must derive from looking in each other's eyes as they take their last breaths—Bob Donohoe had an impulse to ward off the onrushing meteor by raising his hands: an instinctual reaction and a very low-comical definition of futility, if you ask me. But before the neural impulses could jump synapses and pick the appropriate dendritic pathways to Bob's arms, all the atoms in his body lost their affinity for one another in a single spasm of horrible ecstasy and dispersed themselves among other atoms once also organized into complex patterns but now every bit as lost as Bob's former atoms, and all you could see, if you looked down upon the scene from someplace on high, was an enormous depression, along with towering, distending clouds of dust and smoke, which, after a spell, would plunge the world and everything into perpetual wintry darkness.

I watched it all happen: spectacular, I must admit, and not without a certain beauty. Did you ever see a brush fire sweep down out of the mountains on compression-heated sundowner winds and destroy acres of parched chaparral, incinerating or displacing countless reptiles and small mammals and destroying hundreds of homes that lie in its path? If you have any capacity for empathy, you must be appalled and sorry for all the discontinued lives, but at the same time, you can't help admiring the sublime power of nature at its most rampageous, even as the fire takes an abrupt turn and heads your way, with much choking ash in attendance. Watching Bob Donohoe get vaporized by a county-sized meteor was like that, only my own home was never threatened, of course. It's boring sometimes being out of the machine, a benignly insubstantial presence and for all useful purposes dead, but at least you don't need homeowners' insurance.

That's one good thing. Now don't go calling me callous or blaming me or sending letters. Granted, I'm an omniscient sort of narrator, but beyond that my hands are pretty much tied. If you want miracles, give one of those preachers on TV a jingle, or Sai Baba, although I'm not sure how much effect an expensive haircut or a handful of incinerated elephant dung would have in the face of a massive bolide hurtling toward Earth at forty thousand meters per second. It isn't that I don't care—I do, really—but standing in the way of stray celestial bodies never has been part of my job description, and can you imagine how stressed I'd get if I had to intervene every time a disaster threatened to happen? Think what a nuisance it is to water your own house plants, and then factor that by several trillion, every day. Nearly impossible, in other words. Besides, it's a full-time job just to love each one of you and bathe you occasionally in shafts of light, to address you sternly when you discontinue your Thorazine against medical advice, to make those flattened designs in cornfields and knock the china from your shelves sometimes so you think there might be ghosts, and when you die, to put you in that winding, windy duct and create that clever buzzing sound-patch for you to hear, and let you swim weightlessly in the clear ether until your arms get tired. Oh yes, and to leaven the occasional virgin, immaculately. That was a good time for all concerned, you'll have to agree, without which the holidays would be pretty drab and blizzardy. But good times have been getting less frequent of late, and now with this meteor thing, they might be fast drawing to a close. I love arthropods, too, and even viruses, but let's face it: they aren't big on imagination. If I got one of them—say a cockroach—pregnant without her having made love, nobody in the beetle community would twitch an antenna, let alone write books about it. I know them: they'd just go on chomping whatever they could sink their mandibles into and laying their damn eggs. Ah, Me. Well, maybe they'll evolve into something interesting before the sun burns out and I have to start testing the job market. One can only hope.

POINTS TO CONSIDER ABOUT "COCKROACH MIRACLES, SOLVENT DREAMS"

1. How does the author manipulate narrative time in "Cockroach Miracles, Solvent Dreams"? Where does the story proceed at "normal" pace, and where does the reader have a sense of time's expanding or contracting? What is the author's reason for playing with temporality in this way?

2. Describe the narrator in the first portion of the story. Who, in your opinion, is the speaker? Toward the end of "Cockroach Miracles, Solvent Dreams", the speaker shifts to first-person narration, beginning with the statement, "I watched it all happen . . ." Is this the same narrator as in the first part of the

story, or an entirely different person? What is the narrative and thematic effect of this shift from third- to first-person narration?

3. There is one phrase in the "Cockroach Miracles, Solvent Dreams" that trumpets its importance by appearing in all-caps, followed by an exclamation point: "MIRACLE SOLVENT!" The words of this phrase also appear in the story's title. Speculate as to the relevance these words have to the story's implied thematic meaning, as suggested by its resolution.

4. The fourth paragraph of "Cockroach Miracles, Solvent Dreams" gives us a lengthy discussion of the protagonist's background—perhaps more information than we need or want to know about Bob Donahoe. What is the author's intention in providing this overabundance of exposition material? How did you feel as you read it?

5. Does the shift in perspective at the end of "Cockroach Miracles, Solvent Dreams" also occasion a shift in tone? How would you characterize the tone during the first half of the story? How would you describe the tone of the story after the narrator begins speaking in first person? Which section was more engaging for you as a reader, and why?

Selected from The Temple of My Familiar
Alice Walker

"Hello, son."

It was Miss Lissie's voice, yet deeper, and weaker, *older*, than Suwelo remembered it. He adjusted the volume on the cassette player and sat down on the couch in front of it. On the left side of the sofa he'd set up his projector and filled it with the slides of Miss Lissie's work that Mr. Hal had sent him. After listening to her speak, he would have a look.

"By the time you get this," Miss Lissie's deep voice continued, "I will be somewhere and someone else. I have asked Hal to send it to you only upon my death, to which I almost look forward, knowing as I do that it is not the end, and being someone who enjoys hanging around, in spite of myselves. I regret leaving Hal, and am anxious as to our chances of coming to-

Selected chapters from pp. 351–371 of THE TEMPLE OF MY FAMILIAR. Copyright © 1989 by Alice Walker. Reprinted by permission of Harcourt Brace & Company.

gether again; but that is all I do regret, and I have every faith we will meet again, and no doubt soon. For Hal and I have a lot more stuff to work out, and though we have been at it for so many years, and it's been hard labor, I can tell you, we've only just begun.

Miss Lissie cleared her throat.

"I am running on about this, Suwelo, because it is important, and true, but also because I am afraid to tell you how I know all this, to tell you my own news. Which is"—and here she took a long, slow breath—"that I lied when I told you I have always been a black woman, and that I can only remember as far back as a few thousand years.

"Of course I was from time to time a white woman, or as white as about half of them are. I won't bore you with tales of the centuries I spent sitting around wondering which colored woman would do my floors. Our menfolks were bringing them in all the time. You'd go to sleep one night brotherless, husbandless, fatherless, and in the morning more than likely one of them would be back. He'd be leading a string of some of the wretchedest-looking creatures you ever saw. Black, brown, red. Sometimes they looked like Mongols or Chinese. You never knew where in the world they came from. And he wouldn't tell you. 'Got you some help,' was the most he'd say, dropping his end of the chain next to where he kept the dogs tied.

"He'd stick some savagely gorgeous trinket on my neck or arm, surely made by witchcraft, I'd think, but silver or, more likely, gold, and start looking about for breakfast.

"I knew what a lady was supposed to do. I clutched the front of my wrapper shut and went to inspect the savages. I always turned up my nose and made a pukey motion toward their filthy hair. They were so beaten they could barely look at me.

"Over time, if *he* didn't pawn it, the thing on my neck or arm would start talking to me. Especially whenever one of *them* looked at it. It took me years to understand that they knew that on my careless skinny, or fat, white arm I was wearing all the history, art, and culture of their own people that they and their children would ever see."

There was a pause. "Gold," said Miss Lissie thoughtfully, "the white man worships gold because it is the sun he has lost."

There was another pause, during which Suwelo leaned forward slightly and stared into the cassette spinning noiselessly round and round. In a moment, Miss Lissie drew in a labored breath and continued.

"Let me tell you a story," she said. "It is a dream memory, too, like the one I told you about my life with the cousins; but it is more tenuous even than that one, more faded. Weak. And that has been deliberate. I have repressed it for all I am worth. Regardless, it is still with me, because, like the other memories, it *is* me."

She paused, coughed, and said, "This was very long ago, indeed."

Suwelo leaned back against the cushions of the couch, put his feet up on the coffee table in front of him, and placed his hands behind his head.

He thought he was ready.

"We lived at the edge of an immense woods," said Miss Lissie, "in the kind of houses, made of straw, that people built; insubstantial, really flimsy little things, somewhat fanciful, like an anthill or a spider's web, thrown up in a hour against the sun. My mother was queen of our group; a small group or tribe we were. Never more than a couple of hundred of us, sometimes fewer. But she was not 'queen' in the way people think of queens today. No, that way would have been incomprehensible to her, and horrid. I suppose she was what queens were originally, though: a wise woman, a healer, a woman of experience and vision, a woman superbly trained by her mother. A really good person, whose words were always heard by the clan.

"My mother kept me with her at all times, and she was always stroking me, rubbing into my skin various ointments she'd concocted from the flesh of berries and nut that she found. As a small child I didn't notice anything wrong about spending so much time with my mother, nor was it ever unpleasant. Quite the contrary, in fact. Her familiar was an enormous and very much present lion; they went everywhere together. This lion also had a family of his own. There was a lot of visiting between us, and in the lion's little family of cubs I was always welcome.

"This perhaps sounds strange to you, Suwelo. About the lions, I mean. But it is true. This was long, long ago, before the animals had any reason to fear us and none whatever to try to eat us, which—the thought of eating us—I'm sure would have made them sick. The human body has been recognized as toxic, by the animals, for a very long time.

"In the Bible I know there's a line somewhere about a time in the future when the earth will be at peace and the lion will lie down with the lamb. Well, that has already happened, and eventually it was to the detriment of the lion.

"In these days of which I am speaking, people met other animals in much the same way people today meet each other. You were sharing the same neighborhood, after all. You used the same water, you ate the same foods, you sometimes found yourself peering out of the same cave waiting for a downpour to stop. I think my mother and her familiar had known each other since childhood; for that was the case with almost everyone. All the women, that is. For, strange to say, the women alone had familiars. In the men's group, or tribe, there was no such thing. Eventually, in imitation of the women and their familiars, companions, friends, or whatever you want to call them, the men learned to tame the barbarous forest dog and to get the occasional one of those to more or less settle down and stay by their side. I do not mean to suggest that the dogs were barbarous in the sense that we sometimes think of animals today as being 'red in tooth and claw.' No, they were barbarous because they simply lacked the sensibility of many of the other animals—of the lions, in particular; but also of the elephants and turtles, the vultures, the chimpanzees, the monkeys, orangutans, and giant apes. They were opportunistic little creatures, and basically lazy, sorely lacking in integrity and self-respect. Also, they lacked culture.

"It was an elegant sight, I can tell you, my mother and Husa walking along the river, or swimming in it. He was gigantic, and so beautiful. I am talking now about his spirit, his soul. It is a great tragedy today that no one knows anymore what a lion is. They think a lion is some curiosity in a zoo, or some wild thing that cares about tasting their foul flesh if they get out of the car in Africa.

"But this is all nonsense and grievous ignorance; as is most of what 'mankind' fancies it 'knows.' Just as my mother was queen because of her wisdom, experience, ability to soothe and to heal, because of her innate delicacy of thought and circumspection of action, and most of all because of her gentleness, so it was with Husa and his tribe. They were king of creation not because they were strong, but because they were strong and also gentle. Except to cull the sick or injured creatures from the earth, and to eat them, which was their role in creation, just as it is the role of the vulture to eat whatever has already died, they never used their awesome strength.

"We had fire by then. I say this because it was a recent invention; my mother's grandmother had not had it. Husa and his family would come of an evening to visit; they loved the fire; and there we'd all sprawl watching the changing embers and admiring the flames, well into the night, when we fell fast asleep. My mother and I slept close to Husa, and in the morning's chill his great heat warmed us.

"So I was not lonely, though at times I saw that other children regarded me strangely. But then, being children, they'd frequently play with me. I loved this. Our playing consisted very often of finding some new thing to eat. And we would roam for miles in search of whatever was easy to reach and ripe. It seemed to me there was everything anyone could imagine, and more than enough for twenty human and animal tribes such as ours. I wish the world today could see our world as it was then. It would see the whole tribe of creation climbing an enormous plum tree. The little brown and black people, for I had not yet seen myself as different; the monkeys, the birds, and the things that today have vanished but which were bright green and sort of a cross between a skunk and a squirrel. There we'd be, stuffing ourselves on plums—little and sweet and bright yellow. Husa would let us stand on his back to reach the high inner branches. If we were eating for a long time, Husa would lie on the ground yawning, and when we were full, the monkeys, especially, would begin a game, which was to throw plums into Husa's yawning mouth. It was curious to see that no matter how rapidly we threw the plums into his mouth, Husa never swallowed one and never choked. He could raise the back of his tongue, you see, like a kind of trapdoor, and the plums all bounced off it.

"What does not end, Suwelo? Only life itself, in my experience. Good times, specific to a time and place, always end. And so it was with me. The time arrived when I was expected to mate. In our group this was the initiation not only into adulthood, but into separation from the women's tribe—at least from the day-to-day life of it that was all one had ever known. After mating and helping his mate to conceive, a man went to live with men. But this was not a hardship, since the men's encampment was never more than half a day's journey from our own, and there was always, between the two tribes, the most incessant visiting. Why didn't they, men and women, merge? It simply wasn't thought of. People would have laughed at the person who suggested it. There was no reason why they should merge, since each tribe liked the arrangement they had. Besides, everyone—people and other animals—liked very much to visit. To be honest, we loved it. That was our TV. And so it was well to have other people and other animals *to* visit.

"Though I hated the thought of leaving my mother, I knew I could still see her whenever I wanted to, and I also knew that the men in the men's tribe were ready to be my father. For no one had a particular father. That was impossible, given the way the women chose their lovers, freely and variously. The men found nothing strange in this, any more than the women did. Why should they? Lovemaking was considered one of the very best things in life, by women and men; of course it would have to be free. See what I mean about songs?" Miss Lissie chuckled. "Besides, when a young man arrived in the tribe of the men, they were at long last given an opportunity—late, it's true—to mother. Fathering *is* mothering, you know.

"There was a girl I liked, who liked me back. This was a miracle. And at the proper time, the day before the coming up of the full moon, she and I were sent to pick plums together. I remember everything about that day: the warmth of the sun on our naked bodies, the fine dust that covered our feet. . . . Her own little familiar, a serpent, slid alongside us. Serpents then were different than they are now, Suwelo. Of course almost everything that was once free is different today. Her familiar, whom my friend called Ba, was about the thickness of a slender person's arm and had small wheel-like extendable feet, on which it could raise itself and whir about, like some of those creatures you see in cartoons; or, retracting these, it could move like snakes move today. It could also extend and retract wings, for all serpents that we knew of at that time could fly. It was a lovely companion for her, and she loved it dearly and was always in conversation with it. I remember the especially convoluted and wiggly trail Ba left behind in the dust, in its happy anticipation of eating fresh plums. . . . Later that day there was the delicious taste of sun-warmed plums in our mouths. We were, all three of us, chattering right along, and eating, and feeling very happy.

"I was not to be happy long; none of us was. Eventually I had my friend in my arms, and one of her small black nipples, as sweet as any plum and so like my mother's, was in my mouth, and I was inside her. It was everything I'd ever dreamed, and much more than I'd hoped. But it was not, I think, the same for her. When I woke up, she was wide awake, simply sitting there quietly, stroking Ba, who was lazily twisting his full self around and around her beautiful knees. The sun was still above the tree-tops, for I remember that the light was golden, splendidly perfect, but even as I watched, it began rapidly going down.

"And then, when I looked down at myself, I saw that while I was sleeping she had rubbed me all over with the mixture of dark berries and nut fat my mother always used, which I realized had been hidden beneath the plum tree. And for the first time I could ask someone other than my mother what it was for. My mother had said it was to make my skin strong and protect it from the sun. And so, I asked my friend. And *she* said it was to make me look more like everyone else.

"'You look like you don't have a skin, you know,' she said. 'But you do have one.'

"I was thrown completely by this, coming as it did after our first love-making. It seemed to indicate a hideous personal deficiency that I didn't need to hear about just then, on the eve of becoming a man in the tribe of men. Right away I thought: Is this how they'll see me as well?

"She took me gently by the hand and we walked to a clear reflecting pool not far away. We'd often bathed there. And she scooped up a handful of water and vigorously scrubbed my face; then we bent down over the water, and there my friend was, looking very much like my mother and her mother and sisters and brothers and aunts of the village—all browns and blacks, with big dark eyes. And there was I—a ghost. Only, we knew nothing of ghosts, so I could not even make that comparison. I did look as though I had no skin.

"It was the first time I'd truly seen myself as different. I cried out in fear at myself. Weeping, I turned and ran. My friend came running after me. For it had not been her intention to hurt. She was taking over my mother's duty in applying the ointment, and was only trying to be truthful and help me begin to face reality.

"All I could think of was hiding myself—my kinky but pale yellow hair, the color of straw in late summer, my pebble-colored eyes, and my skin that had no color at all. I ran to a cave I knew about not far from the plum tree: And I threw myself on the floor, crying and crying.

"She came in behind me, the mess of berries and nut fat in a bamboo-joint container in her hand. She tried to talk to me, to soothe me, to spread the stuff over me. I knocked it away from me; it rolled over the earthen floor. During this movement, I suddenly caught sight of my member and saw that the color that had been there before we made love had been rubbed off during our contact. The sight shamed me. I ran outside the cave and grabbed the first tree leaves I saw and slapped them over myself.

"But then I realized it was my whole body that needed covering, not just my penis. My friend was still running around behind me, trying to comfort me. She was crying as much as I was, and beating her breasts. For we learned mourning from the giant apes, who taught us to feel grief any-where around us, and to reflect it back to the sufferer, and to act it out. But now this behavior made me sick. I picked up a stick and chased her away. She was so shocked to see me use a stick in this way that she seemed quite happy to drop her sympathies for me and run. But as she turned to run, her familiar, seeing her fright and its cause, extended both its clawed feet and its wings and flew up at me. In my rage I struck it, a brutal blow, with my club, so hard a blow that I broke its neck, and it fell without a sound to the ground. I couldn't believe I had done this. Neither could my friend. She ran back, though she was so afraid, and scooped Ba's broken body up in her arms. The last I saw of her was her small, naked, dark brown back, with Ba's limply curling tail, which was beginning to change colors, dangling down her side.

"I never made it into the men's tribe. I never went back to my mother. The only one from my childhood I ever saw again was Husa. Perhaps he came to look for me as a courtesy to my mother. He found me holed up in a cave far, far from our encampment, my hair in kinky yellow locks, which re-sembled his, actually; my stone gray eyes wild with pain. He came up to me and rested a warm paw on my shoulder and breathed gently into my face. The smell made me almost faint from love and homesickness. Then he pro-ceeded to lick me all over, thoroughly, as he would wash one of his cubs, with his warm pink tongue. I realized that night, sleeping next to Husa, that he was the only father I had ever known or was ever likely to know. And so, I felt, I had left my mother to join the men after all.

"Of course Husa could not stay forever. But he stayed long enough. Long enough to go on long walks with me, just as he did with my mother. Long enough to share fires—which I knew he loved, and so forced myself to make. Long enough to share sunrises and sunsets and to admire giant trees and sweet-smelling shrubs. For Husa greatly appreciated the tiniest particle of the kingdom in which he found himself. He taught me that there was an-other way of being in the world, away from one's own kind. Indeed, he rec-onciled me to the possibility that I had no 'own kind.' And though I missed my mother terribly, I knew I would never go back. It hurt me too much to know that everyone in our group had always noticed, since the day I was born, that I was different from anyone who had ever lived.

"One day, after a kill, Husa brought the remains, a draggle of skin, home to me. With a stone I battered it into a shape that I could drape around myself. I found a staff to support me in my walks and to represent 'my people.'

"Husa left.

"And now I gradually made a discouraging discovery. The skin that Husa gave me, which covered me so much more effectively than bark or leaves, and which I could tie on in a manner that would stay, frightened all the animals with whom I came in contact. In vain did I try to explain how I came by it, how much I needed it. That it was a gift, a leftover, from Husa the lion, who harmed no creature; ever, but was only the angel of mercy to those things in need of death. But what animal could comprehend this new thing that I was? That I, a creature with a skin of its own—for though I looked skinned, they could smell I was not—was nonetheless walking about in one of theirs? They ran from me as if from plague. And I was totally alone for many years, until, in desperation, I raided the litter of a barbarous dog, and got myself companionship in that way."

The tape ran on and on, without Miss Lissie's voice. Suwelo rose from the couch and peered at the spinning cassette. He was about to stop it, and see if it should be turned over, when Miss Lissie's voice continued. She sounded somewhat rested, as if she'd taken a long break.

"You may wonder," she said, "why I repressed this memory. And, by the way, I don't know what else became of me, or of my dog. It is hard to believe my mother never searched for me, never found me. That I lived the rest of my days in that place without a mate. Perhaps my mate did come to me, and perhaps she brought our child, which must have been odd-looking; for she loved me, of that I had no doubt, and perhaps we began a new tribe of our own. That, anyway, is *my* fantasy." She laughed. "It is also the fantasy upon which the Old Testament rests," she said, "but without any mention of our intimacy with the other animals or of the brown and black colors of the rest of my folks.

"I will tell you why I repressed this memory. I repressed it because of Hal. But, Suwelo, there is more; for that is not the only lifetime I have given up, or, I should say, that I have deliberately taken away from myself. In each lifetime I have felt forced to shed knowledge of other existences, other lives. The times of today are nothing, nothing, like the times of old. The time of writing is so different from the so much longer time of no writing. People's very eyes are no longer the same. The time of living separate from the earth is so much different from the much longer time of living with it, as if being on your mother's breast. Can you imagine a time when there was no such thing as dirt? It is hard for people to comprehend the things that I remember. Even Hal, the most empathetic of fellow travelers, up to a point, could not follow some of the ancient and pre-ancient paths I knew. I swallowed past experiences all my life, as I divulged those that I thought had a chance, not of being believed—for no one has truly, truly believed me; at least that is my feeling, a bitter one, most of the time—but of simply being imagined, fantasied.

"Suwelo, in addition to being a man, and white, which I was many times after the time of which I just told you, I was also, at least once, myself a lion. This is one of those dream memories so frayed around the edges that it is like an old, motheaten shawl. But I can still sometimes feel the sun on my fur, the ticks in my mane, the warm swollen fullness of my tongue. I can smell the injured and dying kin who are in need of me to bring them death. I can feel the leap in my legs, the stretch in my belly, as I bound toward them and stun them, in great mercy, with a blow. I can taste the sweet blood as my teeth puncture their quivering necks, breaking them instantly, and without pain. All of this knowledge, all of this remembrance, is just back of my brain.

"But the experiences I best remember were sometime after the life in which I knew Husa. It was, in fact, a terrible, chaotic time, though it had started out, like the eternity everyone knew, peacefully enough. Like Husa I was friends with a young woman and her children. We grew up together and frequently shared our favorite spots in the forest, or stared by night into the same fire. But this way of life was rapidly ending, for somehow or other by the time I was fully grown, and big, as lions tend to be, the men's camp and the women's had merged. And they had both lost their freedom to each other. The men now took it on themselves to say what should and should not be done by all, which meant they lost the freedom of their long, undisturbed, contemplative days in the men's camp; and the women, in compliance with the men's bossiness, but more because they now became emotionally dependent on the individual man by whom man's law now decreed they must have all their children, lost their wildness, that quality of homey ease on the earth that they shared with the rest of the animals.

"In the merger, the men asserted themselves, alone, as the familiars of women. They moved in with their dogs, whom they ordered to chase us. This was a time of trauma for women and other animals alike. Who could understand this need of men to force us away from woman's fire? And yet, this is what they did. I remember the man and the dog who cased me away; he had a large club in one hand, and in the other, a long, sharply pointed stick. And how sad I was to leave my friend and her children, who were crying bitterly. I think I knew we were experiencing one of the great changes in the structure of earth's life, and it made me very sorrowful, but also very thoughtful. I did not know at the time that man would begin, in his rage and jealousy of us, to hunt us down, to kill and eat us, to wear our hides, our teeth, and our bones. No, not even the most cynical animal would have dreamed of that. Soon we would forget the welcome of woman's fire. Forget her language. Forget her feisty friendliness. Forget the yeasty smell of her and the warm grubbiness of her children. All of this friendship would be lost, and she, poor thing, would be left with just man, screaming for his dinner and forever murdering her friends, and with man's 'best friend,' the 'pet' familiar, the fake familiar, his dog.

"Poor woman!

"But to tell you the truth, Suwelo, I was not sorry to go. For I was a lion. To whom harmony, above everything, is sacred. I could see that, merged, man and woman were in for an eternity of strife, and I wanted no part of it. I knew that, even if man had let us remain beside woman's fire he would be throwing his weight around constantly, and woman being woman, every so often would send pots and pans flying over our heads; this would go on forever. An unbearable thought; as a lion, I could not bear loud noises, abrupt changes in behavior, voices raised in anger. *Evilness.* No lion could tolerate such things. It is our nature to be nonviolent, to be peaceful, to be calm. And ever to be fair in our dealings; and I knew this would be impossible in the present case, since the animals, except for the barbarous dogs, clearly preferred woman, and would always have been attempting to defend her. Lions felt that, no matter the circumstance, one must be dignified. In consorting with man, as he had become, woman was bound to lose her dignity, her integrity. It was a tragedy. But it was a fate lions were not prepared to share.

"In subsequent periods lions moved farther and farther away from humans, in search of peace. There were tribes with whom we kept connections, in that we taught, and they learned from us. What did they learn? They learned that rather than go to war with one's own kind it was better to pack up and remove oneself from the site of contention. That as long as there is space in which to move there is a possibility of having uncontested peace. There are tribes living today in South Africa who have never come to blows with each other for a thousand years. It is because of what they learned from the lions.

"For thousands of years our personalities were known by all and appreciated. In a way, we were the beloved 'uncles' and 'aunts'—interesting visitors, indulgent playmates, superb listeners, and thoughtful teachers—of the human tribe, which, fortunately, could never figure out, not for a long, long time, anyhow, any reason why we should be viewed as completely different from them and separate from them. Only gradually did we fade into myth—all that was known of us previously, that is.

"Now," said Miss Lissie, whose voice was again becoming tired, "there were but two things on earth Hal truly feared. He feared white people, especially white men, and he feared cats. The fear of the white man was less irrational than the fear of cats, but they were both very real fears to Hal. You could make him back up twenty miles simply by asking him to hold a cat. And he arranged his life so that if he ever saw a white man, it was by accident, and also very separate from his personal life, an unheralded and unwelcome event. So how could I tell him all of who I was? By now Hal is like my son to me, and I couldn't bear it if he hated me. For such fear as Hal's *is* hatred.

"And so, I never told him. How could I say it? *Yo,* Hal, I was a white man; more than once; they're probably still in there somewhere. *Yo,* Hal, I was also, once upon a time, a very large cat."

Miss Lissie chuckled. Then laughed and laughed. Suwelo did too. Her laughter was the last sound on that side of the tape.

"But if you love someone, you want to share yourself, or, in my case," said Miss Lissie—and Suwelo imagined her wiping her eyes, still smiling—

"you want to share your*selves*. But I was afraid. Maybe there's always a part of the self that we hide, deny, deliberately destroy.

"But oh, how we love the person who affirms even that hateful part of us. And it was for affirming these split-off parts of my memory that I loved your uncle Rafe. Rafe, unlike Hal, was afraid of no one. He thought white people the most pathetic people who ever lived. Ruling over other people, he said, automatically cuts you off from life. And to try to rule over colored people, who, anybody could see, were life itself! He was more puzzled than annoyed when otherwise intelligent-looking and -acting white people called him 'boy' or 'nigger.' He was always hoping for a little better from them than he ever got. But that was because he could easily see some of himself in them, though, when looking back at him, white people apparently saw.... But he often wondered just *what* it was that they saw. What they let themselves see. Were they blind to his very *being*, as he himself was blind to the being of a fly? To him, their constant imperative to 'civilize' us was in fact a need to blind and deaden us to their own extent.

"I told Rafe everything; and he took me north, to Canada, in the summers, to be around white people; and he took me to more zoos than I have the heart to mention. This was part and parcel of his making love to me, you see, taking me to those places of which I was, myself, most afraid. You cannot imagine the feeling I had the first time I sat down to dinner in a restaurant that was filled with white people, white people who only stared at us and whispered among themselves, but did not, as they would have done in the South, rush to throw us out of the building, or perhaps beat us up or even lynch us.

"I remember that Rafe ordered meat. Some kind of duck, I think. And when it came, he saw the look on my face. I could never eat meat among white people; of that I was sure; my stomach heaved at the thought of it. Rafe and I ate mashed potatoes and salad, and he said to me, in that deep, caressing, *sweet* Negro voice of his: 'Well, Lissie, have a *good* look.'

"And I could see how they'd closed themselves off, these descendants, there at the 'top of the heap,' and how isolated they were. They were completely without wildness, and they had forgotten how to laugh. They had also forgotten, I was to discover on our many trips, how to dance and sing. They haunted black people's dance halls and churches, trying to 'pick up' what they'd closed off in themselves. It was pitiful.

"In a way, I preferred the zoos. Though I hated them with all my heart, naturally. But at the zoo, at least there were no illusions about who was free and who was not. The lions were always in cages too small for them. And it had never occurred to anyone that, cut off from life year upon year, as they were, with nothing whatever to do, the least that could be done was to build them a fire. It was heartbreaking—to watch them pace, to smell the sour staleness of their coats and of their cells, to hear the hysteria in their roar, to watch them devour a perfectly healthy animal that had been raised for 'meat' and killed on an assembly line by machine. It was horrible. It was a fate the most imaginative and cynical preancient lion could not have imagined. And now, as a presence in the modern world, I am thankful for this.

"The most abominable thing to see was their faces. Slack, dull, unintelligent, *unthoughtful*. Stupefied from boredom, gross from the degradation of dependency. To every zoo—colored could go even to the one in Baltimore, after a long struggle; but only on maid's day off, Thursday—I carried a large mirror. Anyone else would have thought this strange, but not Rafe. He helped me carry it and hold it up outside the cages. A restless lion would amble up to the bars and have a look at himself. This was usually the first and only look at himself he'd ever had. I held my breath.

"Would there be a flicker of recognition? Even of interest? Did the lion inside the body of the lion see itself? Though I myself had the body of a woman, I could still see my lion inside. Would they see that? Would they see the old nobility, the old impatience with inferiors? The old grace?

"One or two of them saw something. But it only made them sad. They slunk back to a corner of their cages and put their heads down between their paws. Of course, I wanted to leap through the bars to comfort them. I wanted to destroy the bars.

"Rafe carried me back home, a pitiful wreck, after these excursions, and put me to bed. He and Hal and Lulu [our daughter] would come in to kiss me good night; and when Rafe was turning to go, I would grasp his hand—such a good, steady, clean brown hand it was. He would sit down on the bed without a word and take off his shoes.

"Your uncle Rafe was an incomparable lover, Suwelo. And I have missed him so much, I have sometimes longed to meet up with him again, which I know is not likely; there is little need for him to come back. He loved the total me. None of my selves was hidden from him, and he feared none of them. Sometimes, when I would get 'on my high horse,' as he called it, when I was ordering everybody around and complaining that nobody knew anything or could do anything right but me, he'd grin and say, 'You sure are showing your white tonight!' And I'd feel how ridiculous I was being, and laugh.

"Or, sometimes at a party, I'd realize the other people were a bunch of lowlifes, and I'd leave. Just stroll out the door. Rafe would come after me and look at me prowling along the sidewalk aching for distance, and peace, and calm; disgust at the party's members still on my face, and he'd say, 'Baby, the lion in winter's got nothing on you!'

"And of course he knew and appreciated all the other selves, and could call them by name, too.

"So, loving Rafe and being loved by Rafe was the experience of many a lifetime. And very different from being loved by Hal, even when our passion for each other was at its height, Hal loved me like a sister/mystic/warrior/woman/mother. Which was nice. But that was only part of who I was. Rafe, on the other hand, knowing me to contain everybody and everything, loved me wholeheartedly, as a goddess. Which I was."

POINTS TO CONSIDER ABOUT THE SELECTION FROM *TEMPLE OF MY FAMILIAR*

1. We have no way of knowing for sure how Walker constructed this narrative, but what elements in the selection might suggest that she used an organic approach in constructing it? How does the device of the tape recorder ("The tape ran on and on . . .") lend itself to an organic method of story construction? Are there any elements in the story that might hint at a more formal, structural method?

2. What does the speaker mean when she says, "I lied when I told you that I have always been a black woman, and that I can only remember as far back as a few thousand years"? How does this statement set up the plot as it subsequently spins out?

3. How does the character of Suwelo figure in Walker's construction of this story? Is he a cardboard figure, a mere plot device, a sounding-board for Miss Lissie's narrative, or does he serve a more centrally important role than that?

4. Miss Lissie says, "As a small child I didn't notice anything wrong about spending so much time with my mother, nor was it ever unpleasant. Quite the contrary, in fact. Her familiar was an enormous and very much present lion; they went everywhere together." What does she mean by the word "familiar" in this passage . . . and perhaps in the title of her book? How does this word inform the story's plot?

5. All plots involve narrative tension—usually the result of conflict between characters—to some degree. Identify the points of narrative tension in this selection from *The Temple of My Familiar,* and discuss the ways in which Walker relies on patterns of tension and release to keep this story moving forward.

Descent of Man
T. Coraghessan Boyle

I was living with a woman who suddenly began to stink. It was very diffi-cult. The first time I confronted her she merely smiled. "Occupational haz-ard," she said. The next time she curled her lip. There were other problems too. Hairs, for instance. Hairs that began to appear on her clothing, sharp and black and brutal. Invariably I would awake to find these hairs in my mouth, or I would glance into the mirror to see them slashing like razor edges across the collars of my white shirts. Then too there was the fruit. I began to discover moldering bits of it about the house—apple and banana most characteristically—but plum and tangelo or even passion fruit and yim-yim were not at all anomalous. These fruit fragments occurred princi-pally in the bedroom, on the pillow, surrounded by darkening spots. It was not long before I located their source: they lay hidden like gems in the long wild hanks of her hair. Another occupational hazard.

Jane was in the habit of sitting before the air conditioner when she came home from work, fingering out her hair, drying the sweat from her face and neck in the cool hum of the machine, fruit bits sifting silently to the carpet, black hairs drifting like feathers. On these occasions the room would fill with the stink of her, bestial and fetid. And I would find my eyes water-ing, my mind imaging the dark rotting trunks of the rain forest, stained si-enna and mandalay and Hooker's green with the excrements dropped from above. My ears would keen with the whistling and crawking of the jungle birds, the screechings of the snot-nosed apes in the branches. And then, slack-faced and tight-boweled, I would step into the bathroom and retch, the sweetness of my own intestinal secrets a balm against the potent hairy stench of her.

One evening, just after her bath (the faintest odor lingered, yet still it was so trenchant I had to fight the impulse to get up and urinate on a tree or a post or something), I lay my hand casually across her belly and was sud-denly startled to see an insect flit from its cover, skate up the swell of her ab-domen, and bury itself in her navel. "Good Christ," I said.

"Hm?" she returned, peering over the cover of her Yerkish reader.

"That," I said. "That bug, that insect, that vermin."

She sat up, plucked the thing from its cachette, raised it to her lips and popped it between her front teeth. "Louse," she said, sucking. "Went down to the old age home on Thirteenth Street to pick them up."

I anticipated her: "Not for—?"

"Why certainly, potpie—so Konrad can experience a tangible gratification of his social impulses during the grooming ritual. You know: you scratch my back, I scratch yours."

I lay in bed that night sweating, thinking about Jane and those slippery-fingered monkeys poking away at her, and listening for the lice crawling across her scalp or nestling their bloody little siphons in the tufts under her arms. Finally, about four, I got up and took three Doriden. I woke at two in the afternoon, an insect in my ear. It was only an earwig. I had missed my train, failed to call in at the office. There was a note from Jane: Pick me up at four. Konrad sends love.

The Primate Center stood in the midst of a macadamized acre or two, looking very much like a school building: faded brick, fluted columns, high mesh fences. Finger paintings and mobiles hung in the windows, misshapen ceramics crouched along the sills. A flag raggled at the top of a whitewashed flagpole. I found myself bending to examine the cornerstone: Asa Priff Grammar School, 1939. Inside it was dark and cool, the halls were lined with lockers and curling watercolors, the linoleum gleamed like a shy smile. I stepped into the BOYS' ROOM. The urinals were a foot and a half from the floor. Designed for little people, I mused. Youngsters. Hardly big enough to hold their little peters without the teacher's help. I smiled, and situated myself over one of the toy urinals, the strong honest scent of Pine-Sol in my nostrils. At that moment the door wheezed open and a chimpanzee shuffled in. He was dressed in shorts, shirt and bow tie. He nodded to me, it seemed, and made a few odd gestures with his hands as he moved up to the urinal beside mine. Then he opened his fly and pulled out an enormous slick red organ like a peeled banana. I looked away, embarrassed, but could hear him urinating mightily. The stream hissed against the porcelain like a thunderstorm, rattled the drain as it went down. My own water wouldn't come. I began to feel foolish. The chimp shook himself daintily, zippered up, pulled the plunger, crossed to the sink, washed and dried his hands, and left. I found I no longer had to go.

Out in the hallway the janitor was leaning on his flathead broom. The chimp stood before him gesticulating with manic dexterity: brushing his forehead and tugging his chin, slapping his hands under his armpits, tapping his wrists, his tongue, his ear, his lip. The janitor watched intently. Suddenly—after a particularly virulent flurry—the man burst into laughter, rich braying globes of it. The chimp folded his lip and joined in, adding his weird nasal snickering to the janitors' barrel-laugh. I stood by the door to the BOYS' ROOM in a quandary. I began to feel that it might be wiser to wait in the car—but then I didn't want to call attention to myself, darting in and out like that. The janitor might think I was stealing paper towels or something. So I stood there, thinking to have a word with him after the chimp moved on—with the expectation that he could give me some grass-roots insight into the nature of Jane's job. But the chimp didn't move on. The two continued laughing, now harder than ever. The janitor's face was tear-streaked. Each time he looked up the chimp produced a gesticular flurry that would stagger him again. Finally the janitor wound down a bit, and still chuckling, held out his hands, palms up. The chimp flung his arms up over his head and then heaved them down again, rhythmically slapping the big palms with his own. "Right on! Mastuh Konrad," the janitor said, "Right on!" The chimp grinned, then hitched up his shorts and sauntered off down the hall. The janitor turned back to his broom, still chuckling.

I cleared my throat. The broom began a geometrically precise course up the hall toward me. It stopped at my toes, the ridge of detritus flush with the pinions of my wingtips. The janitor looked up. The pupil of his right eye was fixed in the corner, beneath the lid, and the white was red. There was an ironic gap between his front teeth. "Kin ah do sumfin fo yo, mah good man?" he said.

"I'm waiting for Miss Good."

"Ohhh, Miz *Good*," he said, nodding his head. "Fust ah tought yo was thievin paypuh tow-els outen de Boys' Room but den when ah sees yo standin dere rigid as de Venus de Milo ah thinks to mahsef: he is some kinda new sculpture de stoodents done made is what he is." He was squinting up at me and grinning like we'd just come back from sailing around the world together.

"That's a nice broom," I said.

He looked at me steadily, grinning still. "Yo's wonderin what me and Mastuh Konrad was jivin bout up dere, isn't yo? Well, ah tells yo: he was re-latin a hoomerous anecdote, de punch line ob which has deep cosmic impli-cations in dat it establishes a common groun between monks and Ho-mo sapiens despite dere divergent ancestries." He shook his head, chortled. "Yes in-deed, dat Mastuh Konrad is quite de wit."

"You mean to tell me you actually understand all that lip-pulling and finger-waving?" I was beginning to feel a nameless sense of outrage.

"Oh sartinly, mah good man. Dat ASL."

"What?"

"ASL is what we was talkin. A-merican Sign Language. De-veloped for de deef n dumb. Yo sees, Mastuh Konrad is sumfin ob a genius round here. He can commoonicate de mos esoteric i-deas in bof ASL and Yerkish, re-spond to and translate English, French, German and Chinese. Fack, it was Miz Good was tellin me dat Konrad is workin right now on a Yerkish translation ob Darwin's *De-scent o Man*. He is mainly into anthro-pology, yo knows, but he has cultivated a in-ter-ess in udder fields too. Dis lass fall he done undertook a Yerkish translation ob Chomsky's *Language and Mind* and Nietzsche's *Jenseits von Gut und Böse*. And dat's some pretty heavy shit, Jackson."

I was hot with outrage. "Stuff," I said. "Stuff and nonsense."

"No sense in feelin personally treatened by Mastuh Konrad's chieve-ments, mah good fellow—yo's got to ree-lize dat he is a genius."

A word came to me: "Bullhonk," I said. And turned to leave.

The janitor caught me by the shirtsleeve. "He is now scorin his turd opera," he whispered. I tore away from him and stamped out of the building.

Jane was waiting in the car. I climbed in, cranked down the sunroof and opened the air vents.

At home I poured a water glass of gin, held it to my nostrils and in-haled. Jane sat before the air conditioner, her hair like a urinal mop, stinking. Black hairs cut the atmosphere, fruit bits whispered to the carpet. Occasionally the tip of my tongue entered the gin. I sniffed and tasted, thinking of plastic factories and turpentine distilleries and rich sulfurous smoke. On my way to the bedroom I poured a second glass.

In the bedroom I sniffed gin and dressed for dinner. "Jane?" I called, "shouldn't you be getting ready?" she appeared in the doorway. She was dressed in her work clothes: jeans and sweatshirt. The sweatshirt was gray and hooded. There were yellow stains on the sleeves. I thought of the lower depths of animal cages, beneath the floor meshing. "I figured I'd go like this," she said. I was knotting my tie. "And I wish you'd stop insisting on baths every night—I'm getting tired of smelling like a coupon in a detergent box. It's unnatural. Unhealthy."

In the car on the way to the restaurant I lit a cigar, a cheap twisted black thing like half a pepperoni. Jane sat hunched against her door, unwashed. I had never before smoked a cigar. I tried to start a conversation but Jane said she didn't feel like talking: talk seemed so useless, such an anachronism. We drove on in silence. And I reflected that this was not the Jane I knew and loved. Where, I wondered, was the girl who changed wigs three or four times a day and sported nails like a Chinese emperor?—and where was the girl who dressed like an Arabian bazaar and smelled like the trade winds?

She was committed. The project, the study, grants. I could read the signs: she was growing away from me.

The restaurant was dark, a maze of rocky gardens, pancake-leafed vegetation, black fountains. We stood squinting just inside the door. Birds whistled, carp hissed through the pools. Somewhere a monkey screeched. Jane put her hand on my shoulder and whispered in my ear. "Siamang," she said. At that moment the leaves parted beside us: a rubbery little fellow emerged and motioned us to sit on a bench beneath a wicker birdcage. He was wearing a soiled loincloth and eight or ten necklaces of yellowed teeth. His hair flamed out like a brushfire. In the dim light from the braziers I noticed his nostrils—both shrunken and pinched, as if once pierced straight through. His face was of course inscrutable. As soon as we were seated he removed my socks and shoes, Jane's sneakers, and wrapped our feet in what I later learned were plantain leaves. I started to object—I bitterly resent anyone looking at my feet—but Jane shushed me. We had waited three months for reservations.

The maitre d' signed for us to follow, and led us through a dripping stone-walled tunnel to an outdoor garden where the flagstones gave way to dirt and we found ourselves on a narrow plant-choked path. He licked along like an iguana and we hurried to keep up. Wet fronds slapped back in my face, creepers snatched at my ankles, and mud sucked at the plantain leaves on my feet. The scents of mold and damp and long-lying urine hung in the air, and I thought of the men's room at the subway station. It was dark as a womb. I offered Jane my hand, but she refused it. Her breathing was fast. The monkey chatter was loud as a zoo afire. "Far out," she said. I slapped a mosquito on my neck.

A moment later we found ourselves seated at a bamboo table overhung with branch and vine. Across from us sat Dr. and Mrs. U-Hwak-Lo, director of the Primate Center and wife. A candle guttered between them. I cleared my throat, and then began idly tracing my finger around the circular hole cut in the table's center. The Doctor's ears were the size of peanuts. "Glad you two could make it," he said. "I've long been urging Jane to sample some of our humble island fare." I smiled, crushed a spider against the back of my chair. The Doctor's English was perfect, pure Martha's Vineyard—he sounded like Ted Kennedy's insurance salesman. His wife's was weak: "Yes," she said, "nussing cook here, all roar." "How exciting!" said Jane. And then the conversation turned to primates, and the Center.

Mrs. U-Hwak-Lo and I smiled at one another. Jane and the Doctor were already deeply absorbed in a dialogue concerning the incidence of anal retention in chimps deprived of Frisbee coordination during the sensorimotor period. I gestured toward them with my head and arched my eyebrows wittily. Mrs. U-Hwak-Lo giggled. It was then that Jane's proximity began to affect me. The close wet air seemed to concentrate her essence, distill its potency. The U-Hwak-Los seemed unaffected. I began to feel queasy. I reached for the fingerbowl and drank down its contents. Mrs. U-Hwak-Lo smiled. It was coconut oil. Just then the waiter appeared carrying a wooden bowl the size of a truck tire. A single string of teeth slapped against his breastbone as he set the bowl down and slipped off into the shadows. The

Doctor and Jane were oblivious—they were talking excitedly, occasionally lapsing into what I took to be ASL, ear- and nose- and lip-picking like a manager and his third-base coach. I peered into the bowl: it was filled to the rim with clean-picked chicken bones. Mrs. U-Hwak-Lo nodded, grinning: "No on-tray," she said. "Appeticer." At that moment a simian screamed somewhere close, screamed like death itself. Jane looked up. "Rhesus," she said.

On my return from the men's room I had some difficulty locating the table in the dark. I had already waded through two murky fountains and was preparing to plunge through my third when I heard Mrs. U-Hwak-Lo's voice behind me. "Here," she said. "Make quick, repass now serve." She took my hand and led me back to the table. "Oh, they're enormously re-sourceful," the Doctor was saying as I stumbled into my chair, pants wet to the knees. "They first employ a general anesthetic—a distillation of the chu-bok root—and then the chef (who logically doubles as village surgeon) makes a circular incision about the macaque's cranium, carefully peeling back the already-shaven scalp, and stanching the blood flow quite effec-tively with maura-ro, a highly absorbent powder derived from the tamana leaf. He then removes both the frontal and parietal plates to expose the brain . . ." I looked at Jane: she was rapt. I wasn't really listening. My atten-tion was directed toward what I took to be the main course, which had ap-peared in my absence. An unsteady pinkish mound now occupied the cen-ter of the table, completely obscuring the circular hole—it looked like cherry vanilla yogurt, a carton and a half, perhaps two. On closer inspec-tion I noticed several black hairs peeping out from around its flaccid edges. And thought immediately of the bush-headed maitre d'. I pointed to one of the hairs, remarking to Mrs. U-Hwak-Lo that the rudiments of culinary hy-giene could be a little more rigorously observed among the staff. She smiled. Encouraged, I asked her what exactly the dish was. "Much deli-cacy," she said. "Very rare find in land of Lincoln." At that moment the waiter appeared and handed each of us a bamboo stick beaten flat and sharpened at one end.

". . . then the tribal elders or visiting dignitaries are seated around the table," the Doctor was saying. "The chef has previously of course located the macaque beneath the table, the exposed part of the creature's brain pro-truding from the hole in its center. After the feast, the lower ranks of the vil-lage population divide up the remnants. It's really quite efficient."

"How fascinating!" said Jane. "Shall we try some?"

"By all means . . . but tell me, how has Konrad been coming with that Yerkish epic he's been working up?"

Jane turned to answer, bamboo stick poised: "Oh I'm so glad you asked—I'd almost forgotten. He's finished his tenth book and tells me he'll be doing two more—out of deference to the Miltonic tradition. Isn't that a groove?"

"Yes," said the Doctor, gesturing toward the rosy lump in the center of the table. "Yes it is. He's certainly—and I hope you won't mind the pun—a brainy fellow. Ho-ho."

"Oh Doctor," Jane laughed, and plunged her stick into the pink. Beneath the table, in the dark, a tiny fist clutched at my pantleg.

I missed work again the following day. This time it took five Doriden to put me under. I had lain in bed sweating and tossing, listening to Jane's quiet breathing, inhaling her fumes. At dawn I dozed off, dreamed briefly of elementary school cafeterias swarming with knickered chimps and weltered with trays of cherry vanilla yogurt, and woke stale-mouthed. Then I took the pills. It was three-thirty when I woke again. There was a note from Jane: Bringing Konrad home for dinner. Vacuum rug and clean toilet.

Konrad was impeccably dressed—long pants, platform wedgies, cuff links. He smelled of eau de cologne, Jane of used litter. They arrived during the seven o'clock news. I opened the door for them. "Hello Jane," I said. We stood at the door, awkward, silent. "Well?" she said. "Aren't you going to greet our guest?" "Hello Konrad," I said. And then: "I believe we met in the boys' room at the Center the other day?" He bowed deeply, straight-faced, his upper lip like a halved cantaloupe. Then he broke into a snicker, turned to Jane and juggled out an impossible series of gestures. Jane laughed. Something caught in my throat. "Is he trying to say something?" I asked. "Oh potpie," she said, "it was nothing—just a little quote from Yeats."

"Yeats?"

"Yes, you know: 'An aged man is but a paltry thing.'"

Jane served watercress sandwiches and animal crackers as hors d'oeuvres. She brought them into the living room on a cut-glass serving tray and set them down before Konrad and me, where we sat on the sofa, watching the news. Then she returned to the kitchen. Konrad plucked up a tiny sandwich and swallowed it like a communion wafer, sucking the tips of his fingers. Then he lifted the tray and offered it to me. I declined. "No thank you," I said. Konrad shrugged, set the plate down in his lap and carefully stacked all the sandwiches in its center. I pretended to be absorbed with the news: actually I studied him, half-face. He was filling the gaps in his sandwich-construction with animal crackers. His lower lip protruded, his ears were rubbery, he was balding. With both hands he crushed the heap of crackers and sandwiches together and began kneading it until it took on the consistency of raw dough. Then he lifted the whole thing to his mouth and swallowed it without chewing. There were no whites to his eyes.

Konrad's only reaction to the newscast was a burst of excitement over a war story—the reporter stood against the wasteland of treadless tanks and recoilless guns in Thailand or Syria or Chile; huts were burning, old women weeping. "Wow-wow! Eeeeeee! Er-er-er-er," Konrad said. Jane appeared in the kitchen doorway, hands dripping. "What is it, Konrad?" she said. He made a series of violent gestures. "Well?" I asked. She translated: "Konrad says that 'the pig oppressors' genocidal tactics will lead to their mutual extermination and usher in a new golden age . . .'"—here she hesitated, looked up at him to continue (he was springing up and down on the couch, flailing his fists as though they held whips and scourges)—"'. . . of freedom and equality for all, regardless of race, creed, color—or genus.' I wouldn't worry," she added, "it's just his daily slice of revolutionary rhetoric. He'll calm down in a minute—he likes to play Che, but he's basically nonviolent."

Ten minutes later Jane served dinner. Konrad, with remarkable speed and coordination, consumed four cans of fruit cocktail, thirty-two spareribs, half a dozen each of oranges, apples and pomegranates, two cheeseburgers and three quarts of chocolate malted. In the kitchen, clearing up, I commented to Jane about our guest's prodigious appetite. He was sitting in the other room, listening to *Don Giovanni*, sipping brandy. Jane said that he was a big, active male and that she could attest to his need for so many calories. "How much does he weigh?" I asked. "Stripped," she said, "one eighty-one. When he stands up straight he's four eight and three quarters." I mulled over this information while I scraped away at the dishes, filed them in the dishwasher, neat ranks of blue china. A few moments later I stepped into the living room to observe Jane stroking Konrad's ears, his head in her lap. I stand five seven, one forty-three.

When I returned from work the following day, Jane was gone. Her dresser drawers were bare, the closet empty. There were white rectangles on the wall where her Rousseau reproductions had hung. The top plank of the bookcase was ribbed with the dust-prints of her Edgar Rice Burroughs collection. Her girls' softball trophy, her natural foods cookbook, her oaken cudgel, her moog, her wok: all gone. There were no notes. A pain jabbed at my sternum, tears started in my eyes. I was alone, deserted, friendless. I began to long even for the stink of her. On the pillow in the bedroom I found a fermenting chunk of pineapple. And sobbed.

By the time I thought of the Primate Center the sun was already on the wane. It was dark when I got there. Loose gravel grated beneath my shoes in the parking lot; the flag snapped at the top of its pole; the lights grinned lickerishly from the Center's windows. Inside the lighting was subdued, the building hushed. I began searching through the rooms, opening and slamming doors. The linoleum glowed all the way up the long corridor. At the far end I heard someone whistling "My Old Kentucky Home." It was the janitor. "Howdedo," he said. "Wut kin ah do fo yo at such a inauspicious hour ob de night?"

I was candid with him. "I'm looking for Miss Good."

"Ohhh, she leave bout fo-turdy evy day—sartinly yo should be well apprised ob dat fack."

"I thought she might be working late tonight."

"Noooo, no chance ob dat." He was staring at the floor.

"Mind if I look for myself?"

"Mah good man, ah trusts yo is not intimatin dat ah would dis-kise de troof . . . far be it fum me to pre-varicate jus to proteck a young lady wut run off fum a man dat doan unnerstan her needs nor 'low her to spress de natchrul inclination ob her soul."

At that moment a girlish giggle sounded from down the hall. Jane's girlish giggle. The janitor's right hand spread itself across my chest. "Ah wooden insinooate mahsef in de middle ob a highly sinificant speriment if ah was yo, Jackson," he said hissing through the gap in his teeth. I pushed by him and started down the corridor. Jane's laugh leaped out again. From the last door on my left. I hurried. Suddenly the Doctor and his wife stepped from the shadows to block the doorway. "Mr. Horne," said the Doctor, arms folded against his chest, "take hold of yourself. We are conducting a series of experiments here that I simply cannot allow you to—"

"A fig for your experiments," I shouted. "I want to speak to my, my—roommate." I could hear the janitor's footsteps behind me. "Get out of my way, Doctor," I said. Mrs. U-Hwak-Lo smiled. I felt panicky. Thought of the Tong Wars. "Is dey a problem here, Doc?" the janitor said, his breath hot on the back of my neck. I broke. Grabbed the Doctor by his elbows, wheeled around and shoved him into the janitor. They went down on the linoleum like spastic skaters. I applied my shoulder to the door and battered my way in, Mrs. U-Hwak-Lo's shrill in my ear: "You make big missake, Mister!" Inside I found Jane, legs and arms bare, pinching a lab smock across her chest. She looked puzzled at first, then annoyed. She stepped up to me, made some rude gestures in my face. I could hear scrambling in the hallway behind me. Then I saw Konrad—in a pair of baggy BVDs. I grabbed Jane. But Konrad was there in an instant—he hit me like the grill of a Cadillac and I spun across the room, tumbling desks and chairs as I went. I slumped against the chalkboard. The door slammed: Jane was gone. Konrad swelled his chest, swayed toward me, the fluorescent lights hissing overhead, the chalkboard cold against the back of my neck. And I looked up into the black eyes, teeth, fur, rock-ribbed arms.

POINTS TO CONSIDER ABOUT "DESCENT OF MAN"

1. What is Boyle's intended effect in starting his story with the sentence, "I was living with a woman who suddenly began to stink."? What effect does it have on you, if any? How does this statement set the stage for plot events that will follow?

2. "The Descent of Man" was mentioned earlier in this chapter as an example of a story that contains some intentionally shocking elements. What specific plot events might be considered outrageous, shocking? Do these plot events exist for the sole, gratuitous purpose of shocking the audience, or do they help suggest the story's theme and/or develop the characters?

3. Does Boyle want you, as a reader, to believe that Jane is actually turning into an ape, or does he suggest that the narrator is imagining the whole ugly story out of some repressed jealous feelings—or both? If your answer is "both"—that the story works on both the literal and figurative levels—then why does Boyle leave these plot events open to such divergent interpretations?

4. As the plot unfolds, Boyle includes some characterizations that come across to many readers as vile racist stereotypes. What characters in particular might fall into this category? Assuming that Boyle himself is not a vile racist, why would he include these characterizations? What do they tell us about the narrator? What function do the statements of the janitor play in developing the story's theme?

5. How does the character of Konrad figure in the plot? What does the ending of the story suggest in terms of possible thematic interpretations for the story? In addition to its possible intellectual content, how does the story leave you feeling on a visceral level? What is Boyle's point in assaulting the reader on the "gut" level, as he does in " "Descent of Man"? To what "Man" is Boyle referring in the title: all mankind, the narrator specifically, all men . . . or what?

✖ WRITING ACTIVITIES: MAKING STORIES

1. Open a magazine and find an advertisement featuring two models. Imagine those models as characters in a story, the ad's layout as the setting. Let those characters begin interacting with each other, and with any other props that appear in the ad. Take care *not* to plan ahead, because this activity is designed to give you practice in the organic method of plot construction. Instead, let your story's events spin out spontaneously and record them as faithfully as possible, with no thought to "correct" plot structure.

2. Recall a recent real-life interaction between yourself and a friend or family member, or between any two persons of your acquaintance. Ideally, this interaction will involve an element of conflict: an argument about money; a philosophical disagreement over the nature of God, the universe, and everything; an accusation of cheating at gin rummy . . . whatever. Describe the initial conflict as faithfully as you can—including the

setting of the event and any dialogue that actually took place—and then let your imagination take over, creating an entirely new set of consequences that follow from the original conflict. Try not to plan ahead; rather, allow yourself to be "surprised" at the unexpected turns your narrative takes as your subconscious mind directs this organic process.

3. To get the impulse to shock out of your system, use the organic method of plot construction to create a narrative piece whose intent is to disturb as many readers as possible. Feel free to indulge in extended evocations of gore and excreta, racist and sexist stereotypes, irreligious posturings, violent impulses, unpatriotic moods, taboo sexual practices, criminal behaviors, excessive intake of drugs and/or fatty foods. Come up with a central image based squarely in one of these areas and "run with it," allowing the story to spin out spontaneously, ideally building on itself, so that it reaches an orgiastic climax of offensiveness. For an example of a story like this, I append another of my delightful short stories, this one called "The Unluckiest Consumer in the World," which appeared in a recent issue of *Turnstile*. In it, I conceived of a central question—What would happen if one character happened to buy all the defective items on *Consumer Reports'* product recall list?—and then let my fevered imagination direct the narrative toward its gruesome end.

The Unluckiest Consumer in the World
Michael Petracca

You can have binding repaired by manufacturer or authorized dealer—
or, if you make repair yourself, you will get free corduroy hat.
—*Consumer Reports*

It had been a hard year for Mary Grace, and she didn't understand much of it. First her mommy went to heaven in January, when the electrical circuitry in the console of the family's 1988 Saab 9000—the one her father bought Mommy as an anniversary surprise—overheated and caught fire. That made Mommy take her eyes off the road for a second because she thought there was a big bumblebee in the car, but it was really an ash from her burning Fiesta City street map that had been sitting on the console when it overheated. In that moment a bicycle rider came around a corner, and when Mary Grace's mommy saw the man frantically waving and then turning his bike over onto the pavement, she swerved to miss him and slammed the Saab into a parked pickup truck. Mary Grace was in ballerina class when her daddy told her the news. For months after the funeral, Mary Grace imagined her mommy coming through the bedroom door with cool, dry goodnight kisses, her scent like peach soda and jasmine blooms, but she never did.

That was hard, and then Daddy had to go to the hospital after his 1988 Volkswagen Jetta's brake line leaked, causing partial brake failure. Daddy couldn't steer the car very well with the brakes malfunctioning like that, and he bumped into a tree and wrenched his neck so badly that he had to stay in the hospital for a couple of days. Mary Grace stayed with Aunt Rose but got to visit her father. Aunt Rose dropped Mary grace off at the front of the hospital and the doors opened all by themselves. A nice lady in a pink-striped dress accompanied her up the elevator and showed Mary Grace where her daddy was. He was happy to see her, and said he would be out of the hospital soon and they would go to Kiddieland to ride the ponies and the little boats that went around in a circular trough of water.

The day after Clark Spataro got out of the hospital, and with every intention of making good his promise, he buckled Mary Grace into the back seat of a rented 1990 Geo Storm—he had learned from a TV show that children are safer in the back seat. But when he used the release lever to tip his seatback forward, he caught his finger in the hinge mechanism and soon was driving to the emergency room for X rays. Luckily, the finger wasn't broken, and the doctor, whose white plastic lapel tag read, JACK D. HOBBS, M.D., bandaged it up. Mary Grace thought her daddy's finger looked like a big white lollipop with a fudge center.

His finger still throbbing a little and his neck encased in a cloth-covered polyfoam brace, Clark allowed himself to daydream about how he was going to make Mary Grace happy. It had been a heartbreaking year for him, and sometimes he felt as though Mary Grace was the only thing in his life that kept him going. Saturday was her seventh birthday, and he was planning a party to which all her friends would come, the best party ever. He was listening affectionately to his daughter play Barbie-house on the floor of her bedroom when he smelled smoke coming from his Aqua-Hex one-gallon aquarium. The fish were swimming around as usual, but Clark could see that the electric light mounted inside the metal top of the aquarium had gone out. He turned off the light, which made the aquarium stop smoking, and then reached into the water to make sure the Aqua Clear Power Head aquarium pump, model 200, was still working properly—the fish would quickly die without it—and received an electrical jolt of such amplitude that it threw him halfway across the dining room, where he lay stunned on his deep-loop Berber remnant for several moments before regaining full consciousness. When Clark got up and inspected the aquarium, all the fish were floating belly up near the top of the tank, from which a cloud of steam rose and then evanesced into the air. Clark was sad for his fish but cheered himself by listening to Mary Grace, who was still holding pretend conversations with Barbie and Ken and one of their friends whose name he couldn't remember. He thought it might be Whitney.

The next day Clark, who held a middle-management position at a major airborne-delivery service, called in sick. He used his burned hand as an excuse, but really he wanted to spend the day buying prizes for Mary Grace's birthday. Driving the rented Geo Storm all over town, he was so filled with the spirit of celebratory promise that he didn't even notice the traffic or mind the lines at the stores. At the K Mart in the Fairplex Plaza he bought Mary Grace a Ceramic Potpourri House, item #32-67-47, with a special electrical "Tealight Candle" he knew his daughter would like. While he was there he also bought several cans of It's Fun Tyme! String Confetti, taking care to select cans marked, "Safe for the environment, fluorocarbon free," because he knew from another TV show that spray cans were doing something bad to the ozone layer around the earth: either putting more ozone there, or displacing the ozone with aerosol gases, he couldn't remember which. At the Toys "R" Us store in the Paseo Tranquillo mall Clark bought Mary Grace a bright red "Musical Ice Cream Car," model D13/3, which had a rear crank for winding up the music box feature. The ice cream decals on the front, sides, back, and top of the Ice Cream Car reminded Clark of his childhood, when he used to chase the Good Humor man down the street on hot summer days, and it made him feel good. Before leaving the Toys "R" Us store, Clark also bought eight Siren Whistles by Lucky Star Enterprises in a variety of colors—yellow, white, red, blue, orange, green, pink, and black—so that nobody at Mary Grace's party would feel left out of the fun.

Clark made sure to arrive home before the school bus dropped Mary Grace off and stashed his purchased treasures in the bedroom closet behind a collection of dusty wing-tipped oxfords and calf-high side-zipped boots he never wore. When Mary Grace came in the back door and set her metal Jetsons lunch pail on the kitchen counter, Clark gave her a kiss and said, "Honey, I need you to stay out of here for a little while because I'm going to be making a surprise for you. Can you do that for Daddy?" Clark wanted to bake Mary Grace's birthday cake himself, the way his deceased wife, Carin, used to. At first Mary Grace was a bit wounded, but as soon as she realized her daddy was doing something for her birthday, she shouted "Priiiizes!" and bounded out the spring-loaded kitchen door, leaving Clark alone in the kitchen. Clark had never baked a cake before, but he had Carin's wooden recipe box, its flip-top painted with enamel flower designs. The box was packed with blue-lined flashcards and scraps of paper separated by alphabetical dividers. Under G Clark had found "Grandma Comstock's Chocolate Cake," a stained and spotted recipe card that called for sugar, real Vermont maple syrup, baker's chocolate, margarine, baking powder, eggs, flour, and milk—all of which Clark had purchased at the store on the way home from the bicycle store. The first instruction, written in his dead wife's loopy hand (it always made Clark weepy to see his wife's handwriting), was: *Pulp the margarine in the blender to bring it to soft consistency, like tapioca pudding.* Clark had never heard *pulp* used as a verb before, but he knew how to put things in the blender, so he took their La Machine III, model LM5, food processor out and set it on the counter next to Mary Grace's lunch pail. After plugging it into the wall socket, he removed the smoke-tinted plastic cover in preparation for mixing the ingredients in the processor's cylindrical bowl. Unfortunately, removing the cover also overrode the machine's safety interlock mechanism, and the processor whirred unexpectedly to life while Clark's hand was inside. He was merely startled at first by the sound and felt a kind of pulling sensation, but when he saw fine droplets of red liquid misting out of the top of the rotating bowl, he realized he must have cut himself and withdrew his hand. To his horror, the tip of his right index finger was no longer there; blood was pouring forth from the laceration, running down his hand and wrist. Clark was moved to shout, "I cut off my finger!" at the top of his lungs; but he didn't want to alarm Mary Grace and instead hoarsely whispered, "Ahh, my finger, my finger," over and over while he tried to staunch the flow of blood with paper towels.

After the shock of having partially amputated his finger subsided a bit, Clark ran his hand under warm tap water to inspect the damage. It wasn't as bad as he had imagined. True, his finger terminated abruptly and flatly where before it had been rounder and more elongate; and, yes, blood was seeping from exposed capillaries. But, on the up side, the processor blades had missed the bone and sliced off only a cross-section of flesh, leaving the nail intact. It didn't hurt very much, either, which kind of surprised Clark. He remembered hearing about people who had had whole appendages sewed back on after getting them severed in industrial accidents, and looked inside La Machine for the rest of his finger. Sure enough, there inside the red-spattered mixing bowl was the missing tip, looking something like a blanched almond that had been dipped in cocktail sauce. Although Clark felt somewhat queasy at handling his own mutilated appendage, he picked up the fingertip with his better hand—the one with the bandaged finger—and put it inside a Glad sandwich bag, which he secured tightly by pressing its two flaps together at the interlocking ridges. Taking care to compose himself so as not to frighten his daughter, Clark peeked inside Mary Grace's bedroom door and said, "Daddy got a little owwie on his finger, honey. Let's go see the doctor at the hospital."

"The *hostiple?*" Mary Grace whined. "Do we *have* to go there, Daddy?"

"Yes, honey, Daddy cut his finger."

"*Again?*"

"Last time Daddy pinched it. This time I cut a different one in La Machine," Clark explained. "You can bring Barbie and Whitney along if you want to."

"Kimberley," Mary Grace corrected him.

At the emergency room, Clark left Mary Grace, Barbie, and Kimberley in the waiting area, which had a children's annex well-stocked with storybooks and rag dolls and colorful wooden blocks. Dr. Hobbs, a squat, muscular man with a gray-streaked beard and long black hair combed straight back, said, "Back so soon? Maybe you should rent a room," while slipping on a pair of rubber gloves and gesturing for Clark to extend his hand. "Let's have a look," said Hobbs. "Mm-hm, ah-yess," he murmured, turning Clark's hand over several times in his own gloved hands. "I'm afraid there's not much we can do to save the tip," he said finally, explaining the reasons in medical terms that Clark didn't completely comprehend. As he stitched up the wound, Dr. Hobbs went on to predict that Clark might have some permanent loss of feeling in his finger but that the wound would otherwise heal just fine. "It might even be a plus, if you plan to go into burglary," Hobbs appended.

"Burglary?" asked Clark, still shaky from the incident.

"Sure," quipped Hobbs. "No fingerprints."

Saturday morning, while Mary Grace played with her extensive collection of plastic ponies in the TV room, Clark set about making preparations. From his shoe closet Clark retrieved a flat brown paper bag containing party favors he had picked up from the Hallmark store during one of his errand runs. He blew up some Maeno-Ma "Happy Party Balloons," item #B91, tied short lengths of ribbon to the knotted-off valves of the remaining balloons, and taped them up all over the dining area and front room. In the kitchen he stuck nine bud-shaped plastic candle holders into the prepackaged devil's food cake he had picked up on the way home from the emergency room, placed and equal number of pastel-colored helical-twisty candles into the holders, and then put the cake in the refrigerator. As he covered the dining room table with a blue polythene tablecloth and laid out matching paper plates and cups, Mary Grace came in, a plastic chestnut-brown pony in one hand and a grayish foal in the other. Clark, glancing up at the clock, asked, "Don't you think you ought to start getting ready, lambie?"

"For my party?" she asked in a tone of coy expectancy.

"Your friends will be here pretty soon," said Clark, adding a musical lilt to the last two words.

"Oh-*kaay*," enthused Mary Grace, and off she ran, only to return several minutes later, curtseying and twirling theatrically in a pink taffeta dress and shiny black pumps. Clark told Mary Grace she was just about the cutest thing he had ever seen, and she skipped away to play ponies some more.

The first party guests began to arrive just after noon. Marcy Bratton came first, and then Kotsya Nikitin and Ronnette McCullough and Diane Moreling, all bearing gaily wrapped gifts. Nan Carmody and Toni Moniz showed up next, and right behind them Mary Grace's best friend, Emily Wrightson, in a red jumper and black party shoes. Emily's little sister, Carly, came along too, toddling and clutching her Kensington Bears stuffed grizzly cub, which was dressed in a maroon print frock with pink-and-blue trim at the bottom, white lace bloomers, and a straw hat with a pink bow. Emily explained that her parents had to go to some kind of brunch, but that they would be back before the end of the party to take care of Carly and help clean up. Clark liked the part about cleaning up.

Several of the kids immediately moved to Mary Grace's room, where they pretended Ken was a cowboy riding plastic horses. Marcy and Kotsya sat at the spinet and produced a passable four-handed version of "Heart and Soul." Meanwhile, Clark arranged his stackable Virco chairs, series 890, around the table and announced, "All right, children, let's all sit down." The kids took a while to drift into the dining room, but eventually they seated themselves, still chattering, around the table. Clark remained standing. "I'm glad you could all come," he said, filling a waxed-paper cup with apple juice and handing it to Kotsya, who passed it on to Marcy, and so on. As Clark poured juice for all the kids, he told them how much it meant that they could be here on Mary Grace's special day, and then he took a seat away from the table, remembering that as a child he had hated having his parents nearby when his friends were around. He moved his Virco chair next to the sliding glass window leading to the patio, but when he sat on it the Virco leg collapsed. Luckily, it was a front leg, so Clark didn't fall backward through the plate glass window and sever an artery. The girls, who thought Clark was clowning for their benefit, laughed.

Standing up and brushing off his slacks even though there was no dirt on them—he had vacuumed earlier—Clark told the kids it might be a good time to open presents. Everyone cheered in agreement. Mary Grace opened her gifts one by one, commenting briefly on each and thanking the giver, just as her parents had drilled her over the past seven years. The Ceramic Potpourri House was her favorite; when Clark plugged it into the wall and switched on the electric "Tealight Candle" the girls as one said, *"Oooh!"* and *"Pretty!"*

"And now . . ." Clark paused to sustain the dramatic effect already created by the candle. "It's time for cake."

"Yumm," said Nan Carmody.

"It's chocolate," Mary Grace said.

"Chocolate. Num-nummies," said Kotsya Nikitin.

"Yes, but before I bring out the cake, I have a little present for each of *you,* too." Clark reached into a brown paper sack while the children sat open-mouthed with anticipation. When he passed around the Siren Whistles by Lucky Star Enterprises, the kids seemed a bit disappointed; he even thought he heard Diane Moreling mutter, "I'll say it's little" But they soon started blowing the Siren Whistles anyway, and in no time the dining room sounded like a congress of asthmatics in pollen season. Clark didn't mind the noise; if Mary Grace was having a good time, then he was happy.

While the children were wheezing away on their sirens, Clark went into the kitchen and got the cake out of the refrigerator. After lighting the candles one by one, he pushed open the swinging door and began to sing, *"Happy birthday to youuu!"* The girls joined in in merry discord. Clark set the cake on the table, and Nan Carmody told Mary Grace, "Go ahead, make a wish." While Mary Grace closed her eyes solemnly, in the manner of a saint receiving a beatitude, Clark produced the can of It's Fun Tyme! String Confetti from the paper bag and, at the precise moment when his daughter opened her eyes and took a big breath, began spraying aerosol party streamers from the can and shouting "Happy birthday!" Multi-colored streamers jetted from the can's nozzle, twisting and looping in the air before draping themselves on the hanging light fixture over the table. The girls all *oohed* again, and Clark let fly another blast of It's Fun Tyme!, this one aimed a bit lower.

A big mistake, lowering the can: The still-lit birthday candles ignited the aerosol propellant, causing the can to become a sort of blowtorch that set fire to Marcy Bratton's gingham dress. Marcy began screaming and slapping at her right shoulder, which caused her Virco stackable chair to collapse. Unfortunately, because the partiers were paying horrified attention to Marcy's distress, nobody noticed that the "Tealight" candle on the Ceramic Potpourri House had shorted and started a small fire at the other end of the table, beginning with the Ceramic Potpourri House itself and then spreading to the paper tablecloth, which smouldered and then burst into flame—along with the hem of Kotsya Nikitin's dress and petticoat. She, too, started shrieking, slapping at herself, and rolling on the floor. Ronnette McCullough, Diane Moreling, and Nan Carmody were so shocked by the sight of their friends' clothing being incinerated that they breathed a collective sigh of horror and inhaled several small parts from their Siren Whistles in the process. Clutching at their throats, they futilely attempted to expel the intrusive whistle-parts by coughing. Toni Moniz, who had been playing with the Musical Ice Cream Car, was moved to help her stricken friends, but the spectacle of the escalating birthday carnage caused her to squeeze the toy car tightly. The car broke into several sharp pieces that lacerated Toni's hand, and at the sight of blood running down her forearm she, too, began to shriek. Little Carly Wrightson, who had been playing on the floor with the JA-RU "Play to Learn" furniture and had the plastic boy in her mouth, swallowed it when Nan Carmody fell out of her collapsed Virco chair and onto Carly's back. Little Carly started gagging, a look of panic frozen on her reddening face.

Clark had no idea what to do with so many choking, burning, gagging, bleeding, and panicked children, but as fortune would have it Bill and Carol Wrightson arrived at just that moment. At first, Bill and Carol reacted with stunned disbelief, then got busy and tried to calm the terrified children as best they could with soothing words and hasty paramedical action. The Wrightsons helped Clark load all the kids into their 1989 Chrysler LeBaron GTS van with nonturbo 4, and Bill, pale, shaky, and aghast, asked Clark where the nearest hospital was. Clark told him, and Bill gunned the van down residential streets onto the coast highway toward Schooner Valley General. On the way, however, engine oil began to leak from a faulty valve-cover gasket, causing a fire in the van's engine compartment. The fire produced so much smoke, so quickly, that Bill Wrightson was momentarily unable to see, and instead of turning the wheel to follow the big bend in the coastline at Castellamare, he kept the LeBaron going straight. Realizing his error, bill hit the brakes hard, causing one of his Hercules tires, no. UPH-

FKE 179, to blow and the van to skid. When it went airborne after hitting the canted asphalt shoulder, Mary Grace looked out the window and saw a bird flying by at the same speed. For a moment she imagined she was a bird, too, flying heavenward to visit her mommy. Clark also shouted something, possibly the name of his deceased wife, but it was scarcely decipherable because other people started shouting just before the LeBaron hit the granite-scrapple seawall embankment and tumbled all the way down into the Pacific, its waters as gray and craggy as crumpled sheet metal.

A recall notice alerting the Wrightsons to the faulty valve-cover gasket arrived some days later, but nobody was home to read it.

4

Plot Components

THE STRUCTURAL METHOD: PREPARATION

The most effective way to create a workable structure for your story is to start with an *outline:* a preliminary plan, usually organized by headings and subheadings. There are numerous techniques for outlining. Some writers use index cards, others use tables or charts, others use filmic "story boards," complete with rough artistic sketches of scenes to help give them a visual sense of setting. You might experiment with several of these outlining techniques to discover the one that best suits your temperament and creative needs.

Whichever outlining method you use, start the process by writing down the central events of your story as you imagine them at this point. Having accomplished that initial task, place each of your listed events into one of the major structural areas listed below. As you fit your major story events into this framework, you might find yourself moved to develop the events a bit. That's fine—don't be so obedient to the shorthand nature of the traditional outline that you inhibit yourself from composing some actual prose you can use later in your short story or novel.

You will also undoubtedly discover that a certain event in your story will touch off an idea about an event in another part of the story, and you will likewise place that event within the outlined sequence. Plot is frequently thought of as a causally linked series of events, and one plot point will often cause another event or sequence of events, once you start outlining your story. As you develop your outline, keep in mind that it is merely meant to aid you in the composing process, and that it's not set in concrete: As you write your story, you will modify your original story many times, so that your fictional piece may bear little resemblance to the story as you originally conceived it. The rest of this chapter will present the four broad areas around which you will organize your plot: opening, exposition, midpoint(s), and resolution.

DESTROY ALL WOGELFRINS: A FOUR-STEP APPROACH TO STRUCTURAL PLOTTING

1. Opening Sentences

Mystery writers have an axiom: "Always start your story with a smoking gun." Writers of cowpoke fiction have a corollary. "'Shoot the sheriff on the first page, 'is the proverbial western writer's advice," according to author Darrell Schweitzer. These are colorful—if simplistic—ways of suggesting two things: first, that you want your opening to grab and hold the interest of your readers; and second, that a well-structured story should initiate narrative momentum from its very first words.

Some effective stories flaunt this wisdom, by "taking it from the top," developing their plots gradually from moment one. The Bible works this way: "In the beginning God created the heavens and the earth. . . . God saw all that he had made, and it was very good." So does Charles Dickens's classic *Great Expectations:* "My father's family name being Pirrip, and my Christian name Philip, my infant tongue could make of both names nothing longer or more explicit than Pip."

In fact, every story that begins with the phrase, "Once upon a time" is relying on a narrative convention so archetypally familiar that we are almost lulled into following along; "Tell me a story, Mommy," might be the response of our inner kid to such an intro. James Joyce gently satirizes this fictional convention, while still employing it to set off his *The Portrait of the Artist as a Young Man:*

> Once upon a time and a very good time it was there was a moocow coming down along the road and this moocow that was coming down along the road met a nicens little boy named baby tuckoo.

The "from the top" opening—when used in earnest and without the kind of subtle irony Joyce intends here—runs the risk of sounding juvenile or of not being terribly gripping, since exciting things usually don't happen until some narrative tension has been achieved. Still, some contemporary authors use it very effectively and to sophisticated effect. Isabel Allende begins her novel *Eva Luna* this way:

> My name is Eva, which means "life," according to a book of names my mother consulted. I was born in the back room of a shadowy house, and grew up amidst ancient furniture, books in Latin, and human mummies, but none of those things made me melancholy, because I came into the world with a breath of the jungle in my memory. My father, an Indian with yellow eyes, came from the place where the hundred rivers meet . . .

This passage doesn't generate loads of narrative tension, but the sheer literary force of the language, in phrases such as "shadowy house," "human mummies," "breath of the jungle," "yellow eyes," and "where the hundred rivers meet," serve to draw the reader into the story.

Most of today's fiction writers don't start their stories from the beginning. Instead, they use a variety of opening setups to build momentum immediately. One such setup places the main character in a setting that poses some kind of challenge, or suggests a threat or conflict. Pam Houston's short story "Selway," included in this chapter, begins with a foreshadowing of the river encounter that follows:

> It was June the seventh and we'd driven eighteen hours of pavement and sixty miles of dirt to find out the river was at highwater, the highest of the year, and rising.

The implication here is simple and clear: The narrator will soon have to deal with life-threatening danger inherent in the rising river.

Similarly, in beginning her novel *Dogeaters*, Jessica Hagedorn describes a movie theater, another example of the author placing her protagonist in a charged setting:

> 1956. The air-conditioned darkness of the Avenue Theater smells of flowery pomade, sugary chocolates, cigarette smoke, and sweat. *All That Heaven Allows* is playing in Cinemascope and Technicolor. . . .
>   Rock Hudson's rustic gardener's cottage stands next to a frozen lake. The sky is a garish baby-blue, the clouds are ethereal wads of fluffy white cotton. In this perfect picture-book American tableau, plaid hunting jackets, roaring cellophane fires, smoking chimneys, and stark winter forests of skeletal trees provide costume and setting for Hollywood's version of a typical rural Christmas. Huddled with our chaperone Lorenza, my cousin Pucha Gonzaga and I sit enthralled in the upper section of the balcony in Manila's "Foremost! First-Run! English Movies Only!" theater . . .

The depiction of the traditionally chaperoned young Filipino women sitting in the Manila theater, entranced by a stylized Hollywood depiction of American life, initiates the ethnic culture-clash that develops as the theme of Hagedorn's novel.

Another opening setup places the protagonist among characters with whom he or she will have significant interaction later on. Michael Ondaatje's *The English Patient*, for example, immediately establishes the relationship between the nurse, Hana, and the English patient who has been burned during the war,

> Every four days she washes his black body, beginning at the destroyed feet. She wets a washcloth and holding it above his ankles squeezes the water onto him, looking up as he murmurs, seeing his smile. Above the shins the burns are worse. Beyond purple. Bone.
>
> She has nursed him for months and she knows the body well, the penis sleeping like a sea horse, the thin tight lips. Hipbones of Christ, she thinks. He is her despairing saint. He lies flat on his back, no pillow, looking up at the foliage painted onto the ceiling, its canopy of branches, and above that, blue sky.

E.L. Doctorow uses the same method in opening his historical novel *The Waterworks:*

> People wouldn't take what Martin Pemberton said as literal truth, he was much too melodramatic or too tormented to speak plainly. . . . So when he went around muttering that his father was still alive, those of us who heard him, and remembered his father, felt he was speaking of the persistence of evil in general.

This opening passage places the protagonist within a cast of characters—"us," the narrator, his loved ones—with whom he has meaningful contact, and at the same time sets up the possibility of the existence of another key character: the supposedly dead father whose "evil" character poses a threat to all concerned.

A third opening technique initiates the plot at a crisis point. You may have heard the Latin term *in medias res.* It means "in the middle of things," and in literature refers to drama that begins in the middle of a situation or action. This is the category into which the "smoking gun" axiom falls. Stephen King's recent chiller *Desperation* has an opening that serves as an excellent model of this setup method:

> "Oh! Oh, Jesus! Gross"
> "What, Mary, what?"
> "Didn't you see it?"
> "See what?"
> She looked at him, and in the harsh desert sunlight he saw that a lot of the color had gone out of her face, leaving just the marks of sunburn on her cheeks and across her brow, where not even a strong sunblock cream would entirely protect her. She was very fair and burned easily.
> "On that sign. That speed-limit sign."
> "What about it?"

> "There was a dead cat on it, Peter! Nailed there or glued there or
> some damned thing." He hit the brake pedal. She grabbed his shoulder
> at once. "Don't you even *think* about going back."

This opening establishes narrative tension, as the protagonist is immediately presented with an existential dilemma: Peter will either continue driving through Nevada on his pleasant, romantic vacation, or he will eventually find himself confronting the ghastly source of the dead cat nailed to the speed limit sign. Guess which plot direction master suspense-builder King chooses for his characters to follow . . .

The foregoing represents a sampler of the most common techniques by which authors open stories. It's useful to read and internalize these techniques, so when the time comes to begin your own story, you don't have to think about it. Instead, you react instinctually—like my friend Mark Comstock playing a genial riff on his classic pre-CBS Fender Stratocaster guitar—and you make the "right" choice, the one that works . . . effortlessly, and without conscious thought.

2. Exposition

The next stage for you to outline and flesh out is *exposition,* the process of giving your audience crucial background information: narrative history to explain the action at hand, personal history to justify the behavior of your central characters as they respond to charged story situations. Exposition is generally thought to occur toward the beginning of a story. In actuality, though, we learn key information about central characters throughout the entire arc of the plot. Still, it's safe to assume that most of the exposition takes place early in the story. As John Gardner says, "in the novel, as in the short story or novella, what the reader needs to know is everything that is necessary if he is to believe and understand the ensuing action." Additionally, readers need information about characters in order to care about them.

As a mnemonic, you might remember the keys to righteous exposition as all starting with "s," by happy coincidence—subtlety, seamlessness, and subordination. Subtlety, as it relates to exposition, means: Don't hit the reader over the head with background information (fiction Rule #9). This is ungracious and in some cases can be downright painful. I recently heard an advertisement in between segments of the Jim Rome sports radio program. This ad was actually a mini-fiction that included a snippet of dialog between a small boy and an adult female:

> "Hi, Mama. Randy just called."
> "That's nice, honey. What did your older brother, Randy the college student, have to say?"

This passage includes crucial exposition. It establishes the woman as the mother of the young boy, and it introduces a secondary character, the brother. However, it doesn't meet the criterion of subtlety. In reality, a mother would never use the phrase "your older brother, Randy the college student": She would assume that the younger brother knew that Randy was his older brother, and that he was away at school. This phrase is included for the sole purpose of letting the audience know of Randy's relationship to the other characters: an exceedingly unsubtle bit of exposition . . . but then nobody ever accused a radio commercial of subtlety!

For a more literary example of unsubtle exposition, check this example from an old issue of *Tales of Future Fantastic,* a science fiction magazine (the author and title are omitted to save the author any embarrassment):

> "Well, here I am in a time-window, in the year 3050, and I still can't get a good cup of coffee," Captain Newberry said glumly.
>
> He ambled casually up the catwalk of his Space Rover. Then he looked around at the assembled Wogelfrins, the enemy alien creatures that had—amazingly!—become his friends ever since the end of the War of Interstellar Attrition. Their gray-purple eyes (Newberry was amazed for perhaps the thousandth time that these "eyes" lacked lenses to focus as human eyes would focus) looked at him expectantly.
>
> "You, Azmenarg," Newberry called to the one he knew and liked the best, "raise your hairy arm and let me shake your hand, for you are my friend, even though we were bitter enemies during the War of Interstellar Attrition, which ended a year ago."
>
> Of course, Captain Newberry was speaking in Earth years, which would be two of years on the planet Wogelfrin that has a shorter orbit around its sun.
>
> He continued speaking to his Wogelfrin pal, "But it seems we have not come as far as we should have, and that is why I grieve for this year of 3050, this year of the treaty known as the Peace of Sirius Major that you and I signed on behalf of all our peoples, because now you tell me that we will have war again."

This passage overloads the reader with too much background material crammed into a brief fictive space. In so doing, the gradual development of the story's plot grinds to a halt, while we are spoon-fed background information. Worse, the piece shifts points of view, so that we get some background information from the perspective of Captain Newberry, and other material ("Of course, Captain Newberry was speaking . . . ") from an omniscient narrator.

Worst of all, the Captain Newberry excerpt insults the reader's intelligence by delivering its historical material in a glaring, overly conspicuous way. A number of phrases—"these 'eyes' lacked lenses to focus as human eyes would focus"; "Earth years, which would be two of years on the planet Wogelfrin that has a shorter orbit around its sun"; "this year of 3050, this year of the treaty known as the Peace of Sirius Major that you and I signed on behalf of all our peoples"—in no way advance the plot and remind the reader that the story is an artifact, an *un*graceful lie. Louis Auchinloss says of this unfortunate tendency in unsuccessful stories, "Once somebody's aware of the plot, it's like a bone sticking out. If it breaks through the skin, it's very ugly."

Compare the above example of faulty exposition with another passage of science-fictional exposition, this one from Jeff Noon's futuristic novel *Vurt:*

> I couldn't see her lips move and then I realised, Brid was dream-talking, putting thoughts into my mind, which is the gift of the Shadows.
>
> Shadows are the thought-readers. They are born with the powers of telepathy and their mind can by-pass the vocal cords, putting words into your brain, and stealing the secrets that you thought were yours alone. . . . the human Shadow works best when asleep, so that's how you find them, usually, dreaming their dreams of knowledge.
>
> 'Don't let it worry you, Scribble,' Bridget thought.

In contrast to the inelegant Captain Newberry exposition, the *Vurt* passage contains a very concise explanation that is itself stylistically rich and consistent with the tone of the narrator, as seen in the phrases, "stealing the secrets that you thought were yours alone," and "dreaming their dreams of knowledge." Noon's *Vurt* excerpt also makes a graceful transition from one minor plot point (Bridget's dream-talking) to a brief explanation of dream-talking and Shadows—thus exemplifying the second key concern in effective exposition: seamlessness.

When providing background material or an explanation of unfamiliar terms (as in the science fiction subgenre), it's important to have the exposition material fit unobtrusively within the narrative, just as a skillful carpenter's dovetail joint works unobtrusively to hold an armoire or dining table together. Author/writing coach Ansen Dibell says of this quality of exposition,

> To stop the story for long-winded explanations or descriptions is deadly, particularly at the beginning and most especially in the popular genres, where a strong, direct plot that moves along fairly briskly is an absolute necessity.

Notice how seamlessly Don DeLillo delivers crucial information to readers, early in the development of his novel, *White Noise:*

> There is no Hitler building as such. We are quartered in Centenary Hall, a dark brick structure we share with the popular culture department, known officially as American environments. A curious group. The teaching staff is composed almost solely of New York émigrés, smart, thuggish, movie-mad, trivia-crazed. They are here to decipher the natural language of the culture, to make a formal method of the shiny pleasures they'd known in their Europe-shadowed childhoods—an Aris-

totelianism of bubble gum wrappers and detergent jingles. The department head is Alfonse (Fast Food) Stompanato, a broad-chested glowering man whose collection of prewar soda pop bottles is on permanent display in an alcove. All his teachers are male, wear rumpled clothes, need haircuts, cough into their armpits. Together they look like teamster officials assembled to identify the body of a mutilated colleague. The impression is one of pervasive bitterness, suspicion and intrigue.

An exception to some of the above is Murray Jay Siskind, an ex-sportswriter who asked me to have lunch with him in the dining room, where the institutional odor of vaguely defined food aroused in me an obscure and gloomy memory. Murray was new to the Hill, a stoop-shouldered man with little round glasses and an Amish beard. He was a visiting lecturer on living icons and seemed embarrassed by what he'd gleaned so far from his colleagues in popular culture.

"I understand the music, I understand the movies, I even see how comic books can tell us things. But there are full professors in this place who read nothing but cereal boxes."

"It's the only avant-garde we've got."

"Not that I'm complaining. I like it here. I'm totally enamored of this place. A small-town setting. I want to be free of cities and sexual entanglements. Heat. This is what cities mean to me. You get off the train and walk out of the station and you are hit with the full blast. The heat of air, traffic and people. The heat of food and sex. The heat of tall buildings. The heat that floats out of the subways and the tunnels. It's always fifteen degrees hotter in the cities. Heat rises from the sidewalks and falls from the poisoned sky. The buses breathe heat. Heat emanates from crowds of shoppers and office workers. The entire infrastructure is based on heat, desperately uses up heat, breeds more heat. The eventual heat death of the universe that scientists love to talk about is already well underway and you can feel it happening all around you in any large or medium-sized city. Heat and wetness."

When I decided to use this DeLillo passage, I intended to cut it down, to make it less obtrusive in the flow of my own book by replacing certain passages with the *ellipsis:* the handy three-dot tool that writers use for a variety of purposes . . . including the excision of text. But when I tried to remove some material from the DeLillo passage in order to shorten it, I discovered I couldn't. DeLillo joins background material—information about the protagonist's place of employment, his co-workers, the surrounding town, the intellectual climate of the place—so skillfully with narrative elements that there simply is no place to excise phrases without damaging the story in a significant way. Furthermore, there's no variation in tone. It's uniformly ironic and literate throughout.

In the DeLillo passage, important background material never overpowers the story, never impedes the pace of the plot, as happens in the Captain Newberry excerpt. In this way, it also illustrates a third quality of exposition . . . namely, subordination. Only background information that is crucial to an understanding of the characters or to significant advancement of the plot should be included as exposition. Otherwise, we have digression, which may be the soul of some postmodern prose (including, I confess, my own) but can lead to meandering or sluggish plots. None of the material in the DeLillo passage could be called superfluous. Even the extended introduction to Murray Jay Siskind is subordinate to the plot, as Murray turns out to be a central figure in the emerging theme of the novel.

To achieve exposition that is subtle, smoothly incorporated into the story line, and subordinate to foregrounded plot elements, writers employ a number of devices. In some cases, they use dialogue to deliver relevant information, as in this passage from Irish short-story writer Mary Lavin's "The Long Ago":

> The year that Hallie decided to buy a plot for herself in the new cemetery right beside the plot in which Dominie lay, people felt that she was going altogether too far. But again, Ella and Dolly took her part.
> "We know how you feel," Ella said. "If things had gone as they should, we know where your coffin would go by rights—down into the same grave with Dominie!"
> "I thought over it for a long time," Hallie assured her friends, "and I would not have bought the plot if Blossom had stayed a widow."
> After that particular conversation, however, Dolly and Ella felt sadder for her than ever.
> "She doesn't seem to realize that Blossom will have to be buried with Dominie anyway, whether she likes it or not," Dollie said. "A wife is buried with her first husband, no matter how many times she marries."
> "I hope nobody will tell her that," Ella said . . .

Here the dialogue serves to deliver key information about the currents of interpersonal tension running between main characters, and about certain cultural conventions, such as the interesting (and complicating, in terms of plot) proposition that first wives always have dibs on the hubby's underground company.

Another practical method of delivering exposition is by manipulating narrative time, especially through flashback. This is a cinematic technique in which the chronological sequence of the plot is temporarily interrupted, and we are transported to an earlier period, in order to receive some historical material crucial to our comprehending the action at hand. Here's an example of this type of exposition, from Jay McInerney's *The Last of the Savages:*

> "Have you ever heard of the Black Power Solidarity Committee?"
> At first this sounded merely ludicrous, something the director of the FBI dreamed up in an apocalyptic fever. On reflection, however, I realized I'd met the entire politburo of the committee in question, in a hotel suite in Miami a few years before. It *was* ludicrous, but that didn't

prevent it from being frightening—like many things that happened then.

I had just finished my freshman year at Yale and was enjoying a brief vacation . . . I spent my days on the beach with the codgers and the Cuban muscle men . . . Returning to the hotel from a day on the sand, grilled to an unflattering shade of pink, I emerged from the elevator to discover three black men in leather jackets loitering in the turquoise hall.

Lots of writers use flashback, to varying degrees of success. When it works, as in the McInerney excerpt, the reader hardly notices and certainly doesn't object to the temporal shift, because the writer has taken the trouble to make it seamless. The historical passage serves to reinforce the present action and is itself interesting—in the case of the McInerney piece, a brief, tense story within the larger, tense story. When flashback doesn't work, the reader may feel impatient for the plot to pick up again because the historical material doesn't have the same urgency or immediacy as the main plotline, or—even worse—the reader may be physically nauseated by the abrupt veering away from the present. Rule #6 of fiction is: Don't make your readers throw up, unless that's your thematic intention.

Sometimes authors will deliver exposition through the unspoken thoughts of the narrator. The literary term for this is *interior monologue,* and it's perhaps the most common form of exposition. Zora Neale Hurston uses this technique to striking effect in her novel, *Their Eyes Were Watching God:*

. . . Janie waited a bloom time, and a green time and an orange time. But when the pollen again gilded the sun and sifted down on the world she began to stand around the gate and expect things. What things? She didn't know exactly. Her breath was gusty and short. She knew things that nobody had ever told her. For instance, the words of the trees and the wind. She often spoke to falling seeds and said, "Ah hope you fall on soft ground," because she had heard seeds saying that to each other as they passed. She knew the world was a stallion rolling in the blue pasture of ether. She knew that God tore down the old world every evening and built a new one by sun-up. It was wonderful to see it take form with the sun and emerge from the gray dust of its making. The familiar people and things had failed her so she hung over the gate and looked up the road towards way off. She knew now that marriage did not make love. Janie's first dream was dead, so she became a woman.

While typical interior monologue simply relates thoughts and sense impressions from a certain character's point of view (John thought about the pet turtle he had when he was eight; Vanessa reflected on her recently terminated engagement), Hurston here takes creative license with the interior monologue. Instead of having Janie talk to herself, she "spoke to falling seeds"—a more poetic and poignant way of having Janie reflect on the fate of the archetypal feminine in a seemingly male-dominated ("a stallion rolling") world. Furthermore, the passage imparts to the reader Janie's awakening realizations about her past life, especially her marriage, and about changes that are taking place within her ("she began to...expect things,"), and so it artfully serves a practical function as exposition.

As a summary, remember to restrict your own exposition to the barest necessities. Present background information as invisibly as you can, aiming for brevity in a given scene. Distribute necessary background information throughout the first half (or even the first two-thirds) of the story, to avoid interrupting the smooth forward movement of the plot. Be certain the plot is moving forcefully before you digress from it for more than several sentences. Make the active story your priority, and keep it as free from obstructions as you can. Give your plot every chance to flow and to carry the reader along with it.

3. Escalating Midpoints and Crisis

While novels and short stories share many of the same techniques for opening and exposition, they differ greatly in the way they develop through the body of a given piece. Because a novel is relatively long, the author can build tension gradually, through a series of escalating midpoints—mini-climaxes that themselves build to the high point of the novel. In this way, structurally plotted novels resemble motion pictures, whose mini-climaxes are termed "plot points" by the Hollywood establishment.

In movies, the general goal of the scriptwriter is to build narrative tension by consciously (some critics of the Hollywood movie "formula" would say *slavishly)* including plot points at regularly timed intervals—say, every ten or fifteen minutes. In this way, the central characters are regularly experiencing new emotions and understandings, which in turn cause the characters to act in new and different ways...all leading up to the movie's climax. Carefully plotted fiction works in exactly the same way: The author keeps readers interested by piquing their sense of anticipation of the mini-climaxes that occur at regular page intervals. Whether the event is a meeting of two characters who have previously not encountered each other (Nick Carraway meets Jay Gatsby in F. Scott Fitzgerald's *The Great Gatsby),* a romantic pairing (David Copperfield meets and falls instantly in love with Dora Spenlow, his boss' childlike daughter in Charles Dickens's *David Copperfield),* or a violent act (the maid, Rosanna, commits suicide in a pool of quicksand, in Wilkie Collins' nineteenth century proto-mystery/romance, *The Moonstone),* authors manipulate their readers to anticipate the mini-climax with emotions ranging from eager pleasure to terror.

Writers—especially those who use the structural approach to plot construction—cultivate this sense of anticipation very deliberately, through narration, through dialogue between characters' conversations, or through the interior monologue of a key character, usually the protagonist. For example, in *All the Pretty Horses* by Cormac McCarthy, the author provides this piece of narration:

> There was a road on the other side of the fence and a young girl came riding down the road and passed them and they ceased talking. She wore English riding boots and jodhpurs and a blue twill hacking jacket and she carried a ridingcrop and the horse she rode was a black Arabian saddlehorse.... She wore a flatcrowned hat of black felt with a wide brim and her black hair was loose under it and fell halfway to her waist and as she rode past she turned and smiled and touched the brim of the hat with her crop . . .
>
> Rawlins fell back among the riders and alongside John Grady.
>
> Did you see that little darlin? he said.
>
> John Grady didn't answer. He was still looking down the road where she'd gone. There was nothing to see, but he was looking anyway.

The richness of narrative detail in this description, the spoken words, and the actions of the protagonist all cue the reader to anticipate a romantic encounter between John Grady and the Mexican aristocrat's daughter Alejandra—an anticipation which is piqued, teased, deferred and finally fulfilled in the succeeding seventy pages of text.

That's how most novels work: They draw the reader in with a grabber of an opening, they deliver background material gradually and unobtrusively, sometimes over the course of a hundred pages or more, and they hold the reader's interest through a series of complications and small crises. The short story—the form you'll probably begin writing—employs these same techniques. However, because of its limited narrative space, the short story's exposition must be more condensed—sometimes presenting a special challenge to the faithful observance of subtlety—and escalating midpoints fewer in number. Margaret Atwood's wry and much-anthologized story "Rape Fantasies," for example, presents a series of brief, imagined physical encounters, expressed from the point of view of several different women. Each of those encounters might be construed as an escalating midpoint, leading up to the central, mainly nonsexual fantasy of the protagonist. Ernest Hemingway's "The Short Happy Life of Francis Macomber," because it is a longish short story, has the liberty of containing a very novelistic series of mini-climaxes—encounters between the protagonist and wild beasts (including his wife and the male safari guide who lusts after her) in the African bush.

Whether your story builds to a head gradually, through a series of mini-climaxes, or whether its complication leads directly to a single climax, your central scene must pay off. Again, the degree to which you draw out and embellish your crisis point depends in large measure on the extensiveness of your plot up to that point. Hemingway, at the climax of "Macomber," uses the technique of compressing narrative time to foreground the final encounter between the protagonist, the charging buffalo, and the lethal, rifle-toting wife:

> ... the gun-bearer shouted wildly and they saw him coming out of the bush sideways, fast as a crab, and the bull coming, nose out, mouth tight closed, blood dripping, massive head straight out, coming in a charge, his little pig eyes bloodshot as he looked at them. Wilson, who was ahead was kneeling shooting, and Macomber, as he fired, unhearing his shot in the roaring of Wilson's gun, saw fragments like slate burst from the huge boss of the horns, and the head jerked, he shot again at the wide nostrils and saw the horns jolt again and fragments fly, and he did not see Wilson now and, aiming carefully, shot again with the buffalo's huge bulk almost on him and his rifle almost level with the on-coming head, nose out, and he could see the little wicked eyes and the head started to lower and he felt a sudden white-hot, blinding flash explode inside his head and that was all he ever felt.

Hemingway, who is endlessly mocked for writing nothing but short, simple, declarative sentences ("They drank the wine. It was good. It was very good."), had the ability to expatiate with the best of them. He simply reserved his long sentences—some of which rival those of William Faulkner or William Vollman for convolution and complexity—for those points in the narrative development that call for syntactic engorgement. In the above passage, he uses a technique that Burroway likens to cinematic "slow motion": "If you record detail with special focus and precision, it will create the effect of intensity." In this way, he allows the reader to experience every microsensation of his protagonist, up to and including the very moment of his death.

Atwood's climax in "Rape Fantasies" is also richly drawn, although she uses irony, distraction, conversational tone, and pathos, rather than slow motion, to render the scene toward which her story has been pointing:

> ... I explain that I've just found out I have leukaemia and the doctors have only given me a few months to live. That's why I'm out pacing the streets alone at night, I need to think, you know, come to terms with myself. I don't really have leukaemia but in the fantasy I do, I guess I chose that particular disease because a girl in my grade four class died of it, the whole class sent her flowers when she was in the hospital. I didn't understand then that she was going to die and I wanted to have leukaemia too so I could get flowers. Kids are funny, aren't they? Well, it turns out that he has leukaemia himself, and *he* only has a few months to live, that's why he's going around raping people, he's very bitter because he's so young and his life is being taken from him before he's really lived it. So we walk along gently under the street lights, it's spring and sort of misty, and we end up going for coffee, we're happy we've found the only other person in the world who can understand what we're going through, it's almost like fate, and after a while we just sort

of look at each other and our hands touch, and he comes back with me
and moves into my apartment . . .

. . . and she goes on to fantasize about the death, and the funeral and the
mourning, using the same tone, diction, and syntactic features. Even though
the "Rape Fantasies" climax is much less action-packed than Hemingway's
(and contains no corresponding sexual climax, incidentally, as befits her intended theme), it contains a similar payoff for the reader—in this case, a
heightening of the protagonist's imaginative reverie to a near-feverish pitch,
a culmination of the proto-fantasies which the story has been developing as
its midpoints.

When you arrive at the climactic event in your own stories, it's crucial
that you fulfill the expectation you've developed in the reader, just as Hemingway and Atwood have done here. In a piece of "flash" or "sudden" fiction—a story of four pages or less—the climax may be a pithy and richly descriptive sentence or three. However, drawing out and highlighting your
climactic scene is especially important in longer pieces of fiction, such as
novels and novellas, where readers may wait several hundred pages for
that culminating scene. Your climax in those cases should therefore provide
finely rendered description, penetrating emotional insight, and/or extended recounting of physical action, in order to gratify your patient readers. Make the climax worth their wait!

4. Resolution and Theme

We usually grasp what stories are about while we're reading them. Stephen
King's *The Shining*, we gather from the behavior of the protagonist, is saying
something about obsession and dissolution. The subject of J. D. Salinger's
The Catcher in the Rye is adolescent confusion. *Siddhartha* by Hermann Hesse
is about spiritual awakening. Oscar Wilde's *The Picture of Dorian Gray* is
about mutability and the natural tendency to cling to life. Harper Lee's *To
Kill a Mockingbird* is about prejudice. Philip K. Dick's *Do Androids Dream of
Electric Sheep?* is about the nature of humanness. While the subject(s) of a
fictional piece may be clear from a relatively early point in the reading, we
often have to wait until the end of a story to understand what specific point
the author is making about the subject. That specific point is called the *theme*
of a story, and delivering it is one of the main functions of resolution, the
last stage in plot development.

The notion of theme in literature is complicated by the ambiguous nature of artistic constructs. Usually, a complex piece of writing will not have
a single implied meaning. Rather, it will have a multiplicity of possible interpretations, all of which may be "correct," if they are consistently supported by the text. This difficulty is compounded by the wide range of theoretical interests that readers may bring to texts—interests that influence
their interpretation. Marxist cultural critics may find themes of class strug-

gle in certain works; queer theorists may find acting-out of homoerotic impulses in certain characters; eco-critics may find that a given novel implies certain attitudes toward the environment; feminists may find social constructions of gender-role attitudes inherent in a story.

The notion of theme is further complicated by the fact that meanings may emerge that authors did not intend. In my story, "Cockroach Miracles, Solvent Dreams," for example, I wrote the piece organically, with no idea how it would end. I had this cute concept for a piece (meteor kills protagonist, God comments), but beyond that, I let the plot unfold on its own and purposely allowed the meaning of the story to take care of itself. Nevertheless, it's clear from the resolution that a theme does emerge. Even if I hadn't written the thing, I'd still say its main implied meaning is something like: We live in a universe ruled by capricious forces, as emblematized by the wry tone of God at the story's end.

While it's dangerous to make generalizations about anything to do with literature—one of your good friends will point out ten exceptions to the generalization you just made—it's not going too far out on a limb to say that the resolution of the story will carry its main implied message, intended or not. As a maker of coherent plots, you don't have to concern yourself with all the possible interpretations which critics may apply to your stories when you become a national literary treasure. Leave the theorizing to the theorists. You do, however, need to understand that the way you construct—and especially end—your story will very likely suggest its primary meaning.

Even if you consciously intend no theme, be aware that one will probably emerge from your story and its resolution anyway. Human beings are compulsive meaning-makers, and readers naturally instinctively seek meaning in texts. Therefore make sure, during the revision process, that you take time to distance yourself from your first draft, and that you later return to your work with "fresh" eyes, to determine what thematic message your story delivers to readers. If you're not satisfied with the central message or impression that readers will derive from your story, then you may need to re-think the structure and particularly the ending, perhaps taking the story in an entirely different direction than that which you originally intended.

A secondary concern in constructing effective endings is to make them relatively brief. You want to build tension gradually toward your main climax and then, since there will no longer be any narrative tension to keep your readers interested, end the story fairly quickly.

Just like this.

The Short Happy Life of Francis Macomber
Ernest Hemingway
(1899–1961)

It was now lunch time and they were all sitting under the double green fly of the dining tent pretending that nothing had happened.

"Will you have lime juice or lemon squash?" Macomber asked.

"I'll have a gimlet," Robert Wilson told him.

"I'll have a gimlet too. I need something," Macomber's wife said.

"I suppose it's the thing to do," Macomber agreed. "Tell him to make three gimlets."

The mess boy had started them already, lifting the bottles out of the canvas cooling bags that sweated wet in the wind that blew through the trees that shaded the tents.

"What had I ought to give them?" Macomber asked.

"A quid would be plenty," Wilson told him. "You don't want to spoil them."

"Will the headman distribute it?"

"Absolutely."

Francis Macomber had, half an hour before, been carried to his tent from the edge of the camp in triumph on the arms and shoulders of the cook, the personal boys, the skinner and the porters. The gun-bearers had taken no part in the demonstration. When the native boys put him down at the door of his tent, he had shaken all their hands, received their congratulations, and then gone into the tent and sat on the bed until his wife came in. She did not speak to him when she came in and he left the tent at once to wash his face and hands in the portable wash basin outside and go over to the dining tent to sit in a comfortable canvas chair in the breeze and the shade.

"You've got your lion," Robert Wilson said to him, "and a damned fine one too."

Mrs. Macomber looked at Wilson quickly. She was an extremely hand-some and well-kept woman of the beauty and social position which had, five years before, commanded five thousand dollars as the price of endors-ing, with photographs, a beauty product which she had never used. She had been married to Francis Macomber for eleven years.

"He is a good lion, isn't he?" Macomber said. His wife looked at him now. She looked at both these men as though she had never seen them be-fore.

One, Wilson, the white hunter, she knew she had never truly seen before. He was about middle height with sandy hair, a stubby mustache, a very red face and extremely cold blue eyes with faint white wrinkles at the corners that grooved merrily when he smiled. He smiled at her now and she looked away from his face at the way his shoulders sloped in the loose tunic he wore with the four big cartridges held in loops where the left breast pocket should have been, at his big brown hands, his old slacks, his very dirty boots and back to his red face again. She noticed where the baked red of his face stopped in a white line that marked the cir-cle left by his Stetson hat that hung now from one of the pegs of the tent pole.

"Well, here's to the lion," Robert Wilson said. He smiled at her again and, not smiling, she looked curiously at her husband.

Francis Macomber was very tall, very well built if you did not mind that length of bone, dark, his hair cropped like an oarsman, rather thin-lipped, and was considered handsome. He was dressed in the same sort of safari clothes that Wilson wore except that his were new, he was thirty-five years old, kept himself very fit, was good at court games, had a number of big-game fishing records, and had just shown himself, very publicly, to be a coward.

"Here's to the lion," he said. "I can't ever thank you for what you did."

Margaret, his wife, looked away from him and back to Wilson.

"Let's not talk about the lion," she said.

Wilson looked over at her without smiling and now she smiled at him.

"It's been a very strange day," she said. "Hadn't you ought to put your hat on even under the canvas at noon? You told me that, you know."

"Might put it on," said Wilson.

"You know you have a very red face, Mr. Wilson," she told him and smiled again.

"Drink," said Wilson.

"I don't think so," she said. "Francis drinks a great deal, but his face is never red."

"It's red today," Macomber tried a joke.

"No," said Margaret. "It's mine that's red today. But Mr. Wilson's is always red."

"Must be racial," said Wilson. "I say, you wouldn't like to drop my beauty as a topic, would you?"

"I've just started on it."

"Let's chuck it," said Wilson.

"Conversation is going to be so difficult," Margaret said.

"Don't be silly, Margot," her husband said.

"No difficulty," Wilson said. "Got a damn fine lion."

Margot looked at them both and they both saw that she was going to cry. Wilson had seen it coming for a long time and he dreaded it. Macomber was past dreading it.

"I wish it hadn't happened. Oh, I wish it hadn't happened," she said and started for her tent. She made no noise of crying but they could see that her shoulders were shaking under the rose-colored, sun-proofed shirt she wore.

"Women upset," said Wilson to the tall man. "Amounts to nothing. Strain on the nerves and one thing'n another."

"No," said Macomber. "I suppose that I rate that for the rest of my life now."

"Nonsense. Let's have a spot of the giant killer," said Wilson. "Forget the whole thing. Nothing to it anyway."

"We might try," said Macomber. "I won't forget what you did for me though."

"Nothing," said Wilson. "All nonsense."

So they sat there in the shade where the camp was pitched under some wide-topped acacia trees with a boulder-strewn cliff behind them, and a stretch of grass that ran to the bank of a boulder-filled stream in front with forest beyond it, and drank their just-cool lime drinks and avoided one another's eyes while the boys set the table for lunch. Wilson could tell that the boys all knew about it now and when he saw Macomber's personal boy looking curiously at his master while he was putting dishes on the table he snapped at him in Swahili. The boy turned away his face blank.

"What were you telling him?" Macomber asked.

"Nothing. Told him to look alive or I'd see he got about fifteen of the best."

"What's that? Lashes?"

"It's quite illegal," Wilson said. "You're supposed to fine them."

"Do you still have them whipped?"

"Oh, yes. They could raise a row if they chose to complain. But they don't. They prefer it to the fines."

"How strange!" said Macomber.

"Not strange, really," Wilson said. "Which would you rather do? Take a good birching or lose your pay?"

Then he felt embarrassed at asking it and before Macomber could answer he went on, "We all take a beating every day, you know, one way or another."

This was no better. "Good God," he thought. "I am a diplomat, aren't I?"

"Yes, we take a beating," said Macomber, still not looking at him. "I'm awfully sorry about that lion business. It doesn't have to go any further, does it? I mean no one will hear about it, will they?"

"You mean will I tell it at the Mathaiga Club?" Wilson looked at him now coldly. He had not expected this. So he's a bloody four-letter man as well as a bloody coward, he thought. I rather liked him too until today. But how is one to know about an American?

"No," said Wilson. "I'm a professional hunter. We never talk about our clients. You can be quite easy on that. It's supposed to be bad form to ask us not to talk though."

He had decided now that to break would be much easier. He would eat, then, by himself and could read a book with his meals. They would eat by themselves. He would see them through the safari on a very formal basis—what was it the French called it? Distinguished consideration—and it would be a damn sight easier than having to go through this emotional trash. He'd insult him and make a good clean break. Then he could read a book with his meals and he'd still be drinking their whisky. That was the phrase for it when a safari went bad. You ran into another white hunter and you asked, "How is everything going?" and he answered, "Oh, I'm still drinking their whisky," and you knew everything had gone to pot.

"I'm sorry," Macomber said and looked at him with his American face that would stay adolescent until it became middle-aged, and Wilson noted his crew-cropped hair, fine eyes only faintly shifty, good nose, thin lips and handsome jaw. "I'm sorry I didn't realize that. There are lots of things I don't know."

So what could he do, Wilson thought. He was all ready to break it off quickly and neatly and here the beggar was apologizing after he had just insulted him. He made one more attempt "Don't worry about me talking," he said. "I have a living to make. You know in Africa no woman ever misses her lion and no white man ever bolts."

"I bolted like a rabbit," Macomber said.

Now what in hell were you going to do about a man who talked like that, Wilson wondered.

Wilson looked at Macomber with his flat, blue, machine-gunner's eyes and the other smiled back at him. He had a pleasant smile if you did not notice how his eyes showed when he was hurt.

"Maybe I can fix it up on buffalo," he said. "We're after them next, aren't we?"

"In the morning if you like," Wilson told him. Perhaps he had been wrong. This was certainly the way to take it. You most certainly could not tell a damned thing about an American. He was all for Macomber again. If you could forget the morning. But, of course, you couldn't. The morning had been about as bad as they come.

"Here comes the Memsahib," he said. She was walking over from her tent looking refreshed and cheerful and quite lovely. She had a very perfect oval face, so perfect that you expected her to be stupid. But she wasn't stupid, Wilson thought, no, not stupid.

"How is the beautiful red-faced Mr. Wilson? Are you feeling better, Francis, my pearl?"

"Oh, much," said Macomber.

"I've dropped the whole thing," she said, sitting down at the table. "What importance is there to whether Francis is any good at killing lions? That's not his trade. That's Mr. Wilson's trade. Mr. Wilson is really very impressive killing anything. You do kill anything, don't you?"

"Oh, anything," said Wilson. "Simply anything." They are, he thought, the hardest in the world; the hardest, the cruelest, the most predatory and the most attractive and their men have softened or gone to pieces nervously as they have hardened. Or is it that they pick men they can handle? They can't know that much at the age they marry, he thought. He was grateful that he had gone through his education on American women before now because this was a very attractive one.

"We're going after buff in the morning," he told her.

"I'm coming," she said.

"No, you're not."

"Oh, yes, I am. Mayn't I, Francis?"

"Why not stay in camp?"

"Not for anything," she said. "I wouldn't miss something like today for anything."

When she left, Wilson was thinking, when she went off to cry, she seemed a hell of a fine woman. She seemed to understand, to realize, to be hurt for him and for herself and to know how things really stood. She is away for twenty minutes and now she is back, simply enamelled in that American female cruelty. They are the damnedest women. Really the damnedest.

"We'll put on another show for you tomorrow," Francis Macomber said.

"You're not coming," Wilson said.

"You're very mistaken," she told him. "And I want *so* to see you perform again. You were lovely this morning. That is if blowing things' heads off is lovely."

"Here's the lunch," said Wilson. "You're very merry, aren't you?"

"Why not? I didn't come out here to be dull."

"Well, it hasn't been dull," Wilson said. He could see the boulders in the river and the high bank beyond with the trees and he remembered the morning.

"Oh, no," she said. "It's been charming. And tomorrow. You don't know how I look forward to tomorrow."

"That's eland he's offering you," Wilson said.

"They're the big cowy things that jump like hares, aren't they?"

"I suppose that describes them," Wilson said.

"It's very good meat," Macomber said.

"Did you shoot it, Francis?" she asked.

"Yes."

"They're not dangerous, are they?"

"Only if they fall on you," Wilson told her.

"I'm so glad."

"Why not let up on the bitchery just a little, Margot," Macomber said, cutting the eland steak and putting some mashed potato, gravy and carrot on the down-turned fork that tined through the piece of meat.

"I suppose I could," she said, "since you put it so prettily."

"Tonight we'll have champagne for the lion," Wilson said. "It's a bit too hot at noon."

"Oh, the lion," Margot said. "I'd forgotten the lion!"

So, Robert Wilson thought to himself, she *is* giving him a ride, isn't she? Or do you suppose that's her idea of putting up a good show? How should a woman act when she discovers her husband is a bloody coward? She's damn cruel but they're all cruel. They govern, of course, and to govern one has to be cruel sometimes. Still, I've seen enough of their damn terrorism.

"Have some more eland," he said to her politely.

That afternoon, late, Wilson and Macomber went out in the motor car with the native driver and the two gun-bearers. Mrs. Macomber stayed in the camp. It was too hot to go out, she said, and she was going with them in the early morning. As they drove off Wilson saw her standing under the big tree, looking pretty rather than beautiful in her faintly rosy khaki, her dark hair drawn back off her forehead and gathered in a knot low on her neck, her face as fresh, he thought, as though she were in England. She waved to them as the car went off through the swale of high grass and curved around through the trees into the small hills of orchard bush.

In the orchard bush they found a herd of impala, and leaving the car they stalked one old ram with long, wide-spread horns and Macomber killed it with a very creditable shot that knocked the buck down at a good two hundred yards and sent the herd off bounding wildly and leaping over one another's backs in long, leg-drawn-up leaps as unbelievable and as floating as those one makes sometimes in dreams.

"That was a good shot," Wilson said. "They're a small target."

"Is it a worth-while head?" Macomber asked.

"It's excellent," Wilson told him. "You shoot like that and you'll have no trouble."

"Do you think we'll find buffalo tomorrow?"

"There's a good chance of it. They feed out early in the morning and with luck we may catch them in the open."

"I'd like to clear away that lion business," Macomber said. "It's not very pleasant to have your wife see you do something like that."

I should think it would be even more unpleasant to do it, Wilson thought, wife or no wife, or to talk about it having done it. But he said, "I wouldn't think about that any more. Any one could be upset by his first lion. That's all over."

But that night after dinner and a whisky and soda by the fire before going to bed, as Francis Macomber lay on his cot with the mosquito bar over him and listened to the night noises it was not all over. It was neither all over nor was it beginning. It was there, exactly as it happened with some parts of it indelibly emphasized and he was miserably ashamed at it. But more than shame he felt cold, hollow fear in him. The fear was still there like a cold slimy hollow in all the emptiness where once his confidence had been and it made him feel sick. It was still there with him now.

It had started the night before when he had wakened and heard the lion roaring somewhere up along the river. It was a deep sound and at the end there were sort of coughing grunts that made him seem just outside the tent, and when Francis Macomber woke in the night to hear it he was afraid. He could hear his wife breathing quietly, asleep. There was no one to tell he was afraid, nor to be afraid with him, and, lying alone, he did not know the Somali proverb that says a brave man is always frightened three times by a lion; when he first sees his track, when he first hears him roar and when he first confronts him. Then while they were eating breakfast by lantern light out in the dining tent, before the sun was up, the lion roared again and Francis thought he was just at the edge of camp.

"Sounds like an old-timer," Robert Wilson said, looking up from his kippers and coffee. "Listen to him cough."

"Is he very close?"

"A mile or so up the stream."

"Will we see him?"

"We'll have a look."

"Does his roaring carry that far? It sounds as though he were right in camp."

"Carries a hell of a long way," said Robert Wilson. "It's strange the way it carries. Hope he's a shootable cat. The boys said there was a very big one about here."

"If I get a shot, where should I hit him," Macomber asked, "to stop him?"

"In the shoulders," Wilson said. "In the neck if you can make it. Shoot for bone. Break him down."

"I hope I can place it properly," Macomber said.

"You shoot very well," Wilson told him. "Take your time. Make sure of him. The first one in is the one that counts."

"What range will it be?"

"Can't tell. Lion has something to say about that. Won't shoot unless it's close enough so you can make sure."

"At under a hundred yards?" Macomber asked.

Wilson looked at him quickly.

"Hundred's about right. Might have to take him a bit under. Shouldn't chance a shot at much over that. A hundred's a decent range. You can hit him wherever you want at that. Here comes the Memsahib."

"Good morning," she said. "Are we going after that lion?"

"As soon as you deal with your breakfast," Wilson said. "How are you feeling?"

"Marvellous," she said. "I'm very excited."

"I'll just go and see that everything is ready," Wilson went off. As he left the lion roared again.

"Noisy beggar," Wilson said. "We'll put a stop to that."

"What's the matter, Francis?" his wife asked him.

"Nothing," Macomber said.

"Yes, there is," she said. "What are you upset about?"

"Nothing," he said.

"Tell me," she looked at him. "Don't you feel well?"

"It's that damned roaring," he said. "It's been going on all night, you know."

"Why didn't you wake me," she said. "I'd love to have heard it."

"I've got to kill the damned thing," Macomber said, miserably.

"Well, that's what you're out here for, isn't it?"

"Yes. But I'm nervous. Hearing the thing roar gets on my nerves."

"Well then, as Wilson said, kill him and stop his roaring."

"Yes, darling," said Francis Macomber. "It sounds easy, doesn't it?"

"You're not afraid, are you?"

"Of course not. But I'm nervous from hearing him roar all night."

"You'll kill him marvellously," she said. "I know you will. I'm awfully anxious to see it."

"Finish your breakfast and we'll be starting."

"It's not light yet," she said. "This is a ridiculous hour."

Just the lion roared in a deep-chested moaning, suddenly guttural, ascending vibration that seemed to shake the air and ended in a sigh and a heavy, deep-chested grunt.

"He sounds almost here," Macomber's wife said.

"My God," said Macomber. "I hate that damned noise."

"It's very impressive."

"Impressive. It's frightful."

Robert Wilson came up then carrying his short, ugly, shockingly big-bored .505 Gibbs and grinning.

"Come on," he said. "Your gun-bearer has your Springfield and the big gun. Everything's in the car. Have you solids?"

"Yes."

"I'm ready," Mrs. Macomber said.

"Must make him stop that racket," Wilson said. "You get in front. The Memsahib can sit back here with me."

They climbed into the motor car and, in the gray first daylight, moved off up the river through the trees. Macomber opened the breech of his rifle and saw he had metal-cased bullets, shut the bolt and put the rifle on safety. He saw his hand was trembling. He felt in his pocket for more cartridges and moved his fingers over the cartridges in the loops of his tunic front. He turned back to where Wilson sat in the rear seat of the doorless, box-bodied motor car beside his wife, them both grinning with excitement, and Wilson leaned forward and whispered,

"See the birds dropping. Means the old boy has left his kill."

On the far bank of the stream Macomber could see, above the trees, vultures circling and plummeting down.

"Chances are he'll come to drink along here," Wilson whispered. "Before he goes to lay up. Keep an eye out."

They were driving slowly along the high bank of the stream which here cut deeply to its boulder-filled bed, and they wound in and out through big trees as they drove. Macomber was watching the opposite bank when he felt Wilson take hold of his arm. The car stopped.

"There he is," he heard the whisper. "Ahead and to the right. Get out and take him. He's a marvellous lion."

Macomber saw the lion now. He was standing almost broadside, his great head up and turned toward them. The early morning breeze that blew toward them was just stirring his dark mane, and the lion looked huge, silhouetted on the rise of bank in the gray morning light, his shoulders heavy, his barrel of a body bulking smoothly.

"How far is he?" asked Macomber, raising his rifle.

"About seventy-five. Get out and take him."

"Why not shoot from where I am?"

"You don't shoot them from cars," he heard Wilson saying in his ear. "Get out. He's not going to stay there all day."

Macomber stepped out of the curved opening at the side of the front seat, onto the step and down onto the ground. The lion still stood looking majestically and coolly toward this object that his eyes only showed in silhouette, bulking like some super-rhino. There was no man smell carried toward him and he watched the object moving his great head a little from side to side. Then watching the object, not afraid, but hesitating before going down the bank to drink with such a thing opposite him, he saw a man figure detach itself from it and he turned his heavy head and swung away toward the cover of the trees as he heard a cracking crash and felt the slam of a .30-06 220-grain solid bullet that bit his flank and ripped in sudden hot scalding nausea through his stomach. He trotted, heavy, big-footed, swinging wounded full-bellied, through the trees toward the tall grass and cover, and the crash came again to go past him ripping the air apart. Then it crashed again and he felt the blow as it hit his lower ribs and ripped on through, blood sudden hot and frothy in his mouth, and he galloped toward the high grass where he could crouch and not be seen and make them bring the crashing thing close enough so he could make a rush and get the man that held it.

Macomber had not thought how the lion felt as he got out of the car. He only knew his hands were shaking and as he walked away from the car it was almost impossible for him to make his legs move. They were stiff in the thighs, but he could feel the muscles fluttering. He raised the rifle, sighted on the junction of the lion's head and shoulders and pulled the trigger. Nothing happened though he pulled until he thought his finger would break. Then he knew he had the safety on and as he lowered the rifle to move the safety over he moved another frozen pace forward, and the lion seeing his silhouette now clear of the silhouette of the car, turned and started off at a trot, and, as Macomber fired, he heard a whunk that meant that the bullet was home; but the lion kept on going. Macomber shot again and every one saw the bullet throw a spout of dirt beyond the trotting lion. He shot again, remembering to lower his aim, and they all heard the bullet hit, and the lion went into a gallop and was in the tall grass before he had the bolt pushed forward.

Macomber stood there feeling sick at his stomach, his hands that held the Springfield still cocked, shaking, and his wife and Robert Wilson were standing by him. Beside him too were the two gun-bearers chattering in Wakamba.

"I hit him," Macomber said. "I hit him twice."

"You gut-shot him and you hit him somewhere forward." Wilson said without enthusiasm. The gun-bearers looked very grave. They were silent now.

"You may have killed him," Wilson went on. "We'll have to wait a while before we go in to find out."

"What do you mean?"

"Let him get sick before we follow him up."

"Oh," said Macomber.

"He's a hell of a fine lion," Wilson said cheerfully. "He's gotten into a bad place though."

"Why is it bad?"

"Can't see him until you're on him."

"Oh," said Macomber.

"Come on," said Wilson. "The Memsahib can stay here in the car. We'll go to have a look at the blood spoor."

"Stay here, Margot," Macomber said to his wife. His mouth was very dry and it was hard for him to talk.

"Why?" she asked.

"Wilson says to."

"We're going to have a look," Wilson said. "You stay here. You can see even better from here."

"All right."

Wilson spoke in Swahili to the driver. He nodded and said, "Yes, Bwana."

Then they went down the steep bank and across the stream, climbing over and around the boulders and up the other bank, pulling up by some projecting roots, and along it until they found where the lion had been trotting when Macomber first shot. There was dark blood on the short grass that the gun-bearers pointed out with grass stems, and that ran away behind the river bank trees.

"What do we do?" asked Macomber.

"Not much choice," said Wilson. "We can't bring the car over. Bank's too steep. We'll let him stiffen up a bit and then you and I'll go in and have a look for him."

"What do we do?" asked Macomber.

"Not much choice," said Wilson. "We can't bring the car over. Bank's too steep. We'll let him stiffen up a bit and then you and I'll go in and have a look for him."

"Can't we set the grass on fire?" Macomber asked.

"Too green."

"Can't we send beaters?"

Wilson looked at him appraisingly. "Of course we can," he said. "But it's just a touch murderous. You see we know the lion's wounded. You can drive an unwounded lion—he'll move on ahead of a noise—but a wounded lion's going to charge. You can't see him until you're right on him. He'll make himself perfectly flat in cover you wouldn't think would hide a hare. You can't very well send boys in there to that sort of a show. Somebody bound to get mauled."

"What about the gun-bearers?"

"Oh, they'll go with us. It's their *shauri*. You see, they signed on for it. They don't look too happy though, do they?"

"I don't want to go in there," said Macomber. It was out before he knew he'd said it.

"Neither do I," said Wilson very cheerily. "Really no choice though." Then, as an afterthought, he glanced at Macomber and saw suddenly how he was trembling and the pitiful look on his face.

"You don't have to go in, of course," he said. "That's what I'm hired for, you know. That's why I'm so expensive."

"You mean you'd go in by yourself? Why not leave him there?"

Robert Wilson, whose entire occupation had been with the lion and the problem he presented, and who had not been thinking about Macomber except to note that he was rather windy, suddenly felt as though he had opened the wrong door in a hotel and seen something shameful.

"What do you mean?"

"Why not just leave him?"

"You mean pretend to ourselves he hasn't been hit?"

"No. Just drop it."

"It isn't done."

"Why not?"

"For one thing, he's certain to be suffering. For another, some one else might run onto him."

"I see."

"But you don't have to have anything to do with it."

"I'd like to," Macomber said. "I'm just scared, you know."

"I'll go ahead when we go in." Wilson said, "with Kongoni tracking. You keep behind me and a little to one side. Chances are we'll hear him growl. If we see him we'll both shoot. Don't worry about anything. I'll keep you backed up. As a matter of fact, you know, perhaps you'd better not go. It might be much better. Why don't you go over and join the Memsahib while I just get it over with?"

"No, I want to go."

"All right," said Wilson. "But don't go in if you don't want to. This is my *shauri* now, you know."

"I want to go," said Macomber.

They sat under a tree and smoked.

"Want to go back and speak to the Memsahib while we're waiting?" Wilson asked.

"No."

"I'll just step back and tell her to be patient."

"Good," said Macomber. He sat there, sweating under his arms, his mouth dry, his stomach hollow feeling, wanting to find courage to tell Wilson to go on and finish off the lion without him. He could not know that Wilson was furious because he had not noticed the state he was in earlier and sent him back to his wife. While he sat there Wilson came up. "I have your big gun," he said. "Take it. We've given him time, I think. Come on."

Macomber took the big gun and Wilson said:

"Keep behind me and about five yards to the right and do exactly as I tell you." Then he spoke in Swahili to the two gun-bearers who looked the picture of gloom.

"Let's go," he said.

"Could I have a drink of water?" Macomber asked. Wilson spoke to the older gun-bearer, who wore a canteen on his belt, and the man unbuckled it, unscrewed the top and handed it to Macomber, who took it noticing how heavy it seemed and how hairy and shoddy the felt covering was in his hand. He raised it to drink and looked ahead at the high grass with the flat-topped trees behind it. A breeze was blowing toward them and the grass rippled gently in the wind. He looked at the gun-bearer and he could see the gun-bearer was suffering too with fear.

Thirty-five yards into the grass the big lion lay flattened out along the ground. His ears were back and his only movement was a slight twitching up and down of his long, black-tufted tail. He had turned at bay as soon as he had reached this cover and he was sick with the wound through his full belly, and weakening with the wound through his lungs that brought a thin foamy red to his mouth each time he breathed. His flanks were wet and hot and flies were on the little openings the solid bullets had made in his tawny hide, and his big yellow eyes, narrowed with hate, looked straight ahead, only blinking when the pain came as he breathed, and his claws dug in the soft baked earth. All of him, pain, sickness, hatred and all of his remaining strength, was tightening into an absolute concentration for a rush. He could hear the men talking and he waited, gathering all of himself into this preparation for a charge as soon as the men would come into the grass. As he heard their voices his tail stiffened to twitch up and down, and, as they came into the edge of the grass, he made a coughing grunt and charged.

Kongoni, the old gun-bearer, in the lead watching the blood spoor, Wilson watching the grass for any movement, his big gun ready, the second gun-bearer looking ahead and listening, Macomber close to Wilson, his rifle cocked, they had just moved into the grass when Macomber heard the blood-choked coughing grunt, and saw the swishing rush in the grass. The next thing he knew he was running; running wildly, in panic in the open, running toward the stream.

He heard the *ca-ra-wong!* Of Wilson's big rifle, and again in a second crashing *carawong!* and turning saw the lion, horrible-looking now, with half his head seeming to be gone, crawling toward Wilson in the edge of the tall grass while the red-faced man worked the bolt on the short ugly rifle and aimed carefully as another blasting *carawong!* came from the muzzle, and the crawling, heavy, yellow bulk of the lion stiffened and the huge, mutilated head slid forward and Macomber, standing by himself in the clearing where he had run, holding a loaded rifle, while two black men and a white man looked back at him in contempt, knew the lion was dead. He came toward Wilson, his tallness all seeming a naked reproach, and Wilson looked at him and said:

"Want to take pictures?"

"No," he said.

That was all any one had said until they reached the motor car. Then Wilson had said:

"Hell of a fine lion. Boys will skin him out. We might as well stay here in the shade."

Macomber's wife had not looked at him nor he at her and he had sat by her in the back seat with Wilson sitting in the front seat. Once he had reached over and taken his wife's hand without looking at her and she had removed her hand from his. Looking across the stream to where the gun-bearers were skinning out the lion he could see that she had been able to see the whole thing. While they sat there his wife had reached forward and put her hand on Wilson's shoulder. He turned and she had leaned forward over the low seat and kissed him on the mouth.

"Oh, I say," said Wilson, going redder than his natural baked color.

"Mr. Robert Wilson," she said. "The beautiful red-faced Mr. Robert Wilson."

Then she sat down beside Macomber again and looked away across the stream to where the lion lay, with uplifted, white-muscled, tendon-marked naked forearms, and white bloating belly, as the black men fleshed away the skin. Finally the gun-bearers brought the skin over, wet and heavy, and climbed in behind with it, rolling it up before they got in, and the motor car started. No one had said anything more until they were back in camp.

That was the story of the lion. Macomber did not know how the lion had felt before he started his rush, nor during it when the unbelievable smash of the .505 with a muzzle velocity of two tons had hit him in the mouth, nor what kept him coming after that, when the second ripping crash had smashed his hind quarters and he had come crawling on toward the crashing, blasting thing that had destroyed him. Wilson knew something about it and only expressed it by saying, "Damned fine lion," but Macomber did not know how Wilson felt about things either. He did not know how his wife felt except that she was through with him.

His wife had been through with him before but it never lasted. He was very wealthy, and would be much wealthier, and he knew she would not leave him ever now. That was one of the few things that he really knew. He knew about that, about motor cycles—that was earliest—about motor cars, about duck-shooting, about fishing, trout, salmon and big-sea, about sex in books, many books, too many books, about all court games, about dogs, not much about horses, about hanging on to his money, about most of the other things his world dealt in, and about his wife not leaving him. His wife had been a great beauty and she was still a great beauty in Africa, but she was not a great enough beauty any more at home to be able to leave him and better herself and she knew it and he knew it. She had missed the chance to leave him and he knew it. If he had been better with women she would probably have started to worry about him getting another new, beautiful wife; but she knew too much about him to worry about him either. Also, he had always had a great tolerance which seemed the nicest thing about him if it were not the most sinister.

All in all they were known as a comparatively happily married couple, one of those whose disruption is often rumored but never occurs, and as the society columnist put it, they were adding more than a spice of *adverture* to their much envied and ever-enduring *Romance* by a *Safari* in what was known as *Darkest Africa* until the Martin Johnsons lighted it on so many silver screens where they were pursuing *Old Simba* the lion, the buffalo, *Tembo* the elephant and as well collecting specimens for the Museum of Natural History. This same columnist had reported them *on the verge* at least three times in the past and they had been. But they always made it up. They had a sound basis of union. Margot was too beautiful for Macomber to divorce her and Macomber had too much money for Margot ever to leave him.

It was now about three o'clock in the morning and Francis Macomber, who had been asleep a little while after he had stopped thinking about the lion, wakened and then slept again, woke suddenly, frightened in a dream of the bloody-headed lion standing over him, and listening while his heart pounded, he realized that his wife was not in the other cot in the tent. He lay awake with that knowledge for two hours.

At the end of that time his wife came into the tent, lifted her mosquito bar and crawled cozily into bed.

"Where have you been?" Macomber asked in the darkness.

"Hello," she said. "Are you awake?"

"Where have you been?"

"I just went out to get a breath of air."

"You did, like hell."

"What do you want me to say, darling?"

"Where have you been?"

"Out to get a breath of air."

"That's a new name for it. You *are* a bitch."

"Well, you're a coward."

"All right," he said. "What of it?"

"Nothing as far as I'm concerned. But please let's not talk, darling, because I'm very sleepy."

"You think that I'll take anything."

"I know you will, sweet."

"Well, I won't."

"Please, darling, let's not talk. I'm so very sleepy."

"There wasn't going to be any of that. You promised there wouldn't be."

"Well, there is now," she said sweetly.

"You said if we made this trip that there would be none of that. You promised."

"Yes, darling. That's the way I meant it to be. But the trip was spoiled yesterday. We don't have to talk about it, do we?"

"You don't wait long when you have an advantage, do you?"

"Please let's not talk. I'm so sleepy, darling."

"I'm going to talk."

"Don't mind me then, because I'm going to sleep." And she did.

At breakfast they were all three at the table before daylight and Francis Macomber found that, of all the many men that he had hated, he hated Robert Wilson the most.

"Sleep well?" Wilson asked in his throaty voice, filling a pipe.

"Did you?"

"Topping," the white hunter told him.

You bastard, thought Macomber, you insolent bastard.

So she woke him when she came in, Wilson thought, looking at them both with his flat, cold eyes. Well, why doesn't he keep his wife where she belongs? What does he think I am, a bloody plaster saint? Let him keep her where she belongs. It's his own fault.

"Do you think we'll find buffalo?" Margot asked, pushing away a dish of apricots.

"Chance of it," Wilson said and smiled at her. "Why don't you stay in camp?"

"Not for anything," she told him.

"Why not order her to stay in camp?" Wilson said to Macomber.

"You order her," said Macomber coldly.

"Let 's not have any ordering, nor," turning to Macomber, "any silliness, Francis," Margot said quite pleasantly.

"Are you ready to start?" Macomber asked.

"Any time," Wilson told him. "Do you want the Memsahib to go?"

"Does it make any difference whether I do or not?"

The hell with it, thought Robert Wilson. The utter complete hell with it. So this is what it's going to be like. Well, this is what it's going to be like, then.

"Makes no difference," he said.

"You're sure you wouldn't like to stay in camp with her yourself and let me go out and hunt the buffalo?" Macomber asked.

"Can't do that," said Wilson. "Wouldn't talk rot if I were you."

"I'm not talking rot. I'm disgusted."

"Bad word, disgusted."

"Francis, will you please try to speak sensibly?" his wife said.

"I speak too damned sensibly," Macomber said. "Did you ever eat such filthy food?"

"Something wrong with the food?" asked Wilson quietly.

"No more than with everything else."

"I'd pull yourself together, laddybuck," Wilson said very quietly. "There's a boy waits at table that understands a little English."

"The hell with him."

Wilson stood up and puffing on his pipe strolled away, speaking a few words in Swahili to one of the gun-bearers who was standing waiting for him. Macomber and his wife sat on at the table. He was staring at his coffee cup.

"If you make a scene I'll leave you, darling," Margot said quietly.

"No, you won't."

"You can try it and see."

"You won't leave me."

"No," she said. "I won't leave you and you'll behave yourself."

"Behave myself? That's a way to talk. Behave myself."

Yes. Behave yourself."

"Why don't *you* try behaving?"

"I've tried it so long. So very long."

"I hate that red-faced swine," Macomber said. "I loathe the sight of him."

"He's really *very* nice."

"Oh, *shut up*," Macomber almost shouted. Just then the car came up and stopped in front of the dining tent and the driver and the two gun-bearers got out. Wilson walked over and looked at the husband and wife sitting there at the table.

"Going shooting?" he asked.

"Yes," said Macomber, standing up. "Yes."

"Better bring a woolly. It will be cool in the car," Wilson said.

"I'll get my leather jacket," Margot said.

"The boy has it," Wilson told her. He climbed into the front with the driver and Francis Macomber and his wife sat, not speaking, in the back seat.

Hope the silly beggar doesn't take a notion to blow the back of my head off, Wilson thought to himself. Women *are* a nuisance on safari.

The car was grinding down to cross the river at a pebbly ford in the gray daylight and then climbed, angling up the steep bank, where Wilson had ordered a way shovelled out the day before so they could reach the parklike wooded rolling country on the far side.

It was a good morning, Wilson thought. There was a heavy dew and as the wheels went through the grass and low bushes he could smell the odor of the crushed fronds. It was an odor like verbena and he liked this early morning smell of the dew, the crushed bracken and the look of the tree trunks showing black through the early morning mist, as the car made its way through the untracked, park-like country. He had put the two in the back seat out of his mind now and was thinking about buffalo. The buffalo that he was after stayed in the daytime in a thick swamp where it was impossible to get a shot, but in the night they fed out into an open stretch of country and if he could come between them and their swamp with the car, Macomber would have a good chance at them in the open. He did not want to hunt buff with Macomber in thick cover. He did not want to hunt buff or anything else with Macomber at all, but he was a professional hunter and he had hunted with some rare ones in his time. If they got buff today there would only be rhino to come and the poor man would have gone through his dangerous game and things might pick up. He'd have nothing more to do with the woman and Macomber would get over that too. He must have gone through plenty of that before by the look of things. Poor beggar. He must have a way of getting over it. Well, it was the poor sod's own bloody fault.

He, Robert Wilson, carried a double size cot on safari to accommodate any windfalls he might receive. He had hunted for a certain clientele, the international, fast, sporting set, where the women did not feel they were getting their money's worth unless they had shared that cot with the white hunter. He despised them when he was away from them although he liked some of them well enough at the time, but he made his living by them; and their standards were his standards as long as they were hiring him.

They were his standards in all except the shooting. He had his own standards about the killing and they could live up to them or get some one else to hunt them. He knew, too, that they all respected him for this. This Macomber was an odd one though. Damned if he wasn't. Now the wife. Well, the wife. Yes, the wife. Hm, the wife. Well he'd dropped all that. He looked around at them. Macomber sat grim and furious. Margot smiled at him. She looked younger today, more innocent and fresher and not so professionally beautiful. What's in her heart God knows, Wilson thought. She hadn't talked much last night. At that it was a pleasure to see her.

The motor car climbed up a slight rise and went on through the trees and then out into a grassy prairie-like opening and kept in the shelter of the trees along the edge, the driver going slowly and Wilson looking carefully out across the prairie and all along its far side. He stopped the car and studied the opening with his field glasses. Then he motioned to the driver to go on and the car moved slowly along, the driver avoiding wart-hog holes and driving around the mud castles ants had built. Then, looking across the opening, Wilson suddenly turned and said,

"By God, there they are!"

And looking where he pointed, while the car jumped forward and Wilson spoke in rapid Swahili to the driver, Macomber saw three huge, black animals looking almost cylindrical in their long heaviness, like big black tank cars, moving at a gallop across the far edge of the open prairie. They moved at a stiff-necked, stiff bodied gallop and he could see the up-swept wide black horns on their heads as they galloped heads out; the heads not moving.

"They're three old bulls," Wilson said. "We'll cut them off before they get to the swamp."

The car was going a wild forty-five miles an hour across the open and as Macomber watched, the buffalo got bigger and bigger until he could see the gray, hairless, scabby look of one huge bull and how his neck was a part of his shoulders and the shiny black of his horns as he galloped a little be-hind the others that were strung out in that steady plunging gait; and then, the car swaying as though it had just jumped a road, they drew up close and he could see the plunging hugeness of the bull, and the dust in his sparsely haired hide, the wide boss of horn and his outstretched, wide-nostrilled muzzle, and he was raising his rifle when Wilson shouted, "Not from the car, you fool!" and he had no fear, only hatred of Wilson, while the brakes clamped on and the car skidded, plowing sideways to an almost stop and Wilson was out on one side and he on the other, stumbling as his feet hit the still speeding-by of the earth, and then he was shooting at the bull as he moved away, hearing the bullets whunk into him, emptying his rifle at him as he moved steadily away, finally remembering to get his shots forward into the shoulder, and, as he fumbled to re-load, he saw the bull was down. Down on his knees, his big head tossing, and seeing the other two still gal-loping he shot at the leader and hit him. He shot again and missed and he heard the *carawonging* roar as Wilson shot and saw the leading bull slide forward onto his nose.

"Get that other," Wilson said. "Now you're shooting!"

But the other bull was moving steadily at the same gallop and he missed, throwing a spout of dirt, and Wilson missed and the dust rose in a cloud and Wilson shouted, "Come on. He's too far!" and grabbed his arm and they were in the car again, Macomber and Wilson hanging on the sides and rocketing swayingly over the uneven ground, drawing up on the steady, plunging, heavy-necked, straight-moving gallop of the bull.

They were behind him and Macomber was filling his rifle, dropping shells onto the ground, jamming it, clearing the jam, then they were almost up with the bull when Wilson yelled "Stop," and the car skidded so that it almost swung over and Macomber fell forward onto his feet, slammed his bolt forward and fired as far forward as he could aim into the galloping, rounded black back, aimed and shot again, then again, then again, and the bullets, all of them hitting, had no effect on the buffalo that he could see. Then Wilson shot, the roar deafening him, and he could see the bull stagger. Macomber shot again, aiming carefully, and down he came, onto his knees.

"All right," Wilson said. "Nice work. That's the three."

Macomber felt a drunken elation.

"How many times did you shoot?" he asked.

"Just three," Wilson said. "You killed the first bull. The biggest one. I helped you finish the other two. Afraid they might have got into cover. You had them killed. I was just mopping up a little. You shot damn well."

"Let's go to the car," said Macomber. "I want a drink."

"Got to finish off that buff first," Wilson told him. The buffalo was on his knees and he jerked his head furiously and bellowed in pig-eyed, roaring rage as they came toward him.

"Watch he doesn't get up," Wilson said. Then, "Get a little broadside and take him in the neck just behind the ear."

Macomber aimed carefully at the center of the huge, jerking, rage-driven neck and shot. At the shot the head dropped forward.

"That does it," said Wilson. "Got the spine. They're a hell of a looking thing, aren't they?"

"Let's get the drink," said Macomber. In his life he had never felt so good.

In the car Macomber's wife sat very white faced. "You were marvellous, darling," she said to Macomber. "What a ride."

"Was it rough?" Wilson asked.

"It was frightful. I've never been more frightened in my life."

"Let's all have a drink," Macomber said.

"By all means," said Wilson. "Give it to the Memsahib." She drank the neat whisky from the flask and shuddered a little when she swallowed. She handed the flask to Macomber who handed it to Wilson.

"It was frightfully exciting," she said. "It's given me a dreadful headache. I didn't know you were allowed to shoot them from cars though."

"No one shot from cars," said Wilson coldly.

"I mean chase them from cars."

"Wouldn't ordinarily," Wilson said. "Seemed sporting enough to me though while we were doing it. Taking more chance driving that way across the plain full of holes and one thing and another than hunting on foot. Buffalo could have charged us each time we shot if he liked. Gave him every chance. Wouldn't mention it to any one though. It's illegal if that's what you mean."

"It seemed very unfair to me," Margot said, "chasing those big helpless things in a motor car."

"Did it?" said Wilson.

"What would happen if they heard about it in Nairobi?"

"I'd lose my licence for one thing. Other unpleasantness," Wilson said, taking a drink from the flask. "I'd be out of business."

"Really?"

"Yes, really."

"Well," said Macomber, and he smiled for the first time all day. "Now she has something on you."

"You have such a pretty way of putting things, Francis," Margot Macomber said. Wilson looked at them both. If a four-letter man marries a five-letter woman, he was thinking. What number of letters would their children be? What he said was, "We lost a gun-bearer. Did you notice it?"

"My God, no," Macomber said.

"Here he comes," Wilson said. "He's all right. He must have fallen off when we left the first bull."

Approaching them was the middle-aged gun-bearer, limping along in his knitted cap, khaki tunic, shorts and rubber sandals, gloomy-faced and disgusted looking. As he came up he called out to Wilson in Swahili and they all saw the change in the white hunter's face.

"What does he say?" asked Margot.

"He says the first bull got up and went into the bush," Wilson said with no expression in his voice.

"Oh," said Macomber blankly.

"Then it's going to be just like the lion," said Margot, full of anticipation.

"It's not going to be a damned bit like the lion," Wilson told her. "Did you want another drink, Macomber?"

"Thanks, yes," Macomber said. He expected the feeling he had had about the lion to come back but it did not. For the first time in his life he really felt wholly without fear. Instead of fear he had a feeling of definite elation.

"We'll go and have a look at the second bull," Wilson said. "I'll tell the driver to put the car in the shade."

"What are you going to do?" asked Margaret Macomber.

"Take a look at the buff," Wilson said.

"I'll come."

"Come along."

The three of them walked over to where the second buffalo bulked blackly in the open, head forward on the grass, the massive horns swung wide.

"He's a very good head," Wilson said. "That's close to a fifty-inch spread."

Macomber was looking at him with delight.

"He's hateful looking," said Margot. "Can't we go into the shade?"

"Of course," Wilson said. "Look," he said to Macomber, and pointed. "See that patch of bush?"

"Yes."

"That's where the first bull went in. The gun-bearer said when he fell off the bull was down. He was watching us helling along and the other two buff galloping. When he looked up there was the bull up and looking at him. Gun-bearer ran like hell and the bull went off slowly into that bush."

"Can we go in after him now?" asked Macomber eagerly.

Wilson looked at him appraisingly. Damned if this isn't a strange one, he thought. Yesterday he's scared sick and today he's a ruddy fire eater.

"No, we'll give him a while."

"Let's please go into the shade," Margot said. Her face was white and she looked ill.

They made their way to the car where it stood under a single, wide-spreading tree and all climbed in.

"Chances are he's dead in there," Wilson remarked. "After a little we'll have a look."

Macomber felt a wild unreasonable happiness that he had never known before.

"But God, that was a chase," he said. "I've never felt any such feeling. Wasn't it marvellous, Margot?"

"I hated it."

"Why?"

"I hated it," she said bitterly. "I loathed it."

"You know I don't think I'd ever be afraid of anything again," Macomber said to Wilson. "Something happened in me after we first saw the buff and started after him. Like a dam bursting. It was pure excitement."

"Cleans out your liver," said Wilson. "Damn funny things happen to people."

Macomber's face was shining. "You know something did happen to me," he said. "I feel absolutely different."

His wife said nothing and eyed him strangely. She was sitting far back in the seat and Macomber was sitting forward talking to Wilson who turned sideways talking over the back of the front seat.

"You know, I'd like to try another lion," Macomber said. "I'm really not afraid of them now. After all what can they do to you?"

"That's it," said Wilson. "Worst one can do is kill you. How does it go? Shakespeare. Damned good. See if I can remember. Oh, damned good. Used to quote it to myself at one time. Let's see. 'By my troth, I care not; a man can die but once; we owe God a death and let it go which way it will he that dies this year is quit for the next.' Damned fine, eh?"

He was very embarrassed, having brought out this thing he had lived by, but he had seen men come of age before and it always moved him. It was not a matter of their twenty-first birthday.

It had taken a strange chance of hunting, a sudden precipitation into action without opportunity for worrying beforehand, to bring this about with Macomber, but regardless of how it had happened it had most certainly happened. Look at the beggar now, Wilson thought. It's that some of them stay little boys so long, Wilson thought. Sometimes all their lives. Their figures stay boyish when they're fifty. The great American boy-men.

Damned strange people. But he liked this Macomber now. Damned strange fellow. Probably meant the end of cuckoldry too. Well, that would be a damned good thing. Damned good thing. Beggar had probably been afraid all his life. Don't know what started it. But over now. Hadn't had time to be afraid with the buff. That and being angry too. Motor car too. Motor cars made it familiar. Be a damn fire eater now. He'd seen it in the war work the same way. More of a change than any loss of virginity. Fear gone like an operation. Something else grew in its place. Main thing a man had. Made him into a man. Women knew it too. No bloody fear.

From the far corner of the seat Margaret Macomber looked at the two of them. There was no change in Wilson. She saw Wilson as she had seen him the day before when she had first realized what his great talent was. But she saw the change in Francis Macomber now.

"Do you have that feeling of happiness about what's going to happen?" Macomber asked, still exploring his new wealth.

"You're not supposed to mention it," Wilson said, looking in the other's face. "Much more fashionable to say you're scared. Mind you, you'll be scared too, plenty of times."

"But you *have* a feeling of happiness about action to come?"

"Yes," said Wilson. "There's that. Doesn't do to talk too much about all this. Talk the whole thing away. No pleasure in anything if you mouth it up too much."

"You're both talking rot," said Margot. "Just because you've chased some helpless animals in a motor car you talk like heroes."

"Sorry," said Wilson. "I have been gassing too much." She's worried about it already, he thought.

"If you don't know what we're talking about why not keep out of it?" Macomber asked his wife.

"You've gotten awfully brave, awfully suddenly," his wife said contemptuously, but her contempt was not secure. She was very afraid of something.

Macomber laughed, a very natural hearty laugh. "You know I have," he said. "I really have."

"Isn't it sort of late?" Margot said bitterly. Because she had done the best she could for many years back and the way they were together now was no one person's fault.

"Not for me," said Macomber.

Margot said nothing but sat back in the corner of the seat.

"Do you think we've given him time enough?" Macomber asked Wilson cheerfully.

"We might have a look," Wilson said. "Have you any solids left?"

"The gun-bearer has some."

Wilson called in Swahili and the older gun-bearer, who was skinning out one of the heads, straightened up, pulled a box of solids out of his pocket and brought them over to Macomber, who filled his magazine and put the remaining shells in his pocket.

"You might as well shoot the Springfield," Wilson said. "You're used to it. We'll leave the Mannlicher in the car with the Memsahib. Your gun-bearer can carry your heavy gun. I've this damned cannon. Now let me tell you about them." He had saved this until the last because he did not want to worry Macomber. "When a buff comes he comes with his head high and thrust straight out. The boss of the horns covers any sort of a brain shot. The only shot is straight into the nose. The only other shot is into his chest or, if you're to one side, into the neck or the shoulders. After they've been hit once they take a hell of a lot of killing. Don't try anything fancy. Take the easiest shot there is. They've finished skinning out that head now. Should we get started?"

He called to the gun-bearers, who came up wiping their hands, and the older one got into the back.

"I'll only take Kongoni," Wilson said. "The other can watch to keep the birds away."

As the car moved slowly across the open space toward the island of brushy trees that ran in a tongue of foliage along a dry water course that cut the open swale, Macomber felt his heart pounding and his mouth was dry again, but it was excitement, not fear.

"Here's where he went in," Wilson said. Then to the gun-bearer in Swahili, "Take the blood spoor."

The car was parallel to the patch of bush. Macomber, Wilson and the gun-bearer got down. Macomber, looking back, saw his wife, with the rifle by her side, looking at him. He waved to her and she did not wave back.

The brush was very thick ahead and the ground was dry. The middle-aged gun-bearer was sweating heavily and Wilson had his hat down over his eyes and his red neck showed just ahead of Macomber. Suddenly the gun-bearer said something in Swahili to Wilson and ran forward.

"He's dead in there," Wilson said. "Good work," and he turned to grip Macomber's hand and as they shook hands, grinning at each other, the gun-bearer shouted wildly and they saw him coming out of the bush sideways, fast as a crab, and the bull coming, nose out, mouth tight closed, blood dripping, massive head straight out, coming in a charge, his little pig eyes bloodshot as he looked at them. Wilson, who was ahead was kneeling shooting, and Macomber, as he fired, unhearing his shot in the roaring of Wilson's gun, saw fragments like slate burst from the huge boss of the horns, and the head jerked, he shot again at the wide nostrils and saw the horns jolt again and fragments fly, and he did not see Wilson now and, aiming carefully, shot again with the buffalo's huge bulk almost on him and his rifle almost level with the on-coming head, nose out, and he could see the little wicked eyes and the head started to lower and he felt a sudden white-hot, blinding flash explode inside his head and that was all he ever felt.

Wilson had ducked to one side to get in a shoulder shot. Macomber had stood solid and shot for the nose, shooting a touch high each time and hitting the heavy horns, splintering and chipping them like hitting a slate roof, and Mrs. Macomber, in the car, had shot at the buffalo with the 6.5 Mannlicher as it seemed about to gore Macomber and had hit her husband about two inches up and a little to one side of the base of his skull.

Francis Macomber lay now, face down, not two yards from where the buffalo lay on his side and his wife knelt over him with Wilson beside her.

"I wouldn't turn him over," Wilson said.

The woman was crying hysterically.

"I'd get back in the car," Wilson said. "Where's the rifle?"

She shook her head, her face contorted. The gun-bearer picked up the rifle.

"Leave it as it is," said Wilson. Then, "Go get Abdulla so that he may witness the manner of the accident."

He knelt down, took a handkerchief from his pocket, and spread it over Francis Macomber's crew-cropped head where it lay. The blood sank into the dry, loose earth.

Wilson stood up and saw the buffalo on his side, his legs out, his thinly-haired belly crawling with ticks. "Hell of a good bull," his brain registered automatically. "A good fifty inches, or better. Better." He called to the driver and told him to spread a blanket over the body and stay by it. Then he walked over to the motor car where the woman sat crying in the corner.

"That was a pretty thing to do," he said in a toneless voice. "He *would* have left you too."

"Stop it," she said.

"Of course it's an accident," he said. "I know that."

"Stop it," she said.

"Don't worry," he said. "There will be a certain amount of unpleasantness but I will have some photographs taken that will be very useful at the inquest. There's the testimony of the gun-bearers and the driver too. You're perfectly all right."

"Stop it," she said.

"There's a hell of a lot to be done," he said. "And I'll have to send a truck off to the lake to wireless for a plane to take the three of us into Nairobi. Why didn't you poison him? That's what they do in England."

"Stop it. Stop it. Stop it," the woman cried.

Wilson looked at her with his flat blue eyes.

"I'm through now," he said. "I was a little angry. I'd begun to like your husband."

"Oh, please stop it," she said. "Please, please stop it."

"That's better," Wilson said. "Please is much better. Now I'll stop."

POINTS TO CONSIDER ABOUT "THE SHORT HAPPY LIFE OF FRANCIS MACOMBER"

1. What kind of opening does Hemingway choose to employ for "The Short Happy Life of Francis Macomber"? In beginning the story in this way, does he succeed in initiating narrative momentum which impels his plot forward? Does the antagonism between the main characters figure centrally in the plot, or is it merely an interesting but separate story-within-a-story?

2. How does the character of Wilson figure in Hemingway's construction of this story? What specific incidents does Wilson precipitate? What attitudes and/or visceral reactions do you experience as you read about Wilson? Similarly, how does the subject matter—the killing of wild animals for sport—affect you? What is Hemingway's attitude toward this kind of activity? Does he seem favorably disposed toward "big game" hunting, or critical of it? Provide textual evidence for your opinions.

3. What information does Hemingway supply as to the background histories of his central characters? How does he work this material into his story? In what ways does Hemingway's exposition meet the criteria for successful exposition—subtlety, seamlessness and subordination—as explained in this chapter? In what ways might Hemingway's exposition fall short of meeting all these criteria?

4. Does Hemingway make it clear whether Margaret intentionally shoots Francis at the end of the story, or whether it was an accident? What textual clues point to the incident's intentionality, and what might point to its having been an accident? Why does Hemingway choose to structure the story's resolution in this ambiguous way?

5. This story contains a number of shifts in point of view. Sometimes the action is described by a detached third-person narrator, while at other times Hemingway "gets into the head" of his characters (even the animals!), relating directly their thoughts and feelings. Point out specific instances of this shifting point of view. Explain how each of these examples might contribute to the development of the plot, and to Hemingway's ultimate thematic message(s) in "The Short Happy Life of Francis Macomber".

Selway

Pam Houston

It was June the seventh and we'd driven eighteen hours of pavement and sixty miles of dirt to find out the river was at highwater, the highest of the year, of several years, and rising. The ranger, Ramona, wrote on our permit, "We do not recommend boating at this level," and then she looked at Jack.

"We're just gonna go down and take a look at it," he said, "see if the river gives us a sign." He tried to slide the permit away from Ramona, but her short dark fingers held it against the counter. I looked from one to the other. I knew Jack didn't believe in signs.

"Once you get to Moose Creek you're committed," she said. "There's no time to change your mind after that. You've got Double Drop and Little Niagara and Ladle, and they just keep coming iike that, one after another with no slow water in between."

She was talking about rapids. This was my first northern trip, and after a lazy spring making slow love between rapids on the wide desert rivers, I couldn't imagine what all the fuss was about.

"If you make it through the Moose Creek series there's only a few more real bad ones; Wolf Creek is the worst. After that the only thing to worry about is the takeout point. The beach will be under water, and if you miss it, you're over Selway Falls."

"Do you have a river guide?" Jack said, and when she bent under the counter to get one he tried again to slide the permit away. She pushed a small, multifolded map in his direction.

"Don't rely on it," she said. "The rapids aren't even marked in the right place."

"Thanks for your help," Jack said. He gave the permit a sharp tug and put it in his pocket.

"There was an accident today," Ramona said. "In Ladle."

"Anybody hurt?" Jack asked.

"It's not official."

"Killed?"

"The water's rising," Ramona said, and turned back to her desk.

At the put-in, the water crashed right over the top of the depth gauge. The grass grew tall and straight through the slats of the boat ramp.

"Looks like we're the first ones this year," Jack said.

The Selway has the shortest season of any river in North America. They don't plow the snow till the first week in June, and by the last week in July there's not enough water to carry a boat. They only allow one party a day on the river that they select from a nationwide lottery with thousands of applicants each year. You can try your whole life and never get a permit.

"Somebody's been here," I said. "The people who flipped today."

Jack didn't answer. He was looking at the gauge. "It's up even from this morning," he said. "They said this morning it was six feet."

Jack and I have known each other almost a year. I'm the fourth in a series of long-term girlfriends he's never gotten around to proposing to. He likes me because I'm young enough not to sweat being single and I don't put pressure on him the way the others did. They wanted him to quit running rivers, to get a job that wasn't seasonal, to raise a family like any man his age. They wouldn't go on trips with him, not even once to see what it was like, and I couldn't imagine that they knew him in any way that was complete if they hadn't known him on the river, if they hadn't seen him row.

I watched him put his hand in the water. "Feel that, baby," he said. "That water was snow about fifteen minutes ago."

I stuck my foot in the water and it went numb in about ten seconds. I've been to four years of college and I should know better, but I love it when he calls me baby.

Jack has taken a different highwater trip each year for the last fifteen, on progressively more difficult rivers. When a river is at high water it's not just deeper and faster and colder than usual. It's got a different look and feel from the rest of the year. It's dark and impatient and turbulent, like a volcano or a teenage boy. It strains against its banks and it churns around and under itself. Looking at its fullness made me want to grab Jack and throw him down on the boat ramp and make love right next to where the river roared by, but I could tell by his face he was trying to make a decision, so I sat and stared at the river and wondered if it was this wild at the put-in what it would look like in the rapids.

"If anything happened to you..." he said, and threw a stick out to the middle of the channel. "It must be moving nine miles an hour." He walked up and down the boat ramp. "What do you think?" he said.

"I think this is a chance of a lifetime," I said. "I think you're the best boatman you know." I wanted to feel the turbulence underneath me. I wanted to run a rapid that could flip a boat. I hadn't taken anything like a risk in months. I wanted to think about dying.

It was already early evening, and once we made the decision to launch, there were two hours of rigging before we could get on the water. On the southern rivers we'd boat sometimes for an hour after dark just to watch what the moon did to the water. On the Selway there was a rapid that could flip your boat around every corner. It wasn't getting pitch dark till ten-thirty that far north, where the June dusk went on forever, but it wasn't really light either and we wouldn't be able to see very far ahead. We told ourselves we'd go a tenth of a mile and make camp, but you can't camp on a sheer granite wall, and the river has to give you a place to get stopped and get tied.

I worked fast and silent, wondering if we were doing the right thing and knowing if we died it would really be my fault, because as much as I knew Jack wanted to go, he wouldn't have pushed me if I'd said I was scared. Jack was untamable, but he had some sense and a lot of respect for the river. He relied on me to speak with the voice of reason, to be life-protecting because I'm a woman and that's how he thinks women are, but I've never been protective enough of anything, least of all myself.

At nine-fifteen we untied the rope and let the river take us. "The first place that looks campable," Jack said.

Nine miles an hour is fast in a rubber raft on a river you've never boated when there's not quite enough light to see what's in front of you. We were taking on water over the bow almost immediately, even though the map didn't show any rapids for the first two miles. It was hard for me to take my eyes off Jack, the way his muscles strained with every stroke, first his upper arms, then his upper thighs. He was silent, thinking it'd been a mistake to come, but I was laughing and bailing water and combing the banks for a flat spot and jumping back and forth over my seat to kiss him, and watching while his muscles flexed.

My mother says I thrive on chaos, and I guess that's true, because as hard a year as I've had with Jack I stayed with it, and I won't even admit by how much the bad days outnumbered the good. We fought like bears when we weren't on the river, because he was so used to fighting and I was so used to getting my own way. I said I wanted selfless devotion and he took a stand on everything from infidelity to salad dressing, and it was always opposite to mine. The one thing we had going for us, though, was the sex, and if we could stop screaming at each other long enough to make love it would be a day or sometimes two before something would happen and we'd go at it again. I've always been afraid to stop and think too hard about what great sex in bad times might mean, but it must have something to do with timing, that moment making love when you're at once absolutely powerful and absolutely helpless, a balance we could never find when we were out of bed.

It was the old southern woman next door, the hunter's widow, who convinced me I should stay with him each time I'd get mad enough to leave. She said if I didn't have to fight for him I'd never know if he was mine. She said the wild ones were the only ones worth having and that I had to let him do whatever it took to keep him wild. She said I wouldn't love him if he ever gave in, and the harder I looked at my life, the more I saw a series of men—wild in their own way—who thought because I said I wanted security and commitment, I did. Sometimes it seems this simple: I tamed them and made them dull as fence posts and left each one for someone wilder than the last. Jack is the wildest so far, and the hardest, and even though I've been proposed to sixteen times, five times by men I've never made love to, I want him all to myself and at home more than I've ever wanted anything.

"Are you bailing? I'm standing in water back here," he said, so I bailed faster but the waves kept on crashing over the bow.

"I can't move this boat," he said, which I knew wasn't entirely true, but it was holding several hundred gallons of water times eight pounds a gallon, and that's more weight than I'd care to push around.

"There," he said. "Camp. Let's try to get to shore."

He pointed to a narrow beach a hundred yards downstream. The sand looked black in the twilight; it was long and flat enough for a tent.

"Get the rope ready," he said. "You're gonna have to jump for it and find something to wrap around fast."

He yelled *jump* but it was too early and I landed chest-deep in the water and the cold took my breath but I scrambled across the rocks to the beach and wrapped around a fallen trunk just as the rope went tight. The boat dragged the trunk and me ten yards down the beach before Jack could get out and pull the nose of it up on shore.

"This may have been real fuckin' stupid," he said.

I wanted to tell him how the water made me feel, how horny and crazy and happy I felt riding on top of water that couldn't hold itself in, but he was scared, for the first time since I'd known him, so I kept my mouth shut and went to set up the tent.

In the morning the tent was covered all around with a thin layer of ice and we made love like crazy people, the way you do when you think it might be the last time ever, till the sun changed the ice back to dew and got the tent so hot we were sweating. Then Jack got up and made coffee, and we heard the boaters coming just in time to get our clothes on.

They threw us their rope and we caught it. There were three of them, three big men in a boat considerably bigger than ours. Jack poured them coffee. We all sat down on the fallen log.

"You launched late last night?" the tallest, darkest one said. He had curly black hair and a wide open face.

Jack nodded. "Too late," he said. "Twilight boating."

"It's up another half a foot this morning," the man said. "It's supposed to peak today at seven."

The official forest service document declares the Selway unsafe for boating above six feet. Seven feet is off their charts.

"Have you boated this creek at seven?" Jack asked. The man frowned and took a long drink from his cup.

"My name's Harvey," he said, and stuck out his hand. "This is Charlie and Charlie. We're on a training trip." He laughed. "Yahoo."

Charlie and Charlie nodded.

"You know the river," Jack said.

"I've boated the Selway seventy times," he said. "Never at seven feet. It was all the late snow and last week's heat wave. It's a bad combination, but it's boatable. This river's always boatable if you know exactly where to be."

Charlie and Charlie smiled.

"There'll be a lot of holes that there's no way to miss. You got to punch through them."

Jack nodded. I knew Harvey was talking about boat flippers. Big waves that form in holes the river makes behind rocks and ledges and that will suck boats in and hold them there, fill them with water till they flip, hold bodies, too, indefinitely, until they go under and catch the current, or until the hole decides to spit them out. If you hit a hole with a back wave bigger than your boat perfectly straight, there's a half a chance you'll shoot through. A few degrees off in either direction, and the hole will get you every time.

"We'll be all right in this tank," Harvey said, nodding to his boat, "but I'm not sure I'd run it in a boat that small. I'm not sure I'd run it in a boat I had to bail."

Unlike ours, Harvey's boat was a self-bailer, inflatable tubes around an open metal frame that let the water run right through. They're built for high water, and extremely hard to flip.

"Just the two of you?" Harvey said.

Jack nodded.

"A honeymoon trip. Nice."

"We're not married," Jack said.

"Yeah," Harvey said. He picked up a handful of sand. "The black sand of the Selway," he said. "I carried a bottle of this sand downriver the year I got married. I wanted to throw it at my wife's feet during the ceremony. The minister thought it was pretty strange, but he got over it."

One of the Charlies looked confused.

"Black sand," Harvey said. "You know, black sand, love, marriage, Selway, rivers, life; the whole thing."

I smiled at Jack, but he wouldn't meet my eyes.

"You'll be all right till Moose Creek," Harvey said. "That's when it gets wild. We're gonna camp there tonight, run the bad stretch first thing in the morning in case we wrap or flip or tear something. I hope you won't think I'm insulting you if I ask you to run with us. It'll be safer for us both. The people who flipped yesterday were all experienced. They all knew the Selway."

"They lost one?" Jack said.

"Nobody will say for sure," Harvey said. "But I'd bet on it."

"We'll think about it," Jack said. "It's nice of you to offer."

"I know what you're thinking," Harvey said. "But I've got a kid now. It makes a difference." He pulled a picture out of his wallet. A baby girl, eight or nine months old, crawled across a linoleum floor.

"She's beautiful," I said.

"She knocks me out," Harvey said. "She follows everything with her finger; bugs, flowers, the TV, you know what I mean?"

Jack and I nodded.

"It's your decision," he said. "Maybe we'll see you at Moose Creek."

He stood up, and Charlie and Charlie rose behind him. One coiled the rope while the other pushed off.

Jack poured his third cup of coffee. "Think he's full of shit?" he said.

"I think he knows more than you or I ever will," I said.

"About this river, at least," he said.

"At least," I said.

In midday sunshine, the river looked more fun than terrifying. We launched just before noon, and though there was no time for sightseeing I bailed fast enough to let Jack move the boat through the rapids, which came quicker and bigger around every bend. The map showed ten rapids between the put-in and Moose Creek, and it was anybody's guess which of the fifty or sixty rapids we boated that day were the ones the forest service had in mind. Some had bigger waves than others, some narrower passages, but the river was continuous moving white water, and we finally put the map away. On the southern rivers we'd mix rum and fruit juice and eat smoked oysters and pepper cheese. Here, twenty fast miles went by without time to take a picture, to get a drink of water. The Moose Creek pack bridge came into sight, and we pulled in and tied up next to Harvey's boat.

"White fuckin' water," Harvey said. "Did you have a good run?"

"No trouble," Jack said.

"Good," Harvey said. "Here's where she starts to kick ass." He motioned with his head downriver. "We'll get up at dawn and scout everything."

"It's early yet," Jack said. "I think we're going on." I looked at Jack's face, and then Harvey's.

"You do what you want," Harvey said. "But you ought to take a look at the next five miles. The runs are obvious once you see them from the bank, but they change at every level."

"We haven't scouted all day," Jack said. I knew he wanted us to run alone, that he thought following Harvey would be cheating somehow, but I believed a man who'd throw sand at his new wife's feet, and I liked a little danger but I didn't want to die.

"There's only one way through Ladle," Harvey said. "Ladle's where they lost the girl."

"The girl?" Jack said.

"The rest of her party was here when we got here. Their boats were below Ladle. They just took off, all but her husband. He wouldn't leave, and you can't blame him. He was rowing when she got tossed. He let the boat get sideways. He's been wandering around here for two days, I guess, but he wouldn't get back in the boat."

"Jesus Christ," Jack said. He sat down on the bank facing the water.

I looked back into the woods for the woman's husband and tried to imagine a posture for him, tried to imagine an expression for his face. I thought about my Uncle Tim, who spent ten years and a lifetime of savings building his dream home. On the day it was completed he backed his pickup over his four-year-old daughter while she played in the driveway. He sold the house in three days and went completely gray in a week.

"A helicopter landed about an hour ago," Harvey said. "Downstream, where the body must be. It hasn't taken off."

"The water's still rising," Jack said, and we all looked to where we'd pulled the boats up on shore and saw that they were floating. And then we heard the beating of the propeller and saw the helicopter rising out over the river. We saw the hundred feet of cable hanging underneath it and then we saw the woman, arched like a dancer over the thick black belt they must use for transplanting wild animals, her long hair dangling, her arms slung back. The pilot flew up the river till he'd gained enough altitude, turned back, and headed over the mountain wall behind our camp.

"They said she smashed her pelvis against a rock and bled to death internally," Harvey said. "They got her out in less than three minutes, and it was too late."

Jack put his arm around my knees. "We'll scout at dawn," he said. "We'll all run this together."

Harvey was up rattling coffeepots before we had time to make love and I said it would bring us bad luck if we didn't but Jack said it would be worse than bad luck if we didn't scout the rapids. The scouting trail was well worn. Harvey went first, then Jack, then me and the two Charlies. Double Drop was first, two sets of falls made by water pouring over clusters of house-sized boulders that extended all the way across the river.

"You can sneak the first drop on the extreme right," Harvey said. "There's no sneak for the second. Just keep her straight and punch her through. Don't let her get you sideways."

Little Niagara was a big drop, six feet or more, but the run was pretty smooth and the back wave low enough to break through.

"Piece of cake," Harvey said.

The sun was almost over the canyon wall, and we could hear Ladle long before we rounded the bend. I wasn't prepared for what I saw. One hundred yards of white water stretched from shore to shore and thundered over rocks and logjams and ledges. There were ten holes the size of the one in Double Drop, and there was no space for a boat in between. The currents were so chaotic for such a long stretch there was no way to read which way they'd push a boat. We found some small logs and climbed a rock ledge that hung over the rapid.

"See if you can read this current," Harvey said, and tossed the smallest log into the top of the rapid. The log hit the first hole and went under. It didn't come back up. One of the Charlies giggled.

"Again," Harvey said. This time the log came out of the first hole and survived two more before getting swallowed by the biggest hole, about midway through the rapid.

"I'd avoid that one for sure," Harvey said. "Try to get left of that hole." He threw the rest of the logs in. None of them made it through. "This is big-time," he said.

We all sat on the rock for what must have been an hour. "Seen enough?" Harvey said. "We've still got No Slouch and Miranda Jane."

The men climbed down off the rock, but I wasn't quite ready to leave. I went to the edge of the ledge, lay flat on my stomach, and hung over until my head was so full of the roar of the river I got dizzy and pulled myself back up. The old southern woman said men can't really live unless they face death now and then, and I know by men she didn't mean mankind. And I wondered which rock shattered the dead woman's pelvis, and I wondered what she and I were doing out here on this river when Harvey's wife was home with that beautiful baby and happy. And I knew it was crazy to take a boat through that rapid and I knew I'd do it anyway but I didn't any longer know why. Jack said I had to do it for myself to make it worth anything, and at first I thought I was there because I loved danger, but sitting on the rock I knew I was there because I loved Jack. And maybe I went because his old girlfriends wouldn't, and maybe I went because I wanted him for mine, and maybe it didn't matter at all why I went because doing it for me and doing it for him amounted, finally, to exactly the same thing. And even though I knew in my head there's nothing a man can do that a woman can't, I also knew in my heart we can't help doing it for different reasons. And just like a man will never understand exactly how a woman feels when she has a baby, or an orgasm, or the reasons why she'll fight so hard to be loved, a woman can't know in what way a man satisfies himself, what question he answers for himself, when he looks right at death.

My head was so full of the sound and the light of the river that when I climbed down off the bank side of the ledge I didn't see the elk carcass until I stepped on one of its curled hooves. It was a young elk, probably not dead a year, and still mostly covered with matted brown fur. The skull was picked clean by scavengers, polished white by the sun and grinning. The sound that came out of my mouth scared me as much as the elk had, and I felt silly a few minutes later when Harvey came barreling around the corner followed by Jack.

Harvey saw the elk and smiled.

"It startled me is all," I said.

"Jesus," Jack said. "Stay with us, all right?"

"I never scream," I said. "Hardly ever."

No Slouch and Miranda Jane were impressive rapids, but they were nothing like Ladle and both runnable to the left. On the way back to camp we found wild strawberries, and Jack and I hung back and fed them to each other and I knew he wasn't mad about me screaming. The boats were loaded by ten-thirty and the sun was warm. We wore life jackets and helmets and wet suits. Everybody had diver's boots but me, so I wore my loafers.

"You have three minutes in water this cold," Harvey said. "Even with a wet suit. Three minutes before hypothermia starts, and then you can't swim, and then you just give in to the river."

Harvey gave us the thumbs-up signs as the Charlies pushed off. I pushed off right behind them. Except for the bail bucket and the spare oar, everything on the boat was tied down twice and inaccessible. My job was to take water out of the boat as fast as I could eight pounds at a time, and to help Jack remember which rapid was coming next and where we had decided to run it.

I saw the first of the holes in Double Drop and yelled, "Right," and we made the sneak with a dry boat. We got turned around somehow after that, though, and had to hit the big wave backwards. Jack yelled, "Hang on, baby," and we hit it straight on and it filled the boat, but then we were through it and in sight of Little Niagara before I could even start bailing.

"We're going twelve miles an hour at least," Jack yelled. "Which one is this?"

"Niagara," I yelled. "Right center." The noise of the river swallowed my words and I only threw out two bucketfuls before we were over the lip of Niagara and I had to hold on. I could hear Ladle around the bend and I was throwing water so fast I lost my balance and that's when I heard Jack say, "Bail faster!" and that's when I threw the bail bucket into the river and watched, unbelieving, as it went under, and I saw Jack see it too but we were at Ladle and I had to sit down and hold on. I watched Harvey's big boat getting bounced around like a cork, and I think I closed my eyes when the first wave crashed over my face because the next thing I knew we were out of the heaviest water and Harvey was standing and smiling at us with his fist in the air.

I could see No Slouch around the bend and I don't remember it or Miranda Jane because I was kneeling in the front of the boat scooping armfuls of water the whole time.

We all pulled up on the first beach we found and drank a beer and hugged each other uncertainly, like tenants in an apartment building where the fires have been put out.

"You're on your own," Harvey said. "We're camping here. Take a look at Wolf Creek, and be sure and get to shore before Selway Falls." He picked up a handful of black sand and let it run through his fingers. He turned to me. "He's a good boatman, and you're very brave."

I smiled.

"Take care of each other," he said. "Stay topside."

We set off alone and it clouded up and started to rain and I couldn't make the topography match the river map.

"I can't tell where we are," I told Jack. "But Wolf Creek can't be far."

"We'll see it coming," he said, "or hear it."

But it wasn't five minutes after he spoke that we rounded a bend and were in it, waves crashing on all sides and Jack trying to find a way between the rocks and the holes. I was looking too, and I think I saw the run, fifty feet to our right, right before I heard Jack say, "Hang on, baby," and we hit the hole sideways and everything went white and cold. I was in the waves and underwater and I couldn't see Jack or the boat, I couldn't move my arms or legs apart from how the river tossed them. Jack had said swim down to the current, but I couldn't tell which way was down and I couldn't have moved there in that washing machine, my lungs full and taking on water. Then the wave spit me up, once, under the boat, and then again, clear of it, and I got a breath and pulled down away from the air and felt the current grab me, and I waited to get smashed against a rock, but the rock didn't come and I was at the surface riding the crests of some eight-foot rollers and seeing Jack's helmet bobbing in the water in front of me.

"Swim, baby!" he yelled, and it was like it hadn't occurred to me, like I was frozen there in the water. And I tried to swim but I couldn't get a breath and my limbs wouldn't move and I thought about the three minutes and hypothermia and I must have been swimming then because the shore started to get closer. I grabbed the corner of a big ledge and wouldn't let go, not even when Jack yelled at me to get out of the water, and even when he showed me an easy place to get out if I just floated a few yards downstream it took all I had and more to let go of the rock and get back in the river.

I got out on a tiny triangular rock ledge, surrounded on all sides by walls of granite. Jack stood sixty feet above me on another ledge.

"Sit tight," he said. "I'm going to go see if I can get the boat."

Then he was gone and I sat in that small space and started to shake. It was raining harder, sleeting even, and I started to think about freezing to death in that space that wasn't even big enough for me to move around in and get warm. I started to think about the river rising and filling that space and what would happen when Jack got back and made me float downstream to an easier place, or what would happen if he didn't come back, if he died trying to get the boat back, if he chased it fifteen miles to Selway Falls. When I saw the boat float by, right side up and empty, I decided to climb out of the space.

I'd lost one loafer in the river, so I wedged myself between the granite walls and used my fingers, mostly, to climb. I've always been a little afraid of heights, so I didn't look down. I thought it would be stupid to live through the boating accident and smash my skull free-climbing on granite, but as I inched up the wall I got warmer and kept going. When I got to the top there were trees growing across, and another vertical bank I hadn't seen from below. I bashed through the branches with my helmet and grabbed them one at a time till they broke or pulled out and then I grabbed the next one higher. I dug into the thin layer of soil that covered the rock with my knees and my elbows, and I'd slip down an inch for every two I gained. When I came close to panic I thought of Rambo, as if he were a real person, as if what I was doing was possible, and proven before, by him.

And then I was on the ledge and I could see the river, and I could see Jack on the other side, and I must have been in shock, a little, because I couldn't at that time imagine how he could have gotten to the other side of the river, I couldn't imagine what would make him go back in the water, but he had, and there he was on the other side.

"I lost the boat," he yelled. "Walk downstream till you see it."

I was happy for instructions and I set off down the scouting trail, shoe on one foot, happy for the pain in the other, happy to be walking, happy because the sun was trying to come out again and I was there to see it. It was a few miles before I even realized that the boat would be going over the falls, that Jack would have had to swim one more time across the river to get to the trail, that I should go back and see if he'd made it, but I kept walking downstream and looking for the boat. After five miles my bare foot started to bleed, so I put my left loafer on my right foot and walked on. After eight miles I saw Jack running up the trail behind me, and he caught up and kissed me and ran on by.

I walked and I walked, and I thought about being twenty-one and hiking in mountains not too far from these with a boy who almost drowned and then proposed to me. His boots had filled with the water of a river even farther to the north, and I was wearing sneakers and have a good kick, so I made it across just fine. I thought about how he sat on the far bank after he'd pulled himself out and shivered and stared at the water. And how I ran up and down the shore looking for the shallowest crossing, and then, thinking I'd found it, met him halfway. I remembered when our hands touched across the water and how I'd pulled him to safety and built him a fire and dried his clothes. Later that night he asked me to marry him and it made me happy and I said yes even though I knew it would never happen because I was too young and free and full of my freedom. I switched my loafer to the other foot and wondered if this danger would make Jack propose to me. Maybe he was the kind of man who needed to see death first, maybe we would build a fire to dry ourselves and then he would ask me and I would say yes because by the time you get to be thirty, freedom has circled back on itself to mean something totally different from what it did at twenty-one.

I knew I had to be close to the falls and I felt bad about what the wrecked boat would look like, but all of a sudden it was there in front of me, stuck on a gravel bar in the middle of the river with a rapid on either side, and I saw Jack coming back up the trail toward me.

"I've got it all figured out," he said. "I need to walk upstream about a mile and jump in there. That'll give me enough time to swim most of the way across to the other side of the river, and if I've read the current right, it'll take me right into that gravel bar."

"And if you read the current wrong?" I said.

He grinned. "Then it's over Selway Falls. I almost lost it already the second time I crossed the river. It was just like Harvey said. I almost gave up. I've been running twelve miles and I know my legs'll cramp. It's a long shot but I've got to take it."

"Are you sure you want to do this?" I said. "Maybe you shouldn't do this."

"I thought the boat was gone," he said, "and I didn't care because you were safe and I was safe and we were on the same side of the river. But there it is asking me to come for it, and the water's gonna rise tonight and take it over the falls. You stay right here where you can see what happens to me. If I make it I'll pick you up on that beach just below. We've got a half a mile to the takeout and the falls." He kissed me again and ran back upriver.

The raft was in full sunshine, everything tied down, oars in place. Even the map I couldn't read was there, where I stuck it, under a strap.

I could see Jack making his way through the trees toward the edge of the river, and I realized then that more than any other reason for being on that trip, I was there because I thought I could take care of him, and maybe there's something women want to protect after all. And maybe Jack's old girlfriends were trying to protect him by making him stay home, and maybe I thought I could if I was there, but as he dropped out of sight and into the water I knew there'd always be places he'd go that I couldn't, and that I'd have to let him go, just like the widow said. Then I saw his tiny head in the water and I held my breath and watched his position, which was perfect, as he approached the raft. But he got off center right at the end, and a wave knocked him past the raft and farther down the gravel bar. He got to his feet and went down again. He grabbed for a boulder on the bottom and got washed even farther away. He was using all his energy to stay in one place and he was fifty yards downriver from the raft. I started to pray then, to whomever I pray to when I get in real trouble, and it may have been a coincidence but he started moving forward. It took him fifteen minutes and strength I'll never know to get to the boat, but he was in it, and rowing, and heading for the beach.

Later, when we were safe and on the two-lane heading home, Jack told me we were never in any real danger, and I let him get away with it because I knew that's what he had to tell himself to get past almost losing me.

"The river gave us both a lesson in respect," he said, and it occurred to me then that he thought he had a chance to tame that wild river, but I knew I was at its mercy from the very beginning, and I thought all along that that was the point.

Jack started telling stories to keep himself awake: the day his kayak held him under for almost four minutes, the time he crashed his hang glider twice in one day. He said he thought fifteen years of highwater was probably enough, and that he'd take desert rivers from now on.

The road stretched out in front of us, dry and even and smooth. We found a long dirt road, turned, and pulled down to where it ended at a chimney that stood tall amid the rubble of an old stone house. We didn't build a fire and Jack didn't propose; we rolled out our sleeping bags and lay down next to the truck. I could see the light behind the mountains in the place where the moon would soon rise, and I thought about all the years I'd spent saying love and freedom were mutually exclusive and living my life as though they were exactly the same thing.

The wind carried the smell of the mountains, high and sweet. It was so still I could imagine a peace without boredom.

POINTS TO CONSIDER ABOUT "SELWAY"

1. What specific techniques does Houston use to establish narrative tension in the story? Where do the plot points (to borrow a term from Hollywood) occur?

2. At what points does the author include background information regarding the characters of Jack and the narrator? How does Houston keep her expository information from impeding the forward movement of the story?

3. Why does Houston name the story "Selway"? What role does the river play in the story's plot development?
4. At the end of the story, Jack says, "The river gave us a lesson in respect," which certainly seems to be an unambiguous statement of theme. What additional subthemes does Houston introduce in "Selway", to keep it from coming off as didactic or one-dimensional?
5. How does Houston use the subplot of the river encounter to dramatize the relationship between the two protagonists . . . or vice versa? Which ends up being the more important of the two stories?

WRITING ACTIVITIES: PLOT COMPONENTS

1. Pick up a local newspaper and search the metro section for a brief article on a petty crime that took place yesterday. Pick something relatively trivial—a break-in, an act of juvenile vandalism, a phone scam—not a major crime such as murder or armed robbery (you'll get to explore those later, in the mystery chapter). Write a plot outline that first summarizes, then expands on the article's information. Next, write a story by fleshing out that outline with details of character and setting.
2. Using either the news-based story you wrote for Activity #1 or a different story draft you completed recently, rewrite the scenes after the story's climax three times; that is, write three different resolutions that suggest alternative themes for the story—a tragic ending, a they-lived-happily-ever-after ending, and an open-ended or inconclusive one. Pick the ending you like the best, and re-work the entire story, so that it develops smoothly and seamlessly toward your new resolution.
3. Re-read "Selway" in this chapter and make a detailed outline of its plot. Using your own imagination and experience, and substituting your own characters and locales for Houston's, write a new story that "fills in the blanks" of that structural outline. Make the narrative elements so original that even Houston herself wouldn't recognize her story and therefore won't sue you for plagiarism.

5

Storyfolk

You are a real person. If I cut you with my Disneyland souvenir Pirates of the Caribbean jackknife, do you not bleed? If I bore you with lengthy explanations of plot construction, do you not doze? If I irritate you with these questions and their inverted syntactic structure, do you not slam *The Graceful Lie* down on the formica breakfast table, startling Audrey the beagle?

As a card-carrying real person, you are an exceedingly complex aggregation of genetic traits, biochemically influenced moods, subconscious conflicts, buried memories terrible and beautiful, habits born of repetitive gesturing and posturing, regular tides of blood and bowel, nervous tics and shooting lower back pains, responses to astrological alignments, powerful primal urges to copulate, socially constructed attitudes and actions. You may have been called a "character" in your life, but you're not a character in the fictional sense.

Compared to the large, tightly crammed steamer trunk of characteristics that make up real people, fictional characters are a small overnight bag packed (neatly, one hopes) with details imparted by an author, to a reader, through the medium of print. The goal of the writer, then, is to create characters that seem real, given the circumscribed arena of the short story or the novel exposition. This chapter provides you with some suggestions toward that end.

WHERE DO CHARACTERS COME FROM, MOMMY?

As with plot construction, there are two divergent schools of thought regarding characterization. People from the organic camp tend to assert that the most satisfying method for creating believable characters is to "give your characters a very long leash." That is, render your story people roundly, using significant detail, and then let them direct and inform the narrative. Argentine novelist and short story writer Julio Cortazar says of this method,

> It's the characters who direct me. That is, I see the character, he's there, and I recognize someone I knew, or occasionally two who are a bit mixed together, but then that stops. Afterwards, the character acts on his own account. He says things . . . I never know what any of them are going to say when I'm writing dialogue. Really it's up to them.

The advantages of such an approach are that you may find much joy of discovery in the creative process, and your characters will tend to be quirky, surprising, original. "If you give them that kind of long leash and you're very fortunate," observes novelist Richard Russo, "they will take you to some interesting places, and the characters will give the impression of having lives of their own."

In order to make characters appear to have "lives of their own," you must somehow flesh out your story people with individual qualities of appearance, speech, and action. To accomplish this, authors employ a number of strategies. Some—especially those from the organic camp—prefer to draw characters from real-life models. Michael Seidman, who writes extensively on the composition and publishing process, advises,

> Look at the people around you (but not your friends and relatives) and pick those who seem interesting. Create not only their biographies, but predict their futures, based on what you see and know about human nature. What does their dress tell you about them? Their body language? Their mannerisms? Having gone that far, fill in the back story: How do you think they got that way? What is it about people that goes into making them who they are?

Sound practical advice, although I would argue with his exhortation not to use your friends and relatives as models for your fictional characters. In my own experience, loved ones make excellent models, because you know their idiosyncrasies—the way they leave an electric fan on all night to drown out extraneous noise, their unreasonable fear of bees, their recurring nightmares of demonic possession, their tendency to chew through flea collars—as well as their superficial mannerisms. Furthermore, you have intimate knowledge of their personal histories—Brownie medals, rheumatic fever, breach birth, Little League championship, cruel abuses at the hands of their own parents—which can flesh out the characters in your fiction. This will result in story people who have *verisimilitude:* a term academics and palm-court literati sometimes use to indicate a fictional construct that has the appearance of being true or real.

Unfortunately, in creating characters drawn from friends and family, you run the risk of having those "real" people recognize themselves in your work. This can lead to your being dumped by your boyfriend (whom you portrayed unflatteringly in your short story, "The Two-timing, Beer-guzzling, Ultra-macho Rugby Jock Who Never Does the Dishes"), sued for divorce by your third wife, disowned by your parents, written out of your Uncle Jake's will, dissed by your homies. The trick to avoiding any such unpleasantness is to assemble traits of several different people with whom you're acquainted. Prose theorist Elizabeth Bowen says of this method,

> Characters are almost always copies, or composite copies. Traits, gestures, etc., are searched for in, and assembled from, the novelist's memory.... Though much may be lifted from a specific person in "real life," no person in "real life" could supply everything (physical) necessary for the character in the novel.

Rather than basing a given fictional character—say, your protagonist's brother Herman—on single "real-life" individual—say, your own brother Ed—customize Herman like a hot-rod Lincoln from spare parts of many people you know. Take the profession of your childhood best friend's father (he operated a successful laundry and linen rental service until he ran it into the ground with some bad investments), the hobby of somebody you used to play in a cajun band with (he builds button accordions from rare and endangered hardwoods), the facial characteristics of your brother-in-law (who comes from Scotland and has pale skin, a beard the color of a newly-minted penny, a beamy grin, a fetching gap between his front teeth), the vocal mannerisms of Miss Sprewce (your second-grade teacher who had skin that looked like crepe paper and used to *hissss* her *esssssessss),* the private life of your sister's ex-husband (he was a closet prescription painkiller junkie), the physique of your own brother Ed (who eats a few too many health-food bagels every day), the disposition of your dear, sweet spouse (who is dear and sweet except on those days when sleep has eluded her, or her blood sugar is low because she forgot to eat anything for six hours because she was rearranging furniture, or she's trying to stop smoking), and ... *voila!* ... a character none of us has ever seen before or is likely to encounter in any other story, if we're lucky.

Another way to avoid the embarrassments and costly lawsuits that arise when you model your characters after real people is to follow the example of those writers from the structural camp. That is, create your plot first and then assemble a cast of characters to satisfy the requirements of the dramatic situation into which you place them, using imaginary rather than

modeled traits as the atoms that form your story people. A vocal and articulate proponent of this approach, novelist Toni Morrison, criticizes the organic method of plot and character construction, insisting that "you can't let
[the characters] write the book for you. I have read books in which I know
that has happened—a novelist has been totally taken over by a character."

For writers like Morrison, assembling characters from the traits of real
people is tantamount to stealing, an infringement of a living individual's
personality "copyright." Therefore, rather than drawing on actual people
for her characters, Morrison says,

> They are carefully imagined. . . . I never use anyone I know. In the *Bluest
> Eye* I think I used some gestures and dialogue of my mother in certain
> places, and a little geography. I've never done that since. I really am
> very conscientious about that. It's never based on anyone.

These statements suggest a fine but important distinction between inventing characters imaginatively and patterning them after real-life models. To
make an analogy with the visual arts: Those in the "use-your-imagination"
school of characterization might say that modeling one's characters after
real people would be like tracing a photograph with a piece of semi-
transparent paper and then calling it an original artwork. The end product
would have a certain verisimilitude, but would in fact be fraudulent. Writers who advocate this method of characterization believe that the imagination should be the sole source from which one draws storyfolk. It might
help, therefore, to understand just what the imagination is, and how it
works.

THE IMAGINATION: KINASES, PHOSPHATASES, ISOMERASES, AND SO MUCH MORE

The *imagination* is that uniquely human capacity to form a detailed image of
an object not present to the senses. Whether you exalt imagination to be the
"recollective fantasia" of eighteenth-century philosopher Giambattista Vico
or "the living power and prime agent of all human perception, and a repetition in the finite mind of the eternal act of creation in the infinite 'I am,'" as
nineteenth-century poet and critic Samuel Taylor Coleridge put it—or
whether you have a slightly more scientistic twentieth-century view of protein kinases/phosphatases and peptidyl-prolyl-cis/trans-isomerases causing neurons to form recombinant memory—the essential function of the
imagination is synthetic. It instantaneously selects from literally millions of
stored mental records, then combines a number of them into a wholly new
construct: a miraculous (or mechanical, or both) act of creative cold fusion.

Using nothing more than the creative power of the imagination and a
sturdy pair of rubber gloves, a writer who belongs to the Morrison camp

can conjure a wholly original character without using specific models from real life. For instance, pop fantasy author Raymond E. Feist describes a nameless, faceless entity of evil in his novel, *Faerie Tale:*

> Above, in the narrow space between the ceiling and floor, the Bad Thing moved.... With a soft sound, like a baby's sigh, it moved like a spider through the secret crawl space between the floor above and ceiling below, hanging upside down most of the way. At the lintel, at the corner below the boys' room, it pushed aside a narrow board and squeezed out, scampering down the drainpipe. It didn't like being about in the light, for the daylight made it remember vague images of a time long forgotten, when the Bad Thing had been young. Such memories hurt.

This, one assumes, is an imaginative construct, unlike my previous example of Herman, who was a pastiche of qualities observed in a few real-life models. We've never met any Bad Things, supernatural beings who have human-like thought processes, harbor cruel impulses, ambulate like spiders, recoil at daylight (that blind date back in '96 came close, but that's the subject for another story). However, we have been fascinated and perhaps creeped out by fat garden spiders in moonlight, met or heard of some mean people, had Jungian archetypal nightmares of dark spaces and encompassing dread. The imagination can synthesize colorful characters from such disparate life experiences.

Similarly, the imagination enables Hunter S. Thompson to portray a hotel clerk in a wholly original way, in his novel *Fear and Loathing in Las Vegas:*

> There is no way to explain the terror I felt when I finally lunged up to the clerk and began babbling.... The woman's face was *changing:* swelling, pulsing ... horrible green jowls and fangs jutting out, the face of a Moray Eel! Deadly poison! I lunged backwards into my attorney, who gripped my arm as he reached out to take the note. "I'll handle this," he said to the Moray woman. "This man has a bad heart, but I have plenty of medicine. . . ."

We have no way of knowing whether the real-life Thompson lives up to his self-portrayal as a demented taker of Herculean quantities of dangerous mind-altering substances, but it may be that in this case, the imagination was chemically fueled. Historically, writers have been prone to juice their muses with drink, psychostimulants, major tranquilizers, opiates, inhalants, pineal gland extract ... with some spectacular successes (see Ken Kesey's *One Flew Over The Cuckoo's Nest*, Coleridge's "Kubla Khan," Thompson's above-named novel, Burroughs' *Naked Lunch)* and many more crash-and-burn headlines. Whether drug-induced or not, it's probably safe to say that a hotel clerk as Moray Eel is not an everyday perception, that the imagination was somehow successfully engaged in the portrayal of this character.

And, shameless fount of pop-cultural references though I am, I must for credibility's sake provide at least one imaginative characterization from the English literary canon. Here's everybody's main man, Shakespeare, creating a cast of fantastic characters in *The Tempest*: Prospero, the right Duke of Milan, talking with the airy spirit Ariel about the witch Sycorax and her monstrous son Caliban,

> This blue-eyed hag was hither brought with child
> And here was left by the sailors. Thou, my slave,
> As thou report'st thyself, wast then her servant;
> And, for thou wast a spirit too delicate
> To act her earthy and abhorr'd commands,
> Refusing her grand hests, she did confine thee,
> By help of her more potent ministers
> And in her most unmitigable rage,
> Into a cloven pine; within which rift
> Imprison'd thou didst painfully remain
> A dozen years; within which space she died
> And left thee there; where thou didst vent thy groans
> As fast as mill-wheels strike. Then was this island —
> Save for the son that she did litter here,
> A freckled whelp hag-born—not honour'd with
> A human shape.

As West Coast Shakespeare scholar Marshall Sweet notes, "blank verse ain't prose fiction." Nevertheless, this brief excerpt illustrates how the imagination can give rise to a genial list of dramatic personae. You don't have to be the Western world's greatest verbal genius like Shakespeare (or the Western world's greatest doper like Thompson) to engage the imagination in a satisfying way, either. All you need is a willingness to visualize and prophesize, to explore your own nightmare landscapes, to distort perceptions through a painterly lens, to extrapolate from scientific "fact," to sentimentalize excessively, to kick time's lazy ass, to indulge and cultivate your most socially unacceptable thoughts and impulses, to moralize fanatically about the human conscience, to sniff soiled linen and then tell people about it, to feel in every cell the profound joy and suffering of all sentient beings, to drape handmade quilts over dead house pets, to ghostwrite detailed autobiographies of people who never existed, to reinvent your own history, to view the smiling facial features of the crescent moon with a six-inch telescope, to experiment liberally with repetitive nonproductive gesturing and posturing, to celebrate the irresistibly erotic while preaching celibacy to high school students, to bomb the genocidal fascists, to play Barbies once again with the fictitious companions of your childhood, to rant and rant.

Or to be quiet.

Dreaming up story people in this way is endlessly entertaining, but it can also be dangerous. One runs the risk of creating cardboard characters rather than fully developed and believable ones. Working from living models usually circumvents this problem, since your real-life model will always be a unique, complex individual with quirks, tics, and lots of history ... even if he's your most boring friend. By contrast, imaginatively constructed characters may have a subconscious basis in societal stereotypes, or may be rendered incompletely, or superficially. If you're a writer at the beginning of the fiction process, I would suggest experimenting extensively with both techniques of characterization, writing from models *and* from the imagination.

Eventually, as with plotting, you probably will not end up being a fiercely strict adherent to either approach, but will rather combine the elements of each that "ring true" for you. American prose writer Edmund White describes combining techniques of characterization this way:

> I pattern a lot of my characters on people I know, but there is a strictly imaginary element which creeps in after I start writing. I begin by writing a fairly close portrait of somebody I know but then the character begins to seem real to me in his own right. If I'm stuck at some point I try to find something in my own experience that I can use, even if the character is going through something that I've never experienced.

Exercises at the end of this chapter will give you practice in both modes of characterization, so that you can employ either one—or a combination of the two, as Wilson suggests—to meet the demands of narrative situations that arise as you put your stories together.

A GIFT WITH THINGS: THE CHARACTERIZING POWER OF DIALOGUE

In life, we learn about people through the things they say, the things they do, the way they look, feel, smell, sound, and (in some intimate cases) taste. We base our judgments of people on these criteria. If somebody cuts us off on the freeway or borrows five hundred bucks and never returns it or makes an ethnic slur or burns us with a cigarette lighter, those things may engender negative feelings in us. If somebody says our novel is "stylish" or buys us a salmon teriyaki dinner or reminds us of our high school sweetheart or wears the same perfume as our grandmother, we may tend to feel positively about them. Writers develop their fictional characters the same way. Using three techniques—action, appearance, and dialogue—writers give their protagonists and secondary characters the quality of *recognition*: an awareness, on the part of the reader, that the individual being portrayed in print has been perceived before, in the real world.

The characterizing function of narrative action has been covered in our previous discussion of plot, and appearance will be covered in the next chapter, during the discussion of narrative description. Dialogue refers to conversation, the verbal interchange between characters. While characters' speech can serve a narrative function by propelling the plot, it has an equally important role in character development. Dialogue supplies one of the key avenues for the evolving characters on a psychological level, because each word of dialogue will—if done skillfully—deepen our comprehension of the story person who is talking.

Developing characters through dialogue is a tricky business, because you want your dialogue to deliver key descriptive information, but in a manner so subtle, and using speech so natural, that the reader doesn't notice it. As Edith Wharton says, dialogue "should short-circuit description of mental traits." In other words, rather than using blatant exposition to give the reader key information about characters, dialogue can deliver that same information, but in a more elegantly subordinated way. The most leaden dialogue is that in which characters unsubtly explain their feelings. Take a typically charged fictional scene, this one featuring a mother trying to prepare her children for school. The unpracticed writer might have the characters saying,

> "Mother, I am late for school, and I am feeling really pressured, I must say."
>
> "So am I, Mother, I'm all antsy because I don't want to miss the school bus and be late!"
>
> "Oh, you kids, I'm getting so frazzled I could just bust at the seams! I wish your father were here to help get you ready for school right now!!"

This snatch of conversation serves two functions successfully. It lets us know that the protagonist feels overwhelmed by the enormity of her motherly chores, and it provides a certain amount of white space. Modern readers seem to be threatened by large chunks of text—long passages without paragraph breaks—and dialogue serves to lighten up the visual presentation of a page (I'm not kidding!). However, the dialogue in this stupid example—written by myself (with ease, I'm sad to say)—is overly obvious in its narrative intent while sounding pedestrian and unnatural.

A more felicitous way of depicting the same emotions is to have the dialogue allude to them, as illustrated by this passage from Ntozake Shange's novel *Betsey Brown:*

> "Who's got my geography book?"
> "Come on, tie my shoes."
> "That dress is not yours. Give it here."
> "Lord, Lord, help me with these chirren."
> "I'ma tell Daddy you took my books."
> "I bet you won't have no backside side, if he gets holdt to ya."
> "Come tie my shoes, please."

"For God's sake, somebody tie Allard's shoes."
"Margot, you better do something with that mess you call hair."
"You said you would comb it for me."
"She sure 'nough did."
"Where's my geography book?"
"Somebody tie Allard's shoes, fore he trips over himself."
"I'ma tell Daddy."

Rather than stiffly and opaquely explaining the family members' feelings, Shange here embeds their feelings within the dialogue without referring directly to them. In this way, she produces within the reader a visceral reaction to the chaotic early-morning atmosphere—one that is recognizable to anybody who grew up in a family. Furthermore, she recreates real human conversation artfully. The passage has the familiar, colloquial diction and cadence of actual early-morning familyspeak.

Besides its descriptive function, dialogue can also be used to connote emotional and physical changes that take place in a character over the course of a story. The writer of fiction will—subtly, once again—make the reader aware of changes in characters' vocal patterns and choice of words. These conversational changes will mirror changes in the characters' psychological condition, as they respond to the buildup of tension in a given plot. A character who suddenly becomes frightened might develop a halting tone, characterized by sentence fragments, or a rambling, stream-of-conscious vocal pattern, with run-on phrasings. A character who has recently fallen in love might likewise begin speaking more lyrically, using speech sprinkled liberally with poetic metaphors and fugues of fanciful diction.

In John Steinbeck's short story "The Chrysanthemums," notice how the vocal pattern of the protagonist, an isolated Salinas Valley woman named Elisa, changes within the brief span of several pages. Early in the story we read this verbal interchange between husband and wife:

Elisa started at the sound of her husband's voice. He had come near quietly, and he leaned over the fence that protected her flower garden from cattle and dogs and chickens.

"At it again," he said. "You've got a strong new crop coming."

Elisa straightened her back and pulled on the gardening glove again. "Yes. They'll be strong this coming year." In her tone and on her face there was a little smugness.

"You've got a gift with things," Henry observed. "Some of those yellow chrysanthemums you had this year were ten inches across. I wish I you'd work out in the orchard and raise some apples that big."

Her eyes sharpened. "Maybe I could do it, too. I've a gift with things, all right. My mother had it. She could stick anything in the ground and make it grow. She said it was having planters' hands that knew how to do it."

Here Elisa's speech exudes confidence and self-reliance. Compare the rhythm and diction of her speech in this early portion of the story with her conversational patterns toward the end of "The Chrysanthemums," after Elisa has had a humiliating encounter with a traveling handyman:

> He [her husband, Henry] took one hand from the wheel and patted her knee. "I ought to take you in to dinner oftener. It would be good for both of us. We get so heavy on the ranch."
>
> "Henry," she asked, "could we have wine at dinner?"
>
> "Sure we could. Say! That will be fine."
>
> She was silent for a while; then she said: "Henry, at those prize-fights, do the men hurt each other very much?"
>
> "Sometimes a little, not often. Why?"
>
> "Well, I've read how they break noses, and blood runs down their chests. I've read how the fighting gloves get heavy and soggy with blood."
>
> He looked around at her. "What's the matter, Elisa? I didn't know you read things like that." He brought the car to a stop, then turned to the right over the Salinas River bridge.
>
> "Do any women ever go to the fights?" she asked.
>
> "Oh, sure, some. What's the matter, Elisa? Do you want to go? I don't think you'd like it, but I'll take you if you really want to go."
>
> She relaxed limply in the seat. "Oh, no. No. I don't want to go. I'm sure I don't." Her face was turned away from him. "It will be enough if we can have wine. It will be plenty."

Elisa's speech has changed, reflecting an emotional shift in her, one that's thematically significant. This is subtle, controlled characterizing. Steinbeck doesn't come out and say, "Look, dear reader: Here we have a character who has been brutalized during the course of the story by her encounter with a male." Rather, he hints at the effect the encounter with the itinerant handyman has had on Elisa, by portraying subtle but unmistakable changes in her speech.

Where before, Elisa's conversation was dominated by forceful assertions, ("They'll be strong this coming year."; "I've a gift with things, all right."), now it has a much more interrogative tone ("...could we have wine at dinner?" "Do any women ever go to the fights?"). Where earlier, her speech contained mainly words and phrases of affirmation ("Yes," and the following), it now contains words connotative of negation and defeat ("Oh, no. No."). Where before her conversation contained metaphors celebrating life ("...stick anything in the ground and make it grow..." "planter's hands"), now it contains images of human brutality ("the fighting gloves get heavy and soggy with blood") and resignation ("It will be plenty"), which illustrate how Elisa feels she has been brutalized emotionally and physically (she is physically trapped, confined by her wifely role in the Salinas Valley), defeated, and ultimately resigned to her unhappy fate. When change does take place in characters, as happens to Elisa in the above example, it usually illustrates the fictional piece's theme in no uncertain terms. In "The Chrysanthemums," one of Steinbeck's main intended themes is the dehumanizing effect of traditional gender roles and power relationships, and we see that reflected in the dialogue.

An additional—but very important—detail of characterizing dialogue is *attribution:* the "she said," "she asked" sorts of phrases that you can observe in the Steinbeck excerpt above. Writers use these phrases to indicate who is speaking, and how. Ideally, your attribution will not have to contain many descriptive details or modifiers, because the dialogue itself should suggest the speaker's attitude, state of mind, physical condition, circumstance. Gordon Lish, one of the country's foremost fiction editors and himself a composer of leading-edge prose, subscribes to this minimalist approach to attribution. Look at the following Lish story, presented in its entirety because it's a short-short:

My daughter called from college. She is a good student, excellent grades, is gifted in any number of ways.

"What time is it?" she said. I said, "It is two o'clock." "All right," she said. "It's two now. Expect me at four—four by the clock that said it's two." "It was my watch," I said. "Good," she said.

It is ninety miles, an easy drive.

At a quarter to four, I went down to the street. I had these things in mind—look for her car, hold a parking place, be there waving when she turned into the block.

At a quarter to five, I came back up. I changed my shirt. I wiped off my shoes. I looked into the mirror to see if I looked like someone's father.

She presented herself shortly after six o'clock.

"Traffic?" I said. "No," she said, and that was the end of that.

Just as supper was being concluded, she complained of insufferable pain, and doubled over on the dining-room floor.

"My belly," she said. "What?" I said. She said, "My belly. It's agony. Get me a doctor."

There is a large and famous hospital mere blocks from my apartment. Celebrities go there, statesmen, people who must know what they are doing.

With the help of a doorman and an elevator man, I got my daughter to the hospital. Within minutes, two physicians and a corps of nurses took the matter in hand.

I stood by watching. It was hours before they had her undoubled and were willing to announce their findings.

A bellyache, a rogue cramp, a certain nonspecific seizure of the abdomen—vagrant, indecipherable, a mystery not worth further inquiry.

We left the hospital unassisted, using a succession of tunnels in order to shorten the distance home. The exposed distance, that is—since it would be four in the morning on the city streets, and though the blocks would be few, each one of them could be catastrophic. So we made our way along the system of underground passageways that link the units of the hospital until we were forced to surface and exit. We came out onto a street with not a person on it—until we saw him, the young man who was going from car to car. He carried something under his arm. It looked to me to be a furled umbrella—black fabric, silver fittings. It could not have been what it looked to be—but instead a tool of entry disguised as an umbrella!

He turned to us as we stepped along, and then he turned back to his work—going from car to car, trying the doors, and sometimes using the thing to dig at the windows.

"Don't look," I said. My daughter said, "What?" I said, "There's someone across the street. He's trying to jimmy open cars. Just keep on walking as if you don't see him."

My daughter said, "Where? I don't see him."

I put my daughter to bed and the hospital charges on my desk and then I let my head down onto the pillow and listened.

There was nothing to hear.

Before I surrendered myself to sleep, there was only this in my mind—the boy in the treatment room across the corridor from my daughter's, how I had wanted to cry out each time he had cried out as a stitch was sutured into his hand.

"Take it out! Take it out!"

This is what the boy was shrieking as the doctor worked to close the wound.

I thought about the feeling in me when I had heard that awful wailing. The boy wanted the needle out. I suppose it hurt worse than the thing that had inspired them to sew him up.

But then I considered the statement for emergency services—translating the amount first into theater tickets, then into hand-ironed shirts.

Notice how Lish uses the bare minimum attribution—"she/he said"—or no attribution at all. Lish doesn't write this way because his vocabulary lacks adverbs. He knows lots of adverbs, and probably adjectives, too. Rather, Lish has made a conscious stylistic choice *not* to use hack modifiers such as "glumly," "cheerily," "chirpingly," "sorrowfully," but instead to forefront the dialogue, allowing it to stand on its own merit, and to create a crisp, direct, unadorned tone somewhat reminiscent of *noir* forties mysteries or Hemingway's sparse reportage, but also fresh, modern, distinctive.

You will, of course, find well-respected literary authors using a less barebones approach to attribution than Lish, Hemingway et al., with predictably more florid results. Here's Herman Melville, in his "Bartleby the Scrivener":

> "So you have got the word, too," said I, slightly excited.
> "With submission, what word, sir," asked Turkey, respectfully crowding himself into the contracted space behind the screen, and by so doing, making me jostle the scrivener. "What word, sir?"
> "I would prefer to be left alone here," said Bartleby, as if offended at being mobbed in his privacy.

In this passage, Melville relies on his attribution to clue the reader into nuances of narrative action and the affective states of his character, with phrases such as "slightly excited," "respectfully crowding himself," and "as if offended." F. Scott Fitzgerald makes similar use of attribution in his story, "The Diamond as Big as the Ritz":

> "I know," answered John huskily.
> "Don't forget who you are and where you came from," continued his father proudly, "and you can do nothing to harm you. You are an Unger—from Hades."

Fitzgerald here relies on adverbs—"huskily," "proudly,"—to deliver information pertinent to character exposition and development. The hypermodern tendency would be to avoid such attribution as being superfluous, overly demonstrative, and redolent of bad pop writing—"'Gosh, here we are locked in a dungeon with no hope of escape,' said Tom Swift desperately." In his defense, Fitzgerald uses such attribution sparingly, and very precisely. The reader learns much about the characters' emotional state through those few carefully chosen modifiers.

Be aware, also, that while modern literati criticize dialogue with unhip attribution, modern pop writers get millions of bucks for writing it. Check this passage from Stephen R. Lawhead's *In the Hall of the Dragon King* for an example of attribution in the popular genres—in this case fantasy fiction:

> "But you never found the body, did you?" the Prince said firmly.
> "It was snowing, by Zoar!" the knight snapped angrily...."
> "Well it is over. Now to put an end to our other problem, this outlaw leader—what do they call him?"
> "The Hawk," said the knight sullenly.
> "Yes. Strange this Hawk suddenly showing himself—and so close at hand. How do you explain it?" insinuated the Prince in a sly voice.

Lawhead's attribution, with its preponderance of Tom Swift-style adverbs, would be considered artless by contemporary fiction theorists (of whom I am one, I suppose, even though I take guiltless pleasure in pop mysteries and fantasies like Lawhead's). The truth, however, is that The People—the ones who buy entertainment fiction at supermarkets and drugstores and airport terminals—don't care about the niceties of terse attribution, so long as the story has an involving plot with lots of tension and release through-out and a satisfying resolution. As with all of your fictionalizing, this issue turns out to be a matter of taste, and my suggestion would be to err on the side of minimal attribution, following the Lish model. Keep your attribution terse and render your dialogue realistic but not tedious—unless you're try-ing to create the effect of tedium toward some thematic purpose.

Finally, keep in mind that—except in the most extreme, absurdist/postmodern efforts—your dialogue doesn't have to be an exact reproduc-tion of the way people talk in the real world. It would have been much less wonderful if Rick Blaine (the world-weary character played by Humphrey Bogart in *Casablanca)* had said, "It really bothers me that my long-lost love just showed up in this bar," instead of the now-famous "Of all the gin joints in all the towns in all the world, she walks into mine," which is arresting be-cause of its poetic lyricism, its intentional repetition of the phrase "all the" for rhetorical effect, its use of the ultra-cool term "gin joints." Successful dia-logue will generally be a condensed, artful version of actual conversation, with less of the rambling digression, loose association, clichè and humdrum diction typical of our everyday talk. While a bit of artless or pointless blather may be necessary for verisimilitude, too much of it makes a fictional piece *booooo*ring!

KILLED BY HER OWN THOUGHTS: NARRATOR AND POINT OF VIEW

There is one character who occupies a unique position in every piece of fic-tion, by relating the story to the reader. The *narrator* may actually partici-pate in the story's action, or may report/comment on the narrative as a dis-embodied voice—an all-seeing presence commenting from on high—or may assume an attitude somewhere between these two extremes. The liter-ary term *point of view* refers to this attitude or perspective assumed by a story's speaker.

On the "engaged participant" end of the p.o.v. spectrum, the author may create a *first-person narrator*, who speaks in the "I" voice. The first-person narrator is usually the central actor in the story's plot...but not al-ways. For example, in Ken Kesey's *One Flew Over the Cuckoo's Nest*, the first-person speaker, Chief, is secondary to the novel's protagonist, McMurphy... at least until the end of the novel, at which point it could be argued that Chief emerges as the protagonist. More typically, though, the first-person narrator will also be the main character in a story or novel. Amy Tan's nar-rator Jing-Mei Woo is one of these:

> My father has asked me to be the fourth corner at the Joy Luck Club. I
> am to replace my mother, whose seat at the mah jong table has been

> empty since she died two months ago. My father thinks she was killed
> by her own thoughts.

First-person narrators such as Jing-Mei carry certain advantages and disadvantages. On the positive side, they afford the author easy entry into the psyche of the speaker, allowing for much unique, individual roundedness. However, they are also incapable of providing accurate details about the plot and other characters, since their point of view will always be narrow, restricted, personal. Furthermore, all perceptions of story events and other characters will be colored by the first-person narrator's unique (and sometimes inaccurate!) opinions, emotions, and insights.

To counter the limiting point of view typical of the first-person narrator, authors will employ variations on the "I" speaker. In some cases they will use *"multiple-I" narrators*—that is, more than one individual who uses the first person in a given story. This technique has a couple of advantages. It affords different perspectives on the "truth" of the dramatic situation, and it allows for irony in a way that the single first-person usually cannot. John Fowles' *The Collector* employs this technique to stunning effect. In it, his deranged first-person narrator kidnaps a female art student and keeps her captive in his basement. We see the entire event from his point of view, complete with sociopathic rationalizations of all of his behaviors, so that he seems "normal" to himself, if not to the reader. Then Fowles goes back and tells the entire story again, but this time in diary form, from the art student's point of view. By providing a "flip-side" first-person perspective, Fowles is able to underline the monstrosity of the kidnapper's act, which is certainly one of his intended themes.

Occasionally an author will create an *excursive first-person narrator* who "busts through the fourth wall" by addressing the reader directly. The *fourth wall* is a term dramatists use to describe the imaginary barrier between actors and audience at a play. On a typical stage set you will see a room having three walls, the fourth one invisible so that the audience can see what's going on. In plays, a character will occasionally break through the fourth wall by addressing the audience directly, as at the end of Shakespeare's comedies—in this case *As You Like It*:

> I charge you, o women! for the love you bear to men, to like as much of
> this play as please you: and I charge you, o men! for the love you bear to
> women—as I perceive by your simpering none of you hate them—that
> between you and the women, the play may please.

Similarly, in fiction the excursive narrator may interrupt his storytelling to confront the reader directly. Mike Petracca uses this technique to annoying effect in *Captain Zzyzx* ($9.95 or less at your local remainder outlet):

> . . . Being in a poetry group would, I calculated, increase my chances of
> meeting females of character, literacy, taste and construction.

Consider for a moment the state lottery or the dollar slots in Vegas. With either, your chances of making the Big Hit are, to put it optimistically, negligible (unless you consider thirteen mil to one a shoein). But basic probability theory tells us that negligible odds are better than no odds at all, and if you doesn't pay your buck you gots no chance. So it is with meeting members of the opposite sex, and take heed ye readers who are yearning desperately for significant others but don't know how to get yourself one: Put yourself in places which will up your chances of meeting Mr. or Ms. Acceptable. If, for example, you yearn for an outdoorswoman—one who shares your love of tramping up and down hill and dale heedless of sunstroke, snakebite, leaves of three, malaria, encephalitis, or sexual assault at the hands of Beelzebub's Bondsmen or other outlaw bikers you might meet on the trail–then join the Sierra Club. One evening, on returning from a day-long pack into the backcountry, you may find yourself paired up with a robust Nordic wench, a veritable Valkyrie with cheeks like waxed gravensteins, flowing flaxen hair and flanks like a thoroughbred's. You may look into each other's eyes just as the sun dips beneath a violet-hued and jagged horizon, and you'll both know this is finally It, baby. Conversely, if you're more interested in a woman who can free-climb up one side of a sonnet and rappel down the other, who can cook up a villanelle and set it out piping hot and chock full of smiling similes, measured metonymies and feminine rhymes, one who is understated, petite, slightly formal on the exterior but who hides a floe of molten passion beneath her crinolines and stays, then you ought to join a poetry society.

For that reason I said Yes to The Bindhover. I even went so far as to volunteer my drawing room for the regular meeting place of the [poetry group].

Here Petracca interrupts the story to have his narrator, Harmon Nails III, launch into one of his characteristically long-winded digressions during which he addresses the audience directly, to explain some questionable point about meeting chicks. This passage further illustrates the characterizing power of the first-person narrator, by letting us know that Harmon Nails is a neurotic who hides his feelings of inadequacy behind big words.

Having a first-person narrator address the reader directly is not an uncommon practice. In some rare instances, however, an author will take this fourth-wall-busting behavior to an extreme, by having his protagonist address the reader throughout: relating the entire story in the second-person "you," as Jay McInerney does in *Bright Lights, Big City*:

You are the kind of guy who would be at a place like this at this time of the morning. But here you are, and you cannot say that the terrain is entirely unfamiliar, although the details are fuzzy. You are at a nightclub talking to a girl with a shaved head....

and so on, through 182 pages. The advantages of this unusual approach to point of view are its unusualness—*extended excursive narrators* such as Mc-

Inerney's command attention simply because they're as rare as a long-tailed cat in a roomful of rocking chairs—and its ability to place the reader directly in the middle of things. Its disadvantage—and it's a huge one—is that it's frequently viewed as a mere gimmick and not a legitimate narrative stance. As a reader, you're always aware of the narratorial device being used by the author, and this awareness hampers your ability to enter the fictional world. Most writers can't overcome that difficulty as McInerney does successfully in *Bright Lights, Big City*, and so you'll find a small minority of fictional pieces using extended excursive narrators.

To counter the limiting point of view typical of the first-person narrator *and* the disadvantages of multiple or excursive "I" narrators, authors will create an *omniscient narrator* who gives the reader more access to information about the main characters. The omniscient narrator usually speaks in the third person . . . but not always. Remember the story "Cockroach Miracles, Solvent Dreams"? When God spoke directly to the reader at the end of the story, that was an example of the *first-person omniscient narrator.* That technique, however, is extremely rare and even more gimmicky than extended second-person narrators; I'd advise using it only as an exercise in shifting point of view. The more common *third-person omniscient narrator* is constructed as a disembodied speaker who knows and reports everything about the emotions, ideas, past, present, and sometimes future behaviors of all the main characters in a story. The author may tell the story from any perspective, and may shift perspectives freely.

Through the omniscient narrator, the reader learns about characters' thoughts and actions, but also the author's attitudes toward the characters. In Jeff Gomez' recent novel, *Our Noise*, for example, the omniscient narrator relates the lives of a wide variety of twentysomethings, all trying to make their way in a harsh, alienating postcollegial landscape. On one page, the narrator tells us about a central character, Eileen:

> On the corner, at the top of a steep hill, is a place called The Novel Idea Cafe and Bookstore. Over the double doors is a large sign, a Tennielesque illustration of a few stacked books atop which is a steaming teacup. From the sidewalk, Eileen can see couches and chairs, none matching the decor and most of them occupied. So far, Eileen decides, this is obviously the only cool place in this little town to hang out.

Notice the way Gomez' all-seeing, all-knowing narrator shifts perspective numerous times, even within the scope of this brief passage. First the narrator stands outside the character, providing external details of setting ("large sign," "stacked books," "steaming teacup"). Next, the narrator relates the same setting from the character's perspective ("Eileen can see couches and chairs"), and finally the narrator "gets inside" Eileen's head, to tell us her thoughts ("So far, Eileen decides, this is obviously the only cool place . . .").

At another point in *Our Noise*, Gomez' omniscient narrator character-izes Dave, who is plagued by an empty post office box:

> Dave holds his breath, looks through the small window, the yellow wall visible behind it. For a second it feels as though he's been punched in the gut. Tears, a stupid knee-jerk reaction, appear for a second in Dave's eyes before he relentlessly pushes them away. *Why the fuck hasn't anyone written to me? What's going on out there? Doesn't anyone care about what I do? Jesus, I feel like I'm living my life in a black hole.*
>   ...Just as he's turning to leave, he notices a wafer-thin envelope lying flat on the box floor.

Here the narrator has abandoned Eileen as the vantage point and is focus-ing instead on another character, describing him objectively, then relating his thoughts and feelings. Shifting points of view constantly, as Gomez does in *Our Noise*, is typical of *true* or *multiple omniscience*, and is a perfectly legiti-mate and frequently used storytelling technique.

If multiple omniscience gives the author freedom to explore characters from a variety of perspectives, it also presents a challenge to the author, who must skillfully juggle objective descriptions, subjective impressions from numerous central characters, inner thoughts, and feelings. *Coherence*—a desirable quality in fiction, in which all internal elements connect logi-cally, for the sake of aesthetic consistency—is sometimes extremely difficult to achieve while using true omniscience. Because of this, some authors will use a modified form of omniscience, called *limited omniscience*, in which the author will identify with a single major or minor character who acts as the author's intermediary for the duration of the story. As you experiment with different kinds of narrators and alternative points of view, remember that in any given fictional piece you aren't limited to a single narratorial mode. You can shift between two or more kinds of narrators, as long as you maintain coherence.

For example, in John Updike's *The Centaur*, the author alternates be-tween chapters related by a limited-omniscient narrator ("Caldwell turned and as he turned his ankle received an arrow. The class burst into laughter. The pain scaled the slender core of his shin...") and chapters related by a first-person narrator ("My father and my mother were talking. I wake now often to silence, beside you, with a pang of fear, after dreams that leave a sour wash of atheism in my stomach..."), to juxtapose the mythological half-man Chiron with an aging lecturer named George Caldwell. Jess Mowry likewise presents two limited omniscient narrators in his novel *Six Out Seven*, describing first an adolescent African-American's plight in rural Mississippi, then the trials of an inner-city Oakland kid, then alternating chapters between the two points of view until the two eventually meet up in Cali and have life-threatening adventures. There's almost no limit to the ways in which you can manipulate narrator and point of view...as long as you incant, "Coherence, coherence . . ." constantly under your breath while you're doing so.

MINOR CHARACTERS NEED LOVE, TOO

Remember the guys on the original "Star Trek" series, the ones who wear red outfits and beam down with Kirk and Spock to search a class-M planet for survivors of a crashed space craft, only to get killed in two minutes by a creature who looks like he's made with shag remnants from Carpeteria? Those disposable officers are flat characters. We know nothing about them, their tastes in music, their shoe sizes, the brand of toothpaste they use. They are static, neither growing nor changing over the course of the story, aside from the fact that they become molecular vapor before the commercial break. However, such *minor* or *secondary* characters—storyfolk who are not the main focus of a story's narrative action—do serve a narrative function. In the "Star Trek" example, they suggest to viewers that this particular M-class planet is fraught with lethal dangers, thus establishing a climate of narrative conflict—the protagonists (Kirk and Spock) versus the setting.

Some writers—and not just hacks, either—defend the judicious and purposeful inclusion of flat characters in a given fiction, when they play a minor or secondary role. Author and prose theorist E. M. Forster insists that "a novel that is at all complex often requires flat people as well as round . . ." and novelist James Baldwin takes that philosophical stance a step further, asserting that incidental characters

> . . . are the subtext, illustrations of whatever it is you're trying to convey. I was always struck by the minor characters in Dostoyevsky and Dickens. The minor characters have a certain freedom which the major ones don't. They can make comments, they can move, yet they haven't got the same weight, or intensity. . . . They are more a part of the decor—a kind of Greek chorus. They carry the tension in a much more explicit way than the majors.

In certain circumstances it may actually be desirable, Baldwin says, to leave one's minor characters relatively flat, because they can be as evocative and colorful as any other piece of descriptive detail.

However, other prose theorists disagree (surprise!) about the use of flat characters in fiction. Critics with a decidedly literary bent would criticize the shameless use of undeveloped minor characters in the "Star Trek" example as representing the worst kind of hack characterization, because the discerning viewer recognizes the guys in the red uniforms as nothing more than disposable plot vehicles. Some people, such as Elizabeth Bowen, go so far as to insist that "the ideal novel is without 'flat' characters." The more you develop your storyfolk, goes the argument from this camp, the richer, more evocative and thematically layered your stories will be. Why have any flat characters when, with a little effort, you can give all your story people rich, believable selves?

To resolve this exciting debate for students in writing workshops, I make a suggestion that goes something like this: As much as you can, make your characters round. Only fully rounded characters have the capacity to elicit real sympathy in the reader, or to surprise the reader on the deepest levels of implied meaning. Nevertheless, it may on occasion be a valid aesthetic choice and effective narrative strategy to use flat characters when the dramatic situation calls for them, in the manner that Baldwin explains above. If you do create incidental characters who are intentionally flat, however, they should act as plot vehicles while seeming real enough not to draw attention to themselves.

The latter point is crucial. In this excerpt from John O'Brien's novel *Leaving Las Vegas*, from which the movie was made, observe the interaction of the protagonists with a secondary character:

> She follows his prompt and snaps open the box, revealing a pair of black onyx earrings set in white gold. . . .
>
> "I'll wear them tonight. I'll wear one of them tonight," she says. At first she thinks that she may have made a tactless slip, as she is planning to work [as a prostitute] tonight. But then she relaxes, recalling that this issue, when last discussed, was left on a comfortable note.
>
> But Ben has one of those moments that are the liability of any drunk, when the meaning that he is attempting to convey is mismatched with unfortunate words, and by the time the whole thing leaves his mouth even he is unsure of what he feels.
>
> "Yes," he says, looking into his again empty glass, "you'll be able to feel it sharp and hot under your ear as one of the brothers is driving your head, face down, into a penthouse pillow." He tries to look grim, but he is shocked at his own remark. Realizing that she does not deserve this, yet nonetheless disturbed by the image, he stands and walks quickly from the table, unable to bear her gaze.
>
> "Ben, wait!" she calls after him. She fumbles with her purse, trying to leave money for the check. "Please wait for me."
>
> When Ben reaches the door, a large Black man steps into his path and places his hands on Ben's shoulders. "Maybe you should wait for her," says the man.
>
> "Why," says Ben, trying unsuccessfully to shake himself loose from the grip.
>
> The man pauses, as if searching for words that Ben will understand. "Because," he says, "you can hear in her voice that she really wants you to."

This is the last we see of this incidental character. O'Brien portrays him as strong, compassionate, thoughtful, but beyond that we learn no more about him. He is featureless, flat. However, while he clearly serves a crucial function as a plot device—he makes the protagonist alter his behavior, in this case overcoming his instinctive jealousy and cementing his bond with Sera—he also is distinctive. His two brief lines of dialogue inject a centering note of reason in the otherwise chaotic lives of the protagonists, and his featurelessness is consistent with the novel's bleary atmosphere. Furthermore, this incidental character stands in admirable opposition to the debased and freebasing "brothers" of all ethnicities who pay the novel's female protagonist for sex, and so he subtly but effectively delivers one of the novel's central thematic implications: that grace comes in many shapes and forms.

In this way, O'Brien's incidental character differs materially from "Star Trek's" disposable crew, who have no interest or signification beyond their function in advancing the plot. If you're going to use flat and/or minor characters, keep this comparison in mind. Try to make even the most peripheral characters fulfill an expository purpose, and ideally a thematic purpose, as well. Your fiction will be richer if you keep that goal in mind, and your storyfolk will give you a big, wet kiss for the effort.

An-Mei Hsu
Scar
Amy Tan

When I was a young girl in China, my grandmother told me my mother was a ghost. This did not mean my mother was dead. In those days, a ghost was anything we were forbidden to talk about. So I knew Popo wanted me to forget my mother on purpose, and this is how I came to remember nothing of her. The life that I knew began in the large house in Ningpo with the cold hallways and tall stairs. This was my uncle and auntie's family house, where I lived with Popo and my little brother.

But I often heard stories of a ghost who tried to take children away, especially strong-willed little girls who were disobedient. Many times Popo said aloud to all who could hear that my brother and I had fallen out of the bowels of a stupid goose, two eggs that nobody wanted, not even good enough to crack over rice porridge. She said this so that the ghosts would not steal us away. So you see, to Popo we were also very precious.

All my life, Popo scared me. I became even more scared when she grew sick. This was in 1923, when I was nine years old. Popo had swollen up like an overripe squash, so full her flesh had gone soft and rotten with a bad smell. She would call me into her room with the terrible stink and tell me stories. "An-mei," she said, calling me by my school name. "Listen carefully." She told me stories I could not understand.

One was about a greedy girl whose belly grew fatter and fatter. This girl poisoned herself after refusing to say whose child she carried. When the monks cut open her body, they found inside a large white winter melon.

"If you are greedy, what is inside you is what makes you always hungry," said Popo.

Another time, Popo told me about a girl who refused to listen to her elders. One day this bad girl shook her head so vigorously to refuse her auntie's simple request that a little white ball fell from her ear and out poured all her brains, as clear as chicken broth.

"Your own thoughts are so busy swimming inside that everything else gets pushed out," Popo told me.

Right before Popo became so sick she could no longer speak, she pulled me close and talked to me about my mother. "Never say her name," she warned. "To say her name is to spit on your father's grave."

The only father I knew was a big painting that hung in the main hall. He was a large, unsmiling man, unhappy to be so still on the wall. His restless eyes followed me around the house. Even from my room at the end of the hall, I could see my father's watching eyes. Popo said he watched me for any signs of disrespect. So sometimes, when I had thrown pebbles at other children at school, or had lost a book through carelessness, I would quickly walk by my father with a know-nothing look and hide in a corner of my room where he could not see my face.

I felt our house was so unhappy, but my little brother did not seem to think so. He rode his bicycle through the courtyard, chasing chickens and other children, laughing over which ones shrieked the loudest. Inside the quiet house, he jumped up and down on Uncle and Auntie's best feather sofas when they were away visiting village friends.

But even my brother's happiness went away. One hot summer day when Popo was already very sick, we stood outside watching a village funeral procession marching by our courtyard. Just as it passed our gate, the heavy framed picture of the dead man toppled from its stand and fell to the dusty ground. An old lady screamed and fainted. My brother laughed and Auntie slapped him.

My auntie, who had a very bad temper with children, told him he had no *shou*, no respect for ancestors or family, just like our mother. Auntie had a tongue like hungry scissors eating silk cloth. So when my brother gave her a sour look, Auntie said our mother was so thoughtless she had fled north in a big hurry, without taking the dowry furniture from her marriage to my father, without bringing her ten pairs of silver chopsticks, without paying respect to my father's grave and those of our ancestors. When my brother accused Auntie of frightening our mother away, Auntie shouted that our mother had married a man named Wu Tsing who already had a wife, two concubines, and other bad children.

And when my brother shouted that Auntie was a talking chicken without a head, she pushed my brother against the gate and spat on his face.

"You throw strong words at me, but you are nothing," Auntie said. "You are the son of a mother who has so little respect she has become *ni*, a traitor to our ancestors. She is so beneath others that even the devil must look down to see her."

That is when I began to understand the stories Popo taught me, the lessons I had to learn for my mother. "When you lose your face, An-mei," Popo often said, "it is like dropping your necklace down a well. The only way you can get it back is to fall in after it."

Now I could imagine my mother, a thoughtless woman who laughed and shook her head, who dipped her chopsticks many times to eat another piece of sweet fruit, happy to be free of Popo, her unhappy husband on the wall, and her two disobedient children. I felt unlucky that she was my mother and unlucky that she had left us. These were the thoughts I had while hiding in the corner of my room where my father could not watch me.

I was sitting at the top of the stairs when she arrived. I knew it was my mother even though I had not seen her in all my memory. She stood just inside the doorway so that her face became a dark shadow. She was much taller than my auntie, almost as tall as my uncle. She looked strange, too, like the missionary ladies at our school who were insolent and bossy in their too-tall shoes, foreign clothes, and short hair.

My auntie quickly looked away and did not call her by name or offer her tea. An old servant hurried away with a displeased look. I tried to keep very still, but my heart felt like crickets scratching to get out of a cage. My mother must have heard, because she looked up. And when she did, I saw my own face looking back at me. Eyes that stayed wide open and saw too much.

In Popo's room my auntie protested, "Too late, too late," as my mother approached the bed. But this did not stop my mother.

"Come back, stay here," murmured my mother to Popo. "*Nuyer* is here. Your daughter is back." Popo's eyes were open, but now her mind ran in many different directions, not staying long enough to see anything. If Popo's mind had been clear she would have raised her two arms and flung my mother out of the room.

I watched my mother, seeing her for the first time, this pretty woman with her white skin and oval face, not too round like Auntie's or sharp like Popo's. I saw that she had a long white neck, just like the goose that had laid me. That she seemed to float back and forth like a ghost, dipping cool cloths to lay on Popo's bloated face. As she peered into Popo's eyes, she clucked soft worried sounds. I watched her carefully, yet it was her voice that confused me, a familiar sound from a forgotten dream.

When I returned to my room later that afternoon, she was there, standing tall. And because I remember Popo told me not to speak her name, I stood there, mute. She took my hand and led me to the settee. And then she also sat down as though we had done this every day.

My mother began to loosen my braids and brush my hair with long sweeping strokes.

"An-mei, you have been a good daughter?" she asked, smiling a secret look.

I looked at her with my know-nothing face, but inside I was trembling. I was the girl whose belly held a colorless winter melon.

"An-mei, you know who I am," she said with a small scold in her voice. This time I did not look for fear my head would burst and my brains would dribble out of my ears.

She stopped brushing. And then I could feel her long smooth fingers rubbing and searching under my chin, finding the spot that was my smooth-neck scar. As she rubbed this spot, I became very still. It was as though she were rubbing the memory back into my skin. And then her hand dropped and she began to cry, wrapping her hands around her own neck. She cried with a wailing voice that was so sad. And then I remembered the dream with my mother's voice.

I was four years old. My chin was just above the dinner table, and I could see my baby brother sitting on Popo's lap, crying with an angry face. I could hear voices praising a steaming dark soup brought to the table, voices murmuring politely, *"Ching! Ching!"*—Please, eat!

And then the talking stopped. My uncle rose from his chair. Everyone turned to look at the door, where a tall woman stood. I was the only one who spoke.

"Ma," I had cried, rushing off my chair, but my auntie slapped my face and pushed me back down. Now everyone was standing up and shouting, and I heard my mother's voice crying, "An-mei! An-mei!" Above this noise, Popo's shrill voice spoke.

"Who is this ghost? Not an honored widow. Just a number-three concubine. If you take your daughter, she will become like you. No face. Never able to lift up her head."

Still my mother shouted for me to come. I remember her voice so clearly now. An-mei! An-mei! I could see my mother's face across the table. Between us stood the soup pot on its heavy chimney-pot stand—rocking slowly, back and forth. And then with one shout this dark boiling soup spilled forward and fell all over my neck. It was as though everyone's anger were pouring all over me.

This was the kind of pain so terrible that a little child should never remember it. But it is still in my skin's memory. I cried out loud only a little, because soon my flesh began to burst inside and out and cut off my breathing air.

I could not speak because of this terrible choking feeling. I could not see because of all the tears that poured out to wash away the pain. But I could hear my mother's crying voice. Popo and Auntie were shouting. And then my mother's voice went away.

Later that night Popo's voice came to me.

"An-mei, listen carefully." Her voice had the same scolding tone she used when I ran up and down the hallway. "An-mei, we have made your dying clothes and shoes for you. They are all white cotton."

I listened, scared.

"An-mei," she murmured, now more gently. "Your dying clothes are very plain. They are not fancy, because you are still a child. If you die, you will have a short life and you will still owe your family a debt. Your funeral will be very small. Our mourning time for you will be very short."

And then Popo said something that was worse than the burning on my neck.

"Even your mother has used up her tears and left. If you do not get well soon, she will forget you."

Popo was very smart. I came hurrying back from the other world to find my mother.

Every night I cried so that both my eyes and my neck burned. Next to my bed sat Popo. She would pour cool water over my neck from the hollowed cup of a large grapefruit. She would pour and pour until my breathing became soft and I could fall asleep. In the morning, Popo would use her sharp fingernails like tweezers and peel off the dead membranes.

In two years' time, my scar became pale and shiny and I had no memory of my mother. That is the way it is with a wound. The wound begins to close in on itself, to protect what is hurting so much. And once it is closed, you no longer see what is underneath, what started the pain.

I worshipped this mother from my dream. But the woman standing by Popo's bed was not the mother of my memory. Yet I came to love this mother as well. Not because she came to me and begged me to forgive her. She did not. She did not need to explain that Popo chased her out of the house when I was dying. This I knew. She did not need to tell me she married Wu Tsing to exchange one unhappiness for another. I knew this as well.

Here is how I came to love my mother. How I saw in her my own true nature. What was beneath my skin. Inside my bones.

It was late at night when I went to Popo's room. My auntie said it was Popo's dying time and I must show respect. I put on a clean dress and stood between my auntie and uncle at the foot of Popo's bed. I cried a little, not too loud.

I saw my mother on the other side of the room. Quiet and sad. She was cooking a soup, pouring herbs and medicines into the steaming pot. And then I saw her pull up her sleeve and pull out a sharp knife. She put this knife on the softest part of her arm. I tried to close my eyes, but could not.

And then my mother cut a piece of meat from her arm. Tears poured from her face and blood spilled to the floor.

My mother took her flesh and put it in the soup. She cooked magic in the ancient tradition to try to cure her mother this one last time. She opened Popo's mouth, already too tight from trying to keep her spirit in. She fed her this soup, but that night Popo flew away with her illness.

Even though I was young, I could see the pain of the flesh and the worth of the pain.

This is how a daughter honors her mother. It is *shou* so deep it is in your bones. The pain of the flesh is nothing. The pain you must forget. Because sometimes that is the only way to remember what is in your bones. You must peel off your skin, and that of your mother, and her mother before her. Until there is nothing. No scar, no skin, no flesh.

POINTS TO CONSIDER ABOUT "SCAR"

1. What specific qualities of (1) speech, (2) appearance, and (3) action does Tan lend to the character of Popo, in order to give her verisimilitude?

2. Discuss the secondary or incidental characters in "Scar." Who, if anybody, falls into that category in the story? If you discover any secondary characters, what function do they serve?

3. Describe the narrative style of "Scar." In what person is it told? Why does Tan choose to employ this voice for this piece?

4. Notice the way the characterization of the mother changes. At first the narrator—and the reader—learns about the mother through the opinionated statements of Popo (the grandmother), but later the mother makes an appearance. How does this shift contribute to Tan's depiction of the mother as a character?

5. What is the implied meaning of "Scar," as suggested by the passage at the end of the story: "The pain of the flesh is nothing. The pain you must forget. Because sometimes that is the only way to remember what is in your bones"? How does the interaction among the characters—the three generations of women—lead us to this understanding?

The Chrysanthemums
John Steinbeck

The high grey-flannel fog of winter closed off the Salinas Valley from the sky and from all the rest of the world. On every side it sat like a lid on the mountains and made of the great valley a closed pot. On the broad, level land floor the gang ploughs bit deep and left the black earth shining like metal where the shares had cut. On the foot-hill ranches across the Salinas River, the yellow stubble fields seemed to be bathed in pale cold sunshine, but there was no sunshine in the valley now in December. The thick willow scrub along the river flamed with sharp and positive yellow leaves.

It was a time of quiet and of waiting. The air was cold and tender. A light wind blew up from the southwest so that the farmers were mildly hopeful of a good rain before long; but fog and rain do not go together.

Across the river, on Henry Allen's foot-hill ranch there was little work to be done, for the hay was cut and stored and the orchards were ploughed up to receive the rain deeply when it should come. The cattle on the higher slopes were becoming shaggy and rough-coated.

Elisa Allen, working in her flower garden, looked down across the yard and saw Henry, her husband, talking to two men in business suits. The three of them stood by the tractor-shed, each man with one foot on the side of the little Fordson. They smoked cigarettes and studied the machine as they talked.

Elisa watched them for a moment and then went back to her work. She was thirty-five. Her face was lean and strong and her eyes were as clear as water. Her figure looked blocked and heavy in her gardening costume, a man's black hat pulled low down over her eyes, clod-hopper shoes, a fig-ured print dress almost-completely covered by a big corduroy apron with four big pockets to hold the snips, the trowel and scratcher, the seeds and the knife she worked with. She wore heavy leather gloves to protect her hands while she worked.

She was cutting down the old year's chrysanthemum stalks with a pair of short and powerful scissors. She looked down toward the men by the tractor-shed now and then. Her face was eager and mature and handsome; even her work with the scissors was overeager, over-powerful. The chrysanthemum stems seemed too small and easy for her energy.

She brushed a cloud of hair out of her eyes with the back of her glove, and left a smudge of earth on her cheek in doing it. Behind her stood the neat white farmhouse with red geraniums close-banked around it as high as the windows. It was a hard-swept-looking little house, with hard-polished windows, and a clean mud-mat on the front steps.

Elisa cast another glance toward the tractor-shed. The strangers were getting into their Ford coupé. She took off a glove and put her strong fingers down into the forest of new green chrysanthemum sprouts that were growing around the old roots. She spread the leaves and looked down among the close-growing stems. No aphids were there, no sow bugs or snails or cutworms. Her terrier fingers destroyed such pests before they could get started.

Elisa started at the sound of her husband's voice. He had come near quietly, and he leaned over the wire fence that protected her flower garden from cattle and dogs and chickens.

"At it again," he said. "You've got a strong new crop coming."

Elisa straightened her back and pulled on the gardening glove again. "Yes. They'll be strong this coming year." In her tone and on her face there was a little smugness.

"'You've got a gift with things," Henry observed. "Some of those yellow chrysanthemums you had this year were ten inches across. I wish you'd work out in the orchard and raise some apples that big."

Her eyes sharpened. "Maybe I could do it, too. I've a gift with things, all right. My mother had it. She could stick anything in the ground and make it grow. She said it was having planters' hands that knew how to do it."

"Well, it sure works with flowers," he said.

"Henry, who were those men you were talking to?"

"Why, sure, that's what I came to tell you. They were from the Western Meat Company. I sold those thirty head of three-year-old steers. Got nearly my own price, too."

"Good," she said. "Good for you."

"And I thought," he continued, "I thought how it's Saturday afternoon, and we might go into Salinas for dinner at a restaurant, and then to a picture show—to celebrate, you see."

"Good," she repeated. "Oh, yes. That will be good."

Henry put on his joking tone. "There's fights tonight. How'd you like to go to the fights?"

"Oh, no," she said breathlessly. "No, I wouldn't like fights."

"Just fooling, Elisa. We'll go to a movie. Let's see. It's two now. I'm going to take Scotty and bring down those steers from the hill. It'll take us maybe two hours. We'll go in town about five and have dinner at the Cominos Hotel. Like that?"

"Of course I'll like it. It's good to eat away from home."

"All right, then. I'll go get up a couple of horses."

She said: "I'll have plenty of time to transplant some of these sets, guess."

She heard her husband calling Scotty down by the barn. And a little later she saw the two men ride up the pale yellow hillside in search of the steers.

There was a little square sandy bed kept for rooting the chrysanthemums. With her trowel she turned the soil over and over, and smoothed it and patted it firm. Then she dug ten parallel trenches to receive the sets. Back at the chrysanthemum bed she pulled out the little crisp shoots, trimmed off the leaves of each one with her scissors and laid it on a small orderly pile.

A squeak of wheels and plod of hoofs came from the road. Elisa looked up. The country road ran along the dense bank of willows and cottonwoods that bordered the river, and up this road came a curious vehicle, curiously drawn. It was an old spring-wagon, with a round canvas top on it like the cover of a prairie schooner. It was drawn by an old bay horse and a little grey-and-white burro. A big stubble-bearded man sat between the cover flaps and drove the crawling team. Underneath the wagon, between the hind wheels, a lean and rangy mongrel dog walked sedately. Words were painted on the canvas, in clumsy, crooked letters. "Pots, pans, knives, sisors, lawn mores, Fixed." Two rows of articles, and the triumphantly definitive "Fixed" below. The black paint had run down in little sharp points beneath each letter.

Elisa, squatting on the ground, watched to see the crazy, loose-jointed wagon pass by. But it didn't pass. It turned into the farm road in front of her house, crooked old wheels skirling and squeaking. The rangy dog darted from between the wheels and ran ahead. Instantly the two ranch shepherds flew out at him. Then all three stopped, and with stiff and quivering tails, with taut straight legs, with ambassadorial dignity, they slowly circled, sniffing daintily. The caravan pulled up to Elisa's wire fence and stopped. Now the newcomer dog, feeling out-numbered, lowered his tail and retired under the wagon with raised hackles and bared teeth.

The man on the wagon seat called out: "That's a bad dog in a fight when he gets started."

Elisa laughed. "I see he is. How soon does he generally get started?"

The man caught up her laughter and echoed it heartily. "Sometimes not for weeks and weeks," he said. He climbed stiffly down, over the wheel. The horse and the donkey drooped like unwatered flowers.

Elisa saw that he was a very big man. Although his hair and beard were greying, he did not look old. His worn black suit was wrinkled and spotted with grease. The laughter had disappeared from his face and eyes the moment his laughing voice ceased. His eyes were dark, and they were full of the brooding that gets in the eyes of teamsters and of sailors. The calloused hands he rested on the wire fence were cracked, and every crack was a black line. He took off his battered hat.

"I'm off my general road, ma'am," he said. "Does this dirt road cut over across the river to the Los Angeles highway?"

Elisa stood up and shoved the thick scissors in her apron pocket. "Well, yes, it does, but it winds around and then fords the river. I don't think your team could pull through the sand."

He replied with some asperity: "It might surprise you what them beasts can pull through."

"When they get started?" she asked.

He smiled for a second. "Yes. When they get started."

"Well," said Elisa, "I think you'll save time if you go back to the Salinas road and pick up the highway there."

He drew a big finger down the chicken wire and made it sing. "I ain't in any hurry, ma'am. I go from Seattle to San Diego and back every year. Takes all my time. About six months each way. I aim to follow nice weather."

Elisa took off her gloves and stuffed them in the apron pocket with the scissors. She touched the under edge of her man's hat, searching for fugitive hairs. "That sounds like a nice kind of way to live," she said.

He leaned confidentially over the fence. "Maybe you noticed the writing on my wagon. I mend pots and sharpen knives and scissors. You got any of them things to do?"

"Oh, no," she said quickly. "Nothing like that." Her eyes hardened with resistance.

"Scissors is the worst thing," he explained. "Most people just ruin scissors trying to sharpen 'em, but I know how. I got a special tool. It's a little bobbit kind of thing, and patented. But it sure does the trick."

"No. My scissors are all sharp."

"All right, then. Take a pot," he continued earnestly, "a bent pot, or a pot with a hole. I can make it like new so you don't have to buy no new ones. That's a saving for you."

"No," she said shortly. "I tell you I have nothing like that for you to do."

His face fell to an exaggerated sadness. His voice took on a whining undertone. "I ain't had a thing to do today. Maybe I won't have no supper tonight. You see I'm off my regular road. I know folks on the highway clear from Seattle to San Diego. They save their things for me to sharpen up because they know I do it so good and save them money."

"I'm sorry," Elisa said irritably. "I haven't anything for you to do."

His eyes left her face and fell to searching the ground. They roamed about until they came to the chrysanthemum bed where she had been working. "What's them plants, ma'am?"

The irritation and resistance melted from Elisa's face. "Oh, those are chrysanthemums, giant whites and yellows. I raise them every year, bigger than anybody around here."

"Kind of a long-stemmed flower? Looks like a quick puff of colored smoke?" he asked.

"That's it. What a nice way to describe them."

"They smell kind of nasty till you get used to them," he said.

"It's a good bitter smell," she retorted, "not nasty at all."

He changed his tone quickly. "I like the smell myself."

"I had ten-inch blooms this year," she said.

The man leaned farther over the fence. "Look. I know a lady down the road a piece, has got the nicest garden you ever seen. Got nearly every kind of flower but no chrysanthemums. Last time I was mending a copper-bottom washtub for her (that's a hard job but I do it good), she said to me: 'If you ever run acrost some nice chrysanthemums I wish you'd try to get me a few seeds.' That's what she told me."

Elisa's eyes grew alert and eager. "She couldn't have known much about chrysanthemums. You *can* raise them from seed, but it's much easier to root the little sprouts you see here."

"Oh," he said. "I s'pose I can't take none to her, then."

"Why yes you can," Elisa cried. "I can put some in damp sand, and you can carry them right along with you. They'll take root in the pot if you keep them damp. And then she can transplant them."

"She'd sure like to have some, ma'am. You say they're nice ones?"

"Beautiful," she said. "Oh, beautiful." Her eyes shone. She tore off the battered hat and shook out her dark pretty hair. "I'll put them in a flower-pot, and you can take them right with you. Come into the yard."

While the man came through the picket gate Elisa ran excitedly along the geranium-bordered path to the back of the house. And she returned carrying a big red flower-pot. The gloves were forgotten now. She kneeled on the ground by the starting bed and dug up the sandy soil with her fingers and scooped it into the bright new flower-pot. Then she picked up the little pile of shoots she had prepared. With her strong fingers she pressed them into the sand and tamped around them with her knuckles. The man stood over her. "I'll tell you what to do," she said. "You remember so you can tell the lady."

"Yes, I'll try to remember."

"Well, look. These will take root in about a month. Then she must set them out, about a foot apart in good rich earth like this, see?" She lifted a handful of dark soil for him to look at. "They'll grow fast and tall. Now remember this: In July tell her to cut them down, about eight inches from the ground."

"Before they bloom?" he asked.

"Yes, before they bloom." Her face was tight with eagerness. "They'll grow right up again. About the last of September the buds will start."

She stopped and seemed perplexed. "It's the budding that takes the most care," she said hesitantly. "I don't know how to tell you." She looked deep into his eyes, searchingly. Her mouth opened a little, and she seemed to be listening. "I'll try to tell you," she said. "Did you ever hear of planting hands?"

"Can't say I have, ma'am."

"Well, I can only tell you what it feels like. It's when you're picking off the buds you don't want. Everything goes right down into your fingertips. You watch your fingers work. They do it themselves. You can feel how it is. They pick and pick the buds. They never make a mistake. They're with the plant. Do you see? Your fingers and the plant. You can feel that, right up your arm. They know. They never make a mistake. You can feel it. When you're like that you can't do anything wrong. Do you see that? Can you understand that?"

She was kneeling on the ground looking up at him. Her breast swelled passionately.

The man's eyes narrowed. He looked away self-consciously.

"Maybe I know," he said. "Sometimes in the night in the wagon there—"

Elisa's voice grew husky. She broke in on him: "I've never lived as you do, but I know what you mean. When the night is dark—why, the stars are sharp-pointed, and there's quiet. Why, you rise up and up! Every pointed star gets driven into your body. It's like that. Hot and sharp and—lovely."

Kneeling there, her hand went out toward his legs in the greasy black trousers. Her hesitant fingers almost touched the cloth. Then her hand dropped to the ground. She crouched low like a fawning dog.

He said: "It's nice, just like you say. Only when you don't have no dinner, it ain't."

She stood up then, very straight, and her face was ashamed. She held the flower-pot out to him and placed it gently in his arms. "Here. Put it in your wagon, on the seat, where you can watch it. Maybe I can find something for you to do."

At the back of the house she dug in the can pile and found two old and battered aluminum saucepans. She carried them back and gave them to him. "Here, maybe you can fix these."

His manner changed. He became professional. "Good as new I can fix them." At the back of his wagon he set a little anvil, and out of an oily tool-box dug a small machine hammer. Elisa came through the gate to watch him while he pounded out the dents in the kettles. His mouth grew sure and knowing. At a difficult part of the work he sucked his underlip.

"You sleep right in the wagon?" Elisa asked.

"Right in the wagon, ma'am. Rain or shine I'm dry as a cow in there."

"It must be nice," she said. "It must be very nice. I wish women could do such things."

"It ain't the right kind of a life for a woman."

Her upper lip raised a little, showing her teeth. "How do you know? How can you tell?" she said.

"I don't know, ma'am," he protested. "Of course I don't know. Now here's your kettles, done. You don't have to buy no new ones."

"How much?"

"Oh, fifty cents'll do. I keep my prices down and my work good. That's why I have all them satisfied customers up and down the highway."

Elisa brought him a fifty-cent piece from the house and dropped it in his hand. "You might be surprised to have a rival some time. I can sharpen scissors, too. And I can beat the dents out of little pots. I could show you what a woman might do."

He put his hammer back in the oily box and shoved the little anvil out of sight. "It would be a lonely life for a woman, ma'am, and a scarey life, too, with animals creeping under the wagon all night." He climbed over the single-tree, steadying himself with a hand on the burro's white rump. He settled himself in the seat, picked up the lines. "Thank you kindly ma'am," he said. "I'll do like you told me; I'll go back and catch the Salinas road."

"Mind," she called, "if you're long in getting there, keep the sand damp."

"Sand, ma'am? . . . Sand? Oh, sure. You mean around the chrysanthemums. Sure I will." He clucked his tongue. The beasts leaned luxuriously into their collars. The mongrel dog took his place between the back wheels. The wagon turned and crawled out the entrance road and back the way it had come, along the river.

Elisa stood in front of her wire fence watching the slow progress of the caravan. Her shoulders were straight, her head thrown back, her eyes half-closed, so that the scene came vaguely into them. Her lips moved silently, forming the words "Good-bye—good-bye." Then she whispered: "That's a bright direction. There's a glowing there." The sound of her whisper startled her. She shook herself free and looked about to see whether anyone had been listening. Only the dogs had heard. They lifted their heads toward her from their sleeping in the dust, and then stretched out their chins and settled asleep again. Elisa turned and ran hurriedly into the house.

In the kitchen she reached behind the stove and felt the water tank. It was full of hot water from the noonday cooking. In the bathroom she tore off her soiled clothes and flung them into the corner. And then she scrubbed herself with a little block of pumice, legs and thighs, loins and chest and arms, until her skin was scratched and red. When she had dried herself she stood in front of a mirror in her bedroom and looked at her body. She tightened her stomach and threw out her chest. She turned and looked over her shoulders at her back.

After a while she began to dress, slowly. She put on her newest under-clothing and her nicest stockings and the dress which was the symbol of her prettiness. She worked carefully on her hair, pencilled her eyebrows and roughed her lips.

Before she was finished she heard the little thunder of hoofs and the shouts of Henry and his helper as they drove the red steers into the corral. She heard the gate bang shut and set herself for Henry's arrival.

His step sounded on the porch. He entered the house calling: "Elisa, where are you?"

"In my room, dressing. I'm not ready. There's hot water for your bath. Hurry up. It's getting late."

When she head him splashing in the tub, Elisa laid his dark suit on the bed, and shirt and socks and tie beside it. She stood his polished shoes on the floor beside the bed. Then she went to the porch and sat primly and stiffly down. She looked toward the river road where the willow-line was still yellow with frosted leaves so that under the high grey fog they seemed a thin band of sunshine. This was the only color in the grey afternoon. She sat unmoving for a long time. Her eyes blinked rarely.

Henry came banging out of the door, shoving his tie inside his vest as he came. Elisa stiffened and her face grew tight. Henry stopped short and looked at her. "Why—why, Elisa. You look so nice!"

"Nice? You think I look nice? What do you mean 'nice'?"

Henry blundered on. "I don't know. I mean you look different, strong and happy."

"I am strong? Yes, strong. What do you mean 'strong'?"

He looked bewildered. "You're playing some kind of a game," he said helplessly. "It's a kind of a play. You look strong enough to break a calf over your knee, happy enough to eat it like a watermelon."

For a second she lost her rigidity. "Henry! Don't talk like that. You didn't know what you said." She grew complete again. "I'm strong," she boasted. "I never knew before how strong."

Henry looked down toward the tractor-shed, and when he brought his eyes back to her, they were his own again. "I'll get out the car. You can put on your coat while I'm starting."

Elisa went into the house. She heard him drive to the gate and idle down his motor, and then she took a long time to put on her hat. She pulled it here and pressed it there. When Henry turned the motor off she slipped into her coat and went out.

The little roadster bounced along on the dirt road by the river, raising the birds and driving the rabbits into the brush. Two cranes flapped heavily over the willow-line and dropped into the river-bed.

Far ahead on the road Elisa saw a dark speck. She knew.

She tried not to look as they passed it, but her eyes would not obey. She whispered to herself sadly: "He might have thrown them off the road. That wouldn't have been much trouble, not very much. But he kept the pot," she explained. "He had to keep the pot. That's why he couldn't get them off the road."

The roadster turned a bend and she saw the caravan ahead. She swung full around toward her husband so she could not see the little covered wagon and the mis-matched team as the car passed them.

In a moment it was over. The thing was done. She did not look back.

She said loudly, to be heard above the motor: "It will be good, tonight, a good dinner."

"Now you've changed again," Henry complained. He took one hand from the wheel and patted her knee. "I ought to take you in to dinner oftener. It would be good for both of us. We get so heavy out on the ranch."

"Henry," she asked, "could we have wine at dinner?"

"Sure we could. Say! That will be fine."

She was silent for a while; then she said: "Henry, at those prizefights, do the men hurt each other very much?"

"Sometimes a little, not often. Why?"

"Well, I've read how they break noses, and blood runs down their chests. I've read how the fighting gloves get heavy and soggy with blood."

He looked around at her. "What's the matter, Elisa? I didn't know you read things like that." He brought the car to a stop, then turned to the right over the Salinas River bridge.

"Do any women ever go to the fights?" she asked.

"Oh, sure, some. What's the matter, Elisa? Do you want to go? I don't think you'd like it, but I'll take you if you really want to go."

She relaxed limply in the seat. "Oh, no. No. I don't want to go. I'm sure I don't." Her face was turned away from him. "It will be enough if we can have wine. It will be plenty." She turned up her coat collar so he could not see that she was crying weakly—like an old woman.

POINTS TO CONSIDER ABOUT "THE CHRYSANTHEMUMS"

1. Along with dialogue, whose characterizing power is discussed in this chapter, what other characterizing techniques does Steinbeck employ to draw Elisa for his readers? How would you describe Elisa? What textual information compels you to have that "mental picture" of this central character?

2. What kind of man is Henry? What specific clues does Steinbeck provide us in order to form our impression of Elisa's husband? Does Steinbeck portray Henry as a positive or negative personality, or does he purposely

draw Henry in an objective, nonjudgmental way, so that we can draw our own conclusions from his fully rounded characterization?

3. How does the tinker manipulate Elisa to give him some work, overcoming her initial resistance? What does this action suggest about his character? What dimension does Elisa's receptiveness to the tinker's manipulation add to Steinbeck's portrayal of her? What do you make of the quasi-sexual tone in the passage, "Kneeling there, her hand went out toward his legs in the greasy black trousers" and following?

4. What is the significance of Elisa's bathing and admiring herself in the mirror after her encounter with the tinker? How does the character of Elisa change over the course of the story, and what plot events precipitate these changes?

5. How do events at the end of the story—particularly her seeing the flowers discarded in the road—alter the characterization of Elisa? What changes, both in thought and action, does this event cause in her? How is Steinbeck's intended theme for "The Chrysanthemums" embodied in the changes that take place in Elisa at the end of the story?

✄ WRITING ACTIVITIES: STORYFOLK

1. Write a character sketch based exclusively on somebody you know very well: a friend, a loved one . . . even a much-publicized celebrity. Freewrite, in as much detail as you can, everything that individual does in the course of a day, from the moment that person wakes up in the morning until the moment at which he or she goes to sleep at night (you can even go beyond these parameters, if you want to include some description of this person's dreams as well). Include thoughts in the form of interior monologue, repressed desires, mundane chores, dialogue with secondary characters (including yourself). From that extended freewrite, pick one event that took place during the day—ideally an event that's charged with conflict, tension, meaning—and rewrite your freewritten character sketch to lead up to this central event, in the same way that Steinbeck's story leads gradually to her encounter with the tinker.

2. Assemble an "imaginary" character out of traits derived from the following people:
   • your primary care physician
   • your mail carrier
   • one of your parents
   • an animal on the endangered species list
   • a telephone operator
   • a television talk-show host
   • your least-favorite grammar school teacher

- an aunt or uncle
- the person you most admire in the world
- television's Jerry Seinfeld
- the President of the United States . . . and five other people you choose to add to the list. Write a story in which this character gets in a fight (not necessarily physical) with the character you created for Activity #1.

3. You may have noticed that short story and novel writers sometimes have their characters talk to each other. You can tell they're talking, because the author uses quotation marks, along with phrases like, "he said," and "Jane exclaimed gleefully." In fiction (as in life), dialogue serves a number of critical functions. It can advance the plot, reveal character, increase narrative tension, and it's one of the subtlest and most effective means to create ambivalence—that simultaneous pull of opposite feelings which we humans are uniquely doomed to experience. The usual way to write dialogue is to hang it onto a previously conceived framework of plot and characterization. You have a narrative line—boy meets dog, dog gets rabies, boy puts dog to sleep—and you flesh out that story with talk. However, it's possible to begin a fictional piece with dialogue, and then build the other elements around the talking. That's what this activity asks you to do.

Go someplace where people congregate in such a way that you can eavesdrop on them without getting attacked and beaten. Record their conversation as faithfully as possible, including the hesitations, burps, non sequiturs and expletives. Having done that, go somewhere else and do the same thing: Record a completely different conversation, involving entirely different people and dealing with an entirely different subject. Take these two snatches of dialogue back to your solitary writing garret and write a story that interweaves descriptions of setting, characters' appearance, and narrative action into the preexisting conversation. There's only one rule here: Don't alter the words or the sequence of the dialogue. Other than that, you can use your creative license to take this exercise into whatever fictional realm you wish.

6

Ways of Showing

Characters earn their verisimilitude through speech, action, and appearance. The last of these three categories—appearance—happens through the process of *narrative description:* creating a sensory representation of people and things within the framework of a plot's action. Because narrative description transcends characterization—serving to render not only characters' appearances but also physical settings, plot events, and states of mind—it is one of the most important considerations of the fiction writer.

In previous chapters, I promised that I'd get around to talking about the first rule of fiction writing. That time has arrived. Take a few deep breaths. Set fire to a sprig of sagebrush leaves and wave them in the air to chase away distracting spirits. When you're done with the psychic preparations, come back to *The Graceful Lie* and read Rule #1: "Show, don't tell." That's it—the most important single point (or at least the most frequently delivered point) writing teachers tell their students. When you've revived yourself from the shock of this revelation, I'll explain what it means, and why it's a somewhat bogus axiom.

"Show, don't tell" is a phrase you'll read in many, many creative writing books, and which you'll hear in most creative writing classes. Teachers—myself included—hammer away at this simple rule, because the least interesting prose usually features sentences like the following, pulled from a recent student effort:

> She saw him one morning going outside to get the mail, and he looked old. He nearly frightened her with his grungy appearance. . . .

. . . and that's all the description we get of this particular geezer. Grammatically, there's nothing wrong with these two sentences. They demonstrate the student's mastery of basic English mechanical conventions. Furthermore, they're narratively sound. They have a limited third-person speaker, who perceives and relates the action through the eyes of the protagonist ("she"). They also contain some description of a character, the "old" person . . . and here's where the problem lies, and where Rule #1 comes into play. The phrases "looked old" and "grungy appearance" convey some information to us, but it's predigested, lacking power to evoke, impress. It "tells"—describes generally but contains no concrete detail that would ideally allow us to form our own imaginative impression of the individual.

As readers, we instinctively want to be "shown"—presented with specifics that let us form our own pictures and judgments of characters, settings, situations. In this student's case, he might have given us some concrete details of wrinkled flesh, sagging jowls, thinning hair, stooped posture, unsteady gait like a horse that's thrown a shoe, rheumy and world-weary (but also kindly) cast of eye, grim and noble carriage defying time and the elements, malodorous adult diaper, wheezing emphysema and yellowed fingers from too many years of too many smokes, slipping bridgework, dingy and soiled army surplus jumpsuit and wingtip oxfords purchased pre-scuffed and curling at the toes from a thriftstore bargain shelf: details that ideally don't present noxious stereotypes of aging people, but real particularities conspiring to describe one character, so that we readers can conclude on our own that he's old and grungy.

Instead of being *told* he's old and grungy, it's much more satisfying if we readers are *shown* through significant detail that he's old and grungy. That's why we teachers manufactured and continue to market the "Show, don't tell rule." It's a medical bill-reducing measure for writing instructors, who develop eczema, psoriasis, irritable bowel syndrome, migraines, and insomnia when they read too many telling passages.

"Show, don't tell" is good advice, because it promotes writing that elicits sense responses in readers, thus keeping them absorbed in the fictive world of the text. "Show, don't tell" is also, in my experience, confusing to students, because it's impossible advice to follow scrupulously. All fiction writers must "tell" to some extent. Short stories would be two thousand pages long if they didn't. Telling is a shorthand method for collapsing a great deal of specific information—perhaps several pages worth of detail—into a key phrase, so that the writer can get on with the job of spinning out a good yarn. That's why they call it storytelling and not storyshowing.

Certainly there are critically acclaimed writers who have taken "showing" to an extreme, lavishing the reader with pages and pages of evocative detail. Here's a passage from a writer who is, for my money, pound-for-pound, the world's all-time greatest practitioner of showing—Marcel Proust:

> Sometimes, I would stop by the table, where the kitchen-maid had shelled them, to inspect the platoons of peas, drawn up in ranks and numbered, like little green marbles, ready for a game; but what most enraptured me were the asparagus, tinged with ultramarine and pink which shaded off from their heads, finely stippled in mauve and azure, through a series of imperceptible gradations to their white feet—still stained a little by the soil of their garden-bed—with an iridescence that was not of this world. I felt that these celestial hues indicated the presence of exquisite creatures who had been pleased to assume vegetable form and who, through the disguise of their firm comestible flesh, allowed me to discern in this radiance of earliest dawn, these hinted rainbows, these blue evening shades, that precious quality which I should recognize again when, all night long after a dinner at which I had partaken of them, they played (lyrical and coarse in their jesting as the fairies in Shakespeare's Dream) at transforming my chamber pot into a vase of aromatic perfume.

This is an exquisite evocation of veggies. You'll never read a more original, cliché-free and authentic description of the way peas look, or of the way your piss smells like "aromatic perfume" after you eat asparagus. Further, it does a fine job of characterizing the first-person narrator as a sensitive and well-cultured aesthete. However, much as we adore Proust for his lyrical "showing"(*Remembrance of Things Past* has pages and pages of description similar to the above, sometimes with minimal plot, in the traditional sense, to go with it), his prose is a tough read. In his own time, Proust had to deal with endless editorial rejection of his submitted work, so that he ended up self-publishing. I surmise that if Proust sent his work to an agent today, he'd find the postman handing him a rejection letter along the lines of:

> Dear Marcel,
>   We find much to commend in your writing, but we decline to represent it at this time. We love the sensitive-new-male shtick, but you might want to tighten up the four volumes into 150 pages and punch up the plot just a tad. We wish you luck in eventually finding suitable placement for your work.
>   Cheers,
>   Barbzy Civici
>   Transglobal Artistic Management

Proust might receive such a letter because it turns out that a preponderance of showing overwhelms today's average reader, who is increasingly attuned to Website-like bytes of text. Even those readers seeking a high-cultural experience—a quasi-holy submersion in the transformative power of lyrical flights such as Proust's—probably want a relatively even balance between showing and some telling, the latter to keep a plot moving while they're being moved by beautiful figurative language. That's why Steinbeck, in last chapter's quoted example, could get away with the phrase, "In her tone and on her face there was a little smugness." The phrase definitely tells instead of showing—narrates rather than illustrating her smugness—but it allows Steinbeck to deliver key characterizing information in a few words instead of several paragraphs or even several digressive pages.

For that reason, I have come up with Petracca's Modified and Slightly Improved Rule #1: "Show more, tell less." This allows students to daub on a bit of telling as the mortar of a fictional piece—just as Steinbeck does—while reminding them that in most cases, the showing passages should still serve as the hand-molded earthen bricks of their fictional prose. The following section gives you practical suggestions for improving the quality of showing in your own work.

IMAGERY, FIGURATIVE LANGUAGE AND STYLE

When teachers tell beginning writers, "Show, don't tell,"or, "Show more, tell less," we're suggesting that students invest their prose with language constructs more commonly associated with poetry. For example, *imagery* refers to turns of phrase designed to evoke mental images in all the five senses, and corresponding emotional responses as well. As noted in the above "grungy and old" example, much beginning writing suffers from an absence of concrete detail, and in those cases where some detail is included, the imagery is often only visual. Nancy Kress, a prolific and much-published science fiction and fantasy novelist/short story writer, comments on this tendency,

> Writer Poul Anderson once remarked that if his writing didn't have a smell on at least every third page, he went back and put one in. Much fiction could be improved by being smellier.

While the "smell-every-third-page"rule was obviously proposed in a somewhat ironic tone (you actually only need to describe a smell on every fourth page—writers' Rule #5), it's true that you can make your prose stink less by making it smell more . . . and don't stop with smells, either. Include imagistic details that involve all the reader's sensory faculties. The Proust example above is full of imagery. The phrase, " . . . tinged with ultramarine and pink which shaded off from their heads, finely stippled in mauve and azure, through a series of imperceptible gradations to their white feet . . ."appeals to the sense of sight. Similarly, "a vase of aromatic perfume" appeals to smell, and "firm comestible flesh" to touch. For another, more contemporary, example of rich imagistic prose, check this, from T. Coraghessan Boyle's *World's End:*

> ... Jeremias was hoeing up the weeds between the high sweet burgeoning rows of corn in the stand behind the house. It was a messy proposition. The ground was wet as a sponge with the runoff from the previous night's storm, and it tugged at the hoe with a whistling suck and plop and clung to his pegleg like the grip of a dirty hand. He swatted insects, sweat dripped from his nose, there were yellow smears of mud on his face and clothing, on his pegleg and the wooden clog he wore on his left foot. It was only because it was so hot and still—even the birds were at rest till the cool of the evening—that he was able to hear the shudder and whinny of the horses ...

In this brief passage, Boyle manages to appeal to *all* the senses: sight ("yellow smears"); sound ("whistling suck and plop," "shudder and whinny"); touch ("wet as a sponge," "dripped from his nose," "tugged at the hoe," "hot," "grip of a dirty hand"); and smell/taste ("sweet... corn"). While each of your descriptions doesn't have to include every sense, keep in the forefront of your writerly consciousness the goal of images in narrative description: to secure readers' attention by appealing to them on the most basic, sensory levels of apperception.

This passage from *World's End* also contains examples of the other broad "poetic" category of techniques for showing. *Figurative language* refers to expressions in which words are used outside their literal meaning or common usage, in order to increase vividness or to heighten sense impressions imparted by the written text. Figurative language usually operates by comparing or identifying one object or feeling with another object or feeling that is in some way familiar to the reader. Fiction writers use figures of speech continually, to sharpen their descriptions of characters, settings, actions, and to suggest intended themes. In the brief Boyle excerpt above, for example, you'll find a number of figures of speech: *simile* (a comparison using "like"or "as": "wet as a sponge"), *personification* (a figure of speech that invests a nonhuman phenomenon with human-like traits: "the ground ... tugged at his hand"), and perhaps *symbolism* as well (a comparison in which a concrete object—say, a corncob—comes to represent an abstract concept, such as manhood or fertility).

There's technically a difference between simile and another related figure of speech, *metaphor*. The latter is an indirect comparison or renaming of something or someone, as in Thomas Pynchon's *Vineland*—"... the Vaseline of youth has been cleared from your life's lens by the mild detergent solution of time..."—which implies without using "like" or "as" that the passage of time alters one's perceptions of the world in much the same way that a mild soap solution dilutes gloppy accumulations of grease. However, for efficiency's sake, I often use metaphor to describe any comparison of unlike objects or qualities toward some kind of rhetorical effect. Thus, I call the following comparison a metaphor—"I felt myself changing, like a tadpole . . . "(from Lan Samantha Chang, "Pipa's Story")—even though it uses the word "like"and is therefore technically a simile. To my laid-back So-Cal way of thinking, it's less important that you name your figures unerringly than that you understand how they work and why writers use them.

In the previous Chang example, the word "tadpole" has certain connotations that most readers will associate with it: wriggling froggies-to-be perhaps being at the top of the list. When the narrator compares her "changing" to that of a tadpole, the reader automatically links the associated meanings of tadpole to the narrator's current situation and comes up with a mental picture. I imagine an uncomfortable (metamorphosis hurts!) but also necessary (and therefore positive) alteration of lifestyle. You might picture something entirely different. Because your experience is not the same as mine, you may have slightly different personal meanings attached to tadpoles. If you used to keep pet tadpoles in a glass fishbowl and they were continually dying and drifting to the bottom of the bowl, the phrase "like a tadpole" may be more a metaphor of death than the author intended. If you have an environmental bent and have been paying attention to the effects of industrial pollution on frog populations, "like a tadpole" might evoke visuals of grotesque toad mutations with six legs or no eyes. The author always takes a certain risk in creating metaphors, since readers will bring a certain number of idiosyncratic, personal associations to the metaphorical words they read. The author can never predict what the effect a given figure of speech will have on all readers. That's the delight of *ambiguity*—the multiplicity of possible interpretations that a figure can generate—and also the terror of putting your written art out to the world, for all to interpret in their unpredictable ways.

Metaphor does not occur in every successful story. There are plenty of great stories that operate at or near the literal level of narration. Nevertheless, metaphor is a literary device you absolutely need to have at your disposal. The persuasive power of metaphor is unmatched, because it presents a concrete design for comprehending abstract spheres of experience. We don't know what "change" looks like, but we can picture a tadpole. Recent research in language and learning theory has found that "readers consider passages containing metaphor to be more important and find them easier to recall," according to East Carolina University professor Donna M. Congleton. The language in Lawrence Durrell's *Justine*, for example, is striking and memorable because he uses figurative language to stunning effect, while describing the narrator's state of mind and the city of Alexandria, Egypt, during the 1940s:

> That second spring the khamseen was worse that I have ever known it
> before or since. Before sunrise the skies of the desert turned brown as

buckram, and then slowly darkened, swelling like a bruise and at last releasing the outlines of cloud, giant octaves of ochre which massed up from the Delta like the drift of ashes under a volcano. The city has shuttered itself tightly, as if against a gale. A few gusts of air and a thin sour rain are the forerunners of the darkness which blots out the light of the sky. And now unseen in the darkness of shuttered rooms the sand is invading everything, appearing as if by magic in clothes long locked away, books, pictures, teaspoons. In the locks of doors, beneath fingernails. The harsh sobbing air dries the membranes of throats and noses, and makes eyes raw with the configurations of conjunctivitis. Clouds of dried blood walk the streets like prophesies; the sand is settling into the sea like powder into the curls of a stale wig.

Even if you never heard the word "khamseen" before reading this passage, there's no doubt in your mind what it means—a hot, dry springtime wind of the Middle East—and what it feels like. Some of Durrell's metaphors and personifications here are straightforwardly illustrative—"the skies of the desert turned brown as buckram [a coarse, dark cotton fabric—ed.]," "the sand is invading everything"—while others, such as "Clouds of dried blood walk the streets like prophesies," operate at a much more subtle level of thematic suggestion. It's not clear on the literal level what Durrell intends in his depiction of walking clouds of blood. Most likely he is referring to people whose physical selves and very identities become nebulous, cloudy, in the withering hot wind, but the signification is intentionally unclear, as befits the chaotic setting.

Furthermore, the phrase "like prophesies" is an example of *inverse metaphor*, in which a concrete something (walking) is modified by an abstraction (prophesy). This overturns the usual metaphoric structure, in which something concrete (tadpole or buckram) illustrates something relatively abstract (change or brownness), or something concrete lends further depth of description to another concrete something ("sand is . . . like powder in . . . a . . . wig"). The effect of inverse metaphor is not necessarily to make a description more vivid, but to add levels of meaning to a given passage. By saying, "Clouds of dried blood walk the streets like prophesies," Durrell is layering onto the simple physical act of walking all the possible suggestions of prophesy, including mystical revelation, divine inspiration and hoax.

And what about the queer phrase "octaves of ochre"? Ochre is a color, an earthy orangey-yellow, while octave is a group of eight, usually referring to: (a) notes in the musical scale; but also to (b) lines in a poetic sonnet; and to (c) a certain move in the sport of fencing. As a metaphor, "octaves of ochre" is most likely merging color and sound in a kind of *synesthesia* (from the Greek: *syn* = together + *esthesis* = perception, referring to a mystical or psychotic—or both!—mental state in which the excitation of one sensory mode causes a perception in one or more different senses) and at the time making some very sophisticated wordplay on the multiple significations of "octave." In this way, within the twilight space of a three-word metaphor, music becomes color, color becomes poetry, poetry becomes a sword-thrust to the heart.

The variety of metaphoric structures in this one short passage by Durrell illustrates a universe of possibilities for creating figurative language in your own fiction. Before you start dumping ten or twenty metaphors into each paragraph of your fiction, though, a word of caution. Remember how our poor asthmatic friend Proust had trouble getting his stuff published, because the average reader couldn't get past his dense imagery? An overabundance of metaphoric language may have a similar, unwanted effect of limiting your audience. Donna Congleton notes that "over the years ... researchers have attempted to discover the various elements related to readability. Among the factors was figurative language, which ... was found to contribute to reading difficulty." She cites researcher James Cunningham who, in a paper discussing metaphor and reading comprehension, found that prose selections that contain no figurative language are easier to comprehend than those containing metaphor.

Writing for people—that is, for other than purely personal motives—is always a precarious balancing act between being true to your authentic voice and catering to the tastes of your intended audience. If you don't mind pleasing a relatively small group of "literary" readers, then indulge the impulse to load on imagery and metaphor. However, if you want to quit your bartending or car-rental gig by selling lots of books to the mass market, or if you want to develop a *style* characterized by scientific clarity and sparse literal precision, you might want to use imagery and metaphors less frequently. Save them for those points at which they will reveal a character trait or geographical locale or object you want to spotlight.

SETTING: SEVERAL DECADES ON THE HEATH

In discussing ways of showing, we've eased gracefully away from characterization and into the last major fictional area that needs to be addressed: *setting*, the physical place in which a story unfolds. While the foregoing discussions of characterizing detail and metaphor certainly apply to the creation of fictional locales, setting carries with it some unique considerations. Geographic location, if rendered vividly, colors the events and characters placed within it, and often plays an important role in shaping narrative events and revealing/developing central characters. This brings us to the tenth rule of fiction—"Everything happens somewhere"—a saying that may seem obvious but, in fact, summarizes succinctly all the topics we've covered thus far. "Everything" can encompass all the concrete elements that you describe through showing; "happens" recalls all the elements of plot structure and narrative action; and "somewhere" refers to the importance of setting in spatially situating and thematically stratifying the "everything" as it "happens."

Some writers and theorists believe setting should be secondary to plot and therefore played down unless it serves to advance the plot. Elizabeth Bowen says, "Scene is only justified in the novel where it can be shown, or at least felt, to act upon action or a character. In fact, where it has dramatic use. When not intended for dramatic use, scene is a sheer slower-down. Its staticness is a dead weight." According to this school of fiction writing, you want to limit your detailed portrayals of setting to those instances in which the locale of a piece heightens narrative tension and release in a dynamic way.

The terms *local harmony/disharmony* describe the degree to which a story's setting contributes to its plot development by setting up and releasing narrative tension. In this excerpt from *The Stranger*, for example, Albert Camus describes a beach setting during the exposition/complication phase of the plot's development:

> We took the bus and went to a beach I know, some miles out of Algiers. It's just a strip of sand between two rocky spurs, with a line of rushes at the back, along the tide line. At four o'clock the sun wasn't too hot, but the water was pleasantly tepid, and small, languid ripples were creeping up the sand.

This scene illustrates local harmony. Without belaboring the point with three pages of description, Camus makes the setting—an Algerian beach—appear non-threatening in the diminutive phrase "just a strip of sand." The scene is safely bordered by flowering marsh plants ("with a line of rushes at the back"), temperate ("the sun wasn't too hot"), and relaxing ("the water was pleasantly tepid"). To intensify the sense of local harmony in this same scene, Camus actually immerses his characters in the geography:

> Marie taught me a new game. The idea was, while one swam, to suck in the spray off the waves and, when one's mouth was full of foam, to lie on one's back and spout it out against the sky. It made a sort of frothy haze that melted into the air or fell back in a warm shower on one's cheeks. But very soon my mouth was smarting with all the salt I'd drawn in; then Marie came up and hugged me in the water, and pressed her mouth to mine. Her tongue cooled my lips, and we let the waves roll us about for a minute or two before swimming back to the beach.

Here the characters merge happily with the setting, further underscoring the sense of local harmony. They take the warm water into their mouths ("suck the spray off the waves") and interact sensually with it ("spout it out against the sky"), all in the spirit of play ("a new game") and connection ("hugged me in the water").

However, this passage from *The Stranger* also suggests a note of pain ("my mouth was smarting with all the salt"), which foreshadows events that will take place later in the novel. *Foreshadowing* is a dramatic term that refers to building suspense by providing hints at what is to come in future scenes. In this scene, the pain caused by the salt water hints at the novel's climax, in which the narrator will fall into absolute local disharmony with the beach:

> There was the same red glare as far as eye could reach, and small waves were lapping the hot sand in little, flurried gasps. As I slowly walked toward the boulders at the end of the beach I could feel my temples swelling under the impact of light. And each time I felt a hot blast strike my forehead, I gritted my teeth, I clenched my fists in my trouser pockets and keyed up every nerve to fend off the sun and the dark befuddlement it was pouring into me.... For two hours the sun seemed to have made no progress; becalmed in a sea of molten steel. Far out on the horizon a steamer was passing; I could just make out from the corner of an eye the small black moving patch, while I kept my gaze fixed on the Arab. It struck me that all I had to do was to turn, walk away, and think no more about it. But the whole beach, pulsing with heat, was pressing on my back.... The heat was beginning to scorch my cheeks; beads of sweat were gathering in my eyebrows. It was just the same sort of heat as at my mother's funeral, and I had the same disagreeable sensations—especially in my forehead, where all the veins seemed to be bursting through the skin. I couldn't stand it any longer, and took another step forward. I knew it was a fool thing to do; I wouldn't get out of the sun by moving on a yard or so. But I took that step, just one step, forward.

In the preceding sequence of examples, Camus's representation of the seashore typifies the *dynamic* approach to creating fictional settings. When his setting plays a less important role in the plot—as when the narrator and his girlfriend are having a lovely time on the beach—Camus's description of the setting is serviceable but spare, just enough to give us a picture of the beach, and to suggest the harmony between the characters and the locale.

As the setting gains prominence as a plot element, however, it occupies increasing amounts of print-space, so that in the latter example, the beach gets a full-blown, "showing" descriptive treatment, replete with imagery that appeals to the senses (sight: "red glare," "could make out from the corner of an eye the small black moving patch," "gaze fixed on the Arab"; sound: "waves lapping"; touch: "feel my temples," "felt a hot blast strike my forehead," "scorch my cheeks") and figures of speech (the setting "was pressing on my back" like a human antagonist, the sky was like "a sea of molten steel," the veins were "bursting"—the latter a form of figurative language called *hyperbole*, in which events or sensations are exaggerated for rhetorical effect).

In the minds of many writers and theorists, setting should serve as a backdrop to the narrative action . . . until such time as it plays a dynamic role in the plot, as it does in this last Camus example. Other authors take a more atmospheric and less plot-centered approach to setting. *Atmosphere* as a fiction term refers specifically to the mood produced in the reader by a detailed evocation of place. For certain writers and readers, a full soul-and-body immersion in a richly textured local milieu is as important as—or perhaps even more important than—the adrenalin-rush of a gripping plot.

Nineteenth-century novelist Thomas Hardy springs to mind as a prime practitioner and case-in-point example of the atmospheric approach to setting. I hated Hardy's *Return of the Native* when Miss O'Brien made me read it in high school. At the time, I probably didn't think much about why I hated the book—I just found it . . . like, *lame*, and Miss O'Brien definitely lame for assigning it—but now I understand that I had some justification in considering teenage suicide while reading Hardy. Australian critic and fiction writer Elizabeth Jolley notes in Clare Boylan's *The Agony and the Ego,*

> If you read Hardy's novels just for the story you might as well hang yourself. It is often for the passages where the writer dwells with loyalty in his landscape that we read certain authors. This landscape is a setter for the characters and events but it is often more than that. In the time of *dwelling*, looking around at the 'little-trodden spots', the writer can suspend action, add to the portrayal of characters and heighten the drama. Often, too, the landscape parallels some of the characters' hidden aspects, which need to be shown rather than told in straight, flat passages of explanatory narrative.

For atmospheric authors and the people who love them, the "landscape"—and by this Jolley means the setting of a novel or short story—is "often more than" a backdrop for plot. It takes on all the significance of a "dwelling," a place cherished by the human heart, in which one might live comfortably for an extended period.

This discussion should raise a question in your mind: "So am I a local dynamicist, or a local atmosphericist . . . or what?" To discover the degree to which you are a devotee of local color, try a little experiment. Read this long passage of setting description, from the beginning of Thomas Hardy's *Return of the Native*—the very book with which Miss O'Brien tortured me as a youth—and mark the point at which your attention wanders:

> A Saturday afternoon in November was approaching the time of twilight, and the vast tract of unenclosed wild known as Egdon Heath embrowned itself moment by moment. Overhead the hollow stretch of whitish cloud shutting out the sky was as a tent which had the whole heath for its floor.
>
> The heaven being spread with this pallid screen and the earth with the darkest vegetation, their meeting-line at the horizon was clearly marked. In such contrast the heath wore the appearance of an instalment of night which had taken up its place before its astronomical hour

was come: darkness had to a great extent arrived hereon, while day stood distinct in the sky. Looking upwards, a furze-cutter would have been inclined to continue work; looking down, he would have decided to finish his faggot and go home. The distant rims of the world and of the firmament seemed to be a division in time no less than a division in matter. The face of the heath by its mere complexion added half an hour to evening; it could in like manner retard the dawn, sadden noon, anticipate the frowning of storms scarcely generated, and intensify the opacity of a moonless midnight to a cause of shaking and dread.

In fact, precisely at this transitional point of its nightly roll into darkness the great and particular glory of the Egdon waste began, and nobody could be said to understand the heath who had not been there at such a time. It could best be felt when it could not clearly be seen, its complete effect and explanation lying in this and the succeeding hours before the next dawn; then, and only then, did it tell its true tale. The spot was, indeed, a near relation of night, and when night showed itself an apparent tendency to gravitate together could be perceived in its shades and the scene. The sombre stretch of rounds and hollows seemed to rise and meet the evening gloom in pure sympathy, the heath exhaling darkness as rapidly as the heavens precipitated it. And so the obscurity in the air and the obscurity in the land closed together in a black fraternization towards which each advanced halfway.

The place became full of a watchful intentness now; for when other things sank blooding to sleep the heath appeared slowly to awake and listen. Every night its Titanic form seemed to await something; but it had waited thus, unmoved, during so many centuries, through the crises of so many things, that it could only be imagined to await one last crisis—the final overthrow.

It was a spot which returned upon the memory of those who loved it with an aspect of peculiar and kindly congruity. Smiling champaigns of flowers and fruit hardly do this, for they are permanently harmonious only with an existence of better reputation as to its issues than the present. Twilight combined with the scenery of Egdon Heath to evolve a thing majestic without severity, impressive without showiness, emphatic in its admonitions, grand in its simplicity. The qualifications which frequently invest the facade of a prison with far more dignity than is found in the facade of a palace double its size lent to this heath a sublimity in which spots renowned for beauty of the accepted kind are utterly wanting. Fair prospects wed happily with fair times; but alas, if times be not fair! Men have oftener suffered from the mockery of a place too smiling for their reason than from the oppression of surroundings oversadly tinged. Haggard Egdon appealed to a subtler and scarcer instinct, to a more recently learnt emotion, than that which responds to the sort of beauty called charming and fair.

Indeed, it is a question if the exclusive reign of this orthodox beauty is not approaching its last quarter. The new Vale of Tempe may be a gaunt waste in Thule; human souls may find themselves in closer and closer harmony with external things wearing a sombreness distasteful to our race when it was young. The time seems near, if it has not actually arrived, when the chastened sublimity of a moor, a sea, or a mountain will be all of nature that is absolutely in keeping with the moods of the more thinking among mankind. And ultimately, to the commonest tourist, spots like Iceland may become what the vineyards and myrtle gardens of South Europe are to him now; and Heidelberg and Baden be passed unheeded as he hastens from the Alps to the sand dunes of Scheveningen.

The most thoroughgoing ascetic could feel that he had a natural right to wander on Egdon—he was keeping within the line of legitimate indulgence when he laid himself open to influences such as these. Colours and beauties so far subdued were, at least, the birthright of all. Only in summer days of highest feather did its mood touch the level of gaiety. Intensity was more usually reached by way of the solemn than by way of the brilliant, and such a sort of intensity was often arrived at during winter darkness, tempests, and mists. Then Egdon was aroused to reciprocity; for the storm was its lover, and the wind its friend. Then it became the home of strange phantoms; and it was found to be the hitherto unrecognized original of those wild regions of obscurity which are vaguely felt to be compassing us about in midnight dreams of flight and disaster, and are never thought of after the dream till revived by scenes like this.

Damn long, eh? And not an ounce of plot anywhere to be found. If you barely made it through the first fifty words in which Egdon Heath is introduced and then you started thinking about dinner or that cute boy/girl/puppy you saw on State Street this afternoon, then you're definitely a local dynamicist and should devote yourself to creating unique characters and writing great plots onto which you hang some brief place descriptions—nothing that would qualify as descriptive "dead weight," as Elizabeth Bowen would undoubtedly call the Hardy prose. You'll end up rich beyond your wildest dreams.

If you got through the first four paragraphs, then you're naturally inclined to be in the spotlight, you have security, dignity, sexual vigor, and courage, you love the enhanced sense of selfhood that wielding authority gives you, and ... oh wait, I'm confusing this with an astrological chart reading. Sorry. If you got through six paragraphs of Hardy before you started hallucinating about the pet turtle you had in the sixth grade, then you have a pretty even balance between dynamic and atmospheric tendencies, and your prose should reflect that balance. John Mortimer, who wrote the Rumpole of the Bailey lawyer-based novels upon which the BBC/PBS series was based, says of such even disposition, "Places are important to me. I have to know exactly where the action goes on—but I don't like to spend too much time on being atmospheric."

This is the approach that I try to take with my own prose, and that I would recommend as a goal for most writers, without taking style and individual voice into account. In the process of making settings, feel free to interrupt narrative action, but do it toward some purpose. Have locale supplement your depiction of your story's central characters, as Steinbeck did in "The Chrysanthemums," where the Salinas valley, topped with a lid of gray overcast, mirrors the trapped and bored feeling of the female protagonist, Elisa. Likewise, use setting to boost a story's dramatic tension, by putting characters in conflict with the geography, as in the last Camus passage quoted above. With such a balanced approach, the locale will "show" (rather than "telling" in direct, bland paragraphs of expository reportage) crucial story elements without bringing the story to a grinding and boring halt.

Finally, if you made it all the way to the end of the *Return of the Native* excerpt, then you probably feel as though you just spent several decades on the heath and need to change your soiled outergarments. While I've purposely discussed Hardy's extensive use of setting in a mocking *tone*—a literary term referring to the author's implied attitude toward characters or subject—the truth is that I admire the hell out of his prose, for the same reason I admire Proust. These are writers with distinctive voices, who never let assumed public taste influence them to the point that they compromise their literary vision. The difficulty in making fiction is that, much as it's a reflection of a creative process, it's also a *product* which has the potential for garnering big bucks if lots of people buy it. Market surveys reveal that the mainstream reader—who makes up that group known as "lots of people"—doesn't like prose that veers too far from the pop norm: formulaic, Hollywood-style plots, characters with whom we're comfortable because we've seen them many times before, minimal setting that doesn't interfere with the predictable march of plot points. Therefore, beginning writers are often dissuaded from following creative impulses to indulge in extravagant atmospheric description, as Hardy does, or in immoderate imagistic prose, as Proust does, or in wildly digressive plots, as I do, or in nontraditional forms, as Barry Gifford will describe in the chapter on literary fiction at the end of *The Graceful Lie.*

In a recent interview, contemporary fiction writer and instructor Carole Maso describes the problem this way:

> . . . I see . . . in my students, some very raw, extravagant, interesting tendencies, deliberately avoided, consciously swerved away from, because dear God, what would happen if you actually spoke in your own voice, and you sounded like no one else. Looked like no one else, could not be categorized, could not be sold. It's dangerous. Which it should be, of course. But most American writers are unwilling to take the gamble. The price is too high. And American literature suffers a great deal as a result. For me, the price is too high *not* [*italics mine— ed.*] to speak in my own voice. Writing, for me, is a significant human adventure; it is about exploration and investigation and meditation. It's about the search for a le-

gitimate language. It's about the search for beauty and integrity and wholeness. For meaning, where maybe there is none.

If your goal is to raise yourself from poverty by writing popular fiction, then do it earnestly and energetically—I'll take care not to call you a hack. If, however, you want to have a meaningful literary experience—and maybe to make some bucks in the process—then I would side with Maso in urging you to take some risks in experimenting with techniques described above. Write a "story" that is deliberately imagistic to the near-exclusion of plot. Indulge the impulse to write atmospherically, to the point that it sounds like satire. Gradually, from such experimentation, will your unique style and voice—or several unique styles and voices—emerge, and then you'll be on your way to the next chapter: publication.

From Justine
Lawrence Durrell

It is pitch-dark when I awake at the touch of Nessim's gentle hand shaking my shoulder. The alarm clock has failed us. But the room is full of stretching yawning figures climbing from their bunks. The loaders have been curled up asleep like sheepdogs on the balcony outside. They busy themselves in lighting the paraffin lamps whose unearthly glare is to light our desultory breakfast of coffee and sandwiches. I go down the landing stage and wash my face in the icy lake water. Utter blackness all around. Everyone speaks in low voices, as if weighed down by the weight of the darkness. Snatches of wind make the little lodge tremble, built as it is on frail wooden stilts over the water.

We are each allotted a punt and a gun-bearer. "You'll take Faraj," says Nessim. "He's the most experienced and reliable of them." I thank him. A black barbaric face under a soiled white turban, unsmiling, spiritless. He takes my equipment and turns silently to the dark punt. With a whispered farewell I climb in and seat myself. With a lithe swing of the pole Faraj drives us out into the channel and suddenly we are scoring across the heart of a black diamond. The water is full of stars, Orion down, Capella tossing out its brilliant sparks. For a long while now we crawl upon this diamond-pointed star-floor in silence save for the suck and lisp of the pole in the mud. Then we turn abruptly into a wider channel to hear a string of wavelets pattering against our prow while draughts of wind fetch up from the invisible sea-line tasting of salt.

Premonitions of the dawn are already in the air as we cross the darkness of this lost world. Now the approaches to the empty water ahead are shivered by the faintest etching of islands, sprouts of beard, reeds and sedge. And on all sides now comes the rich plural chuckle of duck and the shrill pinched note of the gulls to the seaboard. Faraj grunts and turns the punt towards a nearby island. Reaching out upon the darkness my hands grasp the icy rim of the nearest barrel into which I laboriously climb. The butts consist merely of a couple of dry wood-slatted barrels tied together and festooned with tall reeds to make them invisible. The loader holds the punt steady while I disembarrass him of my gear. There is nothing to do now but to sit and wait for the dawn which is rising slowly somewhere, to be born from this black expressionless darkness.

It is bitterly cold now and even my heavy greatcoat seems to offer inadequate protection. I have told Faraj that I will do my own loading as I do not want him handling my spare gun and cartridges in the next barrel. I must confess to a feeling of shame as I do so, but it sets my nerves at rest. He nods with an expressionless face and stands off with the punt in the next cluster of reeds, camouflaged like a scarecrow. We wait now with our faces turned towards the distant reaches of the lake—it seems for centuries.

Suddenly at the end of the great couloir my vision is sharpened by a pale disjunctive shudder as a bar of buttercup-yellow thickening gradually to a ray falls slowly through the dark masses of cloud to the east. The ripple and flurry of the invisible colonies of birds around us increases. Slowly, painfully, like a half-open door the dawn is upon us, forcing back the darkness. A minute more and stairway of soft kingcups slides smoothly down out of heaven to touch in our horizons, to give eye and mind an orientation in space which it has been lacking. Faraj yawns heavily and scratches himself. Now rose-madder and warm burnt gold. Clouds move to green and yellow. The lake has begun to shake off its sleep. I see the black silhouette of teal cross my vision eastward. "It is time," murmurs Faraj; but the minute hand of my wrist watch shows that we still have five minutes to go. My bones feel as if they have been soaked in the darkness. I feel suspense and inertia struggling for possession of my sleepy mind. By agreement there is to be no shooting before four-thirty. I load slowly and dispose my bandolier across the butt next me within easy reach. "It is time," says Faraj more urgently. Nearby there is a plop and a scamper of some hidden birds. Out of sight a couple of coot squat in the middle of the lake pondering. I am about to say something when the first chapter of guns opens from the south—like the distant click of cricket-balls.

Now solitaries begin to pass, one, two, three. The light grows and waxes, turning now from red to green. The clouds themselves are moving to reveal enormous cavities of sky. They peel the morning like a fruit. Four separate arrowheads of duck rise and form two hundred yards away. They cross me trimly at an angle and I open up with a tentative right barrel for distance. As usual they are faster and higher than they seem. The minutes are ticking away in the heart. Guns open up nearer to hand, and by now the lake is in a general state of alert. The duck are coming fairly frequently now in groups, three, five, nine: very low and fast. Their wings purr, as they feather the sky, their necks reach. Higher again in mid-heaven there travel the clear formations of mallard, grouped like aircraft against the light, ploughing a soft slow flight. The guns squash the air and harry them as they pass, moving with a slow curling bias towards the open sea. Even higher and quite out of reach come chains of wild geese, their plaintive honking sounding clearly across the now sunny waters of Mareotis.

There is hardly time to think now: for teal and widgeon like flung darts whistle over me and I begin to shoot slowly and methodically. Targets are so plentiful that it is often difficult to choose one in the split second during which it presents itself to the gun. Once or twice I catch myself taking a snap shot into a formation. If hit squarely a bird staggers and spins, pauses for a moment, and then sinks gracefully like a handkerchief from a lady's hand. Reeds close over the brown bodies, but now the tireless Faraj is out poling about like mad to retrieve the birds. At times he leaps into the water with his *galabeab* tucked up to his midriff. His features blaze with excitement. From time to time he gives a shrill whoop.

They are coming in from everywhere now, at every conceivable angle and every speed. The guns bark and jumble in one's ears as they drive the birds backwards and forwards across the lake. Some of the flights though nimble are obviously war-weary after heavy losses; other solitaries seem quite out of their minds with panic. One young and silly duck settles for a moment by the punt, almost within reach of Faraj's hands, before it suddenly sees danger and spurts off in a slither of foam. In a modest way I am not doing too badly though in all the excitement it is hard to control oneself and to shoot deliberately. The sun is fairly up now and the damps of the night have been dispersed. In an hour I shall be sweating again in these heavy clothes. The sun shines on the ruffled waters of Mareotis where the birds still fly. The punts by now will be full of the sodden bodies of the victims, red blood running from the shattered beaks on to the floor-boards, marvellous feathers dulled by death.

I eke out my remaining ammunition as best I can but already by quarter past eight I have fired the last cartridge; Faraj is still at work painstakingly tracking down stragglers among the reeds with the single-mindedness of a retriever. I light a cigarette, and for the first time feel free from the shadow of omens and premonitions—free to breathe, to compose my mind once more. It is extraordinary how the prospect of death closes down upon the free play of the mind, like a steel shutter, cutting off the future which alone is nourished by hopes and wishes. I feel the stubble on my unshaven chin and think longingly of a hot bath and a warm breakfast. Faraj is still tirelessly scouting the islands of sedge. The guns have slackened, and in some quarters of the lake are already silent. I think with a dull ache of Justine, somewhere out there across the sunny water. I have no great fear for her safety for she has taken as her own gun-bearer my faithful servant Hamid.

I feel all at once gay and light-hearted as I shout to Faraj to cease his explorations and bring back the punt. He does so reluctantly and at last we set off across the lake, back through the channels and corridors of reed towards the lodge.

"Eight brace no good," says Faraj, thinking of the large professional bags we will have to face when Ralli and Capodistria return. "For me it is very good," I say. "I am a rotten shot. Never done as well." We enter the thickly sown channels of water which border the lake like miniature canals.

At the end, against the light, I catch sight of another punt moving towards us which gradually defines itself into the familiar figure of Nessim. He is wearing his old moleskin cap with the ear-flaps up and tied over the top. I wave but he does not respond. He sits abstractedly in the prow of the punt with his hands clasped about his knees. "Nessim," I shout. "How did you do? I got eight brace and one lost." The boats are nearly abreast now, for we are heading towards the mouth of the last canal which leads to the lodge. Nessim waits until we are within a few yards of each other before he says with a curious serenity, "Did you hear? There's been an accident. Capodistria..." and all of a sudden my heart contracts in my body. "Capodistria?" I stammer. Nessim still has the curious impish serenity of someone resting after a great expenditure of energy. "He's dead," he says, and I hear the sudden roar of the hydroplane engines starting up behind the wall of reeds. He nods towards the sound and adds in the same still voice: "They are taking him back to Alexandria".

A thousand conventional commonplaces, a thousand conventional questions spring to my mind, but for a long time I can say nothing.

On the balcony the others have assembled uneasily, almost shame-facedly; they are like a group of thoughtless schoolboys for whom some silly prank has ended in the death of one of their fellows. The furry cone of noise from the hydroplane still coats the air. In the middle distance one can hear shouts and the noise of car-engines starting up. The piled bodies of the duck, which would normally be subject matter for gloating commentaries, lie about the lodge with anachronistic absurdity. It appears that death is a relative question. We had only been prepared to accept a certain share of it when we entered the dark lake with our weapons. The death of Capodistria hangs in the still air like a bad smell, like a bad joke.

Ralli had been sent to get him and had found the body lying face down in the shallow waters of the lake with the black eye-patch floating near him. It was clearly an accident. Capodistria's loader was an elderly man, thin as a cormorant, who sits now hunched over a mess of beans on the balcony. He cannot give a coherent account of the business. He is from Upper Egypt and has the weary half-crazed expression of a desert father.

Ralli is extremely nervous and is drinking copious draughts of brandy. He retells his story for the seventh time, simply because he must talk in order to quieten his nerves. The body could not have been long in the water, yet the skin was like the skin of a washerwoman's hands. When they lifted it to get it into the hydroplane the false teeth slipped out of the mouth and crashed on to the floor-boards frightening them all. This incident seems to have made a great impression on him. I suddenly feel overcome with fatigue and my knees start to tremble. I take a mug of hot coffee and, kicking off my boots, crawl into the nearest bunk with it. Ralli is still talking with deafening persistence, his free hand coaxing the air into expressive shapes. The others watch him with a vague and dispirited curiosity, each plunged in his own reflections. Capodistria's loader is still eating noisily like a famished animal, blinking in the sunlight. Presently a punt comes into view with three policemen perched precariously in it. Nessim watches their antics with an imperturbability flavoured ever so slightly with satisfaction; it is as if he were smiling to himself. The clatter of boots and musket-butts on the wooden steps, and up they come to take down our depositions in their notebooks. They bring with them a grave air of suspicion which hovers over us all. One of them carefully manacles Capodistria's loader before helping him into the punt. The servant puts out his wrists for the iron cuffs with a bland uncomprehending air such as one sees on the faces of old apes when called upon to perform a human action which they have learned but not understood.

It is nearly one o'clock before the police have finished their business. The parties will all have ebbed back from the lake by now to the city where the news of Capodistria's death will be waiting for them. But this is not to be all.

One by one we straggle ashore with our gear. The cars are waiting for us, and now begins a long chaffering session with the loaders and boatmen who must be paid off; guns are broken up and the bag distributed; in all this incoherence I see my servant Hamid advancing timidly through the crowd with his good eye screwed up against the sunlight. I think he must be looking for me but no: he goes up to Nessim and hands him a small blue envelope. I want to describe this exactly. Nessim takes it absently with his left hand while his right is reaching into the car to place a box of cartridges in the glove-box. He examines the superscription once thoughtlessly and then once more with marked attention. Then keeping his eyes on Hamid's face he takes a deep breath and opens the envelope to read whatever is written on the half sheet of notepaper. For a minute he studies it and then replaces the letter in the envelope. He looks about him with a sudden change of expression, as if he suddenly felt sick and was looking about for a place where he might be so. He makes his way through the crowd and putting his head against a corner of mud wall utters a short panting sob, as of a runner out of breath. Then he turns back to the car, completely controlled and dry-eyed, to complete his packing. This brief incident goes completely unremarked by the rest of his guests.

Clouds of dust rise now as the cars begin to draw away towards the city; the wild gang of boatmen shout and wave and treat us to carved watermelon smiles studded with gold and ivory. Hamid opens the car door and climbs in like a monkey. "What is it?" I say, and folding his small hands apologetically towards me in an attitude of supplication which means "Blame not the bearer of ill tidings", he says in a small conciliatory voice: "Master, the lady has gone. There is a letter for you in the house."

It is as if the whole city had crashed about my ears: I walk slowly to the flat, aimlessly as survivors must walk about the streets of their native city after an earthquake, surprised to find how much that had been familiar has changed. Rue Piroua, Rue de France, the Terbana Mosque (cupboard smelling of apples), Rue Sidi Abou El Abbas (water-ices and coffee), Anfouchi, Ras El Tin (Cape of Figs), Ikingi Mariut (gathering wild flowers together, convinced she cannot love me), equestrian statue of Mohammed Ali in the square.... General Earle's comical little bust, killed Sudan 1885.... An evening multitudinous with swallows ... the tombs at Kom El Shugaffa, darkness and damp soil, both terrified by the darkness.... Rue Fouad as the Old Canopic Way, once Rue De La Porte Rosette.... Hutchinson disturbed the whole water-disposition of the city by cutting the dykes.... The scene in *Moeurs* where he tries to read her the book he is writing about her. "She sits in the wicker chair with her hands in her lap, as if posing for a portrait, but with a look of ever-growing horror on her face. At last I can stand it no longer, and I throw down the manuscript in the fireplace, crying out: 'What are they worth, since you understand nothing, these pages written from a heart pierced to the quick?'" In my mind's eye I can see Nessim racing up the great staircase to her room to find a distraught Selim contemplating the empty cupboards and a dressing table swept clean as if by a blow from a leopard's paw.

In the harbour of Alexandria the sirens whoop and wail. The screws of ships crush and crunch the green oil-coated waters of the inner bar. Idly bending and inclining, effortlessly breathing as if in the rhythm of the earth's own systole and diastole, the yachts turn their spars against the sky. Somewhere in the heart of experience there is an order and a coherence which we might surprise if we were attentive enough, loving enough, or patient enough. Will there be time?

POINTS TO CONSIDER ABOUT DURRELL'S *JUSTINE* EXCERPT

1. Re-read the passage that begins, "Now solitaries begin to pass, one, two, three . . ." Describe the ways in which Durrell uses imagery to evoke multisensory impressions in the reader. Make a list of specific images in that passage and then sort the images by the senses—sight, smell, sound, touch, taste—to which they appeal.

2. What specific techniques does Durrell use to evoke the sense of atmosphere in this excerpt? If you didn't know that *Justine* was set in 1940s Egypt, might you think it was set anywhere else—such as modern-day Malibu, California? Why not?

3. Does this piece suggest a pro-hunting theme, or an anti-hunting theme . . . or is it ambivalent about the issue? If you believe it is ambivalent, taking neither an explicit pro- or anti-stance on the issue, what does that ambivalence "show" us about the personality of the narrator?

4. How does the hunting incident parallel other events in the narrator's life—specifically, emotional issues that are revealed toward the end of this chapter? What has happened between the protagonist and his lover ("the lady")? How are the narrator's feelings about his relationship revealed through Durrell's descriptions of setting?

5. The second-to-last paragraph contains a lengthy list of place-names. Does Durrell include these to make his chapter longer, or might he have a more artistic motive? If so, what is his reason for including those names? How do they contribute to the sense of atmosphere in this excerpt?

Buddah

Susan Straight

"Look at this little Buddha-head dude, man," one of them said. He pushed closer. "He got them Chinese eyes."

"He got a big old head, too, man. I think we should make him say somethin. He don't respect us," another voice said from behind him. Buddah kept his lips pressed warm together and felt the voices slide forward, tighter, taking away the air. He couldn't breathe, and woke from the dream with the dry heat pressing through the walls; hot air seemed to waft into the room as if a giant mouth were hovering around it. A tickle of sweat curled around the skin behind his ear. He lay still, listening for the snores of Rodriguez and Sotelo, the two boys who shared his room. But their beds were empty, he saw, and fear pulled at his ribs. Did Gaines and T.C. make them guys leave so they could jump me? he thought, and when he turned his head and felt the rough pillowcase against his neck he remembered that Sotelo and Rodriguez had gone home to L.A. on a week pass.

It was his seventh day. I can't go on home-pass till I been in this place for a month, he said to himself. They gon talk me to death, bout behavior and pattern of your life, and them Crips gon try and dog me every time I turn around. He opened the door and looked out at the bare land, the stiff yellow grass like dog fur in patches, that surrounded St. Jude's School for Boys. Now everybody on they home-pass, and ain't nobody left but me and them guys that messed up or don't got nowhere to go, he thought. The gray-green weeds close to the fence shivered in the wind. Every day he thought of the miles of desert and boulders he had seen when the social worker drove him in from L.A. "Your program is six months," the man had said.

No one else was awake yet; none of the other boys were roaming the walks in front of the buildings, hanging over the balconies, waiting for an overheated car to pull in off the highway. If a woman ever got out to look for help, they would swarm like dust toward her. Buddah listened to the wind. Must be lettin us sleep cause nobody goin home. He looked down the railing to the other end of the building to see if Jesse, the counselor for the thirteen-to-fifteen-year-olds, was awake, but his door was still closed. A long row of doorknobs glinted in the sun. Third door Gaines and T.C. Sotelo said they ain't got no home-pass. They gon be on me all the time, talkin bout am I gon buy Gaines some pants with my state money. Am I gon give up the ducats.

He thought of the dream, the shapes pressing forward, and he touched the trunk on the floor by his bed. That circle of voices was how he had gotten his name, months ago. A delegation of Bounty Hunters stood around him when he neared the project. "Fuckin Buddha-head, can't even see out them eyes, they so slanty." He'd been waiting for it, and had gifts ready for them: a car stereo, sunglasses from the Korean store, and himself. "I can pull for you," he whispered to them.

At St. Jude's, he had covered the scarred top of his trunk with a sheet of white paper, the way the others had, and written his name in curved letters:

BUDDAH
SOUL GARDENS BOUNTY HUNTER'S

He thought the name might protect him here, but it had been a mistake. He wanted to be left alone, to collect his things invisibly, not to speak. That first night, when they were asked, Sotelo and Rodriguez read the trunk and told the other boys, "New baby? He's red, man." Bounty Hunters wore red bandannas, called each other "Blood." Crips were blue-raggers, and shouted "Cuzz" before they shot someone.

But there were only two other red rags at St. Jude's, and they were in the oldest group. In Buddah's group there were two Crips. Gaines and T.C. Harris had flashed their hands at him, their fingers and thumbs contorted in the signals Buddah had always run from. Gaines fanned his fingers out over his biceps and said, "Oh, yeah."

Now it ain't nobody in the room but me, six more days. Buddah looked at the low, wide windows and imagined the shapes he would see at night, blocking the light from the parking lot when they walked past the curtains; he saw the room as dark and gold-toned as if it were night now, and the crack of light that would cut in as they opened the door.

He let the lock clink against the metal edging of the trunk. It contained everything he had at St. Jude's: the jeans, white T-shirts and cheap canvas shoes Jesse took him to buy with part of the state money. "You got to lock your shit up all the time if you want to keep it," Jesse had said, and Buddah laughed through his nose. Locks ain't about nothin. Shit. They tellin *me* bout locks.

Buddah opened Sotelo's nightstand and saw only paper covered with drawings of heavy-eyed girls. He bent and looked under Sotelo's bed; he'd seen him drop something behind the head one night. This was the first time he'd been alone, able to look. He saw a blunt shape against the wall, lying in the folds of green bedspread. It was a short length of pipe, dull heavy iron. Shit, everybody must got one a these, he thought. He bent to Rodriguez's side and heard Jesse's voice, heard him banging on doors with the flat of his hand, calling, "Get up, hardheads, we got places to go."

Montoya's clipped words came from the doorway next to Buddah's. "Hey, man, Jesse, you wake up so early? You miss me already, man?"

"Yeah, Montoya, I couldn't wait," Jesse said. "Get ready for breakfast."

Buddah slipped to his trunk quickly and dropped the pipe behind it. He heard it land, muffled, on the edge of his bedspread, and then Jesse swung open the door, saying, "Five minutes, Smith. How you like this heat?"

Buddah looked at Jesse's long feet on the hump of the doorway. Ain't here to be likin it.

"Still can't speak, huh?" Jesse said. "Maybe you'll talk at the beach if we cool you off." He turned and Buddah saw the flash of a bird diving to the parking lot for potato-chip crumbs.

They waited for Jesse near the long white van. Montoya, his hair combed smooth and feather-stiff, walked his boxer's walk in baggy *cholo* khakis. Carroll, a white boy, leaned against the van, arms folded under the

"Highway to Hell" that crossed his T-shirt. Buddah stood apart from them, in the shade of a squat palm tree, preparing to be invisible. His arms were folded too, and he pushed down on his feet, feeling the long muscles in his thighs tighten. The ghostly bushes past the fence turned in the wind.

Won't nobody see me. Them Crips be busy talkin shit to Jesse, and I ain't gotta worry bout nobody else. I'ma get me somethin at the beach. It'll be somethin there.

The sound of electric drums, sharp as gunfire, came from the balcony. Buddah waited until they approached. T.C. wore new razor-creased Levis and a snow-white T-shirt, a blue cap set high and slanted on his sunglasses. He carried the radio, a box of cassettes and a can of soda, singing loudly, "It shoulda been *blue*" over the words of the woman who sang, "It shoulda been you."

Gaines followed him, pointing at Buddah when T.C. sang "blue." "If we was at home, nigga, it be a .357 to the membrane," he whispered to Buddah, taking the pointing finger and running it around his ear.

Buddah pulled in the sides of his cheeks, soft and slippery when he bit them with his back teeth. Yeah, but I wouldn't be wearin no red rag, cause I ain't no Bounty Hunter. I'm a independent. Red, blue, ain't about shit to me. He was careful not to let his lips move; he had to be conscious of it, because when he spoke to himself, he would feel his lips touching each other sometimes and falling away as soft and slight as tiny bubbles popping. Probably look like I'm fixin to cry, he thought.

No bandannas were allowed at St. Jude's, no careless hand signals, nothing to spark gang fights. Gaines looked carefully for Jesse, and smiled close to Buddah's face. "The red rag is stained with the blood of disrespectful Hunters, slob. You gon respect us." He got one a them devil peaks, Buddah thought, like Mama say when people hair all in a point on they forehead. Mama say them some evil people with peaks. He glanced away, at T.C., who was uninterested, popping his fingers and singing.

You don't never stop talkin. You always runnin your mouth, that way everybody look at you, know where you are. He saw Jesse appear from the office, and Gaines moved away. Not like me. I'm bad cause you don't see me.

It was easy because he was so small and quiet; he walked into the stores imagining that everything in his face blended together, skin, lips, eyes all the same color. He wasn't hungry with hard rings around his stomach, like when he didn't eat anything for a long time, but he wanted something else in his mouth, a solid taste like he had chosen whatever he wanted. When they still lived in a house, when he was ten, his mother left pots of red beans on the stove when she went to work in the afternoon. Sometimes she left greens and a pan of cornbread, or three pieces of chicken, one each for him, Danita and Donnie.

He used to walk with her to the bus stop, saying nothing, watching her skin begin to shine from the heat, like molasses, with a liquid red sheen underneath the color. Her mouth moved all the time, to smile, to tell him to hurry and get back to the house and damn it, don't be hangin out in the street. Say somethin, David! All right, now. Lock the door.

He always waited until five o'clock had passed and then left the house, saying sternly to his younger brother and sister, "Y'all watch TV. Don't move. I be back."

He stepped over the jagged hole in the wooden porch and walked past children riding bicycles, thin knees angling like iron pipes. The store was five blocks away, a small grocery store with a Korean man behind the register. Women crowded the store then, shopping before they went home from work. They walked around the stacks of cans blocking the aisle, picked over the bright, shiny vegetables and fruit.

Fingering the quarter in his pocket, he brushed past the women near the bread and potato chips. He bent next to one woman, watching, and slid bags of potato chips into the pit of his dark blue windbreaker; they rested silent and light against his stomach. For Danita. He imagined his eyes were like ball bearings, greased, so that he didn't move enough of anything else to rustle. Zingers for himself. At the counter loaded with candy, he knelt to look at the bottom row and beside his knee, pushed a Butterfinger up the sleeve of his jacket. He paid for Donnie's pack of gum, watching the Korean man's eyes, comparing them to his own, holding his plasticlike jacket very still. I got somethin, he thought, looking at the man's hands. I got your stuff.

Walking home quickly, he always touched the food with the same pride. The store was different. He had slipped in and out, and something was changed, missing.

"Oh, man, look who comin, Loco Lopez," T.C. said. "He done lost his home-pass cause they busted him with that paint thinner. My man was *high*."

"*Qué pasa?*" Lopez said to Montoya.

"Shut up, T.C.," Jesse said. "Let's go. Only reason I'm taking you to the beach is cause it's so damn hot out here I can't think."

"I got shotgun," T.C. said.

Jesse looked at him hard and said, "Who are you, ghetto child goes to the beach? Where's your lawn chair and picnic basket?"

T.C. opened the van's front door and said, "I left the caviar at my crib, homes. Too Cool only taking the essentials. And I *been* to the beach, O.K.? Me and my set went to Venice, and it was jammin, all them bikinis and shit."

"Yeah, well, don't expect to pick up any girls at this beach, not dressed like that," Jesse said. He looked at them. Buddah watched Gaines sit alone in the long seat behind T.C. Montoya and Lopez sat together in the back seat; Carroll and Buddah sat far from each other in the middle of the van.

"Anybody gets out of my sight, we go back," Jesse started, turning onto the highway. "Anybody talks shit, like you guys did at the skating rink last week, T.C., we're gone, right back to the Jude's." Jesse paused to look in the rearview mirror. "I'm takin you guys to Laguna. It's not the closest, but it's small, so I can keep an eye on you."

The back of Gaines's neck glittered with sweat. Buddah felt the hot wind from the window scour his face; he watched T.C. rest his hand on the radio and pop his shoulders so they rippled. Buddah felt a tremor in his chest, a settling of his spine, and he touched the window.

The low purplish mountains that rimmed the desert were wrinkled in strange, thin folds and trenches, like his grandmother's neck. He saw her, sitting in her tiny yard in Long Beach the way she'd been the only time he'd ever visited her. She was silent like him, her body rocking slightly all the time, watching her greens and peas grow against the chainlink fence. The velvety skin near her hairline was still tight, and her eyes were slanted upward like his. The mountains came closer as the van began to leave the desert, and soon they were smoother, covered with burnt-gold grass and stunted trees. Buddah was thinking that he hadn't seen a beach in Long Beach when the music began to beat through the van. T.C. drew circles with his hands in the air, and Jesse reached over and turned the radio off. "Man, you ain't got *no* soul," T.C. complained.

"I'm gonna tell you guys, no blasting the box when we get there," Jesse began again. "And something else. Montoya, Lopez, Smith, I don't want you guys even *looking* at anybody's stuff. Montoya, you see what happened to your buddy Jimenez when he took that jacket at the skating rink. Two months added to his program."

"So, man, I been a good boy," Montoya said, and Lopez laughed.

"That's why your mother said she didn't want you home this time, right?" Jesse said. "Last home-pass you took twenty dollars from her purse."

Now he gon start all this talk about behavior and why do you steal, Buddah thought. But Jesse said, "Smith," and looked into the mirror again. "You been doin pretty good, but this is your first off-ground, so don't blow it." Buddah felt them all look at him, and he turned his face to the window, angry, tasting the inside of his cheeks again. Bunk you, man. Don't be tellin me shit. A wine-colored Thunderbird pulled past the van. The faces inside were green behind their windows, staring at the name painted on the van door, at the boys. What y'all lookin at? He felt the glass against his lips. You lookin at me, and I had your T-Bird. Woulda been set.

They had moved to the seventh building of the Solano Gardens housing project, an island run by Bounty Hunters in an ocean of Crips, just after his eleventh birthday. At the welter of railroad tracks behind the junior high, he walked rapidly, seeing the blue bandannas, the watching faces.

But he lived in Soul Gardens; the Bounty Hunters owned him. He had to be occasionally valuable to them, because no one could step outside the project alone, without a protective cadre of red rags. He watched them gather in the courtyard and then walked slightly behind. They left him alone until they needed something.

The dent-puller, long and thin, pierced into car locks easily and pulled the entire silver circles out for him. The cars were like houses, each with its own smell and a push of air that he felt against his face for an instant when he bent to pull the stereo, someone else's smell that he let escape. He learned to start the car if Ellis told him to, and the feel of each steering wheel under his fingers for a moment made his stomach jump. Soft, leather-bound he'd felt once, but cold and ridged usually.

They hadn't gotten caught when they stripped or stole cars in the neighborhood, but Ellis decided he wanted a T-Bird. At the house he finally chose in Downey, where the 7–11 they passed had only white faces inside, a wine-red Thunderbird was parked. Ellis looked at Buddah with a strange smile on his face. Buddah had been waiting for this, too. "Ain't doin no house," Buddah said, and Ellis pushed him. "You know they got a VCR. You better be *down*," Ellis said.

Buddah loved the cars, their metallic shine like crystal sugar on the fruit candy that was his mother's favorite. Some of them even smelled sweet. But the house, even when he stood under the eaves moving the lock, smelled heavy and wrong, and when the door opened and the foreign air rushed at him, he heard the screaming of the alarm and then running.

The ocean glinted like an endless stretch of blue flake on a hood. Buddah had never seen so much water, so many white people. Jesse said, "What you guys think, huh?"

"None a these women got booty," T.C. said. "No ass to hold onto."

Jesse drove down a street that curved toward the water. Clean, shining cars lined both sides: Mercedes, BMWs, station wagons, a Porsche. Buddah looked at the cars, at the chalky clean sidewalks and smooth grass. Jesse circled twice before he found a parking space, and then he said, "Damn, we don't have quarters. We're gonna have to walk to a store to get some, cause if I pull out we won't find another space."

They trailed behind him like fish, swerving and shifting. "Where we goin, man?" Lopez asked. "I don't see no 7–11 or nothin."

Up close, the cars looked even better, a gleaming line unbroken by a parking space as far as they walked, the perfect doors and weak round locks. Ellis would tell me to pull the Mercedes, Buddah thought, and just then Gaines said, "Mercedes, the ladies, when I get one they gon be crazy." Buddah slowed; he'd been thinking about telling Ellis where the cars were, but when he heard Gaines's voice, the same one that had been whispering to him every day for a week, he thought, shit, I don't even know where we are. Ain't tellin Ellis shit when he ax me where I been. Think everything for him.

They walked through an art show that lined the sidewalk, and had to go single file to get past. Buddah watched T.C. rock his shoulders in step to the beat inside his head, passing closely by people to brush them with air, making them move and look at him. Jesse pulled them inside a restaurant lobby and went to get change. "I ain't seen *no* brothers, man," Gaines said to T.C.

"I'm tellin you," T.C. said. "We gon be specks like on a sheet."

At the start of the steep asphalt trail down to the crescent-shaped beach, a large sign read:

Glenn E. Vedder Ecological Reserve
PLEASE DO NOT REMOVE
Shells, Rocks, Plants, Marine Life, or Game Fish
so that others may see and enjoy them
TAKE OUT ONLY THAT WHICH YOU BROUGHT IN

Jesse stopped and read the sign silently for a moment; T.C. said, "Man, it ain't school time," when he read it out loud. After Jesse finished, T.C. said, "Thank you, Mr. Man. How people supposed to know you went to the beach if you don't got no souvenir?"

"You suppose to come back with a suntan, man," Lopez said. "Big problem for you, huh?"

"Man, I'll kick your ass," T.C. said, and Jesse pushed him away.

Buddah stared at the shifting colors, felt the sand against his palm when he sat down. Green plants cascaded from the cliffs behind them, and the bathing suits and water were in motion. He saw a sea gull overhead, hovering. It was clean, thick white, like his T-shirts after his mother bleached them. The gull glided, circled, dipping slightly to turn; it never moved its hard, sharp wings, just bore down on the crowd of people and suddenly pulled up to place its feet on a rock ten feet away. He look just like T.C., Buddah thought. Think he bad, showin off.

T.C. had been watching, too. "That's how we is in the set, man, be swoopin, just like that bird, ain't never move false," he said. "We see what we want and we on it, cool." Buddah looked at Gaines. His shoulders were hunched uncomfortably, like loaves of bread against his neck, and he stared out at the water. "What we suppose to do?" he said to Jesse. "Just sit here?"

"I didn't say you guys couldn't move, I just said you can't disappear," Jesse answered. "Do whatever you want. Look at the scenery. Don't drown." No one moved. "Can any of you swim?"

Carroll said, "I used to know. I went to a lake one time." They looked at him. "A goddamn lake ain't no ocean," Gaines said. He looked back at the water.

"Just go touch it," Jesse said. "It won't kill you." He took off his shoes, and his long feet were ashy gray and rough. Walking toward the water, he said, "Come on, I'll save you if you trip and get your hair wet."

Somebody else gotta move first, Buddah thought. Not me. We specks for sure, like them rocks. T.C. turned up his radio; he and Gaines watched girls walk by and stare. Carroll, Montoya and Lopez had gone to the water's edge, where they stood near Jesse. Buddah saw Jesse gesturing to boats far out on the ocean.

"Forget this shit, man, I ain't sittin with no slob red-ragger," T.C. said. "Ain't shit to do here." He stood over Buddah. Gaines was watching the waves; he seemed to have forgotten Buddah.

You ain't bad now, Too Cool. Nobody payin good attention to you like you want. You just a speck. T.C. picked up the radio and pushed Gaines's foot. "Dude down there sellin sodas, homes. Come on, man, fore I have to fuck this red boy up." Buddah waited. Gaines looked at him and said, "When you givin me my money, punk? I ain't playin." He stood up. It ain't your money. Buddah got up and walked forward slightly, waiting until he heard the music leave.

He looked at the tangle of wet black rocks on the left end of the beach, about twenty yards away, the spray flying from behind them. He felt eyes on him, from the blankets and towels. Now I'm botherin you, cause I ain't movin, I ain't swimmin or nothin. How you know I ain't come to this beach all the time and it's boring?

Three kids made a sand castle, looking up at him now and then. It was plain and round, and the walls sagged because the sand was too wet, too close to the waves. See, I woulda had that castle sharp. Have me some shells line up on the outside, have a whole fence made outta shells. Jesse and the others walked back to the blankets. "Where's Gaines and T.C.?" Jesse said. Buddah lifted his chin toward the soda seller. "Don't get too happy about bein here, man," Jesse said impatiently. "You could be sweatin back at the Jude's."

"I'm goin over here," Buddah said.

Jesse raised his eyebrows. "He says. Don't go past the rocks."

When he made it to the first rock, it was dry and grayish; he ran his hand over the hard warmth. Tiny broken shells were jammed inside the rock's holes. Buddah walked toward the wet, glistening black closer to the ocean. He stood on the edge of the wet sand, feeling his feet sink, and saw the smallest waves, the tiny push of water just at the edge, after the wave had washed up on the beach and before the water pulled back. The dying waves lined the sand with circlets of bright white. He walked forward and smeared the lines with his shoe.

The tall square rock in front of him had a smooth side, from which a fat pale boy climbed down. Buddah stopped, turning away from the boy's staring face. When he had passed, Buddah walked to the wet part and sat on one of the low, flat rocks. From far away, it had looked deep black, but he saw that it was only slightly wet. Green feathery plants hung near the bottom, and he was surprised at the shells and animals clinging to the top. The shells clamped down tightly when he touched them. Lockin up, like you a house. But I could get you if you didn't stay inside.

I could get some a these shells, like them big pretty ones. I go out on them rocks and people only see black, not me. The rocks led to a long formation—a pier, almost, out into the water. Buddah pulled himself up the face of the first rock; at the top, white foam spilled over the end. Small pools of water, still as plastic, were everywhere around him as he walked, picking his way past clumps of seaweed, until he found a dry spot to sit on.

I'm gone. Can't nobody see nothin. He felt his skin warm to the rock. Snails and long insects that looked like roaches dotted the rock. Buddah saw a small snail near his hand; its shell was dull and dry, ashy like Jesse's feet. He touched it with his finger and it didn't move or tighten down like the round shells. He must be dyin, too dry. Must of got left here when the water dried up from one a his holes. A pool of water nearby was empty. He pulled at the snail lightly, wincing at the sucking resistance. Let go. You know you can't be out here all dry. It's some water for you right here. He turned the shell up to look at it; the rim was pink, and a blank, hard eye covered the snail inside. You can open up, let me check you out. But you probably ugly like any other snail.

He dropped the shell into the shallow pool and it was suddenly vivid under the water—the pale dull purple darkened to green, and brighter markings showed in a spiral pattern. The snail came out after a second and rocked its shell. Buddah pulled it from the water. You done lived dry that long. I'ma take you back, get some salt from the kitchen, make you some good water like you need. He waited for the snail to right itself in his palm, but it stayed inside. Cool, stay locked till we get back. Gently, he pushed the shell into his jeans pocket.

The darkness of the rocks made him secure. He turned around slowly, squinting until he could see Jesse and the others. They were drinking sodas. Carroll stood with his feet in the water, arms folded, watching the boats.

Buddah walked farther down the rocks. He sat again near the largest pool of water; whole and broken shells and round, smooth stones waited on the bottom, their colors clear and glossy like red beans soaking in a bowl.

"Slob, man, you been out there playin with yourself?" Gaines said when Buddah approached.

"Shut up, Gaines. That's why we gotta go, cause you guys get bored and talk too much shit," Jesse said. He turned to Buddah. "I was hoping you would see us packin up, Smith."

Jesse started up the beach, talking to Carroll. T.C. and Gaines waited to walk behind Buddah. He felt the shells in his pockets, hard weight against his thighs like money. "You lettin us get behind you, slob, so watch out," Gaines whispered. "You all alone."

Buddah let his head fall back a little so that he looked up the sandy trail. I got something from here. Y'all could be lyin bout bein here, but not me. He felt himself out on the rock, in the spray, listening to the power of the waves, and Gaines's and T.C.'s voices were like bird cries, far away. "Why you look at the water? You can't hide in no water. I'm tired of waitin for my money, pussy."

Buddah fingered the sharpest of the shells and smiled with his head turned toward the cliff.

It was almost ten o'clock, lights out. The noises circled around the courtyard and flew up to his room; through the window screen, Buddah could hear the older boys in the next building shouting something to their counselor and Gaines and T.C. talking out on the balcony, the radio still playing from their doorway. Jesse would come by in a few minutes and make sure they all went into their rooms. Buddah listened in the dark.

"Inside, guys. If you didn't run your mouths so much today, I was thinking of takin you to the Stallone flick next weekend."

"What flick?" T.C. said.

"*First Blood*," Jesse answered.

"Shit, man, why you gotta say that word in my *presence* and shit," T.C. said. Buddah imagined his head jerking violently. "*First Cuzz*, I told you. You disrespectin me."

"You see, T.C.? I'm so tired of that shit. It ain't the real world. You got table clean-up all week."

"Man, Jesse, you the one don't know. You could die for that shit."

"Inside, punks."

Jesse stopped at Montoya's door, and then Buddah heard the feet slide to his. Jesse was wearing house shoes; he'd be going to bed now, and the night man would watch St. Jude's.

Light flashed in the doorway. Buddah sat motionless, but Jesse didn't leave. He walked to the trunk suddenly, where the white paper was brightly lit. He see the pipe, Buddah thought, and pushed hard with his feet on the floor. "Bounty Hunters, shit," Jesse said. "What bounty did you get? Nothin valuable to you, just shit to sell and all this red-rag crap. Soon as you start talkin, you'll probably bore me with all that shit, too." He waited, and then closed the door.

Uh uh, cause I ain't workin no job for the blue, like T.C. and them. But now Jesse got them mad, and they probably come. Buddah got the shells out, arranging them in lines, in fences. He leaned forward and touched the cool pipe on the floor. I could wait and wait, and then what? He went to the sink, where the snail was in the soap dish, and pushed at the tightly-closed shell. You waitin, too, for me to leave you alone. But you could wait forever.

The night man's hard shoes cracked the grit on the balcony when he opened the doors every hour in the beginning. Buddah knew he would quit checking after he heard no noise; he would sit in the room downstairs and watch TV. Buddah waited until the moonlight shifted in the window. He sat, still listening, until the brightest part had gone over the roof. He took off his shirt and opened his door.

His bare feet pressed into the sharp sand. He imagined himself on the black rocks, invisible as he pressed close to the stucco wall. T.C. and Gaines were breathing hard and long, he could hear through their screen. The doorknob turned easily, since it was turned so many times every day and night. Buddah stood in the close air by the wall and listened to them breathe. He had stood by his mother every time, hearing her throat vibrate, before he went out to meet Ellis and the rest of them. Buddah moved away from the wall. The cassettes were on top of T.C.'s trunk, in neat stacks. Buddah lifted off the top four from the closest stack and held them tightly together so they wouldn't click. He pulled the door slowly, straight toward him, and turned the knob. On the balcony, he stood for a moment, looking down the dark tunnel of the overhanging roof to the edge of the stairway and then the flat land past the fence that was exposed, lit silver as flashbulbs by the moonlight coming from behind the buildings, from behind his back.

POINTS TO CONSIDER ABOUT "BUDDAH"

1. What literary technique is Straight using when she has the protagonist, Buddah, think to himself, "We specks for sure . . ." toward the end of the story? How does this "showing" technique contribute to the characterization of the story's protagonist, and to the theme of the story? If you have any knowledge about Buddhism, how does this statement suggest and/or reflect elements of Buddhist philosophy?

2. The author uses a number of similes and metaphors in the story, as in the passage, "The sound of electric drums, sharp as gunfire . . ." How does this simile work to "show" us the protagonist's situation and frame of mind? Find other examples of similes and metaphors in the story, and discuss the ways in which they work together to describe characters and settings, and to create a mood for the story.

3. There are passages in "Buddah" that some ethnic groups and/or women might find offensive. Cite several examples of such passages and discuss the reasons why Straight included this kind of language in the story. Do you feel that these reasons justify the author's use of potentially offensive language? Why . . . or why not?

4. Discuss the scene in which Buddah puts the snail in his pocket. In what ways does Buddah's thinking about the snail—and his treatment of that living creature—work metaphorically to suggest the condition of the human characters in the story?

5. Describe the style of Straight's story. In what ways does Buddah's way of speaking contribute to his characterization? In what ways do imagery and figures of speech help develop the story's central thematic message, as summed up at the end of the story: "... you could wait forever"?

✖ WRITING ACTIVITIES: WAYS OF SHOWING

1. Describe your most recent meal in so much detail that your piece borders on parody. Make sure that your description includes images that appeal to all the senses. You may structure this piece as a simple description—kind of the fictional equivalent of the painter's still-life, if you will—or as a narrative, in which you have a central character interacting with the food. In either case, the reader should end up having a visceral reaction—either positive or negative—to the meal described.

2. Go somewhere in the world where you can sit with your eyes closed without being mugged—the beach, a crowded cafeteria, a mountain stream, a city bus or bus stop, a park. Bring the mandatory yellow legal pad and a pen. Close your eyes and record every sound that you hear, in order. Don't worry about awful penmanship—you'll be able to decipher it well enough later.

   Leave your sound-source location, go to your special writing space, and transcribe what you wrote down, so that you have a list that looks something like this:

   car engine gearing down
   low frequency city hum
   no sound for like two seconds
   kid shout fragments—hey watch this ... my shoe ... hey ... no I don't want to
   bus roar like wounded buffalo?
   passersby talk—this is the end ... beautiful ... what did that guy ask you ... for money I think ... got to move away
   car passing by
   always some noise

   Now, write a two-page narrative which fleshes out your sound images by adding more descriptive detail—some remembered, some imagined—some characters, dialogue, and other imagined sense images as well.

3. Look through a pile of magazines and find a photograph of a setting with which you are unfamiliar—in an advertisement, in a travel article, in a news piece, whatever. Write a three-page description of the place, that includes the following:
   • at least three images that appeal to the reader's sense of sight;
   • at least two images that appeal to the reader's sense of sound;
   • two images that appeal to the reader's sense of smell;
   • at least one image that appeals to the reader's sense of touch;
   • one image that appeals to the reader's sense of taste;
   • at least two metaphors;
   • one instance of personification.

   Feel free to include characters in your description, but try initially to keep the feelings of the narrator out of your description—have it be as dispassionately objective as possible. For a variation on this exercise, however, you can write the same description from the point of view of a narrator who's experiencing an intense emotion: a recent death of a beloved house pet; a satisfying sexual encounter the night before; terror at just having been diagnosed with a serious illness (the latter variation is based on a famous mood-influenced description exercise by John Gardner).

7

Perfection and Print

You should now have some draft material to start revising. If you don't, take a few minutes to write a novel and then come back to this chapter. I'll wait . . .

Nice going. It's possible that you have created, on the first try, a piece of fiction that needs no touching-up. It's perfect, with stylistic congruence throughout, a lucid narrative structure, an admirable spareness of words, balance between speech and thought, and no glaring gaffes of grammar or diction. More likely, though, your story is an example of what Anne Lamott, in her *Bird by Bird,* calls a "shitty first draft." This is Lamott's way of not putting pressure on herself during the initial drafting stage. If you expect your first draft of a story to be less than perfect, then you can disengage the self-critical faculty that causes writer's block. She adds,

> I know some very great writers, writers you love who write beautifully and have made a great deal of money, and not *one* of them sits down routinely feeling wildly enthusiastic and confident. Not one of them writes elegant first drafts. All right, one of them does, but we do not like her very much.

So, unless you're Lamott's friend whom everybody hates, you now have some imperfect work in hand. You're ready to engage in the process of *revision,* by which you turn literary poop into a tasty chocolate pudding.

In putting forth these suggestions for revision, I make the assumption that you're writing for other people. But maybe you're not. If, after reading the first chapter of *The Graceful Lie,* you decided your goal in writing is to have a healthy creative outlet for your feelings and perceptions, then your first draft will also be your final draft, and you're done with this chapter. Skip ahead to Part II of *The Graceful Lie,* and see if any of the fictional sub-genres covered in that portion of the book appeal to you.

If you want other people to read your fiction, though, you might read through the following list of elements for revision, and decide which might apply to the draft material you've produced. The goal of revision is to put forth as polished a final draft as possible, to give it the best chance of being received warmly by readers.

THE SIX C'S (OR IS IT SEVEN?) OF EFFECTIVE REVISION

When I started teaching revision to students, all the individual elements of the rewriting process turned out to start with the letter C. I didn't plan this as a clever *mnemonic* (memory-assisting) device, and frankly I find it just a tad cutesy. Nevertheless, if that happy coincidence helps you to remember the major elements of revision, then use the mnemonic by all means. The first of these elements, *consistency,* refers to a regularity of style that your stories will ideally exhibit. If you started out having your narrator talk like Bertie Wooster in the P. G. Wodehouse "Jeeves" series of aristocratic British comedies—"I turned to Aunt Agatha, whose demeanor was rather like that of one who, picking daisies on the railway, has just caught the down express in the small of the back"—you don't want him to begin talking like the protagonist of an Elmore Leonard *noir* mystery—"Chilly outside. Chili inside. It's a regular fuckin' chili-fest. Hey, waiter—give Mr. Chili Pepper a big fuckin' bowl of chili!"—halfway through the story.

While the Wodehouse/Leonard inconsistency is, of course, an extreme example posited for slight comic effect, writers will often—especially in longer works of fiction—veer by small degrees from the pattern of rhythm, diction, and tone they've established for a story. For instance, I'm one of those Books on Tape commuters. Having endless demands placed on me by my teaching job, writing deadlines, watching *Seinfeld* reruns and Laker games on TV, I have little time to read fiction, which is one of my great joys in life. Therefore I rent unabridged novels and listen to them in the car while I drive. Because the average So-Cal spends approximately fifty hours per week in the car, that means I listen to a lot of recorded fiction—anything from Sue Grafton mysteries to Joseph Conrad's *Heart of Darkness.* It often happens that the style of whatever author I'm listening to influences my own writing style, and I unconsciously insert certain wrinkles of word choice and rhythm. On one page, I'll have a passage of dialogue that sounds suspiciously like Grafton's wisecracking Kinsey Millhone, and several chapters later, I'll have an existential musing on life's dark mysteries, in the somber tone of Conrad.

Oh, the horror! During the consistency phase of my revision process, I may therefore have to decide just what voice I want to establish throughout, and then revise to maintain it. In writing first drafts of shorter pieces, you may find similar kinds of stylistic inconsistencies in your own fiction when you start paying attention to these issues. To revise for consistency, you need to read over your entire draft, decide what the predominant style of the story is (or what you want it to be), modify the tone and atmosphere in certain scenes where they subvert your intended effect, and oftentimes change sentence lengths to conform to the style you want. With practice you'll come to recognize those areas where you're prone to inconsistency, and you'll re-read your draft material with an eye trained on those areas.

Working toward consistency is a somewhat mechanical task, but not an unpleasant one—much like smoothing a piece of maple furniture with fine-grit paper, after several previous sessions of painstaking joinery. To extend the example of my own revision process a bit further . . . besides eliminating unintended resonances from other authors I'm currently reading, my revising for stylistic consistency usually includes chopping up some of my longer sentences to make shorter ones. Rambling—writing sentences that stream over the page like industrious ants seeking out a discarded Tootsie Roll—comes as naturally to me as wheezing. But readers like a short sentence once in a while. They appreciate *conciseness*—another of the core elements of revision. Therefore, I spend much time during the revision phase trying to make my sentences shorter, so that they'll conform to the less digressive style I try to maintain throughout. Working toward conciseness involves aggressively gouging out the "dead wood" that inhabits even the best of first drafts. It may mean working primarily at the sentence level, as in the case of my naturally windy style. Additionally, it may require focusing on specific scenes in your story line and making sure that the plot emerges clearly from details of exposition, and that it proceeds logically. The latter procedure sometimes requires deleting happy turns of phrase: passages you hate to remove, because they contain the most beautiful image or the cleverest metaphor you ever wrote.

Painful as removing inspired draft material may be, you have to do it sometimes, for the sake of your story's *coherence*—another of the rewriting C's. Coherence means making sure that your story has a central narrative thread, and that the supporting elements of the story—characterization, description, and so on, the major topics of this book's middle chapters—serve to advance the plot. In the process of revision, you should retain only those descriptions that count. Fiction Rule #10 is this: If details don't advance the story, hack 'em even if it hurts. I salve this wound somewhat successfully by creating on my computer's hard drive a file of all the wonderful sentences I've cut from my work. Occasionally, late at night, I'll go into my "Brilliant Garbage" directory (as I call it) and turn one of the excised phrases into a flash fiction or a poem. Sometimes I never use the deleted material again, but I still take comfort in knowing it's there—the pack rat in me, I guess. Coherence doesn't involve only deleting material, either. You may run across patches where characterization is sketchy, local atmosphere is not atmospheric enough, or a set-up scene is missing from a piece's plot development. Then you'll have to go back and develop those points, following the guidelines presented in previous chapters of this book.

The revision process is a bit like a tightwire act. You shoot for conciseness, but at the same time you want a certain sophistication, a sense of *charm* and *consequence* that comes about through the use of figurative language, a clear thematic direction, a sense of subtlety, and/or an elegance of style. National Book Award winner Mary Lee Settle, author of numerous acclaimed novels including the *Beulah Quintet*, comments on the joy of revising rough drafts for these qualities:

> When it's out there, apart from me, a thing even roughly formed, I can use my intelligence. I can ask it questions. Is this true? Is this what I mean? Is there too much weight? Too much nervous explanation? Does it balance? And that wonderful slang question—does it fly? For me that means the lightness and connection I seek, all the delicacy and the charm—as in the quality between quarks. Then everything that I've learned, that doesn't consciously help me in the first draft, works for me—it's craft, and it's wonderful, I can do that for hours at a time.

It's hard to teach students how to cultivate "the quality between quarks"—the quantum order that makes a work resonate with the ring of truth and beauty. The key term in Settle's description, I think, is "balance." In the revision stage, work toward making all the previously discussed fictional elements contribute equally, with no single one of the elements crowding the others so that it adds up to "too much weight." You should certainly feel free to write an experimental novel that's all dialogue or a single two-hundred-page-long sentence in the second-person plural. However, you should also be aware that, even in those extreme cases, it would be a good idea to punch up the other narrative elements, for the sake of balance. If you don't, then expect a small, select readership for your story . . . like your mother and your best friend.

Ideally, your prose will convey to readers that it means something: to yourself certainly, and ideally to them as well. You can achieve this sense of consequence by making sure you've applied yourself to creating insightful, well-rounded presentations of characters, painterly rendering of descriptive detail, and carefully layered thematic messages: the meat of previous chapters in *The Graceful Lie*. The amount of care you take in turning out a well-crafted story will relate itself to readers, just as dinner guests will appreciate the work that went into a fine meal—say, a salad of mixed baby field greens, a wild mushroom soup and an artichoke ragout with Thai lemon *jus*—more than a baloney sandwich followed by a Hostess Ding-Dong for dessert. This does not imply that your work has to be ponderous, though. An absurdist satire in the mold of Joseph Heller's *Catch-22*, a light, bright, and sparkling Jane Austen novel, or a well-plotted police procedural may impart as strong a sense of consequence to the reader as a philosophical novel such as Sartre's *Nausea*. The goal here is to give the reader a sense of your commitment to the subject, the characters, the locales you portray.

Care in the *rhythm* of one's prose also determines whether a fictional piece will soar in the manner that Settle suggests. Part of a fictional piece's "charm" derives from the way the prose lines sound when read aloud (or read aloud to yourself, silently). The poetic term *scansion* refers to the process of determining the pattern of accented syllables in a line of poetry. Prose writers would do well to scan their rough drafts for felicity of rhythm as well. Robert Louis Stevenson, who wrote the classic *Treasure Island*, says of this requirement of prose,

> In all ideal and material points, literature, being a representative art, must look for analogies to painting and the like; but in what is technical and executive, being a temporal art, it must seek for them in music. Each phrase of each sentence, like an air or a recitative in music, should be so artfully compounded out of long and short, out of accented and unaccented, as to gratify the sensual ear. And of this the ear is the sole judge.

Whether intentionally or unintentionally, prose writers, like poets, create groups of words that have certain rhythmic patterns. The beginning writer, often not attuned to this issue, may create phrasing patterns that are repetitive or clunky. If you read your first draft out loud to yourself, you will surely identify some awkward, halting, tongue-twisting rhythmic patterns, without having to learn all the rules of poetic scansion. You'll find yourself stumbling over certain phrasings, or becoming tongue-tied when reading others, or running out of breath before the end of a single prepositional phrase. These sentences might want some rewriting, to make them sound more musical, as Stevenson advises.

Such rhythmic clunkiness sometimes results from a preponderance of simple, subject-verb sentences. While you want to hold conciseness in a corner of your mind as a stylistic goal, there will also be instances in which you'll actually need longer sentences, to avoid repeating the same rhythmic pattern over and over. Certain writers, such as Hemingway, have reputations for writing nothing but short sentences. In reality, though, if you examine the rhythm of a writer like Hemingway, you'll discover an admirably concise sentence structure that's broken up by the occasional longer sentence. You may likewise want to develop a style that features more rhythmic variety: some long, complex and compound sentences interspersed with some shorter, more direct subject-verb declarative sentences.

For beginning writers, accustomed to writing mainly simple sentences, a technique called *sentence combining* may be especially useful during revision. Sentence combining is a skill that composition instructors invented to circumvent the amateurish feel of overly choppy and halting short sentences, and to create sentences that may highlight the relationship between several subideas better than a string of short sentences can. Write a short sentence for punch. Maybe even a fragment for emphasis. Then, for the sake of a more sophisticated style, write a longer sentence—maybe one that has an *appositive phrase* (a group of words that explains a noun that precedes it) set off by commas or dashes—while containing a participial phrase (a group of words whose verb ends in "ing," such as "containing") as well. Longer sentences are especially apt for "showing" descriptive passages, as discussed previously. For those of you who may identify your prose as too choppy and simplistic, you will definitely want to vary the rhythm of your prose, for a more consistently charming style.

Another area for consideration during the revision process is called *continuity*. Every plotted story has at least one conceptual thread—a chronological sequence of events that, even if the author doesn't present them in linear order, nevertheless follow one from the next. *Continuity error*, a phrase borrowed from the world of film, occurs when events or details of a particular scene do not follow logically from information imparted in previous scenes. In the recent movie blockbuster *Independence Day*, for example, the President of the United States descends a staircase, a newspaper in hand. The viewer sees a weather map on the back page of the paper, where a color-coded temperature chart shows highs in the near-freezing range, extending into the southern states. Because it's already been established that the action of the movie is taking place on or around the fourth of July, this is clearly a continuity error—especially when the subsequent scene shows the Jeff Goldblum character and his father playing chess, and a nearby radio broadcast proclaims that the temperature in New York is ninety-five degrees!

This type of continuity error is not unusual for big-budget movies, in which many people—director, screenwriter, set designer, costume designer, editor, and so on—may have a hand in the final product. Even though the studios hire editors whose sole job it is to catch these kinds of embarrassing blunders, continuity errors invariably find their way into films, and movie-trivia freaks exalt in sharing these mistakes with one another. With fiction, where only one person is usually responsible for the final artifact, continuity errors occur less frequently, but they do crop up . . . especially in longer pieces. In my first novel, I had a Ford Ranchero pickup truck that magically transformed itself into a VW Rabbit two chapters later, and that error made it all the way through galleys, until an enterprising proofreader caught it before the book went to press. Funny though they may be, continuity errors interfere with the clear progress of narrative development. The difficulty in spotting these kinds of mistakes is that, after reading your own draft material umpteen times, you become desensitized to it. For that reason, continuity errors, along with typos, misspellings and so on, may elude your scrutiny. There are two solutions to this problem. Either have somebody else read your draft—ideally, somebody who cares enough about you (or the money you give them) to read the material with extreme care—or set your draft aside for several weeks or more (really!), so that you return to it with "fresh eyes" that will spot these kinds of mistakes.

And speaking of typos and all things mechanical: The last of the areas for revision is called *correctness*—the final polishing process during which you check for flaws in spelling and grammar, along with the most basic stylistic problems. Once you have removed superfluous description, once you have reordered your plot material to follow a logical sequence, once you've read your material out loud and modified your rhythmic structure . . . then you can begin to proofread. As mentioned earlier, there's no federal statute that says your writing must feature perfect grammar and spelling. You may, for example, have your narrator use street slang and tortured orthography, as in this passage from Irvine Welsh's novel *Trainspotting*, from which the movie was made:

> There were a group a young guys in shell-suits n bomber jaykits whae'd been standin thair longer than us.

Fiction Rule #12 goes: If you're going to break the rules, break them consciously and with clear purpose. In this one short sentence, Welsh has incorrect verb number ("There were a group . . . "), a dangling modifier (". . . jackets who'd been standing . . ."), a faulty objective pronoun (the "us" at the end should be the subjective "we"), and numerous spelling mistakes. Welsh chooses to flaunt the conventions of written English here because it heightens the sense of atmosphere and characterization—the bad spelling, grammar, and dialect tell us much about the speaker and the locale—and because it's natural. Since this is the way urban Scottish punks verbalize, it gives the novel that elusive quality of verisimilitude.

However, if there's no good reason to break the rules, then you might as well follow them and proofread for them as you near the end of the revision process. Some people—especially those who don't consider themselves natural stylisticians or grammarians—may find the proofreading process forbidding. For those people, I suggest checking one group of errors at a time. Begin with stylistic issues first. Eliminate long, freight-train-like strings of prepositional phrases. Cut out redundant phrases and phrases that are redundant. Check your dictionary to make sure your diction is correct throughout, that your words have the correct shadings of meaning.

Eliminate unnecessary qualifiers such as "quite" and "very," which can be quite boring when overused. Likewise, it is suggested that you avoid overuse of passive verb constructions ("The sentence was revised by the editor") when an active construction ("The editor revised the sentence") will give the sentence more punch. Don't indulge in a proliferation of fifty-cent words when a nice short word ("glut" instead of "proliferation," for instance?) will serve just as well, or better.

Having proofread for stylistics, check last for grammar, spelling, typos. If you're a computer user, the latter two you can inspect with the spell-checker that usually comes bundled with word processing software. This isn't a grammar book, so I can't cover each grammatical issue or elaborate on each stylistic point mentioned in the previous paragraph, but there are lots of books on mechanics out on the market, and they work! While all this word-level stuff may seem daunting, it's actually the easiest part of the revision process, because it's a relatively mechanical procedure, like learning to cook an artichoke ragout or program your VCR (actually, the latter is much more difficult than learning the basics of grammar). Besides, if you write a great story and sell it to a major publishing house, they will hire a team of enterprising junior editors to clean up your mechanics for you . . . which transitions us nicely into the last major topic area of *The Graceful Lie*: publication.

PUBLISHING IN THE NEW MILLENNIUM

Recently, I've heard a story circulating in publishing/editorial circles. It involves award-winning (1954 Somerset Maugham Award, 1976 French Prix Medicis for Foreigners for The Golden Notebook, 1982 Austrian State Prize for European Literature, 1985 W. H. Smith Literary Award, 1987 Premio Internazionale Mondello, 1995 Los Angeles Times Book Prize) novelist Doris Lessing, who, as the story goes, sent the manuscript of her most recent book to her publisher under a fake name, only to receive a curt rejection slip in reply.

Whether the story is true or apocryphal is not important. Just the fact that people have been circulating this urban editorial myth indicates an underlying truth that everybody in the business knows: It's hard for unknowns (such as you, dear reader) to get stuff published . . . and it's getting harder all the time. Publishing houses are attuned more than ever to the "bottom line" of sales projections and are therefore less likely to take a chance on an unknown author than they were in previous decades. Not so long ago—say, thirty years—publishers were willing to take on an author who demonstrated some literary talent, and to nurse that individual through several books that didn't make money, in hopes that the author would gradually develop a reputation and a readership. Nowadays, publishers can't afford those initial losses, in many cases because they have to report to the multinational conglomerates who have subsumed the major houses. Publishers have therefore, by necessity, set up roadblocks to new writers, signing contracts with those most likely to be financially successful out of the gate.

Lessing's story illustrates the obstacles built into the accepted procedures of the publishing world. If the first-time author sends a manuscript *over the transom* (directly to a publishing house) or to a literary agency, that piece of fiction has to pass through numerous levels of readership before it gets the golden O.K. At any one of those levels, said manuscript might run afoul of a reader who had a fight with his domestic partner, or who doesn't like the way the author uses the word "amble" on page three. Then comes the dreaded rejection slip. Numerous literary "stars" have suffered through rocky beginnings and accumulated rejections before getting their big breaks. Mary Lee Settle reports that her first book was sent

> ... to literally every major publisher in New York and London, and refused by all of them. While that was going on, I wrote a second novel, *The Love Eaters*. While that too was being refused all over the place, I began to research the first draft of *O Beulah Land*. . . . Finally, after ten years of waiting, and after I had already begun what was to become *The Beulah Quintet*, I had a book accepted.

Although ten years sounds like an impossibly long time to wait for recognition, such stories are not uncommon. The prime directive for you to keep in mind, as you venture into the publishing world, is: Be patient. Be very patient. And while you're being patient, remind yourself that the writing process is itself a joy to be cultivated, regardless of whether your work finds its way into print.

There are, of course, exceptions to the laboring-in-anonymity-for-years scenario. Some writers—on the strength of superb prose that shines through the slush, and/or sheer good luck—get recognized the first time out. John Irving, author of much acclaimed fiction including *The World According to Garp,* says,

> I was lucky from the start. Tom Williams sent a couple of my undergraduate short stories to his agent, Mavis McIntosh. She sold one, "A Winter Branch," to *Redbook* for $1,000 and so I had an agent. She retired less than a year later and passed me along to Peter Mason, who's been my agent ever since.

This is everybody's publishing fantasy. You're twenty years old, as Irving was in the above anecdote, and have written some stories you think are pretty good. You show them to your cousin who knows somebody who goes out with the sister of the agency intern at Transglobal Artistic Management, who likes your stories and raves to the boss, Barbzi Civici, who sends them out to one of her "heavy hitter" publishing contacts. You get a contract accompanied by a big paycheck, and your career is off and running. While things like this do happen sometimes, such happy stories are not the norm. Given that sobering reality, the rest of this chapter is devoted to making it as likely as possible for you to get your work into print . . . ideally, in less than ten years.

OUT OF THE SLUSH: SELLING YOUR NOVEL

Most of you will write short stories before you attempt a novel. Nevertheless, I will begin this section on publication by discussing methods for submitting book-length fiction, because in many cases, the method for submitting short stories is exactly the same. Having finished discussing the specific procedures for novel publication, I'll go on to address short stories separately, pointing out areas in which short fiction submission differs from the procedures used for getting novels into print.

When you've completed a manuscript, you can do one of three things. First, you can decide that your book has some serious flaws and is not ready to send out yet. In that case, you shelve it for future revision. What could be simpler? I have three shelved book-length manuscripts, and someday I may actually get around to fixing them and sending them out (the one about the hermaphroditic spanking-fetishist sex androids with speech impediments I will probably keep permanently shelved).

If you believe your book is worthy of submission, then you can mail it directly to a publishing house or find an agent who will do the submitting for you. To help you make this decision, I suggest the following: If your novel falls squarely into one of the main genres of trade fiction—mystery, romance, science fiction, young adult fiction, and so on (the highly marketable kinds of fiction that comprise the second half of this book)—then find an agent. Agents have direct, personal access to editors at major publishing houses, so they can save your manuscript from becoming buried in the *slush pile:* the hundreds of unsolicited manuscripts that publishers receive from would-be-published authors every month. While literary agents sometimes get stereotyped as venal, tasteless, and pushy, I've met agents who were not tasteless at all. There are lots of smart, caring, enterprising agents who will take on a client because they believe in the merit of his/her prose, and who will "go to bat" for their clients in ways that the average, unconnected author, living in Dubuque and not New York, simply cannot.

To find an agent, you need a list of people to whom you will send query letters. In your local library or bookstore you will find numerous reference volumes that list the major literary agencies in the country, along with pertinent data: education, career history, subjects/categories most enthusiastic about agenting, reading-fee policy, representative titles sold, and more. As you make your "A-list" of agents to whom to submit your work, pay special attention to the genres of fiction in which the agent specializes, and the kinds of titles the agent has recently sold. If you've followed Sue Grafton's advice in Chapter 12 of *The Graceful Lie* and written a well-plotted detective thriller, don't send your book to an agent who says he loves to represent romance fiction. If you've written a futuristic novel using the suggestions of Harlan Ellison and John Landsberg in Chapter 11 of this book, don't send your manuscript to an agent who reports never having sold a science fiction book. Find ten agents who come closest to specializing in the kind of fiction you've written, and send letters to those agents.

A successful query letter should be one to two pages in length, summarize the main points of your book, and provide any relevant information about yourself as well. Submissions editors at major houses read literally thousands of queries a year, so you definitely want to make yours short—that immediately gets the editor on your side!—and error-free. Briefly outline the plot of your story, describe some characteristics that you believe will make it marketable, and perhaps compare it to some successful fiction that is currently on the market. Mention your own credentials also, especially if you have had any significant previous publication. If you haven't published anything before, don't worry about it, and don't spend much letter space trying to sell yourself. Instead, let the description of your story "sell" the piece to your prospective agent.

Eventually, you'll receive some letters back from the agents to whom you sent queries. Some will be form-letter rejection slips with a terse reply: "We feel that we cannot successfully represent your project at this time," or something like that. This leads to Fiction Rule #13, the last one: Don't be disheartened by rejection. While this is almost impossible advice to follow completely (since we're all sensitive people craving acceptance), it's crucial that you develop some psychic mechanisms for coping with the rejection that almost all writers—even the most successful ones—inevitably have, especially early in their careers. Some people build little altars and ritually burn rejection letters when they arrive. I have a friend who whimsically papers her bathroom walls with them. Some vindictive folk hoard their rejection slips, with plans to send the rejecting agents terse letters when those folk become famous writers: "See what a golden opportunity you missed because of your narrow literary paradigms, you vacuous, complacent piece of godforsaken devil-dung." I don't recommend the latter approach. Bitterness—which seems always to accompany the publishing process to some degree—can eat you alive, affect your relationships and your health, and corrupt your writing process. Better to employ some practice—whether it's doing two hours of martial arts or meditating or hiking in the mountains or spending an hour with your favorite psychotherapist—that will get you past the wounds of rejection, so that you can get back to the business at hand: namely, writing stories and enjoying it.

If your project has merit (and if you've followed the prescriptions in the earlier chapters of this book, then it will!), there's a good chance there will be some positive responses in amongst the rejection slips. Maybe you won't get any rejections at all. It happens. When an agent responds positively to a query letter, she typically wants to see a chapter of a manuscript, and occasionally the whole piece. Some authors are reluctant to send copies of their manuscripts out into the world, fearing that an unscrupulous literary type will appropriate their wonderful book idea, leaving the author with two years' worth of grueling composition and revision shot to hell. Such outright theft is extremely rare, but it has been known to occur. What I do to set my mind at ease regarding this concern (some might call it mild paranoia, but I prefer to think of it as healthy precaution) is to seal a copy of my manuscript in a sturdy manila envelope, take it to the post office, and mail it to myself, via registered mail. The post office clerk always gives me a funny look—"You want to mail this to *yourself*? Why don't you just carry it home and save the money?"—but this is recognized by copyright lawyers as the easiest and cheapest way to shelter your work from plagiarism. If you discover that somebody has published your idea or your actual story under his name, you will have that unopened, stamped, signed and dated package as irrefutable proof of your prior authorship. The other way to protect yourself from plagiarism is to send your material to the Library of Congress' Copyright Office, which can be reached by telephone at (202) 707-9100, or by mail at the Library of Congress, Washington, DC 20559. However, registering with the Copyright Office is a more expensive and time-consuming method than mailing your manuscript to yourself . . . and it is often redundant, as your manuscript will be officially registered by your publisher before it comes out.

Having protected yourself in this way, the next question that arises is: Should I submit simultaneously or not? *Simultaneous submission* is a publishing-community term that refers to a process whereby authors send out many copies of their work at the same time, rather than mailing one copy to an agent or editor, and waiting for said agent/editor to respond. The advantages of simultaneous submission are obvious to anybody who's ever taken a basic probability course or played poker for a few hours. As an author, your odds of having your work accepted for publication are much higher if you send out many copies of your work, than if you send out a single copy and wait for a rejection before you send out another copy. This simple logic would seem to suggest that you should always submit simultaneously. Unfortunately, many agents and publishing houses have policies strictly forbidding simultaneous submission, because of the sheer volume of manuscripts they would have to sift through if every author in the world was simultaneously submitting to every potential publisher or agent . . . and because exclusivity prevents agent competition and costly bidding wars between publishing houses.

The simultaneous submission issue can present itself as a moral dilemma to authors who want to play by the rules of the publishing game, but who also want to see their work published in their lifetimes. Many agents insist on having the exclusive right to pass judgment on a story's potential marketability before anybody else has a chance to see it. Since it may take several weeks—and in some cases more than a month—for a given agent to read and respond to submitted work, exclusive submission can be a painfully slow process. If you can't stand the excruciatingly long wait occasioned by single submission, you have a couple of options. You may send your work simultaneously to those agents whose letters say nothing about exclusive reading rights, in which case you'll raise the odds of acceptance by having several people read your work instead of just one. Or, on a slightly less ethical tack, you may waggle a mocking finger or some other mocking appendage in the face of accepted procedure and submit simultaneously, despite the stern injunctions of the publishing community. While I can't publicly advocate such subversiveness (I don't want to come home and find my housecat boiled by an agency goon), there is certainly ample precedent for this behavior, and it's even being encouraged in some reputable publications.

Once you have an agent, you can sit back and let her do the work of getting your manuscript into print, contacting publishers, sending out copies, negotiating advances, handling contracts. Allowing someone—a professional—to do all those onerous chores for you is extremely relaxing and gives you more time to write. For that reason, I suggest that you try to secure an agent, if your project seems obviously marketable. However, if your manuscript ends up being experimental, quirky, densely imagistic or otherwise falls between the cracks of the conventional genres of trade fiction, you may decide that no agent will recognize its fiscal potential, and that you will be wasting your time querying agents. In that case, you still have the option of submitting your work over the transom. Write a query letter similar to the one described above, look through *The Writer's Market* or a similar volume that lists all the publishers in the country, and mail your story off to the publisher (or publishers, if you choose the simultaneous submission route) of your choice.

As you do your publishing research in *The Writer's Market* or a similar book, you'll notice that some houses refuse to receive unsolicited manuscripts. Don't bother sending these editors your fiction. They're serious about not reading unsolicited or unagented work. Fortunately, you will also find plenty of houses—especially the reputable smaller and medium-sized presses—that welcome unsolicited submissions. Be aware, however, that editors at publishing houses are busy people. They may have to edit contracted book projects, negotiate permissions (e.g., how much to pay the guest editors in the second-half of *The Graceful Lie*), develop budget projections, travel to sales meetings, work with book distributors, hire typographers, choose reliable but reasonably priced production services, travel to the annual meeting of the American Booksellers Association, check that work has been satisfactorily completed by contract employees, write promotions copy, help design cover art, shepherd the copyediting and proofreading processes, or check galley proofs. Sheesh! For this reason, editors often assign a relatively low priority to unsolicited work, which may sit for months in their slush pile until somebody gets around to reading it.

Your goal during this phase is to cultivate patience as described above. Editors do eventually get around to reading the material they receive over the transom, but it can take many months. If you want to goose the process a bit, you may send a reminder letter: "Hi, I sent you the manuscript of my novel, *Death Takes a Steam Bath*, on November 9, 1997, and I haven't heard from you since. I was just wondering what you thought about it," or something innocuous like that. To be honest, I'm not sure that such letters have any effect, other than possibly annoying the beleaguered editors or giving them a laugh. My advice is simply to wait . . . and wait . . . and wait.

The good news is that unsolicited and unagented novels do sell. I sent *Doctor Syntax* simultaneously to several publishing houses (I was lucky to have a friend with access to a high-speed Xerox machine in the basement of a local medical facility, which defrayed my photocopying costs), and I received offers on it within two months. This is not an isolated case, because most publishing houses regard unagented prose as a valuable source of saleable material. A recent *Writer's Digest* article reports that Gary Goldstein, an editor at Pocket Books,

> unearthed *Thunder in the Valley*, a first novel by Jim Woolard, in the slush pile at Berkeley four years ago. It went on to win two Golden Spur awards from the Western Writers of America. . . . Before leaving Berkeley, [Goldstein] published *Going Postal*, a first novel by Stephan Jaramillo that came to him as an unagented proposal. "I read the first 30 pages and I thought it was brilliant; a little rough in spots, but it's a first novel," he says. "We signed him for two books."
>
> "I don't even like the expression slush," continues Goldstein. "At Berkeley we regarded them as submissions, even if they came in unagented."

Encouraging words indeed! Despite what you've heard about the major publishing houses being impossible to crack, stories such as these prove that unsolicited manuscripts often find their way to print. Publishers are in the business of finding good work to put out to the public, and they recognize that many promising first authors must resort to sending material over the transom, because of agents' rigorous—and sometimes narrow—standards for taking on new clients. Mary Lee Settle says of agents, "They are not critics, and they are not editors, and their opinions shouldn't be taken too seriously. Remember, they are out to make money, and they want young writers to imitate what has been successful already." Therefore, don't hesitate to send your manuscript directly to publishers if it has been repeatedly rejected by agents. If your project has merit, it will eventually be recognized . . . even if it's "a little rough in spots."

That's the good news. The bad news is that, even when you finally sell your manuscript, you *still* have to be patient. Many unpleasant things can happen between the purchase of your manuscript and its final production. Novelist Cynthia Ozick describes the pre-production wait she had for her book, *Trust:*

> It was a long, hopeless process. I finished it on the day that John Kennedy was assassinated, in November, 1963. Publication wasn't until three years later. Those were three hellish years. . . . At first an option was taken on the novel by [an editor], who procrastinated over a year, and just let the manuscript sit there. . . . The manuscript was finally taken over by his colleague, David Segal, a remarkable editor who . . . sent me a hundred pages with red-pencil marks all over them, and asked for cuts. . . . I had a dilemma: accept the cuts, and be published; refuse and languish forever unpublished. I declined David Segal's cuts. He, amazing man, went ahead and published the novel anyhow.

Life brings joys and hassles, and so does publishing. It just presents you with an especially challenging new set of hassles. Still, one of the great joys in life is seeing one's novel on a bookstore shelf, nestled securely between Walker Percy and Marge Piercy. Viewing your book in print for the first time is sort of like looking in the window of the maternity ward and seeing your newborn snoozing peacefully, swaddled in warm flannel. It's a good feeling, and I hope you have it someday.

FINDING ACCEPTANCE IN MAGAZINES

Meanwhile . . . if you're thinking about submitting short stories rather than novels, many of the procedures are identical. You need to research appropriate journals, make the decision whether to submit simultaneously or not, write a brief but compelling letter to accompany your manuscript, and then wait. I used to think the best way to begin one's career as a published short-fiction writer was to make a list of the most prestigious and high-paying magazines, such as *Harper's, Atlantic, New Yorker,* and then submit material to them. If all the magazines on that list rejected the piece, then I would send the manuscript out to a "B list" of well-respected literary magazines that paid less for a piece . . . and so on, down to the humblest (but still respectable) startup literary mags and college journals. Nowadays, however, I think it's a better idea to start out small, build a reputation, and move gradually toward the big-time. Celebrated short story writer Raymond Carver used the latter approach in his own career:

> I sent my stories and poems to the little magazines and once in a while something was accepted, and I was made happy by the acceptance. I had some kind of audience you see, even though I never met any of my audience.

This philosophy makes more sense to me nowadays, because it seems more reinforcing. Instead of having to weather a shitstorm of rejection slips early in your career, you can start with some modest but still very satisfying acceptances and build toward bigger and more notable successes.

Whichever philosophy you adopt—the start-small or the top-down approach—you'll need to compile a list of magazines to whom you will send your material. There are a number of publications that will have done the preliminary legwork for you. Every year or two, the popular and very helpful *Writer's Digest,* for example, puts out a comprehensive list of fiction publishers, whom they rank according to a point system, evaluating pay rates, simultaneous submissions, free sample copies, individualized rejection letters, and so forth. Other magazine indexes, which you can find in bookstores and libraries, list all the journals in the country, with descriptions of the kinds of work they routinely publish. Finally, certain magazines, such as *Poets and Writers,* contain extensive classified listings of magazines actively seeking short story manuscripts.

Choose some journals appropriate to your work and established reputation (or lack thereof) in the business, make copies of your story (or only one copy if you're not submitting simultaneously), attach your cover letter, and put those stories out there. The happy reality of writing and submitting short stories is that there is an almost infinite number of magazines that publish short fiction. If one editor rejects a given piece, there is always another editor eagerly awaiting your story submission. Keep at it, and (unless you revised your horrible first draft into a horrible third draft) you will see your story in print eventually.

Remember, however, that publishing is not necessarily the ultimate aim of writing; the writing itself is. Many students get caught up in the time-consuming and emotionally draining demands of getting their work into print, only to discover that they've lost the joy of the writing process along the way. Even when they have literary success, many writers feel this sense of loss or dissatisfaction. Anne Lamott says in *Bird By Bird*, "Publication is not going to change your life or solve your problems," and she warns that getting your material into print "will not make you more confident or more beautiful, and it will probably not make you any richer." For some writers, certainly, publication is a means to a fabulous living and/or to a concrete sense of personal accomplishment, and if that's your goal, I support you wholeheartedly in pursuing it. If I didn't have that kind of compulsive drive, I would never have gotten to the end of this chapter in *The Grace-ful Lie,* fifty-five thousand words (give or take a few thousand) since I started. But it's essential for all writers, even the most professional, to culti-vate the heart of an *amateur,* in the truest sense of that word: someone who loves the process intrinsically, without expectation of external reward. Shunryu Suzuki-roshi says of zazen meditation,

> For a while you will keep your beginner's mind, but if you continue to practice one, two, three years or more, although you may improve some, you are liable to lose the limitless meaning of original mind.... In the beginner's mind there are many possibilities; in the expert's mind there are few.... This is also the real secret of the arts: always be a beginner.

If you find yourself losing your amateur's heart, your love of writing, go back to the beginning of *The Graceful Lie* and start over, as though you were writing your first diary toward your first character in your first story, and recall the liberation and sense of promise in those graceful initial steps. Then you will be back on the path to the writer's life.

A Conversation with My Father
Grace Paley

My father is eighty-six years old and in bed. His heart, that bloody motor, is equally old and will not do certain jobs any more. It still floods his head with brainy light. But it won't let his legs carry the weight of his body around the house. Despite my metaphors, this muscle failure is not due to his old heart, he says, but to a potassium shortage. Sitting on one pillow, leaning on three, he offers last-minute advice and makes a request.

"I would like you to write a simple story just once more," he says, "the kind de Maupassant wrote, or Chekhov, the kind you used to write. Just recognizable people and then write down what happened to them next."

I say, "Yes, why not? That's possible." I want to please him, though I don't remember writing that way. I *would* like to try to tell such a story, if he means the kind that begins: "There was a woman..." followed by plot, the absolute line between two points which I've always despised. Not for literary reasons, but because it takes all hope away. Everyone, real or invented, deserves the open destiny of life.

Finally I thought of a story that had been happening for a couple of years right across the street. I wrote it down, then read it aloud. "Pa," I said, "How about this? Do you mean something like this?"

> Once in my time there was a woman and she had a son. They lived nicely, in a small apartment in Manhattan. This boy at about fifteen became a junkie, which is not unusual in our neighborhood. In order to maintain her close friendship with him, she became a junkie too. She said it was part of the youth culture, with which she felt very much at home. After a while, for a number of reasons, the boy gave it all up and left the city and his mother in disgust. Hopeless and alone, she grieved. We all visit her.

"O.K., Pa, that's it," I said, "an unadorned and miserable tale."

"But that's not what I mean," my father said. "You misunderstood me on purpose. You know there's a lot more to it. You know that. You left everything out. Turgenev wouldn't do that. Chekhov wouldn't do that. There are in fact Russian writers you never heard of, you don't have an inkling of, as good as anyone, who can write a plain ordinary story, who would not leave out what you have left out. I object not to facts but to people sitting in trees talking senselessly, voices from who knows where . . ."

"Forget that one, Pa, what have I left out now? In this one?"

"Her looks, for instance."

"Oh. Quite handsome, I think. Yes."

"Her hair?"

"Dark, with heavy braids, as though she were a girl or a foreigner."

"What were her parents like, her stock? That she became such a person. It's interesting, you know."

"From out of town. Professional people. The first to be divorced in their county. How's that? Enough?" I asked.

"With you, it's all a joke," he said. "What about the boy's father? Why didn't you mention him? Who was he? Or was the boy born out of wedlock?"

"Yes," I said. "He was born out of wedlock."

"For Godsakes, doesn't anyone in your stories get married? Doesn't anyone have the time to run down to City Hall before they jump into bed?"

"No," I said. "In real life, yes. But in my stories, no."

"Why do you answer me like that?"

"Oh, Pa, this is a simple story about a smart woman who came to N.Y.C. full of interest love trust excitement very up to date, and about her son, what a hard time she had in this world. Married or not, it's of small consequence."

"It is of great consequence," he said.

"O.K.," I said.

"O.K. O.K. yourself," he said, "but listen. I believe you that she's good-looking, but I don't think she was so smart."

"That's true," I said. "Actually that's the trouble with stories. People start out fantastic. You think they're extraordinary, but it turns out as the work goes along, they're just average with a good education. Sometimes the other way around, the person's a kind of dumb innocent, but he outwits you and you can't even think of an ending good enough."

"What do you do then?" he asked. He had been a doctor for a couple of decades and then an artist for a couple of decades and he's still interested in details, craft, technique.

"Well, you just have to let the story lie around till some agreement can be reached between you and the stubborn hero."

"Aren't you talking silly, now?" he asked. "Start again," he said. "It so happens I'm not going out this evening. Tell the story again. See what you can do this time."

"O.K.," I said. "But it's not a five-minute job." Second attempt:

Once, across the street from us, there was a fine handsome woman, our neighbor. She had a son whom she loved because she'd known him since birth (in helpless chubby infancy, and in the wrestling, hugging ages, seven to ten, as well as earlier and later). This boy, when he fell into the fist of adolescence, became a junkie. He was not a hopeless one. He was in fact hopeful, an ideologue and successful converter. With his busy brilliance, he wrote persuasive articles for his high-school newspaper. Seeking a wider audience, using important connections, he drummed into Lower Manhattan newsstand distribution a periodical called *Oh! Golden Horse!*

In order to keep him from feeling guilty (because guilt is the stony heart of nine tenths of all clinically diagnosed cancers in America today, she said), and because she had always believed in giving bad habits room at home where one could keep an eye on them, she too became a junkie. Her kitchen was famous for a while—a center for intellectual addicts who knew what they were doing. A few felt artistic like Coleridge and others were scientific and revolutionary like Leary. Although she was often high herself, certain good mothering reflexes remained, and she saw to it that there was lots of orange juice around and honey and milk and vitamin pills. However, she never cooked anything but chili, and that no more than once a week. She explained, when we talked to her, seriously, with neighborly concern, that it was her part in the youth culture and she would rather be with the young, it was an honor, than with her own generation.

One week, while nodding through an Antonioni film, this boy was severely jabbed by the elbow of a stern and proselytizing girl, sitting beside him. She offered immediate apricots and nuts for his sugar level, spoke to him sharply, and took him home.

She had heard of him and his work and she herself published, edited, and wrote a competitive journal called *Man Does Live By Bread Alone*. In the organic heat of her continuous presence he could not help but become interested once more in his muscles, his arteries, and nerve connections. In fact he began to love them, treasure them, praise them with funny little songs in *Man Does Live* . . .

> *the fingers of my flesh transcend*
> *my transcendental soul*
> *the tightness in my shoulders end*
> *my teeth have made me whole*

To the mouth of his head (that glory of will and determination) he brought hard apples, nuts, wheat germ, and soybean oil. He said to his old friends, From now on, I guess I'll keep my wits about me. I'm going on the natch. He said he was about to begin a spiritual deep-breathing journey. How about you too, Mom? he asked kindly.

His conversion was so radiant, splendid, that neighborhood kids his age began to say that he had never been a real addict at all, only a journalist along for the smell of the story. The mother tried several times to give up what had become without her son and his friends a lonely habit. This effort only brought it to supportable levels. The boy and his girl took their electronic mimeograph and moved to the bushy edge of another borough. They were very strict. They said they would not see her again until she had been off drugs for sixty days.

At home alone in the evening, weeping, the mother read and reread the seven issues of *Oh! Golden Horse!* They seemed to her as truthful as ever. We often crossed the street to visit and console. But if we mentioned any of our children who were at college or in the hospital or dropouts at home, she would cry out, My baby! My baby! And burst into terrible, face-scarring, time-consuming tears. The End.

First my father was silent, then he said, "Number One: You have a nice sense of humor. Number Two: I see you can't tell a plain story. So don't waste time." Then he said sadly, "Number Three: I suppose that means she was alone, she was left like that, his mother. Alone. Probably sick?"

I said, "Yes."

"Poor woman. Poor girl, to be born in a time of fools, to live among fools. The end. The end. You were right to put that down. The end."

I didn't want to argue, but I had to say, "Well, it is not necessarily the end, Pa."

"Yes," he said, "what a tragedy. The end of a person."

"No, Pa," I begged him. "It doesn't have to be. She's only about forty. She could be a hundred different things in this world as time goes on. A teacher or a social worker. An ex-junkie! Sometimes it's better than having a master's in education."

"Jokes," he said. "As a writer that's your main trouble. You don't want to recognize it. Tragedy! Plain tragedy! Historical tragedy! No hope. The end."

"Oh, Pa," I said. "She could change."

"In your own life, too, you have to look it in the face." He took a couple of nitroglycerin. "Turn to five," he said, pointing to the dial on the oxygen tank. He inserted the tubes into his nostrils and breathed deep. He closed his eyes and said, "No."

I had promised the family to always let him have the last word when arguing, but in this case I had a different responsibility. That woman lives across the street. She's my knowledge and my invention. I'm sorry for her. I'm not going to leave her there in that house crying. (Actually neither would Life, which unlike me has no pity.)

Therefore: She did change. Of course her son never came home again. But right now, she's the receptionist in a storefront community clinic in the East Village. Most of the customers are young people, some old friends. The head doctor has said to her, "If we only had three people in this clinic with your experiences..."

"The doctor said that?" My father took the oxygen tubes out of his nostrils and said, "Jokes. Jokes again."

"No, Pa, it could really happen that way, it's a funny world nowadays."

"No," he said. "Truth first. She will slide back. A person must have character. She does not."

"No, Pa," I said. "That's it. She's got a job. Forget it. She's in that storefront working."

"How long will it be?" he asked. "Tragedy! You too. When will you look it in the face?"

POINTS TO CONSIDER ABOUT "A CONVERSATION WITH MY FATHER"

1. What is the narrator's attitude toward her father's request for "a simple story"? What does he mean by a simple story? How and why are the narrator's typical stories not simple, according to her account in this fictional piece? And speaking of fiction...do you think "A Conversation with My Father" is entirely fictional, or that it's based on the author's real-life experiences? What clues do you have as to the story's degree of "fictionality"?

2. What, according to the father, is the problem with the narrator's first tale, the one about the mother-and-son junkies? What does he suggest that the narrator do to "fix" the story? How does the interaction between

the father and the narrator emblematize the problems with writing—and publishing—for an audience?

3. How does the second version of the story "improve" upon the first? In what ways does the new version conform to the "rules" for revision suggested in this chapter, and in what ways does it diverge from them?

4. What is the author suggesting by the statement, "An ex-junkie! Sometimes it's better than having a master's in education"? How does this statement relate thematically to the rest of "A Conversation with My Father"?

5. Discuss the final conversation between the narrator and the father in terms of its function in "resolving" the story. Does the conversation leave the reader with a sense of narrative closure, or does Paley purposely leave the reader with ambiguities and/or unanswered questions? Why does the author choose this kind of resolution?

Retrospect on My Fictions
Richard Kostelanetz

In a quarter century's exploration of fiction writing, I have produced:

1) a novella with no more than two words to a paragraph (and then, in one published form, no more than two words to a book page),

2) a story with only single-word paragraphs,

3) "minimal fictions" that are no more than three words in length, most having only two words or one before their periods,

4) stories that are narrated through a series of shapes that are composed exclusively of words or letters,

5) stories consisting exclusively of words whose meaning changes with the introduction not of other words but of different configurations of the initial words or nonverbal imagery,

"Retrospect on My Fictions" by Richard Kostelanetz from FORUM:The Future of American Fiction, volume 5, no. 4, New Series (October 1992). Reprinted by permission of the University Press of Kentucky.

6) stories composed entirely of nonrepresentational line-drawings that metamorphose so systematically that each image in the sequence clearly belongs only to its particular place,

7) individual sentences that are either the openings or the closings of otherwise unwritten stories,

8) skeletal stories composed of three words that are not syntactically sequential and have more space between them than is customary,

9) stories composed of just cut-up photographs whose rectangular chips move systemically, as well as symmetrically, through narrative cycles,

10) separate modular fictions of photographs that can be read in any order, of line-drawings whose positions in a sequence are interchangeable (and thus can be shuffled), of sentences that are reordered in systemic ways to produce different emphases of the same words and narrative gestures, if not radically new stories,

11) circular stories that flow from point to point but lack definite beginnings or ends,

12) narratives, one as long as a book, composed exclusively of numerals,

13) a story composed of sixteen different (but complementary) narratives interwoven in print in sixteen different typefaces and on audiotape told in sixteen purposefully different amplifications of a single voice,

14) over two thousand single-sentence fictions representing the epiphanies of otherwise unwritten stories,

15) manuscripts of single-sentence stories that have been offered to periodical editors not to publish *in toto* but as pools from which they may make their own selections that can then be ordered and designed to their particular tastes,

16) a sequence of single-sentence stories that, thanks to structural complexities available in English, are each over two hundred words long,

17) fiction books published in formats ranging from conventional spinebound volumes to such alternatives as tabloid-sized newsprint books, looseleaf books (whose pages are gathered in an envelope), and accordion books that are four inches high and several feet long,

18) one film and a separate videotape whose imagery is nothing other than words telling stories,

19) another film with symmetrical abstract fictions (described in #5 above) that metamorphose in systemic sequence,

20) fictions that exist primarily on audiotape—that cannot be performed live, whose printed version is no more than a score for its realization,

21) books in which abstract sequences are presented both *in toto* and intermixed with other sequences, thereby creating a metastory composed of many individual stories,

22) "skeletal fictions" with horizontal sequences of words, separated by more horizontal space than is customary, without blatant syntactical connections (but narrative implications nonetheless),

23) stories composed entirely of words that rhyme with one another—some two words long, others three, most even more populous,

24) a cycle of one hundred and twenty-seven erotic stories, each successively one word longer than its immediate predecessor until, at sixty-four words in length, each becomes one word shorter than its immediate predecessor,

25) titles with minimal fictions handwritten in large capital letters,

26) a four-hour film composed of verbal and visual epiphanies that have no ostensible connection to each other, either vertically or horizontally, other than common fictional structure,

27) videotapes whose abstract visual syntheses become an accompanying counterpoint to the more concrete audio narration,

28) perhaps a few other departures whose character cannot yet, for better or worse, be neatly encapsulated,

29) the purest *oeuvre* of fiction, as fiction, uncompromised by vulgar considerations, that anyone has ever done,

30) no conventional fiction—absolutely none—which is to say nothing that could pass a university course/workshop in "fiction writing" (and get me a job teaching such), and no familiar milestone from which simple-minded critics could then measure my "departure."

Even though these fictions of mine have appeared in over five dozen literary magazines, and well over a dozen volumes of these fictions have appeared in print (and my critical essays and manifestos were collected as *The Old Fictions and the New*), there have been few reviews of individual books of my fiction, no offers from presses either large or small to do more books of my fiction, no grants for fiction writing, only two passing mentions in purportedly comprehensive surveys of contemporary fiction, little critical acknowledgment of my radically alternative purposes in creating and publishing fiction; only one story was ever anthologized by someone else (Eugene Wildman, in his *Experiments in Prose*, back in 1969). Does anyone care? Should anyone care (other than me)? (Should I care? If so, how? Should I have written this?) What should be made of the fact that no one else—absolutely no one else visible to us—is making fiction in these ways?

POINTS TO CONSIDER ABOUT "RETROSPECT ON MY FICTIONS"

1. How would you characterize the form of "Retrospect on My Fictions": Is it a short story, a piece of journalism, a diary entry, a creative nonfiction piece (the latter receives a full description in Chapter 9 of this book), or an essay? What qualities of each of these subgenres does "Retrospect on My Fictions" exhibit, in your opinion?

2. What is the tone of this piece? From the statement, "these fictions of mine have appeared in over five dozen literary magazines, and well over a dozen volumes of these fictions have appeared in print," it seems as though Kostelanetz has had no small measure of success as a published author. What, then, is the problem, as he describes it in "Retrospect on My Fictions"? Do you sympathize with his complaint, or would you be satisfied with the accomplishments listed here?

3. In what ways, if any, does "Retrospect on My Fictions" compel you to modify the content or output of your own fiction? After reading this piece, do you feel more or less positive about the process of getting your own work published? Why?

4. What is the function of the string of questions, some of them parenthetical—"Does anyone care? Should anyone care (other than me)? (Should I care? If so, how? Should I have written this?)—in the final paragraph of this piece? What is the author's thematic intention in putting these questions at the end of "Retrospect on My Fictions"? How would you answer these questions, based on your own experience?

5. Do you agree with Kostelanetz's contention that "no one else—absolutely no one else visible to us—is making fiction in these ways?" What evidence (or lack of evidence) can you cite to support the author's belief that few, if any, editors and publishers are paying attention to the experimental fiction he describes in "Retrospect on My Fictions"? What examples, if any, can you provide to disprove the author's assertion?

✂ WRITING ACTIVITIES: PERFECTION AND PRINT

1. You are an editor at a major publishing house. The mother of a celebrated author who recently committed suicide brings you a collection of his unpublished writings, including this story fragment, "The Further Adventures of My Atoms." The mother insists that the stories be rewritten into coherent, completed form before she will release them legally. As the public hungrily awaits previously unpublished material from this author, your publishing house wants desperately to acquire the rights to this material. It therefore falls to you to get "The Further Adventures of My Atoms" ready for publication.

Revise this story, following the guidelines presented in this chapter. Also, feel free to add material and/or change the order of paragraphs, if it makes the story hold together better. If you add significant amounts of material, the mother will give you credit as co-author when the piece comes out.

The Further Adventures of My Atoms

Dribbling ball on sidewalk, thunka thunka thunka on concrete dotted with old tossed-away gum like black stars on negative sky. Up the sidewalk by my old grade school, the little kids' water fountains I have to bend way down to reach now. Where I got beat up by Frankie Grillo once a week, on Thursdays, after cotillion dance practice my mom made me go to. He called me "Cow in the family" and "Five eyes" and "Burning taper," whatever that means. I let him pound away awhile. Kids' hands—even big kids like Frankie Grillo—don't hurt that much, in the big scheme.

Now I throw the ball over the chain link, climb up, throw a leg over, make sure not to snag the crotch of my oversize blue Gorilla dungarees. Drop down, hurts the ankles. In a good way.

Two guys on the court already. One with no shirt, tat that says "Jesus" across his flat ripped stomach, another tat looks like a rat's maze on his arms. Other guy in hooded sweatshirt, hood pulled up like a low rent grim reaper playing HORSE with some gangsta con parolee.

Sunny day, with some clouds scudding across the sky. Hot July day. I've got on a red tank top with the inscription "American Zero" in red against the black fabric, and a blue star. Sweat slick glistens on my forearms.

They stop playing when they see me. Sweatshirt guy dribbling the ball idly, behind his back, in front of him, between his legs. Whipping it around and around his waist. Around and around.

They stand next to their stuff on the hot black asphalt. Watching me come up.

Sweatshirt pulls down his hood so I can see his face. Blond kid, maybe fifteen, buzz cut number 2 or 3 clipper setting, by my experience. Bone white skin and acne like somebody splattered butcher paper with tomato paste. Face like a ferret. Real pleasant kid.

No shirt is picking up a stick like a baton that runners use at track meets. Flipping it back and forth in his hands. Watching me come up and flipping that stick.

"Play some ball?" I call across the yard.

"What does it look like?" ferret says.

"Well, your friend has a stick, I thought maybe he was gonna throw it and then you'd go fetch it for him." I can't help myself sometimes.

2. Pretend you're one of the authors whose fiction appears in this book: Ernest Hemingway, Amy Tan, Hunter S. Thompson, Susan Straight. Write a query letter to an imaginary agent, summarizing the marketable points of your fictional piece and making a strong case for your credentials as a writer. As an extension to this activity, pretend you're an agent who's having a bad day—not enough sleep, a desk full of paperwork, nagging authors, fight with the significant other, trying to quit cigarettes—and write a rejection letter that takes out your frustrations on the author's work.

3. Some people—especially those people who believe the printed word will die in the next decade—believe electronic media are the wave of the future. Using a computer with Web-browsing software such as Netscape, check out several of the e-zines (Web-based electronic literary magazines listed below (from Black Star Press, http://www.blackstarpress.com/11zin.shtml):

> *Allegheny Review,* "America's only nationwide literary magazine exclusively for undergraduate poetry and fiction." http://www.alleg.edu/StudentLife/Organizations/AllegReview/
>
> *Chicago Review,* "An international journal of writing and cultural exchange published quarterly in the Division of the Humanities, the University of Chicago." http://humanities.uchicago.edu/humanities/review/
>
> *CrossConnect,* "A tri-annual electronic journal for contemporary art and writing based at the University of Pennsylvania in Philadelphia." http://ccat.sas.upenn.edu/~xconnect/
>
> *ELF: Eclectic Literary Forum,* "E-journal whose editors are all professors of English who have taught creative writing for many years and who are all published authors." http://www.pce.net/elf/
>
> *Enormous Sky,* "Magazine of student poetry, prose, artwork, and photography produced by the students of Temple University." http://www.music.temple.edu/Sky/
>
> *Enterzone,* "A hyperzine of writing, art, and new media. It features criticism, fiction, philosophy, hypertexts, computer graphics, reportage, interactive artforms, scanned photography, sounds, and drawings." http://ezone.org/ez
>
> *Fryburger,* "E-zine with a focus on fiction . . . that is, short stories, poetry, interviews with various authors, and reviews." http://www.uni-freiburg. de/borsch/fryburger/fryburger.html
>
> *georgetown revieWWW,* "An on-line publication edited by the folks at the print edition of 'Georgetown Review'." http://www2.digimag.net/~georgetownreview/
>
> *Gruene Street,* "An Internet Journal of Prose & Poetry." http://ebbs.english.vt.edu/olp/gs/gruene.html
>
> *Highbeams,* "Published and posted quarterly at Beloit College." http:// stu.beloit.edu/~highbe/
>
> *It's a Bunny,* "Emanating quarterly from above a laundromat on Boulevard St. Laurent, Montreal, Quebec, and for now, Canada. It's a Bunny provides shelter for fine new english fiction, poetry, reviews and art in an otherwise cold and brutal climate." http://www.iti.qc.ca/ iti/bunny/current/bunny.html

Kudzu, "A digital quarterly." http://www.etext.org/Zines/Kudzu/index. html

Mississippi Review Web Edition, "Outlet for online fiction, poetry, essays, graphics, sound, video, published monthly by the Center for Writers." http://sushi.st.usm.edu/mrw/

Ploughshares, "Stories and poems, a profile on the guest editor, book reviews, and miscellaneous notes." http://www.emerson.edu/Ploughshares/Ploughshares.html

256 Shades of Grey, "Eau Claire, Wisconsin's Avant-Pop Litarary/Arts 'Zine." http://www.primenet.com/~blkgrnt/

From your examination of these e-zines' content and overall presentation, select five e-zines that look as though they might be appropriate to the kind of work you do, and submit one of your fictional pieces to them.

✖ A WRITER'S DOZEN: THIRTEEN RULES OF SUCCESSFUL FICTION

1. Show more, tell less.
2. Keep writing.
3. Have a healthy fear of taking risks, but take them anyway.
4. Learn the rules so well that you don't have to think about them.
5. Describe a smell on every fourth page, but . . .
6. . . . don't make your readers throw up, unless that's your thematic intention.
7. Write what you know . . . or knew.
8. Hook your readers and keep 'em reading, by whatever means necessary.
9. Don't hit the reader over the head with background information.
10. Everything happens somewhere.
11. If details don't advance the story, hack 'em even if it hurts.
12. If you're going to break the rules, break them consciously and with clear purpose.
13. Don't be disheartened by rejection; instead, strive always to maintain the beginning writer's sense of joyful surprise in discovery.

PART II AN INTRODUCTION
TO THE FICTIONAL GENRES

SASSY, STRONG, AND FULL OF SPUNK:
ROMANCE AND BEYOND

As a fiction writer, you have absolute freedom to move creatively in whatever direction the imagination leads—especially if you aren't concerned with the demands, conventions and accepted procedures of the publishing industry. However, within the popular genres of publishable fiction there are certain "rules" that writers understand and tend to observe. If you work as a romance novelist, for instance, certain publishers will actually send you a list of "dos and don'ts" to follow. Debra Matteucci, senior editor at Harlequin, describes their American Romance line this way:

> . . . a dynamic premise hooks the reader instantly, sweeping her into a 70,000–75,000 word contemporary fairy tale where anything is possible and all dreams come true. . . .
>
> Plot: Show don't tell! We want lively, upbeat action-packed material that is not problem-based or introspective. Aim for fictional credibility, not realism, looking to your imagination and dreams for inspiration, rather than to everyday life. . . .
>
> Hero: He's not the boy next door! This 90's man is a man no woman can resist. Whether he's rough around the edges, or earthy, or

slick and sophisticated, every reader will fall in love with him. He is so dynamic, he may even be the focus in a hero-led story.

Heroine: She's sassy, strong, and full of spunk and never wimps out to her hero . . . in fact, this highly contemporary woman occasionally bests him, which fuels his desire, as so few women have!

Sounds light and lively but somewhat restrictive, no? If you conceive a Woody Allen-esque male character who may fall short of being constantly "dynamic" in a macho sort of way, then forget Harlequin American Romance. Similarly, if you base the female lead in some ways on yourself— and you sometimes wake up in the morning not quite overbrimming with "spunk"—then your character has no place in the "fairy tale" world of the romance.

I don't mean to get into romance-bashing here. Romance fiction, because it's the most widely read and therefore voluminously produced genre of fiction, invites all kinds of authorship, from skilled, reflective practitioners to cliché-mongering butchers of the language. The work of the latter group—and make no mistake: there's plenty of embarrassingly bad writing on the romance shelf at your local drugstore—makes romance fiction an especially easy target for criticism. Yet even within this oft-maligned subgenre, a certain amount of creative license is possible, and many houses are beginning to publish lines of "alternative" romance beyond the traditional historicals and contemporaries. I cite the example of romance fiction not to vilify the people who produce it, but to illustrate that there are certain implicit (and sometimes explicit) codes for writing genre fiction . . . and that it will be useful for you to learn some of them before you start writing a historical short story or a young adult novel.

This section of *The Graceful Lie*, which features celebrated and much-published experts in seven fictional subgenres—prose poetry, creative nonfiction, young adult fiction, science fiction, mysteries, historical fiction, and literary fiction—will provide you with concrete guidelines for writing in many of the genres that interest you. Additionally, the "guest" authors of the following chapters will themselves model a range of prose styles, from the intellectual, to the practical, to the conversational and casual.

I say "many of the genres" rather than "all," because in an introductory text such as *The Graceful Lie*, I can't cover all subgenres of fiction. Instead, I've chosen the ones that my students have historically seemed most interested in producing. In the process, I've had to omit some broad classifications such as romance; there's no point in my giving you guidelines for writing romance fiction, since Harlequin or the other big romance houses will send you explicit guidelines for the price of a postage stamp. Postmodern fiction fell by the wayside as well. I originally planned on devoting a separate chapter to postmodernism as a subset of literary fiction, because it's one of my special interests as a researcher. My own fiction probably falls most neatly into that category, also.[1] However, as I started writing the chapter, I bumped up against the complexity of postmodernism as a literary term and fictional construct. There is little—if any—consensus among critics as to what postmodern fiction is, and so I decided that a twenty-page overview wouldn't do justice to the multiplicity of meanings attached to the term. Instead, I'll let the last chapter in *The Graceful Lie*—Barry Gifford's interview—discuss several aspects of contemporary literary prose, including noir and postmodern fiction. You can use that discussion as a springboard to reading and writing in whatever branch of literary fiction piques your interest.

Another reason I included certain subgenres (to the exclusion of others) is that I wanted to structure the second section of *The Graceful Lie* as a kind of rhetorical sequence, beginning with relatively short, simple and/or personal forms and moving gradually toward specific genre niches. For that reason, I begin this section with a genre that blurs the borders of fiction and other literary forms. Prose poetry provides a short and particularly accessible form by which aspiring writers might ease into the specific activities suggested in this portion of *The Graceful Lie*. Next comes creative nonfiction, a subgenre which incorporates some of the journal work suggested in early chapters of this text and therefore allows for a bit more organic, autobiographical structuring than some of the other, purely fictional, genres. The third subtype in this section, young adult fiction, serves as a transition be-

---

[1]In fact, in *The Graceful Lie,* I purposely incorporated some features of postmodernism, because it's fun and comes naturally to me. One common postmodern feature, for example, is the hoax.[2] I couldn't resist sprinkling earlier chapters with bogus literary allusions and made-up characters, in hopes that you would spot them and laugh . . . or that I would at least entertain myself while writing. Remember the annoying little asides from my editor? All made up; I created an imaginary colleague with whom I could have some heated dialogue, in order to inject a little narrative tension into mainly factual sections. While the character of educational psychologist is real, there is in reality no author named Carlo Zeamba, as I claim in the first sentence of *The Graceful Lie.* I invented him, partly because my inner brat had fun imagining scholars frantically searching their databases for an important writer they'd never heard of, and partially to make a statement—in concrete action—about the viability of the hoax in contemporary writing. Then, of course, I got carried away and started putting in hoaxes all over the place. I never had a student named Dave Pevker (p. 33). I invented Priscilla Lampkin, that noted creative nonfiction writer who loves the yellow pad (p. 35). I worked as a house-cleaner and poker-player— never as a gardener (p. 66)—to help pay my way through college. I made up the Captain Newberry science-fiction example along with the journal it appeared in, *Tales of Future Fantastic.* (p. 115) Shakespeare scholar Marshall Sweet (p. 170) is actually my cousin who loves Shakespeare but is an accountant!

[2]Wacky footnotes are another feature of postmodern fiction, by the way. See, for example, Robert Grudin's novel, *Book,* in which the footnotes become characters that threaten to take over the narrative . . . sort of like my editor threatened to do with this book, before I got tired of all the interruptions and suspended the device.

tween the short and/or personal writing engendered by prose poetry/creative nonfiction and more traditionally narrative genres. While young adult fiction is a sophisticated form that requires a keen knowledge of one's audience and a constant control of tone and diction, it's often (but not always) simpler, in terms of word choice, plot structure, and expressed meaning (i.e., the thematic "moral" of the story), than the forms that follow it: mystery fiction, historical fiction, science fiction, and literary fiction.

To get maximum benefit from this section of *The Graceful Lie*, you might read and work on the exercises in the prose poetry and creative nonfiction chapters, then select one or two succeeding chapters that cover fictional genres you find appealing. Remember: The goal of this section of the text isn't to have you select a niche that you will occupy for the rest of your writing life. To the contrary, I think it's essential that you develop your craft as a writer in a variety of forms before you commit yourself to a single type of fiction. As Sue Grafton says in the mystery fiction chapter that follows,

> In order to write a good mystery novel, I think you first have to try mainstream fiction. You have to teach yourself how to tell a story, the pace of story, how to develop character, how to structure dramatic action. After you have mastered setting and atmosphere, then you can take on the very exotic requirements of the genre. Many people want to try writing for specific genres, when they don't have the basic foundation of writing, which is essential.

The goal of this section, then, is to strengthen your "basic foundation of writing," by introducing you to some of the possibilities inherent in the various genres of fiction, and to give you practice in writing in a variety of styles, voices, and narrative structures.

8

Prose Poetry

Gary Young is a poet and artist whose honors include grants from the National Endowment for the Arts, the National Endowment for the Humanities, the Vogelstein Foundation, and the California Arts Council. He has received a Pushcart Prize, and his book of poems, *The Dream of a Moral Life*, won the James D. Phelan award. He is the author of several other collections of poetry including *Hands, Wherever I Looked*, and the newly released *Days*. He has produced a series of artist's books, most notably *The Geography of Home, Nine Days: New York*, and *My Place Here Below*. His poems have appeared in such magazines as *Poetry, Antaeus, The American Poetry Review, The Kenyon Review*, and *The Nation*. Since 1975, he has designed, illustrated, and printed limited edition books and broadsides at his Greenhouse Review Press. His print work is represented in numerous collections including the Museum of Modern Art, the Victoria and Albert Museum, The Getty Center for the Arts, and special collection libraries throughout the country. In this chapter, Young discusses prose poetry: a subgenre that merges certain qualities of writing that has traditionally been considered "poetic" with qualities typical of narrative fiction.

I have been asked on more than one occasion to defend the prose poem, and to explain in particular how a poem can be a poem without 'the line.' Curiously it is often poets working in free verse who make the most strenuous objection to prose poems, the same poets who argue for the legitimacy of free verse against those who champion poems written in formal meter and rhyme. Both arguments are absurd, and disingenuous as well. One might just as well be asked to defend the sonnet.

The prose poem has a history in the poetry of Europe and America that extends back more than a century-and-a-half. It was appropriated by many nineteenth-century poets who first experimented with other free verse forms, and in China the *fu*, or poem in prose, has a history that stretches back millennia.

There are certain formal elements the prose poem shares with fiction and creative nonfiction, and there are other elements that more closely resemble the tropes and strategies of verse. Brooke Horvath has suggested that poems written in prose attempt to "hide" the poetry behind the prose in part to reclaim an audience that has for the past two centuries been seduced by prose. She also suggests that the prose poem provides a home for fugitive content, and "may well offer a means of saying the no-longer sayable as well as the as-yet unsaid." Certainly the prose poem is enjoying a spirited rise in acceptance and practice. *The Prose Poem: An International Journal* is devoted exclusively to the genre, and two recent anthologies, *The Party Train: A Collection of North American Prose Poetry* (New Rivers Press, 1996), and *Models of the Universe: An Anthology of the Prose Poem* (Oberlin College Press, 1995) are testament to the genre's vitality and acceptance.

There are those who argue that a poem written in prose is neither poem nor prose, but something altogether different. The distinctions, ultimately, are unimportant to the reader, though the writer may wish to position his or her work in one genre, or in one particular philosophical or theoretical camp. This raises the important question of expectation. What preconceptions does a reader bring to any given text, and how do those preconceptions alter the reader's apprehension and appreciation of that text?

Traditional poetic forms create an anticipation of the 'poetic' that prose does not. It is this very lack of expectation which makes the prose poem subversive and supple; the reader may be seduced in wholly unanticipated ways. The prose poem's flexibility is due in part to the fact that the form comes with so little baggage. Readers may be alerted that they are about to experience a poem, and yet they are greeted with comforting, unintimidating prose.

The reader's diminished expectation of a poetic experience also makes the prose poem an especially demanding form. There are no signposts which telegraph: This is a poem. Because it *is* prose—and therefore shares more visual equivalence with the language we use to negotiate newspapers, contracts or personal correspondence—it must work especially hard to embrace the rapture of language we identify as poetry. Ezra Pound once said, "Poetry should be at least as well-written as prose," and we should expect prose poems to incorporate the best elements of both: concision, syntactical intelligence and rhythmical eloquence. By eschewing the ornamental apparatus of received poetic forms, the prose poem must rely wholly on the music and the honesty of its own utterance.

Charles Baudelaire's *Little Poems in Prose* was published in 1869, but even before the term was coined we can find hints of the form in Thoreau, Emerson and Hawthorne, among others. There are even traces of the form in the earliest literature produced in this country. In the mid-seventeenth century, Anne Bradstreet, one of the first poets in the Americas, wrote a series of short prose pieces titled *Meditations Divine and morall*. Their brevity, allusiveness and their lyricism recommend them as prose poems:

> A ship that beares much saile, and little or no ballast, is easily overset, and that man, whose head hath great abilities, and his heart little or no grace, is in danger of foundering.

Walt Whitman may be said to have liberated the poetry of meter and rhyme with the ranging free verse lines we admire in *Leaves of Grass*, but sections of his prose book, *Specimen Days* frequently approach the intensity and focus of his poems, and share more equivalence with his poetry than with his other prose works:

A MEADOW LARK

> March 16.—Fine, clear, dazzling morning, the sun an hour high, the air just tart enough. What a stamp in advance my whole day receives from the song of that meadow lark perch'd on a fence-stake twenty rods distant! Two or three liquid-simple notes, repeated at intervals, full of careless happiness and hope. With its peculiar shimmering slow progress and rapid-noiseless action of the wings, it flies on a ways, lights on another stake, and so one to another, shimmering and singing many minutes.

Whitman has pared his vision and his language to essentials here, and considers a single brief episode with precision, and without haste. He has created a text that is more poetic than prosaic, more poem than story.

Ernest Hemingway punctuated the stories in his collection *In Our Time* with short prose vignettes that also seem closer to poetry than to prose in their condensation, their impact, and their intention. The following piece describes a scene that could be part of a larger story, but it manifests its character, and achieves its power by standing alone. The reader must apprehend this unique offering with undivided attention.

> We were in a garden at Mons. Young Buckley came in with his patrol from across the river. The first German I saw climbed up over the garden wall. We waited till he got one leg over then potted him. He had so much equipment on and looked awfully surprised and fell down into

the garden. Then three more came over further down the wall. We shot them. They all came just like that.

Charles Baudelaire's affection for the work of Edgar Allen Poe is well known, and Poe's *Eureka: A Prose Poem* no doubt influenced Baudelaire's *Little Poems in Prose*. These poems, often moralistic and always a bit fantastic, heralded the modern prose poem in Europe, and were to inform the work of Arthur Rimbaud and countless others. Their fabulist quality is one which has had a particular influence in America. Here is a poem by Baudelaire in which fable and prosaic reality are oddly wedded:

THE SOUP AND THE CLOUDS

My little mad darling was giving me my dinner, and through the open window of the dining-room I was contemplating the moving architectures that god makes out of vapors, those marvelous constructions of the impalpable. And I said to myself, in the midst of my meditation: 'All those phantasmagoria are almost as beautiful as the eyes of my beloved, that monstrous little mad woman with the green eyes.'

And suddenly I received a violent blow on my back, and I heard a charming, raucous voice, a voice hysterical and as though made hoarse by brandy, the voice of my sweet little darling who was saying: 'Well, are you going to eat your soup or aren't you, you bloody dithering cloud-monger?'

Russell Edson, an American master of the prose poem, often creates a fabulous, grotesque world which appears alien and startlingly familiar simultaneously. There is an equivalence in his poems between the animate and the inanimate, between the conjectural and the 'real.'

FATHER FATHER, WHAT HAVE YOU DONE?

A man straddling the apex of his roof cries, giddyup. The house rears up on its back porch and all its bricks fall apart and the house crashes to the ground.

His wife cries from the rubble, father father, what have you done?

The prose poem is particularly well suited to the short fable, and this is a mode frequently exploited by prose poets. This poem by Morton Marcus begins with an extraordinary event, but one that is presented in such a casual, offhanded way that we accept the premise immediately and without reservation:

ANGEL INCIDENT

An angel appeared in my study not long ago: bedraggled, mussed hair, muttering to himself. Both wings lifted like ocean swells with every breath he drew or word he spoke. They seemed to have a life of their own; I couldn't take my eyes off them.

The angel kept muttering to himself. He was studying a crumpled, poorly folded map, the kind bought at gas stations: he opened panels and refolded them, peering repeatedly at the network of red and blue lines inside.

He knew I was there. Several times he looked up and smiled weakly—I nodded in reply—but he never asked me directions before he strolled through the wall near the window and was gone.

Of course, I never asked him if he needed help. It never occurred to me. At the time, I thought it was enough that we were in the same room together. I was wrong. We both were.

Prose is characteristically literal, and we use it to describe, to document and to establish our hold on the everyday world. The prose poem subverts this quotidian use of prose, and employs it to retrieve or reestablish a connection to the poetry of our lives. Two American poets who have exploited this to great effect are James Wright and Robert Hass. Prose poems and lineated verse are juxtaposed in Wright's books *To a Blossoming Pear Tree* and *This Journey*, and he wrenches moments of extraordinary beauty from the most subtle, ordinary prose.

THE ICE HOUSE

The ice house was really a cellar deep beneath the tower of the old Belmont Brewery. My father's big shoulders heaved open the door from the outside, and from within the big shoulders of the ice-man leaned and helped. The slow door gave. My brother and I walked in delighted by our fear, and laid our open palms on the wet yellow sawdust. Outside the sun blistered the paint on the corrugated roofs of the shacks by the railroad; but we stood and breathed the rising steam of that amazing winter, and carried away in our wagon the immense fifty-pound diamond, while the old man chipped us each a jagged little chunk and then walked behind us, his hands so calm they were trembling for us, trembling with exquisite care.

Robert Hass frequently combines prose and lineated verse within the same poem, stretching even further the boundaries between the two genres. The following poem is one of a series of prose poems from his book, *Human Wishes*.

A STORY ABOUT THE BODY

The young composer, working that summer at an artist's colony, had watched her for a week. She was Japanese, a painter, almost sixty, and he thought he was in love with her. He loved her work, and her work was like the way she moved her body, used her hands, looked at him directly when she made amused and considered answers to his questions. One night, walking back from a concert, they came to her door and she turned to him and said, "I think you would like to have me. I would like that too, but I must tell you that I have had a double mastectomy," and when he didn't understand, "I've lost both my breasts." The radiance that he had carried around in his belly and chest cavity—like music—withered very quickly, and he made himself look at her when he said, "I'm sorry. I don't think I could." He walked back to his own cabin through the pines, and in the morning he found a small blue bowl on the porch outside his door. It looked to be full of rose petals, but he found when he picked it up that the rose petals were on top; the rest of the bowl—she must have swept them from the corners of her studio—was full of dead bees.

"A Story About the Body" telegraphs its resemblance to the short story with its title, and the poem possesses those characteristics of plot, discursiveness, and character development we might expect from a short narrative. What sets this poem apart from a short story is its compression, concision, and its lyrical intensity. This is another case in which the particular attention asked of the reader by the poem is rewarded by the poem's subtle movement and final revelation.

The paradox of any poetic form is that it simultaneously liberates and constricts. Any formal strategy will structure a specific logic, and every form accentuates or encourages a particular mode of thinking; I am tempted to say, a particular mode of wonder. Form is merely an architecture necessary to support the ceremony of the poem.

My embrace of the prose poem came as the result of a confluence in my work as a poet and my work as a fine printer. When I published *The Geography of Home*, an artist's book in which the text runs in a single horizontal line across each page, I found myself seduced by a form that literally embodied the semantic landscape I was attempting to inhabit. It proved to be the stylistic and thematic germ for my subsequent book of prose poems, *Days*, and my next collection, *Braver Deeds*. My use of the prose poem is not based on any philosophic projection; it is rather a matter of enthusiasm and practicality.

The poems in *Days* are my attempt to write meaningful utterances that move from beginning to end horizontally rather than vertically. Their measure is emotive rather than syllabic or metrical. My aim has been to write poems that one might figuratively walk along, rather than fall through:

Two girls were struck by lightning at the harbor mouth. An orange flame lifted them up and laid them down again. Their thin suits had been melted away. It's a miracle they survived. It's a miracle they were ever born at all.

My intention was to quiet these poems, not to silence, but to equilibrium, where a calm voice need not interrupt itself with self-consciousness or artifice but speak simply in the knowledge that the breath propelled represents a faithful utterance of the heart:

> She took my two hands in hers, pressed and caressed them as if she were bathing me. I held hers as mine were held, stroked her knuckles, her palms, then realized the finger I lightly traced was my own. How strange to find I could show myself such tenderness.

I have found it more difficult to lie in prose, either through omission or amplification. Poems written in prose encourage—at least in me—a stricter honesty, and as a result the mysteries they reveal seem more genuine and profound. I have tried to write with as much clarity as I can about those brief, disquieting moments that define our lives. Where the impulse might be to reflect and elaborate, to draw a broader reality from the moment at hand, I have tried in my poems to pare away peripheral reflection to touch surely the moment, and to freeze it. The concept of a lyric moment is itself a conceit, of course; even the shortest poem takes time to read. But each instant understood thoroughly—understood as God might understand it—is of a caliber with any other, not because it has been demoted to some lowest common denominator, but because each is a kernel and a mirror of eternity.

> A woman leans against a tall white pine, looks up into the tree, then lowers her head and stares at the horizon. Her son has climbed into the branches high above her. She's called him down twice, but afraid now her voice might distract him, she stands there silently and waits for him to fall. She knows if he does, there is nothing she can do. A cold wind moves through the tree. She can feel her body stiffen, but does not look up when the child cries out, I can see almost forever.

My attraction to the prose poem is emotional rather than critical. The prose poem is a maternal form. It is comforting and embracing, but it can also be smothering, constricting; once inside there is no way out, no place to rest until the poem is finished. It is a clot of language, and must convince through revelation.

> When I was five, I knew God had made the world and everything in it. I knew God loved me, and I knew the dead were in heaven with God always. I had a sweater. I draped it on a fence, and when I turned to pick it up a minute later, it was gone. That was the first time I had lost anything I really loved. I walked in circles, too frightened to cry, searching for it until dark. I knew my sweater was not in heaven, but if it could disappear, just vanish without reason, then I could disappear, and God might lose me, no matter how good I was, no matter how much I was loved. The buttons on my sweater were translucent, a shimmering, pale opalescence. It was yellow.

But in truth, what I treasure most about this form is the moral pressure it exerts. The prose poem encourages a particular kind of modesty. It might even at times achieve a certain humility, a humility which may, through grace, be reflected back upon the poet's own heart.

I put asters in a small blue vase. Each morning they open, and they close again each night. Even in this dark room they follow a light which does not reach them. They have bodies. That is all the faith they need.

Prose Poems
Gary Young

There was dead space behind an upstairs wall where I knew it was safe to hide. I kept a pillow there and a blanket, and I lit the hiding place with candles. Once, I thought I'd left a candle burning there, but when I looked, everything was fine. An hour later, I looked again. I looked every day, and at last, when I only went to look for fire, I emptied the place of candles. That night I heard voices in the other room, angry shouts, breaking glass, and knew I'd left a candle burning, there was no safe place, and I ran from my bed to check again.

The bodies of men and women sometimes ignite from within, and burn from the inside out. Nothing remains but a pile of ash where only minutes before a girl had been lying on the beach, or a young man had complained of the heat and then burst into flame. How can we explain the world? My heart is beating, I can feel it. God loves us more than we can stand.

I discovered a journal in the children's ward, and read, I'm a mother, my little boy has cancer. Further on, a girl has written, this is my nineteenth operation. She says, sometimes it's easier to write than to talk, and I'm so afraid. She's left me a page in the book. My son is sleeping in the room next door. This afternoon, I held my whole weight to his body while a doctor drove needles deep into his leg. My son screamed, Daddy, they're hurting me, don't let them hurt me, make them stop. I want to write, how brave you are, but I need a little courage of my own, so I write, forgive me, I know I let them hurt you, please don't worry. If I have to, I can do it again.

I don't know where the owls go when they leave this place, or if they never leave, but simply leave off calling sometimes in their hollow voices. But tonight they are here: one in a redwood beyond the creek, one high in the fir tree above the house. Rappelled through their voices, those three long vowels the darkness speaks in, I forget my own worthlessness which has troubled me all day.

The stillborn calf lies near the fence where its mother licked the damp body, then left it. All afternoon she has stood beside a large, white rock in the middle of the pasture. She nuzzles it with her heavy neck and will not be lured away. This must be her purest intelligence, to accept what she expected, something sure, intractable, the whole focus of the afternoon's pale light.

The world is made of names; my son is learning to speak. He has faith. He believes in things. Rock, I tell him, leaf. No, *this*, he says, holding the rock. *This*, he says, holding up the leaf.

I had never seen her so angry, and her rage revealed a measure of love I had missed. There were many times she might have hurt me that way, and didn't.

I would live forever if I could, but not like this.

He was drinking in the airport bar, and I asked, are you coming or going? I have been there, he said, and I almost didn't get back. He said, the engines failed, and we seemed to be falling forever; I've never been so afraid. Then he took a sip of his drink, and rolled back his sleeve. He'd printed his name down the length of his arm, and below that he'd written, Honey, I love you. It's strange, he said, what goes through your mind at a time like that. I hope to God this washes off, he said. My wife just loves to worry.

POINTS TO CONSIDER ABOUT GARY YOUNG'S PROSE POEMS

1. Read the first example of Young's prose poetry ("There was dead space...") aloud. What, if anything, do you notice about the rhythm of the writing? Does it seem substantially different from prose fiction you've read, in terms of form and word choice? What, if anything, makes it "poetry" in your mind?

2. Find examples of metaphor and imagery in the above examples of Young's work. Does prose poetry, as exemplified by the writing of Gary Young, seem to contain denser use of figurative language than prose pieces you've read previously?

3. Discuss the "story" structure of Young's third prose poetry example, "I discovered a journal in the children's ward..." In what ways does this piece resemble a very short story? Where, if anywhere, are the exposition, climax, resolution? What thematic message(s) are implied in the poem's narrative line?

4. What do you make of the one-line prose poem that reads in its entirety, "I would live forever if I could, but not like this"? How does this piece explode your notions of prose and poetry form, if at all? What is the author's intention in writing a piece this short; does its very shortness express meaning? If so, what?

5. Describe the ways in which Young's last piece, "He was drinking in the airport bar...", resembles a piece of very short fiction. What is the narrative structure of the poem? How does Young incorporate dialogue to develop meaning. What theme(s) does this prose poem suggest to you?

Prose Poems
Killarney Clary

There will be other falls. When Mama was moved from intensive care, the clock started, pushed aside the seventy-two years before. Now she needs a drink of water. Now she teases the Vietnamese nurse who doesn't understand. I am certain it's a joke, but Mama doesn't smile. She watches me laugh, sort of watches. A voice pages, "Dr. Eisenhower." Mama salutes, says, "Oh, Mrs. Clary, you're so funny."

A bruise, from purple to yellow. A broken bottle in the sand, a danger we might negligently avoid.

We drove north into Donegal, Daddy drank a rum and coke. He said he felt better. We'd done what we had come for.

"Every time I picked up that suitcase with her ashes in it, I remembered carrying her up the stairs of the hotel in Carmel on our honeymoon."

Every time I step into the bathtub, Theresa, I think of you; I think of your foot that was burned when you lived in Michigan. And Claire is on bridges like the Colorado where her mother fell or jumped. I think of Kathy when I see sprinklers turning in roses or I hear the name of her brother, George. Sydne in dime stores. Helen in lavender. Anne Marie with folded notes. Every time I am hit, Jeffrey. I can help, Taka. I cross the border, Billy. When I sleep, large recent faces repeat what they've told me in the past few days then you come toward me with names I haven't said aloud in years, each one of you faint but completed, carrying small stories—where you were once, what it was that happened. And you say, "Here." You see what I have, what you might need to tell someone else.

A pretty woman is showing me how to complete a form. She holds it toward me, against her blouse, and points to it as she talks. She looks down at it until her finger is in the right place, then lifts her eyes to me and taps the paper. Clearly, carefully, she has told me, and now I know what to do.

I'm sorry I brought it up. I'm sorry until I lose my body. I shouldn't have said what I said, not yet or not so late.

I answer, "I love you, too," and think, "for as long as you will believe it." But what I don't say now only thins the travel in and out of my heart, traps me in channels between my one thought and my next. So the one promises I will be new; the other laughs through its nose and says, "Sure."

If I'm daring you to please me, I have to stop somehow, but when I see what I've done wrong I am still wandering disagreeably, doing the wrong thing.

I hope I don't like you, myself, or anyone else. I hope I don't like the next song. If I do, I'll only try to remember it, and I'll have to look forward to hearing it again.

POINTS TO CONSIDER ABOUT KILLARNEY CLARY'S PROSE POETRY

1. It has been said that when we read Killarney Clary's poems, "we connect with a language whose evocative powers, lost through habitual use, have been rehabilitated." What does this statement mean? How can a writer's work "rehabilitate" language that has—through cliché and repetition—lost its power to evoke? Find examples in Clary's work where she finds fresh ways to express timeless and universal human feelings and perceptions.

2. Discuss the ways Clary uses language in the piece that reads in its entirety, "A bruise, from purple to yellow. A broken bottle in the sand, a danger we might negligently avoid." Why does she purposely use grammatical transgressions, such as sentence fragments, here? How does the form of the piece help deliver its thematic meaning?

3. Gary Young says of Killarney Clary's prose: "There is no glamour here, little drama. Clary's subjects are prosaic, but her prose captures the internal rhythms of both memory and casual speech, and has been wrenched into a fierce lyricism." What does Young mean by "prosaic" subjects? Find examples of such subjects in Clary's poems. Likewise, how do memory and "casual speech" figure in the above examples of Clary's work?

4. Consider the notion of fictional characterization in Clary's prose poem that reads, "We drove north into Donegal, Daddy drank a rum and coke. He said he felt better. We'd done what we had come for." What does this small number of words (twenty-three, according to my word processor's Word Count function) tell us about the character of Daddy? Based on those twenty-three words, what do you know, or imagine, about Daddy?

5. What is the function of all the names in Clary's poem that begins, "Every time I step into the bathtub, Theresa..." How does the prose poet use specific details and brief character vignettes to suggest the way memories visit us?

✖ WRITING ACTIVITIES: PROSE POETRY

1. Invent a single, fabulous proposition (for example: people are born, grow old, and die in a single day; street signs can talk; you are the only person on earth who can see color; a dog is elected president) and follow that premise to some conclusion in a single paragraph.

2. Memories, even the most trenchant, are often recalled as brief flashes or mere sensations. Think of a past event, some elusive memory, then transcribe it in a single paragraph... three paragraphs at the most. Try to capture the fleeting details, the odd connections, and the idiosyncratic shifts in consciousness such indistinct memories can induce. Don't force the significance of your associations; let the grammar of your prose make the connections.

3. Describe a single, ordinary occurrence (for example, walking through a door; sipping coffee; peeling an orange) without elaboration or excess. Use a single paragraph of the simplest language possible to explain just what happened and how you felt. As a variation of this exercise, observe a room and write an inventory of the place. Try to achieve a sense of fullness by striking the most salient properties of that space. Do this in exactly five sentences. Alternatively, use two sentences to describe a house by delineating what is *not* there: the things that are missing from the place.

9
Creative Nonfiction

Christopher Buckley is a celebrated, much-published and -anthologized author of creative nonfiction, poetry, and literary criticism. He has published creative nonfiction in such journals as *Creative Nonfiction* and *Crazyhorse*, among many others, and his book of creative nonfiction, *Cruising State: Growing Up In Southern California*, was published in 1994. Buckley's poetry has appeared in *The New Yorker, Antaeus, American Poetry Review, The Hudson Review, The Nation, The Iowa Review, The Sewanee Review*, and *Poetry*, among numerous others. His nine books of poetry include *Last Rites* (1980), *Other Lives* (1985), *Dust Light, Leaves* (1986), *Blue Autumn* (1990), *Dark Matter* (1993), *Camino Cielo* (1997), and *Fall From Grace* (1998). Buckley's criticism and reviews have appeared in such journals as *The Bloomsbury Review, Quarterly West*, and *The Denver Quarterly*. For his writing, Buckley has received an NEA grant, a Fulbright Award in creative writing, an award from the W. B. Yeats Society, four Pushcart Prizes, and many other awards. Buckley is a professor at the University of California, Riverside, where he chairs the creative writing department. Although obviously a multifaceted writer of prose and poetry, Buckley will restrict his comments in this chapter to a single prose subgenre: creative nonfiction.

We all have stories. At a party, in conversation with friends, at work, at a conference, or in serious discussion, we are eager to offer our views, our particular experience, or thoughts, our take on the subject. Someone brings up the horrors of a road trip she recently took, the worst boss she ever had, and most of us are eager to contribute a variation on that theme. We tell the truth as we see it, have seen it, or remember seeing it.

When you write down that story or experience, you are—in the widest sense—a writer of creative nonfiction. The journalist essentially reports, and his/her allegiance is always to the facts, to information. The novelist, short story writer, and poet, all focus on an emotion, or idea—a human truth— and to that purpose they will create plot, character, and event to mix in with fact and experience. Their allegiance is to their creation. Writers of creative nonfiction, however, write accurately about experience and do not invent. They may speculate and make use of fictive strategies to make the meaning of their experience clear and accessible, and interesting; among the facts, events, and details of their lives, they seek to discover a connection to the larger world.

While a portion of creative nonfiction's roots are found in journalism, the genre can also be traced back to the classical personal essays of Montaigne and to the tradition of writing "one's memoirs." Creative nonfiction is a "mixed bag," as the would-be-hip said in the '70s, and its umbrella covers many subsets: science and nature writing, interviews and profiles, some travel writing, "immersion journalism," and more. When journalism, biography, diary writing, and academic/scholarly essays are eliminated, what we have left is creative nonfiction. Creative nonfiction then, is a true "story" told in prose.

Recently in a used bookstore, I asked the clerk for the creative nonfiction section. She half-laughed and said, "Why, that would take up most everything in one section—who are you looking for?" Annie Dillard was in "Health & Nature"; Diane Ackerman was under "Science and Psychology," and John McPhee was housed under "Essays and Literary Criticism." Obviously the popularity of the genre and the term "creative nonfiction" had not reached this store.

CREATIVE NONFICTION: WHAT IS IT?

Despite all the possible styles and focuses of creative nonfiction, it is important to remember that "the story" you are writing is "true" to the best of your ability to research and recall it, and that you are *not* writing an academic/argumentative essay which sets out to "prove" some point. You are out to do what almost all writers are trying to do, regardless of genre—take account and make some sense of their lives and experiences.

Creative nonfiction can, in part, point for its recent beginnings to the essays and books of John McPhee, and Loren Eiseley, and to Tom Wolfe and Joan Didion and the "New Journalism" of the early '70s: fact-based, investigative writing that had something more—some angle of personality or first hand, experiential focus that often used techniques of fiction writing, which was almost always first person, and which shaped the material toward a dramatic view or conclusion or idea.

Joan Didion lets us know what it *feels* like to be in El Salvador; the detail and observation—firsthand, quotidian, political—all work together to put the reader in the place, to feel, experience, then to know the danger she felt during her time living in that conflict-scarred Central American country. With personal, experiential, and sensory detail and imagery, the omnipresent terror of life and death in El Salvador at that time is immediately transmitted to the reader. Through a short but very focused scene, we come to understand that an action as simple and everyday as opening your purse might get you shot, and her recounting of those details gives the reader the larger political overview of the country and times without ever using the vague—and uninteresting—jargon of political ideology:

> Whenever I had nothing better to do in San Salvador I would walk up in the leafy stillness of the San Benito and Escalon districts, where the hush at midday is broken only by the occasional crackle of a walkie-talkie, the click of metal moving on a weapon. I recall a day in San Benito when I opened my bag to check an address, and heard the clicking of metal on metal all up and down the street.

Loren Eiseley's appreciations of nature couple his own experience with a good deal of scientific detail and knowledge. His treks through the world are physical and metaphysical—often almost lyrical—and focus on the essential and democratic force of life. His is a worldview which sees people as only one part of nature, and this outlook is brought to bear in the incidents and observations he recounts. He has compassion for all life, and while he focuses often on animals, in one incident from his last book, *The Star Thrower*, he even directs his embrace toward some of the smallest components of life. After suffering a fall and realizing that he is bleeding, he calls out to his blood cells—"Oh, don't go. I'm sorry, I've done for you." And, as W. H. Auden pointed out in the introduction, Eiseley did this quite unselfconsciously, apologizing to his phagocytes and platelets. In his writing, Eiseley combined his own compassionate and mystical view of the universe with a great deal of scientific knowledge, and that made for writing uniquely his own.

One of the leading promoters of creative nonfiction today, and one of the best writers of that brand of nonfiction that instructs and investigates or offers information, is Lee Gutkind. Gutkind is a Professor at the University of Pittsburgh, where he heads the Creative Nonfiction Foundation, edits the important journal *Creative Nonfiction,* and directs the Creative Nonfiction portion of an MFA program that enrolls about sixty-five graduate students. He has championed the phrase "creative nonfiction" as well as "immersion journalism," which describes the writer who immerses him/herself into a job, profession, or life experience in order to bring some important idea and/or information about it out in his/her prose. Gutkind sends his students to the corner bagel store or the police station to research and "find the story"; they will spend a good deal of time there absorbing details, atmosphere, thoughts and experience. The connections here to journalism are obvious. However, the real difference for this aspect of creative nonfiction is that the writing—if successful—is not just a report and will not be engaging to a reader solely by merit of its details. The last thing creative nonfiction calls for is a *Dragnet*/Sgt. Friday approach, "The facts Ma'am, just the facts." Each writer brings his/her own interest and viewpoint to the subject.

A good example of how this style of nonfiction works is found in Gutkind's book, *Many Sleepless Nights,* a book about organ transplantation. During a recent reading of his own work, Gutkind explained that he researched this subject for two years—scrubbing down and going into surgery, flying at night to pick up donated organs, talking to patients—before he finally realized how he could make his subject "work"—make it immediate and engaging to readers.

He ended up tracing the organs of a young donor to two patients who had been waiting for transplants for some time. After the successful surgeries, he traveled with the two recipients—two years later—to the parents who had donated their son's liver, heart and lungs. Being able to shape and frame the detail and information into an essay of dramatic personal detail and focus made the long project succeed, made all the technical information of the actual transplantation very relevant to a particular life. He began with the life of the donor and at the end of the book, Gutkind was there as the father put his ear to the chest of the woman who had his son's heart beating inside her. He needed all the technical and specific information about the subject, but he finally needed the human and personal story which made it meaningful.

SOURCES FOR WORKS OF CREATIVE NONFICTION

How do you choose your subject for a piece of creative nonfiction? You proceed like any writer, you pursue something that interests you. Diane Ackerman, one of the most popular creative nonfiction writers, just follows her interests, and many of her books and essays have a great deal of scientific investigation involved; *A Natural History of The Senses* was a bestseller and it was later made into a PBS television series. In a *Creative Nonfiction* interview Ackerman put it this way:

> I just try to write about what fascinates me and to contemplate what disturbs me or provokes me in some way, or amazes me. I suppose if I have

> a philosophy on this it's that if you set out to nourish your own curiosity
> and your own intellectual yearnings and use yourself as an object of in-
> vestigation, then, without meaning to, you will probably be touching the
> lives of a lot of people. If you can truly interest yourself, chances are you
> can interest a reader.

If you are a successful professional writer like Diane Ackerman or Annie
Dillard, you can travel to Patagonia or the Galapagos Islands to pursue your
interests. If you are a student or beginning writer, you carry out assignments from a class, or set your own assignments based only on whatever
catches your interest—(in many cases, there is a real freedom in that, almost
as much as a well-paid popular writer). Like most of us, you must rely on
the usual source materials immediately available—library, internet, periodi-
cals, TV and radio reports—and you talk to "experts."

Once you are "immersed," once you have the facts and are knowl-
edgeable in the field, you need to find and present your view of it to the
world. Your writing educates, stimulates, illuminates, rescues from loss and
obscurity, and it focuses—that is, connects that information to the larger
world and to people's individual lives. There will be a good many facts—
most often your final essay will not contain all your research—but they will
be filtered through *your* sensibility and intelligence and so will have an
angle, a theme. Very possibly, another writer in your workshop might take
up the same subject and offer a different point of view or evaluation. With
the bagel shop example, one writer might focus on the people and personalities working there, one on the history of the product, one on the economic
impact to a neighborhood. Who has the truth? All do, to varying degrees.

In just about all creative nonfiction, the writer, even if writing a
"fact/immersion journalism" piece, is intimately involved, is the one conducting the events and shaping the experiences in time. Unlike the journalist, the creative nonfiction writer is often manipulating time, the pace of revelation and event, with flashbacks and other framing strategies; he/she is
creating a structure by omitting some parts of experience that do not fit in
with the focus and finding a balance in action and plot that offers pacing
and a dramatic arc to the event or incident. Unlike the fiction writer, however, the creative nonfiction writer cannot create or add in characters or
change the facts of what happened and to whom.

As compelling as "immersion journalism" often is, the majority of
writers coming to creative nonfiction are interested in writing that is largely
autobiographical, but which need not cover the entire span of a life or reveal
some grand philosophical truth arrived at after decades of struggle. Small
incidents from your childhood or adolescence, from your daily working life,
can offer engaging and subtle revelations about a specific time and way of
life; they can expose whole societies and sets of belief through just a humorous or embarrassing incident. Indeed, the majority of most popular books of

creative nonfiction are about family and growing up in a specific place, or about going out in nature or the world and, through specific experience, seeing how life on the planet—big city or small town—is going. Many writers want to preserve a place and time, particular people or characters in their lives, and they want their experience to "add up," to have some meaningful hold on the world, however small, despite the rush of experience. Very often, the writer is the "hero of the story," and your own life and interests are fine sources!

Now, writing is not compelling simply because it is about the writer. The writer of a personal piece needs to do his/her research just as the writer of a fact piece. But one reason for the widening appeal of creative nonfiction is that what you are reading is a true story and there is a real person narrating it—there is something at stake. Like the fact piece, autobiographical writing makes use of many details and thus preserves and examines experience accurately, concretely, poignantly; details add up to emotional weight. In this way writers use words to understand themselves and make their writing memorable—well-crafted, honest, human expression.

A significant portion of readers—those going into bookstores with the intention of buying nonfiction—are drawn to the autobiographical, for in its specificity, it is, if well written, an emblem and touchstone for their lives as well. I'm reminded again of Lee Gutkind's reading: while the audience was interested in the immersion journalism piece he read and discussed, the personal piece—his newest—was the one that grabbed the attention and emotions of the students, writers, and community members in the audience. He had just finished rewriting it that morning while sitting in a Starbuck's, and he was unsure how it would finally work, as most writers are with very new writing. "Green Horns" was the story of three generations of his family trying to get on a plane for a family vacation. His parents, his brother and his son were all there, and there was a problem with the father trying to bring a heavy box, poorly bound, onto the plane. It was a very specific conflict between these family members and yet a universal conflict for all of us with families. It contained tension and resolution, was never sentimental, and had some great good humor which is almost always a plus. The audience, to a person, was more interested in his memoir than in the fact piece, intense as it was.

And so, in creative nonfiction, especially in the autobiographical mode, you are in a manner of speaking, writing your "memoirs," yet just hearing that term is enough to put many people off the idea. I was at The Bread Loaf Writers Conference several years ago and overheard a writer talking about the big advance he was going to get for writing his memoirs. Most of us were about forty years old at the time, and I wondered what in the world someone that relatively young would have to say that would be important enough to be called "memoirs." Wasn't that something only famous people—*old* famous people—wrote? But this writer had grown up in an unusual place and he remembered it in detail and it gave him ground for some larger speculation about human values. A few years later, his book was a success.

At an earlier Bread Loaf conference, I talked with two fine creative nonfiction writers, Haward Baine and Judith Ortiz Cofer, about writing nonfiction. I had written and published one piece of creative nonfiction in the anthology *California Childhood* edited by Gary Soto, but facing the notion of writing more, writing a collection, I was asking, Who would be interested in my life? Haward and Judy both were very encouraging and pointed out that if you wrote well about some particular incident in or aspect of your life, you would find an audience, that most lives, if closely examined, can make for interesting writing and discovery.

And I had, in an important way, already answered that question for myself, for in the piece I wrote for the *California Childhood* anthology, I centered on a period in my young life that involved playing tennis, my father's obsession with practice and success. While an obsessive parent is hardly a new theme, tennis was the vehicle to get to the relationship (or lack thereof) between my father and myself. Although I succeeded to a large degree with tennis, I abandoned it in favor of surfing just when I could have made a big move forward. This creative nonfictional piece, then, ended up being about will and emotion and self-determination. But all those "big" ideas and emotions came out of the basic incidents and conflicts, the particular details and confrontations between my father and myself. I used scenes, action, and some dialogue and a little evaluation of events, but I never philosophized or used the language of abstraction. I ended up writing my "memoirs"—a collection of essays largely about growing up in Santa Barbara. I received no advance, but the book sold well enough for a university press publication. Books about growing up—a time, a place, a people, a region—comprise a substantial portion of creative nonfiction. Writers such as Annie Dillard (*American Childhood*), Russell Baker (*Growing Up*), Eudora Welty (*One Writer's Beginnings*), Richard Hugo (*The Real West Marginal Way*), Alastair Reid (*Hauntings*), and less senior writers such as Gary Soto (*Living Up The Street*), Judith Ortiz Cofer (*Silent Dancing*), Kim Barnes (*In The Wilderness*), Garrett Hongo (*Volcano*), D. J. Waldie (*Holy Land*), have all written well and variously about where they grew up and the events and people that gave their lives meaning in their own place and time.

The events you never forget, the incidents that remain at the surface of consciousness, the images that return, waking or dreaming: These are the subjects of personal creative nonfiction. You discover, in the process of following that subconscious or emotional trail of events, in the process of writing and rewriting, what the image or event means to you, how that particular incident or story contains its own shining interpretation of the world. Rarely, if ever, in autobiographical writing, do you set out with a Big Idea you are sure you will prove out, a rule for life which everyone should know about and follow.

RESEARCH: GETTING STARTED ON A CREATIVE NONFICTION PIECE

For many creative nonfiction writers, the research/fact-finding part of the writing launches the project, and investigation and interviews often provide an overall direction for the writing, especially if it is a "fact" piece. For the autobiographical writer, just jotting lists of names in a notebook—place names, street names, brand names, names of people—is often a good way to begin.

Either way, research—formal or informal—is a big part of creative nonfiction. Although some shorter vivid writing can be drawn completely from memory, many times an early autobiographical draft will need to be reinforced with details and information not readily accessed by memory. A writer will often have to interview old friends, parents, neighbors, consult encyclopedias, newspapers, and history texts to be sure of the accuracy of memory or to fill in the blanks. On the other hand, in dealing with a general interest in a new subject, or to amplify an experience, to help focus and understand its meaning, a writer may have to do background checks for technical or scientific language and terms, may have to learn the jargon of a particular job or sport.

Sometimes just "reading up" on a new subject and taking notes will be the way to find an entrance to a subject; using the old journalistic questions Who, What, Why, Where, and When, will at least head you in a profitable direction. Freewriting, concentrating on an image or emotion, a memory, scene, or landscape—without any idea of outcome or theme, without any road map, without any editing as you go—is a fine way to start, as the revision and editing process will usually allow thought and emotional investment to bubble to the surface.

In Annie Dillard's third book of creative nonfiction, *Teaching A Stone To Talk: Expeditions and Encounters,* she opens the book with a stunning piece about encountering a weasel while on a walk not far from her home. It is written directly from experience and while technically in the past tense, much of the writing is charged with an immediacy of the encounter between the writer and the weasel, and in fact concludes with a mystical and momentary understanding of the animal brain in the weasel and in us all.

> ...I don't think I can learn from a wild animal how to live in particular—shall I suck warm blood, hold my tail high, walk with my footprints precisely over the prints of my hands?—but I might learn something of mindlessness, something of the purity of living in the physical senses and the dignity of living without bias or motive. The weasel lives in necessity and we live in choice, hating necessity and dying at the last ignobly in its talons. I would like to live as I should, as the weasel lives as he should. And I suspect that for me the way is like the weasel's:

open to time and death painlessly, noticing everything, remembering nothing, choosing the given with a fierce and pointed will.

But before Dillard turned out the finished narrative of her experience, she obviously went to the library and read up on weasels; she wanted to know what she was talking about before pushing through to the larger understanding that the weasel brought to her about herself, about us all. The first page and a half of Dillard's weasel piece reflects her research process, gives us a lot of background information about weasels. This is a base, some ground from where the mind can take off, a solid base for speculation, some authority and expertise:

> A weasel is wild. Who knows what he thinks? He sleeps in his underground den, his tail draped over his nose. Sometimes he lives in his den for two days without leaving. Outside, he stalks rabbits, mice, muskrats, and birds, killing more bodies than he can eat warm and often dragging the carcasses home. Obedient to instinct, he bites his prey at the neck, either splitting the jugular vein at the throat or crunching the brain at the base of the skull, and he does not let go.

I began the book that would become *Cruising State: Growing Up In Southern California* in 1992 when I was loaned a house in Santa Barbara for the summer. This put me in my hometown, where all my memories were, and it gave me access to friends who would provide facts as well as access to the locale to check those facts. I began to see that there really were "stories" behind my memories or feelings about my past and my home, stories that could expand with more detail and characters. I had made a few rough notes about incidents or feelings. Topics and scenes I remembered from childhood and adolescence, and I just sat at a typer those summer mornings and went as fast as I could, never stopping to think of connections, spelling, paragraphing, editing—I just "freewrote" as fast as I could.

I was not then thinking or planning what I would write. Each incident had a lyric impulse, an emotional center—and all my drafts—rough as they were—had me in the center directing traffic and discovering where I wanted it to go as I went. Later on, having revised each one ten or fifteen times, I began to think about what I had done. I realized that a consistent idea or social undercurrent about class and opportunity surfaced in most of the essays and backed up the more prominent theme of cherishing a lost time and environment. I began to trace that initial response to change through each piece and saw that the lyric impulse—the personal emotion of the writer—was really the catalyst for this mode of autobiographical nonfiction, one that had the writer wanting to stop or preserve some event in time as true to that original emotion and vision as possible.

Nevertheless, you may often need to do a good deal of research for facts and dates and place names and street names *et cetera*. I did in writing "Cruising State" and I began a new memoir-type piece, "History of My

Hair" (which is included at the end of this chapter), in the same manner. Whereas most of my writing begins with a few minutes of freewriting in a notebook—jotting down the data of memory as fast as the images appear, writing out a particularly vivid scene and just seeing where it leads without editing or second-guessing myself—this new essay began with more of a research technique. What really got me started was the love of all that language and jargon from the 50s hairstyles—Duck Tail, Jelly Roll, Flat Top, Page Boy, Bee Hive, Fenders—and much more. I wanted to use all those terms in a piece of writing; they were memorable and exotic and I loved the intrinsic power, the nostalgic stardust behind those words, and that got me going . . . that and the image of my friends and myself walking up and down the main street in town, a quarter pound of grease holding the wings on each side of our head in place, as happy as I was ever likely to be. Brylcreem, Butch Wax, Wildroot Cream Oil: I'd carried that language around in my head since I was in fifth grade—like lost incantations—and all I knew when I first started to write was that they wanted to get out on the page and do their work.

I called up friends, had them over for dinner, opened bottles of wine and got them talking. Once their memories were lubricated and running along well, I pulled out a yellow pad and took notes. I wrote to other friends I grew up with and asked them to define terms and check facts for me. I would brainstorm with my oldest friends and we'd try to remember jargon and slang from decades ago that would bring back and convey those times and that experience. I checked the names and location of streets, call letters of radio stations, top-40 hits and movies. While "History of My Hair" is not what I would truly call a *fact piece*—writing that instructs—it is, to a degree, immersion journalism. While it was not a documentary on popular culture, I presented, in as much authentic jargon and language as I could find, the details and facts of that time and that particular lifestyle, and I hoped that all that specificity coupled with dramatic scenes would convey a time and way of life now vanished, make sense of our lives in those days and see the humor in it as well.

I needed to compare notes with my friends regarding differences between a "Waterfall" style of combing the hair forward in front and the jelly roll. I could remember some, but not all of the Rock 'n' Roll Stars who had Big Hair in those days. I checked out some photo calendars and other memorabilia on Elvis, visited a 50s-style restaurant in town that had old record jackets and a Billboard Top 40 on the walls, ate some greasy burgers and did research at the same time.

So, to get started, do your research and freewrite in a notebook following whatever sharp memory or vivid scene presents itself to you, whatever haunting image, language, or piece of dialogue—anything that has been lingering for months or years. Then, start to support your rough notes and interest with some research, whether that is checking with friends or with encyclopedias. Remember that even with personal writing you will have to do some "research" for facts and detail, for confirmation of what was actually said, by whom, at what point in the remembered incident. There will be plenty of time later to revise and focus your writing. The Old Testament tells us that there is nothing new under the sun. Do not worry that the actual subject of your interest or memory has been written about many times before. As long as you write in specific and firsthand detail, it will have your particular mark on it.

THE "CREATIVE" PART OF CREATIVE NONFICTION

O.K., then, where does the "creative" part of creative nonfiction come in? It becomes part of the story in the editing and the later drafts, when you consciously employ some of the strategies of fiction writing and rely as best you can on your memory or the memory of others to fill in the detail or narrative that can no longer be verified as 100 percent true or fully recalled.

Creative nonfiction is not strict history, or autobiography, or journalism. You work from memory as accurately as you can, and as Judith Ortiz Cofer points out in her preface to *Silent Dancing*—as she talks about one of her greatest writing influences, Virginia Woolf—

> She accepts the fact that in writing about one's life, one often has to rely on that combination of memory, imagination and strong emotion that may result in "Poetic Truth." In preparing to write her memoirs Woolf said, "I dream, I make up pictures of a summer's afternoon."

The Nobel poet Pablo Neruda in the preface to his *Memoirs/Confieso Que He Vivido,* tells the reader something similar:

> In these memoirs or recollections there are gaps here and there, and sometimes they are also forgetful, because life is like that. Intervals of dreaming help us to stand up under days of work. Many of the things I remember have blurred as I recalled them, they have crumbled to dust, like irreparably shattered glass.

When gaps present themselves, and you have exhausted all research possibilities, you do what poets do—you fill in the blanks as plausibly and accurately as possible. You remember as best you can, always concentrating on what will advance the piece of writing—the action, the theme—in the best way, and what will stay "close to the bone" emotionally and narratively.

You employ the "creative" part of creative nonfiction when you use the techniques of fiction to shape your piece of writing. You may not be a Nobel-Prize-winning writer, but you have an interior life affected by the world around you, and you can discover the small but meaningful connections between the two. While you remember as accurately as you can, you still *shape* your writing—condense, omit, refocus time and sequence for a fiction-like pace or dramatic movement/arc. This is not documentary writing, this is not journalism in which the focus is just information. Your essay will not be interesting because it is true, but because it is specific and dramatic, and to a degree, reflective.

The use of the techniques of fiction—plot, setting, and dialogue—are very important, then, to creative nonfiction as they work through experience to direct the reader to your emotion/idea/theme. Soon after I sketch the setting of the times in "History of My Hair," for example, I move to action—a memory of my first day at a new school in second grade and of being punched-out by the class tough who has his hair combed in high Hotrod style. Here I was consciously employing a plotting technique, a bit of action to grab some interest.

Most successful creative nonfiction essays develop a sequence of scenes, and as in fiction, you have to be careful not to be too discursive, not to philosophize too much. The old creative writing adage about "show don't tell" still applies for the most part. Gary Soto's short essay "Catholics" opens with action, a vivid detail. He is being punished for fighting; he's in Catholic grade school and the nun is lecturing the class on poverty in the world.

> I was standing in the waste basket for fighting on the day we received a hunger flag for Biafra. Sister Marie, a tough nun who could throw a softball farther than most men, read a letter that spoke of the grief of that country, looking up now and then to measure our sympathy and to adjust her glasses that had slipped from her nose. She read the three-page letter, placed it on her desk, and walked over to the globe to point out Africa, a continent of constant despair. I craned my neck until, without realizing it, I had one foot out of the wastebasket. Sister Marie turned and stared me back into place, before she went on to lecture us about hunger.

This very compact creative nonfictional piece is essentially one scene; as you read it, observe how almost the entire essay is a series of actions and how those actions are emblems for what Soto probably now thinks of that type of educational experience. Notice, too, that Soto never editorializes; the last sentence of the essay subtly sums up, but even there he is sticking to the level of experience and letting the subject, actions, and details add up so that the reader is put almost directly into the scene. This is clearly different in strategy from the academic essay which is purposely unambiguous, with a central thesis and a specific order of ideas and evidence of support/argument. By choosing precise and resonant specifics and action Soto orders the sequence of events so that they indict the callous behavior of the nun toward her students.

You need to decide what to include, what to convey in action or dialogue, and what to leave out. *Simply reporting every detail of a true story will not make for interesting reading.* This is why most writers work in scenes. A scene has a beginning, middle, and end, is charged with action and/or dialogue. In drama, a scene begins when someone comes on stage and ends when someone leaves the stage. You can think cinematically and fictionally in this manner. Ask yourself what happened, what actions and gestures were the most important or significant in your memory of the event. Attempt to see which action or piece of dialogue is the most important and therefore the climax of the scene or incident.

No reader wants a sermon or a lecture. He/she wants as much as possible to experience events along with (or through) the narrator. You can open your piece with a scene, some action, which hints at or echoes the most dramatic point in your narrative, or which is emblematic for the focus of the piece, and then work backward in time to fill in the necessary detail and background. You may omit, rearrange the order of action for greater effect. However, unlike the fiction writer, you cannot invent action—you are telling a true story.

Similarly with dialogue, you cannot make up things for your characters to say, insert something bright or clever you wished you would have said in the circumstance. But dialogue is a very important component of creative nonfiction. Listen to what people say, try to remember as well as you can what was actually said and see how it might contribute to making your point, how it might add irony or resonance. If you hear or remember something said which is very important or particularly phrased, write it down—in your notebook, on a cocktail napkin or hardware store receipt, on anything! Don't let good dialogue/lines slip away.

Note the importance of what the nun says in Gary Soto's "Catholics," how her dialogue reveals a lack of concern for the children directly in her charge.

> "With hunger, heavier people would live longer—they have more fat, you see."...
>
> "If we didn't have any food whatsoever, Gloria would probably live the longest."...
>
> "And Gary . . . well, he would be one of the first to die."

Notice, too, when you read his piece, how accurate and credible the thoughts of Gary as a young student are! Soto moves back into his child's mind and remembers as accurately as he can—using direct and uncomplicated phrasing—what he then might have thought, though when he was writing he no doubt had to reinvent the exact wording.

In "History of My Hair" neither Tuck Schneider nor I can, some thirty-five years later, remember—word for word—what exact phrases and terms were used in fifth grade. But I remembered Tuck calling G. G. Colson off me that first day in second grade and I recalled Tuck explaining how his brother was expelled from high school for combing his hair into a duck tail. The important point is that the dialogue contains the essence of what he said, and it amplifies the visual and experiential quality of the scenes. Overall, however, your writing must all be credible, possible, and accurate in the largest sense. The "creative" aspect then, comes in shaping, structuring—writing in scenes and ordering action and dialogue—and in filling in facts and details.

As importantly, the "creative" aspect of creative nonfiction is found in focus and making linkages, connections between events and their motivations and outcomes, and this gives your writing, as it nears its final draft, its theme or viewpoint. I managed to link an initial interest in the 50s Rock 'n' Roll culture with hairstyles and the underlying social judgments which proved, over time, to be pretty unimportant—an obvious sequence of events it seems to me now. However, the 60s and 70s, the Vietnam war, and subculture in America changed a great deal of our perceptions, personal and social, yet I did not know I was going there when I began writing the piece. I knew I wanted to remember and cherish that time, those friends, and all the rich detail and language that went with that simple but exotic life style.

Creative nonfiction is theme- and voice-driven, not plot- or character-driven as is much fiction. The writer of creative nonfiction does not invent a protagonist, a main character. The writer is the "hero" of the essay most of the time. I wrote "What's Fair" about my friend Peter Sozzi—someone I've known since we were six—and even though he was the subject of the essay, I was right in there in most scenes, and it was my memory of it all, of him, my sensibility through which the events were filtered. The piece was largely flattering, yet even so Peter wrote to me and said, "It's interesting to see how others see you and remember you." Which was a bit of a shock at first, as I was sure that my view of his life was of course the true one and he would agree with every interpretation I had made; after all, I had interviewed him about many incidents in his life. Of course this even further reinforces the idea of "creative" nonfiction—even though you are telling the "truth" to the best of your ability, even though there are objective facts—other writers, readers, participants, might see it differently, put a different "spin" on the same events, if they wrote it!

FOCUS AND VOICE IN CREATIVE NONFICTION

Creative nonfiction is, almost without exception, written in the first person; journalism, as often as not, is written in the third person. The personal cast of the voice colors experience, moves it in a certain direction, and this is in sharp contrast to the objective reporting of journalism. Especially in the case of the autobiographical piece, your voice, your tone and attitude in narrating, is close to the "actual" experience, more real, so that the reader—as in fiction—has a sense of discovery. Moreover, there is a point, a subtle shade of opinion or response to experience detectable in the voice, the writer's attitude; there is an idea or fresh emotional take traveling just beneath the surface of the action. In creative nonfiction that point, that idea is more experientially arrived at through action and dialogue as opposed to the formal arguments and debate of academic essays. Creative nonfiction is more open to your viewpoint and interpretation and is not as objective and quantifiable as the academic essay. What does this mean to the speaker? What has the narrator learned? What have we, as readers, learned? What's at risk? What are the values? These are questions that a reader should be able to answer after reading a piece of creative nonfiction.

In this vein, Natalia Rachel Singer's essay "Nonfiction In First Person, Without Apology" offers good advice for beginning writers in this genre (as well as for any writers, really):

> Nonfiction writing in first person teaches the young writer to sharpen her powers of observation and use of memory, to hone his specificity and finesse for naming concrete things, and to create an honest, living voice.

Honesty and voice are especially important in nonfiction. A reader wants authority for the facts and experience, and he/she wants to be interested and compelled by the particular viewpoint. Creative nonfiction readers are generally not interested in lab reports or lectures; they want to move along with the writer in her/his experience and see the pieces add up to a reasonable interpretation of events. Readers want to believe the writer—the human element—the voice is paramount if a writer wants to persuade a reader that the journey is worth the time and effort.

Likewise, the mood and texture—along with the presentation of the work—must be credible, engaging, singularly identifiable and lyric at the same time. Autobiographical writing especially relies on voice to engage the reader and sustain the emotional undercurrent of the piece. A touch of irony and an honest bit of humility—even humor—help in this regard. Pretentiousness, "wisdom," a superior attitude, will put a reader off from creative nonfiction as rapidly as it will from any other genre. Voice is not a popular subject in academic camps mired in critical theory these days, but a clear, honest, and exact voice is essential for the nonfiction essay. Who is writing this; why then is it interesting or meaningful to my life? are questions that the initial voice of an essay should immediately answer. The audience for creative nonfiction is a very wide one, and it extends far beyond the academy.

TO SUMMARIZE:

- Write small—your interests and life experiences can be compelling/interesting if looked at with honesty and detail. Write in detail in the language of experience using specific concrete nouns and adjectives. If you are particular and accurate the "big idea" will surface necessarily through the force of your detail and facts and actions. It's O.K. to be yourself!

- Use fictive techniques. Write/structure in scenes—use action and dialogue, omit unnecessary information and narration to better make connections. Stick to your focus.

- Don't tell all, don't do too much philosophizing. A reader can understand by example and action—don't be too editorial. Don't summarize.

- What's the point? Remember, this is not journalism; there is an idea or theme or fresh emotional response to which all the elements in your piece should point. It need not be stated in summary prose, but it should be clear finally. Most writers write to try to make sense of some portion of their lives and experience.

HISTORY OF MY HAIR
Christopher Buckley

Hair. In the late 50s and early 60s, it was about all you had. All the consumerism and conspicuous consumption were decades in the future. You were a kid, you wanted to be cool, you had a comb and a little grease and you made the best of it. There were no designer names, few brand names, and, especially if you attended a parochial school, everyone looked the same. Except for their hair. You could be as cool, as way-out as your hair. It was a democracy of sorts for youth—an equal opportunity for radicalization on the smallest scale. But to buck the "I like Ike" society, its lack of hair, and imagination—

"A Living History of My Hair" by Christopher Buckley. Reprinted by permission of Christopher Buckley. Buckley's collection of nonfiction is CRUISING STATE: Growing Up In Southern California was published by University of Nevada Press, 1994. His 9th book of poetry, FALL FROM GRACE, is just out from BK MK Press/University of Missouri, Kansas City. He is chair of the Creative Writing Deparment at the University of California Riverside.

its Robert B. Hall and J.C. Penney simple suit view of the world—was difficult to do. Hair was, as it always has been, a source of vanity, but it was then the one possible way to be yourself, be "with it," and it was the way to be.

1955, and my first day in a new school a kid comes up to me before class and says over his shoulder to a friend, "I wonder what this new kid looks like when he cries." I barely had a second for his salami-breath and crooked nose to register before he sucker-punched me in the stomach. As I was doubling over, I noticed his hair—just a kid and he had it combed like some hot rodder in one of those early teen-hoodlum movies; it was wiry and obviously held in place by Butch Wax, an application so thick that it glistened like lard as the sun struck the side of his head. The top was combed straight forward, tight wings flared back along the sides, and the front worked to a small spit curl in the center of his forehead—a wave working from each side to meet and crash in the middle. G. G. Colson was a "tough" as I immediately learned from his right uppercut, and from the fact that he dared the nuns with a hair style that was basically forbidden.

The kid who called him off after one punch and who later became my friend, Tuck Schneider, also risked a similar waterfall effect and flat-combed top a little later in 5th grade. By then, we had all the examples we were ever gong to need, every one our parents wished we'd never had. Freddy Cannon, Bobby Rydell, Fabian and Eddie Cochran appeared in movies and on Dick Clark's American Bandstand with their huge jelly-rolls, a wave in the front at least three inches high. Elvis had arrived on TV's Ed Sullivan Show and taken it a step further than that big wave in the front rolling back in grease—he'd combed the sides back until they met in the back of his head. This was called a Ducktail; this was going too far for the parents and the self-appointed moral guardians of the society then. On that first Ed Sullivan show the censors had directed the cameras to cut Elvis off at the waist and so avoid his wiggling hips and knees—they had to show the hair! We didn't know much—fashion was not infused into every inch of the media, into the middle and lower middle class as it is now. Just pick up any of the calendars or photo books on Elvis and look at the clothes he was wearing in the 50s and 60s—awful stuff—but so were everyone else's, and no one was looking at the clothes. As kids, we knew uniforms, suits, and blue jeans, with jeans not being allowed at school, restaurants, church, or almost anywhere else. Otherwise, we didn't take much notice. Everyone seemed to have roughly the same gear. There were only two or three brands of tennis shoes, all black high tops and they all cost about two dollars. But if you maneuvered your hair into a Duck Tail as Tuck Schneider's older brother Joe did, you got noticed. Noticed enough to get suspended from Santa Barbara Public High School, a place those of us in Catholic school saw as a bastion of liberal thinking. After three days Joe recombed his hair so the wings on the side of his head did not flare up too much and so they did not meet in the back of his head and returned to school and some modest celebrity. One day after school at Tuck's house, with no one home, we both stood in front of the tall mirror in his brother's room and tried to comb our hair into Duck Tails; Tuck's did not work as he had slightly curly hair, but mine worked perfectly as I already had the wave in front and my hair was straight. Tuck encouraged me to leave it like that, but I didn't have near the nerve. We saw Joe as a minor hero—his hair, just a shade lighter, was exactly like Elvis'. And of course the first thing he did after school, as soon as the first foot touched the public sidewalk on Anapamu or Milpas Street, was to pull out his comb and put the doo-wop back in the wings and rolls there—the Brylcreem, Butch Wax, or Wild Root Cream Oil more than adequate to accommodate the more radical remodeled coif as he stepped out into the world on his own.

One day at the end of lunch period, Schneider, Colson, Fisher, Knapp and Sozzi and myself were all in front of the mirrors in the washroom, and we decided, no doubt at Colson's instigation, to comb our hair like rock-n-roll stars. Colson combed the side wings of his springy hair forward with a duck-tail in the back, something no one had ever done (or would want to do?) so far as we knew. A few went for the waterfall-spit–curl, and forward-combed the top. Sozzi and I tried for the Jimmy Dean style with the jelly-roll wave and high sides winging back—hard to tell from Elvis', really. In we went when the bell rang, thinking we were "really gone" and drawing lots of looks from our classmates. Right out we went as soon as Mrs. Hansen saw us. We would go back to the washroom and comb our hair "properly" or she'd call in the Principal, Sr. Vincent de Paul. VDP we knew would suspend us. Lucky for us, Mrs. Hansen was a lay-person as we called them then. Oh, we realized we'd gone too far, but we thought we were somebody for three or four minutes.

For some reason the small move teens made toward independence with a few hair styles was viewed as downright immoral—as was the music in general of course—the hair guilty as emblem and by association. We returned to Mrs. Hansen's history class with our hair parted properly on the side and modest waves in the front like every Junior Chamber of Commerce man and his son, and sat there quietly waiting for our graduation when we thought we'd be able to wear our hair however we wanted. We'd seen some movies, some posters or clips on TV, seen James Dean or Elvis or Fabian just stop in the middle of what they were doing, spread their feet apart for balance, reach to their back pocket for their comb as smoothly as some gunfighter in a western reaching for his gun, and re-comb and shape their hair before continuing. There was flair to the move—the comb was whisked out and two or three full strokes front to back applied; a small shake of the shoulders and adjustment of the shirt sleeves, then an almost existential (if we'd known that word then) gaze in the eyes was also required. We mimicked this in no time, but only those at the top of the social pecking order could get away with it; those further down or with less flagrant styles were razzed when they tried the same moves.

After the summer, a couple of our friends came to school with Flat-Tops—the newest thing and a style that skirted the taboos as it was essentially a crew cut, the hair cut down to a half inch evenly on the top, but it left the sides and back long enough to comb back into "fenders." High schoolers and hot rodders left the very front of the Flat-Top long so they could comb it toward the middle of their foreheads into a dangling spit curl. Younger kids had the front only slightly longer than the buzzed top and just had it stick straight up and spiky. Lots of the Flat-Toppers carried a little bottle of Butch-Wax that came with a comb which you replaced in the bottle after using, but its popularity didn't last long as it didn't stay closed and so was a very messy proposition. My father absolutely forbade me a Flat-Top and in the summers my mother always argued for a crew cut, the universal buzz.

Only when your parents weren't paying attention, which wasn't often, could you comb your hair in the current fashion and thereby be somebody to yourself and your peers. My father was always after me to comb my hair like his, straight back, no grease. He would only barely sanction the average middle American part on the side. I should—and someday he just knew I'd have the sense to—wear my hair straight back—somehow, that was the only acceptable and moral style. It was serious business then, how you wore your hair—people cared, noticed. Each morning I rubbed enough Wildroot Cream Oil into my hair that it would hold whatever shape I re-figured it to once at school. I then went mainly for the wings along the side and a large Fabian-tall wave in front. I had lots of hair and enough hair oil to be at the top of the fashion in my school group.

But in no time the 50s, which had hung on into the early 60s, were gone. Sure, Elvis was still Elvis, but surfing had come on, was popular in movies, music and dances, and, for some, as an actual sport. But popular culture soon had Elvis and Fabian with their shiny hair completely in place riding twenty foot waves at Sunset Beach, Hawaii, or shooting the pier at Huntington Beach. I'd learned to surf and had been out on some big waves—it didn't take much experience to know how phony those Elvis surf films were with him standing in the middle of a board, feet parallel like a rank beginner, a studio fan blowing in his face and perhaps only two or three strands of his Duck Tail out of place. No real surfers ever went to those films. And then there were the "Ho-daddies"—"Hodads" for short—guys with greasy hair who drove around with boards in or on their cars to parties, or to the surf spots, guys who never went out into the surf.

Right then, what you wanted for the surfer look was dry, shaggy hair, and by all means blond. That left me out on most counts. And for the first year or so I was surfing, ages thirteen and fourteen, I was in a boys' boarding school where you still had to have a short cut and pass inspection for dinner—suit and tie, shoes shined, hair slicked into place. I'd quit the Alberto VO-5 and thicker greases that were still fairly popular in the early 60s.

I'd gone over to Vitalis, a more watery application which, after it dried, left your hair stiff and certainly in place. One friend at that school, Joe Lubin, (a liberal user of VO-5) invited me home to his house in Beverly Hills for a weekend, seemed there was a party with a number of his friends, and he had a date for me—a really cute girl, he said. So we showed up in sport coats, ties and slacks (the Beatles and the rest of the early "British Invasion" of rock-n-rollers would still dress that way in the years right ahead) and met our dates. I could see that Joe was there to meet his girlfriend and they went off immediately to the dance floor and glued themselves together. My date was indeed as attractive as promised, but she wanted nothing to do with me. I thought perhaps it was because I wasn't from her school. But later in the evening, I heard from Joe that the problem was my hair! He had promised her a date with a surfer, and although she herself did not surf she knew that "surfers" did not have black hair like mine. We were introduced and that was basically the last I saw of her. I sat by myself for a while, knowing no one there except Joe who was still leaning into his date on the dance floor. Finally, one of the cheerleaders came over and asked me to dance; she hung around and talked a while as well. Obviously a more mature woman, she still appreciated the hair styles and look of the 50s!

But I could see something had to be done. Here I was, a real surfer with an appropriately beat-up Yater surfboard and surf knots on my knees, but I did not look the part. That summer I tried the lemon routine. A surfing friend told me that another guy we knew, Don Bullock, had actually gotten his dark hair to turn blond by putting lemon on it and staying in the sun for a few hours. We saw Don at one of the beaches and he had this slim streak of light red in the front, miles from blond. Nevertheless, I tried it, but the lemon thing never worked. Lots of kids were trying the peroxide route, which I never did; you could always tell those who had; their hair had a very artificial orange tint. I just went for the surfing and forgot about my hair for a while; besides, my friend and the best surfer in the area, Harry Fowler, had coal black hair—so, so what?

Grease was gone and if you surfed, you just combed your hair once in a while and let it be as dry and floppy as possible. There were unofficial dress codes in high school although there were no uniforms. The Beatles hit in 1963–64 and I can remember thinking how radically long their hair was in that picture on the cover of their first album. Look at that now and John Paul George and Ringo look as if they have very respectable cuts. Of course the late 60s and 70s came with truly long hair for everyone, but then just a touch over the ears with bangs in the front was radical rock-n-roll communist-hippiedom. My friend Francis Orsua—who to this day has a thick mop of hair—and I skipped a few haircuts and headed for the Beatle look. Orsua even got his picture taken and put in the local *Santa Barbara News Press*—he was just walking down State Street and a newspaper photographer, out to capture a newsworthy fringe element loose on our streets, took a photo of Orsua with his hair over his collar. Mine was not so long, but without any hair oil, that huge wave a couple years previously now fell across my forehead, and I had bangs easily as long as Paul McCartney's, or so some girls I knew had told me. On a Friday after school, the disciplinarian, Fr. Bernard, called Orsua and me over from our lockers and without argument or complaint, told us to be sure and see a barber at the weekend or not bother coming to school Monday. What could we do? We got it cut and lost what little notoriety we'd achieved.

For the girls, then, length of hair was not such a critical factor—long or short, any style was acceptable. Many wore a variation on the pageboy, shoulder length hair with bangs. However, when there was a dance, they had to spend hours torturing their hair up into a Beehive, a style that made the top of their heads look like a funnel of cotton candy. Lacquered and sprayed into form, they predated the Coneheads by many years; it was brittle and hard at the same time, but for formal occasions, it was the style. Some girls back-combed or "ratted" their hair to make it poof up and stay poofed, to accommodate the Beehive look beyond the parameters of a dance. There was Gilda Bedola who always had the biggest blond hair at school, and though she was an inveterate "ratter" she was plenty good-looking. She only dated boys from the public high school, though, and whenever we saw her someone always brought up the story of the girl who never took down her ratted Beehive and who was finally killed by black widows that built a nest in there. Surely an apocryphal story, since people at so many different schools knew it. But it says something about the senselessness of style in the first place—what we will put up with or aspire to judging one look better than another.

I went off to college in northern California and within a year or so Orsua went into the Marines, and that was the end of hair considerations for us both. Orsua just wasn't allowed to have any, full stop, and I had too many things to worry about as a freshman in St. Mary's College in Moraga, California. Ours was the last freshman class to be "hazed"—systematically humiliated and tortured by older students. In the past, many freshmen had their heads shaved and painted, but in our class that only happened to one or two. We spent time sneaking around trying not to be apprehended by the upper classmen. There were studies, sports, work on weekends, and just too many people and pressures to worry about hair style then; I just got it cut once in a while in the campus barber shop and didn't think much about it. Didn't think much that is, until our senior year, 1968–69, and some serious opposition to the Vietnam war started to arise nationwide. At our conservative, middle class college, with a student body of about 900, there were only fourteen or fifteen students openly opposed to the war, and only one student in a class below us had long hair—that was it, one guy in the whole school had some outward symbol of protest. I grew a mustache that year, but upon visiting my mother and stepfather on spring break had to shave it off as my mother insisted that my stepfather would not stand for it—after all, he had been good enough to pick up the bills for college tuition after my father bailed out on the entire project. I shaved the mustache that night. How much was hair finally worth?

But the 70s were right around the corner. I took a teaching position at a Catholic school, grades 7 and 8, right out of college. I had decided some time ago to teach, and I also hoped that I would receive a teaching deferment from the war. At Nativity Catholic School in Torrance, I met Doug Salem, the other new hire for 7th and 8th grades, someone who would become a wonderful and important friend to me until he died at age 32 in a car accident. On that first day of meetings before class we became instant friends. He had normal length hair, but also had long sideburns. As the year wore on and we both became involved in opposition to the war, saving the environment, the next Crosby Stills Nash and Young album, his hair became long and he wore striped Levis and looked the part of the counter culture. But he was brilliant, and his ideas on social justice and morality had a great effect on me. A few years later, still with his long hair, he would be appointed dean of a law school at the age of 31. I decided to also grow my hair long then, though in truth it was nothing approaching the shoulder length hair style that would become common in only another year or so. The length of our hair became a problem; parents at Nativity (Torrance was home of the largest Armed Forces Day Parade in the U.S.) were calling meetings, calling Doug and me communists (I had played a Bob Dylan record in class!). By the end of the year neither of us wanted to return.

Doug headed for law school and I took a job teaching the same grades at a Catholic school in Santa Barbara—Mt. Carmel, the same school where G. G. Colson had stood there in his hot-rod hair and punched me out fifteen years before. When I went to see the principal—who really wanted a male teacher for the upper grades, for discipline and for coaching sports—she said the job was mine but I would have to cut my hair, after all, the students were not allowed to have long hair. I pointed out that I was not a student and had just had it cut the day before the interview. Either way, I needed a job and would have to keep it short. When I called a few weeks later about books, contracts, and the like, I was told that I no longer had the job. The other teacher who had agreed to teach the 7th and 8th grade math in trade for the 5th and 6th grade English (I could not teach any math) had backed out of the deal. I suggested that maybe she should lose her job since she had broken our contract, but was told that she lived with another woman who taught at the school and if one were fired the other had threatened to quit. So, goodbye.

I had one month's rent money left and had to find a job pronto. The only thing available to me at the last minute was to go back to the grocery store chain for which I worked in high school and during summers in college. I saw the personnel manager, said nothing about my teaching experience and little about my education and was told I could have a position at just about the lowest level, but first I needed to look at this chart she pulled out from the desk showing allowable grooming for employees, including those who were only going to make $2.50 an hour. If I had a haircut, I could report to my old store on Milpas Street on Monday morning and start mopping and carrying out groceries. I went to see my friend Billy Bonilla who was now a barber and paid him what would be close to three hours grocery wages to cut my hair.

Of course in the 70s, long hair became the norm. TV news anchors, sports announcers, politicians and preachers, everyone and anyone had longer hair. I couldn't see how some baseball players kept their uniform caps on, and many didn't as soon as they moved to make a play. Coast to coast, we had the stage production "Hair" and when something was very difficult or terrifying it was described as "hairy"; if an act required a lot of courage, the idiom had it that "it took a lot of hair" to do it. Go figure. Take out some photos from the 70s, and, if you can get past that truly bizarre Pirates of the Caribbean garb we all wore then, look at our hair. Long, stringy, stacked, frizzy, chunky, you name it. It was there in abundance. I went back to graduate school at San Diego State University and after that at University of California, Irvine. While taking my degrees, I managed to make money in the summers teaching tennis and so there was no need for me not to have my hair long, truly long. I wore head bands, I fit in; I went more or less unnoticed through the times. While staying at my father's house those summers in school, I could see that he was undergoing a hair transplant. Each evening he'd have to retire to the bedroom and put on this shower cap to cover an application of salves and medicines that went over these pencil point plugs of hair that had been cut into his scalp. What a pain, I thought, figuring I'd never have to worry about that—my hair still thick then and long in my late 20s.

I taught part-time at a number of places after graduating from Irvine, longish hair not a problem to get the job. When Proposition 13 passed in California, colleges and community colleges had to cut their part-time teachers and my stint as a freeway faculty between three of them in the area came to an end. I moved to Fresno where it seemed I could pick up some adjunct English classes at the university, and I taught there for two years. In the middle of that time my class at Saint Mary's College was holding a ten year reunion. I decided to attend. I was hitting thirty and thought it a good time to have a good professional cut, a bit shorter than I'd had it for the last number of years. This especially hit home when a student in one of my composition classes at Fresno State called to me after class—a good kid with a sense of humor, and somehow I knew he didn't want to know more about the comma splice. He caught up to me and said, "Hey Mr. Buckley, you've got wavy hair." My hair has always been straight, and so I asked him what he meant. He didn't miss a beat and replied, "It's wavin' goodbye!"

I went to this barber not far from my house, a shop I'd passed by a number of times. In back of the two chairs the shelves were full of gadgets, a microscope-type machine to examine your hair and hair roots, special massagers, charts, and so on. The news was not good; my hair was starting to weaken and thin. I should keep it cut shorter, he said, and avail myself of several potions and processes which he offered. About all I did was pay for the cut and get out, but I could see that I needed now to have a shorter style as it was thinning out in the usual places—something I never thought would happen to me as my hair had always been so thick. Thirty years old and body betrayal had begun and that was pretty much the end of any consideration about hair for me. Keep it short and neat and maybe no one will notice how much light was beginning to reflect off the old dome. I certainly was not going to be one of those guys with a part just above the ear and strands stretching pathetically over the top toward the other side. Nor was I about to go through the cost and ignominy of transplants, though my father's had worked well enough. His hair had gone all white and the transplanted spots on top and in front were O.K. However, they were not near as full as the sides which he had combed into vast swan-like wings, TV Evangelist style. His hair in his 60s was much longer than mine in my 30s, and he probably had more of it. What could I do about that?

What does any of it finally mean? I own more hats than I ever have—I think of skin cancer whereas I never did before. Rogaine can now be had over the counter, and last Christmas a friend—half out of concern and half as a joke—gave me a four month supply of the generic brand she'd picked up mis-marked at a discount store. It's easy to apply, just topical—like a little alcohol—but three months later I can't see a strand of difference. But I don't know, another month and continued applications and it may stop the rapid retreat to the rear? Either way, I pass no moral judgments. By this point in time, I'm either content with who I am or I am not; it's a question of character finally. And health. A great lot of hair like Jim Carrey or Andy Garcia can't change things, won't make you feel any better about yourself . . . will it?

POINTS TO CONSIDER ABOUT "HISTORY OF MY HAIR"

1. How does Buckley use specific scenes of action—including physical violence, both threatened and realized—to keep the reader engaged in his creative nonfictional piece?

2. Examine the ways in which Buckley incorporates researched material into this creative nonfictional piece. What portions of "History of My Hair" appear to be derived from research, what portions appear to be faithful reproductions of memory, and what portions seem like "best

guesses" at the truth? How does Buckley join these elements seamlessly in the piece?

3. In his opening material, Buckley suggests that students "Write/structure in scenes—use action and dialogue, omit unnecessary information and narration to better make connections." Identify the specific scenes in "History of My Hair" and discuss the ways in which they develop the piece's intended theme(s).

4. Speaking of Buckley's opening material . . . what portion of the his opening remarks (not "History of My Hair", but the explanatory material that precedes it) was most interesting/engaging to you as you read this chapter? How does this reaction on your part prove or disprove certain assertions Buckley makes in his chapter?

5. In his opening remarks, Buckley warns the prospective writer of creative nonfiction not to "editorialize" too much in the body of a given piece—to let intended meanings emerge as the piece unfolds. Identify certain points at which Buckley seems to violate this advice and expresses certain value judgments. Is this an oversight on his part, or does he have a reason for inserting these editorial comments? If the latter, what might his reason(s) be? What thematic messages are suggested by the last paragraph of "History of My Hair"?

Living Like Weasels
Annie Dillard

A weasel is wild. Who knows what he thinks? He sleeps in his underground den, his tail draped over his nose. Sometimes he lives in his den for two days without leaving. Outside, he stalks rabbits, mice, muskrats, and birds, killing more bodies than he can eat warm, and often dragging the carcasses home. Obedient to instinct, he bites his prey at the neck, either splitting the jugular vein at the throat or crunching the brain at the base of the skull, and he does not let go. One naturalist refused to kill a weasel who was socketed into his hand deeply as a rattlesnake. The man could in no way pry the tiny weasel off, and he had to walk half a mile to water, the weasel dangling from his palm, and soak him off like a stubborn label.

And once, says Ernest Thompson Seton—once, a man shot an eagle out of the sky. He examined the eagle and found the dry skull of a weasel fixed by the jaws to his throat. The supposition is that the eagle had pounced on the weasel and the weasel swiveled and bit as instinct taught him, tooth to neck, and nearly won. I would like to have seen that eagle from the air a few weeks or months before he was shot: was the whole weasel still attached to his feathered throat, a fur pendant? Or did the eagle eat what he could reach, gutting the living weasel with his talons before his breast, bending his beak, cleaning the beautiful airborne bones?

I have been reading about weasels because I saw one last week. I startled a weasel who startled me, and we exchanged a long glance.

Twenty minutes from my house, through the woods by the quarry and across the highway, is Hollins Pond, a remarkable piece of shallowness, where I like to go at sunset and sit on a tree trunk. Hollins Pond is also called Murray's Pond; it covers two acres of bottomland near Tinker Creek with six inches of water and six thousand lily pads. In winter, brown-and-white steers stand in the middle of it, merely dampening their hooves; from the distant shore they look like miracle itself, complete with miracle's nonchalance. Now, in summer, the steers are gone. The water lilies have blossomed and spread to a green horizontal plane that is terra firma to plodding blackbirds, and tremulous ceiling to black leeches, crayfish, and carp.

This is, mind you, suburbia. It is a five-minute walk in three directions to rows of houses, though none is visible here. There's a 55 mph highway at one end of the pond, and a nesting pair of wood ducks at the other. Under every bush is a muskrat hole or a beer can. The far end is an alternating series of fields and woods, fields and woods, threaded everywhere with motorcycle tracks—in whose bare clay wild turtles lay eggs.

So. I had crossed the highway, stepped over two low barbed-wire fences, and traced the motorcycle path in all gratitude through the wild rose and poison ivy of the pond's shoreline up into high grassy fields. Then I cut down through the woods to the mossy fallen tree where I sit. This tree is excellent. It makes a dry, upholstered bench at the upper, marshy end of the pond, a plush jetty raised from the thorny shore between a shallow blue body of water and a deep blue body of sky.

The sun had just set. I was relaxed on the tree trunk, ensconced in the lap of lichen, watching the lily pads at my feet tremble and part dreamily over the thrusting path of a carp. A yellow bird appeared to my right and flew behind me. It caught my eye; I swiveled around—and the next instant, inexplicably, I was looking down at a weasel, who was looking up at me.

Weasel! I'd never seen one wild before. He was ten inches long, thin as a curve, a muscled ribbon, brown as fruitwood, soft-furred, alert. His face was fierce, small and pointed as a lizard's; he would have made a good arrowhead. There was just a dot of chin, maybe two brown hairs' worth, and then the pure white fur began that spread down his underside. He had two black eyes I didn't see, any more than you see a window.

The weasel was stunned into stillness as he was emerging from beneath an enormous shaggy wild rose bush four feet away. I was stunned into stillness twisted backward on the tree trunk. Our eyes locked, and someone threw away the key.

Our look was as if two lovers, or deadly enemies, met unexpectedly on an overgrown path when each had been thinking of something else: a clearing blow to the gut. It was also a bright blow to the brain, or a sudden beating of brains, with all the charge and intimate grate of rubbed balloons. It emptied our lungs. It felled the forest, moved the fields, and drained the pond; the world dismantled and tumbled into that black hole of eyes. If you and I looked at each other that way, our skulls would split and drop to our shoulders. But we don't. We keep our skulls. So.

He disappeared. This was only last week, and already I don't remember what shattered the enchantment. I think I blinked, I think I retrieved my brain from the weasel's brain, and tried to memorize what I was seeing, and the weasel felt the yank of separation, the careening splashdown into real life and the urgent current of instinct. He vanished under the wild rose. I waited motionless, my mind suddenly full of data and my spirit with pleadings, but he didn't return.

Please do not tell me about "approach-avoidance conflicts." I tell you I've been in that weasel's brain for sixty seconds, and he was in mine. Brains are private places, muttering through unique and secret tapes—but the weasel and I both plugged into another tape simultaneously, for a sweet and shocking time. Can I help it if it was a blank?

What goes on in his brain the rest of the time? What does a weasel think about? He won't say. His journal is tracks in clay, a spray of feathers, mouse blood and bone: uncollected, unconnected, loose-leaf, and blown.

I would like to learn, or remember, how to live. I come to Hollins Pond not so much to learn how to live as, frankly, to forget about it. That is, I don't think I can learn from a wild animal how to live in particular—shall I suck warm blood, hold my tail high, walk with my footprints precisely over the prints of my hands?—but I might learn something of mindlessness, something of the purity of living in the physical senses and the dignity of living without bias or motive. The weasel lives in necessity and we live in choice, hating necessity and dying at the last ignobly in its talons. I would like to live as I should, as the weasel lives as he should. And I suspect that for me the way is like the weasel's: open to time and death painlessly, noticing everything, remembering nothing, choosing the given with a fierce and pointed will.

I missed my chance. I should have gone for the throat. I should have lunged for that streak of white under the weasel's chin and held on, held on through mud and into the wild rose, held on for a dearer life. We could live under the wild rose wild as weasels, mute and uncomprehending. I could very calmly go wild. I could live two days in the den, curled, leaning on mouse fur, sniffing bird bones, blinking, licking, breathing musk, my hair tangled in the roots of grasses. Down is a good place to go, where the mind is single. Down is out, out of your ever-loving mind and back to your care-less senses. I remember muteness as a prolonged and giddy fast, where every moment is a feast of utterance received. Time and events are merely poured, unremarked, and ingested directly, like blood pulsed into my gut through a jugular vein. Could two live that way? Could two live under the wild rose, and explore by the pond, so that the smooth mind of each is as everywhere present to the other, and as received and as unchallenged, as falling snow?

We could, you know. We can live any way we want. People take vows of poverty, chastity, and obedience—even of silence—by choice. The thing is to stalk your calling in a certain skilled and supple way, to locate the most tender and live spot and plug into that pulse. This is yielding, not fighting. A weasel doesn't "attack" anything; a weasel lives as he's meant to, yielding at every moment to the perfect freedom of single necessity.

I think it would be well, and proper, and obedient, and pure, to grasp your one necessity and not let it go, to dangle from it limp wherever it takes you. Then even death, where you're going no matter how you live, cannot you part. Seize it and let it seize you up aloft even, till your eyes burn out and drop; let your musky flesh fall off in shreds, and let your very bones unhinge and scatter, loosened over fields, over fields and woods, lightly, thoughtless, from any height at all, from as high as eagles.

POINTS TO CONSIDER ABOUT "LIVING LIKE WEASELS"

1. How does Dillard begin her piece, with fact or opinion? What specific things do you learn about weasels from the information/ details in the first paragraph?

2. What specific behavioral qualities—personality traits of weasels, if you will—are suggested by the example of the weasel skull attached to the eagle in the second paragraph?

3. In paragraph eight, how many specific images are there *showing* you the weasel? List the examples in order, and discuss the specific senses to which each of these images appeals.

4. In the second half of the piece, do you think Dillard *earns* her fairly mystical connection with the mind of the weasel? How so and where specifically? How has the first half of the writing set this up?

5. How would you sum up what Dillard has learned from her encounter with the weasel? What is she saying about animal life and consciousness versus ours as human beings? How is the final image of "high as eagles" appropriate for her theme and viewpoint?

Catholics
Gary Soto

I was standing in the waste basket for fighting on the day we received a hunger flag for Biafra. Sister Marie, a tough nun who could throw a softball farther than most men, read a letter that spoke of the grief of that country, looking up now and then to measure our sympathy and to adjust her glasses that had slipped from her nose. She read the three-page letter, placed it on her desk, and walked over to the globe to point out Africa, a continent of constant dispair. I craned my neck until, without realizing it, I had one foot out of the wastebasket. Sister Marie turned and stared me back into place, before she went on to lecture us about hunger.

"Hunger is a terrible, terrible thing," she began. "It robs the body of its vitality and the mind of its glory, which is God's."

Sister Marie cruised slowly up and down the rows, tapping a pencil in her palm and talking about death, hunger, and the blessed infants, which were God's, until the students hung their heads in fear or boredom. Then she brightened up.

"With hunger, heavier people would live longer—they have more fat, you see." She tapped her pencil, looked around the room, and pointed to Gloria Leal. "If we didn't have any food whatsoever, Gloria would probably live the longest." Hands folded neatly on her desk, Gloria forced a smile but didn't look around the room at the students who had turned to size her up.

Sister Marie walked up another row, still tapping her pencil and talking about hunger, when she pointed to me. "And Gary . . . well, he would be one of the first to die." Students turned in their chairs to look at me with their mouths open, and I was mad, not for being pointed out but because of that unfair lie. I could outlive the whole class, food or no food. Wasn't I one of the meanest kids in the entire school? Didn't I beat up Chuy Hernandez, a bigger kid? I shook my head in disbelief, and said "nah" under my breath.

Sister Marie glared at me, almost bitterly, as she told the class again that I would be the first one to die. She tapped her pencil as she walked slowly up to me. Scared, I looked away, first up to the ceiling and then to a fly that was walking around on the floor. But my head was snapped up when Sister Marie pushed my chin with her pencil. She puckered her mouth into a clot of lines and something vicious raged in her eyes, like she was getting ready to throw a softball. What it was I didn't know, but I feared that she was going to squeeze me from the waste basket and hurl me around the room. After a minute or so her face relaxed and she returned to the front of the class where she announced that for the coming three weeks we would collect money daily for Biafra.

"The pagan babies depend on our charitable hearts," she said. She looked around the room and returned to the globe where she again pointed out Africa. I craned my head and pleaded, "Let me see." She stared me back into place and then resumed talking about the fruits of the world, some of which were ours and some of which were not ours.

POINTS TO CONSIDER ABOUT "CATHOLICS"

1. From your reading of the first three paragraphs, how would you say Sister Marie is treating her own students? To what economic and social class of students is she speaking?

2. In the second paragraph, do you see any irony in the fact that Sister Marie is telling the students about the problems associated with hunger? How do you imagine some of those students might be responding in their own minds?

3. In the next-to-last paragraph, what sort of portrait of Sister Marie emerges? How does Gary (the character in the story, not necessarily the author) respond to her? Which specific words convey his attitude?

4. Does "Catholics" present a realistic portrait of a childhood educational setting? Which specific details lend this creative nonfictional piece the ring of truth? Is there anything in your own experience that supports this view of Sister Marie or people like her?

5. Do you find any irony in the last sentence of the piece? What might Soto be implying regarding words versus actions? Where, as the cliché has it, should charity begin, according to the implied theme of "Catholics"?

✂ WRITING ACTIVITIES: CREATIVE NONFICTION

1. For an "immersion journalism" essay, try spending some time at a seemingly mundane place of employment: a pizza parlor, a gas station, a hair salon. Find out what goes on beyond the obvious and write about it. Alternatively, write about a job you've done and know well—ideally a job you loved or hated. What did you learn? What did you not get that you expected to? Pay special attention to the "language" of the place/job, and to the individuals who populated that place of employment.

2. For a short, experiential essay, write about a grade school or high school event that you remember vividly. Concentrate initially on just writing out the scene and memory as it presents itself. On a second draft, add in details, events, people, and dialogue that you left out initially. In subsequent drafts, see if, as in Gary Soto's "Catholics," a thematic point of view emerges or surfaces from the actions and scene you present. If not, revise the piece to point to a theme without "hitting the reader over the head" with it.

3. Try a "nature writing" piece. Take a walk in the woods, by a river or creek, along the beach, through the fields. Make some notes as you go or when you return from your walk. Later, do some research and look up names of animals and plants you observed in the environment. Try to work in present tense as much as possible, to give your piece a sense of immediacy. Finally, look inside—see if the exterior landscape reflects something about interior landscape, your thoughts, feelings, preoccupations. See what you might have learned from the experience and/or from the subsequent research: a very small lesson perhaps, a personal revelation, an increased environmental or social awareness, or a point that deserves further consideration.

4. Complaint! For a fact piece, try some investigation into politics, water resources, the environment in your area. What specific individuals/organizations are responsible for causing an environmental problem, or for not dealing adequately with a pre-existing problem. How does this directly impact your life? What solutions can you propose, from the far-fetched to the practical?

5. Write an extension of Buckley's "History of My Hair", bringing it up to date. What were your hair considerations as you grew up, the tonsorial fads of your generation as you were growing up? What hair styles—both for men and women—are in vogue today, and what social-political-economic implications might these styles have?

10

Young Adult Fiction

Francess Lantz describes herself—accurately, I think, judging from her stories' strikingly real depictions of adolescents—as "an adult who remembers what it was like to be fifteen years old." She has used this knowledge to become an award-winning author of twenty books for young readers, including *Stepsister From The Planet Weird, Neighbors from Outer Space, Spinach With Chocolate Sauce,* and *Dear Celeste, My Life Is a Mess.* Lantz's young adult novel *Varsity Coach: Doubleplay* was chosen a Recommended Book For Reluctant Readers by the American Library Association. Her latest novels for young adults are *Someone to Love* and *Fade Far Away*, both published by Avon Books; *Someone To Love* was recently chosen a "Best Book For Young Adults" by the American Library Association and one of the year's best "Books For The Teen Age" by the New York Public Library. In this chapter, Lantz will give you the inside scoop on how to target your fiction to a young adult readership.

WRITING FICTION FOR YOUNG ADULTS

Young adult literature is not a genre, at least not in the same way mysteries, science fiction, and romances are. You can write a mystery story (for example) that is targeted for any age group, from toddlers through senior citizens. As long as you meet the requirements of the genre, it qualifies as a mystery. But you can't write a young adult novel for preschoolers or second graders or adults. YA fiction is by definition fiction for and about teenagers. It can be in any style, any genre, with any amount of literary merit, but if it isn't written with young adults in mind, it isn't young adult fiction.

However, this doesn't mean that YA fiction is always read by teenagers. Most kids over the age of fifteen are reading adult novels exclusively, if they haven't given up reading altogether. In fact, the target audience for most YA fiction is girls between the ages of ten and fourteen. Boys also read YA fiction, but don't expect your average American boy to read books with a female protagonist (at least not in public; they certainly might sneak a peek at *Forever*, Judy Blume's novel about a couple's first sexual encounter, in the far reaches of the library stacks). Most girls, however, have no qualms about picking up an interesting-looking novel with a male main character.

Some adults, especially adult women, also read YA novels. This may be due to the fact that many libraries shelve their YA fiction near (or with) the adult fiction. Other adults discover YA novels when their own children begin reading them, then stick with them because they enjoy the writing, not to mention the length (usually less than two hundred pages), the lack of profanity, and the mainly upbeat endings.

It is interesting to note that many of the YA novels that earn good reviews and win prestigious awards are not especially popular with teenagers. *M. C. Higgins the Great* by Virginia Hamilton (winner of the Newberry award—the Oscar of children's literature), *The Thief* by Megan Whalen Turner (a Newberry Honor Book) and *Missing May* by Cynthia Rylant (another Newberry winner) are rarely sought out by young adult readers. Nevertheless, many teens will eventually read these books in school because English teachers like to assign them.

As an aspiring writer of YA fiction, you must be aware that even if you write a story teenagers want to read, it will not fly directly from your computer into the hands of America's youth. It must first pass before the critical eyes of editors, reviewers, and parents, not to mention religious watchdog groups who want to censor anything they consider provocative. This means you must follow the accepted rules of YA fiction (more on this later) or find a way to break the rules so artfully that nobody minds. Or—and this happens may be once a decade—you can write a book that breaks every rule but is so original, so compelling, so unique (think *The Outsiders, The Chocolate War, Weetzie Bat*) that it succeeds despite (or because of) the fact that adults are outraged by it.

How do I do that? I hear you asking. The first step is to study the genre. Go to the library, find the Young Adult section, and start reading. Visit your local bookstore, read the trade journals, and find out what's new and hot. Learn where the young adult novel has been and where it's going.

To get you started, here's a brief history of the field.

BEYOND *NANCY DREW*

There have always been stories written for teenagers, but the young adult novel as we know it began in the late-1960s with the publication of *The Outsiders* and a few other ground-breaking novels. Written by a seventeen-year-old girl named S. E. Hinton, *The Outsiders* told the story of a group of lower-class gang members and their fight for acceptance and survival. Adults had little to do with their world. They were their own family, hanging out together, taking care of each other, dealing with hatred, loneliness, and violence. The story was current, realistic, and hard-hitting, and for that reason teenagers found it irresistible.

With the success of *The Outsiders,* publishers were eager to buy more timely, relevant YA novels. No subject was off-limits, no dialogue was too frank. Authors wrote about drugs, murder, homosexuality, divorce, and domestic violence. Publishers—and teenagers—couldn't get enough.

The Pigman by Paul Zindel told the story of two teens who befriended and ultimately betrayed a lonely, elderly man. *The Cat Ate My Gymsuit* used humor to explore the feelings of an overweight, unhappy girl who was inspired by her anti-establishment English teacher. *The Chocolate War* by Robert Cormier was the first YA novel with a downbeat ending—a boy who refused to be bullied into selling chocolates for his school was tormented, beaten up, and ultimately defeated.

Throughout the seventies, the "problem novel"—books about contemporary teen problems—sold well. Novels by authors of color (including Virginia Hamilton, Walter Dean Myers, and Lawrence Yep) also became commonplace. Meanwhile, chain bookstores like Waldenbooks and B. Dalton sprang up in malls all over the country, and kids began buying their own paperbacks instead of checking out hardcover books from the library. YA fiction was hotter than ever.

Then in the 1980s, the mood of the country grew more conservative. Adults decided they didn't want their teenagers reading about abortions, interracial marriages, and premarital sex. At the same time, publishers figured out that there was an audience for original paperbacks, and that books marketed as a series (either a number of titles with the same characters or separate books with a common theme) sold well.

Enter the young adult romance novel. Packagers (independent book producers who create series of books for major publishers) began churning out squeaky-clean romance titles faster than teens could say, "First kiss." Bantam's *Sweet Dreams* series rose to the top of B. Dalton's bestseller list in 1982. Other YA series, like the soap opera-ish *Sweet Valley High,* also sold millions.

Meanwhile, authors writing challenging, literary YA fiction found it difficult—if not impossible—to get published. A few top name authors survived (usually by writing high quality love stories), but many mid-list authors either succumbed to the lure of series books or stopped writing young adult novels altogether.

Eventually, the market became glutted with romance novels and in the nineties, publishers moved on to the next trend—horror fiction. By the second half of the decade, the market was once again glutted and sales of *Goosebumps, Fear Street,* and other horror series declined. What will be the next "hot" topic? No one knows, but historical YA fiction appears to be doing well.

Throughout the eighties and nineties, authors have continued to write and sell serious YA fiction, but in much smaller numbers than they did in the late sixties and seventies. A startling, unique novel like Robert Cormier's *Fade,* Francesca Lia Block's *Weetzie Bat,* or Karen Cushman's *Catherine Called Birdy,* can still cause a sensation, but without excellent reviews and a prestigious award or two, YA fiction authors can forget about living off their earnings.

"YA books will rise from the ashes," Olga Litowinsky says in her book *Writing And Publishing Books For Children In The Nineties,* "and they will be better than ever." Wishful thinking? With the advent of cable TV, video games, and the Internet, teenagers have more entertainment choices than ever before. How can we convince them to choose reading?

The answer is inside of you. It's up to today's promising young writers to start the next trend—the 21st-century version of *Sweet Dreams* or *Goosebumps*—that will lure teens into bookstores and put YA fiction on the top of the bestseller lists again. Or maybe you will write a novel as powerful as *Slake's Limbo* or *Hatchet* or *Go Ask Alice*—a book that is added to reading lists, assigned in English classes, and never goes out of print.

If you care about young people, if you care about the future of reading, perhaps you will be inspired to rise to the challenge.

OF ANGST AND ACNE

What do teenagers want to read? Teenagers love to read about themselves and their world. Therefore, if you can figure out what adolescents care about, worry about, dream about, what inspires and bores them, thrills and disgusts them, you'll have a good idea of what sort of fiction they want to read.

In *Writing Books For Young People,* editor James Cross Giblin calls young adult novels "transitional novels" because readers between the ages of ten and fourteen are making the transition from children's fiction to adult fiction—and by extension, from childhood to adulthood. Making that transition is not easy in an industrially advanced country like ours. Unlike adolescents in primitive societies, where specific accepted rituals were used to facilitate a quick, smooth passage from childhood to adulthood, modern teens are condemned to spend years living in a vast, gray no-man's-land. Adult society considers them too mature, too sophisticated, too *big* to be treated as children, but not experienced or responsible enough to be treated as grownups.

Adrift in their no-man's-land, teens search for clues that can help them understand what it means to be an individual, a man or woman, an adult. They look to the media for role models, to adults, and to their peers. The two people they *don't* look to—at least consciously—are their mother and father. And why should they? They have viewed at close range their parents' failures and hypocrisies, observed their every foible and inadequacy. What's worse, they have had to take orders from these losers for the last twelve years. "I may not know much," teenagers across the country are thinking, "but I do know I'd rather die than grow up to be like Mom and Dad."

As teens move away from parents, as they rebel against their mother and father's seemingly irrelevant values, they move toward each other. They discover a way to dress, to talk, to think, to live that is different from adults but exactly like each other. Together with other teens, they try out roles, test their boundaries, experiment with drugs and alcohol and sex. They might shoplift, spraypaint their names on water towers, join a gang, or run away from home. It's all part of testing the waters, searching for meaning, finding out what they—and society—will condone and condemn.

In short, the adolescent's life theme is the search for identity, and not surprisingly, that's the theme of most young adult novels. Other related themes include: facing and dealing with corruption and hypocrisy; learning to view parents and other adults as three-dimensional people; facing peer pressure and learning to trust one's own judgment.

If you can write about these issues in an honest and compelling way, teenagers will want to read your fiction.

HANGING WITH THE MALL RATS

So much for the grand themes of YA fiction. Now for the specifics. Young adults have extremely sensitive "bullshit detectors." If you write a story with corny dialogue or unbelievable situations they'll toss your book aside without a second glance. If you want to get through to teenagers, you have to know their world. And that means spending time with them.

If you're a teacher, a coach, or the parent of a teenager—or if you're a teenager yourself—then you've got a leg up on the rest of us. If you don't currently have any teens in your life, you might want to consider volunteering at your local library, junior high school, or YMCA. If that's not an option, you can still observe teens in their natural habitat. Hang out at the mall, at video arcades, at movie theaters and skateboard parks and beaches. Check out what kids are wearing, how they move, their facial expressions.

Eavesdrop on their conversations and make note of their curse words, their slang.

On the way home, buy copies of *Seventeen, Rolling Stone,* and *Skateboarding,* and read them from cover to cover. Watch MTV and Nickelodeon and take notes. And of course, keep reading young adult novels. They'll show you how authors take the chaotic, absurd, profane reality of adolescence and turn it into fiction that is both acceptable to school librarians and interesting to real-life teenagers.

Even more important, perhaps, is spending time remembering your own adolescence. If you still have your old yearbook, class notes, or diaries, take them out and read them. What memories do they conjure up? What emotions? Keep a journal and write down everything you can remember about being a teenager. What was your most embarrassing moment? Your proudest? What was your first sexual experience like? How did you rebel against your parents? What scared you? Excited you? Bored you?

Music, hairstyles, and slang may change, but the basic feelings and attitudes of adolescents remain the same. All teens know how it feels to be embarrassed by their parents, to fall madly in love (or is that lust?), to be ridiculed by their peers. If you can remember your own version of those experiences and the emotions that went along with them, then update them to make them relevant to today's youth, you'll be well on your way to writing a successful young adult novel.

GETTING STARTED

Okay, you've studied the world of young adults, come up with some characters, a plot, and a theme, and now you're ready to start writing. But how can you make sure that what you're producing is a *bona fide* young adult novel, and not an adult novel with a teenage protagonist? In other words, what makes YA fiction different from adult fiction? Both can be about adolescents and their problems. Both may be read and enjoyed by teenagers and adults. But that is where the similarities end.

Most young adult novels are shorter than adult novels. The average length of a YA novel is 150–200 manuscript pages. Furthermore, the stories usually span a shorter time period than do novels for adults. One summer or one school year is typical. *Hatchet* takes place over fifty-four days; my novel *Fade Far Away* starts at the beginning of the school year and ends in early November.

In the world of teens, a year is a lifetime. The changes that take place in a human being between thirteen and seventeen could fill volumes. Furthermore, young readers generally like to read about a protagonist who is older than they are; therefore a fifteen-year-old who picked up a book about a girl aging from twelve through seventeen would probably be turned off unless the younger years were told in flashback.

Of course, there are always exceptions. *Crash* by Jerry Spinelli is narrated by a teenager, but the story begins when the two main characters are young children. The use of humor—and a distinctive first-person narrator—makes it work.

SETTING THE TONE

One of most obvious differences between adult and young adult fiction is the vocabulary and sentence structure. YA fiction is usually simpler and less densely written than adult fiction. However, it is a mistake to consciously "write down" to teens. If you do, you'll end up sounding condescending and turn off your reader. Instead, I advise you to read a number of popular young adult novels and get a feel for the style.

An Almost Perfect Summer is a light novel for younger teens, and consequently author Rona S. Zable keeps her vocabulary basic and her sentences simple:

> I don't know if a fifteen-year-old girl can actually have a heart attack, but on Friday afternoon, I thought for sure I was going to be a statistic.
>
> I had just spotted Todd for the first time since he'd gotten back from Maine. He was washing his Mustang in the driveway, so I ran over to ask him what time he'd be coming by for me Saturday night.
>
> He just stared at me blankly. "Saturday night? What's happening Saturday night?"

On the other hand, Lynn Hall's *The Solitary* is a more literary work, written for older teens, and the author's vocabulary reflects that:

> She let out her breath in a long sigh and moved forward for a closer look. The wire mesh of the cages was crusted with ancient filth. The crockery water dishes were full of dust and dead flies; many were cracked. Wisps of twelve-year-old hay still lay in some of the cages. But it was there, the precious equipment! It was all workable, cleanable, possible. She emerged into the winter sunlight with a smile of triumph illuminating her face.

Young adult fiction is almost always written from the main character's point of view. We're inside his head, viewing the world through his eyes. It's a very personal, intimate point of view, and to achieve it many authors choose to write in the first person.

Here's an example from my novel, *Someone To Love:*

> I've been a vegetarian for over six months and Mom still refuses to alter her cooking one bit to accommodate me. "Just eat the rice and vegeta-

bles and leave the meat," she says, even though I've told her a thousand times I need rice and beans to have complete protein. I think she figures that eventually I'll see that meat sitting on the plate and become over-whelmed with carnivorous desire. Yeah, right. I'm a human being, Mom, not a wolf.

First person works well in YA fiction because it sets a hip, youthful tone and accurately reflects the teenager's somewhat self-absorbed world view. On the other hand, it can also be claustrophobic and limiting. In his novel *Hatchet*, Gary Paulsen chooses the third-person-limited point of view. The novel, which tells the story of a thirteen-year-old boy stranded in the wilderness with only the clothes on his back and a hatchet, emphasizes ac-tion. There is internal dialogue, but not the endless stream of thoughts a teenage girl usually has:

> He could do nothing, think nothing. His tongue, stained with berry juice, stuck to the roof of his mouth and he stared at the bear. It was black, with a cinnamon-colored nose, not twenty feet away from him and big. No, huge. It was all black fur and huge. He had seen one in the zoo in the city once, a black bear, but it had been from India or some-where. This one was wild, and much bigger than the one in the zoo and it was right there.

In *Slake's Limbo*, author Felice Holman uses the third-person omni-scient point of view to comment on the predicament of her main character, Aremis Slake, and to show us the inner thoughts of the novel's secondary character, subway driver Willis Joe:

> The excellence of Slake's hideout—Slakes' new home—was the result of (1) misjudgment; (2) a hot summer's day; (3) the evil influences of alco-hol, and other fortuitous circumstances which Slake did not know and would never know. But nevertheless, it may just as well be told that Slake's room no longer had anything to do with the subway. It really had more to do with the Commodore Hotel, against whose wall he now leaned.

Holman's style is very unusual for a young adult novel, but it works well and it also helps to make the novel stand out among the hundreds of first-person narratives on the library shelves. The same goes for Jeannette Eyerly's *See Dave Run* which tells the saga of a fifteen-year-old runaway and uses twenty-three different narrators.

DOWN AND DIRTY

Most young adults curse. Many are sexually active, or at least curious about sex. Some drink and take drugs. All these things are realities of teenage life;

it makes sense to find them mentioned in a young adult novel. Nevertheless, few parents want their teenagers reading explicit descriptions of lust or drunkenness or drug addiction, even if the ultimate message of the novel is abstinence.

My first novel, *Good Rockin' Tonight,* told the story of a fifteen-year-old aspiring rock star. In the course of the novel, my heroine smokes grass and lets her boyfriend grope her, but eventually decides he's a jerk and marijuana isn't for her. Despite this message, the Fulton County (Georgia) Board of Education gave *Good Rockin' Tonight* the following review: "The story as well as the reading level and style are excellent, but there are several passages describing heavy petting and making out as well as the use of drugs. Not recommended."

So what's an author to do? Once you become well-known and respected, you can get away with almost anything. (Judy Blume is a perfect example. She could probably write a young adult porno novel and get it published!) Until then—well, you can't please everybody, especially not in Fulton County. Your best bet is to keep the sex and drugs scenes in your fiction to a minimum. No subject should be considered taboo, but it must be presented tastefully, not explicitly.

An example is *Abby, My Love,* a novel about incest by Hadley Irwin. In order to deal with the subject honestly while still staying clear of sensationalism, the author tells the story from the point of view of Abby's best friend, a girl who senses something is wrong but never actually views the incestuous behavior.

In Richard Peck's novel about rape, *Are You In The House Alone?* the author cleverly describes a pornographic letter left in a locker without using one word of profanity:

> My mind kept rejecting the words. Instead I noticed the even margins, the accurate punctuation. But the words. All the things someone thought I was. And all the things someone planned to do to me, to make me do. Every perverted, sadistic, sick, and sickening ugly act. A twisted porno movie playing in somebody's brain.

Sometimes it's almost impossible to avoid profanity, but you must use it sparingly. *Center Line* by Joyce Sweeney tells the story of five brothers who run away from home to escape their alcoholic, abusive father. Avoiding profanity whenever possible, she still manages to make the brothers sound like real teenagers:

> "What's this?" Mark demanded without really looking at it.
> Chris sat down opposite him. "It's your lunch. Eat it."
> Mark narrowed his eyes at the sandwich. "I don't like it. I don't want it. Can I have something else?"
> Chris frowned. "Eat it. I worked hard to get you that sandwich. I had to kill a man to get you that sandwich."

Mark played with his hair, pulling it back and letting it fall in his eyes again. "If I eat all of this, can I have some cookies or something?"

Christ nodded. "If you eat all this and if you drink a glass of milk."

"Jesus," said Mark. "Where's you-know-who?"

GIMMICKS GALORE

Reviewers of young adult fiction may turn a jaundiced eye on racy subject matter, but when it comes to style and form, anything goes. In Virginia Euwer Wolff's *Make Lemonade,* the text lines break at natural speaking phrases, and the protagonist's first-person prose is peppered with misspellings (for example, *sposed* for supposed). In my novel, *Someone To Love,* the plot unfolds in a series of letters written by the main character to her unborn sibling-to-be. In Robert Cormier's intriguing *I Am The Cheese,* the first-person present-tense chapters alternate with transcriptions of a mysterious interview and a third-person past-tense narrative.

Of course, gimmicks for the sake of gimmickry are not recommended, but creativity most definitely is. Young adults are eager to read books that are unique, arresting, even shocking. They delight in the hip, off-the-wall humor of Francesca Lia Block (*Weetzie Bat,*) and Ron Koertce (*Confess-O-Rama*); they are fascinated by the unique writing styles of Robert Cormier and M. E. Kerr (*The View From Saturday*).

So go wild. If you can find an unusual way to tell a story and make it work, your readers will respond.

CURRENT BUT NOT TRENDY

Young adults are instantly turned off by dated prose. If your novel is set in 1997 and your main characters says, "Golly gee!" or "That's groovy!" your reader will roll his eyes and toss the book aside. Likewise, you must not put your 1990s characters in 1970s clothes, or have them listening to supposedly popular records by Chicago or Traffic. In fact, they shouldn't be listening to records at all, unless they were purchased at a used record store. Today's youth listen to tapes and CDs.

So how up-to-the-minute must you be? It depends on what you're writing. Original paperbacks, especially series books, are disposable. They stay in print a few years, then disappear. Readers of these books like to read timely descriptions of clothes, hairstyles, and pop culture. By the time the trend is gone, the book will be, too.

Literary novels are a different story. If you're lucky, you'll write a classic that will be in print for decades. Therefore, it's best not to get too specific. Tell us your character is wearing jeans, but don't mention the brand. Tell us he went to see an action movie, but don't name the star. Name your characters John and Mary or even Fido and Esmerelda, but not the celebrity baby name of the hour.

REALISTICALLY EVER AFTER

Lastly, there is the question of endings. Authors of young adult novels want to inspire and motivate their readers. They want to present the world realistically, but they also want to give their readers the courage to face their problems and the hope that things can and will get better. For that reason, the vast majority of YA novels have positive, hopeful endings. This should not be confused with happy endings, in which all problems are resolved and the protagonist lives "happily ever after." What you're after is an ending which leaves some issues realistically open-ended, some problems unsolved, but still allows the reader to feel that the main character has survived and grown and that his future will not be quite as difficult and challenging as his past.

An example is *The Midwife's Apprentice* by Karen Cushman. Set in fourteenth-century England, the novel tells of a homeless orphan who struggles to find a place for herself in the world. She eventually becomes a midwife's apprentice but leaves in shame after trying and failing to deliver a baby on her own. After many tribulations, she returns to the midwife, a wiser, stronger person.

> She marched up to the midwife's door and knocked firmly.
> "Jane Sharp! It is I, Alyce, your apprentice. I have come back. And if you do not let me in, I will try again and again. I can do what you tell me and take what you give me, and I know how to try and risk and fail and try again and not give up. I will not go away."
> The door opened. Alyce went in. And the cat went with her.

In *After The Rain*, Norma Fox Mazer describes the growing relationship between Rachel and her difficult, dying grandfather. After the elderly man's death, Rachel searches for the initials he carved into a bridge he helped build. When she finds them, she understands that although her grandfather is gone, he will always be with her.

> Here is the proof. Here the handprint, here the initials. Nothing can remove them.
> They are here now, she thinks, and they will still be here years from now, when she, herself, is old. And then, though today the whole

sky is covered by gray clouds, for a moment she feels the sun on her head, as warm as a living hand.

It is also possible to end your story on a slightly more downbeat note. Like life, YA fiction doesn't always end with a smile. In *Remembering The Good Times* by Richard Peck, Trav, a teenager who seems to have everything going for him, commits suicide. No one can bring him back, but a public meeting held at the school to discuss the suicide draws the community together and helps Trav's friends mourn his death.

A Good Courage by Stephanie S. Tolan tells the story of Ty, a teenaged boy whose mother joins a religious cult. Eventually, Ty must leave his mother behind in order to escape the fanatical, dangerous cult. At the end of the novel, the reader has no doubt that Ty has made the right choice.

In Jenny Davis's *Sex Education*, the horror of watching her boyfriend die has sent Livvie into a mental hospital. At the end of the novel, things are still grim but we know Livvie will survive:

> Both David and Mrs. Fulton taught me a lot about caring. About sex. About love. I taught myself about pain. It has to mean something, to be put to use, caring use. Otherwise it just kills you. And I don't want to die.

BREAKING THE RULES

Some of the best young adult fiction ever written breaks the rules I've just discussed. How do the authors get away with it? By writing a story that is so unique, so arresting, so compelling that an editor is willing to take a chance on it. That, along with good reviews, will turn a much-rejected manuscript into a classic.

A good example is Robert Cormier's *The Chocolate War*. Its depiction of a corrupt parochial school and its violent, downbeat ending frightened off editors. As a result, Cormier received dozens of rejections before being published by Pantheon. But the novel's central question, *Do I dare disturb the universe?* struck a chord with reviewers who called it "complex, brilliant, and uncompromising." The book is now required reading in many high schools.

A unique perspective—and a generous dose of humor—helped make *Weetzie Bat* by Francesca Lia Block a success despite the fact that the novel includes homosexuality, drugs, premarital sex, and a whole lot more. The wild, breezy, charming tone of the novel is set in the first paragraph.

> The reason Weetzie Bat hated high school was because no one understood. They didn't even realize where they were living. They didn't care that Marilyn's prints were practically in their backyard at Graumann's;

that you could buy tomahawks and plastic palm tree wallets at the Farmer's Market, and the wildest, cheapest cheese and bean and hot dog and pastrami burritos at Oki Dogs; that the waitresses wore skates at the Jetson-style Tiny Naylor's; that there was a fountain that turned tropical soda-pop colors, and a canyon where Jim Morrison and Houdini used to live, and all-night potato knishes at Canter's, and not too far away was Venice, with columns, and canals even, like the real Venice but maybe cooler because of the surfers. There was no one who cared. Until Dirk.

Reviewers called the book "weird, bizarre, strange" but also "a rare treat," and "an ingeniously lyrical narrative." Two sequels have been published.

READY IF YOU ARE

At this point, most of your questions about young adult fiction should be answered. But maybe the real question is, why write for young adults in the first place? Publishers pay less for young adults novels than they do for adult novels. For the most part, adolescent fiction sells poorly, and YA authors receive little respect from the writing community, the media, or even their readers.

The answer is that YA novelists write because they want to reach young adults. They feel a connection to teenagers, they know how teens think and feel, they care passionately about them. Often, they are still in touch with the teenager inside them. They remember their adolescence well, and they can easily summon up the intense and confusing feelings they experienced as teenagers. Perhaps they are writing books which are based on their own adolescence, and which are concerned with issues they are still dealing with in their adult lives.

If you care about teenagers, if you remember how it feels to be one, if you want to communicate with young adults, move them, shake them up, maybe even change their lives for the better, then writing YA fiction is for you. If you're lucky, you'll also write a book which wins awards and is added to every high school English curriculum in the country. You'll be read by generation after generation of kids. Who knows? You might even make some money.

Fade Far Away
Francess Lantz

Silence.

That's the first thing I notice when I walk into Hugh's studio. It's so unnaturally quiet.

The crack of my boot heels against the concrete floor sounds like a series of small explosions. I walk to the center of the room and sit cross-legged beside a neatly-stacked pile of bronze ingots. The place smells of stale smoke and plaster dust. The big barn doors haven't been opened for days; the ceiling fans haven't been turned on.

Less than a month ago, this building was alive with sound and motion. Miles Davis blasting through the speakers as Hugh and his assistants, Eric and Mason, mixed plaster. The amazed gasps of the onlookers as Hugh lifted a crucible of molten bronze from the red-hot furnace. The grinding wail of the electric hammer as he broke open the investment mold, revealing the bronze sculpture within.

I had thought this studio was my father's version of paradise. The place he felt most happy, most alive. How strange to find out it was really his prison.

I place my sketch book on the floor in front of me. The cardboard cover is frayed and smudged. A few grains of sand are still lodged in the binding. "I've brought the island back with me," I whisper.

I've brought memories back, too.

I close my eyes and images assault me. Caleb's lobster boat bobbing on the gray-green sea, Hugh's face squinting into a Manhattan streetlight, hand-carved wooden flowers in the snow. My head feels light, my heart races.

I clench my fists and force my brain to go blank. It's easy to let the images overwhelm me, but I don't want to remember like that. That's why I'm here, alone, in Hugh's studio. That's why the sketch book is lying at my feet. It will be my road map, leading me page by page, day by day, through the last two months. Forcing me to relive it all from start to finish, just the way it happened.

What the result of this little exercise will be, I have no idea. I may never be able to make sense of everything that's happened, let alone accept it. Still, I know I have to try. I owe to my father, to my mother. I owe it to me.

And so . . . I draw a deep breath and prepare myself. Sunlight streams through the skylights. The floor feels cold beneath my open palms. I reach for the sketch book, open it, and begin.

PART I: THE FARMHOUSE

I'm in my room, trying to capture on paper the patches of sunshine and shadow that play tag across my legs. I put down my pencil and open the window, breathing in the warm, too-sweet smell of Indian Summer. In a week or two the breezes will turn cold, and the handyman will come to put up the storm windows. But for now, I wear sleeveless T's to school and sweat my way through P.E., wondering if summer will ever end.

I finish my sketch and close the notebook. As usual, I feel a peculiar sense of relief. It's as if the things I saw with my eyes had somehow crawled inside me and started an itch I just had to scratch. Until I got them down on paper, I couldn't concentrate on anything else, couldn't distract myself, couldn't relax.

I stand up and walk downstairs, ghost-like, silent, hugging the sketch pad to my chest. Liesel, our housekeeper, is in the kitchen, making dinner. She's not from this family, not even from this country, but she seems to have a lot more purpose around here than I do. She can make a souffle, get microcrystalline wax off blue jeans, and she knows how to brew that swampy herb tea Marianna swears gets rid of her indigestion.

Marianna Scully is my mother. My father is Hugh Scully. I've never called them Mom and Dad, never even thought of it. I suppose it's because they never referred to themselves that way. I came fairly late into their lives—Hugh was forty-five, Marianna forty—and I don't think they ever viewed themselves as parents. They were too absorbed in the art world, and in each other.

I hear Marianna talking on the phone in her office. In December, the Los Angeles Museum of Contemporary Art is holding a retrospective of my father's work. As his business manager, it's her job to act as liaison between Hugh, his gallery, and the museum.

"Did you speak to Kurt at the museum?" she says into the receiver. "Yes . . . yes . . . no, absolutely not. The pieces have to be free-standing. Look, have the inspector call me directly. Yes, as soon as possible."

I try to slink by, unnoticed, but she's hanging up and she sees me. "The city is trying to tell the museum they have to attach the pieces to the wall," she says. "Something about earthquake standards." She shakes her head, stunned by their stupidity. "How was school?"

"Okay."

"I'm thinking of signing you up for art classes at Tyler."

"Marianna, no!"

"You're always scribbling in that sketch book. You need to develop your talent, learn about color, design. . . . "

"I haven't got any talent. I'm just screwing around."

"Well, it's about time you stopped screwing around and got passionate about something. What are you going to do after high school? Get married and become a soccer mom?"

"It's an option. Collecting coupons, getting my hair done, maybe popping out a couple of kids . . . hey, I think I've found my calling."

The phone rings. Marianna shoots me a withering look and answers it. I take advantage of the distraction to head for the side door. I know she won't follow. She's much too busy.

I walk across the lawn to the high grass and into a stand of birch trees. Beethoven's Seventh Symphony is blasting out of Hugh's studio. I wonder what the original owners of this place would say if they could see it now. The farmhouse hasn't changed all that much, if you don't count the addition of electricity and indoor plumbing. But the barn—that's another story. It once housed animals and plows; now it's an art studio and bronze foundry. The place where Hugh Scully creates. The place where his heart lives.

I see cars in the driveway, so I know Hugh is holding an open studio. People wait months for the chance to watch him pour bronze. I'm lucky. I can watch him work any time I want. So long as I don't bother him or get in his way. So long as I remain invisible.

I open my sketch pad, study a slender, gray mushroom growing beside my foot, and think back to the first time I became aware that my father was famous. I was six years old, a precocious reader who viewed books as sacred treasures. I spent hours reading children's books, and hours more pouring through the books in our house, searching for words I knew.

Then one day, in a fat, oversized book of pictures, I discovered my own name, Scully. I showed it to Marianna who explained that what I was seeing was actually my father's name and that he was the creator of the sculpture pictured in the book. I was astonished, and so proud to think that my father had done something important enough to have his name in a book.

Now it's Hugh's talent that amazes me, not simply the fact that he's represented in books of twentieth century art. But the feelings I had that day have never left me. I'm still astonished by him, and still proud.

The murmur of voices brings me back to the present, and I turn toward the barn. Hugh and his assistants have come outside, along with maybe twenty visitors. Hugh is pacing in front of the sand pit, shouting directions at Eric and Mason.

I stand up and move closer, silently positioning myself behind a tree. Now I can see the wild glow in Hugh's eyes, the throbbing vein on his neck. His thick salt and pepper hair is mussed, his heavy leather jacket, apron, and boots do nothing to slow him down. As always when he's about to pour bronze, the can't stand still.

He motions the crowd back as Eric and Mason, wearing heat-resistant jackets and thick gloves, carry the heavy plaster investment molds out from the kiln. Using shovels, they pack the molds into the sand pit. Then Hugh walks to the melting furnace where the bronze ingots are heating. He waits while Eric and Mason don helmets with plastic masks that cover their faces.

Hugh slips on a pair of leather gloves, but his face is unprotected. He grabs the handle on the furnace lid and smiles in anticipation. The crowd can't take their eyes off him. Neither can I.

Hugh slides open the lid of the furnace, revealing the crucible of blazing yellow-orange bronze within. The crowd moves back, feeling the heat even from twenty feet away. They stare, open-mouthed, stunned by the color and consistency of the bronze, like Day-Glo liquid sunshine.

With Eric and Mason's help, Hugh uses tongs to lift up the two-hundred pound crucible of molten bronze. The crowd sucks in a collective breath as the men lug it to the sand pit. Slowly, carefully, Hugh pours the spitting yellow liquid into the first mold.

A moment later, the bronze rises in the vents and oozes to the surface of the mold. Hugh makes a fist and lets out a triumphant grunt. The crowd responds, exclaiming and applauding, but my father doesn't notice. He's moving on to the next mold, judging the heat of the bronze, deciding how long it will remain hot enough to pour.

Then suddenly, he grimaces and raises a hand to his head. No one notices except me. He takes a step, stumbles, and drops the handle that supports his side of the crucible. Eric and Mason stagger under the unexpected weight. The crucible falls into the sand pit, splattering molten bronze across the tops of the investment molds. At the same instant, Hugh collapses.

Someone must have dragged him away from the pit, but I don't remember anything except my heart throbbing, my breath coming in gasps as I run toward him. It isn't until I get there that I realize his body is stiff, his arms and legs are twitching uncontrollably. I fall to my knees, then hesitate. I never touch Hugh when he's awake and aware; how can I touch him now when he's so vulnerable, so not himself?

"Get Marianna!" I shout to Eric and Mason, surprised at the power of my voice. "Marianna!" I shriek, not waiting for their response. "Marianna!"

She appears a moment later, running out of the house with Liesel behind her. I back away as she kneels down beside him. She touches his shoulder and his body miraculously stops twitching, stops moving entirely. He's breathing deeply, eyes closed and mouth open, like a man in a deep sleep.

Marianna is scared, I can see it in her eyes. But as usual, she takes control. "Liesel, call an ambulance," she says. "Eric, please escort the people to their cars. Mason, clean up this mess."

She has forgotten about me, or so I think. Then she turns and says in a voice that's both reassuring and commanding, "Sienna, go inside now. Go on."

That's it. There's no job for me to do, no reason for me to be there. So I walk away. At the side door I turn back. From this angle, I can't see my father's face. There's only Marianna leaning over him, whispering intimate words in his ear.

I'm sitting on a stool at the kitchen counter, drawing to keep from thinking. The distant whine of a siren grows louder as I sketch the tulips in the vase by the sink, capturing the shapes, adding the shadows. And then I hear the ambulance pull into the driveway. I'm scared to look, but I walk to the window. I don't know what I'm expecting—anything but what I see. Hugh is on his feet, talking to the paramedics. Marianna is at his side, looking up into his face, nodding, smiling.

The paramedics get back in the ambulance and drive away. Then Hugh and Marianna climb in the Range Rover and follow them down the driveway. A moment later, Liesel walks into the kitchen.

"What's happening?" I ask.

"Mr. Scully wouldn't get in the ambulance," she explains. "Mrs. Scully is driving him to the doctor."

"What's wrong with him?" I ask.

She frowns, considering. "It looked like some kind of seizure. Perhaps . . ." She shrugs, shakes her head. "The doctor will know."

I turn back to the window. Eric and Mason are reheating the bronze, preparing to pour it into the plaster molds that didn't get cast. It's a strange sight to see them working without my father. He's always nearby, giving orders, grabbing a shovel or a hack saw and stepping in when he feels someone isn't doing things right.

"Come, Sienna," Liesel says, appearing at my shoulder. "I was about to make Mr. Scully an omelette. No need for it to go to waste."

I'm not hungry, but I let her lead me back to the stool. I want to be comforted, cared for, and right now this is the best I can hope for.

Hugh and Marianna come home late, after I'm already in bed. I hear them moving in the hallway and I sit up, straining to overhear some scrap of conversation. But they say nothing. Then I hear the door to their bedroom close and the house goes dark.

The next morning, it's as if nothing out of the ordinary ever occurred. Liesel is in the kitchen. "Would you like some pancakes?" she asks as I walk in.

I shrug, searching her face for clues, but she's as blank as a new sketch pad. If she knows anything, she isn't telling.

I walk down the hall to Marianna's office. She's sitting with her back to me, sipping coffee and typing a letter on the word processor. I hesitate, wondering if I should speak. But I'm frightened of what I might find out. So I slip past the door and head outside.

The morning sun is golden; the grass is wet with dew. I walk over to the barn, then stop and listen. A Mozart string quartet is singing through the speakers so I know Hugh is inside. I lean my body against the barn door, letting the music wash over me and wishing I was listening to it at his side.

Long ago, I used to enter my father's studio as if it were my playhouse. That was when I was in pre-school, eager and thoughtless and certain that the world revolved around me. Hugh was still painting sometimes back then, and I remember sitting on the floor beside him, scribbling with crayons while he worked. Even then my drawings were small and careful; even then Hugh didn't approve. He used to grab the crayon from my hand and tell me to loosen up, relax, think big and broad and bold. Then he'd fill the paper with color and line and hand it to me. "See?" he'd say. "That's how you do it. Now go on, Sienna. You try it."

So I'd start over, but the results never seemed to satisfy him. They were too timid, too monochromatic, too realistic. As his criticisms continued, my frustration grew, until finally I would throw the crayons aside, stamp my foot, and shout, "You're a bad bear! I don't like you!" Then Marianna would come and carry me, kicking and sobbing, out of the studio and back to the house.

After one too many tantrums, the barn was declared off limits to me. I missed the smell of turpentine, the sun flooding through the skylights, the solid strength of my father standing beside me, doing important things with paint and clay and steel. But I didn't complain. In my four-year-old way, I understood I didn't belong there anymore. I understood a test had been given me, and I had failed it.

Since that day, no one has ever told me to keep out of the studio. No one has had to. I watch from the doors, sometimes take Hugh a drink or a sandwich that Liesel has made for him, but I don't stay. I'm too old for crayons, and besides, my sketches are still small and careful. Only now Hugh doesn't disapprove. Now he doesn't notice.

Liesel's voice brings me back to the present. "Sienna, breakfast is ready."

I turn and head back across the grass. Marianna is waiting for me at the door. She meets my eye and my stomach tightens in anticipation of what she might tell me. But all she says is, "The bus will be here any minute."

"I know," I say. It's Friday, a school day. I walk toward the kitchen.

Then she says something else, speaking so softly I almost wonder if I've imagined it. "It's a brain tumor."

A sick, unsteady feeling floods through me. "What?"

I turn around to find her smiling. "It's not as bad as it sounds. We can lick this thing. Hugh's going to start radiation therapy right away."

"Radiation?" I repeat stupidly.

She nods. "To eradicate the tumor. Our goal is to get Hugh completely healthy in time for the opening of the L.A. retrospective."

She sounds so confident, so certain everything is under control that I don't think to question her, don't even bother to ask if the tumor is benign. It must be; the retrospective is only three months away and she said Hugh will be well by then, didn't she? Of course she did.

So I take all the questions, all the doubts and fears that are spinning around inside me, force them into a little box, and close the lid. My brain is full of boxes, neatly stacked away so they won't cause anyone any trouble. One more won't matter.

I nod to show Marianna that I understand, that she doesn't have to worry about me, but she's already turned away and is walking back to her office. I wait until she steps inside and closes the door. Then I walk back outside, avoiding Liesel and the pancakes, and head down the driveway to wait for the bus.

POINTS TO CONSIDER ABOUT *FADE FAR AWAY*

1. This excerpt is from the opening section of a new novel by Francess Lantz, *Fade Far Away*. How long does it take for the reader to figure out who Hugh is, and the narrator's relationship to this character? Why does Lantz draw out her novel's exposition in this way? Could one use this same kind of opening technique in a short story? Why, or why not?

2. How would you describe the language of the first-person narrator? Does this sound like any teenager you've ever met? What does Sienna's choice of words tell you about her; how does Lantz use the narrator's diction to develop the characterization of her protagonist? Cite specific examples from this section of *Fade Far Away* to support your assertions.

3. What function does the sketch pad serve for Sienna? What function does it serve in the narrative development of *Fade Far Away*? Discuss the role that secondary characters play in the story's plot.

4. Sienna mentions early in the story that she has never thought to call her parents Mom and Dad. She further explains that she came to them late in their lives, and that she believes they never really viewed themselves as parents. How does this shared information contribute the plot development of *Fade Far Away*? Have you felt (or can you imagine feeling) the same way toward your parents? What specific factors might contribute to such a feeling? How might this attitude of Sienna's relate to the title of the story?

5. In the chronology provided by subsequent chapters of *Fade Far Away*, Sienna idolizes her father, then resents him, then gets to know him and

develops a new, more mature attitude toward her relationship with him
. . . all of which prepares her to feel at peace with his death at the end of
the book (Sorry if I spoiled the read for you!). What are the thematic implications of this plot; what "message" does Lantz intend to send to
young people via *Fade Far Away?* How does this intended message conform to the "requirements" of YA fiction, as explained by Lantz in Chapter 10 of *The Graceful Lie?*

50% Chance of Lightning
Cristina Salat

"I wonder if I'll ever have a girlfriend." Robin stamps her sneakers against
the wet pavement, tired of waiting.

Malia laughs. "Is that all you think about?"

"Well, what's the point of being gay if I'm never going to *be* with anybody? Robin shifts the big umbrella they are sharing to her other hand. Fat
silver drops of rain splatter above the plastic dome. She wishes the bus
would run on time for once.

"Independent women. We vowed, remember? No guy chasing," Malia
says.

Robin shoots Malia a look.

"Or girl chasing," Malia adds quickly.

"You can't talk," Robin says, trying not to feel each strand of her hair
as it frizzes. "You have someone."

"That's true." Malia smiles.

Robin looks at the gray, wet world through her clear umbrella. It's hat
weather. Black baseball hat and hair gel. She uses both, but nothing really
helps on damp days like this. "It's silly to worry how you look. Rain can
make you alive if you let it!" Robin's mother used to say. She loved stormy
weather almost as much as Robin didn't.

"It's Friday! How come you're so quiet?" Malia asks. "You're not ob-
sessing about your hair, are you? It looks fine. I'd trade you in a second . . .
so don't start in about my perfect Filipino hair!" She grins, reading Robin's
mind.

Robin can't help smiling. They've know each other a long time.

"Guess what!" Malia changes the subject. "Tomorrow is me and Andrew's six-month anniversary. That's the longest I've ever gone out with anybody."

Robin sighs. "You guys will probably get old together." And I'll be the oldest single person on the face of the planet, she thinks gloomily.

Malia's forehead wrinkles into a slight frown. "No. I'm leaving. I can't wait to get out of here." A large electric bus lumbers to the curb and stops with a hiss. "I sent my applications out yesterday. NYU, Bryn Mawr, Hampshire, and RIT, in that order," Malia says as she boards.

They squeeze onto the heated bus between packed bodies in steaming overcoats. The bus lurches forward.

"Where did you decide?" Malia asks, grabbing onto a pole near the back.

Robin shrugs.

Malia raises one eyebrow. "It's almost Thanksgiving. You are still going to try for NYU and Hampshire with me, aren't you?"

"I guess," Robin says. "I haven't had time to decide anything yet." It's not like she hasn't been thinking about it. College catalogs are spread across the floor of her bedroom. All she has to do is figure out where she wants to spend the next four years of her life. New York? Massachusetts? Zimbabwe? There's an endless stream of choices.

"You better make time," Malia says. "You shouldn't wait until the deadlines."

"Give me a break, okay?" Robin stares past the seated heads in front of her.

"Cranky, cranky." Malia elbows Robin's arm.

A woman wipes one hand across a steamed window for an outside view and pulls the bus cord. She vacates her seat and Malia and Robin squeeze past someone's knees to claim it. With Malia balanced on her lap, Robin turns her head toward the window and watches the city swish by. She tries to picture herself next fall, suitcases packed, excited to be going. She's almost eighteen; she should want to leave home. A new room. New city. New friends.

I can't leave, not yet! The air in the bus is thick and warm; it's hard to breathe enough in. Outside the window, sharp-edged buildings and signs fly past. Robin's head feels light and disconnected. She presses her face against the cold glass. She doesn't have to leave. She can apply to San Francisco State or USF right here in the city. Or she won't go at all. Malia's mom didn't go to college. Robin's dad didn't go either, but he wants her to. "You're smart, like your mother," he's always saying. But what if she doesn't want to go?

It's okay, Robin repeats to herself. No one can make me.

Outside the window she watches a small, mixed terrier approach the curb, sniffing the ground. Its fur is wet and matted, standing up in points. The dog steps into the stilled, waiting traffic. Robin scans the sidewalk for the dog's person. Don't they know it's dangerous to let their puppy wander into the street?

Robin stares through the window, her mind racing. Maybe it's lost. She could help. She could get off the bus and . . . A car honks loudly. Something inside her shrinks up. Malia's weight is heavy on her lap. The dog looks up and scampers back to the curb as traffic surges and the bus rumbles forward. Robin cranes her neck. She should get off, before it's too late. But she can't.

"What is it?" Malia asks, feeling Robin's shift.

Robin forces herself to lean back in the seat and breathe slowly. She's being stupid. The dog won't get run over. Its owner is probably just down the block.

They hang their jackets over the chair in Malia's small, neat room and Robin drops her baseball cap onto the desk.

"You want to see my list of goals?" Malia asks. "I read in *New Woman* if you know exactly what you want, you're more likely to get it." She hands Robin an open, spiral-bound notebook and drops next to her on the bed.

Malia Manansala
Goals for Now
Get into a good college, far away
Major in computer science or business
Get another part-time job for clothes, makeup, etc.
Have fun!
Eventually
Dressy job where I make a lot of money and get respect
Nice apartment with classy things
Old BMW or Jeep Cherokee (depending where I live)
Great friends
Marry someone loyal, sexy, and successful

"Money." Robin shakes her head. "Even if we get scholarships, we're going to be paying off college loans forever."

Malia nods. "That's why I need a big career. I'm not going to suck up to some man for money. You should make a goal list," she suggests, handing over a pen. "I need a snack."

Robin flops onto her side. Why not? At the top of a clean page, in slow, careful letters, she writes:

Goals
Figure Out Who I Am
Be Proud of Myself
Fall in Love
Do Something Good

Robin frowns at her list. How does Malia know exactly what she wants?

"Hand it over." Malia comes back into the room with a tray of hot cocoa and microwaved pork buns.

"Okay, but it's not like yours."

"Do something good?" Malia makes a face. "Can you be more specific?"

"Hey, I didn't pick on your list!"

"I don't get it. When you want to do something, you just do it. This year you start telling everyone, 'I'm a lesbian, deal with it.' Why can't you be like that about college?"

"It's different," Robin says, thinking, I didn't tell everyone. My mother never got to know. Her mom drove a red Honda CRX with African pendants dangling from the rearview mirror. She took the highway a lot, to avoid city traffic. Route 101 South. Robin yanks her mind away.

"You are going to do more with your life than just be a lesbian, aren't you?" Malia prods.

Robin gets to her feet, shaking the damp bottoms of her baggy jeans away from her ankles. "Can I borrow something dry?"

"Come on. Seriously. What kind of job do you want?" Malia sounds like Robin's mom and dad used to—always excited about plans.

"I don't know. Something to help people," Robin says, looking through the closet.

"Peace Corps? Lawyer? Social worker?" Malia suggests.

"No," Robin says, a faded memory seeping into her mind. She used to play medicine woman when she was little, healing stuffed toy rabbits and her plastic Ujima dolls with bowls of grass-flower soup. "I always pictured myself in a funky office," she tells Malia, "where people or animals would come when they didn't feel well."

"You want to be some kind of doctor!" Malia enthuses.

Robin shakes her head. Playing medicine woman was a kid thing. "You know I can't stand blood and guts." Robin focuses her attention in the closet, taking out a black lace top and black leggings.

"How about a therapist? You could help people's minds."

"And listen to people complain all day?" Robin asks as she changes.

Malia sighs, shutting the notebook. "Well, what do you want to do tonight? I told Andrew I'd call him by four. Oh, I forgot! My mother and the jerk are going out after work. They won't be home till late. Do you want to have a party?"

"Yes!" Robin says. "Go rent some movies. I'll call for a pizza and invite everybody."

Andrew arrives first with a soggy Safeway bag tucked into his aviator jacket.

"Hey, Robbie!" he says, unpacking jumbo bottles of root beer and 7Up on the living-room table.

The doorbell rings again. Robin runs to let in Malia's friend Dan, who has brought his sister, Cybelle—a junior—and another girl. Malia has plenty of friends. Most of them are at least part Filipino.

Being a mix (African and Polish), Robin doesn't care what her friends are. She only has a few anyway, though she knows a lot of people. When her mother died at the end of sophomore year, nobody knew what to say, so they acted like nothing happened. Robin still hangs out with the same people, but just because it's something to do; not because she cares.

When Malia returns from the video store, fifteen people are sprawled on the couch and floor with paper plates of mushroom and garlic pizza.

"Party woman," Andrew teases Malia, leaning down for a kiss. "You're soaked."

"It was only drizzling when I left. Sorry I took so long. I couldn't decide!" Malia takes two video cassettes out of a plastic bag. "I got a vampire movie and *The Best of Crack-Up Comedy.*"

"I love vampires!" Cybelle adjusts one of the five rhinestone studs on her left ear. "Let's get scared first."

"Go change," Andrew tells Malia. "I'll set up the movie." He nudges her toward the bedroom.

Robin watches, wondering if anyone will ever care like that about her. For some reason the wet dog she saw from the bus pops into her mind. Nobody cared enough to keep it safe.

"Hi. You're Robin Ciszek, right?" A white girl in ripped jeans and a "Save the Planet" sweatshirt sits down next to Robin on the couch. "I read your article in the school paper! I'm April, Cybelle's friend. I never thought what it feels like to be gay until I read your essay. Do you know a lot of gay people, or was the story mostly about you?" April's slate-colored eyes are wide and curious.

Robin takes a big bite of pizza. It's still hard to believe she wrote an article about being gay and submitted it to the school paper. She must have been crazy.

"I hope you don't mind me asking," April says quickly. "I'm just interested."

"The story's mostly about me," she tells April. "I don't know a lot of other gay people."

"I guess you will next year," April says. "My sister goes to UC Berkeley, and she says there's like three different gay groups on campus."

Robin feels her shoulders clench up. Is college the only thing anyone can talk about? Of course, it'll be worth it to be out of high school just to get away from the stupid notes guys are taping on her locker door: *All you need is a real man* and *Robin C. and Malia M. eat fish.*

"Personally, I'm glad I don't have to think about college for another year," April continues.

"Really? Why?" Robin asks, surprised.

April looks away, embarrassed. "It's dumb. I have this cat. I don't want to leave her."

"Guess what I brought!" Cybelle calls out as Andrew dims the living-room light. She takes a half-full bottle of brandy from her tote bag.

"I'll have a little of that," Malia says, coming back into the room in overalls and a fluffy white sweater. "To warm me up."

"Quiet—it's starting," Gary yells from the easy chair as a bold, red title flashes across the television screen.

"I want to sit on the couch," Tara giggles. "Move over, Danny."

April moves toward Robin to make room for another person. Her hip rests against Robin's. The couch armrest presses into Robin's other side.

"Oh, hold me, Andrew!" Cybelle teases Malia as eerie music fills the darkened room. Malia laughs.

April's leg relaxes against Robin's. Out of the corner of one eye, Robin looks at the girl sitting next to her. April is watching the screen. Robin's thigh sizzles.

Robin nonchalantly eases sideways until their arms and legs are touching. A faint scent of perfume tinges the air. April doesn't move away. Robin's whole left side buzzes. She sinks into the couch, holding her breath. It would be so amazing if—

If what? Just because this girl liked the article doesn't mean she's interested. Robin moves her leg away, mad at herself. On screen, a shadowy figure suddenly whirls around and grins evilly. April leans softly against Robin.

Warm drops of sweat trickle down Robin's side. The room feels dark and red. Robin could reach out, take April's hand, trace one finger over the knuckle bumps and pale, freckled skin. . . .

Halfway through the vampire movie, Robin has to go to the bathroom, bad. She is tempted, but restrains herself from squeezing April's leg as she gets up.

Away from everyone, she splashes cold water on her face, smiling. Could April really be interested? I could go back and sit away from her to see if she follows me.

Feeling hot and wild, Robin unlocks the door. It doesn't budge. She pulls harder, leaning backward, and opens it a foot.

"Hi, Robin." Cybelle grins, peeking around the corner.

"What's with you? Get away from the door," Robin says.

"Okay." Cybelle runs one hand through her porcupine patch of short, black hair. "C'mere. I want to ask you something." Cybelle pulls Robin into Malia's room. She shuts the door without flicking on the light.

"Smell my breath," she says, leaning close.

A warm rush of brandy air tickles Robin's face.

"I can't go home wasted. Do I smell like pizza or alcohol?" Cybelle asks. Her lips touch the side of Robin's mouth.

"What are you doing?" Robin asks.

Cybelle nuzzles Robin's face, tracing her lips along Robin's. "Don't you like me? Kiss me back."

Robin's heart stutters. Is this for real? Cybelle slides one hand under Robin's hair and grips the back of her neck, kissing harder.

I've wanted this for so long, Robin thinks, awkwardly moving her arms around Cybelle. It's weird not being able to see. Robin touches sharp shoulder blades through the thin cotton of Cybelle's turtleneck.

I should have helped that dog. The thought scuttles into Robin's head. Why is she thinking about that now!

Cybelle sucks on Robin's lower lip. I should have gotten off the bus and helped. I could have taken it to the pound, or home. Why didn't I do something?

Cybelle's small tongue slides into Robin's mouth. Why am I doing this? I've seen Cybelle around school and never wanted to. She's got a boyfriend. She'll probably tell everyone, "I made out with the lesbian at Malia's house," for a laugh.

Robin shifts sideways. "I have to go."

"What?"

"I'm going back to the living room." Robin feels for the wall switch and flicks on the light.

Cybelle blinks. "How come? It's okay. Nobody misses us." She smiles and tugs on Robin's arm, moving closer.

"I want to see the rest of the movie," Robin says, pulling away. It's a lame excuse, but what else can she say? "I want to kiss somebody I'm really into, and you're not it"?

Cybelle stops smiling and drops Robin's arm. "Oh sure," she laughs. "You're scared! Writing that story and you don't even know what to do! What a joke." She yanks open the door and walks out before Robin can respond.

Robin follows Cybelle to the living room and watches her take the small, open spot on the couch next to April. She glares at the back of Cybelle's spiked head. Who does she think she is? I don't have to make out if I don't want to!

Whirling around, Robin heads back to the bedroom and jams her feet into her sneakers.

"You okay?" Malia asks, coming in.

"Sure." Robin doesn't look up.

"Are you leaving? What's going on?"

"Nothing I want to talk about right now." Robins zips up her jacket. They walk to the front door. Robin flings it open. She can't wait to be outside.

"Call me tomorrow, okay? Hey." Malia grabs Robin's jacket.

Robin looks back over her shoulder. "What?"

"We're best buddies forever, right?"

If Malia moves to New York and Robin stays here . . . Nothing's forever.

"Sure," Robin says, looking away.

Malia smiles and reaches out for a hug. "I'm sorry you didn't have a good time. Let's go shopping tomorrow morning, just you and me. Okay?"

As soon as Robin steps away from Malia's house, she realizes she's forgotten her baseball cap. Angrily, she pops open her umbrella. It doesn't matter. There's a bus stop at the corner and she's just going home.

Water drops drum against the plastic shield above her head as cars zip by, their rubber tires splashing against wet asphalt. Robin glares at each car that passes. She will never own one. What if that dog got run over? She should have helped. A bolt of light illuminates the night. Robin looks helplessly down the empty street for a bus. She hates being out alone after dark, even when it's not very late.

Whenever someone worried, her dad used to say: "There's a fifty-fifty chance of something good happening." Robin's mother loved that saying. Her father hasn't said it much lately. It's hard to believe in good stuff when you're dealing with the other fifty percent. At least she ended the thing with Cybelle. That's something. Robin might want experience, but she's not desperate.

Thunder swells, filling the night. Robin cranes her neck, looking down the street. No bus. So it's fifty-fifty. Should she wait here, hoping no weirdos show up and bother her before the bus comes, or should she start walking in this lousy weather? Her parents used to take walks in the rain. They were nuts . . . but happy.

Robin starts to walk. A sharp wind whips by, threatening to turn her umbrella inside out. Okay, why not? She has nothing to lose. Robin clicks the umbrella shut. Rain falls cold against her face and settles onto her thick hair, expanding it. She walks fast, with the wooden umbrella handle held forward, staying near the streetlamps. Water trickles down her face and soaks into her clothing. She licks her lips. The rain tastes strangely good.

When she reaches the place where she saw the dog, Robin stops and studies the black road. A few torn paper bags. No blood or fur. It could be dead somewhere else. Or it could be off foraging in a garbage can or sleeping under a bush.

I'm sorry I didn't get off the bus to see if you needed help, she thinks. Next time I will. I hope you're safe. But maybe the dog didn't need help. Maybe it wasn't even scared. Maybe it was totally pleased to be out exploring and taking care of itself. Robin decides to picture the terrier that way.

From down the block a bus approaches, grumbling to a stop a few feet ahead. Robin hurries over. As the doors squeal open, she looks behind at the dark, empty street. She is afraid, but she doesn't want to be. Slowly, Robin turns away.

It is a long walk home under the wide, electric sky.

At the warm apartment on Guerrero Street, Robin finds her father asleep on their living-room couch. A paperback novel is spread open across his chest and his glasses are pushed up onto his forehead. Standing over him, dripping onto the brown shag rug, Robin feels tender and old. She removes his glasses and places the book on the glass coffee table, careful not to lose his page.

In her room, Robin drops her wet clothing to the floor and changes into an old set of flannel pajamas. Then she sits down at her drafting table desk. Nothing's forever, and that's just the way it is. Moving college applications aside, she lifts two thick San Francisco phone books from the floor.

Robin thumbs through the thin A–L yellow pages slowly. There is something she can do. Something right.

Attorneys, Automobile . . . Bakers, Beauty . . . Carpets, Collectibles . . . Dentists, Divers . . . Environment . . . Florists . . . Health. Health clubs, health and diet, health maintenance, health service. A boxed ad catches Robin's eye.

Holistic Health Center
Dedicated to the well-being of body and mind
Licensed: nutritionists, massage therapists, acupuncturists
Courses in herbal healing, yoga, natural vision, Tai Chi

Medicine without blood and guts. Smiling to herself, Robin reaches for some looseleaf paper and a pen. There's a new life out there, waiting for her. She just has to find it. She moves A–L aside and flips open M–Z. By ten P.M. three looseleaf pages are filled with numbers and addresses. At the top of the first page, she writes: *Call for info.*

Robin stretches and climbs into bed with her new list. She rubs the soles of her bare feet against the chilled sheets. Maybe life is like rain. Alive if you let it be; lousy and depressing if you don't. She rolls onto her stomach. Under the information for the Shiatsu Institute, the College of Oriental Medicine, and the School for Therapeutic Massage, she writes: *Tell Malia to get April's number from Dan. Call her?!?!?!*

POINTS TO CONSIDER ABOUT "50% CHANCE OF LIGHTNING"

1. Enumerate the qualities of "50% Chance of Lightning" that make it fall squarely within the subgenre of young adult fiction. By contrast, what qualities does this story—and, by extension, all young adult fiction—share with fiction written to a more mature readership?

2. What is the thematic message implied by this story? Do you feel that stories with these kinds of themes should be read by young people? If so, what might young adults gain by reading such stories? If not, what are the dangers, in your opinion, in allowing/encouraging young people to read stories such as "50% Chance of Lightning"?

3. "50% Chance of Lightning" is a story that makes a definite point about gender and sexual identity, and yet it's still a *story* first and foremost. How does Salat manage to deliver her political/social message without "hitting the reader over the head" with it?

4. How old are the central characters, Robin and Malia? What other details of youth culture lend credibility to "50% Chance of Lightning"? Does this story convincingly capture the concerns of young people, based on your experiences of having been a young person, and on your observations of today's teens?

5. Is "50% Chance of Lightning" a story in the traditional, Aristotelian sense; does it have narrative tension that moves the plot toward a climax and resolution? If so, identify the specific elements of plot development; if not, explain why Salat chose not to follow the so-called "rules" of successful plotting.

✖ WRITING ACTIVITIES: YOUNG ADULT FICTION

1. Recall the turmoil of your adolescence. The issues and hardships you had to confront as a teenager are no doubt similar to the experiences and hardships of today's teens. Isolate a specific issue—sexual awakening, peer pressure, sports, change in body image, changes in relationship to parents, drugs—and recall an instance in which you had to confront this issue. Try to place yourself into the memory and write about the emotions and feelings as you dealt with then. Having done that, go back and write about the same incident from your (hopefully!) more mature perspective of the present. Finally, fuse these two writings into a story written in a first-person voice (from the teenager's perspective), but which subtly embeds the insights and truths attained through your more adult experience.

2. There are numerous current topics that receive much discussion in the media, due in part to their possible negative influences on young adults. Focus on one of these topics as it related to you in your own adolescence—smoking? television violence? heavy metal music with satanic messages? domestic abuse?—and write about an incident that illustrates your having to deal with this issue. Write several endings to your story—including entirely fictional ones that did not happen to you in real life—and then select the ending that best conforms to Francess' Lantz's guidelines for effective resolutions in YA fiction. In the process of undertaking this activity, don't be afraid to unveil painful truths to your audience.

3. Remember a person you didn't like in junior high or high school. It could be a bully, a person who was very popular at a time when you weren't, a person who turned you in to the principal for cheating on a math test, someone who "trash-talked" to you continually on the basketball court, a person well-known for cruel gossip. Imagine a scenario in which your adolescent self gets into an elevator with this person and confronts him/her directly, in a way that you never could when you were a teenager. Write the confrontation primarily in the form of dialogue. Take that passage of dialogue and frame a story around it, so that your protagonist's risk-taking behavior in confronting this individual seems perfectly justified, given the narrative situation. Try several resolutions: perhaps one in which the two characters end up having the potential for being friends, and another in which the object of your youthful dislike ends up with fewer teeth than before the elevator encounter.

11

Mystery Fiction

Best-selling author Sue Grafton has sold over 2 million copies of her books in hardcover and over 16 million copies in paperback to date in the United States alone. Her books are in print in the United Kingdom, as well as in 20 other languages: Bulgarian, Chinese, Croatian, Czech, Danish, Dutch, Finnish, French, German, Hebrew, Icelandic, Indonesian, Italian, Japanese, Korean, Norwegian, Polish, Portuguese, Spanish, and Swedish. Grafton came to the book publishing world after working for fifteen years in Hollywood as a screen writer. She wrote numerous movies for television, including "Walking Through Fire" (1979), for which she won a Christopher Award; "Sex and the Single Parent"; "Mark, I Love You"; and "Nurse." With her husband Steve Humphrey, Sue adapted two Agatha Christie novels, *Caribbean Mystery* and *Sparkling Cyanide,* and co-wrote "Killer in the Family" and "Love on the Run." She began her "alphabet series" of Kinsey Millhone mysteries in 1982 with *A is for Alibi,* and her most recent is *N is for Noose.* In this interview, Sue Grafton discusses techniques and concerns unique to the mystery genre, her writing process specifically... along with issues pertinent to writers of *all* genres of fiction, including some fascinating discussion of the role of the subconscious in the creative process.

AN INTERVIEW WITH SUE GRAFTON

MP: Why don't we start out by talking about the *M is for Malice* chapter included at the end of this interview. What specific narrative tasks do you try to accomplish in the initial chapters of your books?

SG: The conceit of these books is that Kinsey Millhone, when she finishes a case, sits down and does an account for her own purposes. Generally there is a prologue and an epilogue, which are sort of bookends. The prologue, whether it is separated out or folded into the first chapter itself, is meant to set the tone of the book, so that I have a feel for whether it's going to move toward action, humor, reflection . . . whatever the case may be.

MP: How does the journal help you accomplish this?

SG: Often, I find that in those first pages of the journal is the true thread of the story, although I often misunderstand it in its purity. Some of the journal is my process of discovering what the story really is. I sometimes imagine it in one form and discover that it's really coming to me in another form. Most of the journal doesn't end up in the book itself, but it is a way of going up roads and coming back, of finding cul-de-sacs and dead ends. There's a lot of backing up and moving forward and stumbling in the journals.

MP: In the journal do you make a structural outline for the book and then plug material into it later?

SG: I generally do not begin with a total, detailed outline, because I personally can't figure out who my characters are until I reach them in the narrative. Occasionally, if I have a sequence coming up that's unclear to me, or if I'm not sure where I'm going next, I will stop and begin to break down sequences of action, and that just gives me a little confidence. I think, "O.K., I know the order in which things need to occur." In the journals I also keep a running account of each book—what Kinsey Millhone is hired to do, the sex of the victim, the sex of the perpetrator, and the nature of the climax—because I think we have a tendency to repeat ourselves, even at a subliminal level. In the creative process I think we tend to return to some comfortable format, and I have to be very careful that my psyche—who is always presenting things to me as new, fresh, original and different—is not sneakily trying to recycle a story I've already written. When I have an idea for a book, I analyze it and break it down into that very simple question of who does what to whom. That way I can say, "Ah, wait a minute, this is moving too much toward something I've done before."

MP: I remember reading in a *Good Housekeeping* article that you said it was actually getting harder to write the books, because you kept running into stuff that you had written earlier . . . ?

SG: . . . which is not to say one can't do some repetition or variation on a theme or development of an idea, but I don't want to fall into an unconscious pattern whereby the reader goes, "Oh, here's the car chase, O.K., we know whodunit because she always sets it up this way." Prior to *M is for Malice*, people had been saying they wanted to see Robert Dietz again, which I had promised to do. Generally I'll promise these things for several books and finally I'll say to myself, "Ms. Grafton, you *have* to do what you said you would do!" So the front end of the journal is my chat with myself about where to cut into a story, which I think of as the angle of attack. Job number one is to figure out what *is* the story, and then, when I have some of that established, I need to figure out how close to the beginning I start. Do I try a flashback, do I cut straight into the heart of it? I'm always trying to do an action opening, which I notice Dick Francis does often; I can't seem to pull it off! I'll try an action opening where you just jump into the heart of it, and by the time I finish explaining how she got to where she's currently embroiled, I just think, "Oh, cut it out and do it in a straight, linear fashion." Many times I've abandoned my tricky opening and done it in a much more straightforward manner.

MP: Because you're working in a series, it seems to me that you frequently want Kinsey to tell the reader who she is, and establish each book as separate from the rest, so that a reader who hasn't read the entire series can still find entry into the current novel.

SG: That is always the tricky thing to do. You don't want to bore the reader who's been with you from the beginning. Sometimes, too, when people discover the series, they read them in a row, so that when I get to *N is for Noose*, or O is for whatever, I am sometimes dealing with a reader who has everything fresh in his mind, or her mind, and you don't want to come up with the same paragraph, because people will jump right over it. But coming up with ninety-nine new ways to describe Henry Pitts is about to do me in! Sometimes I get bored with Henry Pitts, or bored with Rosie, or bored with Santa Teresa, and that's when I cut away or take her out of town.

MP: You go on the road.

SG: That's right. And then, having done that, and having gotten a slew of complaints from readers who feel everything should be exactly the same, who want Kinsey in Santa Teresa, I will do one for them. I try not to let my readers dictate too much to me, but they do have some effect.

MP: The germ of the idea for your alphabet series of mystery novels is well documented: You were reading a book of Victorian illustrations featuring twenty-six pictures of children who expire by various means—"A" is for Amy who fell down the stairs, "B" is for Basil assaulted by bears, and so on. How do you come up with ideas for the individual books in the series?

SG: I will sometimes have a very basic notion of something I might like to try at some point. For instance, for *I is for Innocent*, I thought to myself, "Wouldn't it be interesting to do a courtroom drama?" I quickly realized that I hadn't the confidence or the information to write about that judicial process. My initial idea was to have Kinsey in some way involved in a court case, but when I realized how horrified I was at the agony of actually learning all that stuff, I thought, "Why don't I set up what would in essence be a courtroom drama without the courtroom?" The first third of *I is for Innocent* is the prosecution's case, the middle third is the defense, and the last third is sort of the rebuttal and the resolution of the story. That was fun for me; it was such a fun way to structure a book. But when I began, I had only that rudimentary notion of what I wanted to accomplish. With *K is for Killer*, I had been thinking it would be fun to do a book set entirely at night. Given that, I began to think about who was awake at night, what they might be doing, how I could in fact move Kinsey Millhone from herself as a day person into that other atmosphere. I also started to think about what it might do to her. *K is for Killer* has a lot of Jungian symbolism attached to it—not, I hope, in any obnoxious manner.

MP: I think of that as the scariest of your books, actually.

SG: It is about night creatures, and the unreal. The man on the bicycle is not anybody. That is just almost an hallucination, the recurrent figure, but it isn't a person. Many readers have written to say, "Who was that?" and I have to write back and say, "That was a night creature." If you analyze that book, it moves in its description of night from the quite benign, velvety and soft images down to the two mimes she sees on the corner, and toward the end, when she's going back to the water treatment plant, she hears the coyotes howling as they chase down some hapless creature. It was fun, too, to graduate that transition: night as enveloping to night as something threatening.

MP: Was the ghost in *M is for Malice* in your mind a hallucination also?

SG: I had thought to myself that it would be fun to do a ghost story, but that's a tricky business because I don't literally believe in ghosts, and yet I have in my mind had occasions where I felt there was a presence. I thought, "Well, we don't have to explain everything. Kinsey is subject to the same emotional states that the rest of us are."

MP: That's a very archetypal, primal kind of fear, whether you believe in it or not.

SG: Yes, that's right. And I think what saved me in that instance was that I did not try to explain it. She experiences something that she can't explain— maybe it was something and maybe it was nothing—and the reader can decide for herself, if she chooses to.

MP: You've said that, after rereading *J is for Judgment*, you realized it was a perfect mystery. What is it about that particular book that makes it "perfect" in your mind?

SG: My object in life is to write one perfect mystery. I'd hate to think I've done it, because then I'd have to quit! But when I was writing *J is for Judg-*

ment, I felt in the first few chapters that the work, the writing, was getting very flat. Part of that was because I had received so many letters about my "wild" language from people who objected to my four-letter words that I had begun to self-censor. Without even being aware of it, I was just substituting the words "heck" and "oh, shoot" for the other, more wicked versions. I think, in truth, Kinsey Millhone was pouting, because I was putting her in a bind. I was forcing her into some sanitized version of herself.

At a certain point I got a phone call from a friend of mine. "Do you remember," said she, "when you said if I ever found a perfect therapist for creative people, I should tell you?" Now the truth is I had no recollection of having said that to her, but I said, "Sure." She said, "I have this fellow who is at this moment very magical. I don't know how long it will last, but right now he's very magical." I called him up within twenty minutes—that was on a Wednesday or Thursday—I met with him on Saturday down in Los Angeles, and for three months we did this phone therapy which was generally Jungian in its foundation. He taught me the difference between Ego and Shadow—he taught me many, many concepts—and what I did finally was to give that book over to Shadow. Why I think it is a perfect book is that, because it is a Shadow-written book: I gave up any attempt to control it.

At a certain point, in the dead of night, Shadow woke me up, and she said to me, "You have never understood what this book is about, I will now tell you what this book is really about." That's where the epilogue came from—I could suddenly see that it was never Wendell Jaffe's story, it was Renata's story—and that was stunning to me, to watch how you could tell a story entirely from one point of view, based on one set of facts, and at a certain point the same set of facts would support an entirely different point of view. That was such fun for me, it was such a revelation.

MP: You're lucky that your shadow actually says things to you. Mine usually lurks in the background.

SG: Oh, I'll tell you how to do this—it's so easy! First of all, the shadow does not jump to your schedule. The shadow will give you answers in . . . I think men's shadows are male . . . in his own time. What you need to do is pose the question and then allow quite a lot of space for Shadow to respond. Shadow will not always answer directly. My Shadow, for instance, will wake me in the middle of the night and say, "Don't forget it's raining." I'll think, "Shoot, that's right, it's raining in the narrative, and I haven't mentioned that." Or she'll say to me, "Don't forget that Kinsey changed into the black, all-purpose dress," and I'll think, "Shoot, I forgot she has to change clothes." I think of them as roses on my pillow. I wake up and find a rose on the pillow. Your Shadow will wake you up in the night, when your Ego or your Left Brain is down and asleep. That's when Shadow comes out. Your

Shadow will tell you things if you listen. Your Shadow is telling you things all the time; you're just not listening. What I do often, if I'm stuck or blocked, I'll drink coffee in the afternoon, and then Shadow wakes up at 2 A.M, and you'd be amazed at the amount of information you get.

MP: Pepperoni pizza at midnight works also.

SG: That's right. Literary inspiration is often mistaken for indigestion.

MP: You're a prime practitioner of what readers and critics call the "female private detective genre." To what degree does your awareness of writing not only for a fictional genre, but perhaps for a social movement as well, affect your writing process . . . if at all?

SG: "If at all" is the answer. When I began *A is for Alibi*, I honestly didn't realize there weren't female private investigators being written about. I knew there were some in the real world, but I didn't know there was no fictional counterpart. I knew about Marcia Muller's books, because I had read *Edwin of the Iron Shoes*, but I just thought she was one of many. I didn't think I was doing any groundbreaking, pioneering, effort. I made Kinsey Millhone female because I am female.

When I began *A is for Alibi*, I knew nothing about how to write mysteries, I knew nothing about police procedurals, I didn't even know clearly what a private investigator did. While I was in the process of learning everything I needed to learn to write the first book, I thought, "I'm not writing from a man's point of view, I don't have a clue about how men think or how they reason." So I thought, "At least I know about being female," and I made her a version of myself, because that was the only thing I felt like I had any confidence about. You'll find the word "confidence" creeping up often in my talking about these things; every book has a crisis of confidence.

At any rate, at this point I am not interested in Kinsey Millhone toeing the line in terms of feminist theory. I feel she should be flawed and inconsistent. I don't want her to be superwoman, I don't want her to be larger than life. She is by her nature rebellious and strong and independent; she's not into male-bashing. I understand there are conventions at which they discuss my work and heated arguments erupt because some feel that Kinsey Millhone is a feminist, and others feel she is not hard-core enough. I just don't believe that it is the purpose of fiction to persuade anybody of anything, except that I hope my books are about not killing each other . . . and going to therapy instead. My basic message is: Let's just quit killing each other. But given the fact that people are murdered every day, I think to myself, "Why? Where does that come from?" I think we're all capable of murder, so I look at that in myself and I look at it in the people I know, to see if I can ever understand it.

MP: There does seem to be a strong sense of social justice underlying all of your books. In fact, I recall Kinsey using the phrase, "I know it's not up to me to solve the world's problems, but I'd like to believe there's a hidden order somewhere." That implies to me that you have some social message—at least in your subconscious—when you're writing your mysteries . . . or, are you simply telling a story and letting readers derive what meaning they will from the text?

SG: I obey the law. I pay my taxes. I don't cheat, and I don't think other people should cheat, either. I'll grant you the law is not perfect, and certainly the judicial system is not perfect, but it is all we have for the time being . . . so I support that, and I sometimes wish it were more effective than it happens to be. Given the fact that sometimes the police know whodunit and they can't prove it, or they prove it and a mistrial is declared, or someone is convicted of murder and is out of prison in a few years, I think that is the reality we deal with. In the fictional world of Kinsey Millhone, sometimes we create a different form of justice just as satisfying . . . if not more so, because it's quicker.

MP: Following that thread, I'm thinking of a quote Jermiah Healy said in *Writing Mysteries,* which you edited: "There must be some violence in a private investigator book." This is one element which separates mysteries from young adult fiction or Jane Austen novels. What is your attitude toward violence in your own writing?

SG: I'm not sure it needs to be violence, although that's what it often looks like. I think it needs to come down to a physical contest. That's archetypal: It is the battle between good and evil, plain and simple. You can't end a mystery novel with the heroine arguing with the villain, "Did too," "Did not," "Did too," "Did not." You don't want to get into this lengthy, arch discussion of who done what to whom. You can have that, but I try to lay it in, so that when I get to the climactic moment, we're not having to stop and gather all the suspects and have an endless reiteration of the story line. You try to set it up so that by the time you get to that final chase, or the gun battle, or whatever it happens to be, the reader understands all of the ramifications of the action itself. To me, it is most satisfying if there is a rising action, if you have things moving toward some moment of suspense and resolution. In that respect, violence is sometimes a byproduct. It's not like I aim for that, it's not like I celebrate violence—violence scares to me to death—but I recognize that in terms of how you lay out a story, it comes down to some kind of high moment that, for the detective, has some kind of violence attached to it.

MP: A review of *E is for Evidence* in the San Francisco *Chronicle* called the book "exceptionally entertaining" and said that you have "an offbeat sense of humor." How important is humor in your fiction—and in your life?

SG: I think humor is terribly important, but I don't think you can try to be funny. If you put a gun to my head and said, "Now let's see you be terribly amusing and witty," I couldn't do it. I watch other writers try to be funny, and it is so strained and so excruciating to me. "Humorous" mystery novels are generally to me very flat and false. What I think is funny is the truth. I always get tickled by the truth. A good comedian doesn't tell jokes; a good comedian tells you something that is true, and it makes you laugh because you recognize the truth. Whatever humor exists in my books comes from Shadow, or from Kinsey Millhone, which may be one and the same thing, some variation. I just focus on what I'm saying, and I try to say it as truly as possible. Sometimes that little voice pipes up and says, "Oh, put this in. Oh, go ahead and write this down," and sometimes it is so wicked I have to put it down and take it back out. I sit there and go, "I can't say that!" But sometimes I do anyway. I just think, "I'm not responsible for every single line of this. If people disagree, then so be it." I think the humor comes from Shadow, that repressed piece of us. Sometimes I think Kinsey's humor is a function of the fact the she thinks and says things the rest of us repress. It's funny to hear somebody actually say it.

MP: As you talk about Kinsey, it sounds as though you see her in a way as an embodiment of your own shadow.

SG: She is to some extent. Shadow, by its nature, is something you cannot see, that is often behind you. But insofar as it is possible to incorporate at any kind of conscious level, she is certainly another of my personalities.

MP: You've said, "I think of mystery writers as the brain surgeons of literature. I also think of us as the moralists and the magicians." Can you explain what you mean by that?

SG: In part what I refer to is the fact that mystery writing is very intellectual, and it's at some levels very left-brain, analytical, and exacting. People will launch themselves into a novel, never having written a word in their lives, but they've read mystery novels, and they think, "Well, I can do this." What they fail to understand is that the mystery novel is an exalted form. In order to write a good mystery novel, I think you first have to try mainstream fiction. You have to teach yourself how to tell a story, the pace of story, how to develop character, how to structure dramatic action. After you've mastered setting and atmosphere, then you can take on the very exotic requirements of the genre. Many people want to try writing for specific genres, when they don't have the basic foundation of writing, which is essential.

The reason I refer to it as "brain surgery" is that I think brain surgeons work at a most exacting and delicate level, which I think mystery writers do, too. I think we are magicians because we are always working with sleight of hand. It is like performing magic tricks before a willing audience. The game is: I pull a rabbit out of a hat, and you see if you can figure out how I do it, but I have to show you "nothing up my sleeve," I have to show you "no wires, no gimmicks"... and then, of course, I use every wire and gimmick at my disposal. I think we are moralists because we are dealing with life and death and murder and truth and justice.

MP: The magician aspect, I suppose, is the one I concern myself with most as a writing teacher.

SG: The thing about mystery writing is that you can never tell what the reader is picking up, because many forms of communication in the writing of a mystery take place at a subliminal level. For instance, in this book I just finished, *N is for Noose,* my husband was reading it, and he said, "I knew on page 314 who did it." We went back and we looked at that page, and there was nothing on the page that even pertained. But somehow through the lines and between the lines he got the message. Well, it was way too early, so I had to go back and really work to figure out how he got that subliminal message. He doesn't consider himself a sophisticated mystery reader. He doesn't even read to figure out whodunit, and he still got it. Sometimes there will be a reader who gets it on page four—bang! they know—and sometimes you get to the end of a book and they still don't know. You can tell them, "Here's whodunit," and they'll say, "I didn't get that!"

MP: Do you typically show your work to people before you finish a manuscript?

SG: Steve reads it when it is finished. He's the first reader. Once in a while, I get scared in the middle. I think, "I could be so far off base, so let's figure it out right now, before I commit another year to this book." In the middle of *G is for Gumshoe* I said, "I just have to know if you think I'm off base." He read the first half and said, "Oh, you're fine. Go back to work." Once in a while I get paranoid. So he reads it first, and then it goes straight to my editor at Holt. She'll have it back to me in a day and a half, completely edited, with all the notes attached. I'm barely out from under the thing, and it's back on my doorstep.

But back to the issue of being a good magician . . . some of that is trial and error. Some of that is knowing exactly what the story is and then pretending you don't . . . sort of voluntary amnesia. Part of it is understanding the process of reading. For instance, in a mystery novel I always think to myself, "No means yes." If a character looks particularly sinister, and squinting and drooling, they couldn't possibly be the killer. If a character looks completely loving and benign and goodhearted, you might start getting suspicious about that character.

MP: In poker, it's called misdirection.

SG: Right! But if you overplay your hand, then you've flipped it again. You have to be very careful how much you're showing of the scarf up your sleeve or the rabbit in the hat. You can never quite be sure. You can only hope to fool most of the people some of the time.

MP: You had Kinsey say in one of your books, "Honesty will get you nowhere, especially with these law-and-order types." Do you consciously use humor to take the hard edge off the law-and-order message?

SG: Probably. I recognize that there are times when obeying the letter of the law or being scrupulously honest can occasion disaster. Many people fudge slightly on many fronts. I don't think we need to be Nazis about these things, and there is a sense that the world is probably softer in its reality than it is on the printed page.

MP: I remember reading in one of your books, "Too much virtue has a corrupting effect," or something along those lines.

SG: It can be just as damaging to be too pious, for instance. I get a lot of letters from pious people, and under the piety is a lot of anger. I think, "What is that about? Why wag a finger at me, pretending you're better than I am, when in fact you're just as pissed off as I am?"

MP: Let's just talk about your plotting, getting back to that for a second. You worked as a screenwriter before you started writing fiction. Do you consider elements such as Hollywood-style "plot points" when constructing your Kinsey Millhone stories?

SG: Sometimes I do. Actually, I had written seven mainstream novels, of which only three were published, before I went to Hollywood. I started as a solo writer doing "mainstream fiction," whatever the fuck that is, and then I got into screenwriting and learned absolutely everything. I've learned so much from screenwriting in terms of laying out a story, and being economical with dialogue. I value that tutelage. I think it is fabulous training. I just didn't want to do it when I grew up.

MP: And you don't want to lend your stories to Hollywood, apparently.

SG: Right. I don't want to lend them, lease them, rent them—none of the above—because I don't like those people, and I don't want their help.

MP: What is it specifically about the Hollywood system that makes you want to avoid it so strenuously?

SG: I am basically not a collaborator. I once said to somebody, "I'm too much of a prima donna and not enough of a star for Hollywood." I wanted my way, and I want control, and I want to make the decisions, which in the publishing world is mine as long as I make money for people. It's economics, pure and simple. When my books make money, I get to be the boss. If I stray and my books start losing money, then somebody else is going to be the boss. But in Hollywood, the minute money changes hands, you've given up every piece of power you had, and I'm not willing to do that anymore. I don't think those people were good for me, I don't think they were good for my work.

MP: The funniest comment I ever read on your work was on the internet. Amazon.com, one of the on-line booksellers, has readers' comments on many different books. One of your readers said—I believe it was about *L is for Lawless*, "This book has TV movie written all over it . . . Valerie Bertinelli IS Kinsey Millhone!" And I thought, "Sue Grafton would just *die!*"

SG: It's funny! And here's another thing: people are not aware that these books are actually set ten years back. They get sequential, they start in '82, so Kinsey Millhone is currently living in 1986...

MP: ...and she's still only thirty six.

SG: She isn't even thirty-six yet! But I got this huffy letter from a woman who said, "Well, clearly your dates are all completely out of whack. I understand taking a manuscript out of the drawer and dusting it off ten years later, but you could have at least changed the dates." She literally believed that I had had this manuscript sitting around for ten years, and had just hauled it out as a piece of aesthetic laziness. I would never do such a thing. So in response to the comment about *L is for Lawless* being like a TV movie, probably the writer of that imagined that I had some old screenplay that I quick-converted into a novel.

MP: No, I think the comment was actually intended as very high praise for your work, that it could be converted into a TV movie starring Valerie Bertinelli.

SG: Hollywood is full of good ideas like that.

MP: Back to the writing process... I've heard you say, "The early days in a writer's life, before you first break into print, are very, very tough. In some ways, survival is more about strength of character than it is about talent." Can you give aspiring writers some tips to surviving the early stages of the writing—and even publishing—game?

SG: My father was a writer in addition to being a municipal bond attorney. He would say, "Bend with the wind. A tree that is too stiff or too rigid, when adversity comes along, that tree will topple or crack. If you can be flexible and bend with the wind, then you can right yourself again." He would just say, if you are disappointed because your manuscript comes flying back in with one of those nasty form letters, "Go ahead and weep. Of course it is disappointing. Don't pretend you don't feel the disappointment. But once you get done being disappointed, get mad. Pick yourself back up and say, 'Goddamnit, I will do this.'"

Also—and this I learned the hard way—you have to ask yourself how much you have learned from a piece of writing, and when it is time to move on. Many people will do one book, and they're so worried that they don't have another book, that they endlessly tinker with that one book, they endlessly send that one book out. That's all well and good, but at a certain point you have to say, "I have learned everything there is to learn from this piece of writing. Let me take that lesson and move on to the next piece of writing and learn what I need to learn from that." I wrote three completed manuscripts before I reached the fourth, which was the first novel I had published. I didn't devote my life endlessly to one piece of work. My big gripe about novice writers is that they will do one draft of one book and then call me up and want to know who my editor and my agent are. I'm going, "Don't even discuss it. How dare you?"

Writing is about the journey, it is not about the destination. So many novice writers only want the fame and the glory and the money. They don't understand that what it is about is survival and hardship and how you take rejection and how you deal with adversity . . . which is what character is about. If you have no backbone and if you have no resiliency and if you have no capacity to learn from what's happening to you in the world, you cannot make it as a writer. The exception to this are those poor souls who reach fame and fortune on the basis of one slender volume and never can repeat it, because they've had no learning process. Those early years as a writer are critical, and sometimes I think the harder they are, the better they are, if you can prevail. Also, while you're at it, you'd better learn the rules of grammar, because that's crucial.

MP: Who were your early influences as a mystery writer?

SG: Probably Agatha Christie, because I thought she was so clever. I realize now she did not develop character. Many times her books would hinge on one small idea, and if you got the idea, you got the whole shootin' match. But I still think she was very ingenious as a writer. And of course I'm crazy about Raymond Chandler and Ross McDonald, not so much Dashiell Hammett. James M. Cain I like. And I love Elmore Leonard's work.

MP: I know that you read Nancy Drew mysteries as a kid.

SG: Yes . . . but just until I discovered Mickey Spillane!

MG: Any last words you can give to young writers who are thinking about writing mysteries?

SG: I think writers need to have a very clear respect for professionalism. It takes a long time. A little revelation I had when I was twenty-two years old was that I thought to myself, if I wanted to be a doctor, I would understand that I would have to go to four years of medical school and a year of internship and a year of residency. You're looking at six years. I thought of my development as a writer in terms of five years—and not five years of idling about, but five years of very hard, constant, intense work. At the end of that five years, then you can reevaluate your situation. What makes me most impatient is the haste and the sloppiness with which some writers go about their business. Writing is a very exacting craft, and I think you have to give yourself enough time and enough energy and enough bad writing to teach yourself. You cannot take classes or get M.F.A. degrees and learn how to write. All those educational programs do is give you the opportunity to write. There's no getting around the fact that you have to write hundreds and hundreds and hundreds of thousands of words, many of which are very bad. If you have a little humility and a little respect for the craft, maybe you can move to what is your own true voice and your own truth that you have to offer up to the world.

M is for Malice
Sue Grafton

CHAPTER 1

Robert Dietz came back into my life on Wednesday, January 8. I remember the date because it was Elvis Presley's birthday and one of the local radio stations had announced it would spend the next twenty-four hours playing every song he'd ever sung. At six A.M. my clock radio blared on, playing "Heartbreak Hotel" at top volume. I smacked the off button with the flat of my hand and rolled out of bed as usual. I pulled on my sweats in preparation for my morning run. I brushed my teeth, splashed water on my face, and trotted down the spiral stairs. I locked my front door behind me, moved out to the street where I did an obligatory stretch, leaning against the gatepost in front of my apartment. The day was destined to be a strange one involving as it did a dreaded lunch date with Tasha Howard, one of my recently discovered first cousins. Running was the only way I could think of to quell my uneasiness. I headed for the bike path that parallels the beach.

Ah, January. The holidays had left me feeling restless and the advent of the new year generated one of those lengthy internal discussions about the meaning of life. I usually don't pay much attention to the passing of time, but this year, for some reason, I was taking a good hard look at myself. Who was I, really, in the scheme of things, and what did it all add up to? For the record, I'm Kinsey Millhone, female, single, thirty-five years old, sole proprietor of Kinsey Millhone Investigations in the southern California town of Santa Teresa. I was trained as a police officer and served a two-year stint with the Santa Teresa Police Department before life intervened, which is another tale altogether and one I don't intend to tell (yet). For the last ten years, I've made a living as a private investigator. Some days I see myself (nobly, I'll admit) battling against evil in the struggle for law and order. Other days, I concede that the dark forces are gaining ground.

Not all of this was conscious. Much of the rumination was simmering at a level I could scarcely discern. It's not as if I spent every day in a state of unremitting angst, wringing my hands and rending my clothes. I suppose what I was experiencing was a mild form of depression, triggered (perhaps) by nothing more complicated than the fact it was winter and the California sunlight was in short supply.

I started my career investigating arson and wrongful-death claims for California Fidelity Insurance. A year ago, my relationship with CFI came to an abrupt and ignominious halt and I'm currently sharing space with the law firm of Kingman and Ives, taking on just about anything to make ends meet. I'm licensed, bonded, and fully insured. I have twenty-five thousand dollars in a savings account, which affords me the luxury of turning down any client who doesn't suit. I haven't refused a case yet, but I was strongly considering it.

Tasha Howard, the aforementioned first cousin, had called to offer me work, though the details of the job hadn't yet been specified. Tasha is an attorney who handles wills and estates, working for a law firm with offices in both San Francisco and Lompoc, which is an hour north of Santa Teresa. I gathered she divided her time just about equally between the two. I'm normally interested in employment, but Tasha and I aren't exactly close and I suspected she was using the lure of business to insinuate herself into my life.

As it happened, her first call came on the day after New Year's, which allowed me to sidestep by claiming I was still on vacation. When she called again on January 7, she caught me off guard. I was at the office in the middle of a serious round of solitaire when the telephone rang.

"Hi, Kinsey. This is Tasha. I thought I'd try you again. Did I catch you at a bad time?"

"This is fine," I said. I crossed my eyes and pretended I was gagging myself with a finger pointed down my throat. Of course, she couldn't see that. I put a red eight on a black nine and turned up the last three cards. No play that I could see. "How are you?" I asked, perhaps a millisecond late.

"Doing well, thanks. How about you?"

"I'm good," I said. "Gee, your timing's uncanny. I was just picking up the phone. I've been making calls all morning and you were next on my list." I often use, the word gee when I'm lying through my teeth.

"I'm glad to hear that," she said. "I thought you were avoiding me."

I laughed, ha-ha-ha. "Not at all," said I. I was about to elaborate on the denial, but she plowed right on. Having run out of moves, I pushed the cards aside and began to tag my blotter with a little desktop graffiti. I block-printed the word BARF and gave each of the letters a three-dimensional cast.

She said, "What's your schedule like tomorrow? Can we get together for an hour? I have to be in Santa Teresa anyway and we could meet for lunch."

"I can probably do that,"' I said with caution. In this world, lies can only take you so far before the truth catches up. "What sort of work are we talking about?"

"I'd rather discuss it in person. Is twelve o'clock good for you?"

"That sounds fine," I said.

"Perfect. I'll make reservations. Emile's-at-the-Beach. I'll see you there," she said, and with a click she was gone.

I put the phone down, set the ballpoint pen aside, and laid my little head down on my desk. What an idiot I was. Tasha must have known I didn't want to see her, but I hadn't had the nerve to say so. She'd come to my rescue a couple of months before and though I'd repaid the money, I still felt I owed her. Maybe I'd listen to her politely before I turned her down. I did have another quick job in the works. I'd been hired to serve two deposition subpoenas in a civil case for an attorney on the second floor of our building.

I went out in the afternoon and spent thirty-five bucks (plus tip) on a legitimate salon haircut. I tend to take a pair of nail scissors to my own unruly mop about every six weeks, my technique being to snip off any tuft of hair that sticks out. I guess I must have been feeling insecure because it wouldn't ordinarily occur to me to pay real bucks for something I can do so handily myself. Of course, I've been told my hairstyle looks exactly like a puppy dog's backside, but what's wrong with that?

The morning of January 8 inevitably arrived and I pounded along the bike path as if pursued by wild dogs. Typically, I use my jog as a way to check in with myself, noting the day and the ongoing nature of life at the water's edge. That morning, I had been all business, nearly punitive in the energy I threw into the exercise. Having finished my run and my morning routine, I skipped the office altogether and hung around my place. I paid some bills, tidied up my desk, did a load of laundry, and chatted briefly with my landlord, Henry Pitts, while I ate three of his freshly baked sticky buns. Not that I was nervous.

As usual, when you're waiting for something unpleasant, the clock seems to leap forward in ten-minute increments. Next thing I knew I was standing at my bathroom mirror applying cut-rate cosmetics, for God's sake, while I emoted along with Elvis, who was singing "It's Now Or Never." The sing-along was taking me back to my high school days, not a terrific association, but amusing nonetheless. I hadn't known any more about makeup in those days than I do now.

I debated about a new outfit, but that's where I drew the line, pulling on my usual blue jeans, turtleneck, tweed blazer, and boots. I own one dress and I didn't want to waste it on an occasion like this. I glanced at the clock. It was 11:55. Emile's wasn't far, all of five minutes on foot. With luck, I'd be hit by a truck as I was crossing the street.

Almost all of the tables at Emile's were occupied by the time I arrived. In Santa Teresa, the beach restaurants do the bulk of their business during the summer tourist season when the motels and bed-and-breakfast establishments near the ocean are fully booked. After Labor Day, the crowds diminish until the town belongs to the residents again. But Emile's-at-the-Beach is a local favorite and doesn't seem to suffer the waxing and waning of the out-of-town trade.

Tasha must have driven down from Lompoc because a sassy red Trans Am bearing a vanity license plate that read Tasha was parked at the curb. In the detective trade, this is what is known as a clue. Besides, flying down from Lompoc is more trouble than it's worth. I moved into the restaurant and scanned the tables. I had little appetite for the encounter, but I was trying to stay open to the possibilities. Of what, I couldn't say.

I spotted Tasha through one of the interior archways before she spotted me. She was seated in a small area off the main dining room. Emile had placed her by the front window at a table for two. She was staring out at the children's play equipment in the little beach park across the street. The wading pool was closed, emptied for the winter, a circle of blue-painted plaster that looked now like a landing pad for a UFO. Two preschool-age children were clambering backward up a nearby sliding board anchored in the sand. Their mother sat on the low concrete retaining wall with a cigarette in hand. Beyond her were the bare masts of boats slipped in the harbor. The day was sunny and cool, the blue sky scudding with clouds left behind by a storm that was passing to the south of us.

A waiter approached Tasha and they conferred briefly. She took a menu from him. I could see her indicate that she was waiting for someone else. He withdrew and she began to peruse the lunch choices. I'd never actually laid eyes on Tasha until now, but I'd met her sister Liza the summer before last. I'd been startled because Liza and I looked so much alike. Tasha was cut from the same genetic cloth, though she was three years older and more substantial in her presentation. She wore a gray wool suit with a white silk shell showing in the deep V of the jacket. Her dark hair was streaked with blond, pulled back with a sophisticated black chiffon bow sitting at the nape of her neck. The only jewelry she wore was a pair of oversized gold earrings that glinted when she moved. Since she did estate planning, she probably didn't have much occasion for impassioned courtroom speeches, but she'd look properly intimidating in a skirmish nonetheless. Already I'd decided to get my affairs in order.

She caught sight of me and I saw her expression quicken as she registered the similarities between us. Maybe all the Kinsey girl cousins shared the same features. I raised a hand in greeting and moved through the lunch crowd to her table. I took the seat across from hers, tucking my bag on the floor beneath my chair. "Hello, Tasha."

For a moment, we did a mutual assessment. In high school biology, I'd studied Mendel's purple and white flowering peas; the crossbreeding of colors and the resultant pattern of "offspring." This was the very principle at work. Up close, I could see that her eyes were dark where mine were hazel, and her nose looked like mine had before it was broken twice. Seeing her was like catching a glimpse of myself unexpectedly in a mirror, the image both strange and familiar. Me and not me.

Tasha broke the silence. "This is creepy. Liza told me we looked alike, but I had no idea."

"I guess there's no doubt we're related. What about the other cousins? Do they look like us?"

"Variations on a theme. When Pam and I were growing up, we were often mistaken for each other." Pam was the sister between Tasha and Liza.

"Did Pam have her baby?"

"Months ago. A girl. Big surprise," she said dryly. Her tone was ironic, but I didn't get the joke. She sensed the unspoken question and smiled fleetingly in reply. "All the Kinsey women have girl babies. I thought you knew."

I shook my head.

"Pam named her Cornelia as a way of sucking up to Grand. I'm afraid most of us are guilty of trying to score points with her from time to time."

Cornelia LaGrand was my grandmother Burton Kinsey's maiden name. "Grand" had been her nickname since babyhood. From what I'd been told, she ruled the family like a despot. She was generous with money, but only if you danced to her tune—the reason the family had so pointedly ignored me and my aunt Gin for twenty-nine years. My upbringing had been blue collar, strictly lower middle class. Aunt Gin, who raised me from the age of five, had worked as a clerk/typist for California Fidelity Insurance, the company that eventually hired (and fired) me. She'd managed on a modest salary, and we'd never had much. We'd always lived in mobile homes—trailers, as they were known then—bastions of tiny space, which I still tend to prefer. At the same time, I recognized even then that other people thought trailers were tacky. Why, I can't say.

Aunt Gin had taught me never to suck up to anyone. What she'd neglected to tell me was there were relatives worth sucking up to.

Tasha, likely aware of the thicket her remarks were leading to, shifted over to the task at hand. "Let's get lunch out of the way and then I can fill you in on the situation."

We dealt with the niceties of ordering and eating lunch, chatting about only the most inconsequential subjects. Once our plates had been removed, she got down to business with an efficient change of tone. "We have some clients here in Santa Teresa caught up in a circumstance I thought might interest you. Do you know the Maleks? They own Malek Construction."

"I don't know them personally, but the name's familiar." I'd seen the company logo on job sites around town, a white octagon, like a stop sign, with the outline of a red cement mixer planted in the middle. All of the company trucks and job-site Porta Potties were fire engine red and the effect was eye-catching.

Tasha went on. "It's a sand and gravel company. Mr. Malek just died and our firm is representing the estate." The waiter approached and filled our coffee cups. Tasha picked up a sugar pack, pressing in the edges of the paper rim on all sides before she tore the corner off. "Bader Malek bought a gravel pit in 1943. I'm not sure what he paid at the time, but it's worth a fortune today. Do you know much about gravel?"

"Not a thing," I said.

"I didn't either until this came up. A gravel pit doesn't tend to produce much income from year to year, but it turns out that over the last thirty years environmental regulations and land-use regulations make it very hard to start up a new gravel pit. In this part of California, there simply aren't that many. If you own the gravel pit for your region and construction is booming—which it is at the moment—it goes from being a dog in the forties to a real treasure in the 1980s, depending, of course, on how deep the gravel reserves are and the quality of those reserves. It turns out this one is on a perfect gravel zone, probably good for another hundred and fifty years. Since nobody else is now able to get approvals . . . well, you get the point I'm sure."

"Who'd have thunk?"

"Exactly," she said and then went on. "With gravel, you want to be close to communities where construction is going on because the prime cost is transportation. It's one of those backwater areas of wealth that you don't really know about even if it's yours. Anyway, Bader Malek was a dynamo and managed to maximize his profits by branching out in other directions, all building-related. Malek Construction is now the third-largest construction company in the state. And it's still family owned; one of the few, I might add."

"So what's the problem?"

"I'll get to that in a moment, but I need to back up a bit first. Bader and his wife, Rona, had four boys—like a series of steppingstones, all of them two years apart. Donovan, Guy, Bennet, and Jack. Donovan's currently in his mid-forties and Jack's probably thirty-nine. Donovan's the best of the lot; typical first child, steady, responsible, the big achiever in the bunch. His wife, Christie, and I were college roommates, which is how I got involved in the first place. The second son, Guy, turned out to be the clunker among the boys. The other two are okay. Nothing to write home about, at least from what Christie's said."

"Do they work for the company?"

"No, but Donovan pays all of their bills nonetheless. Bennet fancies himself an 'entrepreneur,' which is to say he loses great whacks of money annually in bad business deals. He's currently venturing into the restaurant business. He and a couple of partners are opening a place down on Granita.

Talk about a way to lose money. The man has to be nuts. Jack's busy playing golf. I gather he's got sufficient talent to hit the pro circuit, but probably
not enough to earn a living at it.

"At any rate, back in the sixties, Guy was the one who smoked dope
and raised hell. He thought his father was a materialistic, capitalistic son of
a bitch and told him so every chance he could. I guess Guy got caught in
some pretty bad scrapes—we're talking criminal behavior—and Bader finally cut him off. According to Donovan, his father gave Guy a lump sum,
ten grand in cash, his portion of the then-modest family fortune. Bader told
the kid to hit the road and not come back. Guy Malek disappeared and he
hasn't been seen since. This was March 1968. He was twenty-six then, which
would make him forty-three now. I guess no one really cared much when
he left. It was probably a relief after what he'd put the family through. Rona
had died two months before, in January that same year, and Bader went to
his attorney with the intention of rewriting his will. You know how that
goes: 'The reason I have made no provision for my son Guy in this will is
not due to any lack of love or affection on my part, but simply because I
have provided for him during my lifetime and feel that those provisions are
more than adequate-blah, blah, blah.' The truth was, Guy had cost him
plenty and he was sick of it.

"So. Fade out, fade in. In 1981, Bader's attorney died of a heart attack
and all of his legal files were returned to him."

I interrupted. "Excuse me. Is that common practice? I'd assume all the
files would be kept by the attorney's estate."

"Depends on the attorney. Maybe Bader insisted. I'm not really sure. I
gather he was a force to be reckoned with. He was already ill by then with
the cancer that finally claimed him. He'd also suffered a debilitating stroke
brought on by all the chemo. Sick as he was, he probably didn't want to go
through the hassle of finding a new attorney. Apparently, from his perspective, his affairs were in order and what he did with his money was nobody
else's business."

I said, "Oh, boy." I didn't know what was coming, but it didn't sound
good.

"'Oh, boy' is right. When Bader died two weeks ago, Donovan went
through his papers. The only will he found was the one Bader and Rona
signed back in 1965."

"What happened to the later will?"

"Nobody knows. Maybe the attorney drew it up and Bader took it
home for review. He might have changed his mind. Or maybe he signed the
will as written and decided to destroy it later. The fact is, it's gone."

" So he died intestate?"

"No, no. We still have the earlier will—the one drawn up in 1965, before Guy was flung into the Outer Darkness. It's properly signed and fully

executed, which means that, barring an objection, Guy Malek is a devisee, entitled to a quarter of his father's estate."

"Will Donovan object?"

"He's not the one I'm concerned about. The 1965 will gives him voting control of the family business so he winds up sitting in the catbird seat regardless. Bennet's the one making noises about filing an objection, but he really has no proof the later will exists. This could all be for naught in any case. If Guy Malek was hit by a truck or died of an overdose years ago, then there's no problem—as long as he doesn't have any kids of his own."

"Gets complicated," I said. "How much money are we talking about?"

"We're still working on that. The estate is currently assessed at about forty million bucks. The government's entitled to a big chunk, of course. The estate tax rate is fifty to fifty-five percent. Fortunately, thanks to Bader, the company has very little debt, so Donovan will have some ability to borrow. Also, the estate can defer payment of estate taxes under Internal Revenue Service code section 6166, since Malek Construction, as a closely held company, represents more than thirty-five percent of the adjusted gross estate. We'll probably look for appraisers who'll come up with a low value and then hope the IRS doesn't argue too hard for a higher value on audit. To answer your question, the boys will probably take home five million bucks apiece. Guy's a very lucky fellow."

"Only nobody knows where he is," I said.

Tasha pointed at me. "That's correct."

I thought about it briefly. "It must have come as a shock to the brothers to find out Guy stands to inherit an equal share of the estate."

Tasha shrugged. "I've only had occasion to chat with Donovan and he seems sanguine at this point. He'll be acting as administrator. On Friday, I'm submitting the will to the probate court. In essence, all that does is place the will on record. Donovan's asked me not to file the petition for another week or so in deference to Bennet, who's still convinced the latter will surface. In the meantime, it makes sense to see if we can determine Guy Malek's whereabouts. I thought we'd hire you to do the search, if you're interested."

"Sure," I said promptly. So much for playing hard to get. The truth is, I love missing-persons' cases, and the circumstances were intriguing. Often when I'm on the trail of a skip, I hold out the prospect of sudden riches from some recently deceased relative. Given the greediness of human nature, it often produces results. In this case, the reality of five million dollars should make my job easier. "What information do you have about Guy?" I asked.

"You'll have to talk to the Maleks. They'll fill you in." She scribbled something on the back of a business card, which she held out to me. "This is Donovan's number at work. I wrote the home address and home phone number on the back. Except for Guy, of course, the 'boys' are all still living together on the Malek estate."

I studied the back of the card, not recognizing the address. "Is this city or county? I never heard of this."

"It's in the city limits. In the foothills above town."

"I'll call them this afternoon."

SUE GRAFTON'S WORKING JOURNAL
FOR M IS FOR MALICE

4-29-95

Starting all over again because I think I was on the wrong track. Today is Jay's birthday and I'm going to call him in a bit and wish him a Happy Happy Birfday to He!

Bringing data over from the other journal . . .

BOOK:	VICTIM	MOTIVE	KILLER	FINALE
'A'	one male, two female	to prevent exposure and revenge	male & female	K. kills killer
'B'	female	money	female & male	K. in fisticuffs
'C'	male	extortion	male	K. subdues killer
'D'	male	revenge	male	killer commits suicide
'E'	male, female, & female	to prevent exposure and jealousy	male	killer blows himself up accidentally
'F'	female	jealousy	female	killer subdued by her own father
'G'	male, male	revenge	male	killer shot by ex-wife
	female	old murder for money	male	killer killed by killer
'H'	male	to prevent exposure	male	K. subdues killer
'I'	female	money	male	K. kills killer
'J'	male	money	female	killer commits pseudocide, gets away with murder
'K'	female male male female	money	male	K. makes a phone call to the Mafia who dispose of the guy themselves

BOOK:	VICTIM	MOTIVE	KILLER	FINALE
'L'	male	money	male	One guy kills another & K. gets knocked out

LOG LINES

In 'A' ... Kinsey's hired to prove the innocence of a woman just out of prison after serving seven years for the murder of her husband.

In 'B' ... Kinsey's hired to find a woman whose signature is required on a minor document.

In 'C' ... Kinsey's hired by a kid to find out who's been trying to murder him.

In 'D' ... Kinsey's hired to deliver a twenty-five thousand dollar cashier's check to a fifteen year old boy.

In 'E' ... Kinsey's hired to do an arson investigation at a manufacturing plant and she's framed in the process.

In 'F' ... Kinsey's hired to prove an escaped inmate is innocent of the murder he's been convicted of 17 years earlier.

In 'G' ... Kinsey, at the top of Tyrone Patty's hit list, is hired to drive down to the Mojave desert to find a woman's missing mother.

In 'H' ... Kinsey's hired to go undercover, investigating a case of automobile insurance fraud after a colleague at CF gets murdered in the parking lot.

In 'I' ... Kinsey's hired to finish an investigation in an upcoming 'civil' murder trial after the P.I. on the case drops dead of a heart attack.

In 'J' ... Kinsey's hired by California Fidelity to locate a 'dead' man whose 'widow' has just collected half a million dollars in insurance benefits.

In 'K' ... Kinsey's descent into the underworld is triggered when she's hired by a murder victim's mother to find her daughter's killer after the police have been unable to resolve the case in the ten months since the girl's death.

In 'L' ... Kinsey's hired to help recover stolen money and ends up crossing the country in pursuit of it.

All I know about 'M' at this point is that Robert Dietz comes back. What he wants and how he gets there I do not know yet.

Last night in the dead of night Shadow suggested the following:

Robert Dietz calls or shows up just as Kinsey's on her way to an interview/appointment at a very classy address.

Talks to a glamourous woman who says she's met a man, etc. She's been taken advantage of in the past and she's vowed not to be taken again. She'd like Kinsey to do a deep background check.

"How deep?"

During the course of this interview, the woman says she's just on her way to the Bahamas . . . or some place posh. She'll be back on the . . . th but she'll check with Kinsey by phone, etc.

Receives a phone call . . . missing earring . . .

Must talk to Westec about what kind of records are kept by security companies. For instance, is a record kept every time someone punches the code in or out even if there's no alarm going off? In this case, someone at the alarm company has been paid off . . . or tricked . . . must think on this depending on what the guy at Westec says . . .

Also must find out from the phone company if they have logs of calling numers for every incoming call received. That might be a nice lead later.

Also the missing earring.

Kinsey gets home. Interacts w/Dietz who is recovering from knee surgery. She hopes he doesn't think she's going to play nurse maid. Not at all. He thought of coming here because he knew she wouldn't fuss. She's going to be busy anyway. She tells him about the case. He says she should connect up with a bigger company this round & take advantage of computer technology. He's burned out, doesn't want to do another piece of investigation if his life depended on it. That suits Kinsey because she's halfway ticked off at him anyway for his long absence.

Kinsey contacts a Ventura firm. Drives down. The guys do a computer check & come up blank.

She goes about it the old-fashioned way, thinking they're not so hot.

She turns up a lead . . . figures out where the guy is in due course. Reports back to her employer who pays her handsomely.

She's feeling smug until the guy turns up dead.

She backtracks.

Realizes she's been set-up.

Dietz pitches in because she's got her tit in a wringer.

The two of them begin to investigate the missing woman.

Must, of necessity, figure out what the back story is. This is just structure.

FIRST THIRD OF THE BOOK IS KINSEY'S INVESTIGATION.

SECOND THIRD IS HER INVESTIGATION OF THE SCAM ARTISTS.

THIRD IS HER TURNING THE TABLES ON THEM.

(7-4-95) Actually I just realized in re-reading this that it's the plot line for a short story I wrote called 'NON-SUNG SMOKE.' I guess my psyche thought she could recycle that one.

5-8-95

Still trying to hit a vein here. Over derby week-end, Laura Swain suggested 'M' IS FOR MISSING which is kind of nice I think. At least it suggests some story beats. I'm not sure I want to start with a 'who' missing, but I might like a 'what.' I'm still attracted to the idea of Kinsey's being hired by an elegant woman in an elegant house. The woman says she's met a man, etc. She's been taken advantage of in the past and she's vowed not to be taken again. She'd like Kinsey to do a deep background check. Kinsey finds the guy who turns up dead shortly thereafter. When she returns to the house, she realizes she's been had.

Why do 'they want this guy?
>He's cheated them out of money.
>He knows or has discovered something that would prove disastrous to them.
>He blew the whistle on them & they want revenge.
>He made a deal with them & then reneged on his end.

How did they track him to Santa Teresa?
>Rumor: Someone saw him in the area.
>Speculation: He has relatives in the area.
>>He used to live in ST.
>Evidence: Phone records indicate several calls to the area.

Why don't they just find him & kill him themselves?
>They don't want to be associated with the man's death.

Why do they need Kinsey?
>They've tried two other agencies.

And why her & not someone else?
>They've tried others & she's next on the list.

How come Kinsey finds him when nobody else can do it?
>Intuition . . . common sense . . . old-fashioned leg-work. She tries the new-fangled methods w/computers, etc. but comes up with nothing, like everybody else.

What does she have to go on?
>Name.
>Photograph.
>Approximate age, height, weight, & build.

This guy has money because he stole it from them.
He needs a new identity . . .
>Why would he take the chance of going to an area where he's been before or has relatives?

This looks like a woman who wants Kinsey to do a background check on a guy who's proposed.
>Wouldn't the woman have to give her quite a bit of information? Like an address, etc.
>Maybe the woman claims this guy took advantage. They were engaged. He borrowed money & then skipped.
>Why would she have to be in a big fancy house? To lend credence to her story.

Maybe she claims she has two homes or three.

Maybe she just has a hunch he's in the area.

Maybe she met him here when she was in town househunting.

How could this tie in with a Medicare scam?

Who is this woman?

How does she really connect?

Is she the wife of the hospital administrator?

Would somebody actually kill for this?

Is she the bookkeeper?

Is she the cashier?

Has she managed to 'cook' the books & blame it on someone else?

Did this guy figure it out & skim off the money before she could get to it?

Is she a doctor's office manager?

Is he the accountant?

Is she operating out of the doctor's house?

No, because then she'd be too easy to identify.

Why wouldn't Kinsey spot her if she went to the doctor's office?

Maybe she works in the accountant's office.

Kinsey goes in. There's a new 'girl' at the desk.

It doesn't occur to Kinsey at first that this 'girl' is replacing the woman who absconded w/the money.

When the guy shows up dead, Kinsey would start to back-track. It would soon be obvious that she's been completely misled.

She goes to Westec or their equivalent.

They check their records. No one by that name living in the house. Computer check shows someone was in the house that night. Would they give Kinsey a copy of the list of authorized persons? Probably not. Unless she knows the guy & talks him into it.

Kinsey goes down the list. No one knows anything.

The couple was out of town for two months.

Cops doing a homicide investigation . . .

Or may be it looks like an accident.

Maybe Kinsey talks Dolan into checking out the house.

They dust the phone for prints, but it's been wiped clean.

She spots the earring in the drawer or on the rug nearby.

Hand-made?

She tracks the jeweler . . .

Suppose Kinsey catches up w/the woman.

Woman admits to lying. Saw the notice in the paper & she panicked . . .

Who else could look guilty & how would Kinsey ever twig to the fact that there's a fiddle going on?

I'd love to find a way to work in this business about the court reporter . . .

How is the guy killed?

   Mugging? Watch & wallet stolen . . . along w/his office keys?

By the time Kinsey checks his office, the relevant files are gone.

   She gets the passbook to the savings account he's opened to hide the
   money. Or does he pull it out of the account little by little & keeps it on
   the premises.

      There's been an audit . . .

      Or there's an audit coming up.

         The guy's death delays everything just long enough for this
         woman to skip town.

5-9-95

I've ordered some books on Medicare scams and Leslie's going to give me
the telephone number of a hospital consultant who knows the system. I
need to talk to Lori about how claims originate, what the process is, and
where it's vulnerable. In the back of my mind, I'm not sure I'm barking up
the right tree, but I don't know what else to do at this point. The subject
may be like forgery, in that I explore it and then can't find a way to make
the story work.

Hmmm. I'm realizing some of the above is the frame-work for a short story
I wrote called "NON-SUNG SMOKE" in which a woman hires Kinsey to
track down some guy she's met. Kinsey does so and then the guy turns up
dead.

All right . . . skip that.

Found a quote from Henry Kissinger that I thought deserved entry here in
my journal. "Each success only buys an admission ticket to a more difficult
problem."

Last Names

Ahearn	Chase	Fannin	Kagan	Shackelford . . .
Adkins	Cheslet	Finn	Littenberg	'Shack'
Alpert	Christie	Ginger	Loftin	Toth
Backman	Copley	Hagen	Lukehart	Worn
Bacon	Dillard	Hayhurst	Ostrom	Wray
Bader	Dixon	Hobb	Peoples	Wylie
Balentine	Donnelly	Kahn	Rink	Sedgewick
			Ringwald	Woody

Men's First Names

Dennis	Thomas	Wesley	Wayne	Trinidad
Joseph	Alan	Rex	Pick	Clancy
Roy	Jerrold	Foster	Toby	Guy

Women's First Names

Jackie	Vicki	Peggy	Lynette	Elsie ...
Fay	Amber	Connie	March	someone young
Stephanie	Ariel	Judith		Dodie
				French

You can spend a lifetime wondering what would have happened if a rock hadn't rolled down a hill. I thought about all the lives that had been changed by that one event ... my own primarily.

5-9-95

Still trying to see if I can make this work ...

STORY POSSIBILITY #1:

A woman in her late sixties has worked for thirty years for the same law firm ... a two-man operation. One old partner dies & the other retires.
She's overworked, underpaid, has access to client information & client files. Wanted to be a lawyer, but never had the money to go to law school. An unfortunate family background prevented her from realizing her ambition. Bitterly angry and determined to get her own.
Has data and equipment she's stolen from the law firm ... typewriter she took when the computer system was installed.

Retires and then finds she can't live on her income.
Goes to work as a companion for someone represented by her former law firm ... the dead partner's client.

It occurred to me in the dead of night that I don't have to screw around with a forged will at all. I can either have the will still mention the errant son & his issue OR I can have a new will in which the father says he's eliminating this son because of his death and lack of issue, or something to that effect. From what I've read, the law would reinstate the inheritance of the son's son.

Then I realized that as long as probate takes, the companion would be long gone. BUT I then realized that if this is a mansion & there's megabucks at stake, she might find a way to stay on at the house as the housekeeper. One of the sons or daughters could move in.

I was worried about the issue of the missing grandchild. If this person presents himself with his hand out, the reader will know he's a fake. But if the family attorney hires Kinsey to go looking for him, there won't be the same suspicion aroused about his true identity.

But if the bum lives in town, wouldn't everyone know about him?
Someone from San Francisco might contact lawyer who contacts Kinsey.
In 1932, the guy was said to be traveling to ST, never heard from again.
She actually tracks him down, but he's been dead for . . . years.
His portion goes to several nieces & nephews.
Aunt Beatty dies . . . brothers being dead, etc.
Her only brother O.G. hasn't been heard from for years.
Passel of nieces & nephews.
Kinsey's hired to find out if the old guy is alive.

He's a transient . . . found dead some months before in ST.
No one's been able to identify him.
Known by his nickname, but no i.d. & no prints on file.
Prints being run through FBI.
Shortly after Kinsey 'finds' him, the prints are confirmed.
She thinks he was murdered.
Where are the nieces & nephews?

Seems like the family unit should consist of two sisters. The one w/money has one son who's a black sheep and has disappeared from view. The other has five kids who are set to inherit if the black sheep turns up dead. The old woman dies and Kinsey's hired to search about for word of the black sheep.
She hunts him down . . . a bum & homeless, living in his car.
He's killed . . . or turns up dead.
Turns out he has a wife & child living at a shelter.
The child then is set to inherit many million bucks.

I like the Cinderella aspect of the story. The down & out turn out to be millionaires.
The first revelation could come when Kinsey actually tracks this guy down.
The second revelation is his death either shortly before she arrives or afterwards. He either dies of acute alcohol poisoning . . . which would look 'natural' . . . or he's killed in the say way some other bums.
The third revelation is the existence of the wife & kid.
I think Kinsey has to save this kid and cross the ice, metaphorically speaking.

She probably hears about the case through an attorney.
I'm thinking Tasha would be perfect, just to tie off a loose end.
Maybe she has to track the guy from Lompoc to . . . to . . . to ST.
Or ST . . . to Perdido . . . and back again.
I'd just as soon talk about the homeless somewhere else. I hate to set off the locals.

I also want Kinsey to get to know this family so I don't want her straying too far from home base.

If they're local, her search could take her somewhere else.

Las Vegas?

Where haven't I gone that might be interesting.

Bakersfield? Venice? Sacramento?

Maybe the deceased has a brother and a sister . . . each of whom have one or two or three kids.

Nice cast of suspects.

Actually, it's the sister who does the deed.

One suggestion is the use of old high school annuals to find former class-mates who might still live in the area.

Also mentioned was the use of a Criss Cross to find an old address when all you have is an old telephone number.

> Suppose Kinsey finds a school book with the name & number written in pencil . . .

BJ mentioned that if you check the computer terminal at the voter registra-tion office, one of the 'prompts' as you exit is 'cancelled' registrations which will pop up on the screen.

What is the point of a story in which Kinsey searches out a missing heir?

> Someone nicks in ahead of her & kills the guy, then tries to kill his kid . . .

>> The suspects in this instance would be narrowed down to the re-maining heirs . . . wouldn't they?

>> Might be enough of 'em to be interesting . . .

> Someone kills the guy for some other reason, alerted to his where-abouts by Kinsey's investigation.

>> Kinsey would have to figure out that money wasn't the motive.

STORY POSSIBILITY #2:

Did the missing guy steal/forge something years ago & that was the dis-grace that got him barred from the family.

> Someone knows he stole these valuable papers.

> If he isn't found, then how can the papers be recovered.

>> What if he stole something thought to be valuable that in fact was forged . . .

>> The guilty party's been waiting all these years for the other shoe to drop . . .

>>> so . . . either Kinsey has to be prevented from finding this guy & hearing what he has to say . . .

>>> or . . . the guy has to be found & silenced.

If the guy stole something he thought was valuable, that in fact, was a forgery ... wouldn't he have already tried to hawk it and thus discovered its lack of value?

Forgery substituted for the genuine ...

  or the other way around?

I don't want to get into art forgeries ...

What about documents or signatures ...

The dead father has pulled off a scam in his past ... examines a document for which a curator has paid megabucks. He substitutes a forged copy and keeps the original. He retains this document among some papers in his possession. The curator meanwhile suffers disgrace. When the expert dies, the document goes to his wife & on her death, it's left to the errant son ...

  Why? Because this son ... who's disgraced himself ... will know the difference. He'll realize it's genuine & take the proper steps ...

    which are?

      sell it for his personal fortune.

      return it to the museum.

      burn it ... thus covering his father's crime.

      turn it over to the experts.

The father can't bear to do this during his lifetime because he can't bear the disgrace. The wife doesn't know the difference, but the errant son would.

  Who would benefit from interfering with this discovery?

    Wouldn't the museum/document's owner have the forgery verified by another expert?

    Has someone else colluded w/the old man?

    Is it the errant son who later disgraces himself & takes off?

From my book on questioned documents, it's clear that quite sophisticated forgeries have been detected for a number of years ... since 1911 given one case cited. So it's not just a matter of high tech equipment. In other words, a forgery is probably going to be detected, that is, if a document is forged and the suspicion comes to light, the forgery will also come to light in fairly short order.

So.

What if this were an instance in which a proclaimed forgery turned out to be genuine ...

Documents switched ...

  don't see how anyone could pull this off.

  "Expert" testifies that a genuine document is forced.

  In truth, it's not.

  But if there were any question, the document would be submitted to a host of experts.

Wait . . . museum calls in an expert to examine a document which he greatly lusts after. He switches it for a fake and then proceeds to document the fakeness of the fakery. Other experts concur. The museum curator who has staked his reputation & large portions of the museum's money on the purchase is forced to resign in disgrace. Is the curator later murdered because he's figured it out? His death looks like suicide, but it's really not. Many years pass & the thief dies, willing his papers to his wife. On her death, everything passes to his several children . . . one of whom has been thought dead.

In truth, he's alive & homeless, living in. . . . He's a hopeless alcoholic who mistreats his wife & son. Kinsey locates him, but he's dead or soon murdered.

Or Kinsey locates him & he cleans himself up . . . comes home for the funeral. He doesn't inherit money, but he does inherit his father's document collection . . . in which is the priceless genuine.

Why would dad leave this to the son?
Has the son disgraced himself after daddy's death. Was this guy his favorite? Was this kid w/him when he switched the papers? The old man can't own up to his skullduggery, but he knows this guy will know the difference. He's been a respectable fellow until the demon rum gets the better of him and now he's on a downward spiral to the grave.

What if . . .
The genuine/forged document issue was related to typewritten matter.
And . . .
What the old man leaves the black sheep is the typewriter in question that could prove the point. Looks like a footlocker full of junk. The old man claims the typewriter is one he used in college . . . but he knows the errant son will remember the critical occasion . . .

Does the typewriter belong to a famous novelist?
Has the expert discredited a posthumous manuscript?

He has the machine . . . he retypes the questioned document & forges the signature. Declares the document a fake.
typewriter is genuine.
he proves the material was typed by someone different.

Other experts concur.

The curator kills himself.

The old man dies w/the genuine machine & the real document among his effects.
How has the old man come across this machine?
Maybe it's like Ralph Sipper's relationship with Ross McDonald . . .
the writer dies & his widow disposes of his belongings . . .

How could the old man profit from such a scam?

It 'makes' his reputation.

It establishes the 'gullibility' of a man he hates, causing his disgrace & death.

It throws into question the skills and abilities of his rival . . . a man who bested him on some other occasion.

But would I talk about a real writer or his/her fictional counterpart?

Can't use real w/o permission . . .

Scholar?

Some fellow who's based his career on a matter later proved to be 'false.'

Why would the old guy do it?

What if . . . the middle page of a three page document has been done on a different machine?

Or what if . . . it's the same machine, but a different typist?

That way the signature on the document could be genuine.

The experts determine that a different typist, same machine, produced page two, but there's no way to identify who actually did the work. Maybe what Kinsey finds is a sample from the same machine, same second typist, that would fully identify the 'forger.'

Were huge sums of money paid at the time the document was authenticated?

I have to make sure the significance registers when it turns out the alleged fake is actually genuine.

Maybe it's a letter that disclaims or verifies authorship of something . . .

Again, it has to be apparent on the surface because I don't want characters to have to sit around explaining the import.

Shadow pointed out last night that if the document were a will, where the middle page had been replaced, there would still be the original copies on file in the attorney's office.

There's nothing wrong with the idea of Kinsey being hired to determine if the family black sheep, last heard of ten years ago, now believed dead, ever had any offspring. Maybe Kinsey gets the case from a PI in another geographic area. He's been contacted by the family attorney who says the guy was last heard of in Santa Teresa. Can she get a line on him? No contact.

She locates him . . . he has an ex-wife & kid. Calls in a report.

Next thing you know the guy's dead. Police tell her the ex-wife & kid have both disappeared. Kinsey's pissed. She thinks she's been had.

Who hires her next?

The family matriarch?

She's the only one who's actually seen and talked to the wife & kid. Kid will inherit money. Can she locate him?

Not if he's going to end up the same way his father did.

STORY POSSIBILITY #3:

I still like the idea of a partnership agreement, three to five pages in length where the signatures appear on the last page of the document. "Someone" carefully extracts the middle page/s on all the copies of the document and substitutes an amended page or pages which, in effect, changes the impact or the substance of the agreement. Once the business fails, the 'victim' has no recourse. He swears he'd never sign an agreement containing such a clause, but he's made some poor judgments in the past and everyone just assumes he didn't read it carefully enough.

> His life is ruined . . . he loses all his money. Plus this is the last in a long string if failures. He can't face his family so he kills himself.
> Daughter has to drop out of law school & go to work.
> Big house sold.
> Wife's health fails.

Daughter blames . . .

> his two partners

She's determined to wreck their lives as she felt hers was wrecked.

She forges death certificate which she leaves among her parents' effects. When her mother dies, she inherits nothing anyway. (Question: Where does she tuck the phony death certificate? How does she assure that Kinsey Millhone will find it? Must find a way for the trail to lead back.)

Wonder if she comes across an electric typewriter ball in what looks like a ring box.

> Why would anybody keep such a thing?

The typewriter itself would be long gone.

I still need to decide where the journey takes her. If the case originates in Santa Teresa . . . where was the missing heir last seen or heard from? Where does she go? I don't want the case to originate from out of state because then she'd do the skip trace & that would be the end of it. Also, if the case originated here & the guy was last heard from in Arizona or Nevada or some place else, why wouldn't she just call an investigator in that area & save the client some dough? The client could insist I guess . . . but I'm wondering why. I want the home base to be here. I guess she could call an investigator in another state & the client could be unhappy when the guy turns nothing up. I was thinking in the dead of night that her tracing of him is a geographical record of his decline & fall. Does he end up right back in Santa Teresa?

5-10-95

Let's think what I like here . . .
And what I don't like . . .
Don't like the will.
Do like the housekeeper taking revenge.
    Revenge for what?
        For the disgrace brought down on her father by the theft of a rare
        document years before.
            Why wouldn't she simply work to see her father's name
            cleared? Because he killed himself (or was ruined by the
            disgrace) and because she lost her chance to make some-
            thing of her life. Mother turned to drink & died. She feels
            victimized & therefore feels justified in her persecution of
            the family.
        Does she kill someone?
            Maybe the black sheep who participated in the crime . . . or
            was present . . .
How does she come up with her own obit? When has she done this?
Was it years before? Kinsey could come across the clipping among the
old man's effects.
How long has this woman been planning this crime?
        It isn't about the will . . . it's about finding the black sheep . . .
        Did he do the deed? Is he the focus of her rage?
        If he's got this valuable document, why not sell it for hard cash?
        Because he obtained it illegally and it's been his ruination. But
        where is it now? Among his father's effects? Why there? Why not
        buried in a safe deposit box.

His father was training him. He knew his father coveted this document. He
made the switch & his father documented the fraud, thus ruining his rival.
The father, however, would never have countenanced such a move so in the
end, the kid has nothing. The father's conscience troubles him. Perhaps he's
secretly blamed for the misfortunes that befall the curator's family. If the father finds out what his son has actually done, he'll expose the kid. Kid can't
even present his beloved dad with the prize. He acts without understanding
the true consequence and then he can't undo it. He's desperate for his dad's
approval and all he nets is disdain. He's a hot-shot in his twenties . . . all
flash and no substance. His father's been training him, but he has no apti-
tude.

Meantime, the rival's life has been ruined & his daughter wants a pay-back.
        Does the dying father know? Is he troubled & guilty? Does he feel re-
        sponsible? Does he suspect his kid? Does the document come to light
        among the old man's effects?

Where is the thing? Has the son concealed it in a picture frame . . . sandwiched between a photograph & the matting . . .

Does he come back to steal it once his father dies? Has he kept in touch? Does Kinsey track him down?

I like the idea of the obit because it deflects suspicion. The woman could probably acquire a copy of a death certificate. She'd have a way to fake the notary seal. She either has one herself or the paralegal in the office has one.

She takes a 'married' name & uses her middle name as her first.

I'm liking this crime & I'm liking the kid's motive. I'm liking the McGuffin.

Does the companion fake out the will so that someone will track him down? She knows if she includes the clause about the deceased & it turns out to be untrue, that the kid will inherit . . . which means the attorney would make an effort to track the kid down. Why can't she do that? Because she has no skills. She wants someone to do it for her. That way she can get to him without a trace back to her.

She has access to the new will & access to the one before. All she has to do once she goes to work for the sick man is to substitute one for the other . . . the fake for the genuine. When the fakery comes to light, the previous will is enforced.

5-11-95

Still playing with this one. What I'm liking is that this appears to be about an inheritance when it's really about revenge. The companion is using her knowledge of the legal system to institute a search for the kid she wants to kill. On the surface, it will look like this guy is murdered to prevent his inheriting of money.

The story line seems cleaner than the version in which the companion is trying to pass someone off as the real grandchild when, in fact, there's no relation.

Other family members are bound to resent the guy. He's always been trouble. He's never lifted a finger. Now it would appear, he's going to inherit equally with the others.

Is this the guy's only son?

Are the other beneficiaries, the nieces & nephews?

Does this guy have a kid?

Is he down & out, living in his car, but he has a wife & daughter living in a shelter somewhere.

That would be an irony. The guy commits a crime that results in the ruin of an entire family. When he finally pays for his sins, his own destitute family is lifted out of the miry pit.

Those due to collect money should probably be unpleasant . . . but maybe not. Maybe outrage is sufficient. They could be brothers and sisters. Nephews & nieces probably wouldn't have that great a stake in this business. This reflects some of the sentiment in 'F' IS FOR FUGITIVE in which the 'good' daughter bitterly resents the esteem in which her no-good brother is held. Except, of course, that this isn't the motive for the murder.

Would the wife look guilty, too? I'm reluctant to play with the idea of battering. Maybe the guy is down and out . . . a real loser. Maybe he gambles and everytime they get a little bit ahead, he throws it all away. He knows where the document is hidden. Does he think there's some way to retrieve it and sell it?

That would seem odd . . . if some old black and white photograph were stolen.

Must think about the document . . .

Kinsey would consult other experts, but she wouldn't understand the connection. She'd suspect there was a link, but how could she put her finger on it? As far as she can tell, the curator and his family are all gone.

What does she think about the obit she finds?

Maybe the companion plants the articles about the scandal among the old guy's effects. But why would she do that? Why call attention to the situation? The obit would be nice.

"Who's this?"

"Oh . . . that's another story," she said.

"You want to tell me about it?"

How would the story lay out?

First third is Tasha's hiring her and Kinsey's search . . .

Second is the murder and the realization that something doesn't fit.

Kinsey would believe that she'd been used to get this guy taken out.

Maybe everybody ends up with an air-tight alibi.

Backend of the book is her search for the 'dead' killer and her realization of who it is.

Would the companion want to kill the kid?

Is the black sheep the only male and she wants to wipe out the line?

I'll need my books on probate & wills.

The murder would occur at the end of Chapter 7.

By the end of Chapter 14, she'd find herself at a dead-end and she'd have to start at the beginning.

Meanwhile, a little Lompoc . . . a professional truce with Tasha . . . Dietz' arrival and the progress of their renewed relationship.

The companion would be on the scene throughout. Kinsey would go to the house to see the daughter.

She'd search the old man's effects.

She'd talk to his other kids.

Companion would be unobtrusively cleaning, serving tea, seeing to the running of the house. She might have listening devices planted all over the house. She'd know everything.

Kinsey might even chat with her about the comings & goings of the various siblings.

"I feel like I've been used. If I hadn't done my job so well, this guy would be fine. Who set this in motion?"

"Nobody. This is just the way the system works. Any will entered into probate would be handled the same way."

"What about this business you mentioned about a previous will, etc."

"Well, I guess that was somewhat unusual . . . "

"Why would anyone imagine the guy was dead in the first place?"

"I don't know. Maybe it was wishful thinking. Nobody'd heard from him for ten years. Last anybody knew, he was on a downward spiral, etc."

I like the fact that Kinsey's never been hired to find an heir.

I like it that the case can come through Tasha and that they begin to mend their fences.

I like it that Kinsey ends up feeling she's been used to set up a murder.

I like it that Dietz, who resists, is drawn into the case by her distress.

Must think about the ending. I really don't want Dietz saving her.

Maybe she could save him. that would be a nice turn of events.

7-1-95

It's Saturday, July 1 and I'm settling into work on 'M' . . . thinking about names for the prime family. Also need to decide on the breakdown of ages & sex . . . and the time table. How old are these people?

This is 1985 . . .

Must name the prodigal son first . . .

Christie Malek

Bader Malek

Dillard Malek . . . Dill Malek

Dixon

Guy Malek

My brother, Guy . . .

For the time being, we'll call the prodigal son, Guy Malek . . .

He must have been in his twenties when he left . . . 1968

He was into one scrape after another . . . drugs, hippiedom . . .

Charming, charismatic, crooked . . . a chronic liar and thief.

In 'E' . . . the family consisted of Hazel and Woody Wood . . .

Ebony

Olive

Ash

Bass

and another brother? Whose name I forget.
Shit . . . he worked at the company and Kinsey went to see him. Lance.
So there were five kids . . . three girls & two boys.

Let's make this look different . . .
Three sons & a daughter?
Christie is the daughter
Guy is the prodigal son
Dillard and Bader . . .
Is Guy really the PS?
Where does Guy fit into the constellation.
Don't want him to be the youngest because I did that in 'E'
Maybe he's the oldest . . . rebellious . . .
Father was very tough on him & he turned like a chow dog, doing just the opposite.
Guy Malek sounds like the head of the family . . .
Have I used the name Guy before?
Greg?
Maybe I should get that book on birth order . . .
What's the dysfunction in this family?
Did the mother die young & dad raised the kids all by himself?
Ham fisted, authoritarian . . .
Dillard is the only name I question at this point.
If Guy was 26 in 1968, he'd have been born in 1942 . . . which would make him 43 in 1985 . . .
Is he the oldest? Is that name right?
Don't like Dillard. How about Don.
Maybe the oldest son was named after his father . . . Donnelly

Must think, too, about the back story.
Guy Malek . . . the dishonest one . . . has a summer job in 1968 which his father gets for him. He's working as a gopher/courier for a manuscript library . . .
The manuscript library is asked to appraise a manuscript collection, discovered in a trunk passed down to the family by an eccentric aunt. The family consists of mom, dad, & 2 daughters. This is 1968 and the younger daughter is 18 . . . a top level student with her heart set on a good college.

> Dad has provided little or nothing for his family, but he has letters & papers which he believes to be very valuable. He has the manuscript library appraise the collection. Valued at $52,000. Not a fortune by any stretch, but sufficient to send his younger daughter through college and the older one through med school. He dies, leaving everything to Mom. She's one of those wives who never learned to drive, never learned to balance a checkbook, etc. Guy (or Jack) shows up at the door & says there's reason to believe the documents are fraudulent.

He needs to borrow them & send them off for scientific analysis . . .
paper & ink . . . promises to return them unharmed. Instead he makes
copies, a series of clever forgeries, which he returns, keeping the genuine documents, which he sells on the open market. Mom still believes
she has a priceless collection, but when she offers them for sale, the
dealers recognize them as forgeries & decline to buy. The fraud comes
to light & Mom and her two daughters are left with nothing.

      Wouldn't Mom renounce the son on sight? Maybe so, but before
charges can be filed he's skipped . . . aided by his father who
doesn't believe he's done it . . .

POINTS TO CONSIDER ABOUT CHAPTER 1
OF *M IS FOR MALICE*

1. Look over Grafton's working journal for *M is for Malice* and discuss the
   ways in which she uses the journal to create characters, to generate a
   gripping and believable plot, to research specific subjects with which
   she is unfamiliar, to come up with names for her story people. In what
   ways does Grafton's journal resemble the mystery novel itself, as Grafton
   describes it in the interview?

2. In the interview with Sue Grafton, she says that each of her books begins
   with a "prologue" which gives the reader necessary background material
   regarding Kinsey Millhone, her job, circumstances, surroundings.
   Grafton says of this prologue material, which she places at the beginning
   of every novel in her "alphabet series" of mysteries, "You don't want to
   bore the reader who's been with you from the beginning . . . and you
   don't want to come up with the same paragraph, because people will
   jump right over it." After reading the portion of the second paragraph
   that begins with the phrase, "For the record . . . ," what do you feel about
   the prologue material: If you have read any of Grafton's earlier novels, is
   this material repetitive to the point of being intrusive; if you've never
   read any of Grafton's novels, does this prologue section give you adequate historical material? Does her prologue weaken or strengthen the
   opening, in your opinion; why?

3. Grafton says in the interview, "Sometimes I think Kinsey's humor is a
   function of the fact the she thinks and says things the rest of us repress.
   It's funny to hear somebody actually say it." Point out examples in the
   first chapter of *M is for Malice* where Grafton has her protagonist say humorous things—both in narrative and in dialogue. What functions do
   these humorous statements serve in the novel, in terms of setting tone,
   establishing character, and perhaps even suggesting thematic meaning?

4. What role does dialogue—in this case, between Kinsey and Tasha—play in the exposition stage of this novel's development? How does Grafton use dialogue as a tool for developing narrative tension between her characters?

5. Re-read the following paragraph, concentrating specifically on its tone:

> I went out in the afternoon and spent thirty-five bucks (plus tip) on a legitimate salon haircut. I tend to take a pair of nail scissors to my own unruly mop about every six weeks, my technique being to snip off any tuft of hair that sticks out. I guess I must have been feeling insecure because it wouldn't ordinarily occur to me to pay real bucks for something I can do so handily myself. Of course, I've been told my hairstyle looks exactly like a puppy dog's backside, but what's wrong with that?

What words would you use to characterize the tone of this paragraph. By what means does Grafton accomplish this tone, and why does she choose to lend this kind of tone to her mystery novels? How does the tone of *M is for Malice* compare to that of other mysteries you've read—hard-boiled police procedurals, antic Carl Hiaasen romps, and so on?

Karen Makes Out
Elmore Leonard

They danced until Karen said she had to be up early tomorrow. No argument, he walked with her through the crowd outside Monaco, then along Ocean Drive in the dark to her car. He said, "Lady, you wore me out." He was in his forties, weathered but young-acting, natural, didn't come on with any singles-bar bullshit buying her a drink, or comment when she said thank you, she'd have Jim Beam on the rocks. They had cooled off by the time they reached her Honda and he took her hand and gave her a peck on the cheek saying he hoped to see her again. In no hurry to make something happen. That was fine with Karen. He said "Ciao," and walked off.

Two nights later they left Monaco, came out of that pounding sound to a sidewalk café and drinks and he became Carl Tillman, skipper of a charter deep-sea fishing boat out of American Marina, Bahia Mar. He was single,

---

married seven years and divorced, no children; he lived in a ground-floor two-bedroom apartment in North Miami—one of the bedrooms full of fishing gear he didn't know where else to store. Carl said his boat was out of the water, getting ready to move it to Haulover Dock, closer to where he lived.

Karen liked his weathered, kind of shaggy look, the crow's-feet when he smiled. She liked his soft brown eyes that looked right at her talking about making his living on the ocean, about hurricanes, the trendy scene here on South Beach, movies. He went to the movies every week and told Karen—raising his eyebrows in a vague, kind of stoned way—his favorite actor was Jack Nicholson. Karen asked him if that was his Nicholson impression or was he doing Christian Slater doing Nicholson? He told her she had a keen eye; but couldn't understand why she thought Dennis Quaid was a hunk. That was okay.

He said, "You're a social worker."

Karen said, "A *social* worker—"

"A teacher."

"What kind of teacher?

"You teach Psychology. College level."

She shook her head.

"English Lit."

"I'm not a teacher."

"Then why'd you ask what kind I thought you were?"

She said, "You want me to tell you what I do?"

"You're a lawyer. Wait. The Honda—you're a public defender." Karen shook her head and he said, "Don't tell me, I want to guess, even if it takes a while." He said, "If that's okay with you."

Fine. Some guys, she'd tell them what she did and they were turned off by it. Or they'd act surprised and then self-conscious and start asking dumb questions. "But how can a girl do that?" Assholes.

That night in the bathroom brushing her teeth Karen stared at her reflection. She liked to look at herself in mirrors: touch her short blond hair, check out her fanny in profile, long legs in a straight skirt above her knees, Karen still a size six approaching thirty. She didn't think she looked like a social worker or a schoolteacher, even college level. A lawyer maybe, but not a public defender. Karen was low-key high style. She could wear her favorite Calvin Klein suit, the black one her dad had given her for Christmas, her Sig Sauer .38 for evening wear snug against the small of her back, and no one would think for a moment she was packing.

Her new boyfriend called and stopped by her house in Coral Gables Friday evening in a white BMW convertible. They went to a movie and had supper and when he brought her home they kissed in the doorway, arms slipping around each other, holding, Karen thanking God he was a good kisser, comfortable with him, but not quite ready to take her clothes off. When she turned to the door he said, "I can wait. You think it'll be long?"

Karen said, "What're you doing Sunday?"

They kissed the moment he walked in and made love in the afternoon, sunlight flat on the window shades, the bed stripped down to a fresh white sheet. They made love in a hurry because they couldn't wait, had at each other and lay perspiring after. When they made love again, Karen holding his lean body between her legs and not wanting to let go, it lasted and lasted and got them smiling at each other, saying things like "Wow," and "Oh, my God," it was so good, serious business but really fun. They went out for a while, came back to her yellow stucco bungalow in Coral Gables, and made love on the living room floor.

Carl said, "We could try it again in the morning."

"I have to be dressed and out of here by six."

"You're a flight attendant."

She said, "Keep guessing."

Monday morning Karen Sisco was outside the federal courthouse in Miami with a pump-action shotgun on her hip. Karen's right hand gripped the neck of the stock, the barrel extending above her head. Several more U.S. deputy marshals were out here with her, while inside, three Colombian nationals were being charged in District Court with the possession of cocaine in excess of five hundred kilograms. One of the marshals said he hoped the scudders liked Atlanta as they'd be doing thirty to life there pretty soon. He said, "Hey, Karen, you want to go with me, drop 'em off? I know a nice ho-tel we could stay at."

She looked over at the good-ole-boy marshals grinning, shuffling their feet, waiting for her reply. Karen said, "Gary, I'd go with you in a minute if it wasn't a mortal sin." They liked that. It was funny, she'd been standing here thinking she'd gone to bed with four different boyfriends in her life: an Eric at Florida Atlantic, a Bill right after she graduated, then a Greg, three years of going to bed with Greg, and now Carl. Only four in her whole life, but two more than the national average for women in the U.S. according to *Time* magazine, their report of a recent sex survey. The average woman had two partners in her lifetime, the average man, six. Karen had thought everybody was getting laid with a lot more different ones than that.

She saw her boss now, Milt Dancey, an old-time marshal in charge of court support, come out of the building to stand looking around, a pack of cigarettes in his hand. Milt looked this way and gave Karen a nod, but paused to light a cigarette before coming over. A guy from the Miami FBI office was with him.

Milt said, "Karen, you know Daniel Burdon?"

Not Dan, not Danny, Daniel. Karen knew him, one of the younger black guys over there, tall and good looking, confident, known to brag about how many women he'd had of all kinds and color. He'd flashed his smile at Karen one time, hitting on her. Karen turned him down saying, "You have two reasons you want to go out with me." Daniel, smiling, said he knew of one reason, what was the other one? Karen said, "So you can tell your buddies you banged a marshal." Daniel said, "Yeah, but you could use it, too, girl. Brag on getting *me* in the sack." See? That's the kind of guy he was.

Milt said, "He wants to ask you about a Carl Tillman."

No flashing smile this time, Daniel Burdon had on a serious, sort of innocent expression, saying to her, "You know the man, Karen? Guy in his forties, sandy hair, goes about five-ten, one-sixty?"

Karen said, "What's this, a test? Do I *know* him?"

Milt reached for her shotgun. "Here, Karen, lemme take that while you're talking."

She turned a shoulder saying, "It's okay, I'm not gonna shoot him," her fist tight on the neck of the twelve-gauge. She said to Daniel, "You have Carl under surveillance?"

"Since last Monday."

"You've seen us together—so what's this do-I-know-him shit? You playing a game with me?"

"What I meant to ask, Karen, was how long have you known him?"

"We met last week, Tuesday."

"And you saw him Thursday, Friday, spent Sunday with him, went to the beach, came back to your place . . . What's he think about you being with the marshals' service?"

"I haven't told him."

"How come?"

"He wants to guess what I do."

"Still working on it, huh? What you think, he a nice guy? Has a sporty car, has money, huh? He a pretty big spender?"

"Look," Karen said, "why don't you quit dickin' around and tell me what this is about, okay?"

"See, Karen, the situation's so unusual," Daniel said, still with the innocent expression, "I don't know how to put it, you know, delicately. Find out a U.S. marshal's fucking a bank robber."

Milt Dancey thought Karen was going to swing at Daniel with the shotgun. He took it from her this time and told the Bureau man to behave himself, watch his mouth if he wanted cooperation here. Stick to the facts. This Carl Tillman was a *suspect* in a bank robbery, a possible suspect in a half-dozen more, all the robberies, judging from the bank videos, committed by the same guy. The FBI referred to him as "Slick," having nicknames for all their perps. They had prints off a teller's counter might be the guy's, but no match in their files and not enough evidence on Carl Edward Tillman—the name on his driver's license and car registration—to bring him in. He appeared to be most recently cherry, just getting into a career of crime. His motivation, pissed off at banks because Florida Southern foreclosed on his note and sold his forty-eight-foot Hatteras for nonpayment.

It stopped Karen for a moment. He might've lied about his boat, telling her he was moving it to Haulover; but that didn't make him a bank robber. She said, "What've you got, a video picture, a teller identified him?"

Daniel said, "Since you mentioned it," taking a Bureau wanted flyer from his inside coat pocket, the sheet folded once down the middle. He opened it and Karen was looking at four photos taken from bank video cameras of robberies in progress, the bandits framed in teller windows, three black guys, one white.

Karen said, "Which one?" and Daniel gave her a look before pointing to the white guy: a man with slicked-back hair, an earring, a full mustache, and dark sunglasses. She said, "That's not Carl Tillman," and felt instant relief. There was no resemblance.

"Look at it good."

"What can I tell you? It's not him."

"Look at the nose."

"You serious?"

"That's your friend Carl's nose."

It was. Carl's slender, rather elegant nose. Or like his. Karen said, "You're going with a nose ID, that's all you've got?"

"A witness," Daniel said, "believes she saw this man—right after what would be the first robbery he pulled—run from the bank to a strip mall up the street and drive off in a white BMW convertible. The witness got a partial on the license number and that brought us to your friend Carl."

Karen said, "You ran his name and date of birth . . . "

"Looked him up in NCIC, FCIC, and Warrant Information, drew a blank. That's why I think he's just getting his feet wet. Managed to pull off a few, two three grand each, and found himself a new profession."

"What do you want me to do," Karen said, "get his prints on a beer can?"

Daniel raised his eyebrows. "That would be a start. Might even be all we need. What I'd like you to do, Karen, is snuggle up to the man and find out his secrets. You know what I'm saying—intimate things, like did he ever use another name. . . . "

"Be your snitch," Karen said, knowing it was a mistake as soon as the words were out of her mouth.

It got Daniel's eyebrows raised again. He said, "That what it sounds like to you? I thought you were a federal agent, Karen. Maybe you're too close to him—is that it? Don't want the man to think ill of you?"

Milt said, "That's enough of that shit," standing up for Karen as he would any of his people, not because she was a woman; he had learned not to open doors for her. The only time she wanted to be first through the door was on a fugitive warrant, this girl who scored higher with a handgun, more times than not, than any marshal in the Southern District of Florida.

Daniel was saying, "Man, I need to use her. Is she on our side or not?"

Milt handed Karen her shotgun. "Here, you want to shoot him, go ahead."

"Look," Daniel said, "Karen can get me a close read on the man, where he's lived before, if he ever went by other names, if he has any identifying marks on his body, scars, maybe a gunshot wound, tattoos, things only lovely Karen would see when the man has his clothes off."

Karen took a moment. She said, "There is one thing I noticed."

"Yeah? What's that?"

"He's got the letters f-u-o-n tattooed on his penis."

Daniel frowned at her. "Foo-on?"

"That's when it's, you might say, limp. When he has a hard-on it says fuck the Federal Bureau of Investigation."

Daniel Burdon grinned at Karen. He said, "Girl, you and I have to get together. I mean it."

Karen could handle "girl." Go either way. Girl, looking at herself in a mirror applying blush-on. Woman, well, that's what she was. Though until just a few years ago she only thought of women old enough to be her mother as women. Women getting together to form organizations of women, saying, Look, we're different from men. Isolating themselves in these groups instead of mixing it up with men and beating them at their own men's games. Men in general were stronger physically than women. Some men were stronger than other men and Karen was stronger than some too; so what did that prove? If she had to put a man on the ground, no matter how big or strong he was, she'd do it. One way or another. Up front, in his face. What she couldn't see herself playing was this sneaky role. Trying to get the stuff on Carl, a guy she liked, a lot, would think of with tender feelings and miss him during the day and want to be with him. Shit . . . Okay, she'd play the game, but not undercover. She'd first let him know she was a federal officer and see what he thought about it.

Could Carl be a bank robber?

She'd reserve judgment. Assume almost anyone could at one time or another and go from there.

When Karen did, she came home and put a pot roast in the oven and left her bag on the kitchen table, open, the grip of a Beretta nine sticking out in plain sight.

Carl arrived, they kissed in the living room, Karen feeling it but barely looking at him. When he smelled the pot roast cooking Karen said, "Come on, you can make the drinks while I put the potatoes on." In the kitchen, then, she stood with the refrigerator door open, her back to Carl, giving him time to notice the pistol. Finally he said, "Jesus, you're a cop."

She had rehearsed this moment. The idea: turn saying, "You guessed," sounding surprised; then look at the pistol and say something like "Nuts, I gave it away." But she didn't. He said, "Jesus, you're a cop," and she turned from the refrigerator with an ice tray and said, "Federal. I'm a U.S. marshal."

"I would never've guessed," Carl said, "not in a million years."

Thinking about it before, she didn't know if he'd wig out or what. She looked at him now, and he seemed to be taking it okay, smiling a little.

He said, "But why?"

"Why what?"

"Are you a marshal?"

"Well, first of all, my dad has a company, Marshall Sisco Investigations. . . . "

"You mean because of his name, Marshall?"

"What I am—they're not spelled the same. No, but as soon as I learned to drive I started doing surveillance jobs for him. Like following some guy who was trying to screw his insurance company, a phony claim. I got the idea of going into law enforcement. So after a couple of years at Miami I transferred to Florida Atlantic and got in their Criminal Justice program."

"I mean why not FBI, if you're gonna do it, or DEA?"

"Well, for one thing, I liked to smoke grass when I was younger, so DEA didn't appeal to me at all. Secret Service guys I met were so fucking secretive, you ask them a question, they'd go, 'You'll have to check with Washington on that.' See, different federal agents would come to school to give talks. I got to know a couple of marshals—we'd go out after, have a few beers, and I liked them. They're nice guys, condescending at first, naturally; but after a few years they got over it."

Carl was making drinks now, Early Times for Karen, Dewar's in his glass, both with a splash. Standing at the sink, letting the faucet run, he said, "What do you do?"

"I'm on court security this week. My regular assignment is warrants. We go after fugitives, most of them parole violators."

Carl handed her a drink. "Murderers?"

"If they were involved in a federal crime when they did it. Usually drugs."

"Bank robbery, that's federal, isn't it?"

"Yeah, some guys come out of corrections and go right back to work."

"You catch many?"

"Bank robbers?" Karen said, "Nine out of ten," looking right at him.

Carl raised his glass. "Cheers."

While they were having dinner at the kitchen table he said, "You're quiet this evening."

"I'm tired, I was on my feet all day, with a shotgun."

"I can't picture that," Carl said. "You don't look like a U.S. marshal, or any kind of cop."

"What do I look like?"

"A knockout. You're the best-looking girl I've ever been this close to. I got a pretty close look at Mary Elizabeth Mastrantonio, when they were here shooting *Scarface?* But you're a lot better looking. I like your freckles."

"I used to be loaded with them."

"You have some gravy on your chin. Right here."

Karen touched it with her napkin. She said, "I'd like to see your boat."

He was chewing pot roast and had to wait before saying, "I told you it was out of the water?"

"Yeah?"

"I don't have the boat anymore. It was repossessed when I fell behind in my payments."

"The bank sold it?"

"Yeah, Florida Southern. I didn't want to tell you when we first met. Get off to a shaky start."

"But now that you can tell me I've got gravy on my chin . . . "

"I didn't want you to think I was some kind of loser."

"What've you been doing since?"

"Working as a mate, up at Haulover."

"You still have your place, your apartment?"

"Yeah, I get paid, I can swing that, no problem."

"I have a friend in the marshals lives in North Miami, on Alamanda off a Hundred and twenty-fifth."

Carl nodded. "That's not far from me."

"You want to go out after?"

"I thought you were tired."

"I am."

"Then why don't we stay home?" Carl smiled. "What do you think?"

"Fine."

They made love in the dark. He wanted to turn the lamp on, but Karen said, no, leave it off.

Geraldine Regal, the first teller at Sun Federal on Kendall Drive, watched a man with slicked-back hair and sunglasses fishing in his inside coat pocket as he approached her window. It was 9:40, Tuesday morning. At first she thought the guy was Latin. Kind of cool, except that up close his hair looked shellacked, almost metallic. She wanted to ask him if it hurt. He brought papers, deposit slips, and a blank check from the pocket saying, "I'm gonna make this out for four thousand." Began filling out the check and said, "You hear about the woman trapeze artist, her husband's divorcing her?"

Geraldine said she didn't think so, smiling, because it was a little weird, a customer she'd never seen before telling her a joke.

"They're in court. The husband's lawyer asks her, 'Isn't it true that on Monday, March the fifth, hanging from the trapeze upside down, without a net, you had sex with the ringmaster, the lion tamer, two clowns, and a dwarf?"

Geraldine waited. The man paused, head down as he finished making out the check. Now he looked up.

"The woman trapeze artist thinks for a minute and says, 'What was that date again?'"

Geraldine was laughing as he handed her the check, smiling as she saw it was a note written on a blank check, neatly printed in block letters, that said:

> THIS IS NO JOKE
> IT'S A STICKUP!
> I WANT $4,000 *NOW!*

Geraldine stopped smiling. The guy with the metallic hair was telling her he wanted it in hundreds, fifties, and twenties, loose, no bank straps or rubber bands, no bait money, no dye packs, no bills off the bottom of the drawer, and he wanted his note back. Now.

"The teller didn't have four grand in her drawer," Daniel Burdon said, "so the guy settled for twenty-eight hundred and was out of there. Slick changing his style—we *know* it's the same guy, with the shiny hair? Only now he's the Joker. The trouble is, see, I ain't Batman."

Daniel and Karen Sisco were in the hallway outside the central courtroom on the second floor, Daniel resting his long frame against the railing, where you could look below at the atrium, with its fountain and potted palms.

"No witness to see him hop in his BMW this time. The man coming to realize that was dumb, using his own car."

Karen said, "Or it's not Carl Tillman."

"You see him last night?"

"He came over."

"Yeah, how was it?"

Karen looked up at Daniel's deadpan expression. "I told him I was a federal agent and he didn't freak."

"So he's cool, huh?"

"He's a nice guy."

"Cordial. Tells jokes robbing banks. I talked to the people at Florida Southern, where he had his boat loan? Found out he was seeing one of the tellers. Not at the main office, one of their branches, girl named Kathy Lopez. Big brown eyes, cute as a puppy, just started working there. She's out with Tillman she tells him about her job, what she does, how she's counting money all day. I asked was Tillman interested, want to know anything in particular? Oh, yeah, he wanted to know what she was supposed to do if the bank ever got robbed. So she tells him about dye packs, how they work, how she gets a two-hundred-dollar bonus if she's ever robbed and can slip one in with the loot. The next time he's in, cute little Kathy Lopez shows him one, explains how you walk out the door with a pack of fake twenties? A half minute later the tear gas blows and you have that red shit all over you and the money you stole. I checked the reports on the other robberies he pulled? Every one of them he said to the teller, no dye packs or that bait money with the registered serial numbers."

"Making conversation," Karen said, trying hard to maintain her composure. "People like to talk about what they do."

Daniel smiled.

And Karen said, "Carl's not your man."

"Tell me why you're so sure."

"I know him. He's a good guy."

"Karen, you hear yourself? You're telling me what you feel, not what you know. Tell me about *him*—you like the way he dances, what?"

Karen didn't answer that one. She wanted Daniel to leave her alone.

He said, "Okay, you want to put a wager on it, you say Tillman's clean?"

That brought her back, hooked her, and she said, "How much?"

"You lose, you go out dancing with me."

"Great. And if I'm right, what do I get?"

"My undying respect," Daniel said.

As soon as Karen got home she called her dad at Marshall Sisco Investigations and told him about Carl Tillman, the robbery suspect in her life, and about Daniel Burdon's confident, condescending, smart-ass, irritating attitude.

Her dad said, "Is this guy colored?"

"Daniel?"

"I *know* he is. Friends of mine at Metro-Dade call him the white man's Burdon, in account of he gets on their nerves always being right. I mean your guy. There's a running back in the NFL named Tillman. I forget who he's with."

Karen said, "You're not helping any."

"The Tillman in the pros is colored—the reason I asked. I think he's with the Bears."

"Carl's white."

"Okay, and you say you're crazy about him?"

"I like him, a lot."

"But you aren't sure he isn't doing the banks."

"I said I can't believe he is."

"Why don't you ask him?"

"Come on—if he is he's not gonna tell me."

"How do you know?"

She didn't say anything and after a few moments her dad asked if she was still there.

"He's coming over tonight," Karen said.

"You want me to talk to him?"

"You're not serious."

"Then what'd you call me for?"

"I'm not sure what to do."

"Let the FBI work it."

"I'm supposed to be helping them."

"Yeah, but what good are you? You want to believe the guy's clean. Honey, the only way to find out if he is, you have to assume he isn't. You know what I'm saying? Why does a person rob banks? For money, yeah. But you have to be dumb, too, considering the odds against you, the security, cameras taking your picture. . . . So another reason could be the risk involved, it turns him on. The same reason he's playing around with you. . . . "

"He isn't playing around."

"I'm glad I didn't say, 'Sucking up to get information, see what you know.'"

"He's never mentioned banks." Karen paused. "Well, he might've once."

"You could bring it up, see how he reacts. He gets sweaty, call for backup. Look, whether he's playing around or loves you with all his heart, he's still risking twenty years. He doesn't know if you're on to him or not and that heightens the risk. It's like he thinks he's Cary Grant stealing jewels from the broad's home where he's having dinner, in his tux. But your guy's still dumb if he robs banks. You know all that. Your frame of mind, you just don't want to accept it."

"You think I should draw him out. See if I can set him up."

"Actually," her dad said, "I think you should find another boyfriend."

Karen remembered Christopher Walken in *The Dogs of War* placing his gun on a table in the front hall—the doorbell ringing—and laying a newspaper over the gun before he opened the door. She remembered it because at one time she was in love with Christopher Walken, not even caring that he wore his pants so high.

Carl reminded her some of Christopher Walken, the way he smiled with his eyes. He came a little after seven. Karen had on khaki shorts and a T-shirt, tennis shoes without socks.

"I thought we were going out."

They kissed and she touched his face, moving her hand lightly over his skin, smelling his after-shave, feeling the spot where his right earlobe was pierced.

"I'm making drinks," Karen said. "Let's have one and then I'll get ready." She started for the kitchen.

"Can I help?"

"You've been working all day. Sit down, relax."

It took her a couple of minutes. Karen returned to the living room with a drink in each hand, her leather bag hanging from her shoulder. "This one's yours." Carl took it and she dipped her shoulder to let the bag slip off and drop to the coffee table. Carl grinned.

"What've you got in there, a gun?"

"Two pounds of heavy metal. How was your day?"

They sat on the sofa and he told how it took almost four hours to land an eight-foot marlin, the leader wound around its bill. Carl said he worked his tail off hauling the fish aboard and the guy decided he didn't want it.

Karen said, "After you got back from Kendall?"

It gave him pause.

"Why do you think I was in Kendall?"

Carl had to wait while she sipped her drink.

"Didn't you stop by Florida Southern and withdraw twenty-eight hundred?"

That got him staring at her, but with no expression to speak of. Karen thinking, Tell me you were somewhere else and can prove it.

But he didn't; he kept staring.

"No dye packs, no bait money. Are you still seeing Kathy Lopez?"

Carl hunched over to put his drink on the coffee table and sat like that, leaning on his thighs, not looking at her now as Karen studied his profile, his elegant nose. She looked at his glass, his prints all over it, and felt sorry for him.

"Carl, you blew it."

He turned his head to look at her past his shoulder. He said, "I'm leaving," pushed up from the sofa and said, "If this is what you think of me . . . "

Karen said, "Carl, cut the shit," and put her drink down. Now, if he picked up her bag, that would cancel out any remaining doubts. She watched him pick up her bag. He got the Beretta out and let the bag drop.

"Carl, sit down. Will you, please?"

"I'm leaving. I'm walking out and you'll never see me again. But first . . . " He made her get a knife from the kitchen and cut the phone line in there and in the bedroom.

He *was* pretty dumb. In the living room again he said, "You know something? We could've made it."

Jesus. And he had seemed like such a cool guy. Karen watched him go to the front door and open it before turning to her again.

"How about letting me have five minutes? For old times' sake."

It was becoming embarrassing, sad. She said, "Carl, don't you understand? You're under arrest."

He said, "I don't want to hurt you, Karen, so don't try to stop me." He went out the door.

Karen walked over to the chest where she dropped her car keys and mail coming in the house: a bombé chest by the front door, the door still open. She laid aside the folded copy of the *Herald* she'd placed there over her Sig Sauer .38, picked up the pistol, and went out to the front stoop, into the yellow glow of the porch light. She saw Carl at his car now, its white shape pale against the dark street, only about forty feet away.

"Carl, don't make it hard, okay?"

He had the car door open and half turned to look back. "I said I don't want to hurt you."

Karen said, "Yeah, well . . . ," raised the pistol to rack the slide, and cupped her left hand under the grip. She said, "You move to get in the car, I'll shoot."

Carl turned his head again with a sad, wistful expression. "No you won't, sweetheart."

Don't say ciao, Karen thought. Please.

Carl said, "Ciao," turned to get in the car, and she shot him. Fired a single round at his left thigh and hit him where she'd aimed, in the fleshy part just below his butt. Carl howled and slumped inside against the seat and the steering wheel, his leg extended straight out, his hand gripping it, his eyes raised with a bewildered frown as Karen approached. The poor dumb guy looking at twenty years, and maybe a limp.

Karen felt she should say something. After all, for a few days there they were as intimate as two people can get. She thought about it for several moments, Carl staring up at her with rheumy eyes. Finally Karen said, "Carl, I want you to know I had a pretty good time, considering."

It was the best she could do.

POINTS TO CONSIDER ABOUT "KAREN MAKES OUT"

1. Compared to Sue Grafton's tone in the Kinsey Millhone mysteries (see Points to Consider about Chapter 1 of *M is for Malice*, #5), how would describe the tone Elmore Leonard creates for this story? What specific literary elements work together to create this tone? What qualities of style place this story squarely within the genre of mystery fiction? Cite examples from the story to support your assertions.

2. In the interview with Sue Grafton, she says, "I just made Kinsey Millhone female because I am female." In "Karen Makes Out," Leonard also creates a protagonist who is female, despite the fact that he is male. In your opinion, how well does Leonard accomplish the task of creating a central character of the "opposite" sex? Are there points at which his characterization of Karen Sisco suffers because Leonard is a male writer trying to imagine the psychological workings of a woman?

3. Leonard uses quite a bit of crude, sometimes sexually explicit language in this story. Identify specific examples. What is the function of that sort of speech is this narrative context? In your opinion, does this language enhance the tone of the story or detract from it?

4. What is the "mystery" element in "Karen Makes Out"? What specific techniques does Leonard use to create suspense, and how does he eventually reveal the "truth"? Can you find any instances of "yes means no," as Grafton describes, in Leonard's short story?

5. In this brief fictional piece, Leonard manages to incorporate the same major plot stages—opening, exposition, escalating midpoints and climax, resolution—that he uses in his novels. Identify each of these elements in the story, and explain how they work to create a satisfying narrative arc. What theme(s)—implied meaning(s)—is (are) suggested by the story's resolution?

✖ WRITING ACTIVITIES: MYSTERY FICTION

1. This first activity is a general process suggestion, rather than an exercise in writing mysteries . . . although a mystery story may emerge from this exercise. Following Grafton's suggestions to cultivate the "Shadow" faculty of the subconscious mind, begin a journal practice in which you record your dreams each night. Some people write down their dreams in the morning, but I prefer to keep a microcassette recorder by my bed and speak my dream-narratives into it the moment I wake up, sometimes at three in the morning, sometimes when I get up; that way, I make sure not to forget the details of my dreams. Using this journal, write a fictional piece based on a dream (or series of dreams). Don't try to make too much sense of the imagery or storyline—just flesh out the dream as faithfully as you can, following the promptings of your Shadow voice. Alternatively, modify a story currently in process, if any such voice emerges as you pay closer attention to the workings of your subconscious.

2. Here is a list of guidelines for an eight- to ten-page mystery story you will write:
   - Your hero will be the same gender as you are.
   - Your setting will be the town in which you spent the most time during your life—make your setting descriptions brief but rich with detail that makes your local vivid and unique.
   - The mystery will center on a relative or close friend who mysteriously disappears.
   - Your narrator will not be a professional private investigator and will be reluctant to get involved in the case.

- Your narrator will tell the story from the first-person perspective.
- Your piece will involve at least one act of violence, in which somebody ends up hurt or bleeding; death is optional.
- Your narrator cannot end up being the guilty party at the end of the story.
- One of the secondary characters will be a romantic interest, to inject an element of sexual tension into the story.
- None of your characters will speak in dialects, but at least one of your characters will use lots of slang—and perhaps curse words, if you're so inclined.
- Your dialogue attribution will be minimal: he said, she said, or nothing at all.
- Your story will contain at least two descriptions of the weather outside.
- You must have introduced three secondary characters, including the guilty party, by page five.
- You will base the guilty party on somebody who has been your supervisor at work during your life.
- All of your scenes will involve your narrator by him/herself, or with one other character; never more than two characters.
- None of your sentences will be more than ten words long, except for one sentence at the story's climax. That sentence must be longer than twenty-five words.

Have at it. Depending on your temperament, you can begin by describing your protagonist and secondary characters, and let the plot develop organically from their interaction, or you can begin with a structural outline/working journal, roughing out the plot scene-by-scene before you actually begin writing the story. Feel free to modify any of these ingredients if healthy creative impulses take you in unexpected directions.

12

Reinventing *Was:* Writing Historical Fiction

Leonard Tourney is the author of eight critically-acclaimed mystery novels set in Shakespeare's England: *The Players' Boy is Dead, Low Treason, Familiar Spirits, The Bartholomew Fair Murders, Old Saxon Blood, Knaves Templar, Witness of Bones,* and *Frobisher's Savage,* along with numerous scholarly books and articles. Tourney has taught writing at the university level for over thirty years and in this chapter offers his insights—as both teacher and author—into the process of writing historical fiction.

Serious fiction writers understand what makes their work tick. Stories are not just stories: they're narrative languages or codes requiring interpretation. They fall, sometimes not so neatly, into genres or categories—literary types the "rules" of which form a communicative bond between writer and reader. These rules or "conventions" give a certain shape to the plot, characters, incidents. Your first question then is what are the conventions of your chosen genre? What do readers—and editors—expect of your story or novel?

If you're writing a mystery, you need to understand how to create a knotty puzzle, full of intrigue and suspense. That's what readers expect of a mystery. If you choose to write science fiction, you need to know how to make believable technology, events, even worlds that exist only in the outer space of your imagination. Readers want to believe your speculation is real.

If historical fiction is your choice, your concern is how to recover—even reinvent—the past and make its dry bones live again in a story that has the momentum and dramatic impact of a contemporary tale. My purpose here is to suggest ways you can do this. The advice I give below I haven't gotten out of books; it's come from my experience as a reader and writer of historical fiction.

WHAT IS HISTORICAL FICTION?

In a sense, all fiction is historical, in that it is situated in a place and time that, if not history today, will be so tomorrow. Generally, however, the term "historical" applies to fiction whose setting is more deeply rooted in the past. So, while it is readily evident that a novel set in ancient Rome, or Renaissance Italy, or Victorian England is *historical*, so too is a novel set in the "Roaring Twenties," the Great Depression, or the Vietnam era. Writers who choose to set their stories in these more recent periods face challenges not unlike those who elect a more remote time and place.

In history fiction worthy of the name, *history* should form a significant part of the theme as well as provide the story with a chronological setting. That is, the story is not merely incidentally set in the past, but purposely so. The writer wants to feature as part of the story's theme the component of time: the era or age featured. The characters move around in a distinctive time zone, and the sights, sounds, beliefs, and preoccupations of that era shape the characters' personalities, motivations, and fate.

While historical fiction is generally thought to be a tributary of so-called mainstream literature, it is not a literary backwater. Many classic works of fiction are "historical": Mark Twain's *Huckleberry Finn*, for example, written in the 1880s but dealing with events in the American South prior to the Civil War; Charles Dickens' *Tale of Two Cities*, set during the French revolution but written a generation later; and Nathaniel Hawthorne's *The Scarlet Letter*, set in Puritan New England but written in the mid-nineteenth century. Leo Tolstoy, Sir Walter Scott, Robert Louis Stevenson, and Alexandre Dumas all wrote historical fiction, and historical novels have proven to be some of the great bestsellers of our time, like Margaret Mitchell's *Gone With the Wind* and Lew Wallace's *Ben Hur*. To these "classics" we can add the more recent historical excursions of major British and American writers such as Anthony Burgess' *Nothing Like the Sun* (Elizabethan England), John Barth's *The Sot-Weed Factor* (Colonial United States), and Gore Vidal's *Aaron Burr* (American Revolution).

Historical novels have not only been literary prize winners and best-sellers, but also highly successful films, such as Irwin Shaw's *The Young Lions* (Germany and U.S. World War II) John Fowles' *The French Lieutenant's Woman* (nineteenth-century England), E. L. Doctorow's *Ragtime* (Early twentieth-century United States), and more recently, Michael Ondaatje's *The English Patient* and Thomas Keneally's *Schindler's List*, both set during World War II.

Historical fiction also has strong ties to other subgenres: to the superb period mysteries of Anne Perry, Steven Saylor, Sharan Newman, Kate Ross, and Ellis Peters; to the large corpus of Western dime novels and the more serious "Westerns" of A. B. Guthrie, Larry McMurtry, and Cormac Mc-Carthy; to romance fiction, much of which employs historical atmosphere; to the wonderful maritime novels of Patrick O'Brian; and action/adventure novels of wars and political intrigues of yesteryear by writers too numerous to mention.

For writers, then, history is not a nightmare from which they have struggled to awaken—as James Joyce described Ireland's heavy-handed past in his *Portrait of the Artist as a Young Man*—but a dream they have worked to revive from the dust and share in the furtherance of a great literary tradition.

PICKING THROUGH THE TAILINGS OF TIME

You can choose any period you like as a setting for your story or novel, which gives you dozens if not hundreds of possibilities. But unless you are a polymath with a vivid imagination and catholic tastes, you will lean toward only a few times and places. Perhaps you read a thousand Westerns as a child, or majored in French history in college, or wrote a Master's thesis on the Balkan Wars, or have always been intrigued by the Medieval life and know Arthurian legend like the back of your chainmail-gloved hand. My own academic training in English literature furnished me with grist for historical fiction when in the late 1970s I started to write about an Elizabethan clothier named Matthew Stock who, with his wife, Joan, found his duty as town constable involving him in one homicide investigation after another. I already knew the basic facts of the period, a good deal about customs, costumes, and laws. I had to learn more.

But while facts are important and a solid historical foundation is useful *before* you start that first draft, equally important is temperamental affinity, the sympathetic bond that causes a writer to find one time period appealing while others hold no interest or are downright repellent. One period differs from another not only in its technology and politics, but also in its world view, social atmosphere, and characteristic preoccupations. The age of Shakespeare, for example, is characterized by a certain intellectual adventurousness, moody spirituality, and rambunctious wit and vulgarity—all wrapped up in one diverse and paradoxical sensibility. That era requires characters of many words, and a writer who prefers the strong, silent type might be more comfortable setting his or her scene among the laconic cow-boys of the Old West. By the same token, some writers may find the Middle Ages too gloomy, the eighteenth century too artificial, the Victorians too staid, the Romans too bombastic, the First World War—and indeed all wars—a crashing bore. There's no arguing with taste, and while some periods are more trendy and thus more marketable than others, the choice is yours.

But remember: writing is the kind of work bearable only when you're having a good time with it. Neither fame nor fortune can compensate for drudgery. So choose wisely. Writer, know thyself! What kind of a person are you? With what sort of folks do you feel comfortable? Remember, if you're planning to write a novel, you may be living with your characters and in their historical moment for years. You want to enjoy both.

HISTORICAL RESEARCH—GETTING YOUR FACTS STRAIGHT

All writers must do some research, even those who write about their own time and place. However, as a writer of historical fiction you have a greater burden. First, unless you are writing about the recent past and depending on your memory, your knowledge of history is almost entirely second- or third-hand, a garnering of information from old documents—diaries, journals, yellowing newspapers, faded photographs, and maps, as well as scholarly histories. You may also travel to observe directly the artifacts of the past—churches, cathedrals, castles, and palaces, old ships, period clothing, and weaponry safely displayed behind the glass at museums.

Second, you will use your imagination and intuition too, guessing intelligently how our ancestors thought and spoke and inventing some facts—for almost all historical fiction is a blend of what *was* and *what might have been*.

But don't be discouraged by the spectre of spending years of your life in the library or raiding the Internet. Historical fiction is not primarily about history, but about the people who lived it. For that reason, many successful writers do their research *while* they are writing, not before. Why? Because it is only as the story unfolds that you have any concrete idea of what you actually need to know about the past.

So what are the best sources of historical information?

For the broader facts of the period (the reign of kings, the size of cities and towns, the dates of battles, discoveries, inventions) a good encyclopedia—in print or on the computer screen—is more than adequate. Readers of historical fiction assume that a historical novel will merge historical fact with the author's imagination (distaste for such merging is why some readers prefer their history straight), but they do require that the basic facts of the period be accurate.

That means also you must verify dates, locate battles on the right field, and not extend a king's reign beyond the dictum of the history books.

That means the technology of the period must also be correct. Don't have a character fly off into the sunset if planes weren't invented until a generation later! Put your characters in the historically correct clothing, equip them with the proper eating utensils, and let them have dreams and fears characteristic of the time in which they lived.

All this should go without saying, yet you'd be surprised how often an author's anachronisms spoil the mood for the discerning reader.

CHARACTERS, REAL AND IMAGINED

Some historical fiction takes as its subject the life of a real person—a famous general or president, actor or writer, artist or musician. The idea is that the movers and shakers of history have enough appeal that readers can't get enough of them in history books but also want to see their lives and achievements under color of fiction. Such fictional biographies are a variety of the basic historical fiction genre. To write such a novel, you must have a scholar's knowledge of your central characters and the details of their lives. Readers will expect, even demand, accuracy. Don't expect to dash off a fictional biography of a Mussolini, Babe Ruth, or Bach in six months or less. It took years for Robert Graves to write *I, Claudius,* his saga of the Roman Emperors.

Much historical fiction mingles real and invented persons. Imagine this: you're writing a novel about Theodore Roosevelt, a very real American president well known to the general reading public. In your novel, you have Roosevelt carry on a conversation with a veteran of the Rough Riders, a wounded soldier who is purely the figment of your imagination. You put words in Teddy's mouth, create a conversation that never happened on an occasion that never happened. Are you playing fair?

Most readers will say yes. Mingling fact with fiction is a convention of the genre, but it is not a license to abuse the historical record. An invented scene or character requires a slight incision in the fabric of actual events. Well and good. But the more facts one alters for the sake of the plot, the more you're likely to invite criticism that you've abused history, not used it.

As for imputing thoughts to real historical personages, they should be generally consistent with what is known about the personage. This doesn't mean that you're not entitled to your own opinion of what kind of person character X *really* was. It does mean that if you go too far you'll lose credibility. That is, your Roosevelt need not represent the party line, but he should be a Roosevelt who's not so inconsistent as to suggest you've confused him with Ghengis Khan or Oscar Wilde.

A final caution. Don't bring famous persons on stage as window dressing. Characters should have some legitimate function in the story to earn their keep. And don't cast too many characters either real or imagined. Have mercy on the poor reader struggling to remember who's who. One *War and Peace* (one of the great historical novels, which features no less than ten central characters and a seemingly endless number of secondary characters) is enough.

THE PLOT'S THE THING WHEREIN WE CATCH
THE CONSCIENCE OF THE READER

I've bent Prince Hamlet's famous words to my own ends. I want to stress the importance of plot, a much maligned and misunderstood element of the storyteller's art.

The plot is the backbone of fiction. It is the sequence of events, the structure of conflict, rising action, and resolution, the story's own unique chronology and armature. When we say that a certain book is a whopping good story, we are talking about more than plot; yet plot is an important contributor to our enjoyment, and it's hard to imagine a reader approving of a novel where the plot's a dud.

Constructing the plot of a historical fiction involves basically the same skills used by a writer of any genre, for the historical setting is usually a *background* for the actions and relationships of individual characters, not the foreground. Theoretically, then, any narrative thread—love, revenge, frustrated or perverse ambition, personal heroism or malignity, domestic discord, dissolution, or restoration—can be placed in a historical setting, can become the "main plot" of the story. The larger historical events provide a framework or context for the evolving present action. They may even achieve the status of a subplot if sufficiently dramatic.

For example, suppose you are writing a novel about the American Civil War. Suppose the action occurs during a specific battle. And suppose the plot involves two rivals—they both love the same woman—who enlist in the same cavalry unit. They extend their rivalry into their military experiences, becoming friends at last, but only after one deserts and is brought back forcibly by the other. The heroic one dies in his efforts, thus allowing the other to return home, marry the object of their rivalry, and presumably live happily ever after.

I won't argue this is a particularly original story. It is, however, a workable outline involving conflict, suspense, and resolution, the essential elements of plot. The same plot could take place against the background of any battle, any war, but you have chosen, say, the Battle of Gettysburg, so you must make that historical event earn its keep in your book.

To do this, you integrate the structure of the personal rivalry and its final resolution with the events of the battle, the positioning of the Union and Confederate troops, the specific phases of the conflict, and its ultimate resolution in the Union victory. The plot of the novel, then, is an intertwining of private events and public, the story of fictional rivals in love and the larger conflict of rival armies whose quarrel is not about the claims of love but about states' rights, slavery, and political power. The personal tragedy of the dying hero echoes the greater one of a nation divided against itself.

The Battle of Gettysburg has earned its keep.

To sum up: as you construct your plot, think of the ways historical background echoes the novel's foreground—the central characters and their actions. Look for mirrored images, ironic parallels. Let background and foreground interact with each other and teach you meanings that had not occurred to you previously. You spin a complex web when you unite real and imagined lives. Make sure that becoming ensnared in the web is worth the reader's time and effort.

BACKGROUND: THE "NEED TO KNOW" PRINCIPLE

Most beginning writers make the mistake of assuming that their first job is to provide the reader with a full understanding of the historical setting, as though the writer were a history professor preparing the student for a final exam. This mistake is based on several dubious assumptions: first, that the novel is chiefly about history; second, that readers cannot engage in the story unless they know everything there is to know about the American revolution, or the Edwardians, or the Franco-Prussian war—whatever the background may be—and up front.

Both these assumptions are dangerous, if not outright false. Historical novels are not about history but about people in history. Readers are not only perfectly able to commit to a book without knowing certain so-called essentials; they generally do not get interested in a story unless they are hooked by an engaging foreground.

Let's begin with the essential background.

Most of the background information that beginning writers consider essential . . . isn't. This is because either readers already know it, or the readers don't and their ignorance makes no difference to the evolving plot. Readers were not born yesterday, despite the lamentable state of public education. Even when information is essential, downloading a lot of expository prose at the beginning of the story is unwise. The successful storyteller is much like a successful general. Victory depends not just on what equipment and troops you have at your disposal but *where* and *how* you position them. If you begin your story with a lot of historical background, or if you feel compelled to tell all you know about your research because you don't want to waste it, or feel that it's your duty to educate, you run the risk of boring readers. If readers wanted that kind of history, they would have consulted an encyclopedia or a university press book.

Don't expect readers to be patient while they wade through thirty pages of background information. Patience is a virtue rarely found in modern readers. It is virtually nonexistent in editors and agents.

I recommend this principle: Provide readers with only the background they absolutely *need* to know and *when* they need to know it. An arresting beginning is one where the reader is intrigued by characters in action, not facts and figures. If the foreground commands attention, readers will not only endure history lessons; they'll hunger for them. But don't be professorial. *Integrate* background information:

> Do it in dialogue.
> Do it in short passages of exposition.
> Do it in action.

When you write about history, think drama. Imagine you're making a movie, not giving a lecture.

WHEN IN ROME, THINK AS THE ROMANS THINK

In the past, life was different from what it is today. It was harder, simpler, usually shorter, often brutish. I'm not talking merely about the absence of computers, indoor plumbing, and the internal combustion engine. People dressed differently (and admired what they wore, regardless of how ridiculous it may seem to us!); they also thought differently, living in a world that was smaller than our own, and yet in some ways larger too. All this should go without saying, you think; and yet it must be said, because beginning writers often forget this fundamental truth.

For example, through most of antiquity, in the so-called Christian world at least—and even until recent times—all might not be right with the world but God was in His Heaven, the Devil in his Hell, and mankind in between, destined for judgment and an afterlife. Thus, religion played a much greater part in the average person's thought, activities, and conversation than it does in today's largely secular world. Gender roles were often quite different from what they are today, as were courtship practices and attitudes toward marriage and childrearing, table manners, and politics. I do not mean to suggest that there were no atheists in Elizabethan foxholes, or that everyone in Colonial America believed in witchcraft, or that no citizen of Imperial Rome questioned sending Christians to the lions (except of course the Christians). I am not saying that in the past women were always subservient to their men, that no one married for love rather than power or convenience, or that no one wanted to climb above his social station. But in each time and place there were prevailing views and practices, and often a degree of homogeneity in attitude lacking in today's diverse society. So while you're telling the story, tell the truth about its world. A writer who imposes modern attitudes upon a past age runs the risk of seriously undermining the credibility of the story. The same writer also deprives readers of one of the pleasures of historical fiction, a tour of the real past, not of a cardboard cutout with modern folks parading in period costumes.

How can you avoid imposing anachronistic values on your characters? Sound research is a start. When I suggest above that you know your period, I mean that you know its prevailing thought—the attitudes, values, and myths that give it a distinct identity and social order as well as dates and names. Writers dress their characters' minds as well as their bodies. They give them a world view to inhabit as well as a certain kind of house or castle.

Consider your characters. Do they *think* like persons of their time and place? If individual characters are exceptions to the cultural rule, is their nonconformity acknowledged in the story and accounted for? Dramatic conflict in fiction often arises from a character's nonconformity with his neighbors. A rebel against the authority of the Church, the control of parents, the divinity of the king, or the existence of God, might be quite interesting and credible, too—even in the most socially submissive of ages. But the rebel's values need to be seen as contrary and controversial by other characters, not misrepresented as the norm.

THEME: WHAT THE READER MAKES OF THE STORY

In historical fiction, as in fiction in general, theme is the wisdom, the knowledge of life, that readers infer from the story's action. I use the word *infer*. Good writers don't spell out the themes of their stories as though they were providing readers with embroidered samplers to hang on the wall. They are concerned not with the moral of the tale but its drama, content to let readers take from the story what they will and can. Beginning writers, on the other hand, spend too much time making sure the reader gets the point, makes the right interpretation, doesn't miss the writer's political or social agenda. They trust the reader too little, explain too much, and often ruin the story's vitality and credibility by editorializing.

This is the sugarcoated pill theory of literature in which the reader is thought to receive a beneficial dose of enlightenment for his pains. At least that's the idea. But there is such a thing as a bitter pill, and some stories and novels are so heavily programmed to make a point or advocate a doctrine that the story becomes too hard to swallow.

Using a story as a pulpit is a mistake and writers who do so run the grave risk of producing dull, didactic tracts, most of which never get published. They fail to understand that whatever a good story is, it absolutely must be a *story*, not a sermon, and while fiction can be an instrument of political and social change, when ideology is the writer's commanding imperative, the story wallows in self-consciousness, the reader dozes, and art degenerates into propaganda.

The moral? Don't preach, don't lecture, don't explain. Show your story and let the theme take care of itself. The inference of the theme is the reader's business, not yours.

STYLE

Style is the distinctive expression of a story as opposed to its paraphrasable content. Style is where writers exercise their options and make choices from an array of possibilities not dictated automatically by the demands of grammar, syntax, or conventional form.

Special stylistic concerns rear their heads in historical fiction: (1) whether the narrative style reinforces the period setting; and (2) whether dialogue suggests the speakers live in the past rather than the present. Failure in either of these areas can produce a story that denies its own basic premise: that events occurred and people lived when the writer claims.

Let's consider first how narrative style mirrors, or deflects, the time period of the novel.

Style is servant of story, not its master. A good style is one that doesn't get in the way of the novel's narrative flow or emotional impact and actually enhances the work's illusion of a bygone time. Writers of period fiction sometimes imitate the more elaborate literary style of the past. A. S. Byatt's novel *Possession* is an example of a novel that purposely imitates the elegant manner of late Victorian prose, as do the current host of lesser literary lights producing sequels of the novels of Jane Austen and Emily Bronte. Anthony Burgess' brilliant *Nothing Like the Sun* and John Barth's *The Sot-weed Factor* give us the intellectual wordplay and salacious wit of the Elizabethan age. Similarly, Patrick O'Brian's seagoing adventures might well have been written by the nineteenth-century gentlemen the novels feature.

Most writers, however, serve up history in a straightforward modern prose style, not that different from that of mainstream fiction. In fact, some writers believe that a more contemporary narrative style enhances historical fiction by making characters and events as immediate, gritty, and credible as fiction set in today's world. George Garrett, for example, sets his much-admired novels in the age of Shakespeare (*Death of a Fox* and *The Succession*) in a style that is more contemporary and much less complicated than Burgess' and yet still manages to enthrall us with a world gone by.

The "Elizabethan" style in my own novels—and in the excerpt provided in this chapter—strives for a similar effect: to suggest the period without overwhelming the reader with it; to use language expressively as Shakespeare's generation did; and at the same to time keep the sense crisp and clear for modern readers. You may choose among these approaches, but keep in mind that it is easier to get a novel published if its readers aren't turned off by an excessively mannered style.

Period dialogue presents its own special challenge.

Let's suppose that, fond of early English literature and history, you decide to write a novel set in medieval England. You have read around in the literature of that period—Langland, Chaucer, the Paston Letters—and have realized that "Middle English" is quite different from modern. Not exactly a foreign language, but largely incomprehensible without a glossary. Novel readers traditionally hate footnotes, not unreasonably associating them with dry-as-dust textbooks and boring research papers. Daunted by the prospect of representing Middle English to a modern English audience, you decide to advance your novel in time, say the great age of Elizabeth I. Here you have also done extensive reading—Shakespeare, Marlowe, Jonson. But even here the language is difficult and if you were able to represent it accurately, the reader would balk. Reading your story wouldn't be a labor of love; only a labor.

At the same time, you realize that if the language of your characters is too contemporary, it undermines the illusion you are at pains to create: a story written today about persons and events of yesteryear. Stuck on the horns of a dilemma, you realize that a linguistic compromise is in order.

Historical novelists usually create a language for their characters that *suggests* the period without reproducing it in its archaic fullness. They may use everyday expressions, oaths, terminology, names, greetings—all culled from old diaries and plays—but at the heart of the style of dialogue is a simple, straightforward English not readily identifiable with any particular period. They do avoid metaphors, slang, buzzwords, or colloquialisms evoking the contemporary scene, so that no sixteenth-century milkmaid comes across as a California surf chick or no noble Roman talks quite like a Washington bureaucrat.

Some writers, of course, deliberately modernize the speech of their historical characters, either to shock or to make the past seem more "relevant." They rarely do so, however, without criticism. A safer bet is to make sure your characters' speech is compatible with the novel's period. Readers know when they read a historical novel that the author has massaged the language—taken off the rough edges of its diction and syntax to give readers a break. They can live with the imitation of antique speech rather than its reality. What they cannot abide is talk that rings jarringly untrue because it yanks them from the past of the novel into the present without warning or reason.

THE ONE READER WHO MUST ABSOLUTELY ENJOY THE BOOK IS YOU

I've described some of the problems in writing historical fiction, I hope not at the expense of its pleasures. The past is six feet under, and making it live and breathe again is not so much a matter of *unearthing* it as *reinventing* it. Historical fiction offers its readers history in a highly palatable form, but that's not all it offers. It also gives us the insight and delight of envisioning the human drama against a larger backdrop of a remote time and place. From that conjunction of plot and history comes insight into what is universal in human nature and what is peculiar to one historical moment. Reinventing the past, populating it with living characters, and setting them in motion with a credible and engaging plot are well worth the trouble. It can sharpen your sense of language, broaden your understanding of culture, history, and psychology, and give you and your readers a real adventure in the world that was.

The Hangman's Apprentice
Leonard Tourney

The Three Ravens had been a small manor house, probably built before King Henry's time by the pitch of its roof and rough, warped timbers, but fallen into decay in this year of Grace 1602. Now fitted out as an inn, it sat weather-beaten and forlorn in the Kentish countryside, and was the first habitation the clothier and his wife had come upon after an evil hour of increasingly dangerous travel on a road virtually impassable, a nightmare of flooded ruts, mud, and gathering darkness. When the lights of the inn appeared in the distance, their stopping there was a foregone conclusion, despite its dilapidated appearance and its portentous sign: three ravens feasting on a hanged man's skull.

This clothier, Matthew Stock by name, was a portly, square-faced man of about thirty-five or forty, given to blunt speech and plain manners. In his town of Chelmsford, Essex he was a well-respected clothier and constable.

His wife, Joan, had a pretty oval face, dark hair and eyes, and a tongue that could be as sharp as a razor when she was riled. They had come into these parts to pay a last visit to Joan's dying uncle, a prosperous tailor of advanced years and large posterity. The uncle had given up the ghost in a timely fashion, and then the multitude of relations feasted on the relics of his larder, congratulated themselves that they remained among the living, and began the division of the deceased's earthly goods, which gross spoilage the Stocks found so offensive that they took leave of these greedy cousins and swore never to let their shadow fall upon Kentish countryside again.

The host of the Three Ravens was a tall, broad-shouldered, saturnine man of about fifty, with a ruddy beard and brooding, melancholic eyes. He said very little upon the Stocks' arrival, seeming content to let his wife handle the business of guests. She was a shrunken, timorous woman, with sharply molded features and so grave a pallor that she looked as if she had been exhumed for the occasion. It was the woman who led them to an upstairs chamber, found the roof leaking, and then conveyed them to a more commodious chamber on the same floor that by its gaping hearth and mullioned windows the Stocks supposed must have at one time been the principal bedchamber of the house.

The woman's daughter, a girl of about sixteen with the sharp, pale features of her mother, now appeared, and the woman of the house wished them a good night. Meanwhile the girl set about to light a fire, explaining awkwardly that the chamber had been unused for some time but not why. The girl, who did not give her name, was with child if the roundness of her belly was any indication, although no mention was made of a husband and she wore no ring upon her finger. She left two candles, an extra blanket for the large four-poster bed, showed them where the chamber pot lay, and promised to fetch them the remains of a steaming pork pie she had that day made should they be hungry.

Matthew and Joan declined in unison, professing to be too weary to eat. Matthew wondered if the girl were cook as well as housemaid. She replied that she regularly prepared the meals for the household and their infrequent guests.

The girl's remark about the infrequency of guests prompted Matthew to ensure that the horses were well cared for before turning in. Telling Joan he would return presently, he headed for the stable.

The stable was long and dark and Matthew's candle illuminated little of the space ahead of him. He was aware of several horses not his own in the stalls, and then beyond heard the sound of soft, raspy snoring, mixed with the occasional plop of rain leaking through the roof. Presently he came to where a very old man lay fast asleep. He was wrapped in a horse blanket and had a beard of such generous growth that only his old rheumy eyes, very red and bloody at the rims, appeared out of the matted hair. At Matthew's approach he had awakened with a sudden start and looked around him wildly, crossing himself, and keening in a high-pitched voice, "Avaunt you devil. Oh Jesus God in heaven protect me from such."

Matthew did his best to assure the hunched old man that his nocturnal visitor was no more than an innocent guest of the inn come down to see to the well-being of his horses, and in due time the old man appeared more calm and talkative.

"Your horses lie at the other end, sir," croaked the old man who said his name was Oswald. "I have fed and watered them and if my screams have not alarmed them, they stand as safely asleep as they would in their own paddock. The roof does not leak a drop I assure you and I have five doughty cats to keep the mice at bay."

Matthew decided to have a look for himself despite Oswald's assurance, since Oswald's comment about the integrity of the roof in the face of obvious signs of leaks gave him little faith in the old man's judgment. Matthew saw that indeed the horses had been fed and water was available. He patted both of the beasts on their withers, called them good faithful creatures, and returned to Oswald.

"The inn is somewhat remote from its neighbors," Matthew observed, curious about the inn's isolation.

"It is," said Oswald, situating himself in his blanket as though he intended to return to sleep despite Matthew's candle in his face. "Such remoteness was much of its appeal to the innkeeper." Oswald laughed a little at this.

"Indeed," said Matthew.

"Edward Garnett. Do you recognize the name?"

Matthew did not. He knew no Garnetts in Chelmsford or its environs. In his infrequent excursions to London he had met none.

The old man smiled in his beard. "Well God's truth is that few knew his name, but himself, although he was a fine public man, a true servant of Her Majesty, and a merry if not pious fellow in his own right."

"How is it that he can be a public man and few know his name?" Matthew asked hesitantly, not sure he wanted to hear the story that he sensed would be forthcoming. It was late, and he was damp and tired.

"Now I'll tell you a riddle, sir, if you can endure the wait. I think it unlikely you will answer it."

"Say on," Matthew said, more interested now for he enjoyed a good riddle as much as any.

The old man sucked in air and wiped his rheumy eyes as though anticipating the joy of his riddle. "What man of business is he who has most to gain when he's known for sharp practice, deals his customers a heavy blow, and yet receives their forgiveness as well as gold for his purse?"

Matthew thought for a moment and then said, "I think it is not a lawyer whom you speak of, nor a greengrocer. For when they lose customers, their fortune diminishes and when either does wrong to another they receive little thanks."

"Right you are," cackled Oswald. "Right in admitting your being wrong that is, for the riddle's answer is neither lawyer nor greengrocer though both be worthy callings."

"Give me more of this riddle," Matthew said.

"Very well, sir, since I grant it is no easy one, but what follows should put you in the right way of a better answer. What man is he who bears his face at home, hoods it at his work, and kills but takes the sacrament on Sundays?"

Matthew thought for a long minute. "The hangman."

This answer brought another explosion of laughter from Oswald. The old man shook so hard Matthew thought for a moment he was suffering a seizure and could not breathe. But Oswald recovered, nodding his head enthusiastically. "Oh you are right as rain, sir. It's God's very truth, for Edward Garnett is, or was, the hangman. Did you not like the riddle, sir, especially the part about sharp practice? Did you understand that, *sharp practice*, for the hangman's skill is all in severing the organs with great delicacy and exactness."

"My host is a hangman?" Matthew asked incredulously.

Oswald said, "Why, you noticed the sign did you not, the ravens dining on a hanged man's skull? Your host, though of melancholy nature, is not without his humor. He retired from his post, having received the Queen's pension about a year hence, came to this place with a wife, daughter, and handsome young apprentice to his trade he had kept about him in London. He bought the inn from the previous owner who could not make a good living here."

"But Master Garnett could?" Matthew asked, thinking of the dilapidated condition of the house and stable and the poor business, even on such a night as it was.

"Between you and me, sir, he did not need income from the Inn, only a roof above his head for himself, wife, and his daughter, for his pension sufficed, enough to supply his reasonable wants until Death sever body and soul."

"With so little to do," Matthew said. "I'm surprised that you have stayed. How can your employer pay you?"

The old man laughed his creaky laugh and exposed toothless gums. "Oh, he pays me neither silver nor gold. I ask only my board and room, here in this stable. It is warm enough in the winter and straw makes a good bed for an honest man. Besides, sir. I be a native of this shire, born in the town not a dozen leagues since, where my father was a hostler afore me and his father afore him even until Adam, I think."

"And this handsome servant, this apprentice hangman?" Matthew asked. "I saw none about."

"Nor will you," said Oswald. "For he's gone away, gone away these nine months. To sea, says Master Garnett; to London, says his wife. Their daughter laments his loss as does many a young girl of the neighborhood, but knows not whether to credit her father's opinion or her mother's."

Matthew wished the old man goodnight, oppressed by his new knowledge of his host's former occupation and considering whether he should present a true report of the conversation to Joan or let this sleeping dog lie.

He thought to find Joan asleep but she was up and stirring about the chamber, sniffing and making a face of adamant disapproval. Matthew instantly recognized her concern. A subtle but distinctly unpleasant smell was evident in the room. Given his wife's sharp senses, he knew she would experience the sensation more strongly than he.

"We can't sleep here," he agreed, after Joan had explained that she first detected the odor not long after the fire had been laid. The smell had grown worse in the intervening minutes.

"Where were you, husband? You were so long seeing about the horses that I began to worry. The night is black as the devil's heart, the storm dreadful. The whole house shakes at every blast of wind. And then this noisome stench."

"I had some talk with the hostler, a venerable old man with a story to tell about the inn." Matthew said, deciding to come out with it.

"Tell me no stories now," Joan said. "What are we to do about this foul stink? Why, I cannot live with it, much less sleep. Our hostess must find the cause of this annoyance or provide us with a chamber with healthier air."

Matthew said he would wake their host.

Master Garnett and his family had a chamber below them. The wife had told him that when they had arrived, should the Stocks want anything, she had said. Matthew descended there now with his candle and knocked five times on the door, calling out the husband's name and hoping that the wife would answer. Matthew had begun to wonder if he had knocked at the wrong room when he heard voices and footfalls from within. The door opened slightly and the daughter peered forth. She looked startled to see Matthew standing there, although he was at a loss to understand why she should be. Were they not the Three Ravens' only guests?

Matthew apologized for waking her and explained about the smell. Behind the daughter, the mother's face materialized, although the door remained only partly open as though they feared Matthew would invade their room. She too was dressed in nightgown and night cap, clothing that given her pallor made her look even more corpselike than before. The mother said, "There's a smell in your room, sir? Well, now it is an old house and the mildew is the worse when the weather is damp."

"This isn't mildew," Matthew said firmly. "It smells as though something is rotting. Perhaps an animal fell into the chimney and died there. It sometimes happens."

"I can do nothing now. My husband is asleep. Perhaps in the morning."

Matthew grew impatient. "The morning? We shall not live with this stench until then. If you can do nothing now to discern the cause of the annoyance, at least allow us to move to more healthful air."

"Anon, sir," the woman said.

The door closed while Matthew waited. After a few minutes the woman reappeared with a candle and said, "There's another chamber above, sir. But there's no bedding and it's not half as pleasant as the first you occupied."

"All well and good," Matthew said. "We can carry the bedding from the first room to the new."

The woman closed the door behind her. Matthew went to the chamber where Joan was still searching for the source of the odor. He advised her to give over the search. It wasn't after all as if the odor was their business. All they needed was a good night's sleep.

"It does smell as if something died," Joan said stonily. "Decaying flesh, that's what it is—as when our good cat Marcus died in the barn and after many a day we sniffed his body out in the corncrib."

"I suppose," Matthew said, "That such a fate has befallen our hostess' cat—or dog. Or perhaps rats or other vermin have died within the chimney. The hostler told me the room has not been used for many a month."

"Has it not?" Joan said, giving up her probing with a sign of resignation. "And why not? There is no other inn within miles upon this lonely road. And the next town is too small to provide much convenience for travelers."

Joan drew from him the hostler's history of their host as they transported the bedding from their old chamber to a smaller and even danker one down the long corridor. Matthew saw to his dismay that this chamber had no fireplace, yet although it was far from sweet-smelling neither was it redolent of decay as their former accommodation. He decided to lodge no complaint although remembering the cost of the lodgings he full well intended to ask the mistress of the house for a return of part of the cost for the more modest chamber and the inconvenience of moving in the middle of the night.

They undressed, said prayers, and climbed in bed. Matthew, weary from the day, rolled over and was nearly asleep when Joan started from the bed and cried: "Matthew? Are you awake?"

He was now again awake. "What is it?"

"I fell asleep and dreamed."

"You what?" Matthew murmured sleepily.

"I had a dream. Of something dreadful up the chimney. Something that did not belong there."

"Tell our hostess in the morning. It's her chimney, not ours. Let her look to it."

"The hostler's story you told me brought it to my mind."

Matthew sat up in bed and looked at the reclining form of his wife. She didn't move, only spoke in whispers, as though she were afraid of being overheard by someone in the next room or lurking outside their door. But of course there was no one, not at this hour, not in this desolate place.

Her voice came again. "I think it may have been a dead man."

"A what?"

"In my vision I saw a dead man in the chimney."

"You saw that?" Matthew exclaimed.

Joan rolled over. He could see her white face in what little natural light that came in the window. Outside the storm had abated. It was very quiet now. The moon had revealed itself.

"God in Heaven, Joan. This is a fine bedtime matter."

He imagined reporting Joan's finding to Mistress Garnett, imagined the conversation: "Oh, good Mistress Garnett, by the way, my wife has dreamed there is a rotting corpse within your chimney, and therefore the stench whereof we so complained."

"I did not," she said resolutely, sitting up in bed. "I know what I saw in my dream. A hangman as a host! Sweet Jesus, Matthew, I would rather have spent the night in the storm than found refuge in a hangman's house with God knows what ghastly victim of his violence cooking within a chimney like a smoked herring."

To Matthew the image that Joan had conjured up was so disgusting that he knew sleep would never come to him now, and perhaps for many nights after, even in the comfort of his own house and bed. Joan often had dreams and visions. It was her nature. Over the years, he had learned not to scoff.

"If I go look, will you be at peace?"

"And leave me here alone?" she asked with sudden alarm. "I think not, husband."

"Are you not afraid of these bones you saw?"

"I don't fear the dead but the living and now no longer feel safe within the house."

There was no use arguing with her on this point. Matthew got up and slipped his cloak over his nightgown. He lit the candle while Joan dressed similarly. "Walk softly," he said. "We don't want to wake the house. I liked not the look of Master Garnett when we arrived. He regarded me as though he thought I'd steal the silver."

They tiptoed down the corridor, the floor squeaking with each step despite their care and came to the chamber they had occupied before. The fire still burned within the grate, the unpleasing smell was still detectable.

"The stench of hell," Joan muttered over his shoulder. Matthew took the water from the wash basin and doused the remnant of fire until it was quite out.

It was not a fireplace large enough to stand upright but he could crouch there and hold the candle aloft. In such close quarters the smell was stronger but he endured it long enough to hold the candle up into the flue and taking the staff Joan had seen in the corner, thrust it upward once, twice, and yet again, but without results. While he did this Joan stood upon the flat stones by the hearth and suddenly let out a sharp cry of surprise. Matthew withdrew from his crouching position and looked at Joan.

"The stone moved," she said. "See, husband, there's something here. A false door perhaps, a hiding place, a priest's hole."

Matthew examined the smooth stones of the hearth and the wooden panel just above it, found the one that indeed moved, and pushed it down. At the same moment a part of the stone gave way to reveal a cavity in the floor about the size of a large chest.

Husband and wife peered down into the cavity at the same time. From the darkness below came the offensive smell like an exhalation from the mouth of hell.

In his time as constable, Matthew Stock had seen more than one dead man in the deplorable condition of decay: bloated corpses drowned in ditches, victims of highwaymen left to the mercy of ravenous creatures of the woods, even hoary skeletons exhumed to make room for new occupants of their graves—not to mention all the dead from mere age or disease taken from their beds and loaded in the dead cart to be conveyed like cordwood to their common burial in quicklime. But what was stuffed within the priest's hole, the shrunken, half-skeletalized mockery contorted into a position that appalled his imagination and must have alone been enough to kill the miserable wretch so unceremoniously handled shocked him more than any. Not the least of the abominations was that the wretched man's head nestled in the crook of his arm, rudely severed.

"You see I was right," Joan announced triumphantly when they had returned to their other chamber.

"You were right," he said, struggling still to keep his bile down, "although not in the chimney."

"Chimney or priest's hole, it makes little difference. My dream is vindicated. Now, what shall you do?" she asked. "Is this not our host's work, this murder?"

"The body hidden, the head cruelly severed. There were stab wounds in the poor wretch's chest and a deal of dried blood. I make it that his head was removed off after he was dead."

Joan made a noise of disgust and said she didn't stay to look that closely.

"He was a young man, beardless," Matthew went on. "His body so decayed his mother wouldn't know him now."

"How long do you think he lay there? Was he a priest, do you think?"

"Surely not," Matthew said. "It's been a generation since priests were hunted. This body has not lain in the box above a year, by my judgment."

"The hangman's apprentice, do you think?"

"Possibly, but it could have been others, a guest of the inn perhaps, although no local farmer or shepherd. His clothes are too fine for that."

"I shall not sleep in a house of murderers," Joan said firmly.

"We don't know for a fact that the hangman murdered the man." Matthew said, not savoring the prospect of journeying forth into the night, a dead body notwithstanding.

"What's that noise?" Joan asked suddenly.

Matthew listened too. A sound of steps upon the stairs, then the creaking floorboards. Heavy steps. A man's steps.

Matthew snuffed out the candle and held his breath, signaling to Joan to do likewise. The steps drew nearer; there was the grace of a few moments of silence; then the steps retreated.

"Garnett," she whispered. "He'll think us asleep."

Matthew got out of bed and moved quickly to the door, not bothering to wrap himself in anything. He opened the door and looked down the corridor, watching the retreating shadow. It was Garnett, Matthew could discern that much. The lumbering bulk of the man was unmistakable. He continued to watch while Garnett walked into the chamber where the body was concealed and shut the door behind him.

Matthew did not dare wait for Garnett to come out again, but returned to Joan and reported what he had seen.

"He knows we know, Matthew, Oh God," Joan said. "He knows we know. And what shall he do with us when morning comes, for no murder suffers a witness to broadcast his act?"

"He may not know, Joan. That we have been annoyed by foul odor, yes, but not necessarily that we have discovered its source."

"You said he went back into our first chamber."

"We replaced the lid to the hole."

"But we may have disturbed the dust or done some other thing amiss. He'll know what we found, Matthew. Will he not?"

Matthew had no immediate answer to Joan's question. Husband and wife held each other close, neither knowing which of their two hearts beat the faster with dread and confusion. At length, Matthew said. "Come, Joan, let's pray together, then sleep if we can. It's but a few hours until cockcrow. Perhaps if we can fathom this mystery we shall find the means of our salvation."

Matthew rose before Joan and went at once to the stable to ensure that the horses would be ready. The talkative hostler told him all he needed to know. Then he returned to the room and woke Joan.

"I have had another talk with the hostler and I think I have unraveled the matter at hand."

She urged him to tell her at once, for she was dying of fright.

"Calm yourself, Joan. The story is a long and complicated one, and yet to be put to the final proof. Still I think I have the means for us to escape the hangman's wrath. Trust me that by mid morning we'll be on our way home again without harm to either of us. For now, get yourself dressed straightway. I will not have our host grow even more suspicious of us than he now stands."

When shortly thereafter they descended to breakfast they found all the inhabitants of the inn in the common room, where the daughter served her parents, and even the old hostler with his rheumy eyes had been given something to eat in the corner. Mistress Garnett wished them good morrow, said it promised to be a better day than the one before, and asked them if they would eat. Their host, dour as usual, said nothing but occupied himself by munching on cheese and bread, apparently all that was to be served for breakfast in addition to some strong brown ale.

Matthew accepted her invitation, and he and Joan set down at the table.

Mistress Garnett apologized again about the great chamber. "Old houses ever have these musty smells," she said, smiling encouragingly. "I trust the air was fresher in your second room?"

"Oh it was fresh enough," Joan said. She looked nervously at Garnett, who to this point had said nothing nor did he seem to have as much as noticed their presence, but continued to tear at the bread with his teeth.

"I think it was something up the chimney," Matthew said, "for when I stirred it with a stick, the obstacle fell down into the grate."

Upon making this announcement, Matthew studied the faces of each person present but especially that of his host. Garnett had stopped eating. He turned to Matthew with a dark glower of a man who has just been challenged by another to a duel.

"Some creature," Matthew continued before he could be interrupted and directing his remark to Mistress Garnett. "Perhaps, your husband can remove it, bury it properly. Just bones and some veneer of flesh. A dangerous animal I surmise, one who concealed himself within the chimney to do harm to your family and having been caught there, died as he undoubtedly deserved."

Matthew paused, breathed in as though his concluding phrase required effort. "A traitor's death."

Now Matthew looked directly at Garnett. "No one need know it was ever there or why, for my wife and I shall speak nothing of it. Then all will be well and your guests will have the joy of so commodious a chamber."

There was a dull silence in the room now. Both wife and daughter were looking at Garnett, who sat as stony-faced as before, his eyes leaden with some indiscernible emotion. Finally Garnett broke silence.

"A vicious animal, you say?"

"Yes, Master Garnett, indeed it was, vicious indeed. No creature so betrays its nature as to betray him to whom it owes its chief loyalty. Now it has paid for its viciousness."

"And so amen to him and his kind," Garnett said. The former hangman turned to his wife and motioned for her to pass the plate of cheese to the Stocks.

Matthew and Joan ate, but neither with much appetite. All the while there was silence at the table with each of the strange family of Garnetts not looking at the other and not saying a word and the rheumy-eyed hostler in the corner leaning against the wall like a rag doll watching all of this and mumbling something inaudible in his beard.

The hostler had hitched their horses to the wagon, Matthew had settled his account with his host, and having bundled up, the Stocks set out. When the Three Ravens was far in the distance, and the horses moving at a steady pace, Joan said. "What justice is this, Matthew? We have discovered a murder, the murderer, and his accomplices in the crime, and yet no one is to pay for the outrage."

"Ah, payment is always forthcoming in such matters," Matthew said, not taking his eyes from the road. "My whole concern was to get us from there in without harm. Did you see the look I had from Garnett when I talked of my discovery?"

"If looks could kill, I would be a widow," Joan said. "At least until you started speaking of vicious animals and traitors. Pray, what was that all about, husband? Unless my eyes deceived me, that thing in the priest's hole was no animal."

"For reasons I will straightway explain. As for our host, Garnett is no murderer."

Joan regarded her husband with amazement. "No murderer? What say you, husband, no murderer indeed? A rotting corpse in one of his bedchambers with his head severed and you say the hangman is not answerable?"

"This morning I asked the hostler to describe the apprentice, what he was wont to wear. Flesh rots and stinks, but cloth decays at a much slower rate. I have not spent my life as a clothier for naught, but observe such details, as you well know."

Joan agreed that he did. A sharp eye her husband had for cloth.

"I saw the dead man was dressed in good broadcloth and despite the blood stains I could discern the color of his garment and the design of his buttons and the cut of his sleeves. An apprentice is not so well furnished with clothing that a fellow servant wouldn't have recalled a doublet or jerkin he had seen the man wear a dozen times or more."

"So it was the apprentice?"

"Without a doubt."

"And his treason?"

"The hostler said it was nigh onto nine months since the boy disappeared. You saw the condition of Garnett's daughter?"

"As ripe with child as a sweet plum ready to drop."

"And wears no wedding ring nor speaks of a husband."

"The apprentice? Yes, Matthew, but all the more reason for the hangman to chop off his head. Why even a man of more peaceful disposition might have sought to avenge the deflowering of his daughter."

"Granted, but consider the manner of the young man's murder. First he was stabbed and bled to death—"

"Then his head was struck off."

"Not struck, Joan, there's enough of the poor wretch left to discern that. The act was ineptly done, the head severed with some cruder instrument than a broadsword or headsman's ax, which bone and sinew cleanly and squarely cuts when expertly administered. That thing in the priest's hole is not the work of a practiced executioner such as Garnett was. Besides, you well know that beheading is reserved for high born persons, not mere apprentices, even if they are traitors to their masters. Garnett would never have dignified the man by cutting off his head. He would have been satisfied to see him bleed from his former wounds or sever some nether, private part more germane to the man's offense. And Garnett would have removed the body from the house, not deposited it in a priest's hole, for he would have had the strength and cunning. A man of judgment knows that murder is not finished until the body is concealed."

"What are you saying, Matthew?"

"That the murder was apprentice work itself, a crime of bedeviled passion. Accomplished by one with a will but no art."

"Then who? The mother? She hardly looks as though she had the strength to wield a needle, much less kill a man with such hideous savagery. Surely the hostler—"

"Too old and decrepit, with limited access to the house. As for the passion—"

"But that leaves only—"

Matthew nodded.

"Oh, Matthew, I cannot think . . . and she a mother and of such tender years."

"There is precedent for it, Joan. Make me not recount the horrors we have come to know of in our time. But consider this, the hostler reports the apprentice to have been a saucy and lecherous servant. One kind of traitor betrays his master. Another sort betrays his mistress. Say the girl found out about the betrayal. Or say he took her by force. Either way, his seed was planted in her womb, and with it grew her hatred for his treason."

"By which hatred she stabbed him and then severed his head." Joan said.

"She had her father's violent instincts, but not his sense of decorum or his precision instruments. A kitchen knife served her purpose, such a one we observed her use with skill this very morning, although she put it down quick enough when I mentioned the vicious creature we had discovered. She knew about the priest's hole; she put his body there and prayed it would not compete too successfully with the other rank odors of the house. Evidently the heat our fire generated in the chamber stimulated those noxious vapors into renewed vigor."

"But her father and mother must have known."

"I don't know that they did," Matthew said. "At least not until last night when Garnett, suspicious of our complaint, discovered the body as did we and did in truth as you surmised, know that we knew the horrid fact."

"He must have also known who killed his apprentice then?"

"He surely must."

"But how could you be sure he would not kill us to conceal his daughter's crime?"

Matthew sighed. "I didn't know that, Joan. Therein I acted in simple faith, trusting that, though an executioner and a severe and melancholy man, Garnett was no murderer, but chosing my words with great care so to allay his doubts about our secrecy."

"You might have been wrong, Matthew, overestimated his virtue."

"We had little to lose by giving his virtue the benefit of the doubt." Matthew said.

They drove on in silence, the road widened ahead of them, improved in condition. It had not rained so heavily in the region through which they now travelled.

After a while Joan shook her head and said. "Yet I like not private vengeance, husband."

"Nor I," Matthew said. "In the judgment both the executed and his executioner will answer before the bar of God's justice. May God have mercy upon them all."

"And upon us," Joan said, deciding that she had learned as much as she wanted to know that day about priests' holes, headless corpses, and the secret sins of men and maids.

POINTS TO CONSIDER ABOUT
"THE HANGMAN'S APPRENTICE"

1. How does the initial description of the characters help to establish the time period of "The Hangman's Apprentice"? If you had not been provided with the year in the first sentence, what clues throughout the piece would have clearly set the time period in the reader's mind?

2. In his discussion of the way historical fiction writers use language, Tourney says one can write a story in the language of the time, or can elect to

use more modern word choice and syntactic structures. How would you characterize the language in this story's descriptive passages? Do the word choices and sentence structures seem to fit within the era or are they more modern . . . or some of each? Provide examples from the story to support your assertions.

3. In what specific ways is Matthew Stock a man of his historical period? In what other ways might he be a man of any historical period, including ours; which of Matthew Stock's traits are timeless and universal?

4. Here are some non-contemporary-sounding phrases from the dialogue in "The Hangman's Apprentice": "Avaunt you devil"; "I be a native of the shire, born in the town not a dozen leagues since, where my father was a hostler afore me and his father afore him even until Adam, I think"; "this noisome stench"; "no murder suffers a witness to broadcast his act"; "a few hours until cockcrow"; "No creature so betrays its nature as to betray him to whom it owes its chief loyalty." What does each of these phrases mean, and how—based on your reading of his previous introductory material— did Tourney come up with these archaic-sounding phrases? Cite other examples of dialogue that is *not* so distinctively Elizabethan.

5. Describe the tone of "The Hangman's Apprentice." What words/phrases work to create this tone? Does this story's tone remind you of any other writers you have read? If so, which one(s)? Tourney injects humor— sometimes subtle, sometimes purposely blatant—periodically into the story. Cite examples of humor, and explain the ways in which humor contributes to the story's tone.

Every Night for a Thousand Years
Chris Adrian

He dreamed his brother's death at Fredericksburg. General Burnside appeared as an angel at the foot of his bed to announce the tragedy. "The Army regrets to inform you that your brother George Washington Whitman was shot in the head by a lewd fellow from Charleston." The General alit on the bedpost and drew his dark wings close about him, as if to console himself. Moonlight limned his strange whiskers and his hair. His voice shook as he went on. "Such a beautiful boy. I held him in my arms while his life bled out. See? His blood made this spot." He pointed at his breast, where a dark stain in the shape of a bird lay on the blue wool. "I am so very sorry," he said, choking and weeping. Tears fell in streams from his eyes, ran over the bed and out the window, where they joined the Rappahannock, which had somehow come north to flow through Brooklyn, bearing the bodies of all the battle's dead.

In the morning he read the wounded list in the *Herald*. There it was: "First Lieutenant G. W. Whitmore." He knew from George's letters that there was nobody named Whitmore in the company. He went to his mother's house. "I'll go find him," he told and his sister and his brothers.

So he went. Washington, he quickly discovered, was a city of hospitals. He looked in half of them before a cadaverous-looking clerk told him he'd be better off looking at Falmouth, where most of the Fredericksburg wounded still lay in field hospitals. In Falmouth he wandered outside the hospital tents, afraid to go in and find his mangled brother. He stood before a pile of amputated limbs, arms and legs of varying lengths, all black and blue and rotten in the chill. A thin layer of snow covered some of them. He circled the heap thinking he must recognize his brother's hand if he saw it. He closed his eyes and considered the amputation: his brother screaming when he woke from the chloroform, his brother's future contracting to something bitter and small.

But George had only got a hole in his cheek. A piece of shell pierced his wispy beard and scraped a tooth. He spit blood and hot metal into his hand, put the shrapnel in his pocket, and later showed it to his worried brother, who burst into tears and clutched him in a bear hug when they were reunited in Captain Francis's tent, where George sat with his feet propped on a trunk and a cigar stuck in his bandaged face.

"You shouldn't fret," said George. But he could not help fretting, even now that he knew his brother was alive and well. A great fretting buzz had started up in his head, inspired by the pile of limbs and the smell of blood in the air and ruined Fredericksburg across the river, all broken chimneys and crumbling walls. He stayed in George's tent and, watching him sleep, felt a deep satisfaction. He wandered around the camp, sat by fires with sentries who told him hideous stories about the death of friends.

Ten days later he still couldn't leave Falmouth. Even after his brother moved out with the healthy troops on Christmas Day, he stayed and made himself useful, changing dressings, fetching for the nurses, and just sitting with the wounded boys, with the same satisfaction on him as when he watched George sleep. In Brooklyn a deep and sinister melancholy had settled over him. For the past six months he had wandered the streets, feeling as if all his vital capacities were sputtering, about to die. In the hospital that melancholy was gone, scared off, perhaps by all the misery, and replaced by something infinitely more serious and real.

He finally went back to Washington in charge of a transport. With every jolt and shake of the train a chorus of horrible groans wafted through the cars. He thought it would drive him insane. What saved him was the singing of a boy with a leg wound. The whole trip he sang in a rough voice indicative of tone-deafness. His name was Henry Smith. He'd come all the way from divided Missouri, and said he had a gaggle of cousins fighting under General Beauregard. He sang "Oh! Susanna" over and over again, and no one told him to be quiet.

All the worst cases went to Union Square Hospital, because it was closest to the train station. He went with them, and kept up the service he'd begun at Falmouth—visiting, talking, reading, fetching and helping. Months passed.

He went to other hospitals. There were certainly enough of them to keep him busy—Finley, Campbell, Carver, Harewood, Mount Pleasant, Judiciary Square. And then there were the churches and public buildings, also stuffed with wounded. Even the Patent Office held them: boys on cots set up on the marble floor of the model room. He brought horehound candy to an eighteen-year-old from Iowa, who lay with a missing arm and a sore throat in front of a glass case that held Ben Franklin's printing press. Two boys from Brooklyn had beds in front of General Washington's camp equipment. He read to them from a copy of the *Eagle* his mother sent down, every now and then looking up at the General's tents rolled neatly around their posts, his folded chairs and mess kit, sword and cane, washstand, his surveyor's compass, and, a few feet down, in a special case all to itself, the Declaration of Independence. Other boys lay in front of pieces of the Atlantic Cable, ingenious toys, rattraps, the razor of Captain Cook.

He could not visit every place all in a day, though he tried at first. Eventually he picked a few and stuck with those. But mostly he was at Union Square, where Hank Smith was.

"I had my daddy's pistol with me," said Hank Smith. "That's why I got my leg still." I wasn't the first time he'd been told how Hank had saved his own leg from the "chopping butchers" in the field hospital. But he didn't mind hearing the story again. It was spring. The leg was still bad, though not as bad as it had been. At least that was the impression that Hank gave. He never complained about his leg. He'd come down with typhoid, too, a gift from the hospital. "I want my pistol back."

"I'll see what I can do." Walt always said that, but they both knew no one was going to give Hank back the pistol with which he threatened to blow out the brains of the surgeon who had tried to take his leg. They had left him alone then, and later another doctor said there wasn't any need to amputate. They would watch the wound. "Meanwhile, have an orange." Walt pulled the fruit out of his coat pocket and peeled it. Soldiers' heads began to turn in their beds as the smell washed over the ward. Some asked if he had any for them.

"Course he does," said Hank. In fact, he had a coatful of them. He had bought them at Center Market, then walked through the misty, wet morning, over the brackish canal and across the filthy Mall. The lowing of cattle drifted toward him from the unfinished monument as he walked along, wanting an orange but afraid to eat one lest he be short when he got to the hospital. He had money for oranges, sweets, books, tobacco from sponsors in Brooklyn and New York and elsewhere. And he had a little money for himself from a job, three hours a day as a copyist in the Paymaster's office. From his desk he had a spectacular view of Georgetown and the river, and the three stones that were said to mark the watery graves of three Indian sisters. They had cursed the spot: anyone who tried to cross there must drown. He would sit and stare at the rocks, imagining himself shedding his shirt and shoes by the riverside, trying to swim across. He imagined drowning, the great weight of water pressing down on him. Inevitably his reverie was broken by the clump-clump of one-legged soldiers on their crutches, coming up the stairs to the office, located perversely on the top floor of the building.

Union Square was under the command of a brilliant drunk named Canning Woodhull. Over whiskey he explained his radical policies, which included washing hands and instruments, throwing out sponges, swabbing everything in sight with bitter-smelling Labarraque's solution, and an absolute lack of faith in laudable pus.

"Nothing laudable about it," he said. "White or green, pus is pus, and either way it's bad for the boys. There are creatures in the wounds—elements of evil. They are the emissaries of Hell, sent earthward to increase our suffering, to increase death and increase grief. You can't see them except by their actions." They knocked glasses and drank, and Walt made a face because the whiskey was medicinal, laced with quinine. It did not seem to bother Woodhull.

"I have the information from my wife, who has great and secret knowledge," Woodhull said. "She talks to spirits. Most of what she hears is garbage, of course. But this is true." Maybe it was. His hospital got the worst cases and kept them alive better than any other hospital in the city, even ones that got casualties only half as severe. Woodhull stayed in charge despite a reputation as a wastrel and a drunk and an off-and-on lunatic. Once, he was removed by a coalition of his colleagues, only to be reinstated by Dr. Letterman, the medical director of the Army of the Potomac, who had been personally impressed by many visits to Union Square. "General

Grant is a drunk, too," he would say in response to a charge against Dr. Woodhull.

"They are vulnerable to prayer and bromine, and whiskey and Labarraque's. Lucky for us." He downed another glass. "You know, some of the nurses are complaining. Just last Tuesday I was in Ward E with the redoubtable Mrs. Hawley. We saw you come in at the end of the aisle and she said, 'Here comes that odious Walt Whitman to talk evil and unbelief to my boys. I think I would rather see the Evil One himself—at least if he had horns and hoofs—in my ward. I shall get him out as soon as possible!' And she rushed off to do just that. She failed, of course." He poured again.

"Shall I stop coming, then?"

"Heavens, no. As long as old Horse-Face Hawley is complaining, I'll know you're doing good. God keep some dried-up old shrew from driving you away."

Two surgeons came into Woodhull's makeshift office, a corner of Ward F sectioned off by three regimental flags.

"*Assistant* Surgeon Walker is determined to kill Captain Carter," said Dr. Bliss, a dour black-eyed man from Baltimore. "She has given him opium for his diarrhea and, very foolishly, in my opinion, withheld ipecac and calomel." Dr. Mary Walker stood next to him, looking calm, her arms folded across her chest. She held the same rank as George did. Their uniforms had the same gold stripes, the same gold braid on the hat.

"Dr. Walker is doing as I have asked her," said Woodhull. "Ipecac and calomel are to be withheld in all cases of flux and diarrhea."

"For God's sake, why?" asked Dr. Bliss, his face reddening. He was new in Union Square. Earlier the same day, Woodhull had castigated him for not cleaning a suppurating chest wound.

"Because it is for the best," said Woodhull. "Because if you do it that way, a boy will not die. Because if you do it that way some mother's heart will not be broken."

Dr. Bliss turned redder, then paled, as if his rage had broken and ebbed. He scowled at Dr. Walker, turned sharply on his heel, and left. Dr. Walker sat down.

"Buffoon," she said. Woodhull poured whiskey for her. It was an open secret in the hospital that they were lovers.

"Dr. Walker," said Woodhull, "why don't you tell Mr. Whitman about your recent arrest?" She sipped her whiskey and told how she'd been arrested outside her boarding house for masquerading as a man. Walt only half listened to her talk. He was thinking about diarrhea. It was just about the worst thing, he had decided. He'd seen it kill more boys than all the miniés and shrapnel, and typhoid and pneumonia—than all the other afflictions combined. He'd written to his mother. "I think we ought to stop this war, however we can. Just stop it. War is nine hundred and ninety-nine parts diarrhea to one part glory. Those who like wars ought to be made to fight in them."

"I did my best to resist them," said Dr. Walker. "I shouted out, 'Congress has bestowed on me the right to wear trousers!' It was to no avail." She was silent for a moment, and then all three of them burst out laughing.

In the summer he saw the President almost every day, because he lived on the route the President took to and from his summer residence north of the city. Walking down the street, soon after leaving his rooms in the morning, he'd hear the approach of the party. Always he stopped and waited for them to pass. Mr. Lincoln, dressed in plain black, rode a gray horse, surrounded by twenty-five or thirty cavalry with their sabres drawn and held up over their shoulders. The got so they would exchange bows, he and the President, he tipping his broad, floppy felt hat, Lincoln tipping his high stiff black one and bending a little in the saddle. And every time they did this the same thought bloomed large in Walt's mind: A sad man.

With the coming of the hot weather Dr. Woodhull redoubled his efforts to eradicate the noxious effluvia. They threw open the windows and burned eucalyptus leaves in small bronze censers set in the four corners of each ward. The eucalyptus, combined with the omnipresent reek of Labarraque's solution, gave some of the boys aching heads, Dr. Woodhull prescribed whiskey.

"I want a bird," Hank Smith said one day late in July. The weather was hot and dry, Hank had been fighting a bad fever for a week. Walt helped him change out of his soaked shirt, then wiped him down with a cool wet towel. The wet shirt he took to the window, where he wrung out the sweat, watching it fall and dapple the dirt. He lay the shirt to dry on the sill, and considered his wet, salty hands. In the distance he could see the Capitol, gleaming magnificently in the late-afternoon sun.

"I want a bird," Hank said again. "When I was small, my sister got me a bird. I named it for her—Olivia. Would you help me get one?" Walt left the window and sat on a stool by the bed. The sun lit up the hair on Hank's chest, and made Walt think of shining fields of wheat.

"I could get you a bird," he said. "I don't know where, but I will get you a bird."

"I know where," said Hank, as Walt helped him into a new shirt. With a jerk of his head he indicated the window. "There's plenty of birds out in the yard. You just get a rock and some string. Then we'll get a bird."

He came back the next day with rock and string, and they set a trap of bread crumbs on the windowsill. Walt crouched beneath the window and grabbed at whatever came for the crumbs. He missed two jays and a blackbird, but caught a beautiful cardinal by its leg. It chirped frantically and pecked at his hand; the fluttering of its wings against his wrists made him think of the odd buzz that still thrilled his soul when he was in the wards.

He brought the bird to Hank, who tied the string to its leg, and the rock to the string, then set the rock down by his bed. The cardinal tried to fly for the window, but only stuck in midair, its desperate wings striking up a small breeze that Walt, kneeling near it, could feel against his face. Hank clapped and laughed.

They called the bird Olivia. She became the ward's pet. Other boys would insist on having her near their beds. It did not take her long to become domesticated. Soon she was eating from Hank's hand and sleeping at night beneath his cot. They kept her secret from the nurses and doctors, until one morning Hank was careless. He fell asleep having left her out in the middle of the aisle while Woodhull was making his rounds. Walt had just walked into the ward, his arms full of candy and fruit and novels.

"Who let this dirty bird into my hospital?" Woodhull asked. He very swiftly bent down and picked up the stone, then tossed it out the window. Olivia trailed helplessly behind it. Walt dropped his packages and rushed outside, where he found the bird in the dirt, struggling with a broken wing. He put her in his shirt and took her back to his room, where she died three days later, murdered by his landlady's cat. He told Hank she flew away. "A person can't have anything," Hank said, and stayed angry about it for a week.

At Christmas, Mrs. Hawley and her cronies trimmed the wards; evergreen wreaths were hung on every pillar and garlands strung across the hall. At the foot of every bed hung a tiny stocking, hand-knitted by Washington society ladies. Walt went around stuffing them with walnuts and lemons and licorice. Hank's leg got better and worse, better and worse. Walt cornered Dr. Woodhull and said he had a bad feeling about Hank's health. Woodhull insisted he was going to be fine; Walt's fretting was pointless.

Hank's fevers waxed and waned, too. Once Walt came in from a blustery snowstorm, his beard full of snow. Hank insisted on pressing his face into it, saying it made him feel so much better than any medicine had, except maybe paregoric, which he found delicious, and said made him feel like he was flying in his bed.

Walt read to him from the New Testament, the bit about there being no room at the inn.

"Are you a religious man?" Hank asked him.

"Probably not, my dear, in the way that you mean." Though he did make a point of dropping by the Union Square chapel whenever he was there. It was a little building, with a quaint onion-shaped steeple. He would sit in the back and listen to the services for boys whom he'd been visiting almost every day. He wrote their names down in a small leatherbound notebook that he kept in one of his pockets. By Christmas he had pages and pages of them. Sometimes at night he would sit in his room and read the names softly aloud by the light of a single candle.

Dr. Walker came by and asked to borrow his Bible. She said she had news from the War Department.

"What's the news?" he asked her.

"Nothing good," she said. "It is dark, dark everywhere." She wanted to read some Job, to cheer herself.

Sometimes when he could not sleep, which was often, he would walk around the city, past the serene mansions on Lafayette Square, past the President's house, where he would pause and wonder if a light in the window meant Mr. Lincoln was awake and agonizing. Once he saw a figure in a long, trailing black crêpe veil move, lamp in hand, past a series of windows, and he imagined it must be Mrs. Lincoln, searching forlornly for her little boy, who had died two winters ago. He walked past the empty market stalls, along the ever stinking canal. He would pause by it, looking down into the dirty water, and see all manner of things float by. Boots and bonnets, half-eaten vegetables, animals. Once there was a dead cat drifting on a little floe of ice.

Walking on, he would pass into Murder Bay, where the whores hooted at him, but he was otherwise left alone. From a distance he was large and imposing, not an easy target, and up close he looked so innocent and sweet that even the most heartless criminal would not raise a hand against him. He would peek into alleys that housed whole families of "contraband." Sometimes a dirty child would rush out of a dank shanty and ask him a riddle. He got to keeping candy in his pockets for the children. He would cut back along the canal, then across, sometimes watching the moon shine on the towers of the Smithsonian castle, and on the white roofs of Union Square. He would walk among the shrubs and trees of the Mall, sometimes getting lost on a footpath that went nowhere, but eventually he would cross the canal again and walk up to the Capitol. The great statue of General Washington was there, the one that everyone ridiculed because he was dressed in a toga. It was said that his sword was raised in a threat to do harm to the country if his clothes were not returned.

He liked the statue. He would crawl up into its lap and sprawl out, Pietà-like, or else put his arms around the thick marble neck and have a good wrenching cry. At dawn he would stand outside the Capitol, writing his name in the snow with his foot, and he could smell the bread baking in the basement. He had a friend in the bakery, who loaded him down with countless hot loaves. He'd walk back to Union Square, warmed by the bread in his coat, and sometimes he'd have enough so that every full-diet boy in a ward would wake with a still-warm loaf on his chest.

"They want to take my leg," Hank told him. It was early May, and still cold. "I ain't going to let them. You've got to get me a gun."

"Hush," said Walt. "They won't take your leg." Though in fact it looked as if they would have to. Just when he had seemed on the verge of good health, just when he had beaten off the typhoid, the leg flared up again and deteriorated rapidly. Dr. Woodhull cleaned the wound, prayed over it, swabbed it with whiskey, all to no avail. A hideous, stinking infection had taken root and was growing.

He went looking for Dr. Woodhull, to discuss Hank's case. He did not find him in his office. There was a pall of silence and gloom over all the wards. News of the horrible casualties accrued by General Grant in his Wilderness campaign had reached the hospital. Dr. Bliss and Mrs. Hawley were having a loud discussion as she changed dressings. "Trust a drunk not to give a fig for our boys' lives," said Dr. Bliss. "This was is an enterprise dominated by inebriates, charlatans, and fools." He gave Walt a mean look. Walt asked if either of them had seen Woodhull. Neither of them replied, but the young man whose dressings were being changed told him he had gone out to the deadhouse.

Walt found him there, among the bodies. There were only a few, just the dead from the past few days. He was weeping over a shrouded form. Dr. Walker stood beside him, her hand on his shoulder.

"Canning," she said. "You've got to come back now. We've got boys coming from Spotsylvania."

"Oh, darling," said Woodhull. "I just can't stand it." He was leaning over the shrouded body, dropping tears onto the face. As the fabric became wet Walt could make out the boy's features. He had a thin mustache, and a mole on his cheek. "There's such an awful lot of blood. You'd think they could do something with all that blood. A great work. Oughtn't something great to be coming?"

Dr. Walker noticed him standing by the door. "Mr. Whitman," she said. "If you would assist me?" He put his arm around Dr. Woodhull and bore him up, away from the body and out of the deadhouse. They put him on an empty cot, in a half-empty ward.

"Oh, darling," said Woodhull. "I don't even want to think about it." He turned over on his side and began to breathe deeply and evenly. The odor of urine began to rise from him.

Dr. Walker took a watch from her pocket and looked at it. "We got a wire," she said. "They're moving a thousand boys from the field hospitals." Then she leaned down close to Woodhull's snoring face and said, "You had better be well and awake in five hours, sir."

"I will do whatever I can," said Whitman.

"I am glad to hear it." She adjusted her hat on her head and uttered an explosive sigh. "General Stuart has died," she said. "Did you know that? Shot by a lowly infantryman. I had a dream once that he came for me on his horse, with garish feathers in his hat. 'Come along with me, Mary,' he said. 'We'll ride away from it all.' 'Not by your red beard, General Satan,' said I.

'Get thee behind me.' Do you suppose I did the right thing? Would you have gone with him?"

Walt thought about it: He pictured himself riding west with General Stuart to a place where the war could not touch them. He imagined the tickly feeling General Stuart's feathers would make in his nose as they rode to the extreme end of the continent. And he thought of the two of them riding shirtless through sunny California and of reaching out their hands to pick fat grapes.

"I've got to get out," said Hank. A week had passed, and Union Square was stuffed to the gills with new patients. Hank's leg was scheduled to come off in two days. In the deadhouse there was a pile of limbs as high as Walt's head.

"Settle down," said Walt. "There's no cause for alarm."

"I won't let them have it. You've got to help me get out. I won't make it if they take my leg. I know I won't." He had a raging fever and had been acting a little delirious.

"Dr. Walker is said to wield the fastest knife in the Army. You'll be asleep. You won't feel it."

"Ha!" said Hank. He gave Walt a long, wild look. "Ha!" He put his face in his pillow and wouldn't talk anymore. Walt walked around the wards, meeting the new boys. He went to the chapel. The limbs piled higher in the deadhouse, many of them joined there soon by their former proprietors.

That night, unable to sleep, he made his usual tour of the city, stopping for a long time outside Union Square. He found himself outside Hank's window, and then inside, next to his bed. Hank was sleeping, his arm thrown up above his head, his sheet thrown off and his shirt riding up his belly. Walt reached out and touched his shoulder.

"All right," Walt said. "Let's go." It was not a difficult escape. The hardest part was getting Hank's pants on. It was very painful for him to bend his knee, and he was feverish, disoriented. They saw no one on their way out; the night attendants were in another ward. They stole a crutch for Hank. He fell on the Mall, and the crutch broke under him. He wept softly with his mouth in grass. Walt picked him up and carried him on his back, toward the canal and over it, then into Murder Bay. Hank cried to be put down. They rested on a trash heap teeming with small crawly things that were unidentifiable in the dark.

"I think I want to sleep," said Hank. "I'm so tired."

"Go ahead, my dear," said Walt. "I shall take care of you."

"I would like to go home." He put his head against Walt's shoulder. "Take me back to Hollow Vale. I want to see my sister." He slowly fell asleep, still mumbling under his breath. They sat there for a little while. Some people passed them but did not disturb them. If this heap were a horse, thought Walt, we could ride to California. "Never mind General Stuart," he said aloud, taking Hank's wet hand in his own. "In California there is no sickness. Neither is there death. On their fifth birthday, every child is made a gift of a pony." He looked at Hank's drawn face glowing eerily in the moonlight and said, "In California if you plant a dead boy under an oak tree, in just one day's time a living hand will emerge from the soil. If you grasp that hand and pull with the heart of a true friend a living body will come out of the earth. Thus in California death never separates true friends." He looked for a while longer into Hank's face. His eyes were darting wildly under the lids. Walt said, "Well, if we are to get there soon we had best be going now." But when he picked him up he brought him back to the hospital.

"You will wash that beard before you come into my surgery," said Dr. Woodhull. Walt stank of garbage. He went to a basin, and Dr. Walker helped him scrub his beard with creosote, potassium permanganate, and Labarraque's solution. Walt held a sponge soaked with chloroform under Hank's nose, even though he hadn't woken since falling asleep on the heap. He kept his hand on Hank's head the whole time, though he could not watch as Dr. Walker cut in and Dr. Woodhull tied up the arteries. He looked down and saw blood seeping across the floor, into mounds of sawdust. Looking up, he fixed his attention on a lithograph on the far wall. It had been torn from some book of antiquities, a depiction of reclining sick under the care of the priests of Ascelpius, whose statue dominated the temple. There was a snake-entwined staff in his hand, and a big friendly-looking stone dog at his feet. A large caption beneath the picture read, "Every night for a thousand years the sick sought refuge and dreams in the Temple of Asclepius." He closed his eyes and heard the saw squeak against Hank's bones.

Hank woke briefly before he died. "They got my leg," he said. "You let them take it."

"No," said Walt. "I've got it right here." In fact, he did. It lay in his lap, bundled in two clean white sheets. It could have been anything. He would not let them take to the deadhouse. He put it in the bed. Hank hugged it tight against his chest.

"I don't want to die," he said.

He packed his bag and sat on it, waiting at the station for the train that would take him back to Brooklyn. The train came and went; he stayed sitting on his bag. Then he got up and went back to Union Square. It was night. Hank's bed was still empty. He sat down on it and rummaged for a pen and paper. When he had them, he wrote in the dark:

Dear Friends,

I thought it would be soothing to you to have a few lines about the last days of your son, Henry Smith—I write in haste, but I have no doubt anything about Hank will be welcome.

From the time he came—there was hardly a day but I was with him a portion of the time—if not in the day then at night—(I am merely a friend visiting the wounded and sick soldiers). From almost the first I felt somehow that Hank was in danger, or at least was much worse than they supposed in the hospital. As he made no complaint they thought him nothing so bad. I told the doctor of the ward over and over again he was a very sick boy, but he took it lightly and said he would certainly recover; he said, "I know more about these fever cases than you do—he looks very sick to you, but I shall bring him out all right—" Probably the doctor did his best—at any rate about a week before Hank died he got really alarmed, and after that he and all the other doctors tried to help him but it was too late. Very possibly it would not have made any difference.

I used to sit by the side of his bed generally silent, he was opprest for breath and with the heat, and I would fan him—occasionally he would want a drink—somedays he dozed a great deal—sometimes when I would come in he woke up and I would lean down and kiss him, he would reach out his hand and pat my hair and beard as I sat on the bed and leaned over him—it was painful to see the working in his throat to breathe.

Some nights I sat by his cot far into the night, the lights would be put out and I sat there silently hour after hour—he seemed to like to have me sit there—I shall never forget those nights in the dark hospital, it was a curious and solemn scene, the sick and the wounded lying around and this dear young man close by me, lying on what proved to be his death-bed. I did not know his past life, but what I saw and know of he behaved like a noble boy—Farewell, deary boy, it was my opportunity to be with you in your last days. I had no chance to do much for you; nothing could be done—only you did not lie there among strangers without having one near who loved you dearly, and to whom you gave your dying kiss.

Mr. and Mrs. Smith, I have thus written rapidly whatever came up about Hank, and must now close. Though we are strangers and shall probably never see each other, I send you all Hank's brothers and sisters my love. I live when at home in Brooklyn, New York, in Portland Avenue, fourth floor, north of Myrtle.

He folded up the letter and put it in his shirt, then lay down on his side on the bed. In a while a nurse came by with fresh sheets. She thought she might scold him and tell him to leave, but when she looked in his face she turned and hurried off. He watched the moon come up in the window, listening to the wounded and sick stirring in the beds around him. It seemed to him, as he watched the moon shine down on the dome of the Capitol, that the war would never end. He thought, In the morning I will rise and leave this place. And then he thought, I will never leave this place.

He slept briefly and had a dream of reaching into Hank Smith's dark grave, hoping and fearing that somebody would take his groping hand. He woke with the moon still shining in his face. Somewhere down the ward a boy began to weep.

POINTS TO CONSIDER ABOUT "EVERY-NIGHT FOR A THOUSAND YEARS"

1. How does Adrian use the physical setting of "Every Night for a Thousand Years" to set the story's time period? What details of setting and/or characterization help establish the time period for this piece of historical fiction?

2. How does the passage of dialogue—"There are creatures in the wounds—elements of evil. They are the emissaries of Hell, sent earthward to increase our suffering, to increase death and increase grief."— help situate "Every Night for a Thousand Years" in its historical context? How does it simultaneously help develop the story's intended theme(s)?

3. What is the significance of the brief glimpses of President Lincoln within the story? Do these scenes add more credibility to "Every Night for a Thousand Years", or does the mention of President Lincoln act merely as a "window dressing" as Tourney mentions in his introductory remarks to this chapter? Explain.

4. There is, within "Every Night for a Thousand Years", a relatively long story-within-the-story about a bird named Olivia. What happens in the Olivia anecdote? Is this story merely a diversion—at first whimsical, then quasi-tragic—or does it have some significance relative to character development and/or theme?

5. What is the symbolic significance of the description of Walt and the statue of George Washington: "He would crawl up into its lap and sprawl out, Pietà-like, or else put his arms around the thick marble neck and have a good wrenching cry."? What does the phrase "Pietà-like" mean? How does this image relate to the story's intended thematic message(s)? Is the notion of a man having a "good wrenching cry" distinctly modern (and therefore anachronistic, a no-no in historical fiction), or is it consistent with values of the Civil War period as well?

✖ WRITING ACTIVITIES: HISTORICAL FICTION

1. Have a conversation with someone older than yourself, if you can find somebody older than yourself. In your conversation, ask that individual about "hot" social issues that confronted young people during a previous decade. Explore the topic with your older interviewee, having him

or her recount a brief narrative that illustrates this social issue. Next, turn this anecdote into a short story, which you write in the first person, present tense. For example, one of my students recently wrote a piece of historical fiction set in the 1960s, based on a conversation with her aunt, who said that many people during that time believed that sex and drugs were a means to liberate the soul. The aunt related a story about her first experience with LSD, which my student (who has never used LSD and never intends to) turned into an engaging tale: sometimes amusing, sometimes harrowing, and always fleshed out with details of that distant historical period, such as bell-bottom pants, guys with long hair and big moustaches, Volkswagen bugs, slang phrases such as "groovy" and "far-out," and so on.

2. Write a scene in which a period character first views an object, machine or other piece of "technology" (e.g., first view of a steam engine, sky-scraper, horse and rider, submarine). Consider how the character's lack of experience or cultural background would influence his perception, and thus your description, of the object.

3. Do a fifteen-minute freewrite about a major event in history. Instead of describing the event as an encyclopedia might do, try to be more evocatively descriptive, personal, engaged. Who is there? What are they wearing? What is the scenery like? What season of the year is it? What smells/sounds are incorporated in the scene? After doing the freewrite, go to the library and/or search the World Wide Web to find out specific supplementary information about the period and event in question. Do another freewrite, this time focusing on a central character—or maybe two characters—who live at this time and are affected by the historical events surrounding them. Based on that freewrite, create a short story that is set in the historical period in question, and which prominently features the character you envisioned in the second freewrite.

4. Write a dialogue between two contemporary characters discussing a current issue or event. Then write a dialogue turning the characters into persons from an earlier time period, using as their subject a parallel topic. How might the change in chronological setting alter the tone and style of the dialogue, as well as its content?

5. Write a story about a historical conflict with which you are relatively familiar: World War II, the Vietnam conflict, Gulf Storm, Mafia turf wars . . . or even (more recently but still in the past) a local gang conflict. Imagine that your story's plot involves two rivals in love who enlist in the same military unit (or wear the same gang colors or belong to the same Mafia family). They extend their rivalry into the conflict situation, becoming friends at last, but only after one deserts and is brought back forcibly by the other (Does this sound familiar? If not, re-read "The plot's the thing . . . " section of Leonard Tourney's introduction to this chap-

ter.). The heroic one dies in his efforts, thus allowing the other to marry the object of their rivalry, and presumably live happily ever after. Supplement your knowledge of this historical situation with some research, using at least one book, one newspaper or magazine article, and several World Wide Websites.

13

Science Fiction

One of the world's most celebrated contemporary authors, Harlan Ellison has written or edited seventy-four books, and approximately seventeen hundred short stories, scripts, essays, and reviews. His work has been translated into thirty-seven languages, and his television credits include scripts for episodes of "The Outer Limits," "The Alfred Hitchcock Hour," "Star Trek," and "The Twilight Zone," (1985 CBS revival). He has won more World Science Fiction Convention Hugo Awards than any other living author (8½). Ellison is also the recipient of three Nebula Awards (Science Fiction Writers of America), five Bram Stoker Awards (Horror Writers of America)—including a Lifetime Achievement Award—two Edgar Allan Poe Awards (Mystery Writers of America) and four Writers Guild of America Awards for Most Outstanding Teleplay. Additionally, he is a two-time winner of the World Fantasy Award, the British Fantasy Award and the Silver Pen of P.E.N. for journalism. In 1993, Ellison was awarded the rare and coveted World Fantasy Lifetime Achievement Award and was included in **The Best American Short Stories.**

John M. Landsberg's science fiction career began in earnest when he created, edited, and published *UNEARTH, The Magazine of Science Fiction Discoveries.* Landsberg (with co-editor Jonathan Ostrowsky) used the magazine to discover and publish the first stories of numerous new writers who have since become shining lights in the field, including William Gibson, S. P. Somtow, James P. Blaylock, Richard Bowker, and others. While editing *UNEARTH,* he also published work by legendary author Harlan Ellison.

Landsberg's fiction has appeared in the premier magazines and anthologies in the science fiction field, including *The Magazine of Fantasy and Science Fiction*, and both the *Universe* and the *Full Spectrum* series of anthologies. Landsberg is a member of the Science Fiction and Fantasy Writers of America and has been a professional guest panelist at various science fiction conventions. Most recently, Landsberg has been working on a short science fiction film, *These Few Weapons Against Death*, which he wrote and directed, and which stars Emmy-winning actress Barbara Babcock.

In this chapter of *The Graceful Lie,* Ellison and Landsberg collaborate to discuss the central concerns of the science fiction genre. Ellison examines three crucial topic areas—titles, characters, and narrative openings—while Landsberg "moderates" the chapter, introducing/discussing Ellison's points and then presenting additional information relevant to the creation of successful science fiction stories. The chapter begins, appropriately enough, with Ellison's insightful discussion of an issue too often overlooked by instructors and workshop directors: the story's title.

"First, There Was the Title"
Harlan Ellison

Like most comfortable, familiar old-shoe clichés, there is an important and irrefutable kernel of truth in this one: people, schmucks though they may be for doing it, *do* judge a book by its cover. Even I do it once in a while. I bought a recent Bantam paperback, APELAND, because of the cover. There was a mystery novel I spent seven dollars to purchase, in hardcover, because of the cleverness of the cover art. It was called DEAD PIANO. It wasn't that good a novel, but what did the author or the publisher care by that time . . . they had me. Not to mention my seven dollars.

And after judging by the cover, readers judge by the title. Many times they read the back spine of the book, or the title on a table of contents if it's a shorter story in question, so it's judged *before* the cover. What you *call* a story is important.

I'll try to tell you why. And how to do it well.

Here's a sample group of titles. I've made them up on the moment. Say they're arrayed on a contents page, each bylined with a name you don't know, so you have no preference based on familiarity with an author's previous work. Which one do you read first?

THE BOX
HEAT LIGHTNING
PAY AS YOU GO
HEAR THE WHISPER OF THE WORLD
THE JOURNEY
DEAD BY MORNING
EVERY DAY IS DOOMSDAY
DOING IT

Now, unless you're more peculiar than the people on whom I tried that list, you picked "Hear the Whisper of the World" first, you probably picked "Doing It" next, and "Dead By Morning" third. Unless you've led a *very* dull life, you picked "The Box" next to last, and would read everything else before selecting "The Journey." If you picked "The Journey" first, go get a bricklayer's ticket, because you'll never be a writer. "The Journey" is the dullest title I could think of, and believe me I *worked* at it.

It wasn't the length or complexity of "Hear the Whisper of the World" that made it most intriguing. I'll agree it may not even be the most exhilarating title ever devised, but it has some of the elements that *make* a title intriguing, that suggest a quality that will engender trust in the author. He or she knows how to use words. S/he has a thought there, an implied theme, a point to which the sub-text of the story will speak. All this, on a very subliminal level as far as a potential reader is concerned. And (how many times, to the brink of exhaustion, must we repeat *this!?*) trust is the first, the best thing you can instill in a reader. If readers trust you, they will go with you in terms of the willing suspension of disbelief that is necessary in *any* kind of fiction, but is absolutely mandatory for fantasy or science fiction.

The second thing it possesses is a quality of maintaining a tension between not telling too little and not telling too much. Remember how many times you were pissed off when a magazine editor changed a title so the punchline was revealed too early: you were reading along, being nicely led from plot-point to plot-point, having the complexity of the story unsnarl itself logically, and you were trying to outguess the writer, and then, too soon, you got to a place where you remembered the title and thought, *oh shit, so that's what it means!* And the rest of the story was predictable. The title stole a joy from you.

So a title should titillate, inveigle you, tease and bemuse you . . . but not confuse you or spill the beans. Titles in the vein of "The Journey" neither excite nor inform. "Hear the Whisper of the World," I hope and pray (otherwise it's a dumb example), fulfills the criteria.

The BLANK of BLANK titles are the kinds of titles away from which to stay, as Churchill might have syntactically put it. You know the kind I mean: **THE DOOMFARERS OF CORAMONDE, THE DANCERS OF NOYO, THE HERO OF DOWNWAYS, THE SHIPS OF DUROSTORUM, THE CLOCKS OF IRAZ.** That kind of baroque thing.

Naturally, I've picked examples of such titles that include another sophomoric titling flaw. The use of alien-sounding words that cannot be readily pronounced or—more important—when the reader is asking to purchase the book or recommending it to someone else, words that cannot be remembered. "Hey, I read a great book yesterday. You really ought to get it. It's called the something of something . . . THE REELERS OF SKOOTH or THE RAVERS OF SEETH or . . . I dunno, you look for it; it has a green cover . . . "

Asimov believed in short titles, because they're easy to remember by sales clerks, bookbuyers for the chain stores, and readers who not only don't recall the titles of what they've read, but seldom know the name of the author. On the other hand, both Chip Delany and I think that a cleverly constructed long title plants sufficient key words in a reader's mind that, even if it's delivered incorrectly, enough remains to make the point. Witness as examples, "Time Considered as a Helix of Semi-Precious Stones," "The Beast that Shouted Love at the Heart of the World," "Repent, Harlequin!' Said the Ticktockman" or "The Doors of His Face, the Lamps of His Mouth." There is strong argument both ways. "Nightfall," "Slan," "Dune" and "Killdozer" simply cannot be ignored. But then, neither can DO ANDROIDS DREAM OF ELECTRIC SHEEP?

The rule of thumb, of course, is simply: if it's clever and catchy enough, short or long doesn't make a bit of difference.

But try to avoid being *too* clever. You can bad-pun and out-clever yourself into annoying a reader before the story is ever considered. I NEVER PROMISED YOU A ROSE GARDEN makes it, but YOUR ERRONEOUS ZONES simply sucks. The original title for Roger Zelazny's "He Who Shapes," published in book form as THE DREAM MASTER, was "The Ides of October," which seems to me too precious by half, while the title Joe Haldeman originally wanted to put on his *Star Trek* novelization— SPOCK, MESHUGINAH!—caroms off into ludicrousness. But funny. I know from funny, and *that* is funny. Thomas Disch is a master at walking that line. GETTING INTO DEATH is masterful, as is FUN WITH YOUR NEW HEAD. But the classic example of tightropewalking by Disch was the original title of his novel MANKIND UNDER THE LEASH (the Ace paper-

back title, and a dumb thing it is), which was originally called THE PUP-
PIES OF TERRA. (That's its title in England.)

Arthur Byron Cover has a flair for the utterly ridiculous that is *so*
looney you have to buy the book to see if he can pull it off. Witness: THE
PLATYPUS OF DOOM.

Until the very last tick before production, the title of Margaret
Mitchell's GONE WITH THE WIND was MULES IN HORSES' HARNESS;
and though I truly love the hell out of it, sufficiently to have appropriated it
half-a-century later for an essay I wrote, I think Scott Fitzgerald was well-
pressured when his publisher badgered him into retitling TRIMALCHIO IN
WEST EGG as THE GREAT GATSBY.

The name of a character, if interesting, can be a way out when you're
stuck for a title. It's surprising how few sf novels have done this, indicating
the low esteem most traditional sf writers have placed on characterization,
preferring to deal with *Analog*-style technician terms such as "Test Stand,"
"Flashpoint," "Test to Destruction" or "No Connections." We have so few
novels with titles like THE GREAT GATSBY, BABBITT, ADVENTURES OF
HUCKLEBERRY FINN or LORD JIM. Delany scored with DHALGREN,
I've had some success with "Knox," and Gordon Dickson's best-loved story
is "Black Charlie."

Ideally, a title should add an extra fillip when you've finished reading
a story. It should capsulize it, state the theme, and make a point after touch-
down. It should, one hopes, explain more than you cared to state baldly in
the text. Judith Merril's "That Only a Mother" is a perfect example, as is the
double-entendre of her "Dead Center." It is an extra gift to the alert reader,
and makes the reader feel close to you.

By the same token, you dare not cheat a reader with a clever title that
doesn't pay off. The one that pops to mind first is "The Gun Without a
Bang," one of the best titles from the usually satisfying Robert Sheckley.
Great title. The only thorn on that rose was that it was a dumb story about
some people who find a gun that didn't make any noise, which says a whole
lot less than the symbolic, metaphysical, textual or tonal implications pas-
sim the title's promise.

One of the most brilliant title-creators sf has ever known, is Jack
Chalker. I'm not talking about the actual stories, just the titles. Beauties like
MIDNIGHT AT THE WELL OF SOULS, AND THE DEVIL WILL DRAG
YOU UNDER, PIRATES OF THE THUNDER, and "Forty Days and Nights
in the Wilderness" are to die for.

But when—way back in 1978—Jack saw publication of a short story
with the absolute killer title "Dance Band on the *Titanic*," everybody wanted
to assassinate him. First, because the title was utterly dynamite; and second,
because the stupid story was *about* the dance band on the Titanic!

No! we screamed at him, *you great banana,* you don't waste a prime
candidate for beautiful allegory on a story that is about the very thing
named in the title. Man was lucky to escape with his life!

For myself, I cannot begin a story until I have a title. Sometimes I have titles—such as "The Deathbird" or "Mefisto in Onyx"—years before I have a story to fit. Often a story will be titled in my mind, be the impetus for writing that particular piece, and then, when I've finished, the title no longer resonates properly. It is a title that has not grown to keep pace with more important things in the story, or the focus was wrong, or it was too frivolous for what turned out to be a more serious piece of work. In that case, painful as it may be to disrespect the spark that gave birth to the work, one must be bloody ruthless and scribble the title down for later use, or jettison it completely. That is the mature act of censorship a writer brings to every word of a story, because in a very personal way that is what writing is all about: self-censorship. Picking "the" instead of "a" means you not only exclude "the," but all the possible storylines proceeding from that word. You kill entire universes with every word-choice. And while it's auctorial censorship, it is a cathexian process forever separating the amateurs from the professionals.

I cannot stress enough the importance of an intriguing and original title. It is what an editor sees first, and what draws that worthy person into reading the first page of the story.

No one could avoid reading a story called "The Hurkle is a Happy Beast" or "If You Was a Moklin," but it takes a masochist to plunge into a manuscript titled "The Wicker Chair."

I leave you with these thoughts.

Right now I have to write a story called "The Other Eye of Polyphemus."

Landsberg: The clarity of Ellison's message in the preceding essay precludes any need for restatement, but this is an instructive text in which a certain amount of repetition is valuable, so I will restate what he just told you: Every element of a work of fiction is crucial to accomplishing its overall effect. The title of the work takes its place shoulder-to-shoulder with every other tool the writer can use to make the work wholly satisfying to the reader. In fact, in at least one way, the title is the most important element . . . first impressions being crucial, after all. Would you want to read a story called "The Beast that Shouted Love at the Heart of the World"? Or "'Repent, Harlequin!' Said the Ticktockman"? How about "I Have No Mouth and I Must Scream" or "Objects of Desire in the Mirror are Closer than they Appear"?

Of course you would! Confronted with such examples of Ellison's genius at creating masterful titles, how could you *not* want to read the stories they adorn? Each story, by the way, is one of Harlan's numerous winners of the Hugo or Nebula Award, the highest honors in the science fiction field, given by the Science Fiction and Fantasy Writers of America or the World SF Convention. I wouldn't claim that the titles assured the awards, but they sure didn't hurt!

You may have noticed something else about Harlan's essay. Although it includes frequent references to science fiction, as well as a powerful point about the special importance of titles to the craft of science fiction, the essay is not exclusively about writing science fiction as opposed to writing any other kind of fiction. This will hold true through the two more essays that Harlan is going to give us; dressed up in science fictional allusions and examples, his teachings here are nevertheless concerned primarily with writing fiction—any kind of fiction, no matter what label you stick on it. I am claiming an editor's prerogative to reveal Harlan's cunning here, because it is essential that you do not miss this point: Fiction is fiction is...you guessed it, fiction. The fundamental techniques of creating an effective story do not vary from genre to genre, and you ignore them at your own peril. There are, of course, elements unique to each genre, but these elements must be constructed atop a sound foundation. In reading Harlan's essays, you can see how this sound foundation is built under science fiction as well as any other kind of fiction. Later in this chapter, I will discuss some of the genre-specific techniques that are unique within, and necessary to, science fiction.

Which brings me back to Harlan's point about the special importance of titles in science fiction. He said a good title can instill within the reader a sense of trust, and trust is essential to the "willing suspension of disbelief that is necessary in *any* kind of fiction, but is absolutely mandatory for fantasy or science fiction." In other words, a good title helps the reader cross the bridge between daily reality and the world of the story. No matter how realistic a story is, it is not reality; between a reader's reality and a writer's brave new world, science fiction creates an abyss that can be immense. If the reader is not eager to be a partner in crossing that gap, the story cannot succeed. This is what is meant by the "willing suspension of disbelief." Disbelief is natural and even expected when a reader confronts a work of fiction, because after all, fiction is a lie—a graceful lie, as suggested by the title of this text, but a lie nevertheless—isn't it? You have to get the reader to go along with the lie, which means you first have to get the reader to *want* to go along with the lie. The reader must willingly suspend his or her natural tendency to disbelieve. Put another way, if you don't tell a good enough lie, the reader won't want to believe it.

Nothing is more important to a good lie—I mean a good story—than a well-constructed character. A writer can't really write a decent story if none of the characters is worth the effort it takes to write it, and a reader won't read it if the characters are not worth the effort of getting to know them. Let me throw this back to Harlan, then, so he can relate some key points about creating flesh-and-blood characters who make us care about their lives.

"Tell-tale Tics and Tremors"
Harlan Ellison

Under the pseudonym "Frederick R. Ewing," the late, multifarious Theodore Sturgeon once wrote a serio-comic historical romp titled I, LIBERTINE, the protagonist of which had an interesting character trait. The novel was a swashbuckler, and the hero was a much-vaunted swordsman. The only trouble with him was that when he was in a dangerous situation, he became petrified with fear. When that happened, his mouth went dry and his upper lip invariably stuck to his teeth, forcing him to draw his mouth up to loosen it. It was a nervous tic, but the effect it had was to make him appear to be smiling. He became famous, therefore, as a man who "smiles in the face of danger." This minor infirmity was taken for what it was not, he was counted fearless, and frequently escaped being killed because it generated a wholly undeserved reputation for his being foolhardily dangerous to the point of lunacy; and it terrified the bejeezus out of his attackers.

Scott Fitzgerald foreshadowed the totality of the basic theme of THE GREAT GATSBY in his portrayals of Tom and Daisy Buchanan as people who "... smashed up things and creatures and then retreated back into their vast carelessness ... and let other people clean up the mess they had made. ..." The concept of "careless people" is one that applies perfectly to whole groups of young people one meets today. For instance, the wife of a friend of mine has managed to accumulate one hundred and thirteen parking tickets in a year in Beverly Hills alone. Most of them have even gone to warrant. Unlike New York City, where, if you are a scofflaw and have a pile of tickets, they settle with you annually ... or states where they refuse to renew your license until you clean up your outstanding tickets ... in California, they simply bust you and toss you in the tank till you're paid up. So last week, when this woman's husband was himself stopped for some minor traffic infraction, the Highway Smokey ran the car's registration through the computer, found there were warrants outstanding, and tossed *him* in the slam till several thousand dollars were shelled out. He spent the night in the Beverly Hills penal pen, with other high-end felons, and the next day they started to ship him off to one jail after another in the jurisdictions where *she* had picked up bad paper. Her carelessness caused an entire cadre of us, their friends, to waste an entire day, and many dollars, trying to pry *him* loose from the coils of the Law. And she just laughed it off. Careless. And that's the key to her character. She is a woman terrified of growing up, of becoming an adult who must accept responsibility not only for her own life, but for that part of the lives of others that is involved with hers.

Pinocchio's nose grows when he tells a lie.

Archy the cockroach avers he is the reincarnation of a *vers libre* poet.

Uriah Heep wrings his hands, dissembles, and deprecates himself when he is being disingenuous.

Scarlett O'Hara captures the totality of her character, in the denouement of her story, in the microcosm of a single phrase as she keeps repeating, "I'll think of it all tomorrow . . . After all, tomorrow is another day."

Chaucer's pilgrims all have mannerisms and physical attributes that speak to their basic nature. The wife of Bath, as an example, is gap-toothed, meaning lusty. She has five husbands.

In the series of novels about the actor-thief Grofield, Donald Westlake (writing under the name Richard Stark) has his bemusingly melodramatic hero hearing film background music as he has his adventures. He'll be going into a dangerous caper and the soundtrack in his brain is playing, say, the Korngold theme from the Errol Flynn film, *The Sea Hawk*. It is a mild and antic way of showing how Grofield is able to laugh at himself, even at a precarious moment; and it explicates his character fully.

Grofield's interior soundtrack, Uriah's dry-washing, Scarlett's refusal to deal with pragmatic reality when it soils her fantasies, Pinocchio's priapean proboscis, the Buchanans' (and my friend's wife's) amoral thoughtlessness, the swordsman's daunting grin . . . they are all examples of a writing skill that *must* be present in the work of anyone who wishes to create characters that live. They are the minute mannerisms and attributes that create an instant flare of recognition in the reader. They are the core of character delineation; and writers who think they can deal only with gimmicks and sociology and gadgets and concepts, without breathing life into the players on whom gimmicks, sociology, gadgets and concepts have their effect, is doomed to frustration . . . and worse, shallowness.

I've quoted this before, and will no doubt quote it many times more, but for me the most basic thing ever said about the important material for stories was said by William Faulkner in his Nobel Prize acceptance speech. He said: ". . . the problems of the human heart in conflict with itself which alone can make good writing because only that is worth writing about, worth the agony and the sweat."

What I've just said is so obvious to any professional, that it must seem a ludicrous redundancy. Yet my experience with young writers has shown me that an astonishing number of talented people conceive of the writing of a story as an exercise in conundrum: a problem situation that, like a locked-room mystery, must be solved. They relate to the work the way computer programmers relate to an "heuristic situation." They simply do not comprehend, as each of you reading this *must* comprehend, on almost a cellular level, so it becomes basic nature with every story you attempt, that the only thing worth writing about is people.

I'll say that again. The *only* thing worth writing about is people. *People.* Human beings. Men and women whose individuality must be created, line by line, insight by insight. If you do not do it, the story is a failure. It may be the most innovative sociological insight or scientific concept ever promulgated, but it will be a failure. I cannot stress this enough. Doesn't matter if it's a novel or a hundred-word short-short: no character that breathes... you got no story. There is no nobler chore in the craft of writing than holding up the mirror of reality and turning it slightly, so we have a new and different perception of the commonplace, the everyday, the "normal," the obvious. *People* are reflected in the glass. The fantasy situation into which you thrust them is the mirror itself. And what we are shown should illuminate and alter our perception of the world around us. Failing that, you have failed totally.

Melville put it this way: "No great and enduring volume can ever be written on the flea, though many there be who have tried it."

I had not meant, in this brief exegesis, to get too deeply into the arcane philosophy of writing. I leave that to pedants and academics who all-too-often worry such concepts into raggedness, like a puppy shaking a Pooh cuddly. Nonetheless, I am pressed to it; there is such a fractionalizing of the genre currently, with many writers opting for obscurantism and convoluted, insipid cleverness in aid of the smallest, most familiar point... or wallowing in smug arrogance that they write "heroic" fiction that masters mind-numbing concepts, but do not reveal the presence of a single living, identifiable human being... that I find I must belabor the *people* concept a moment longer.

One of the least defensible rationales for the "validity" of science fiction as a worthy genre of literature, handed down to us from the 1920's, is that it is a "problem-solving fiction." This bogus apologia, handservant to the more exploitable (but no less phony) asseverative justification that sf predicts the future, is a bit of paranoia left over from a long-gone time when the writing and the reading of sf was considered tantamount to being certifiably tetched.

But those days are far behind us. The sophistication and craft-upgrading that has come to sf through the works of writers such as Silverberg, Disch, Wilhelm, Wolfe, Harrison, Moorcock, Tiptree and Le Guin has put it forever out of the line of contempt of all but the most purblind and reactionary critics. (This does not save us, however, from the moronic effusions of *Time's* Peter Prescott, or the lamebrains who work on rural dailies, who think they're being hip when they call it "sci-fi." Nor does it filter any light into the murky caverns wherein dwell holdovers from the "Golden Era" who are now counted as great historians and critics of the field, who continue to suck up to every pitiful monster flick or limp-logic deigning of notice from Establishment journals, chiefly because their lack of ego-strength refuses to permit them to understand that sf has long-since arrived. We must suffer with these benighted few, but we need not allow *their* hangups to be *our* hangups.)

Summation, then: outdated attitudes continue to prevail throughout the genre. Bad writers justify their work and the Brobdingnagian publisher's advances they get by puffing up with assertions that they write "true science fiction." Well, they're welcome to it, if they believe the value of the work lies in nothing but thunderous concepts flung through enormous vistas of space, sans emotion, sans people, sans wit, sans anything but necromancy and/or hardware. It is writing more allied with the preparation of technical journals than it is with the heritage of Melville, Twain, Shelley, Kafka and Borges.

I urge all of you seeking careers as writers, to eschew this dead end. Leave it to the amateurs who make their livings as technicians or engineers, with an occasional foray into fiction that is merely the mythologizing of their current "heuristic situation." Ten years from now their stories will be as forgotten, as unreadable, as the entire contents of issues of 60's and 70's Campbell *Analogs* are today.

The only stories that live on, that are worth "the agony and the sweat" of writing, are the ones that speak with force to the human condition. *Star Wars* is amusing, but please don't confuse it with *Citizen Kane*, *Taxi Driver*, or *The Conversation*.

Writing about people should be your mission.

Which brings us back to the proper place for this essay, after a digression informed more by anger and impatience than a sense of propriety. I beg your pardon.

If you'll accept my messianic fervor as regards the *reason* for writing, then it follows that creating (not real, but) verisimilitudinous people—go look up the word verisimilitude *now*—is mandatory. It also requires very nearly more art than any other aspect of writing. It entails keen observation of people, attention to detail, the eschewing of cynicism, the total flensing from your mind of any kind of bigotry, wide knowledge of habit patterns and sociological underpinnings for otherwise irrational or overfamiliar habits, cultural trends, familiarity with dress and speech and physical attributes, fads, psychology and the ways in which people say things other than what they mean.

It devolves upon being mature enough, and empathic enough, and tough enough to be able to encapsulate a human being of your own creating, in a line or, at most, a paragraph. A single act or habit would be ideal.

Lean! Lean and fatless, a minimum of words! The fewest possible words, where more would obfuscate that moment of recognition. The writing must be lean and hard!

Read this:

> *A man has a shape; a crowd has no shape and no color. The massed faces of a hundred thousand men make one blank pallor; their clothes add up to a shadow; they have no words. This man might have been one hundred-thousandth part of the featureless whiteness, the dull grayness, and toneless murmuring of a docile multitude. He was something less than nondescript—he was blurred, without identity, like a smudged fingerprint. His suit was of some dim shade between brown and gray. His shirt had gray-blue stripes, his tie was patterned with dots like confetti trodden into the dust, and his oddment of limp brownish mustache resembled a cigarette-butt, disintegrating shred by shred in a tea-saucer.*

That was the late Gerald Kersh, my favorite writer, now-forgotten giant of great, great storytelling ability, describing the indescribable: a man with no outstanding characteristics, a plain man, an invisible man, a little soul never examined and a presence instantly forgotten. The words sing the song, of course, but consider the images. Precise. Lean. Hard.

Not cynical, but utterly pragmatic. Confetti in the dust, a smudged fingerprint, a cigarette butt disintegrating in a saucer. Exact. Evocative. And in sum the images and the choice of words—self-censorship at its most creative and intelligent and productive level—give us a description of that which cannot be described. The only other example of this I've ever encountered was Coppola's cinematic characterization of the professional electronic bugger, Harry Caul, in *The Conversation.* As critic Pauline Kael described him, he is "a compulsive loner (Gene Hackman), a wizard at electronic surveillance who is so afraid others will spy on him that he empties his life; he's a cipher—a cipher in torment. There's nothing to discover about him, and *still* he's in terror of being bugged." Coppola's writing, combined with Hackman's subtle sense of his own anonymity, described the indescribable: a man who is a shadow. And both Kersh and Coppola did it with the barest possible delineation. Lean, hard, precise!

Get it: what I'm suggesting as an imperative for the writer who wishes to create stories of power and immediacy, is the tough and unrelenting process of describing characters in a few words, by special and particular attributes. The swordsman's grin, Heep's hand-washing, Scarlett's interior will to survive even in the face of consummate disaster. I'll give you a few more examples.

In Edmund Wilson's justly famous story "The Man Who Shot Snapping Turtles" we have a character named Asa M. Stryker (note the name as descriptive tool) who is obsessed with the predatory chelonians that lurk in his pond and drag down the little ducklings he admires. The obsession grows until Stryker goes into the turtle soup business. He becomes more and more snapperlike until his movements and manner become paradigmatic of the very creatures he has devoted his life to vanquishing. Here is a bit from the story:

> ... *Stryker, at ease in his turbid room, upended, as it were, behind his desk, with a broad expanse of plastron and a rubbery craning neck, regarding him with small bright eyes set back in the brownish skin beyond a prominent snout-like formation of which the nostrils were sharply in evidence* ...

Wilson uses the device of direct analogy to demonstrate the subtext of the story: Stryker became what he beheld. It is one method of characterizing a player. It is a variation of the Disney Studios manner of humanizing animals or inanimate objects like pencils or garbage cans by anthropomorphizing them. Wilson's technique, technically known as anthroposcopy, character-reading from facial features, can be used as straight one-for-one value-judgment or as misdirection, where precisely the *opposite* of what a person looks like indicates his or her nature. Take Victor Hugo's Quasimodo, the hunchback of Notre Dame, as an example.

Chekhov once admonished young playwrights, "If, in act one you have a pistol hanging on the wall, be assured it is fired before the end of act two." The same goes for character traits.

Take the gorgeous novella BILLY BUDD, FORETOPMAN, for instance. Herman Melville tells us that Billy stammers. But only at certain times. When he is confronted by mendacity, duplicity, evil. Symbolically, we can take this to mean that Billy, as a corporeal manifestation of Goodness in a Mean World, is rendered *tabula rasa* by Evil Incarnate. That would be the academic view. But as a writer ensorcelled by "process," I choose to see the stammer as a plot-device. The inability to defend himself verbally is used near the climax of the novella as the mechanism by which Billy's fate is sealed. Herman Melville was a great writer, but he was a *writer* first. He knew how to plot. He knew the pistol had to be fired.

Historically, such physical infirmities were used by writers such as Hawthorne to indicate inner flaws. The Reverend Dimmesdale, in THE SCARLET LETTER, has a burning scar on his chest. He is an adulterer. The scar is the outward manifestation of what he feels is his inner sin. When he bares his bosom to the entire congregation, it is a shocking moment. The pistol has been fired.

Shakespeare goes even further. Probably because his talent was greater than anyone else's. More than merely using physical mannerisms or frailties, he uses the forces of Nature in all their unleashed passion to reflect the viewpoint character's state of mind. In Act II, scene *iv* of *King Lear*, at the very moment that he wanders out onto the heath, having renounced his power while trying to retain his title, having been driven to the point of madness by his daughters, who have thrown him out of their homes, we find the following:

> LEAR
> . . . You think I'll weep;
> No, I'll not weep:
> I have full cause of weeping;
> But this heart
> Shall break into a hundred
> thousand flaws,
> Or ere I'll weep. O fool,
> I shall go mad!

At which point the storm and tempest break. Shakespeare mirrors Lear's instant of going insane with Nature's loosing of all its mad passion. He tells us that Lear realizes, in that moment of final lucidity before the plunge into madness, that in his life there can be no separation of title from power. That to retain the former, one must have the latter to buttress it. He is alone, beaten, tragic, defenseless before Man *and* Nature.

It is mythic characterization on a cosmic level.

Less grand in its scope, but as revealing in its placement of a human being within the context of his society, is the little trick Turgenev uses to show us that Paul Petrovich of FATHERS AND SONS feels discontiguous. The novel was written at the fracture-point in Russian history when the serfs were in revolt, and it is a time of ambivalence; dichotomous; vacillating between the traditions of the aristocracy and the pull of rule by the common man. To demonstrate Petrovich's uncertainty, Turgenev has a meeting between Petrovich and his young adult student nephew, after many years, containing a moment in which the elder not only shakes hands in the "European" manner but kisses him "thrice in the Russian fashion, that is to say, he brushed his cheeks thrice with his scented moustaches, exclaiming, 'Welcome home!'"

Alfred Bester's THE STARS, MY DESTINATION is a classic novel to read and re-read for such minutiae of characterization. Gully Foyle, the protagonist, for instance, has his progression and growth of character from near-bestial lout to cultured avenger epitomized by his language and manner of speech. At first he speaks only the gutter slang of the future invented by Bester to micromize the era, but as Gully grows and buys himself an education, he declares himself in very different, more cadenced patterns. This is paralleled by the visibility of the "tiger mask" that covers his face. When he is a beast, it shows easily; later, it becomes almost invisible, manifesting itself only when his rage makes him revert for a moment. Literary resonance in simple impossible-to-misinterpret, dramatic imaging: *show, don't tell.* Heinlein's DOUBLE STAR is another limitless source-reference, jam-full of this kind of technique. Which is why these two books continue to be thought of as "classics" long after books that made bigger initial splashes have faded from memory.

Algis Budrys once wrote a story, the title of which escapes me right now, in which a very fat man, an official of some bloated interstellar military-industrial organization, stuffs his mouth with candy bars all through conversations with the hero. Thus, by miniaturized example—arguing from the smaller to the greater—Budrys led us to a perception of the fat man in paradigm, as one with the fat organization.

A horde of examples from my own work pop to mind, but a sense of propriety prevents my dealing with them in detail. I use a hare-lip sometimes to indicate that a character is a born victim; and men who are punctilious about their hair and clothes usually turn out, in my stories, to be men who get their comeuppance or who are shallow. "Pretty Maggie Moneyeyes" has two characters I think are well formed using the techniques I've enumerated here, and if you get a moment you might look it up.

In the script I wrote for *Blood's a Rover*, the 2-hour pilot movie for what was to have been an NBC series, based on the novella and the film of "A Boy and His Dog," I introduce a female solo who is as tough as the amoral Vic. Her name is Spike, and at one point in the film she joins up with the dog, Blood. Vic returns, after having split up with Blood, and wants to get together again as partners. But the Spike character is now Blood's partner. To demonstrate that she thinks very little of Vic, when she gets angry, she never talks to *him,* she talks to the dog. "Tell it to shut its mouth before I blow its head off," she says to the dog, referring to Vic. Blood then repeats what she's said to Vic, who has heard it, of course. This goes on till Vic is driven into a rage. It is a mannerism that will be a continuing in-joke for the film pilot and the series. By talking to a dog about a human, and referring to the human as "it" instead of the animal, I hope to make a point about the way in which men treat women as objects. This, done subtly, because the networks would never permit it if they knew what I was doing ... that is, actually putting in a sub-text and symbolism, heaven forbid ... will serve to deepen the subject matter as visually presented.

I've offered all these examples of minute character traits—tics and tremors—in an attempt to demonstrate that it is possible with extreme economy to create a fully fleshed player, even if that player is only a walk-on. And when you're getting into the story, touches like these can set up the reader through many pages of plot and concept, action and background, permitting the reader to identify with the viewpoint character. It is a tone that will inform the story throughout.

As a final note, let me hit once again at the core fact that no matter what it is you *think* you're writing about, the best and most significant thing to write about, what you're *always* writing about, is *people!*

Building people who are believable, verisimilitude being the operative word, not *real people* but *believable people,* is a product of the touches and techniques discussed here.

Or, as John le Carré, the novelist who wrote THE SPY WHO CAME IN FROM THE COLD and THE LOOKING GLASS WAR, among others, has said, "A good writer can watch a cat pad across the street and know what it is to be pounced upon by a Bengal tiger."

Whether pounced upon by a giant cat, explaining why a coward's smile makes his enemies flee, how a careless person can destroy those around her, what hypocrisy lies in an idle drywashing motion of a sycophant's hands, or how a beautiful and kindly man can condemn himself to death because he stammers, if you intend to write well, and write for posterity, or even simply to entertain, you must remember . . .

Fire the pistol.

Landsberg: If you now see the importance of creating believable characters, you can understand why most of your thoughts should be devoted to this task before you actually sit down to write. This does not mean that you have to have your characters delineated in every last detail before you begin writing—much of that comes in the writing itself—but you have to have the essence of the central characters in mind before you begin. If you don't, you probably don't have much of a story in mind. What does a bridge across the Atlantic, or a nuclear holocaust, or even a new fangled coffee bean grinder *mean*, if there isn't someone *to whom it can be meaningful*? Of what value is whatever science-fictional thingie or situation you've invented for your story if you don't create someone whose life is significantly affected by it?

Having at least a darn good idea of your plot, characters, and setting, you sit down to write and find yourself faced with what classically was called "the blank page." Nowadays it's more likely to be "the blank screen" of your computer, but whatever blankness you are facing, it can seem massive and daunting. And yet, if you could only get started, you would find that writing begets writing—whatever you've already written inspires further writing, and before you know it, you have a story. Therefore, Harlan is now going to explain a thing or two about the crucial skill of beginning a story effectively.

"How Do We Get Into This Mess?"
Harlan Ellison

On a dead run, that's how.

One of the most common reasons for the rejection of a story has virtually nothing to do with the overall impact of that particular piece of writing. An otherwise excellent story can find itself being stuffed back into the SASE and being dropkicked into the mail chute because it had a slow, an obscure, a confusing, or redundant opening section. Though the characterizations are strong, the concepts imaginative, and the action sequences motor right along, if the story crawled on all fours from page one through, say page eight, before it got to its feet and started sprinting, chances are good that the editor grew impatient and decided the reading of one unsolicited manuscript should not become his or her life's work.

No sense railing at this seeming callousness. The editor is only human. And to be absolutely pragmatic about it, freed of the maudlin self-pity and justifications unpublished writers substitute for logic, the editor is *only* a reader, albeit a more trained reader than the casual magazine-buyer. If you can't grab the editor's interest, odds are heavily against your being able to grab Joe or Joan Reader with that slow opening.

To state that communication is the bottom line of all writing would be to jackhammer a truism into the tarmac. If the communication isn't there from the git-go, the reader has—it seems to me—an unconscious reluctance to trust the writer. That means the writer must work ever so much harder to get the reader *into* that mind-warp I mentioned earlier, the "willing suspension of disbelief." The longer it takes a writer to nudge, push or pull a reader into that state, the more chances the reader has of escaping the web of the fiction.

So it becomes clear that we must cherry-bomb the reader as quickly and as completely as possible, to the self-serving end of snaring the twisty beast. To that purpose, here are three devices I've found universally present in good writing. The first is the title, and we've already masticated *that* one. The second is the literary hook, the beguiling opening line, about which I'll discourse some other time. The third device is no device at all, but is one of the plimsoll-line measurements of craftsmanlike writing. It is knowing how and where to *begin* the story.

In editing the *Dangerous Visions* anthologies I read more than my share of stories that I eventually published, but often only after asking the writers for revisions that dealt with the opening pages of the work. And I've read many stories that made it into print even though they suffered from the same flaccid lack of muscle tone. In working Clarion, and other prestigious writing conferences, I've seen much the same thing. (And much less of that slow pacing at the beginning when I've bludgeoned my students into writing a story a day. When they have to write fast, they automatically understand that there is limited time available to them to grind out a complete story, so they instinctively reject superfluous or repetitious backstory, compress rambling scenes, find side-roads that shortcut lumbering, dead patches of exposition and, in the words of the television industry, they "cut to the chase" immediately. In most cases it tightens the plot and drags the reader along.)

Understanding where to begin a story is a facility that comes with years of writing *many* stories. It's a mugg's game, trying to set down hard-and-fast rules, because it's different every time; and no set of rules really works. The best I can do, I guess, is try to give some examples and then examine them, and hope that I'm being clear enough so you can apply the lessons to specific stories on which you're working. But do please take this *caveat* into consideration as you read these comments: this is just a general rule of thumb, and you must take the Cortical-Thalamic Pause (as dear A.E. van Vogt put it), noodle this information for individual assimilation. Not to put too fine a point on it, do as I suggest, not as I frequently don't do it myself.

All right, then. To it, with vigah!

Let's suppose a story. Um. Okay, how's this:

Bizarre story about a guy who has nothing but shitty relationships with women, who cannot cop to his own fractured persona. Argues with his lovers, brutalizes them, intimidates them. But though he's given to some low-level self-analysis—he's rather bright—he always manages to rationalize the encounters so he comes off looking good and the women always come off, in his mind, as immature or castrating or just plain fucked-up. So he sinks deeper and deeper into despondency, until he decides he'll never be able to find a woman who is good enough for him. Meaning, of course, a woman whom he can dominate while she manages to retain a sense of her own identity that doesn't threaten him. From this lightless perception of the world, skewed as it is, he comes across an advertisement for android companions, programmed to suit every need. So he gets one, a beautiful woman who seems just right, because he has gone through extensive bio-medical brain-scanning that has pulled out of him and his needs a template that forms the basis of her identity. He marries her. Everything goes well for a "honeymoon" period of six months, and then he discovers that his android wife is having an affair with another man. He is so enraged by this, that he plans to kill her. But is it murder if you kill an android? Is it rational? Should he take her back into the shop to be re-programmed? Or will he finally understand that the flaws are in *him*, that he sows the seeds of interpersonal destruction because of his narrow view of other human beings?

(Yes, I know, I know . . . Bradbury did exactly this story, and then it was adapted for *The Twilight Zone* . . . but it's a place to start for a paradigm, so shut up and stop being such a pecksniff smartass.)

Now. That's the basic idea. It's *not* a story, friends. (That's something else I'll belabor at length in the future: knowing the difference between an "idea" and a "story." But not now, not now; stop pestering me.) But it's all we need to examine the point of entry *into the story.*

There is a kind of literary magic, the inarticulate power of certain auctorial magicians to transmute base metal ideas into the pure gold of a compelling story opening. Sheckley has the power, as did Phil Dick; so does Kotzwinkle, and Ann Beattie, and Ron Goulart; so did Alice Sheldon before she killed herself, her ailing beloved husband, and James Tiptree, Jr. and Raccoona Sheldon, all on the same dark day. I could list dozens who lack that power, but I don't need to; you can do it for yourself. So where do we tap with that magic finger to start our story?

Well, here's one way:

Walter Nesterman tried desperately not to hate women. He walked away from Francine's monad cursing her, cursing himself, cursing his inability to have said what he wanted to say to her. The French called it l'esprit d'escalier, *the spirit of the stairs, or as close to translation as could be managed in English, the mood of thinking retrospectively, as one walked down the stairs away from the argument, what one* should *have said. I should* have told her, you stupid bitch, if you weren't having all these fights . . . I *should* have said, you're just flat out immature, that's *your problem . . .*

But he hadn't. He had raged and fumfuh'd and gotten red in the face, and now another affair was over. It was the fifth lousy liaison he'd been involved in over the past year.

And he felt at once furious and guilty.

Okay. Now there's nothing much wrong with that. I took pains to write it well, so I couldn't be accused of loading the gun in favor of an alternate method that I think is better.

Here's another way of doing it:

A snake uncoiled in Walter Nesterman's gut and the first thing he thought, a kind of inarticulate scream of rage within him, was I'll kill that android bitch!

Married less than six months and she was busily humping some other guy. His mind reeled across a surreal landscape of impossible possibilities. How could a pre-programmed android created specifically to his needs be unfaithful? Was it a human she was fucking, or another chemical construct? How was she slipping out to see him? Could it be a "her"? Was the flaw in himself, in the brain-scan that had been pulled out of him to form her template?

But most of all, mournfully whistling like an Autumn wind across his mind, was the cry Am I never *to find a woman I can love?*

And the certain knowledge: I gotta kill that android bitch!

Now that's closer to it. But even though we've eliminated all the back-story of Nesterman's unhappy relationships and an examination of his personality *in situ*, it's still wrong. Or, more exactly, it ain't right. (*Nothing*, if written well and intriguingly, is *wrong*. See what I mean about how hard it is to pinpoint this problem? The rules simply don't hold.) Whoever Francine was, she's out of it as we open the story, so we don't need to lumber the reader with a reference to someone we're not going to see again. And *both* of these open on interior monologue of one sort or another. Granted (he said humbly), notwithstanding they're both moderately interesting, passionate interior monologues, they are, nonetheless, essentially passive. And we want to start at a dead run if we can. So I'd suggest something short and sharp like this:

Nesterman looked down at his wife asleep in the waterbed. Her eyes were closed, her breathing was shallow, and the recharger plugged into her right hip was glowing bright red. He held the laser knife tightly and warred within himself. Cut her lying android throat, or simply take her back to the shop and have them turn her into slag?

He couldn't escape the awful reality: not even an android, built to satisfy his every need, could be faithful to him. His beautiful chemical construct of a wife, beautiful charming Charlene was having an affair! And all he could think was: I've gotta kill this bitch!

Okay. Now, can you see the variations? In the first, we start six and more months before the nub of the story, with a lot of backplot and soul-searching that is pretty much dead time as far as plot progression is concerned. In the second, we bring the story six months into the present, but it's right at the moment when he's come to his decision to kill Charlene. And that might seem a pivot point in his life, which it is, but again we're dealing passively with a passionate, action-filled situation.

The third opening brings us to the moment that he's standing right over this sleeping, helpless woman, with murder in his heart. Now, if we want to have him back off because he's torn, because he's starting to realize the problem lies with *him*, not *her*, we have the basis for a subsequent series of scenes in which he has to disguise his feelings, in which he tries to draw out of her an admission of what's been going on, in which he seeks out the man or woman or artificial life-form she's having an affair with, in which he goes back to the company that made her and tries to find out what went wrong (nice idea: a psychologist who ministers to the fluxes and flows of both human and android principals) . . . an infinitude of possibilities for examination of the human condition, not to mention an expansion of the basic plot situation.

Or if we want to have him kill her, right then and there, we can run it like Poe's "The Tell-Tale Heart" and have the miserable fucker going bananas because of what he's done.

Don't' forget, what we're dealing with in this story is the moment of realization on the part of a complex and tormented human being that he is incapable of decent warmth and a lasting relationship. *Therein* lies the story, not the amusing conceit of what is entailed when one murders something that isn't really alive. That's the furniture. The theme is human travail.

I'm not sure if you get what I'm saying in these three examples, but I'll bat it around a little more and hope that one or more comments will concretize the rigor I'm suggesting you adopt as a religion.

Look: a novice would go with the question "Is it murder to kill an android?" Wrong. That's been done. Dozens of times, all the way back to Eando Binder's famous short story, "I, Robot" in the January 1939 issue of *Amazing Stories.* And it's a moot point at this stage of recombinant DNA research in our lives. It's no longer extrapolative when we're all reading a *Time* essay on the moral and philosophical conundrums inherent in such a real-life case. But right now all we have to work with is human beings, and this kind of story (it seems to me) is only valuable for us if it explores the labyrinthine byways of the human heart. It's an allegory, if you will. A paradigm. Using it as such, we can find out—if not for the entire world, then at least for ourselves as writers—what messes with *human* relationships. And to do that in a storytelling way, we have to get into the situation when it's already fully formed. Building to it *can* be interesting, but diving in while the action is transpiring around us makes it *immediately* arresting.

One way to do this sort of thing would be to start it at whatever point your own skill dictates, write on for a couple of thousand words, and then set it aside for a day, or even a few hours, whatever your work-habits require.

When you go back, re-read it and ask yourself, *How much of this tells itself through context? How much is revealed by the actions of the characters without telling the reader through static narration? How much can I show with scenes, rather than dropping in lumps of undigested exposition? How much of this is stuff I needed to know, as background, but is also stuff the reader need* not *see specifically?*

Then cut. And once you've cut it, cut it again. And when it is clear that nothing else can be cut . . . cut it again. Go to the muscle and the bone. Strip away the rhetorical flab. And then. . . .

Cut it again.

Boil down that first two thousand words of bibble and self-revelation to a paragraph of hard, mean prose. And you will very likely have gotten to a place in the story that originally appears on page eight.

Take the writing of screenplays as a model. Never write a scene where someone sits alone in a room and there is a knock on the door, the person gets up and goes to the door, answers it, meets the visitor, invites the visitor in, they seat themselves and begin to have a long discussion that ends with a fist fight. Cut to the chase. Open the story with the first punch being thrown. Fredric Brown did that sitting alone in a room routine, and called it "Knock." Except his first line was a technical masterpiece: *The last man on Earth*—or in the universe, for that matter—*sat alone in a room. There was a knock at the door . . .*

So unless you can beat what a dead man did perfectly, you can forget it, chum.

I've digressed on that man-alone-in-a-room situation, because I know sure as the insensate Universe made little green apples, that some wiseass fan would take my using it as an example of dull writing and say, "Yeah, but what about the Fred Brown story?" And it's a perfect example, so I wanted to close up the rat hole.

What I'm suggesting is that *any* scene you use to launch a narrative can be cut in half, opened like a ripe orange, and the flesh in the middle has *got* to be tastier than the pith. So go to the middle of a situation, go past the backstory material that got you interested in the first place, the stuff you can slide in as slivers of enlightenment throughout the first third of the story, the stuff that formed the original plot epiphany, when you said to yourself, "Hey, wouldn't it be interesting if . . ." It's what happens *after* that initial idea the world has come to call "a story."

Cut to the chase. Go to the first punch. Start at the instant the fire ignites. Disabuse yourself of the misconception that to write well, to write interestingly, to write with class and verve, one must try to emulate Proust or James. Those were storytellers of a different time, who worked in a medium that has changed enormously. We read faster now, we think more quickly, and clarity can be as complex as obtuseness. Now you must snare them immediately!

The job is to tell the story feelingly, and at a dead run if at all possible. To do that, you must consider the point of entry and make certain it is one edged with fishhooks. Once having impaled the reader, you'll find you're telling a story that has snagged *you* too.

And by the way, I may eventually wind up writing that story about Nesterman and Charlene, because if I call Ray and say, "Hey, kiddo, I've got an alternative take on 'Marionettes, Inc.', d'you mind if I go at it, if I drop a 'thank you' to you at the end?" my friend Bradbury will say, "It's an honor to be plagiarized by a talent as great as yours, Harlan!" So stay away from it, you geeks.

Landsberg: Harlan Ellison has now explained three of the most important elements of crafting a competently written work of fiction. Armed with at least this much information, anyone with a modicum of talent who works hard enough for long enough *should* be able to write a decent story. If you want it to be a science fiction story, however, there are distinctive elements and characteristics that you must utilize to establish your story as an example of this genre, and not any other. So without further ado, let's take a detailed look at what I call the Special Demands of Writing Science Fiction

A LITERATURE OF CHANGE

The central concern of science fiction is the creation and exploration of universal situations which differ from our own. In simplest terms, science fiction asks what would happen if something in our world were different from the way we know it to be.

Typically, science fiction uses extrapolation into the future as its most common source of variations from everyday reality. Although many types of changes can be grist for the science fiction mill, the most popular and most potent generative focus of science fiction has been the study of changes *that might possibly occur* as the world moves forward in time. But whether a science fiction story explores change over time, or change across dimensions, or change in social circumstances, or change to a different pattern of the development of earthly civilizations, or any other change a writer can dream up, science fiction is the literature of change.

And because change is inevitable, ongoing, and inextricably entwined with each and every human life, sf (use the abbreviation most acceptable to professional science fiction writers—we hate the term sci-fi, by the way!) is at heart a reflection of what we undergo every day, even if superficially transposed to distant times or distant planets. For example, in my story, "Embodied In Its Opposite," an ambassador from Earth is sent alone to a planet so far away that no other Earth ship will land there for twenty years. The inhabitants he encounters are so strange to him that he can find almost no point of similarity between them and humans. But his quest to understand them mirrors the struggle each of us wages to understand each other—especially those who seem on the surface most different from us—and to understand ourselves. The theme is the need for interracial understanding, right here on Earth; this message is made more palatable (i.e., less dogmatic) and more poignant (hence more persuasive) by the strange setting.

Let's go back to the opening sentence of this section. Notice this: I claim that sf postulates different *universal* situations. Do I mean that sf postulates changes in the entire universe? The answer is yes, I mean exactly that, because there is no such thing as one small change. Any change from what we know, no matter how trivial (or how portentous), must necessarily be a change in the entire universe—because a universe without pencil sharpeners *is not the same universe* as one with pencil sharpeners, even if everything else in that universe is apparently the same.

Every element (every *thing*, every *situation,* every *whatever*) you put into a story must have both causes and effects—not in the sense of daily causality, such as that swinging a hammer causes a nail to go into wood. No. I'm talking about causes and effects that logically are connected to your central proposition—things that are more *philosophically* connected—such as that a hammer is logically connected to a nail because nails probably wouldn't exist in a world without hammers, and vice versa. Each element of your story therefore *implies* the existence of logically connected causes and effects—and these causes and effects are therefore *implications*.

For example, if you write that a rocket crashed on Venus, the implications of this event, in logical story terms, include who sent the rocket there and why (causes), as well as the crater that results, and who died, and which aliens heard the crash (results). Another logical result of a rocket crashing on Venus is *the presence of rocket fuel in the universe of your story*. Do you see how rocket fuel is a necessary part of that universe in which a rocket flies to Venus and crashes, and therefore is a *result of* you writing that the rocket crashed? Do you see then how the "implications" I am talking about are not indicative of *causal* relationships, but *logical* ones?

Many of the implications of any given story element are profound and far-reaching. You can't write about all of them, so you have to ignore some. And if a writer chooses to ignore some broader implications, he or she must be aware of *what is being ignored.* In the story as written, we—alert readers that we are—can deduce some of the unmentioned implications for ourselves. We can fill in the blanks that the writer has left for us. The writer, therefore, has to stay one step ahead of us; the writer can stay that step ahead only if he or she has figured out the implications before we do. Moreover, what the writer leaves unsaid affects what *is* said; a writer must write a story in a certain way because of things that are left unsaid, and might accidentally write something that doesn't fit the story if things left unsaid are never taken into consideration.

Consider this brief sentence from top sf author Michael Bishop's imaginative novel, *A Funeral for the Eyes of Fire*: "Eventually, in a manner I'm not going to describe here, we escaped the Urban Nucleus, fled to Unified Europe, and in the free city of Scandapol bought passage aboard the probeship *Edvard Grieg* for Glaparcus." The book was published in 1975, prior to any serious suggestion that Europe would unite in any way. The prediction, however, that Europe would someday unite requires the writer to consider whether Europe would be likely to be united *in the universe he is postulating*, and if so, what would be the factors that would lead to it and result from it? Consider the spaceship's name, *Edvard Grieg*. Bishop chose to use the Norwegian composer's name intentionally, not randomly. He was considering unmentioned implications such as these: Perhaps there is a pan-European council that determines the names of spaceships, following a mandate to choose names that culturally represent each of the different national groups that make up this new Europe. Bishop is not required to discuss this existence of this council, and his actual explanation for the source of the spaceship's name is probably something other than such a council, but whatever the explanation, it must fit the logic of the story as a whole.

Let's go further. Why is there a city named Scandapol? Is it an outgrowth of a previously known city, or a new one constructed from the ground up with a huge explosion of population? And take note of the fact that Bishop slips "free city" right past us while we're thinking about all this other stuff. Well, okay—if it's a free city, that *implies* that there are cities that are *not* free. And what does *that* mean to the story? How did it come to be, and how does it affect the actions of the protagonist? Bishop has to have *some* answers in mind, even if he never gives them to us explicitly, so that he doesn't wind up calling his probeship The Machu Picchu, a name that might give us the vague sense that something was not quite consistent, or even force us to stop and ask, "Why would a European ship be named that?" (I hope you're beginning to see that Bishop's sentence is a good example of how complicated an apparently simple sentence in sf can actually be.)

Let's illustrate the point further by varying the data embedded in the sentence; we'll quickly see how much the implications are affected. For example, if Bishop had called Scandapol a "guarded city", it might then have seemed awkward if he didn't write, "we debated the size of the bribe required to get us on the ship," or some other statement that would respond to the implication that the city was in some way guarded, instead of free. And consider what happens to the story if somewhere else within it we were to find the statement, "He knew all too well his grandfather's stories about the problems that had come when probeships were docked at the free cities." In such a case the alert reader will note that the protagonist could not then have boarded a ship at Scandapol—and if the writer didn't know this as well (long before the reader), he might not have eliminated the internal contradiction, leaving the story with a big hole in the plot. A writer as skilled as Michael Bishop would never let such a thing happen.

Bishop makes certain kinds of statements because Scandapol is a free city rather than any other kind of city. He does not want to spend a lot of story time on this one minor item, however, so he ignores many implications of Scandapol's status as a free city. Let's say, just for the sake of argument, that one implication turns out to be this: A free city is one in which sausages are handed out on every street corner just for the asking. (We're pretending that Bishop figured this out by delineating all the interrelated characteristics required by his scenario of what he wants a "free city" to be.) But does it matter that the protagonist can get a free sausage any time he wants? No, it doesn't matter; it doesn't affect the action in the story, and therefore Bishop ignores it—doesn't even mention it—knowing that even if a reader deduces that the protagonist can get a free sausage, it won't make any of the story's action implausible. (As in, "Hey, wait a minute! He wouldn't have to *steal* a sausage; he could just *ask* for one!")

And so we see that the danger for an sf writer lies not in the act of ignoring the implications of a postulated change, but in not being aware of, and therefore not compensating for, the effect of ignoring them. What this means is that if you ignore implications, you'd better be doing it intentionally, *knowing* which implications you're ignoring. If you are not aware you are ignoring implications, then all you can do is hope that no big plot-wrecking implications are waiting in the wings for a reader to discover.

All of this does not mean that you are better off simply NOT ignoring implications, even intentionally. In fact, it is almost always necessary when writing sf to ignore many or most of them. The implications of any postulated change can be so vast that it would take an entire series of novels to contemplate them all, which means that if you are writing a short story of three thousand words, you had better know what to leave out. It is possible, and quite commonly done, to keep most of the substantive elements of a story very similar to those in the world we know, changing only one element, and then to examine the impact—the immediate, relatively obvious, and more or less direct effects—of that small change within a very limited section of the universe, simultaneously ignoring the vast and profound implications of that change. Therefore, often an sf writer merely ignores implications of change, when it will do no harm simply to leave them out. Sometimes, however, it is necessary to *suppress* implications of change.

Why *suppress* implications? The reason is that very often there are implications that would force the story to move in a direction different from that which the writer wants to explore. Perhaps the plot would be altered, or perhaps a character might be compelled to act in an undesirable (from the writer's point of view) manner, if the writer allowed us to consider implications that are not germane to the story's point. Sometimes a writer can see implications that would even contradict the point he or she is trying to make.

Compensating for these sorts of implications, then, is a process of hiding them so effectively that the reader will not be likely to come upon them. This is done by presenting the *desired* implications with enough complexity in the details of both their logical existence and their physical existence that they attain the apparent force of *inevitability* (the sensation in the reader's mind that, *of course*, things just have to be this way). In this way the desired implications become plausible, and the story line is supported. The necessary level of complexity required to achieve this effect is demanded by the circumstances of the particular story. A writer would not create a ten-page quasi-scientific treatise on "hyperspace drive" to be included in what would otherwise be a fifteen-page thriller about a rocket race between Earth and Mars. Nor would a writer toss off a mere one-paragraph description of the protagonist's home planet if the story is a thousand-page tale of her trek across three continents to find the only source of all known magic, which in fact turns out to be a heretofore misunderstood elemental force of physics that has shaped the planet itself.

Alternatively, rather than directing us away from undesirable implications, the writer may include story material that anticipates and guides the reader's inferences. The writer can shape a reader's deductions by answering the reader's questions in a convincing way in advance, thus preventing the reader from coming up with any other answer—the reader won't need any other answer if the writer's answer is good enough. To do this, the writer must first identify the most likely question a reader would be expected to pose when that reader spots a buried implication. As a shining example of this, Bob Shaw's classic story, "Light of Other Days," creates a richly intriguing new world out of one stunning change, all the while staying one step ahead of the reader. From the opening sentence, "Leaving the village behind, we followed the heady sweeps of the road up into a land of slow glass," we are transfixed. What could slow glass be? We try to figure it out, but before we can, we learn that it is a type of glass that transmits light very, very slowly, so that images passing into it do not emerge from the other side for months or years. Having absorbed this amazing concept, we begin to wonder what implications it would have for the world. But here Shaw uses a classic distracting technique to perfection: By designing his story around a trip being taken by a married couple in the Scottish countryside, he distracts us from the broader implications of this technological marvel, and forces us to consider its impact in one small region of the world. He nevertheless makes a few statements about the overall condition of the world, proving that he knows what slow glass means to the world in general, but he focuses our attention on the situation of the protagonists, and by doing so it is as if he says, "I could easily tell you everything that has changed as a result of slow glass, but that's not important at the moment. Look at what's happening to these people right here and now." And so we put aside any questions about what slow glass might mean to someone in Indiana or Rangoon.

Then Shaw moves back into a beautiful sequence of elements that illustrate how to stay one step ahead of the reader: Just as we're barely beginning to wonder what slow glass is used for, Shaw shows us that our couple is driving through a region of *slow glass farms*, and we are startled again as we start to realize, "Oh, these pieces of glass capture images, but there must then be images to be captured, and so the glass is set out in picturesque locations until it has stored up a few months or years of beautiful images," and by now Shaw is already on to the next issue. He's saying, "Yes, that's good, isn't it? You see, I figured all that out, and aren't you clever to have figured it out, too, but now take a look at this." And breathlessly we try to keep up with him, as we find out more and more about it, until the final twist, when he proves how well he has stayed ahead of our deductions all the way. Of course I can't reveal the ending because that would spoil everything, but I can tell you it will make you say, "But of course, why didn't I think of that?!" at the same time you are feeling your heart wrenched around in your chest by the genius and beauty of what Shaw has done. Here's a tip: Read the story if you want to see just how meaningful, powerful, and entertaining—all at once—the best sf can be. (It has appeared in many collections, including *Alpha 6*, edited by Robert Silverberg, and *The Road To Science Fiction #4*, edited by James Gunn. I leave you to seek it out, because if you are serious about writing sf, you will.)

To reiterate, the writer must always be able to say to the reader, in a manner that is not at all condescending, "See, I'm ahead of you here. I thought of that already." A writer who is unable to convince a reader of this has little to offer the reader. In sf particularly, the reader wants to be taken somewhere he or she has never been, to a world (no matter how much or how little different from ours) that he or she has never experienced. If the reader is never surprised, or can pick apart the structure of that fictional world so that it is not convincing as a place worthy of exploration, then the story is a failure. This can happen in numerous ways; I'll mention only a couple here, just to give you the idea.

One common error in the stories of novice sf writers is to place a story in the near future, and then write about changes that could not possibly happen until much later, such as when a writer postulates intergalactic travel sometime in the early twenty-first century. Hmm . . . the twenty-first century sounds pretty far in the future, but as I write this, it's only a few years off, and you, dear reader, may already be in the twenty-first century as you read this. Is there intergalactic travel happening while you read this? Even if you're reading this near the *end* of the twenty-first century, say in the year 2099, I'll bet there isn't. Another neophyte's error is making alien species all too human, such as entirely human creatures who just happen to have pointy ears. Hmm . . . does this sound familiar? Well . . . the famous Mr. Spock is not a *plausible* alien at all from a scientific viewpoint, but television and film sf, in some cases, still provides a haven for some of the devices that were found in printed sf of a less evolved form. Of course, we forgive *Star Trek* numerous scientific inaccuracies, because of the many other pleasures it provides. Moreover, *Star Trek* uses devices like Mr. Spock to illuminate aspects of human nature in revealing ways, and thereby justifies—no, even more than justifies, *Star Trek* makes us delight in our acceptance of— an otherwise preposterous character.

To be fair, it must be noted that the demands of filmed (or videotaped) sf are very different from those of printed sf. Primarily, filmed sf is interested in visual dynamics (including special effects), powerful plot lines, and a (low) level of story complexity that can be grasped by most viewers just as quickly as the images and scenes fly by. Remember, you don't get a chance to stop and linger over an interesting or challenging paragraph when you're watching a film! This does not mean that complex, sophisticated sf does not

exist in the filmed medium, only that it is still in the minority. As the sophistication of the audience increases, we are seeing more and more of it all the
time. What's more, the delights of great special effects and powerful plot
lines are not to be discounted (there aren't many of us who don't love *Star
Wars*, right?) but for the purposes of this chapter I will simply say that you
need to learn how to write sf that is intended to be *read* before you write sf
that is intended to be *seen*. The point is that once you know how to build really solid sf, you can break it down, and even flaunt the rules, to suit your
purposes.

And building good sf means creating a convincing new world while at
the same time compensating for ignored or suppressed implications of the
change that got us into that world. If, as you construct an sf story, you ne-
glect the need to accomplish both ends of this task, you can blunder horren-
dously.

LET'S BUILD A STORY AND SEE WHAT KIND OF MESS WE CAN MAKE!

Let's say you decide to create a universe in which dogs have a very poor
sense of hearing. And let's say you are doing this because you want to tell a
story about a man who has a dog that he loves very much. One day the dog
runs into the street and is hit by a car because the dog didn't hear the car
coming, even with its horn blaring. And the man is stricken because he
couldn't save his beloved dog from every possible danger, and now he is
lost—bereft of friendship, doomed to spend his days alone.

Ignoring for a moment the obvious and overblown melodrama of this
situation, we can see that the story fails in structure because we have neglected to consider what the world would really be like if dogs couldn't
hear very well. The reader immediately asks, Wouldn't dogs have found another way to avoid cars? Or if not, wouldn't people have found a way to
protect them? It could be that dogs, being so treasured by humans, would
have become the recipients of special doggie hearing aids, and so to accomplish the plot as stated, the situation would require the dog losing his hearing aid and *then* getting run over. Or perhaps the man is too destitute to afford a hearing aid for his dog. Right away, you can see how we are finding
ways to make a lot more sense. What's more, you can also see that we have
moved slightly in the direction of legitimate pathos, and away from godaw-
ful melodrama—not that we have improved things all that much, but at
least we're taking steps in the right direction.

But consider further. If dogs really did have poor hearing, we should
probably trace this change all the way back to its origin, thus: If dogs have
poor hearing, they must have evolved that way, which means they *never*
had good hearing, and were therefore never very useful as companions to

humans . . . in which case they never underwent the level of domestication that they did in the world as we know it, and remained essentially wild animals, and eventually became targets for big game hunters before the ecology movement put a stop to that—and in the meantime, cats became our number one most trusted and domesticated animal. And where do you, dear sf author, go with the implications of all of *that*?

You can postulate a lot more fallout to the changes mentioned here; this barely scrapes the surface. But you can see from this analysis that even one small change necessitates some very careful thinking about consequences (implications!).

Before I leave our story about hearing-impaired dogs, let me point out that a writer can, and very often does, throw a monkey wrench (or a Milk-Bone) into the deductions that derive from his or her own universe-building. For example, let's start our chain of assumptions and conclusions all over again, *and then break it*, thus: If dogs have poor hearing, then they must have evolved that way—but wait! Maybe they didn't evolve that way. Maybe they were just as we know dogs to be today, noble creatures with excellent hearing, but they lost their hearing somewhere along the way. And if so, what might have caused them to lose their hearing? Perhaps in the process of polluting our world we introduced an environmental neurotoxin that attacks the nervous system of dogs and destroys their hearing. Therefore, dogs' hearing loss is our fault, and yet since there seems to be no other negative effect of this neurotoxin, no one cares to devote lots of energy and money to remove it from the environment. And maybe the protagonist of our story is an activist who is fighting to get the governments of the world to eliminate this toxin, but they won't, until the day his beloved dog sees the President of the United States about to be assassinated. The dog rushes across the street to attack the assassin, but doesn't hear the car coming, and gets run over, and the President is assassinated. And finally everyone sees the value of removing that toxin from the face of the earth.

Wow! Now there's a story. Actually, it's pretty awful, too, but many worse have been written. And the point is that now we have generated a more complexly constructed story that has some inherent tension and a genuine plot. More importantly, despite its shortcomings, it does make some kind of sense. A pattern of logical and physical inevitability is being built, so that the story doesn't make you say, "But wait a minute, if dogs can't hear, *why* can't they hear? And wouldn't people have given them hearing aids?" And whatever other questions you naturally would want to fling at the original version of our story.

At this point, it is natural to wonder how it is possible to deal with every implication of the changes you might wish to postulate in any given story. If any change generates such a wealth of implications, how can any writer determine what all of them are, decide which ones to eliminate, explore the chosen ones, and compensate for the excluded ones?

Obviously, it would be impossible to accomplish this process with every conceivable implication. And the reader does not expect a writer to do so. What a reader expects is a level of reasonability that makes him or her comfortable with the story. In this way, all fiction writing is alike. For an sf writer, contemplating the possible implications of any change is akin to any other writer contemplating the possible outcomes of any plot element in any genre. For the most part, this is done not by trying to discern every question that could possibly be posed in any given story situation, but by asking the obvious questions, the ones that naturally spring to mind *when the reader is inside the story*.

INTERNAL VS. EXTERNAL CONSISTENCY

How can a reader be inside the story? In this way: The reader wants to be inside the story anyway (that's why the reader is reading your story in the first place), and so a thoroughly convincing context for all the elements of a story will be persuasive to the reader, and the reader will then be *absorbed*— the reader will be drawn in, vicariously living in the world depicted therein. At this point, the reader will not question anything that makes sense in that world, even though an objective observer, one who is outside that world, might be able to spot an ignored implication. It should be emphasized that this principle applies no matter what type or genre of fiction you are writing, because no story can be the real world; every story, no matter how close to our known reality, creates its own reality, and must be internally consistent. I emphasize *internally* consistent—consistent within itself. For a work of fiction, consistency outside itself—consistency with known reality—is only another writing tool to be used to varying degrees depending on the purposes of the story. The spy fiction of John Le CarrÈ, for example, depends heavily on a massive infusion of verisimilitude, or the simulation of known reality. His fictional world must seem to be very much the world we know in order to be gripping to the fans of that sort of fiction. Fantastic fiction, on the other hand, intentionally breaks with known reality to serve its purposes, which are often allegorical.

Let's look at an example of how a fictional world can be internally consistent, thereby eliminating a willing reader's potential complaints about ignored implications, even though an objective observer from outside that fictional world can easily spot an ignored implication. Consider a scene from a romance novel set in the year 1830. The heroine (I use the older term here, rather than "protagonist", to fit the genre under discussion) has lost her house, her farm, and all her money, and is about to sign onto a sailing ship as a scullery maid. The evil ship's captain holds out the contract for her to sign, proffering a quill pen along with it. Trembling, she takes the pen and signs, but suddenly shots are fired, and the hero, his pistol blazing, comes riding up on powerful stallion and sweeps her away.

Once the writer has created this scene, he or she must stop and consider: If the ship's captain offers her a pen, it would be a quill pen, wouldn't it? Yes, the writer thinks—not a ballpoint. And might the heroine actually go to work as a scullery maid? Well, yes, says the writer, I've set this in New Orleans, where there are indeed ships, and in the previous chapter I've given her no other means of support, and I've pointed out that no other work is available, so her choice is not unreasonable. Now what about the hero? Oops! There is no such thing as multi-shot weapons in this world, so we wouldn't hear more than one shot being fired unless someone was returning fire, and moreover his pistol would not be blazing as he rides to the rescue, because he would already have fired his single shot, and he wouldn't have been able to reload while riding at full gallop—unless I want to make him the most astounding pistol-shot ever known!

And so the writer fixes that whole mess. But there's something else the writer does not need to fix: Neither the heroine, nor the hero, nor the writer, nor (if the writer has succeeded) the reader, is troubled by the fact that the heroine signed a contract and is legally bound to serve on that ship. The contract becomes nothing more than a point that emphasizes her need to be rescued, if it is even considered at all. This is because the world of the story, which we are assuming the writer did indeed create with sufficient complexity, has achieved a life of its own, *and it is not exactly the world as it was once known*, even though it *appears* to be New Orleans in the early nineteenth century. The point is this: In the real world, that contract would have some meaning, and couldn't be simply brushed aside as the hero sweeps the heroine away, but this fact has been suppressed in the world of the story, *and no one cares*.

Similarly in sf, the writer must consider only those implications of the postulated changes which are relevant to the context of the story. In my story, "And of the Earth, A Womb," a jet fighter pilot captures a creature from another world and attempts to communicate with it. But years of war precede this climactic event. In the following excerpt, the protagonist has just used his jet fighter to lay floating mines in the sky; these will interrupt the Earthward plunge of the attacking aliens, who fall from the sky as they attack, and whom the humans have dubbed "Orbs":

> He rolls ninety degrees and clears to a safe distance. Hovering, he gazes at the mines suspended in the sky like buoyant pearls the size of beach balls. Above, the Orbs tumble downward like spherical brown meteors. As always, he is amazed that they can fall so peacefully, even thought they *must* be aware of their fate. And as always, he marvels at the strange beauty of this frightening ballet.
>
> The sky catches flame as the rain of Orbs ignites the proximity-fused mines. Tongues of fire lick the clouds. Seconds later the shock waves, with a roar like the yell of a giant, buffet his plane. The hull tem-

perature peaks at nearly one hundred eighty degrees, then gradually
slides down to a more normal fifteen.

If you were to stop and think for a moment, one possible implication of
thousands of battles like this is that the weather might be affected, but the
story does not consider that. It would be distracting and irrelevant to what
the story is trying to say. Notice how I provide a wealth of detail about the
second to second progress of the battle, and more importantly, I personalize
the story intensely with a searching consideration of the protagonist's
thoughtful and troubled reaction to the war. Faced with so much gritty reality and so much emotional depth, no reader would ever stop to consider the
weather.

     This example, then, depicts two of the most common and most effec-
tive techniques for focusing a reader's attention on desired implications and
away from non-desired ones. The first technique is to provide just enough
detail about the depicted world that the reader has no time to think about
what might be missing, and in any case the quantity of detail leaves him or
her feeling satisfied that the information provided is sufficient, and that
there is no need to look for more. The second technique is to keep the
story's point of view very closely allied to that of the main character, so that
the reader identifies with that character, and allows that character's view
of the world to stand in for the reader's. And since the protagonist is
not spending any time worrying about the weather, the reader doesn't,
either.

     Now, remember I said that the writer must compensate for suppressed
implications of change *in a manner that is not at all condescending*. How, then,
does a writer avoid being condescending?

     By not being obvious. And the greatest sin of obviousness in sf is bla-
tantly telling the reader the facts and circumstances of the story situation as
if the story were a travelogue or an encyclopedia article—unless that is
specifically what the writer is mimicking. But aside from such gimmicks,
the vast majority of sf must be written in a natural way. A sense of palpable,
plausible reality must be created, just as with any fiction, but remember that
it is a plausible *internal* reality, married to external, known reality only to
whatever degree the writer needs to make the story work. The story I have
just described is set in the relatively near future on Earth, and so its
verisimilitude depends on a close simulation of what we can expect the
world to be like only a few years from now. A story like Michael Bishop's,
cited above, set in the far future on far planets, depends on a huge departure from our current known reality in order to establish its own plausibil-
ity.

     In all cases, however, the writer must never reveal the circumstances
of the story in an obvious or insulting way. Again, this is a rule that applies
to all genres. For example, in a mystery story, when the detective says, "The

punk leveled his gat, aiming at a spot somewhere between my nostrils," you know what he means, even if you have never seen the word "gat" before. The context explains it to you. The writer would have insulted you if the detective had said, "The punk aimed his gat, which means his gun." Even worse, the punk might have said, "All right, you. I'm going to pick up this gat, you know, this gun, and shoot you."

The proper method of being non-obvious can be described as *creating well-constructed context in which new information is embedded*. It is a key technique in sf writing, because the sf reader must be introduced to a new "reality" that may contain huge amounts of unfamiliar material, and all that information simply cannot be plunked down in blunt exposition.

So we see that, just as in the mystery story above, an sf writer must never write, "All right, you! I'm going to pick up this *ganzick*—you know, this sort of ray gun thing that shoots energy beams—and shoot you." The strength of *well-constructed context in which new information is embedded* is evident if we do a little experiment: What if the mystery writer had written, "The punk leveled his ganzick, aiming at a spot somewhere between my nostrils"? Amazingly, this works fairly well; even if nothing in the story up to that point had told you what a ganzick is, you would have a pretty good idea from the context. And the writer hasn't insulted you; the writer has said, "I know you're pretty clever; you'll get the idea." Now in science fiction, it works the same: "The Feldoran leveled his ganzick, aiming at a spot somewhere between my nostrils."

This principle is so important in sf that I will reiterate it: Give the reader clear but detailed context, from which he or she can infer the meaning of new information embedded therein. Look at the quote from Michael Bishop again. What about "probeship"? That's not a word we use every day, but I'll bet none of you even thought about it until I just mentioned it. Bishop slipped that one in on us without causing us to bat an eye, and we understood it from the context of the sentence—and not only that, but the word itself even generates its own internal context, so that we grasp it right away. We don't know everything there is to know about a probeship yet, but we get the gist.

This rule of context can occasionally be sidestepped in the case of a first-person narrative, or a story in which there is some type of narration (for example, the report of a scientific expedition sent to explore a new planet). In such a case, some new information can be imparted directly to the reader, but the writer must be very judicious about this, because narration usually bogs down a story.

Most important of all, NEVER have a character impart information bluntly to another character *who should already know that information!* Example: "Well, Ed, I'm just going to turn on my jet pack, which I use to fly home every night, and head out of here. See you tomorrow." This is Sin Number One in writing sf, and cannot be tolerated in the slightest.

THE HUMAN HEART IN CONFLICT WITH ITSELF:
REQUIREMENTS OF THEME IN SCIENCE FICTION

The concerns of science fiction are different from those of every other genre. In a sense, that is exactly what defines a genre. If mysteries did not have a set of concerns different from the set that defines romance stories, they would not be different genres. But let me be more specific. The concerns to which I have referred so far are those of subject matter. Mysteries are concerned with crime, romance stories with love, science fiction with change. There are many other concerns with which a writer struggles, and many of them are, for the sf writer, exactly the same as those found in any other field of writing. Many of these concerns *must be* the same, or else there is little validity to the writing.

Let me discuss only one of these concerns, the one that is by far the most important.

It is this: The human heart in conflict with itself. Harlan Ellison mentioned this in his discussion of characterization. It is taken from William Faulkner's Nobel Prize acceptance speech, and I wish to discuss it here for a moment. The best fiction, no matter what category you choose to stick it in, has this essential element as its primary and central concern. Science fiction, as much as any form of fiction, must track the pathways of human emotion if it is to have any claim to significance. The particular angle that sf usually takes, as we have seen, is an exploration of the human heart in conflict with itself as it faces the future, and after all, aren't all of us always—and I do mean at every moment—facing the future?

A few more words on "the human heart in conflict with itself": This condition is most pointedly revealed within any situation in which a person is faced with two or more courses of action, each one of which in some way excludes the others, and in which the person has good reasons to follow each course, but *must* choose only one. In making this choice, the character illuminates something about himself or herself, and by extrapolation, something about all of humankind and the human condition.

In the second of the two stories you are about to read, a piece I wrote called "Conditioning" which was first published in what has traditionally been the most literary of the sf magazines—namely *The Magazine of Fantasy and Science Fiction*—I tried to crystallize a moment of the human heart in conflict with itself, delineating that moment so precisely that we can see the parameters of the conflict clearly, feel the agony of the protagonist's decision, see the consequences to the entire world of the protagonist's actions, and understand the factors that led him to his climactic action. I suggest you read it once for enjoyment, and then go back and see how each of the concerns and techniques discussed in this chapter was used to build an effective, engaging story. And then I hope you will also notice how the possibilities for making creative use of the writing techniques discussed in this chapter are limitless, because you are also going to see that this story makes use of one major device, one particular writer's tool, not even discussed in this chapter, that helped me accomplish the essential task of *creating well-constructed context in which new information is embedded*, while at the same time forcing the reader to accept the implications that the protagonist sees, rather than any others that might disrupt the story. (The device I mean has to do with the way I linked the narrative voice with the protagonist's state of mind; you'll notice it immediately.)

And in the first of the two stories you are about to read, Harlan Ellison's classic "All the Sounds of Fear," you cannot help but notice that Ellison utilizes the essential element of *change* in a wholly startling and original way. Ellison is both a mind-blowing artist and a master craftsman; he is a brilliant fantasist, and certainly the most unique voice ever to be associated with science fiction, even though his work goes far beyond what most of us do within the borders of the science fiction field. He proves that fiction is fiction is fiction, and that genres are, in the last analysis, meaningless. Harlan Ellison is no more a "science fiction writer" than Raymond Chandler is a "detective fiction writer" or Fyodor Dostoyevsky is a "crime fiction writer" or Jorge Luis Borges is a "fantasy fiction writer". He is simply a great writer, but he deigns at times to tolerate having his work categorized as science fiction, and for this we who write science fiction are honored.

So now read "All the Sounds of Fear", and think of all the ways that *change* is a meaningful element of this story. For one, wholesale changes in a human being drive the plot. For another, the world depicted in the story is changed from the one we know, in a crucial way—I will leave it for you to identify and then define your own interpretation of what change this is. And for a third, I will ask you to notice how the power and artistry of Ellison's writing style in and of itself creates a world that is not like our own. Could you read this story and not feel as if you had entered another dimension?

Both stories, then, demonstrate examples of taking elements essential to science fiction and using them in creative and original ways. Let them inspire you to find new ways of your own to take these same essential elements and expand the horizons of science fiction as it moves onward, ahead through time.

All the Sounds of Fear

Harlan Ellison

"Give me some light!"

Cry: tormented, half-moan half-chant, cast out against a whispering darkness; a man wound in white, arms upflung to roistering shadows, sooty sockets where eyes had been, pleading, demanding, anger and hopelessness, anguish from the soul into the world. He stumbled, a step, two, faltering, weak, the man returned to the child, trying to find some exit from the washing sea of darkness in which he trembled.

"Give me some light!"

Around him a Greek chorus of susurrating voices. Plucking at his garments, he staggered toward an intimation of sound, a resting place, a goal. The man in pain, the figure of *all* pain, all desperation, and nowhere in that circle of painful light was there release from this torment. Sandaled feet stepping, each one above an abyss, no hope and no safety; what can it mean to be so eternally blind?

Again: "Give me some light!"

The last tortured ripping of the words from a throat raw with the hopelessness of salvation. Then the man sank to the shadows that moved in on him. The face half-hidden in chiaroscuro, sharp black, blanched white, down and down into the grayness about his feet, the circle of blazing white light pinpointing him, a creature impaled on a pin of brilliance, till closing, closing, closing it swallowed him, all gone to black, darkness within and without, black even deeper, nothing, finis, end, silence.

Richard Becker, Oedipus, had played his first role. Twenty-four years later, he would play it again, as his last. But before that final performance's curtain could be rung, twenty-four years of greatness would have to strut across stages of life and theater and emotion.

Time, passing.

When they had decided to cast the paranoid beggar in *Sweet Miracles*, Richard Becker had gone to the Salvation Army retail store, and bought a set of rags that even the sanctimonious saleswomen staffing the shop tried to throw out as unsalable and foul. He bought a pair of cracked and soleless shoes that were a size too large. He bought a hat that had seen so many autumns of rain its brim had bowed and withered under the onslaught. He bought a no-color vest from a suit long since destroyed, and a pair of pants whose seat sagged baggily, and a shirt with three buttons gone, and a jacket that seemed to symbolize every derelict who had ever cadged an hour's sleep in an alley.

He bought these things over the protests of the kindly, white-haired women who were *doing their bit for charity,* and he asked if he might step into the toilet for a few moments to try them on; and when he emerged, his good tweed jacket and dark slacks over his arm, he was another man entirely. As though magically, the coarse stubble (that may have been there when he came into the store, but he seemed too nice-looking a young man to go around unshaved) had sprouted on his sagging jowls. The hair had grown limp and off-gray under the squashed hat. The face was lined and planed with the depravities and deprivations of a lifetime lived in gutters and saloons. The hands were caked with filth, the eyes lusterless and devoid of personality, the body grotesquely slumped with the burden of mere existence. This old man, this skid from the Bowery, how had he gotten into the toilet, and where was the nice young man who had gone in wearing that jacket and those slacks? Had this *creature* somehow overpowered him (what foul weapon had this feeble old man used to subdue a vital, strong youth like that)? The white-haired Good Women of Charity were frozen with distress as they imagined the strong-faced, attractive youth, lying in the bathroom, his skull crushed by a length of pipe.

The old bum extended the jacket, the pants, and the rest of the clothing the young man had been wearing, and in a voice that was thirty years younger than the body from which it spoke, he explained, "I won't be needing these, ladies. Sell them to someone who can make good use of them." The voice of the young man, from this husk.

And he paid for the rags he wore. They watched him as he limped and rolled through the front door, into the filthy streets; another tramp gone to join the tide of lost souls that would inevitably become a stream and a river and an ocean of wastrels, washing finally into a drunk tank, or a doorway, or onto a park bench.

Richard Becker spent six weeks living on the Bowery; in fleabags, abandoned warehouses, cellars, gutters and on tenement rooftops, he shared and wallowed in the nature and filth and degradation of the empty men of his times.

For six weeks he *was* a tramp, a thoroughly washed-out hopeless rum-dum, with rheumy eyes and palsied hands and a weak bladder.

One by one the weeks mounted to six, and on the first day of casting for *Sweet Miracles,* the Monday of the seventh week, Richard Becker arrived at the Martin Theatre, where he auditioned for the part in the clothes he had worn for the past six weeks.

The play ran for five hundred and eighteen performances, and Richard Becker won the Drama Critics' Circle Award as the finest male performer of the year. He also won the Circle Award as the most promising newcomer of the year.

He was twenty-two at the time.

The following season, after *Sweet Miracles* had gone on the road, Richard Becker was apprised, through the pages of *Variety*, that John Foresman and T. H. Searle were about to begin casting for *House of Infidels*, the new script by Odets, his first in many years. Through friends in the Foresman and Searle offices, he obtained a copy of the script, and selected a part he considered massive in its potentialities.

The role of an introspective and tormented artist, depressed by the level of commercialism to which his work had sunk, resolved to regain an innocence of childhood or nature he had lost, by working with his hands in a foundry.

When the first night critics called Richard Becker's conception of Tresk, the artist, "a pinnacle of thespic intuition" and noted, "His authority in the part led members of the audience to ask one another how such a sensitive actor could grasp the rough unsubtle life of a foundry-worker," they had no idea that Richard Becker had worked for nearly two months in a steel stamping plant and foundry in Pittsburgh. But the makeup man on *House of Infidels* suspected Richard Becker had once been in a terrible fire, for his hands were marked by the ravages of great heat.

After two successes, two conquests of Broadway, two characterizations that were immediately ranked with the most brilliant Shubert Alley had ever witnessed, Richard Becker's reputation began to build a legend.

"The Man Who *Is* 'The Method,'" they called him, in perceptive articles and interviews. Lee Strasberg of the Actors Studio, when questioned, remarked that Becker had never been a student, but had the occasion arisen, he might well have paid *him* to attend. In any event, Richard Becker's command of the Stanislavski theory of total immersion in a part became a working example of the validity of the concept. No mere scratcher and stammerer, on a stage Richard Becker *was* the man he pretended to be.

Of his private life little was written; he let it be known that if he was to be totally convincing in a characterization, he wanted no intrusive shadow of himself standing between the audience and the image he offered.

Hollywood's offers of stardom were refused, for as *Theatre Arts* commented in a brief feature on Richard Becker:

> *The gestalt that Becker projects across a row of footlights would be dimmed and turned two-dimensional on the Hollywood screen. Becker's art is an ultimate distillation of truth and metamorphosis that requires the reality of stage produc-*

tion to retain its purity. It might even be noted that Richard Becker acts in four dimensions, as opposed to the merely craftsmanlike three of his contemporaries. Surely no one could truly argue with the fact that watching a Becker performance is almost a religious experience. We can only congratulate Richard Becker on his perceptiveness in turning down studio bids.

The years of building a backlog of definitive parts (effectively ruining them for other actors who were condemned to play them after Becker had said all there was to say) passed, as Richard Becker became, in turn, a Hamlet that cast new lights on the Freudian implications of Shakespeare... a fiery Southern segregationist whose wife reveals her octaroon background... a fast-talking salesman come to grips with futility and cowardice... a many-faceted Marco Polo... a dissolute and totally amoral pimp, driven by a loathing for women to sell his own sister into evil... a ruthless politician, dying of cancer and senility....

And the most challenging part he had ever undertaken, the recreation, in the play by Tennessee Williams, of the deranged religious zealot, trapped by his own warring emotions, into the hammer-murder of an innocent girl.

When they found him, in the model's apartment off Gramercy Place, they were unable to get a coherent story of why he had done the disgusting act, for he had lapsed into a stentorian tone of Biblical fervor, pontificating about the blood of the lamb and the curse of Jezebel and the eternal fires of Perdition. The men from Homicide East included in their ranks a rookie, fresh to the squad, who became desperately ill at the sight of the fouled walls and the crumpled form wedged into the tiny kitchenette; he became violently ill, and was taken from the apartment a few minutes before Richard Becker was led away.

The trial was a manifest sadness to all who had seen him onstage, and the jury did not even have to be sent out to agree on a verdict of insanity.

After all, whoever the fanatic was that the defense put on the stands, he was not sane, and he was certainly no longer Richard Becker, the actor.

For Dr. Charles Tedrow, the patient in restraining room 16 was a constant involvement. He was unable to divorce himself from the memory of a night three years before, when he had sat in an orchestra seat at the Henry Miller Theater and seen Richard Becker, light and adroit, as the comical Tosspot in that season's hit comedy, *Never a Rascal.*

He was unable to separate his thoughts from the shape and form of the actor who had so immersed himself in The Method that for a time, in three acts, he *was* a blundering, maundering larcenous alcoholic with a penchant for pomegranates and (as Becker had mouthed it onstage) "barratry on the low seas!" Separate them from this weird and many-faceted creature that lived its many lives in the padded cell numbered 16? Impossible.

At first, there had been reporters, who had come to inteview the Good Doctor in charge of Becker's case; and to the last of these (for Dr. Tedrow had instituted restrictions on this sort of publicity) he had said, "To a man like Richard Becker, the world was very important. He was very much a man of his times; he had no real personality of his own, with the exception of that one overwhelming faculty and need to reflect the world around him. He was an actor in the purest sense of the word. The world gave him his personality, his attitudes, his façade and his reason for existence. Take those away from him, clap him up in a padded cell—as we were forced to do— and he begins to lose touch with reality.'

"I understand," the reporter had inquired carefully, "that Becker is re-living his roles, one after another. Is that true, Dr. Tedrow?"

Charles Tedrow was, above all else, a compassionate man, and his fury at this remark, revealing as it did a leak in the sanitarium's security, was unlike him. "Richard Becker is undergoing what might be called, in psychiatric terms, 'induced hallucinatory regression.' In his search for some reality, there in that room, he has fastened onto the method of assuming characters' moods he has played onstage. From what I've been able to piece together from reviews of his shows, he is going back: from the most recent to the next and the next and so on."

The reporter had asked more questions, had made more superficial and phantasmagoric assumptions, until Dr. Charles Tedrow had concluded the interview forcibly.

But even now, as he sat across from Richard Becker in the quiet office, he knew that almost nothing the reporter had conceived could rival what Becker had done to himself.

"Tell me, Doctor," the florid, bombastic traveling salesman who was Richard Becker asked, "what the hell's new down the line?"

"It's really very quiet, these days, Ted," the physician replied. Becker had been this way for two months now: submerged in the part of Ted Rogat, the loudmouthed philandering protagonist of Chayefsky's *The Wanderer*. For six months before that he had been Marco Polo, and before that the nervous, slack-jawed and incestuous son of *The Glass of Sadness*.

"Hell, I remember one little chippie in, where was it, oh yeah, hell yes! It was K.C., good old K.C.! Man, she was a *goodie!* You ever been to K.C., Doc? I was a drummer in nylons when I worked K.C. Jeezus, lemme tell ya—"

It was difficult to believe that the man who sat on the other side of the table was an actor. He looked the part, he spoke the part, he *was* Ted Rogat, and Dr. Tedrow would catch himself from time to time contemplating the release of this total stranger who had wandered into Richard Becker's cell.

He sat and listened to the story of the flame-hipped harlot in Kansas City whom Ted Rogat had picked up in an Armenian restaurant, and seduced with promises of nylons. He listened to it, and knew that whatever else was true of Richard Becker, this creature of many faces and many lives, he was no saner than the day he had killed that girl. After eighteen months in the sanitarium, he was going back, back, back through his acting career, and re-playing the roles; but never once coming to grips with reality.

In the plight and the flight of Richard Becker, Dr. Charles Tedrow saw a bit of himself, of all men, of his times and the thousand illnesses to which mortal flesh was heir.

He returned Richard Becker, as well as Ted Rogat, to the security and tiny world of room 16.

Two months later he brought him back and spent a highly interesting three hours discussing group therapy with Herr Doktor Ernst Loebisch, credentials from the Munich Academy of Medicine and the Vienna Psychiatric Clinic. Four months after that, Dr. Tedrow got to know the surly and insipid Jackie Bishoff, juvenile delinquent and hero of *Street of Night*.

And almost a year later—to the day—Dr. Tedrow sat in his office with a bum, a derelict, a rheumy-eyed and dissipated vagabond who could only be the skid from *Sweet Miracles*, Richard Becker's first triumph, twenty-four years before.

What Richard Becker might look like, without camouflage, in his own body, Tedrow had no idea. He was, now, to the most agonizing scrutiny, the seedy old tramp with the dirt caked into the sagged folds of his face.

"Mr. Becker, I want to talk to you."

Hopelesness shined out of the old bum's eyes. There was no answer.

"Listen to me, Becker. Please listen to me, if you're in there somewhere, if you can hear me. I want you to understand what I'm about to say; it's very important."

A croak, cracked and forced, came from the bum's lips, and he mumbled, "I need'a drink, yuh got uh drink fuh me, huh . . ."

Tedrow leaned across, his hand shaking as he took the old bum's chin in his palm, and held it fixed, staring into this stranger's eyes. "Now listen to me, Becker. You've got to hear me. I've gone through the files, and as far as I can tell, this was the first part you ever played. I don't know what will happen! I don't know what form this syndrome will take after you've used up all your other lives. But if you can hear me, you've got to understand that you may be approaching a crisis point in your—in your life."

The old bum licked cracked lips.

"*Listen!* I'm here, I want to help you. I want to *do* something for you, Becker. If you'll come out for an instant, just a second, we can establish contact. It's got to be now or—"

He left it hanging. He had no way of knowing *if—what*. And as he lapsed into silence, as he released the bum's chin, a strange alteration of facial muscles began, and the derelict's countenance shifted, subtly ran like mercury, and for a second he saw a face he recognized. From the eyes that were no longer red-rimmed and bloodshot, Dr. Charles Tedrow saw intelligence peering out.

"It sounds like fear, Doctor," he said.

And, "Goodbye, once more."

Then the light died, the features shifted again, and the physician was staring once more at the empty face of a gutter-bred derelict.

He sent the old man back to room 16. Later that day, he had one of his male nurses take in an 80-cent bottle of muscatel.

"Speak up, man! What in the name of God is going on out there?"

"I—I can't explain it, Dr. Tedrow, but you'd better—you'd better get out here right away. It's—it's, oh Jee-zus!"

"What *is* it? Stop crying, Wilson, and tell me what the hell is *wrong!*"

"It's, it's number 16 . . . it's . . ."

"I'll be there in twenty minutes. Keep everyone away from that room. Do you understand? Wilson! Do you understand me?"

"Yessir, yessir. I'll—oh Christ—hurry up, Doc . . ."

He could feel his pajama pants bunched around his knees, under his slacks, as he floored the pedal of the ranch wagon. The midnight roads were jerky in the windshield and the murk that he raced through was almost too grotesque to be a fact of nature.

When he slewed the car into the drive, the gatekeeper threw the iron barrier back almost spastically. The ranch wagon chewed gravel, sending debris back in a wide fan, as Tedrow plunged ahead. When he screeched to a halt before the sanitarium, the doors burst open and the senior attendant, Wilson, raced down the steps.

"This way, th—this way, Doctor Te—"

"Get out of my way, you idiot, I know which direction!" He shoved Wilson aside, and strode up the steps and into the building.

"It started about an hour ago . . . didn't know what was happ—"

"And you didn't call me immediately? Ass!"

"We just thought, we just thought it was another one of his stages, *you* know how he is . . ."

Tedrow snorted in disgust and threw off his topcoat as he made his way rapidly down the corridor to the section of the sanitarium that housed the restraining rooms.

As they came into the annex, through the heavy glass-portaled door, he heard the scream for the first time.

In that scream, in that tormented, pleading, demanding and hopelessly lost tremor there were all the sounds of fear he had ever heard. In that voice he heard even his own voice, his own soul, crying out for something.

For an unnameable something, as the scream came again.

"Give me some light!"

Another world, another voice, another life. Some evil empty beseeching from a corner of a dust-strewn universe. Hanging there timelessly, vibrant in colorless agony. A million tired and blind stolen voices all wrapped into that one howl, all the eternal sadnesses and losses and pains ever known to man. It was all there, as the good in the world was sliced open and left to bleed its golden fluid away in the dirt. It was a lone animal being eaten by a bird of prey. It was a hundred children crushed beneath iron treads. It was one good man with his entrails in his blood-soaked hands. It was the soul and the pain and the very vital fiber of life, draining away, without light, without hope, without succor.

"Give me some light!"

Tedrow flung himself at the door and threw back the bolt on the observation window. He stared for a long and silent moment as the scream trembled once more on the air, weightlessly, transparently, tingling off into emptiness. He stared, and felt the impact of a massive horror stifle his own cry of disbelief and terror.

Then he spun away from the window and hung there, sweat-drenched back flat to the wall, with the last sight of Richard Becker he would ever hope to see, burned forever behind his eyes.

The sound of his sobs in the corridor held the others back. They stared silently, still hearing that never-spoken echo reverberating down and down and down the corridors of their minds:

"Give me some light!"

Fumbling beside him, Tedrow slammed the observation window shut, and then his arm sank back to his side.

Inside room 16, lying up against the far wall, his back against the soft passive padding, Richard Becker looked out at the door, at the corridor, at the world, forever.

Looked out as he had in his first moment of life: purely and simply.

Without a face. From his hairline to his chin, a blank, empty, featureless expanse. Empty. Silent. Devoid of sight or smell or sound. Blank and faceless, a creature God had never deigned to bless with a mirror to the world. His Method now was gone.

Richard Becker, actor, had played his last part, and had gone away, taking with him Richard Becker, a man who had known all the sights, all the sounds, all the life of fear.

POINTS TO CONSIDER ABOUT "ALL THE SOUNDS OF FEAR"

1. In "All the Sounds of Fear," what specific qualities of writing support Landsberg's assertion that "Ellison is both a mind-blowing artist and a master craftsman . . . "—a gifted writer of fiction, no matter what the genre? What elements within this story place it within the science fiction genre as described by Landsberg?

2. Describe the ways in which significant change plays a central role in "All the Sounds of Fear." How does change, as outlined by Landsberg, affect the story's protagonist? In what ways does this change suggest thematic implications inherent in the story? What "crucial" changes have

taken place in the world as described by Ellison here? How do those changes impact Richard Becker . . . and humanity in general?

3. Do you find any irony in the titles of the plays in which Richard Becker performs: *Sweet Miracles, House of Infidels, Never a Rascal, The Wanderer, The Glass of Sadness*—or are they just titles selected randomly by Ellison, in your opinion? What is "The Method," an acting theory and practice that receives some subtle commentary in "All the Sounds of Fear"? What points might Ellison be suggesting about The Method, or about acting in general, in this story?

4. Dr. Charles Tedrow says of the story's protagonist, "He was very much a man of his times; he had no real personality of his own, with the exception of that one overwhelming faculty and need to reflect the world around him." To what "overwhelming faculty" is the fictional reporter referring here? What is overwhelming about it? Looking at possible thematic implications embodied in "All the Sounds of Fear", how is Richard Becker "a man of his times"—the quintessential product and reflection of our modern (some might say postmodern) age?

5. Late in the story, the "real" Richard Becker emerges momentarily from his role-imposed persona to respond to Dr. Charles Tedrow's plea, "If you'll come out for an instant, just a second, we can establish contact." Becker responds, "It sounds like fear, Doctor." What, in your opinion, is Becker saying here? How does this statement, and the story's title, help deliver some of the underlying message(s) of "All the Sounds of Fear"?

Conditioning
John M. Landsberg

You ain't never gonna do that again, are ya, Shermie?"

Shermie Brooks dragged the back of his arms across his face where it was sore. Some blood leaked out of his nose and messed his sleeve. He tried to rub it off, but it only smeared worse. Mom would be pretty mad at him for getting that blood there, but after she was mad, she probably would give him a little kiss on the tip of his nose to make it all better, and maybe she'd even let him have a choco-chip cube, if they still had some left this month. His stomach grumbled more than usual, just from thinking about that.

He squinted up at Gritch, who was making a mean face. Gritch looked kind of swirly because there was a lot of water in Shermie's eyes.

"No, Gritch," Shermie said. "No, I won't. I won't never do that again."

Gritch smiled, a big smile with his mouth, but his eyes still looked kind of mean. His mouth had some brown teeth and some black spaces in between. "That's real good, Shermie," he said real slow, and when he was saying it, he was making Shermie's pocket knife jump and down in his hand the same slow way he was talking. Four words, four jumps.

Gritch rubbed his thumb on the side of the knife. "This is a real nice one," he said. A long time ago maybe the knife had some paint on it, but that was all scraped off now. "Yeah," Gritch said, "real neat. You shouldn'ta tried to keep it away from me."

Shermie stood up slow, and then hunched over, so Gritch wouldn't get mad from looking up at him. "Now, Gritch?"

"Now."

"Thanks for—for letting me give you my pocket knife, Gritch."

Gritch tilted back his head and laughed real loud. "What did I tell you, Sly?"

Shermie looked at Sly, who was standing there with Gritch. Sly had greasy hair that made Shermie kind of sick to look at it. Sly chuckled and stuck his thumbs in his pants pockets. "You said it, Gritch. You got him trained real good."

"Yeah," Gritch said. He pulled out the blade, which was the only blade that was still left in the knife, and he waved it up and down and sideways like a little sword. The point of the blade was broken off. "I got him, you know, *conditioned.*" He laughed again. "That's what. Conditioned." He folded the blade inside again and stuck the knife in his back pocket. "C'mon, I'm starvin' to death; let's go see who we can get some ration cards off of."

Gritch and Sly walked away slow, kind of rocking their shoulders from side to side. "That's really somethin'," Sly said. "He gonna be like that all his life? Ain't he never gonna get any smarter?"

The way Sly said that—it made a kind of hot feeling shoot up in Shermie's chest. "Gritch!" he yelled.

Gritch and Sly stopped walking and turned around.

"I *am* gonna get smarter. Someday I'll be smarter."

Gritch made a mean face again. "Did I hear you *actually* raise your voice at me?" he said, in a real nasty way.

"No, Gritch," Shermie said. Now look what he did. Gritch was gonna get mad again, which made Shermie kind of scared. "I didn't raise my voice. Really. I—I just didn't remember—I didn't remember how old—I just wanted to remember how old you said I hafta be to keep my own things."

Gritch smiled. "I said when you turn forty, and don't ask me one more time." He went walkign away again. He laughed some more.

"O.K., Gritch," Shermie called. "I won't ask you that."

Shermie rubbed his knee, which felt sore from bonking on the ground when Gritch hit him. His face was scrunched up because he was trying to think. He was thinking he could remember what Gritch said before, so he wouldn't have to ask Gritch anymore. Before, Gritch said he could keep his own things when he was thirty-nine, *and* Gritch said when he was thirty-eight, and maybe—yeah, Gritch definitely said when he was twenty—he could definitely remember that—maybe. But how could that be right? Because Gritch just now said when he was forty. Yeah. When he was forty, Gritch would let him keep his own things. It wasn't time for him to keep his own things. He wasn't smart enough. He shouldn'ta tried to keep the knife.

Shermie turned around and went walking the other way. He scraped his feet over the sidewalk cracks and pushed his feet sideways around all the big holes, except sometimes he stepped down in the holes for fun. He was going the way to his private place, a place that Gritch didn't even know about.

Gritch don't know about it, he thought. But right away when he thought that, his stomach got sick, and his breathing got going too fast. This was the first time he ever thought how Gritch didn't know about his private place. Maybe Gritch would be angry if he knew. Maybe Gritch would beat him up again.

But that couldn't be right. This was a *place,* not a *thing.* So that was O.K. Because how could he give it to Gritch? He couldn't give a *place* to Gritch; he couldn't anyway. A place just had to always stay where it was.

His breathing got O.K. then, and he kept walking. He sniffled a little because he could feel some blood trying to come out from his nose, and he didn't want some to come out, because that would make him think about Gritch taking his knife, and he didn't want to think about that. He wished Gritch would let him keep something, like maybe his rabbit's foot. That rabbit's foot was pretty neat. Why didn't he let him keep his rabbit's foot, or that beat-up piece of leather? Well, O.K., so leather was super special *real* hard to find, he knew that, so for sure he couldn't keep some leather. And so what about the rabbit's foot? He didn't care about the rabbit's foot anyway, because it was older than he was, and Mom said there weren't rabbits around anywhere since about the twenties, which was longer ago than he could even think about.

He went through the alley, kept going down a dirt road, and kept going more until there weren't even any trees, just lots of dirt all around. He liked it out here, not in the city, because he didn't like trees anyway. He didn't like the way the leaves clicked when it was windy. In the winter, it wasn't so bad, because the leaves had snow on them, so they didn't blow around and click so much. Mom said the way it used to be was that the leaves would fall off the trees before the snow came, but Shermie couldn't figure out how that could be true, unless maybe they used to have crummier glue for holding the leaves on, a long time ago.

It was a whole lot of walking, and then he got to the rocks that were the front of his private place. He squeezed between two of the rocks and looked around. His private place was pretty big, bigger than even about ten or a hundred living cubicles like the cubicle that was his and Mom's, and his private place didn't have anything in it except dirt, and nothing around it except rocks, and nothing over it except regular brown sky. The thing was, he could be in it without Gritch or anybody.

He walked around a little bit and said, "This is my private place," and that made him smile some. He pushed his feet in the dirt when he walked. Then he stopped and got down on the ground, got down flat on his back, and he looked up at the sky and opened up his hands flat, and patted his hands up and down on the ground. He could feel the dirt puff out under his hands when he patted it. "Well," he said, kind of quiet, "here I am."

He patted the ground some more, and after he patted it enough, he said, "Well, what do you think? I think maybe now it's time to climb the big rock. O.K. That sounds good."

One thing he liked to do was climb up on the tallest rock and look at the city, which was exciting to look at from there because it was very far away, which he could tell because he almost couldn't see the city with so much air in the way. And then he would pretend he was the king of the whole city, and he owned it all, and he was so many years old that Gritch would really let him keep it.

But he didn't get to climb up the rock this time because something funny happened. Some kind of tickly tingly feelings jumped around on his neck and his back, and that made him turn around, which was when he saw something that wasn't supposed to be in his private place, but it was. It was a big giant ball, like the little one Mom used for sticking all her pins and needles in, but this was a giant one that filled up almost his whole private place, and it had a million zillion giant needles sticking out from it.

There was a thing in front of the ball that looked kind of like—like something he saw in a picture once—like a *dog,* that's what, a dog, except different. He couldn't remember for sure—did a dog have lots of arms, and was it painted all over with lots of colors? Mom said dogs were nice, real nice. She said she wished she had one if only they still had some in the world. She said they used to call them a name like somebody's best friend.

This dog thing was holding a little box, and it was waving one arm at Shermie. Maybe it wanted to give him the box, but why would it? It sure was a strange thing with its strange giant ball, but that wasn't so strange as that somebody would for real want to give him something. But if that was what it wanted, to give the box to him, maybe he better take it. Maybe if he didn't take the box, the dog thing would get mad like Gritch.

So he went and got over there and stuck out his hand. The dog thing put the box in his hand and waved all its arms a lot. It turned around about five times fast—real, real fast—and some weird sounds came out from it, and then it kind of slipped inside a hole in the giant ball that wasn't there before. Then the hole in the ball got smaller and smaller and wasn't there anymore, and the giant ball went up in the air fast and went in the clouds, and Shermie couldn't see it anymore.

"Huh!" he said.

Then he looked at the box. It had about a million buttons on it. He pressed one, and what do you know? Some soft green stuff pushed up from the dirt in his private place, all around him and even under his feet, too. It was like a green rug, but it had a smell that he couldn't figure out. He bent over and rubbed his hands on it, and it was made from lots of little pieces all glued to the ground, sort of like the grass in the park, except different, because these pieces were soft and they bent when he touched them. Plus, the grass in the park sure didn't have a small like this. The grass in the park didn't have any smell. But this green stuff smelled. It smelled kind of good.

"Huh!" he said again. He pressed another button, and big green sticks jumped up from the ground. They were taller than the top of his head, and they had long green leaves sticking off that bent over, and they smelled a little bit like something he had smelled a couple of times, which was corn. But this wasn't corn, because where were the cans that had little yellow cubes in them to eat?

He shrugged. This was sure a strange box. He pressed another button, and that one made the green rug rip open in some places, and some trees jumped up, but he couldn't figure out how they did it because he didn't see anybody building them. And these trees didn't have only green leaves. They also had a lot of round, shiny balls that were red hanging on the branches. He never saw things like that on a tree. He went over to see them better, and they had a smell, too—a *real* good smell, kind of prickly and cold in his nose. It made him feel tingly, and kind of like he wanted to smile, and—and it made him feel even *more* hungry, too. That smell made him feel more hungry, but why would it? He never ate anything like those red things, but gosh, he was sure hungry now. Maybe Mom would give him something to eat if he went home right now and asked real nice, even if it wasn't time for today's meal.

But even if Mom didn't give him something to eat now, this wasn't such a bad day after all. Now he had a box that made stuff, which was pretty neat stuff even if he didn't know what it all was, and it all made him feel good, and there was still lots of other buttons left to push.

His nose itched, so he scratched it, and some blood dropped out and made a spot on the box. And he looked at the blood spot that was on the box, and he thought, Oh no, that's not my box. I have to give it to Gritch. Because I am *conditioned*. He didn't know what that meant, but he remembered when Gritch said it—he remembered all about what was happening then, and all of a sudden he didn't like to hear it in his head the way Gritch said it. All of a sudden he didn't like it at all.

He felt funny inside his stomach, but not hungry like all the time, and not sick like a lot of times, but some other funny feeling he never had before, kind of like getting punched real hard. And that funny feeling was making his breathing go too fast, and his eyes felt kind of burning like they wanted to cry, and his teeth were grinding like they were mad—real mad at Gritch. Which was scary and wasn't good because he wasn't allowed to ever be mad at Gritch. But all he could think was, it was the worst thing ever if Gritch took the box, because this box was maybe the specialest thing he ever had, and maybe he wouldn't ever be old enough or smart enough if Gritch took away something this special. And he didn't like to feel so scared and so mad, but when he thought about Gritch owning this box, he got more scared and more mad, like there was even something else wrong with Gritch just even having the box, but he didn't know what it was, and it scared him even more to think something like that, something that he didn't even understand why he was thinking it. And he was really crying then because he didn't know how to stop being so scared.

He put the box down on the ground, and he picked up the biggest rock he could find, and he smashed the box, and smashed and smashed, and then it was just a bunch of very, very tiny pieces. And then he made a hole in the dirt and stuck all the pieces in. And he wouldn't ever, ever, tell anybody about it. Because then Gritch wouldn't ever even know about the box, and if he didn't know about it, then it didn't count the same way as trying to keep it and not give it to Gritch.

Which was maybe cheating a little, so it made him feel a little bad.

But he wasn't scared anymore. And he wasn't crying. He thought maybe he felt kind of good.

Kind of like—like he had done something real special.

Kind of like maybe he really was old enough now. And smart enough, maybe he was really smart enough now, because he had figured out how it could be that Gritch wouldn't have the box, but he wasn't keeping it away from Gritch. He must have been real smart to figure that out.

So he even smiled a little bit when he started walking away from the trees and stuff in his private place, which he thought maybe he wouldn't go back to again, because it was different and scary now, but he didn't have to think about it if he didn't look at it again, and he could find another private place anyway.

But there was one more thing he thought, one more thing he thought for sure when he was running back home, and it was this:

The next neat thing he found, the very next one, he was gonna keep it.

POINTS TO CONSIDER ABOUT "CONDITIONING"

1. When and where does this story take place? What clues does Landsberg provide to establish setting and historical period? Describe the world in which Shermie Brooks lives, and the secondary characters with whom

he interacts. What is Shermie's world like, and how did it get to be the way it is, according to details provided in "Conditioning"?

2. Of "Conditioning", Landsberg says, "I tried to crystallize a moment of the human heart in conflict with itself, delineating that moment so precisely that we can see the parameters of the conflict clearly, feel the agony of the protagonist's decision, see the consequences to the entire world of the protagonist's actions, and understand the factors that led him to his climactic action." What are the "parameters of the conflict" in this story? Where do the external conflicts lie, and what is the conflict within the heart of Shermie? How does this internal conflict resolve itself . . . or does it?

3. How would you describe the voice of this story's narrator? Why does Landsberg choose to use this kind of diction as his narrator relates the unique situations confronting Shermie Brooks? How old is Shermie—what clues do you have as to his age? Why does Shermie talk and act the way he does? How old is Gritch, and what are his motivations as Landsberg establishes his character?

4. What is meant by the story's title? Is Shermie Brooks the only product of conditioning in the story, or are all the characters conditioned to some extent? Explain. Does any character manage to break free from his/her/its conditioning at some point during the story? Does this story embody "change"—or the potential for change—as Landsberg describes it in his introductory material? Does Shermie manage to understand and overcome his conditioning? How does the story resolve itself, and what does its resolution suggest about the human condition during our own historical period?

5. What is the "dog thing" that appears toward the end of the story? Where does it come from, and what does it look like? What is the function of the "dog thing" in the story's narrative structure? What is the "little box" that the "dog thing" brings with it? How does the "little box" function symbolically within "Conditioning", contributing to Landsberg's ultimate thematic message(s)?

�֎ WRITING ACTIVITIES: SCIENCE FICTION

1. Your agent calls one day and says, "Quick! I've got to have a short short story involving the following elements by next week, to enter into the *Galaxy Busters Science Fiction Magazine* contest." She gives you these two elements:

   A. A team of two police officers, one of whom is an android, and one of whom is human.

B. A gun which can be set to fire either of these (but not both at the same time): bullets that will penetrate android flesh but not human flesh, and bullets that will penetrate human flesh but not android flesh.

First, write a brief synopsis of the plot of a story based on these two premises. Using your synopsis as a guide, write your agent a story in five hundred words or less.

2. Continue this dialogue as far as you wish, but for at least one more page. Remember to embody the principle of internal consistency, as described by John M. Landsberg in his introductory remarks, as you undertake this activity.

> "Do you see the moon?"
> "How could I miss it?"
> "You could miss it if you don't let go of the throttle in about ten seconds."

3. The following paragraph is chock full of errors and stupidities that violate basic principles of science fiction as explained by John M. Landsberg . . . along with some egregious sentence-level errors as well. Rewrite it, doing anything that you can possibly do to make it better:

> "Now that I'm here, Commander Blangelbin," he said. "He" referred to the "man" which was "standing" with his foot on the neck, if anyone might call it as a neck, of the first guard who dared to lay a paw on him. "Ha!" chortled in return that very Blangelbin, who was the Lord High Execution Person of The Forces of Plinky-Plinky, chortling merrily to himself, because chortling was what he did a lot, on this planet called F. That's right, F, and only F. "Because I am Harry," he said,"that is Harry of F, Conqueror of The West End of The Known Universe."

Additionally, write your own science fiction story that takes off on settings/characters presented in this paragraph and write your own, much better, story.

4. Following the precepts set out by Harlan Ellison in his earlier discussions, begin a science fiction story by writing the most intriguing opening sentence you can. Give yourself five minutes to do so and no more! To extend the activity, do the same thing for the last sentence, then go back to the beginning and write a second sentence, then to the end and write the second-to-last sentence, and so on until you eventually meet at the story's center, which should be a narrative high-point or mini-climax. If you want the creative pump primed, here is an example of the first and last two sentences of a sf story based on this activity prompt.

First two:

> I saw myself in a window. It had fallen out of its seventeenth-floor casing, and I with it.

Last two:

> I never saw that damned prextile again. And in that hot sundowner wind I was born.

14

Literary Fiction

Barry Gifford was born in Chicago and raised there and in Key West and Tampa, Florida. He has received awards from PEN, the National Endowment for the Arts, the Art Directors Club of New York, and the American Library Association, and his book *Night People* received the Premio Brancati, the Italian national book award established by Pier Paolo Pasolini and Alberto Moravia. His writing has appeared in such publications as *Punch, Esquire, Cosmopolitan, Rolling Stone, Sport*, the *New York Times*, and the *New York Times Book Review*. Mr. Gifford's novels, including *Arise and Walk, Baby Cat-Face, Perdita Durango, Wild at Heart: The Story of Sailor and Lula*, and *Port Tropique*, have been translated into seventeen languages, and *Wild at Heart* was made into an award-winning film directed by David Lynch, who directed and co-wrote the recent film *Lost Highway*. *Perdita Durango* was also made into a feature film, for which Gifford co-wrote the screenplay. In the following interview, Gifford discusses specific qualities that distinguish literary fiction from other fictional subgenres, and describes some of the joys and sorrows of writing for an ever-shrinking literary fiction market, along with his work as a screenwriter.

AN INTERVIEW WITH BARRY GIFFORD

MP: Are you working on a new project with David Lynch?

BG: We're chatting. Basically, David gets all this stuff submitted to him, and my feeling is that it's not worth doing anything together unless it's original. That's how I felt about *Lost Highway,* and that's how I feel about anything.

MP: He gets scripts thrown at him?

BG: Oh, sure, if he wants to remake the Three Stooges, he can. He'd probably do something interesting with it, too. The good thing about David is that when it comes down to doing it, he's going to do something that's audacious and original. So we may do something again, and that's all I have to say about that.

MP: O.K. Let's talk about the ways in which your fiction fits into the literary tradition. I've heard you described by some critics as a postmodern writer, by others as a *noir* writer. What do you think about these categories?

BG: I'm a literary writer whose work is sometimes identified—especially in France—as *noir*. Choosing not to be very analytical myself, I leave that kind of categorizing to those to whom that's important. I don't necessarily have an objection to it. My idea of *noir* had to do with the R.K.O. movies of the late-forties and early-fifties. That was the label that was put on those kinds of films. The distinguishing quality of *noir*, for me, is desperation. There has to be a feeling of desperation and/or despair, and that would identify *noir*.

MP: The R.K.O. films that you're talking about have a certain atmosphere that's created by the cinematography itself, it seems to me. When these French folks describe your fiction as *noir*, do you agree with it?

BG: It's a funny thing. In France, the category of thriller or *noir* is just as legitimate literarily as "straight" fiction of any kind. Some of my books in France are published as straight literature, some are published as *noir*, but both are considered equally literary . . . whereas they're not in this country. In this country, if you are classified as mystery writer, then you're thrown in the mystery section. My books are certainly not in the mystery section here or anywhere else in the world . . . only in France. At first I had an objection, frankly, to being classified as a *noir* writer in France and being part of this *polar* group. It's sort of an interchangeable term over there. *Polars* include Chandler, Hammett, Cain, and all kinds of people you wouldn't think of as *noir* writers fall into this group, including myself. Is Faulkner's *Sanctuary* a *noir* novel? It is in France! The thing is, I'm published in something like seventeen languages now, which is really great, because I like having that kind of global currency. It doesn't matter to me how my books are published or what they're called. To me, I'm just a literary novelist, and I leave it at that. I really refuse in a certain way to analyze what I do. The writing process itself is mysterious, and I don't like to tamper with it.

MP: James Morley, a professor at St. Joseph's College in West Hartford, has described postmodernism this way:

> Postmodernism is characterized by a rejection of the sovereign autonomous individual with an emphasis upon anarchic collective, anonymous experience. Collage, diversity, the mystically unrepresentable,

dionysian passion are the foci of attention. Most importantly we see the dissolution of distinctions, the merging of subject and object, self and other. This is a sarcastic playful parody of western modernity and the "John Wayne" individual and a radical, anarchist rejection of all attempts to define, reify or re-present the human subject.

Given this brief and admittedly incomplete definition, how does your writing fit the criteria for postmodernism?

BG: Some people seem to consider me a postmodern writer, since I was recently included in the *Norton Anthology of Postmodern Fiction*. What this means, I'm not exactly clear about. Capote's in there, and Mailer's in there, and Vonnegut's in there, but I just think we're all writers. I do disagree with one of the professor's points, though, at least in relation to my own work. The individual is very important to me. Everything I've ever done is based on the individual. My models in writing were Jack London and Joseph Conrad—writers who were concerned with the plight of the individual, and the fate of the individual.

Furthermore, the word I object to most strenuously—insofar as it might be applied to my work—is "sarcastic." Everything that I do is serious and intentional and as straightforward and as sincere as it could possibly be. It's easy for people to pigeonhole others, and I object to this kind of pigeonholing. I don't think it can be easily done. I am a literary writer, and beyond that, I think my work resists neat classification. I remember, when was I was starting out as a poet, I wrote a book called *Coyote Tantras*, which did quite well for a book of poetry; in 1973 it sold three thousand copies. A lot of it was nature poetry, but it was involved with the trickster myth. It had a lot of Native American allusion and information in it—basically came out of the fact that I'd been living in the woods for two years. But the thing about it was, I'll never forget someone saying, "You're part of that Gary Snyder school, and you'll always be thought of in this way." They knew nothing about me, where I was headed or what was likely to happen. I remember thinking, "How foolish!" I've always resisted this business of being typed.

MP: "Hero eradication" seems to be one of the hallmarks of postmodernism, and that's something you could be interpreted as doing in your writing. The Bill Pullman character becomes a twentysomething garage mechanic a third of the way into *Lost Highway*, and Sailor Ripley and Lula Fortune, who are protagonists of earlier books of yours, make an appearance in *Baby Cat-Face* and then disappear.

BG: When Bill Pullman's character, Fred Madison, is transformed, it's really in his own mind. It's his helplessness, his psychogenic fugue. So really, it's a fantasy. In my fiction, I start out by being interested in one person. If I'm writing in, say, *Baby Cat-Face*, I'm interested in Esquerita Reyna, how she came to be where she is and all that. What I recognize—and this might be something for the postmodern theorists—is that I see the world as being a very random kind of place. That's why there's so much violence in these books: because I've seen it and felt it. What I'm really doing is satirizing it, but it's also a sad commentary on where we're at here at the beginning of the twenty-first century. So one character devolves into another. One character gives way for another. In the novels—and you'll see in again in the new novel, *The Sinaloa Story*—one character passes out of the picture for a while and may come back—that's how I see real life, and that's why I think I'm a very realistic writer—but he may come back in a different form, a different guise, years later . . . or not. Sailor and Lula appear in *Baby Cat-Face*, but they appear as a prequel to *Wild at Heart*. What I've done is to create a universe, not unlike, say, Yoknapatawpha County *[a fictional location of William Faulkner's fiction—ed.]*, but a different sort of universe, certainly, which is populated by all these people, and I can move them in and out as I see fit.

MP: "All these people" in your fictional universe have funny names: Ray Bob Realito, The Reverend Cleon Tone, Gaspar DeBlieux, Wilbur "Damfino" Nougat, Klarence Kosciusco Krotz, a perfume called "Paroxysme," Croesus "Spit" Spackle, Demetrious "Ice D" Youngblood, and my personal favorite, Zvatiff Thziz-Tczili (pronounced, "So vat if this is silly?"). What are you doing with names in your fiction?

BG: The same thing that Nabokov, another writer of literary fiction, was doing. His names were filled with triple-entendres. The names really inform the characters, and they give you some information if you're sharp enough to pick up on it. They'll give you a picture. If you hear a name like Perdita Durango, you get a visceral feeling about this character immediately. Romeo Dolorosa—he's bad news, man. These names do mean a lot.

MP: Writing with names like that tends to be satirical, in my experience.

BG: Well, somebody once described the names that Jack Kerouac gave to people as "funny hats" that he put on their heads, and they did have meaning. I was influenced by Kerouac, whose work I loved—in spirit and tone more than anything else—and who was a real inspiration to me, because there were a lot of similarities between our lives. I saw something there—with Kerouac and Nabokov both—in terms of names, of how characters are named and why. As time went on, I guess beginning with the Sailor and Lula novels, it just made sense: this is who the character is.

MP: Speaking of Kerouac, there's a conversation in one of your recent books that goes:

> "Remember what Jack Kerouac said: 'I'd rather be thin than famous.'"
> "Who is this person who speaks such absurdities?"
> "A novelist."
> "Ach . . . novels! I never read them."

Is this a satirical commentary on the general public's lack of literary taste, or what?

BG: I'm speaking through a particular character who represents a point of view that certain people do have. It's clear that the general public in the United States doesn't read literary fiction. There may be more books being sold now than ever, but what are the books? They're mysteries, romance, cookbooks, how-to books. There's very little commerce when it comes to literary fiction, and this is just a fact. The evisceration of the independent bookstores has guaranteed this kind of awful future, and I can't help but feel any other way. There was a time when you went into a bookstore, and you weren't sure what to read, but there was a bookseller there who would hand-sell you a book: "Look, here's the new novel by this guy Mike Petracca. It's really very beautiful." The bookseller would know the kind of books you like to read, and what you were interested in, or maybe how your mind worked. The whole idea of reading any writer, for me, on a consistent basis is: the guy or woman might write better books sometimes than other times, but I'm interested in the way the person's mind works. It's like having a conversation with them. Jack Spicer, a poet, once said that poems are the way dead men write to one another—he talked about certain pieces being letters to Shakespeare, for instance—and I take that seriously. You're not writing just for the immediate audience, but you're really communicating with those people with whom you feel something in common, and who've come before you.

MP: If the market for literary fiction is so bleak right now, what do you—or I, as a teacher—tell to twentysomethings who want to write literary fiction?

BG: Well, I hope that this, like most other things, is cyclical. You can go back to Lady Murasaki and *The Tale of Genji* and say that was the beginning of the novel—or Sei Shonagon and *The Pillow Book*—and say for a thousand years the novel had a nice run. Or you can go to Cervantes and say we had a nice four hundred-year run. With the coming of television, and now computers and the internet, people spend less time reading serious fiction. They don't use their imaginations the same way. In fact, their imaginations are being eviscerated. It's like twisting people's arm to get them to sit down and read a literary title like Balzac's *Lost Illusions,* say, that they could buy in paperback for four or five bucks. I think it's a difficult time if you're thinking about writing literary fiction. Probably—and I say this in all candor—if I were starting today, I would be writing screenplays. I would have a video camera and a little self-editor, and be out there making movies, because that's the language of the time. You can get to so many people through that form—look, I work in the medium myself. I go back and forth between novels and film, and I think that's entirely valid. Meanwhile, it seems to me that the literary novel is becoming more and more the province of academia and soon may only be published by academic presses . . . although the academic presses, the university presses themselves want trade-type books. Even they want literary novels less and less.

MP: Yet you used the word "cyclical," which suggests you think public taste may swing back in a literary direction . . .

BG: That's my hope. I don't know whether the fuses have to blow, so that the people can't get to their computers and TVs, and then they'll be left with the written word . . . or what. But I hope it will happen, and I certainly don't want to discourage young writers from creating literary fiction, because there's always a readership for it even in these discouraging times. You just may have to move to France!

MP: From reading your most recent book [*The Phantom Father: A Memoir* is Gifford's literary reconstruction of his father, a man well-known in Chicago of the 1930s through the 50s as the proprietor of an all-night liquor and drugstore adjacent to a popular nightclub, and as a reputed gangster], I gather you had a somewhat unconventional childhood. How did that contribute to your becoming a writer?

BG: When I was a small child, I lived mainly in the company of adults. In a peripatetic kind of childhood like I had, moving from hotel to hotel, being in the company of adults, being around my father's friends who spoke elliptically and symbolically, I really had nothing to do but sit and listen and observe . . . which is the greatest university for a writer. I would listen to what they said, and then wonder what they were really saying behind the words they were using. I also listened to the dialects, the way they spoke. Often they were from somewhere in Europe, or parts of the United States that I was unfamiliar with, so I began to pick up on the language. It was the language as much as the stories that interested me. Often, when I didn't know what it was they were talking about, I could make it up. I would invent it in my own mind. So I was unconsciously inventing fictional scenarios even at five or six years old. Also, as early as I can remember, I was a voracious reader. I was a very physical kid, though—fishing, swimming, then later playing every sport imaginable. But I was often left to my own devices—I didn't have, as Sailor Ripley says, "a lot of parental guidance." When I wasn't being physically active, I was reading, listening. It all goes into the writing.

MP: With regard to listening: some writing teachers advise students *not* to use dialect, because it can unintentionally ridicule the character who's talking, or simply because it's hard to get dialect to sound right. You seem to have a lot of dialect in your fiction, though: rural American cracker, African-American, New Orleans *patois*, Hispanic, and so on.

BG: That's what I was hearing. I listen to the way people speak and try to record it accurately, that's all. Faulkner said that he was frightened by the movies, because he felt that what it would regularize the way people spoke, and it would diminish—or ultimately do away with—regional speech. Little did he know about television, which enables you to be in New

Orleans, or San Francisco, or New York, and the person reading the news to you speaks in the same uninflected voice! That's what Faulkner was referring to. He liked the idea of regional differences in speech. In *Night People* I put in one character, a jail guard, who speaks totally in dialect. I did it all phonetically, because I wanted one time, in one place, to represent the way certain people really speak, and to make it almost unidentifiable as speech. I did this on purpose. I was taken to task for it, I remember, in a review in the New Orleans *Times-Picayune*. The guy said, "This is absurd, nobody speaks this way." What I was doing, in fact, was recreating the way people in a particular Louisiana parish speak. I know that speech; I lived there! The amazing thing about it is that this book has been translated into ten languages. How do they translate it? It's impossible for them to get it. But you can approximate it. I wanted to capture regional speech, just one time, in that purest possible way, just to show this is the way certain people speak. This kind of thing does take a well-attuned ear, though; maybe that's what those writing teachers are warning their students about.

MP: Well, most of the reviews of your dialogue tend to be much more favorable that the one from the *Times-Picayune*. In fact, I have a quote here from Jonathan Wilson in The *New York Times Book Review,* who recently said of your prose, "His short, imagistic chapters have the quality of tableaux—Mr. Gifford is adept at establishing atmosphere . . . He also has a fine ear for dialogue and an ability to sketch character economically."

BG: I don't spend a lot of time with reviews. I do what I'm sure you do with newspaper reviews of your books: I scan it and then put it in a box. In fact, though, I've mostly been praised for my dialogue, and I work very hard at it.

MP: How do you construct plots? Do you do it differently in your films than you do it in your books, or is the process essentially the same? Do you outline ahead of time, or do you let it spin out organically?

BG: The only thing that the writing of screenplays and the writing of fiction have in common is that both necessitate the use of words. Otherwise they are entirely different disciplines. Being good at one certainly does not guarantee that you can be even mediocre at the other. It takes a while to learn one or the other, and writing novels is, of course, much, much more difficult than writing screenplays. Insofar as plots are concerned in the novels, I never know what's going to happen. I don't get an idea, now I'm going to write a novel about the holocaust, now I'm going to write a novel about serial killers in Bolivia. Everything I do is visual. It comes from an image, a very particular image. For instance, in the new novel, *The Sinaloa Story*, I had an image of a car driving across a desert landscape. It was at night, and there was a bolt of cloud-to-ground lightning behind the car. I actually saw this, a kind of photograph in my mind. I wondered, "Who is this person in this car, and why is he or she driving across the desert?" That's how the novel got started. I said, "O.K., here's who the person is, and here's what's going on in his mind, he's listening to the radio in the car, and so it proceeds from there." I had *no idea* that the book was going to be about prostitution on the U.S.-Mexico border, child prostitution, and the *campesino* rebellion in Mexico. No idea. None. In other words, it was an adventure for me. I try to keep the writing process entertaining for myself, in that sense.

When I wrote *Wild at Heart*, I was staying in a little hotel on the Cape Fear River in North Carolina, and I woke up one day and heard voices—a conversation going on—and I sat down and wrote the conversation. Some people have misquoted me in various places, saying that I overheard a conversation coming from another room. It wasn't coming from another room, it was in my head. There were two people talking, and it was Sailor and Lula. They were having this conversation. At first I thought it just a little short story—kind of Tennessee Williams-ish—but the conversation continued, and then I as well as the characters got a little claustrophobic, so I had to get them out of that hotel room and on the road. Most of the time, though, what happens is that I will have a visual image, and I usually write to an image. I usually have a cover for a book—sometimes it's even been used for the novels!—where the image will represent something for me, and there it goes. With Perdita Durango, here was a character who came in toward the end of *Wild at Heart*, who began to dominate my thoughts. I became very, very interested in this character, and so I had to do my best to suppress her and finish that episode—which was the first of the Sailor and Lula novels, *Wild at Heart*—and then go onto the second one, which is the story of Perdita Durango. She took over, because I realized she needed her own voice and her own stage. I just wanted to see what was going to happen with her. I might make notes as I go along. I'll think of something, and I'll write something in the margins and keep it for later—sometimes I do incorporate it and sometimes I don't—but the characters carry the narrative. I never know what they're going to do or say next, and I prefer it that way.

MP: You're describing an organic process, as some people might call it, for writing fiction. Do you use the same method for movies, which by their nature have to be less digressive and more structured?

BG: Much as I hate advocating a lack of spontaneity, you pretty much have to know where you're going in a screenplay. However, that said, writing a screenplay like *Lost Highway* is another experience. If you're writing a screenplay based on a novel, you know how the novel ends. You might have your three acts already. But when you're doing a completely original piece of work, then other things happen that *are* more organic. Each situation dictates its form and process. If you're working with a director like David Lynch, of course, with whom I get along so well because we let our imaginations run, then that becomes a different sort of organic process. Remember that films are collaborations, and novels usually aren't. Writing a novel, you're sitting in your little room, you're in your cell, you're the only one who's responsible for anything that goes on that page, and then

they're going to publish the book. The thing is, you're entirely responsible
for everything. With a film, a screenplay is something like a blueprint. Yes,
you write the screenplay, and if the dialogue is good, then they're going to
keep it—one hopes—but you have so many different people saying something about your screenplay—producers and studio executives and actors,
not to mention the director—that you know it's going to go through a lot of
changes. Even if you're working with someone who has complete control,
the screenplay's still going to change in the editing. And when you're on
the set, and people say something, it may sound a little wrong for that situation. It may have been right on the page, but in fact it's wrong coming
out of somebody's mouth. So that becomes an organic process, also. The
film is really going to develop and change until the thing is up there on the
screen.

MP: Speaking of your little writing cell...do you have a regular
writing routine? Do you use a typewriter or word processor?

BG: I write in longhand.

MP: Yellow pad?

BG: Yes. I like to write in the morning. When I'm on a project, I'll
work every day. I'll go from eight to one in the afternoon or something.

MP: Do you ever get writer's block?

BG: It's funny, because I think I've always had it and not had it.
There are times when I simply don't write, and I don't think about it.

MP: It doesn't worry you that the words will never come again?

BG: I could go sell soda pop and bait on a dock in West Florida, and
I'd be all right! I've written a lot. I've probably written enough for a lot of
people. It's another thing that I do. I don't identify myself entirely with
being a writer. I *am* a writer, I've always been a writer, it's something I've
always done, but I've done a lot of other things, too. The lifestyle suits me,
certainly, and it's a wonderful thing to get paid for something you love to
do. It's like being a baseball player, which is really the only other thing I
ever wanted to do. But, yes, I write in longhand, and then I'll make a correc-
tion on that, and then I'll put it on a manual typewriter, and that's sort of
like the third draft, and then I'll correct that by hand—that's a fourth draft—
and then I'll make a clean copy, again on the manual typewriter, so that's a
fifth draft.

MP: And you're revising as you're typing these additional drafts?

BG: Sometimes I don't do much revision, and sometimes I make
more extensive changes, but it's usually in the way of additions. What I'll
often do—even with a screenplay—is write what I call a "skeleton draft." In
other words, I'll write it straight through, and then I'll go back and put
some meat on the bones. I like to get through to the end, I do like to know
what's going to happen. The skeleton draft may be only seventy-five pages
long, but then I'll go back and write another hundred and fifty pages.

MP: I've heard you say that the opening chapters of *Baby Cat-Face*, which appear after this interview, are among your "truest" writing.

BG: The openings of two of the books, *Perdita Durango* and *Baby Cat-Face*, have the most uncompromising openings. You're in the soup right away. When Perdita has that conversation in the airport in San Antonio, that sets the tone: there's no compromise. The same thing is true with the conversation between Baby and Jimbo. You know right where you're at . . . or you don't; you're at sea. Who are these people who speak like this? What are they talking about? What they say is not uninteresting, they're not unintelligent. There's a great deal of wisdom in what they say. It's honest, and what follows is certainly unusual. It even gets a bit otherworldly.

MP: Yes, when extraterrestrial wasp-people start figuring in the plot, I'd call that otherworldly.

BG: But here's the question: how much of that "surreal" narrative can be taken literally? It's interesting. Kirkus recently gave *The Phantom Father* a really nice review, and I think the only good review they ever gave me before that was for *The Neighborhood of Baseball: A Personal History of the Chicago Cubs*. Same with a *New York Times* reviewer taking me to task for writing all these woefully bizarre novels but loving *The Phantom Father*. It's like they want you to be a certain way: "The guy can write, but why does he waste his time with this bullshit?" In any case, that's their problem; I write what I'm moved to write, and my novels reflect that. So in the opening chapters of *Baby Cat-Face*, I wanted to show the reader what this person's life was like by jumping right into the middle . . . and let the reader sink or swim, because I wanted the reader really with me. I wanted the reader to be intrigued. I've often heard people describe my writing as very *different*. I like to think that it *is* different, and maybe that's why it gets called literary fiction—it resists formula, traditional structures, contains unusual perspectives.

MP: What fiction—especially literary fiction—do you read these days?

BG: I've been doing a lot of re-reading. It's not that I don't read contemporary work, I just don't read much of it. I try to read work by friends of mine whose writing I respect. I've found that in the last few years, when I'm writing I don't read much. I'll read informationally, anything from *Natural History* magazine to biographies. Lately, I've gone back, and I'll reread Stendhal, *The Charterhouse of Parma*, or go back to Balzac and *Les Illusions Perdues*. I want to go back and reread things that I miss, and characters that I loved, and situations that thrilled me. I've always been pretty reflective—maybe, being a writer, that's part of the business—but lately I seem to be going back and looking at the people who inspired me to be a *real* writer, who made me realize that this is an old profession, that telling a story is a difficult but rewarding job—who legitimized literary fiction for me.

Baby and Jimbo
Barry Gifford

"Take here dis lady in Detroit bludgeon her husban', chop up da body, den cook it. Talkin' 'bout payback! Whoa!"

"Baby, you oughtn't be readin' dem kinda lies is put inna newspaper. Ya know dat shit jus' invented, mannipilate y'all's min'. Make peoples crazy, so's dey buy stuff dey don't have no need fo'. Stimmilate da 'conomy."

"Wait up, Jimbo, dis gal got firs' prize. She skin him, boil da head, an' fry his hands in oil."

"What kinda oil? Corn oil? Olive oil?"

"Don't say. Lady be from Egyp', 'riginally. Twenny-fo' years ol'. Name Nazli Fike. Husban' name Ralph Fike. Police found his body parts inna garbage bag, waitin' be pick up. Whoa! Ol' Nazli was stylin'! Put onna red hat, red shoes an' red lipstick befo' spendin' hours choppin' on an' cookin' da body. Played Ornette Coleman records real loud while she's doin' it. Tol' police her ol' man put her onna street, shot dope in her arms, an' was rapin' her when she kill him in self-defense."

"Bitch was a hoojy, begin wit'."

"Jimbo, how you know? Plenty guys lookin' turn out dey ol' ladies."

"Was a hoojy."

"Aw, shit!"

"What?"

"She ate parts da body."

"Cannibal hoojy."

"Dis disgustin'."

"What else it say?"

"Can't read no more."

Jimbo Deal got up from the fake-leopard-skin-covered sofa and snatched the newspaper out of Baby Cat-Face's hands. He and Baby had been living together for six weeks now, since the day after the night they had met in Inez's Fais-Dodo, and he wasn't certain the arrangement was going to work out. She had a tendency to talk too much, engage him in conversation when he

---

was not in a conversational mood. At thirty-four years old, Deal was used to maintaining his own speed. Since Baby Cat-Face, who was twenty-three, had come into his life, he had been forced to *adjust.*

"Woman ain' be clean fo'way back, Baby, you read da res'. Run numbers on guys since she come from Egyp', seven years ago. Car thef', drug bus', solicitin' minors fo' immoral purpose. A hoojy, like I claim. *Foreign* hoojy."

"Husban' put her up to it," said Baby. She lit a cigarette and stood looking out the window down on Martinique Alley. "She been abuse' as a chil', too."

"Dat's what dey all usin', now. Abuse dis, abuse dat. Shit. Says she be foun' sane an' sentence to life imprison. Shit. She prob'ly be queen da hive, have hoojies servin' on her in da joint. Big rep hoojy like her."

"Quit, Jimbo! Cut out dat 'hoojy' shit, all ri'? Tired hearin' it."

"Troof, is all. Since when you don't like to listen da troof?"

Baby sucked on an unfiltered Kool, then blew away a big ball of smoke.

"Swear, Mister Deal, you da mos' truth tellines' man in New Orleans."

Jimbo tossed the newspaper on the coffee table.

"I got to get ready fo'work," he said, and left the room.

Baby Cat-Face smoked and stared out the window. The sky was overcast. It was almost six o'clock in the evening and Baby was not sure what she was going to do while Jimbo pulled his night shift at the refinery in Chalmette. She saw two boys, both about twelve years old, one white, one black, run into the alley from off Rampart Street. They were moving fast, and as they ran, one of them dropped a lady's handbag.

"Baby!" Jimbo Deal shouted from the bathroom. "You gon' make my lunch?"

Baby took a deep drag of the Kool, then flicked the butt out the window into the alley. It landed, still burning, next to the purse.

"We got some dat lamb neck lef', darlin', ain' we?"

Rat Tango

"'What you want, baby I got it. What you want, baby I got it.'"

"Say, what?" Baby Cat-Face said to the red-haired, café au lait woman who was singing and dancing the skate next to the jukebox, her back to Baby.

"Huh?" the woman said, doing an about-face, keeping her skates on. "How come there ain't mo' Aretha on this box? 'R-e-s-p-e-c-t, find out what it mean to me.'" She sang-shouted, beginning to swim and shimmy. "Sock-it-to-me sock-it-to-me sock-it-to-me!"

The woman wiggled and shook, causing Baby and another patron of the Evening in Seville Bar on Lesseps Street to grin and clap.

"Down *to* it, Radish!" shouted a fat man standing next to the pay phone. He banged his huge right fist on the top of the black metal box. "Be on time! Ooh-ooh-ooh!"

The dancing woman looked at Baby, and asked, "You say somethin'?"

"Thought you was talkin' to me, was all," said Baby. "You say 'baby.'"

"Yeah, so?"

"That's my name, Baby."

The woman smiled, displaying several gold teeth, one with a red skull painted on it. "Oh, yeah? Well, hello, Baby. I'm Radish Jones. Over here playin' the telephone's my partner, ETA Cato."

The fat man nodded. He was wearing a porkpie hat with a single bell on the top with DALLAS printed on a band around the front of it, and a black silk shirt unbuttoned to the beltline, exposing his bloated, hairy belly.

"Happenin', lady?" he said.

"ETA?" said Baby.

Radish laughed. "Estimated time of arrival. Cato's firs' wife name him, 'count of his careless way 'bout punctchality. Come we ain't seen you in here before, Baby?"

"Firs' time I been, Radish. My ol' man, Jimbo Deal, tol' me check it out."

"Shit, you hang wit' Jimbo? Shit, we know da man, know him well. Don't we, Cato?"

"Who dat?"

"Jimbo, da oil man."

Cato nodded. "Um-hum. Drink Crown Royal an' milk when he up, gin when he down."

"Dat him," said Baby.

"Where he at tonight?" Radish asked.

"Workin'."

"Well, glad you come by, Baby. We front you a welcome by."

"Rum an' orange juice be nice."

"Say, Eddie Floyd Garcia," Radish called to the bartender, "lady need a rum an' OJ."

The bartender mixed Mount Gay with Tang and water and set it up for Baby.

"Thanks, Eddie Floyd," said Radish. "This here's Baby."

"Hi, Baby," the bartender said. "Round here we call dis drink a Rat Tango, as in 'I don't need no rat do no tango at my funeral.'"

Eddie Floyd Garcia, a short, wide, dark blue man of about fifty, winked his mist-covered right eye at Baby. Up close, she could see the thick cataract that covered it.

ETA Cato traded off dancing with Radish and Baby to the juke over the next couple or three hours, during which time they consumed liquor at a steady clip, Eddie Floyd making sure to keep their drinks fresh. It was a

slow night in the Evening in Seville. Other than a few quick-time shot and
beer customers, the trio and Eddie Floyd had the place to themselves. Baby
learned that Cato worked as a longshoreman on Celeste Street Wharf, and
Radish did a thriving nail-and-polish business out of her house on the corner of Touro and Duels called The Flashy Fingers Salon de Beauté.

Sometime past two A.M., Radish decided that ETA Cato had danced
one too many times in a row with Baby Cat-Face. Johnny Adams, "The Tan
Canary," was seriously wailing "I Solemnly Promise" when Radish flashed
a razor under Cato's right ear, cutting him badly.

"Damn, woman!" Cato yelled. "What you do that for?!"

Radish Jones shook a Kool from a pack on the bar, stuck it in her
mouth, but couldn't quite hold her lighter hand steady enough to fire up the
cigarette.

Eddie Floyd Garcia grabbed a rag, vaulted over the counter, and knelt
next to ETA Cato, who had slid to the floor, holding his right hand over the
cut. Blood was jumping out of his neck.

"King Jesus! King Jesus!" screamed Baby, backing away.

Eddie Floyd applied pressure to Cato's wound with the rag, but the
bleeding did not abate.

"Call a ambulance!" Eddie Floyd cried. "Look like a artery be sever'."

Radish did not pay any attention to Cato's predicament, absorbed as
she was in her attempt to torch the Kool. Baby grabbed the phone and di-
aled 911. When a voice answered, she started to talk, then stopped when she
realized it was a recorded message requesting that the caller please be patient and hold the line until an operator became available.

Baby forced herself to look at Cato. He coughed, lurched forward, and
fell back against Eddie Floyd. Cato turned toward Baby and opened his
eyes wide. She thought he was going to say something, but he died with his
mouth half open, staring at her. A human being came on the line and asked
Baby, "Is this an emergency?"

Only the Desperate
Deserve God

"In Yuba City, California, two severed hands were found in a K-mart shopping cart. The grisly discovery was made at about four P.M. Sunday by a
clerk collecting carts, a Yuba City police spokesman said. The hands are
being treated as evidence in a crime, but it will take a forensics expert to determine for sure that the body parts found are, in fact, human and whether
homicide is indicated."

"There just ain't no end to human mis'ry," Baby said out loud to herself, as she switched off the radio next to her and Jimbo's bed.

Baby Cat-Face had spent most of the previous three days drifting in and out of sleep, depressed by thoughts of the incident she had witnessed in the Evening in Seville Bar. After Radish Jones slit the throat of her boyfriend, ETA Cato, who expired on the barroom floor, flooded by his own blood, Baby had gone stone-cold with shock. Jimbo Deal told Baby later that the police had brought her home and that he had put her to bed after feeding her the Valium mints the NOPD nurse had safety-pinned in a tiny plastic bag to Baby's blouse.

She had eaten sparingly during this time, only rice Krispies and dry toast with tea. Jimbo had stayed home from work for two days, "baby-sittin'," as he called it; but today he had had to go, afraid that he would be fired if he did not. Jimbo placed a loaded Ruger Bearcat in Baby's bedside drawer and told her to protect herself with it if she had to until he came home.

Baby reached over with her right hand and switched the radio back on, tuning it until she found an interesting voice, and left it there.

"People, when I say you got to *stand up* to God, I *mean* you got to *challenge* his word!" said the voice. "You got to be *bold* enough for Him to pay you any mind. Only the *desperate* deserve God, don't you know? Hallelujah! Are you *desperate* yet? Are you *ashamed* yet? Are you *frightened* next to death yet? Well, well, well—you *should* be! Yes, you should, you should! This is the *time*, people, the *only* time you got to hear God's word. It don't matter what your name is, what color you are, what *size* or financial condition, no! You got to *stand up* to him right now or it's snake eyes for the planet! Yeah, we got to do this little thing together, people, make it work *right*. Get our neighbor to *admit* how desperate he or she is so we can get *on* with this holy war, 'cause that's what it is, a *holy* war! Standin' up to God means standin' up to the beast in the street, the one soon's spit poison in your eyes as look at you. You *got* to know what I'm talkin' about, people, or *die stupid!*"

"I know," Baby said. "I know what you sayin'."

"*All right*, then!" said the voice from the radio. "*Stand up* to God! Do what's necessary! Most of you desperate and don't know it!"

Baby turned off the radio. She heard the front door to the apartment open and then quietly close.

"Jimbo?" Honey, that you home already?"

A short person wearing a red ski mask stepped into the bedroom. The intruder held a .45 automatic pistol with both black-gloved hands and pointed it at Baby. Baby threw a pillow at the gun and rolled off the bed onto the floor, pulling down the bedside table as she fell. She grabbed Jimbo's Ruger from the drawer, swung it toward the intruder, closed her eyes, and pulled the trigger twice. Baby opened her eyes and saw that she was alone in the room. She held the Bearcat straight out in front of her as she got to her feet.

"Come on, muthafuck!" Baby yelled. "I stand *up* to God now!"

Baby crept stealthily from the bedroom into the living room. The front door was closed. The kitchen, which was in full view from the living room, was empty. The only other place a person could be hiding was the bathroom.

"Come out of there!" Baby shouted, pointing the Ruger at the closed bathroom door. "Or sure as shit I gon' bust a cap up yo' butt!"

There was no sound from the bathroom, so Baby Cat-Face fired two rounds through the door. She kicked it open and charged inside, firing two more shots into the shower stall. Baby looked around: there was nobody but her in the bathroom. She saw her reflection in the mirror above the washbasin. Her eyes were slashes of red on her face.

"King Jesus," she said, "am I hallucinatin'?"

A police siren wailed and Baby heard a car screech to a stop in Martinique Alley. She sat down on the toilet seat and let the handgun drop to the floor.

"Maybe I be *too* desperate," said Baby.

POINTS TO CONSIDER ABOUT THE OPENING CHAPTERS OF *BABY CAT-FACE:* "BABY AND JIMBO," "RAT TANGO," AND "ONLY THE DESPERATE SERVE GOD"

1. Michael W. Foley, a political science professor, observes a distinction between two categories of postmodernists. The "skeptical postmodernists," he says, argue that the postmodern age is one of fragmentation, disintegration, malaise, meaninglessness, a vagueness or even absence of moral parameters and societal chaos. Foley argues, "In this period no social or political 'project' is worthy of commitment. Ahead lies overpopulation, genocide, atomic destruction, the apocalypse, environmental devastation, the explosion of the sun and the end of the solar system in 4.5 billion years, the death of the universe through entropy." He contrasts postmodern skeptics with "affirmatives" who are generally optimistic; they are either open to positive political action [that is, revolutionary struggle and resistance] or "content with the recognition of visionary, celebratory, personal, nondogmatic projects that range from New Age religion to New Wave life styles and include a whole spectrum of post-modern social movements." Based on your readings of these three short chapters at the beginning of Barry Gifford's *Baby Cat-Face,* where do you think Gifford fits into this skeptical/affirmative split?

2. A character in one of Gifford's novels says, ". . . time peoples get a clue. Organize religion be dangerous to dey health. Ought to da gov'ment put warnin' signs on churches, same as on cigarettes." What does this quote

suggest about Gifford's attitude toward organized religion? Do you find echoes of this sentiment in "Baby and Jimbo," "Rat Tango," and/or "Only the Desperate Serve God"?

3. Discuss Gifford's use of dialect in these selections. How do the speakers' inflections contribute to their development as characters? Do you object to the fact that Gifford writes in a regional African-American dialect, despite the fact the Gifford spent extended time in that geographic locale and himself has an ethnically mixed family? Explain your position with regard to Gifford's regional speech.

4. "There ain't no end to human mis'ry," Baby Cat-Face says near the beginning of "Only the Desperate Serve God." How does this statement support Gifford's view of the world, as he expresses it in the interview? Find other examples in "Baby and Jimbo," "Rat Tango," and/or "Only the Desperate Serve God" that might also develop/support Gifford's worldview.

5. In the interview, Gifford says of these chapters at the beginning of Baby Cat-Face, "There's a great deal of wisdom in what they say," referring to the protagonists of the story. Find specific examples of "wisdom" in these stories' dialogue passages.

Vasiliy Shishkov
Vladimir Nabokov

The little I remember about him is centered within the confines of last spring: the spring of 1939. I had been to some "Evening of Russian Émigré Literature"—one of those boring affairs so current in Paris since the early twenties. As I was quickly descending the stairs (an intermission having given me the opportunity to escape), I seemed to hear the gallop of eager pursuit behind me; I looked back, and this is when I saw him for the first time. From a couple of steps above me where he had come to a stop, he said: "My name is Vasiliy Shishkov. I am a poet."

Then he came down to my level—a solidly built young man of an eminently Russian type, thick-lipped and gray-eyed, with a deep voice and a capacious, comfortable handshake.

"I want to consult you about something," he continued. "A meeting between us would be desirable."

I am a person not spoiled by such desires. My assent all but brimmed with tender emotion. We decided he would see me next day at my shabby hotel (grandly named Royal Versailles). Very punctually I came down into the simulacrum of a lounge which was comparatively quiet at that hour, if one discounted the convulsive exertions of the lift, and the conversation conducted in their accustomed corner by four German refugees who were discussing certain intricacies of the *carte d'identité* system. One of them apparently thought that his plight was not as bad as that of the others, and the others argued that it was exactly the same. Then a fifth appeared and greeted his compatriots for some reason in French: facetiousness? swank? the lure of a new language? He had just bought a hat; they all started trying it on.

Shishkov entered. With a serious expression on his face and something equally serious in the thrust of his shoulder, he overcame the rusty reluctance of the revolving door and barely had time to look around before he saw me. Here I noted with pleasure that he eschewed the conventional grin which I fear so greatly—and to which I myself am prone. I had some difficulty in drawing together two overstuffed armchairs—and again I found most pleasing that instead of sketching a mechanical gesture of cooperation, he remained standing at ease, his hands in the pockets of his ancient trench coat, waiting for me to arrange our seats. As soon as we had settled down, he produced a tawny notebook.

"First of all," said Shishkov, fixing me with nice, furry eyes, "a person must produce his credentials—am I right? At the police station I would have shown my identity card, and to you, Gospodin Nabokov, I must show this—a cahier of verse."

I leafed through it. The firm handwriting, slightly inclined to the left, emanated health and talent. Alas, once my glance went zigzagging down the lines, I felt a pang of disappointment. The poetry was dreadful—flat, flashy, ominously pretentious. Its utter mediocrity was stressed by the fraudulent chic of alliterations and the meretricious richness of illiterate rhymes. Sufficient to say that such pairs were formed as, for example, *teatr-gladiator, mustang-tank, Madonna–belladonna.* As to the themes, they were best left alone: the author sang with unvarying gusto anything that his lyre came across. Reading his poems one after the other was torture for a nervous person, but since my conscientiousness happened to be reinforced by the author's watching closely over me and controlling both the direction of my gaze and the action of my fingers, I found myself obliged to stop for a few moments at every consecutive page.

"Well, what's the verdict?" he asked when I had finished: "Not too awful?"

I considered him. His somewhat glossy face with enlarged pores expressed no ominous premonition whatever. I replied that his poetry was hopelessly bad. Shishkov clicked his tongue, thrust the notebook back into the pocket of his trench coat, and said: "Those credentials are not mine. I mean, I did write that stuff myself, and yet it is all forged. The entire lot of thirty poems was composed this morning, and to tell the truth, I found rather nasty the task of parodying the product of metromania. In return, I now have learned that you are merciless—which means that you can be trusted. Here is my real passport." (Shishkov handed me another, much more tattered, notebook.) "Read just one poem at random, it will be enough for both you and me. By the way, to avoid any misapprehension, let me warn you that I do not care for your novels; they irritate me as would a harsh light or the loud conversation of strangers when one longs not to talk, but to think. Yet, at the same time, in a purely physiological way—if I may put it like that—you possess some secret of writing, the secret of certain basic colors, something exceptionally rare and important, which, alas, you apply to little purpose, within the narrow limits of your general abilities— driving about, so to speak, all over the place in a powerful racing car for which you have absolutely no use, but which keeps you thinking where could one thunder off next. However, as you possess that secret, people must reckon with you—and this is why I should like to enlist your support in a certain matter; but first take, please, a look at my poems."

(I must admit that the unexpected and uncalled-for lecture on the character of my literary work struck me as considerably more impudent than the harmless bit of deception my visitor had devised. I write for the sake of concrete pleasure and publish my writings for the sake of much less concrete money, and though the latter point should imply, in one way or another, the existence of a consumer, it always seems to me that the farther my published books, in the course of their natural evolution, retreat from their self-contained source, the more abstract and insignificant become the fortuitous events of their career. As to the so-called Readers' Judgment, I feel, at that trial, not as the defendant, but, at best, as a distant relative of one of the least important witnesses. In other words a reviewer's praise seems to me an odd kind of *sans-gêne,* and his abuse, a vain lunge at a specter. At the moment, I was trying to decide whether Shishkov tumbled his candid opinion into the lap of every proud writer he met or whether it was only with me that he was so blunt because he believed I deserved it. I concluded that just as the dog-gerel trick had been a result of his somewhat childish but genuine thirst for truth, so the voicing of his views about me was prompted by the urge of widening to the utmost the frame of mutual frankness.)

I vaguely feared that the genuine product might reveal traces of the defects monstrously exaggerated in the parody, but my fears proved unfounded. The poems were very good—I hope to discuss them some other time in much greater detail. Recently, I was instrumental in getting one published in an émigré, magazine, and lovers of poetry noticed its originality.[1] To the poet that was so strangely gourmand in regard to another's opinion, I incontinently expressed mine, adding, as a corrective, that the poem in question contained some tiny fluctuations of style such as, for instance, the not quite idiomatic *v soldatskih mundirah;* here *mundir* (uniform) should rather be *forma* when referring as it did to the lower ranks. The line, however, was much too good to be tampered with.

"You know what," said Shishkov, "since you agree with me that my poems are not trifles, let me leave that book in your keeping. One never knows what may happen; strange, very strange thoughts occur to me, and—Well, anyway, everything now turns out admirably. You see, my object in visiting you was to ask you to take part in a new magazine I am planning to launch. Saturday there will be a gathering at my place and everything must be decided. Naturally, I cherish no illusions concerning your capacity for being carried away by the problems of the modern world, but I think the idea of that journal might interest you from a stylistic point of view. So, please, come. Incidentally, we expect" (Shishkov named an extremely famous Russian writer) "and some other prominent people. You have to understand—I have reached a certain limit, I absolutely must take the strain off, or else I'll go mad. I'll be thirty soon; last year I came here, to Paris, after an utterly sterile adolescence in the Balkans and then in Austria. I am working here as a bookbinder but I have been a typesetter and even a librarian—in short I have always rubbed against books. Yet, I repeat, my life has been sterile, and, of late, I'm bursting with the urge to do something—a most agonizing sensation—for you must see yourself, from another angle, perhaps, but still you *must* see, how much suffering, imbecility, and filth surround us; yet people of my generation notice nothing, do nothing, though action is simply as necessary as, say, breath or bread. And mind you, I speak not of big, burning questions that have bored everybody to death, but of a trillion trivia which people do not perceive, although they, those trifles, are the embryos of most obvious monsters. Just the other day, for example, a mother, having lost patience, drowned her two-year-old daughter in the bathtub and then took a bath in the same water, because it was hot, and hot water should not be squandered. Good God, how far this is from the old peasant woman, in one of Turgenev's turgid little tales, who had just lost her son and shocked the fine lady who visited her in her isba by calmly finishing a bowl of cabbage soup 'because it had been salted'! I shan't mind in the least if you regard as absurd the fact that the tremendous number of similar trifles, every day, everywhere, of various degrees of importance and of different shapes—tailed germs, punctiform, cubic—can trouble a man so badly that he suffocates and loses his appetite—but, maybe, you will come all the same."

I have combined here our conversation at the Royal Versailles with excerpts from a diffuse letter that Shishkov sent me next day by way of corroboration. On the following Saturday I was a little late for the meeting, so that when I entered his *chambre garnie* which was as modest as it was tidy, all were assembled, excepting the famous writer. Among those present, I knew by sight the editor of a defunct publication; the others—an ample female (a translatress, I believe, or perhaps a theosophist) with a gloomy little husband resembling a black breloque; her old mother; two seedy gentlemen in the kind of ill-fitting suits that the émigré cartoonist Mad gives to his characters; and an energetic-looking blond fellow, our host's chum—were unknown to me. Upon observing that Shishkov kept cocking an anxious ear—observing, too, how resolutely and joyfully he clapped the table and rose, before realizing that the doorbell he had heard pertained to another apartment—I ardently hoped for the celebrity's arrival, but the old boy never turned up.

"Ladies and gentlemen," said Shishkov and began to develop, quite eloquently and engagingly, his plans for a monthly, which would be entitled *A Survey of Pain and Vulgarity* and would mainly consist of a collection of relevant newspaper items for the month, with the stipulation that they be arranged not chronologically but in an "ascending" and "artistically unobtrusive" sequence. The one-time editor quoted certain figures and declared he was perfectly sure that a Russian émigré review of that sort would never sell. The husband of the ample literary lady removed his pince-nez and, while massaging the bridge of his nose, said with horrible haws and hems that if the intention was to fight human misery, it might be much more practical to distribute among the poor the sum of money needed for the review; and since it was from him one expected that money, a chill came over the listeners. After that, the host's friend repeated—in brisker but baser terms—what Shishkov had already stated. My opinion was also asked. The expression on Shishkov's face was so tragic that I did my best to champion his project. We dispersed rather early. As he was accompanying us to the landing, Shishkov slipped and, a little longer than was required to encourage the general laughter, remained sitting on the floor with a cheerful smile and impossible eyes.

A fortnight later he again came to see me, and again the four German refugees were discussing passport problems, and presently a fifth entered and cheerfully said: "*Bonjour, Monsieur Weiss, bonjour, Monsieur Meyer.*" To my questions, Shishkov replied, rather absently and as it were reluctantly, that the idea of his journal had been found unrealizable, and that he had stopped thinking about it.

"Here's what I wanted to tell you," he began after an uneasy silence: "I have been trying and trying to come to a decision and now I think I have hit upon something, more or less. *Why* I am in this terrible state would hardly interest you; I explained what I could in my letter but that concerned mainly the business in hand, the magazine. The question is more extensive, the question is more hopeless. I have been trying to decide what to do—how to stop things, how to get out. Beat it to Africa, to the colonies? But it is hardly worth starting the Herculean task of obtaining the necessary papers only to find myself pondering in the midst of date palms and scorpions the same things I ponder under the Paris rain. Try making my way back to Russia? No, the frying pan is enough. Retire to a monastery? But religion is boring and alien to me and relates no more than a chimera to what is to me the reality of the spirit. Commit suicide? But capital punishment is something I find too repulsive to be able to act as my own executioner, and, furthermore, I dread certain consequences undreamt of in Hamlet's philosophy. Thus there remains but one issue: to disappear, to dissolve."

He inquired further whether his manuscript was safe, and shortly afterwards left, broad-shouldered yet a little stooped, trench-coated, hatless, the back of his neck needing a haircut—an extraordinarily attractive, pure, melancholy human being, to whom I did not know what to say, what assistance to render.

In late May I left for another part of France and upon returning to Paris at the end of August happened to run into Shishkov's friend. He told me a bizarre story: some time after my departure, "Vasya" had vanished, abandoning his meager belongings. The police could discover nothing—beyond the fact that *le sieur Chichkoff* had long since allowed his *karta*, as the Russians call it, to run out.

That is all. With the kind of incident that opens a mystery story my narrative closes. I got from his friend, or rather chance acquaintance, bits of scant information about Shishkov's life and these I jotted down—they may prove useful someday. But where the deuce did he go? And, generally speaking, what did he have in mind when he said he intended "to disappear, to dissolve?" Cannot it actually be that in a wildly literal sense, unacceptable to one's reason, he meant disappearing in his art, dissolving in his verse, thus leaving of himself, of his nebulous person, nothing but verse? One wonders if he did not overestimate

> The transparence and soundness
> Of such an unusual coffin.

NOTE

[1]To relieve the dreariness of life in Paris at the end of 1939 (about six months later I was to migrate to America) I decided one day to play an innocent joke on the most famous of émigré critics, George Adamovich (who used to condemn my stuff as regularly as I did the verse of his disciples) by publishing in one of the two leading magazines a poem signed with a new pen name, so as to see what he would say, about that freshly emerged author, in the weekly literary column he contributed to the Paris émigré daily *Poslednie Novosti*. Here is the poem, as translated by me in 1970 (*Poems and Problems*, McGraw-Hill, New York):

THE POETS
From room to hallway a candle passes
And is extinguished. Its imprint swims in one's eyes,
until, among the blue-black branches,
a starless night its contours finds.
It is time, we are going away: still youthful,
with a list of dreams not yet dreamt,
with the last, hardly visible radiance of Russia
on the phosphorent rhymes of our last verse.

And yet we did know—didn't we?—inspiration,
we would live, it seemed, and our books would grow
but the kithless muses at last have destroyed us,
and it is time now for us to go.

And this not because we're afraid of offending
with our freedom good people; simply, it's time
for us to depart—and besides we prefer not
to see what lies hidden from other eyes;

not to see all this world's enchantment and torment,
the casement that catches a sunbeam afar,
humble somnambulists in soldier's uniform,
the lofty sky, the attentive clouds;

the beauty, the look of reproach; the young children
who play hide-and-seek inside and around
the latrine that revolves in the summer twilight;
the sunset's beauty, its look of reproach;

all that weighs upon me, entwines one, wounds one;
an electric sign's tears on the opposite bank;
through the mist the stream of its emeralds running;
all the things that already I cannot express.

In a moment we'll pass across the world's threshold
into a region—name it as you please:
wilderness, death, disavowal of language,
or maybe simpler: the silence of love;

the silence of a distant cartway, its furrow,
beneath the foam of flowers concealed;
my silent country (the love that is hopeless);
the silent sheet lightning, the silent seed.
                          Signed: Vasiliy Shishkov

The Russian original appeared in October or November 1939 in the *Russkiya Zapiski*, if I remember correctly, and was acclaimed by Adamovich in his review of that issue with quite exceptional enthusiasm. ("At last a great poet has been born in our midst," etc.—I quote from memory, but I believe a bibliographer is in the process of tracking down this item.) I could not resist elaborating the fun and, shortly after the eulogy appeared, I published in the same *Poslednie Novosti* (December 1939? Here again the precise date eludes me) my prose piece "Vasiliy Shishkov" (collected in *Vesna v Fialte*, New York, 1956), which could be regarded, according to the émigré readers' degree of acumen, either as an actual occurrence involving a real person called Shishkov, or as a tongue-in-cheek story about the strange case of one poet dissolving in another. Adamovich refused at first to believe eager friends and foes who drew his attention to my having invented Shishkov; finally, he gave in and explained in his next essay that I "was a sufficiently skillful parodist to mimic genius." I fervently wish all critics to be as generous as he. I met him, briefly, only twice; but many old literati have spoken a lot, on the occasion of his recent death, about his kindliness and penetrativeness. He had really only two passions in life: Russian poetry and French sailors.

V.N., *Tyrants Destroyed and Other Stories*, 1975

POINTS TO CONSIDER ABOUT "VASILIY SHISHKOV"

1. As mentioned in the opening remarks to Part II of *The Graceful Lie*, the hoax is a considered by many critics to be a valid component of postmodern literary fiction. How does "Vasiliy Shishkov" fit into this category? What are your own feelings about "playing tricks" on readers by deliberately misleading them with assertions that turn out to be false, such as the authoritative-sounding "quotation" of the fictional Carlo Zeamba in Chapter 1 of *The Graceful Lie?*

2. In what ways does this story exhibit certain qualities of literary fiction, as Gifford describes them in his interview? What distinguishes this story from, say, one of the examples of historical fiction in the previous chapter?

3. Another of the qualities of postmodern fiction, as described by James Morley (and quoted in the Gifford interview), is "the merging of subject and object, self and other." Where do you see this kind of blurring of the boundaries between characters, and/or between the author and his characters, in "Vasiliy Shishkov"?

4. This short story is about a fictional poet and contains some sly commentary about the nature of language. What specific points does "Vasiliy Shishkov" suggest about "good writing" specifically, and about language more generally?

5. What do you make of the last lines: *"The transparence and soundness/Of such an unusual coffin"?* What does the phrase mean on the literal level? What does it imply on a more metaphoric level of interpretation? How might this concluding phrase help suggest Nabokov's intended theme in "Vasiliy Shishkov"?

✳ WRITING ACTIVITIES: LITERARY FICTION

1. Using the method described by Gifford in his creation of *The Sinaloa Story,* do whatever it takes—pepperoni pizza at midnight? forty-eight hours without sleep? three cans of Jolt Cola? a ten-mile uphill run? meaningful tunes cranked at top volume? an extended session of prayer and/or meditation? a quiet afternoon in nature?—to get yourself a vision: a mental picture, an imagined dialogue so real that it sounds like the people are in the next room, whatever emerges. Then, write a "short, imagistic chapter," in the mold of "Baby and Jimbo," "Rat Tango," and/or "Only the Desperate Serve God," that evolves organically from the vision, with no preconceptions of plot or form.

2. Author Carole Maso said in a recent interview,

   > ...I see...in my students, some very raw, extravagant, interesting ten-dencies, deliberately avoided, consciously swerved away from, because dear God, what would happen if you actually spoke in your own voice, and you sounded like no one else. Looked like no one else, could not be categorized, could not be sold. It's dangerous. Which it should be, of course. But most American writers are unwilling to take the gamble. The price is too high. And American literature suffers a great deal as a result. For me, the price is too high *not* [*italics mine: ed.*] to speak in my own voice. Writing, for me, is a significant human adventure; it is about explo-ration and investigation and meditation. It's about the search for a legiti-mate language. It's about the search for beauty and integrity and whole-ness. For meaning, where maybe there is none.

   Do a focused freewrite in response to this quote by Maso. Consider the ways in which, as you write fiction, you might compromise your vital, unique personal voice to conform to others' expectations. Having done this, then write a brief fictional piece in which you intentionally in-dulge—ideally, to absurd excess!—in the very practices you usually avoid.

3. Write a piece of "hoax" scholarship. Amuse yourself by pretending you're a professor in a given academic field and writing an extended treatise on a given topic—a made-up poem? a psychological disorder? a geologic discovery? an environmental disaster?—complete with bogus quotes, invented bibliographic references, nonexistent institutions, foot-notes that go nowhere. Try to be subtle enough in tone that it takes a while for the reader to realize you're making all this stuff up, but outra-geous enough for this to emerge finally as a parody of some "real" pro-fessors' ramrod-stiff scholarly posturing and tortured academic jargon.

Index